Contextualizing Teaching

Joe L. Kincheloe
*CUNY-Brooklyn College and The
Pennsylvania State University*

Patrick Slattery
Texas A&M University

Shirley R. Steinberg
Adelphi University

Introduction to Education and Educational Foundations

LONGMAN

An imprint of Addison Wesley Longman, Inc.

New York • Reading, Massachusetts • Menlo Park, California • Harlow, England
Don Mills, Ontario • Sydney • Mexico City • Madrid • Amsterdam

Marketing Manager: Renée Ortbals
Full Service Production Manager: Mark Naccarelli
Project Coordination and Text Design: Nesbitt Graphics, Inc.
Electronic Page Makeup: Nesbitt Graphics, Inc.
Cover Designer/Manager: Nancy Danahy
Cover Illustration: "Dagger Eyes" (1998) by Craig R. Johanns
Senior Print Buyer: Hugh Crawford
Printer and Binder: The Maple-Vail Book Manufacturing Group
Cover Printer: Coral Graphic Services

Library of Congress Cataloging-in-Publication Data

Kincheloe, Joe L.
    Contextualizing teaching: Introduction to education and educational foundations   /
Joe L. Kincheloe, Patrick Slattery, Shirley R. Steinberg.
        p.   cm.
    Includes bibliographical references and index.
    ISBN 0-8013-1504-2
    1. Teaching.   2. Education—Philosophy.   3. Effective teaching.
  I. Slattery, Patrick, 1953–   II. Steinberg, Shirley R., 1952–
  III. Title.
  LB1025.3.K583   2000
371.102—dc21   99–18229
                                                               CIP

Please visit our website at http://www.awlonline.com

ISBN: 0–8013–1504–2

2345678910—MA—02010099

for Bill Pinar

Brief Contents

Contents

Chapter 3 Engaging Students in Philosophical Reflection   89

PART 2 Historical Context: How Did We Get Here?   109

Chapter 4 The Ambiguities and Contradictions in Early American Schooling   111

Chapter 5 Common Schools and Beyond: Education for Social Control versus Education for Democratic Citizenship   134

PART 3 Economic Context: Power, Work and Schooling   173

Chapter 6 Labor and Economics in a Democratic Society   175

Chapter 7 Political Debates about Work   204

Chapter 8 Empowering Teachers   225

PART 4 Teaching Context: Teachers as Reflective Thinkers, Curriculum Leaders and Action Researchers 265

Chapter 9 Teachers as Researchers 267

Chapter 10 Curriculum Issues and Debates 300

PART 5 Social Context: Students as Learners in Contemporary Culture   339

Chapter 11 The Impacts of Race, Class and Gender on Education   341

Chapter 12 Youth Culture   378

Chapter 13 Educational Futures   403

Preface

We have written *Contextualizing Teaching* for undergraduate teacher education students who are preparing for careers in elementary and secondary schools. We have also written this book for master's degree students who are returning to college to explore the complexity of teaching and learning in contempory U.S. society. Specifically, this book is designed as a general introduction to education and/or a reading for courses in the foundations of education. Thus we have included chapters on the philosophy of education, the history of education, the economics and politics of education, the sociology of education and the teaching and learning process. Although the structure of this book resembles a traditional foundations of education textbook, the contents of each chapter challenge many of the assumptions about education in such books. In fact, as we have taught courses in education at many universities in the United States over the past twelve years, we have become increasingly frustrated with the textbook selection available on the market for our students. Thus, we decided to write a book that offered a different approach.

So what are our concerns, and how is this book different from other education textbooks? Our first concern is that traditional textbooks are decontextualized. They too often present data and information that are divorced from the human experience. In every chapter of this book we connect philosophy, history, economics, teaching and sociology to examples and case studies that illuminate the concepts we present. We pause often to tell stories about our students, our schools and ourselves. We encourage our readers to add their own stories to broaden their understanding. In short, we seek to contextualize teaching and learning.

Our second concern is that traditional textbooks present data and information uncritically. They present an unchallenged philosophical, historical and sociological viewpoint, assuming that they are presenting the whole truth and nothing but the truth. We begin with a different premise. We invite our students and our readers not only to challenge and critique the traditional data in education textbooks, but also to raise questions about the material in this book as well. We believe that all assumptions and theories must be challenged and questioned. We do not believe that truth and knowledge are fixed and final; knowledge is constructed, evolving and tentative. In short, we raise challenging questions throughout this book, and we encourage our readers to do the same.

Our third concern is that the modern world has created a system of beliefs that will no longer be completely useful in the twenty-first century, and these modern beliefs permeate traditional educational foundations textbooks. We do not dismiss the positive contributions of the arts and sciences in the modern era;

we do not propose a revolt to overthrow the schools and society. However, we do propose a critical and constructive postmodern philosophy as an alternative way of looking at the world and thinking about teaching and learning in the schools. In short, this book incorporates contemporary postmodern thinking from philosophy, history, economics, political theory, sociology and curriculum theory.

Our final concern deals with multiculturalism and diversity. Traditional educational foundations textbooks often avoid the difficult issues surrounding diversity and refuse to explore the complexity of these topics. We lament this deplorable situation; we believe that it contributes to the oppressive silence in our society about injustices. We have written a book that addresses diversity at every possible turn. Yes, we do have a chapter dedicated to race, class and gender, but long before you read the material in Chapter 11 you will have been thoroughly immersed in issues related to diversity in the following arenas:

Feminist critiques of schools and society

Racism and racial diversity discourses

Gender bias in schools and society

Marginalization of students

Multicultural education

Gay, lesbian and sexuality issues

Social class bias and economic injustice

The effects of political and power theories

Ethnicity and cultural diversity

Education and handicapping conditions

Students with physical and psychological challenges

Deception and distortion in the curriculum

Multiple forms of teacher research

Empowerment of teachers and students

We are committed to promoting a constructive postmodern world in which diversity, justice, critical analysis, compassion and ecological sustainability are hallmarks of a new education. We invite you on a journey through the foundations of education from a contextualizing perspective.

Introduction

CONTEXTUALIZING TEACHING

Education is the lifelong process of coming to understand ourselves as individuals and members of our local communities in the constantly changing global society. *Education* requires passion, a humanist vision and a critical posture. It can stir the soul; expand the imagination; impart critical skills; energize the body; and secure justice, compassion, empathy and ecological sustainability. Critical educators do more than simply study and transmit subject matter; they examine social structures, explore community issues and help others to live meaningful lives. By contrast, formal institutional *schooling* too often reduces learning to codification and memorization, and it too often takes place in settings isolated from the society and cultures that surround it. As a result, schooling becomes education without *context*. This book discusses the need to *contextualize* teaching, reinvigorated with a passionate, humane and critical vision of the promise of contemporary society.

Throughout this book we insist that everyone involved in the process of education—students, teachers, parents, administrators, staff members and the community—must commit themselves to the exploration of the meaning of knowledge. By this we mean the investigation of the relevance of historical, cultural and scientific information in the various subjects schools teach; the process of challenging assumptions and sedimented perceptors—that is, deeply entrenched biases that individuals are not even aware exist—in textbooks, the media and schools; and the reenchantment of justice, compassion and sustainability in the world.

In other words, education must above all help us understand the context that connects us as individuals to our sociocultural environment. Therefore, we emphasize *autobiography, community relationships, reflective and interdisciplinary practices, creative problem solving* and *social action in the schooling process*. These emphases make education an active, dynamic and empowering process rather than a passive, static and credentialing function. A close study of the social foundations of education should reveal information and questions that help students to reconceptualize the role of education in creating a just, caring and ecologically sustainable world, rather than the ratification of inert ideas and the status quo.

YOUR LIFE AS A TEACHER IN CONTEXT

Teachers currently face increasing expectations with diminishing support and resources in an increasingly confrontational and sometimes violent atmosphere. The emotional stress and psychological pressure teachers find in contemporary schools can stifle and oppress them. More than ever before, then, educators must understand the social, economic, ideological, philosophical, historical, psychological, theological and political contexts of the culture beyond the schools in which they teach if they expect their work to be meaningful. When teachers approach their tasks lacking an awareness of the context in which they teach, they simply exacerbate frustration, anxiety and injustice in today's society. Accordingly, the process of contextualization is crucial to meaningful and consequential education.

While it is essential in the education of learners, contextualization is also vital for the education of teachers. The process of contextualization invites us to understand and assess the complexity of the learning process in schools. This process informs this book as we begin our journey toward understanding the foundations of education.

As we proceed, we consider the sociocultural context and the social foundations of education. Unfortunately, fragmentation now thoroughly infects the structures of contemporary schooling and social life; learning is divided into distinct subjects with specialized information and formulas that ignore interdisciplinary connections, just as labor is divided into discrete tasks performed by passive workers who are seen by themselves and others as contributing little to the organization's goals. Our social and political lives, too, seem divided into opposing parties and confrontational ideologies warring for dominance and control; even human aspirations become compartmentalized into various categories and possibilities manipulated by the media. In short, we lack a vision of interrelationships in broader humanistic contexts.

Teachers without a vision of the interconnectedness of educational purposes and global social issues often become alienated from and cynical about their role. We have spent hours with colleagues who dread coming to work. A frequent conversation we hear among teachers centers on the careers they should have chosen or would like to try. As a running joke, whenever he has a bad day at school one of our colleagues repeats his desire to find employment elsewhere: "I'm calling Fuller Brush," he threatens at least once or twice a week. Another colleague reminds the faculty daily of her approaching retirement: "I only have eleven years, three months, and sixteen days to freedom," she sighs with frustration, indicating her disgust with her profession, her students, her colleagues and her life. These teachers seem to enjoy no larger vision of educational purpose; they do not yet understand the contextualized dimension of teaching. In effect, they see their lives and their work as meaningless drudgery. Philosophically and pedagogically, they are lost and confused, and this disorientation exacts a professionally and emotionally damaging toll.

By contextualizing the teaching and learning experience we hope to clarify the connections among your political, religious, familial, environmental, social, economic, athletic, aesthetic and academic lives. In other words, we support the idea of education as a holistic experience that can bring all of the dimensions of our lives together without compartmentalizing the learning experience.

Thus, contextualization rather than fragmentation is the focus of our investigation of the social foundations of education. More specifically, we contend that the traditional elements of the foundations of education—philosophy, history, sociology, anthropology, politics, curriculum and teaching—can be understood only in relation to each other and in relation to the experiences of individual students and teachers. The division of these topics into independent subjects to be studied in isolation perpetuates the frustrating segmentation teachers and students too often find in school. Each section of this book, then, brings these elements of the foundations of education together. Specifically, each chapter draws connections between professional life and everyday life to illustrate the need for teachers to understand their larger educational purpose and their relationships with students. We challenge you as a prospective teacher to understand your own potential and your place in the web of reality. We explain theoretical examples with concrete teaching and learning experiences, remembering the need for humor and humility throughout education. Finally, we take the process of preparing to become a teacher as our opportunity to engage you in a metaconversation about the nature of educational theory and practice. This process involves an exciting search for a new and better way of living in our complex and often confusing global society.

CONTEXTUALIZING PHILOSOPHY

To contextualize education we will focus first on philosophy. As we explore the purpose of education, we ask you to join us in the search for wisdom and understanding. Here we try to understand philosophy—along with history, politics, curriculum and sociology—as a strategy for encouraging student self-reflection and emancipation, and not as a category offering only abstract information.

The role of the teacher that emerges from these inquiries transcends the traditional linear model of the "teacher in the school hierarchy": the superintendent to the supervisor, the supervisor to the principal, the principal to the department chair, the chair to the teacher, and at last the teacher to the student. Rather, we portray teachers as mentors, reflective practitioners, diagnostic professionals, facilitators of personal growth, social activists, action researchers and lifelong scholars who study schools, subjects, students and self, all in relation to the educational process. In addition, we portray students less as objects of instruction or empty vessels waiting to be filled with certified knowledge than as dynamic participants in the construction of knowledge.

Teachers and students are, of course, contextualized persons, self-constructed beings within a sociocultural milieu. But teachers and students are also subjects of history, constructed by contemporary society, media and youth cultures, as well as by the dynamic interplay of race, social class, religion, language, gender, sexuality and place. In this sense we acknowledge and affirm students and teachers as historical subjects who actively construct knowledge and meaning. The social foundations of education—philosophy, history, sociology, anthropology, politics, curriculum and teaching—represent dynamic and organic areas of investigation each student and teacher in his or her context constructs, reconstructs and reconceptualizes. How we understand the contextualization and social construction of our "selves" influences the way we come to see ourselves as teachers, citizens and community members.

Philosophy, therefore, is far more than just one among several elements of the foundations of education with precepts to be categorized, memorized and repeated on standardized exams. In its etymological tradition, philosophy is the love (*philo*) of wisdom (*sophia*). Join us in the process of discovering, affirming and refining your philosophy of education, reflecting on the many ways teachers, writers, artists, theologians, musicians and scientists experience and understand philosophy. We invite you on a journey that leads to a love of wisdom and understanding.

UNDERSTANDING THE CONTEXT OF THIS BOOK

As you begin to read this book, we caution that you will be reading a text like none you have ever read. It is our intention not only to explore teaching and the foundations of education from a critical and contextual posture, but to do so in a way that is radically different from traditional education textbooks. Modern textbooks have assumed neutrality with an implied authoritarian tone. Students have been taught to believe that the written text contains incontestable facts and data. Citizens today are constantly deceived by politicians, salespersons, journalists, preachers and teachers because they do not have the critical skills and creative reflection to challenge what they read or watch on television. There is something very wrong with our society when democratic participation is replaced with sheepish subservience or inane media gratification. It is also very dangerous. The racism, sexism, heterosexism, economic injustices and environmental degradation in our communities flourish because so many citizens are silent, fearful and uncertain. Students often lack imagination and sit back passively, refusing to take action to advance justice and equality. We wrote this book with the hope that more teachers and students would become empowered and emboldened to think and act. In a sense, we call on teachers to speak with a prophetic voice and, as the Catholic social activist Dorothy Day often said, "to comfort the afflicted and afflict the comfortable." In other words, our job is to teach, guide, support and comfort students who are in need in any way—intellectually, psychologically, physically, emotionally, spiritually or economically—and to raise difficult and challenging questions to powerful people who remain smug in their positions of dominance while ignoring the needs of others. Literally, we will have to become advocates for appropriate educational environments and services for our schools and our children. Thus, teachers are not simply curriculum dispensers, but rather are cultural workers committed to addressing the contextual issues facing our students, our schools and our communities.

Teachers are not functionaries in a bureaucratic system of information transmission. Nor are they passive dispensers of inert ideas. Rather, teachers who understand the context of the learning experience offer students inspiration, compassion, multiple perspectives, multicultural sensitivity, rigorous intellectual debates, critical analysis and, ultimately, hope for a better world and a fulfilling life. This cannot be accomplished when teacher education students are not empowered by professors, supervisors and textbook authors to contextualize their experiences. We wrote this book to challenge you to take control of your own learning and career. Thus we have not included staged pictures of idyllic classrooms and playgrounds full of smiling children with perfect teeth. Look around your campus and the various neighborhoods in your community—factories, churches, farms, bars, shopping malls, laundromats, shelters for battered women and abused children, school lunch rooms, unemployment offices, social clubs, concert halls, free health clinics for the poor, private HMOs or hospitals for the wealthy, pristine golf clubs, chemically polluted rivers, wildlife preserves, museums, manicured athletic fields in some neighborhoods, playgrounds with broken glass and weeds in others, locker rooms and gyms, crack houses, prostitution corners and drug infested alleys—notice the contrasts and note that this is the context of the lives of your students. Look carefully at faces, expressions and gestures. Create your own pictures of your community—maybe even set out to capture them with a camera, VCR or tape recorder. And then look, listen, smell, taste and feel the pulse of your community.

Be committed to stepping out of your comfort zones. Explore several newspapers and look for the variety of events in your community, especially in the free underground newspapers, music and art listings and social action advertisements. Visit the AIDS task force or Planned Parenthood center in your community. Attend a rally or revival in an orthodox and a progressive synagogue, mosque, temple or church you have never visited before. Inquire about sweat lodges and holistic healing centers. Spend some time in a jazz, zydeco, grunge or blues club. Attend a poetry reading. Go to a retirement home or a gathering place of senior citizens and ask folks to tell you about their lives—and enjoy listening to the stories. Walk or ride your bike along a nature trail and listen to the wind and the trees. Join a civic action group. Talk to people of various racial and ethnic identities, sexual orientations, religions or socioeconomic classes on their turf; listen to their hopes, concerns and fears. Critically and empathetically analyze all that you observe. Look for a common humanity with people and a kindred spirit with the earth.

Inquire about educational programs—or lack thereof—for the children of migrant or displaced workers (did you ever notice the migrant families in your community and have you ever stopped to listen to them?); for students with ADD, ADHD, MMR, Tourette's syndrome or dyslexia (have you ever heard these terms? have you ever inquired about them? do you have one of these conditions yourself?); for youth in prisons, juvenile homes or foster care systems (do we really make any effort to rehabilitate or address the needs of abandoned, orphaned, troubled or mentally ill children?); for talented children in the arts or sciences (do we nurture creativity in our schools? do we provide appropriate funding for academic programs, field experiences, labs and the arts?); for physically challenged, deaf, blind or mentally impaired students (is there appropriate access to buildings and programs? are equitable educational services provided? do people complain about these students? why or why not?); for quiet and compliant academic students who do not excel but are seldom recognized or asked to participate (is anyone noticing? will anyone give "average" kids attention and encouragement?); for young women who do not have equal access to sports, technology, advanced placement courses and other activities because counselors, administrators and board members refuse to fund programs for both genders equally or continue to harbor condescending and patriarchal attitudes (who will challenge such sexism? will young women and men be treated fairly in your school and classroom?); for lesbians, gay, bisexual and transgendered kids (will you support these students and intervene if they are taunted?); for racial, ethnic, religious or linguistic minority students (will they all be affirmed in their diversity in your school and classroom?). This list could continue at length to include so many others. These will be your students. Are you willing to accept, teach and nuture all of them in each unique context?

JOE SPANGLER: A STUDENT IN CONTEXT

At this point we pause to contextualize our philosophy by introducing Joe Spangler and allowing him to share his story with you. We will pause often in this book because we want you to realize that the questions and issues we raise are not simply theoretical; our ideas apply to the lived context of real people. Joe Spangler is studying to become a teacher. He is an adult who has returned to school in a master of education program. This, in itself, is a miracle, considering all that it took for Joe to get to this point in his life. Let's listen to his story in his own words. Remember, you will have many students like Joe in your classroom.

> *In the past children with disabilities did not receive proper diagnosis and treatment. Most children with disabilities were given tests without any special accommodation. After failing, most children were discouraged and gave up or dropped out of school. Great numbers of learning disabled children were passed through the school systems without learning to read and write. After graduation the cycle of failure continued because without developing the proper learning tools the person often fails. Children with disabilities have been treated like bruised bananas that are less valuable than the rest. However, with just the right amount of sugar, water and flour bruised bananas can turn into wonderful tasting banana bread. How many students are the bruised bananas who will never be given the chance to become banana bread and are thrown out with the rest of the trash? As a graduate student in special education I work and study with other professional educators. During conversations with fellow teachers, I often hear them reflect back to the "good old days" when they were young and life was perfect. They wish*

that they could have taught "back then." However, when I think back to the "good old days" I remember a crowded classroom with 45 students. My teacher is trying to teach me to read but is unsuccessful. I ran away because I could not learn to read. In desperation, my parents transferred me to another school where I repeated first grade. My third grade teacher did not know how to teach me and she put me in the corner because I had trouble understanding how to read and spell. Once again I was retained in third grade. This was very devastating because my friends were moving on and I was all by myself. All through elementary I had to learn how to get around my difficulty in spelling. Most of the time I would take assignments home and my mother would write them out for me. In high school I learned how to survive. I never missed a class, and I would try to answer any questions during class time. Because I realized I had trouble taking exams, I had to show the teacher that I knew the material during class or I would fail the course. Playing sports in high school was my salvation and prevented me from becoming a complete failure. However, because I was retained in elementary school, I lost my eligibility in my senior year. For four years in high school I played the dumb jock role because people would not accept me in the group if they knew I had a problem. Once I graduated from high school I thought my problems were behind me, but to my surprise they got worse. One professor who was teaching me how to write said to me that "I was a poor excuse for our educational system because I graduated without learning to read or spell." She went on to say that "I was a dumb jock and that she would see to it that I was expelled from college." After losing my track scholarship, I transferred to Ohio State where I continued to struggle only to fail courses. A professor noticed that I was highly motivated, and she could not understand why I was failing. She suggested that I be tested for dyslexia. Then, after testing I was diagnosed as dyslexic, and I started to adapt myself in order to overcome my disability. While studying biology, for example, I would use the biology book as a reference but would learn by discussing issues with classmates and thinking of kinesthetic experiences. I taped lectures and used the notes of my classmates to study. I received oral exams from my professors so that I could explain my answers clearly. If I had to memorize difficult material I would use flash cards or picture images. Computer technology helped sometimes. By using DragonDictate *voice activated software from* Dragon Systems *I was able to keep up with my fellow students academically. I have tried to change the word "no" to "yes" when it comes to reaching my life goals. My disability has been challenging, but it has made me the person I am today. I am prepared to be a better teacher because I understand the needs of children with disabilities. I hope to be a teacher who will always be on the lookout for ways to help children in need.* (Spangler, 1998)

Joe Spangler certainly understands contextualization. We must all continue to find ways to understand the context of human beings in the educational process. As we have emphasized, Joe is representative of the students you will teach in your classroom. Contextualizing teaching offers the opportunity to ensure that all students are provided with the opportunity to learn and grow. Would you agree that this is what a democratic community must be all about?

DIVERSITY AND QUESTIONS IN CONTEXT

Think about the diversity of students in your context. Investigate until you get weary or angry or confused or frustrated, and then do something positive! We challenge you to create your own picture of education to stuff between the pages of this book. Maybe you will create mental images, or maybe you will take photographs. However you choose to visualize education, it must come from your context. We will do the same in our communities, and we can compare images with each other at another time in another book—just do not expect us to paint a picture of your context in this book.

We will not provide summary questions or Internet sites for you to explore at the end of each chapter, as do so many of today's textbooks. We find such material insulting and debilitating. It gets in the way of critical thinking and creative problem solving. Instead, you must create your own questions as you read each chapter. Authentic questions that come from the passion of your own context will lead to fruitful responses. If we provide the questions, students will be less likely to generate their own ideas and solutions. As you read, agree with us at times, and get angry with us at other times. Challenge what we say. Add your own examples. Rewrite sections that miss the point. Let us hear from you with suggestions and critiques. But by all means, do not seek to answer our questions—you will not find any at the ends of chapters or at the end of the book. Rather, if you follow our advice to explore your community to create your own picture of education, then plenty of important questions will emerge as you read this book.

We purposely did not write a teacher's guide for this book. Your professor does not have all of the answers, and neither do we. So why should we pretend to give your professor the answers we do not have? A major mistake in schooling is the assumption that the teacher is the expert who has all of the answers and the student is the empty vessel—what John Locke called the *tabula rasa* (blank slate)—who passively absorbs information and experiences. The best teachers are those who are continually reading, traveling, exploring ideas, attending artistic and musical events, engaging in philosophical discussions and political action, exercising their bodies—in short, searching for wisdom and understanding. Conversely, the best students are those who are actively engaged in sharing ideas, conducting experiments and teaching others about their insights and visions. It may seem ironic, but good teachers are perpetual students and good students are active teachers. We reject the notion of a teacher's guide, answer key or resource manual because it perpetuates the notion of fixed meaning and authoritarian expertise. We will return to many of these ideas throughout this text.

Another word of caution concerns the words we use when we write. Throughout this book we provide examples and stories to help explain the difficult concepts we discuss. However, there is no getting around the fact that you will encounter new words and ideas. We suppose that words like *hermeneutics, hegemony, postmodernism, sedimented perceptors, existentialism* and *historiography* are unfamiliar to some readers; we will do our best to define these terms within the context of our discussions and examples, but we also urge you to be prepared to expand your vocabulary. Just because you have not heard of a term or an idea—perhaps dyslexia and ADHD, above—does not mean that they are impossible to understand. Remember, the best teachers are always looking for ways to expand their knowledge and understanding.

The final important introductory information concerns our philosophical assumptions. Every author has accumulated years of insights from many sources that lead to certain worldviews. In fact, one French philosopher of the twentieth century, Jacques Derrida, contends that there is no singular original author of any book because the voices of other people have so permeated and blended with every author's voice that it is impossible to distinguish among them. Consider your own religious and political beliefs, as well as your social and cultural practices. Are there people who influence the way you think and the beliefs you espouse? Have you ever felt manipulated into believing something out of obligation rather than conviction? Have you ever rejected a value or political view that had been ingrained in your thinking since childhood? Have you ever adopted a political or religious position after carefully reading and listening to others speak? Where do their ideas end and yours begin? We do not have answers to these questions, yet we raise them with good reason. We have been influenced by a worldview called *postmodernism*, a philosophy we will discuss in detail throughout this book. However, we want to comment now on some of the postmodern ideas that permeate our thinking.

CRITICAL CONSTRUCTIVE POSTMODERN PHILOSOPHY

The postmodern movement in art, architecture, philosophy, science, literature and education that started in the 1960s has emphasized eclecticism, parody, irony, deconstruction, indeterminacy, ambiguity, complexity and multiple forms of understanding the world and texts. Some of the ideas that postmodern philosophies have articulated (most are much more complex than our brief introduction here and will be addressed further in later chapters) are as follows:

1. The death of the author (Derrida, 1981, 1982) and the death of the subject (Foucault, 1972, 1977b), concepts that put in the foreground self-deception and the limitations and contradictions of truth statements by individuals, thus revealing a "fictional self" capable of many complex meanings rather than an "authentic self" capable—in the Enlightenment sense—of being wholly knowable and rational. In other words, we never fully "know" ourselves because we are always in the process of learning and are continually influenced by many complicated factors we are not even consciously aware of. Sometimes we wear masks; sometimes we repress feelings and experiences. Sometimes our unconscious influences us.

2. The repudiation of depth models of psychology that provide a body of disciplinary knowledge to explain the world while acting detached and objective—thus, we cannot escape our context and speak with absolute certainty. We are influenced by our place in the web of the global society.

3. The rejection of grand narratives or universal explanations of history that propose to have the whole story and absolute solution because there are many different versions of any event, depending on who is telling the story and from what vantage point (Lyotard, 1984; Knobel, 1998).

4. The illusion of the transparency of language where words are merely signs always pointing with precision to the signified object (Foucault, 1983). Thus, the possibility of linguistic certainty is eliminated because ambiguity and uncertainty will always be present because words have many interpretations and nuances (Kristeva, 1987).

5. A communication and media revolution in which the distinction between reality and the word or image that portrays it breaks down into a condition of hyperreality and signs—*simulacra*—that come to replace reality (Baudrillard, 1988).

6. The impossibility of giving any final meaning to any idea because words have no fixed or stable relationship to the concepts or things they are meant to signify—the meanings of words can only be described by more words—so meaning is endlessly deferred (Derrida, 1976).

7. The effects of power on the objects it represents (Ellsworth, 1997; Rouse, 1987) as associated with "identity politics"—movements that represent the empowerment and civil rights agendas of groups marginalized by their racial, gender, sexual, physical or other identities—and queer theory—philosophies that investigate notions of identity by "refusing normal practices and the practice of normalcy," by "exploring those things that education either dismisses or cannot bear to know," and by "imagining a sociality unhinged from the dominant conceptual order" (Britzman, 1995). These theories can be understood as protesting the idea of "normal" behavior, emphasizing instead diverse forms of individual and social identity (Slattery & Morris, 1999).

8. The failure of pure reason to understand the world (Pinar, 1997), along with the importance of intuition, imagination, emotion, arts and spirituality in understanding complex issues (Greene, 1995).

9. The decentering of the Western logos and with it the dethroning of the colonizing "first world" so that multicultural global communities are validated along with Western cultures (Banks & Banks, 1997; Gandhi; 1998).

10. The end of a belief in progress as a natural and neutral panacea that assumes that things are always getting better as a result of technology or communication (Bauman, 1992; Lyotard, 1992).

11. A celebration of difference and multiplicity leading to a revolutionary multiculturalism that unites critique and action in liberatory practices (McLaren, 1997) and affirms diversity from an antiracist position (Nieto, 1996) as we move toward equity in both the process and outcomes of education (Gay, 1994).

12. An understanding of the importance of the indigenous knowledges of African, Latin American, Asian, First Nations, Native American and Australian Aboriginal peoples. In this context Westerners learn profound

lessons from the ways indigenous peoples come to understand themselves in relation to their environment, the physical world, their cultural beliefs, their history and their spirituality (Semali & Kincheloe, 1999).

13. The belief that a quality education emerges from an evolving understanding of the complexity of social, cultural and psychological phenomena. "Postmodern rigor" in education involves moving past reductionistic views of reality and appreciating the interrelationships, the emerging processes and the effects that characterize human endeavor (Kincheloe, Steinberg, & Tippins, 1999; Kincheloe, Steinberg, & Hinchey, 1999).

14. The necessity of the search for new and exciting forms of intelligence that move us to new and exciting forms of intelligence that move us to new understandings of ourselves and the world around us. Such critical postmodern intelligences understand the tendency of modernist definitions of intelligence to privilege Western, European, male, upper middle class, ways of thinking as the model all other peoples around the world should emulate (Kincheloe, Steinberg, & Villaverde, 1999).

We realize that this introduction to our postmodern philosophy may be difficult; remember that new ideas are often both challenging and challenged by traditionalists. Think of great musicians, sports figures, scientists, religious leaders and inventors whose creative work was ridiculed or rejected because it challenged long-held beliefs and practices. Just as Copernicus and Galileo provided a new perspective on the position of the Earth in the universe more than five hundred years ago, twentieth-century space exploration and photographs of the Earth from space have provided a stunning perspective of the relation of human life to the cosmos. The Italian religious and political leaders who silenced and excommunicated Galileo did not stop the emergence of the modern cosmology, so why should we expect negative reactions to silence the emerging postmodern worldview? Even though these introductory ideas may seem complex, refusing to engage in the postmodern dialogue on the issues outlined above, as well as a stubborn entrenchment in the limited tenets of a modern worldview, are futile attempts to silence new concepts that have already emerged at the beginning of the third millennium. We hope you will join us in the process of investigating and understanding our postmodern world—and critically evaluating potential problems with postmodern philosophy as well—as we journey through the foundations of education in this book.

Part 1

Philosophical Context

Asking Questions about Purpose

A Conversation about Educational Philosophy

INTRODUCTION

Sooner or later all teachers study the philosophy of education. They often dread their philosophy courses. You may even wonder yourself how such ancient ideas could possibly relate to your life today and to your goal of becoming a teacher. Professors sometimes present the philosophy of education as a sacred vault of immutable ideas and relics from the golden ages of human thought. These timeless truths and values are seen as latent in the mind, waiting to be brought to consciousness by studying objects in the natural world and applying the scientific method of collecting data and building formulas. Perennial truths and values thought to lie beyond reproach like stones too often become inert ideas or scientific facts to be categorized and memorized. Too rarely do we think of them as tentative discourses to be challenged and reformulated in each new era and each new context. Moreover, we tend either to enshrine individual thinkers and writers who articulate perennial philosophies as icons of humanity or to castigate them as subversive destroyers of the truth—depending, of course, on our political and religious preferences and prejudices.

We begin this study of the philosophy of education with a different premise: Philosophy is an emergent and autobiographical love of wisdom and understanding constantly in need of reflection and revision. Thus, your own philosophy of education is constantly evolving, and you can—you must—develop it in a community context rather than feel it imposed uniformly on you by a school district, professor or textbook. By all means, keep a daily journal and take notes about your philosophy of education as you read this chapter and share these ideas with your classmates, professors, family and friends. Compare and contrast your philosophy with the ideas contemporary and historical writers, thinkers, politicians, theologians and ordinary citizens lend you. Recognize yourself as both a consumer of ideas and a creator of a philosophy of education, as well as a participant in the ongoing construction of knowledge and wisdom. Our schools and society desperately need citizens willing to attempt an understanding of the major issues that confront us at the dawn of the twenty-first century and then contribute economic, environmental, social and psychological solutions to these difficult problems. Understanding and contributing are crucial steps in becoming a reflective—and successful—teacher, coach, director and mentor. In fact, a reflective educator who contextualizes teaching and engages in the philosophic dialogue expresses the voice of compassion, justice and prophecy in the dysfunction of modern society.

ARTICULATING YOUR PHILOSOPHY

Inspiring teachers continually articulate, evaluate and revise their philosophies of teaching and learning as they relate to their particular situation. These teachers devote a lot of thought to the meaning and purpose of what they do with students in their classrooms and the ways they express their creative energies. They constantly search for books, people, art, stories, literature, music, metaphors and cultural artifacts to help them convey the principles that inspire and guide their work. The best teachers have many interests and hobbies; they read journals and newspapers, write prose and poetry, attend plays and concerts, travel, organize community events, support social causes, meditate and dream, volunteer in churches, lead youth athletics and cultural programs, visit museums, exercise and play sports, sing and play musical instruments, protect the environment, care for senior citizens and young children, nurture friendships, attend lectures, paint, plant, dance, carve, take photographs and much more.

Unfortunately, these teachers are the exceptions; many more remain inactive and uninspired. They ignore philosophical reflection. They lack the passion and courage for intellectual expansion. They have been conditioned either to avoid questions or to resist exploring their inner motivations. Philosophical reflection challenges this modern malaise and affirms the importance of community solidarity, lifelong learning, autobiographical excavation and social activism. It also puts us in touch with our context, our "selves," other human beings and the natural world.

As teachers engage in the philosophic process and share their ideas with their students, opportunities for further reflection and insights increase and understanding improves. As evidence of this process, we provide four examples of philosophic statements below. Practicing teachers composed the first two statements, an undergraduate education major the third, and a public school board member the fourth. But rather than simply imitating these statements as you develop your own philosophy of education, read them instead for inspiration and as examples of the autobiographical nature of the philosophic process we have described.

Philosophy Statement One

An artist and art educator wrote the first statement. She explains her approach to drawing, as well as to her art itself. Those who read this statement and see her art generally understand the philosophy that guides her approach to art, education and life. As you read her statement, imagine yourself a student in her art class or a visitor to a gallery showing her work. What impact does this statement have on you?

> *I believe in beauty. Awe, mystery, reverence and ancient memory are all aspects of my working attitudes. I understand that an important attribute of any art is humility.*
>
> *I believe in direct experience. Drawing is the most immediate and unmediated link between eye, heart, hand and surface.*
>
> *I believe in dichotomy and paradox. I choose to work solely in black and white. This apparently limited palette contains a range that is vastly complex and layered that endlessly reveals itself. A Chinese saying expresses it best: "Knowing the white, keep the black, and illumination of spirit will come of itself."*
>
> *I choose to work on paper. Its inherent sensuousness holds a strength and power matched by its fragility. It is skin.*
>
> *I believe in paying attention. I work in cycles and series, relentlessly scrutinizing a shape or pattern from numerous perspectives, both literal and metaphorical. This requires an open listening as the work often directs a particular direction or passage. My task is to respond appropriately to the readiness of time.*
>
> *I believe in claiming space. Often, the physical parameters of my work are the scale of my body—stretching as high and as wide as I can. A teacher once told me to walk as if my head held up the sky and my feet held down the earth. My work comes from the place in between.*
>
> *I believe in life. Seed pods and eggs are recurrent shapes in my work. They open, disclose, enfold, again and again. Movement, energy and time are liberated and become one.*
>
> *My work explores experiencing time as a spiral rather than a linear progression. A seemingly new and unexplored event is actually one of long standing. Infused with new information, insight and awareness, my work accesses memory; it does not record it. (Barbara Bernstein, 1994)*

Can you sense the autobiographical nature of this philosophical statement about art and aesthetics? Can you sense that this artist brings both her knowledge of art and her entire life experiences to the construction of her philosophy? No other teacher could write this statement, and no classroom could replicate the uniqueness of this teacher's approach to the aesthetic experience. While her philosophy can inform and inspire us, her context cannot. It is unique, and we could hardly impose it on another classroom setting. Every philosophy is a dynamic and organic understanding of life, wisdom and knowledge constructed within its own context.

Philosophy Statement Two

The second example of a teacher's philosophy of education reflects the vision of a high school social studies department chairperson. Again, as you read the statement, imagine yourself a student in this teacher's history classroom or an educator reflecting on this philosophy in your own classroom, studio, gymnasium, stage or laboratory.

> *I didn't become a history teacher because I thought it important; I became a history teacher because there's nothing more fun than history. I was preventing a confrontation with my great fear in life—boredom—by casting my lot with the story of humankind. . . . There is no better story than history. The cast of characters in the human race gives us plenty of sex, violence, and knavery, with occasional acts of genius and nobility that propel the race forward in spite of itself. In fiction, who could come up with people as intrinsically good as Jesus, Mohammed and the Buddha? Who do we find today as noble as Socrates, Abraham Lincoln, Chief Joseph, Clara Barton or Frederick Douglass? Who has the complexities of nature of a King David or Thomas Jefferson? How can we contemplate through the imagination the horrors that befell the 14th and 20th centuries. . . . No doubt, history has to include rational analysis to strengthen one's ability to make logical conclusions, create intellectual order out of the material and develop a healthy skepticism. However, history is also the intuitive, the visceral, the imaginative. . . . We can all share in the glory and disasters that are our own. Refusing to share in either risks the loss of our own humanity, for the lens to our individual soul becomes unfocused. Kenneth Clark said that we need to learn from history because it is ourselves. But without a leap of the imagination and a willingness to be part of the collective human race, there is little that history can do for us. I want to experience that true story and to make the ultimate connection with someone in another place and time. If I am not careful, I might in the process learn a little more about who I am. And God forbid, I might have more fun than academia should allow. But don't tell anyone. (Howard G. Hunter, 1994)*

This philosophy statement about teaching history exemplifies the principles of autobiography, complexity, imagination and context so essential to the educational process. The next statement provides another example of such contextualization.

Philosophy Statement Three

An undergraduate student wrote the third example of an autobiographical philosophy statement. Like you, she is studying to become a teacher. This elementary education major wrote her statement at the end of her junior year, after completing a philosophy of education course. As you read her statement, reflect on your own philosophy of education. Do you find any similarities or differences between this student's philosophy and your own?

> *Every child has the potential to learn. It is our job as educators to encourage learning. A child's progression of learning is like a fire. The kindling and the*

spark are already present in natural curiosity. When we feed the fire with intuitive and discovery learning situations such as experiments, field trips, interactions with guest speakers and "real life" experiences, roaring flames of curiosity come to life. However, when we spoon-feed information to students through constant lectures, dry textbook chapters and busy work, the flames of curiosity are doused with an ocean of water. In order to be successful teachers, we must make sure that our students do not drown in boredom and irrelevant paperwork. We must ensure that the curriculum is applicable to each student's environment. The more students can apply a lesson to their lives, the more engaged they will be in learning. Teachers create successful learning environments when they nurture caring communities which focus on student interests and experiences. (Sara L. Goodman, 1996)

Philosophy Statement Four

The fourth and final philosophy statement was written by a school board member, a white woman in a racially diverse urban district, the home of Lorain High School (near Cleveland) from which African American author Toni Morrison graduated (in fact, it was in her high school English class that Morrison began a draft of what would become *The Bluest Eye*). This philosophy statement was written as the board was attempting to come to terms with issues related to inadequate funding for schools, the recent closing of an automobile plant in the community, racial diversity in the district and pressure to raise scores on the state proficiency tests. All of these issues were framed in the following statement about diversity.

Embracing diversity may be the key to educational development in the postmodern world. To embrace diversity is to promote unbiased education through a broader base of understanding of human, institutional and group behavior, relationships and interactions; to understand history without the ethnocentric focus of white western culture; to examine learning and teaching as a culturally impacted phenomenon that needs to accommodate multiple styles and perspectives; to open our lives to sights, sounds and ideas that have never crossed our paths; and, very important, to bring people into our lives who lived and learned somewhere outside of our majority American culture.

Such an education is not only crucial to our children's chance for peace and freedom, but is, moreover, a joy and a privilege to experience. The goal of education is not the accumulation of a body of information, just as the purpose of life is not the accumulation of possessions. The goal of education is to spark lifetime learning and growth in understanding one's self, others and one's world and the formation of values by which to live. (Ann Mensendiek Jensen, 1998)

These four autobiographical statements articulate the ideologies, beliefs, practices and hopes that guide the work and lives of educators who pursue their careers as artists, historians, preservice education students and school board members. This philosophy then translates into the schooling context, where teachers create situations, spaces and possibilities that reflect their beliefs and values. Every educator should become involved in the creation, evaluation, ongoing revision and articulation of his or her philosophy. We encourage you to begin this process now, for your aspirations and beliefs already shape your life and work. When educators consciously construct an autobiographical philosophy statement they become confident, inspired and energized.

FROM INDIVIDUAL TO COMMUNITY PHILOSOPHIES

Beyond those educators who articulate individual philosophies, throughout history women and men have come together to formulate manifestos reflecting a common creed or worldview. These manifestos can energize communities and inspire action. Sometimes they expand freedom and dignity; at other times they initiate fear and repression. In either case, they reflect the contextual experience that compels their composition. Over time their applications in new historical settings change as they are adjusted, reconstituted and understood in different contexts. Courts, for example, regularly interpret, alter and amend political documents and constitutions. Manifestos, like autobiographical philosophies, are malleable documents. In fact, we ought to examine all written artifacts and philosophies critically and assess their shortcomings and historical contingencies.

Read the list of manifestos that follows. Take some time to visit the library or an Internet site and review a few of these documents in detail, considering the philosophy that informs each statement. Or, as a class, divide the list and investigate all of these manifestos. Can you identify both benefits and tragedies that have visited societies upon the political implementation of these philosophical documents? In Chapters 4 and 5 we reflect more specifically on possible responses to this question, but for now simply note that all of these documents are human constructions designed to affirm particular assumptions about the nature of reality in human societies. Also note that there have been many interpretations and applications of these manifestos—sometimes in conflict with and in contradiction to other interpretations—over time in various cultures and nations. Religious and political schisms, revolutions, constitutional crises and court battles all testify to the complex and volatile nature of interpreting human constructions of reality. All of these manifestos are evaluated and reinterpreted contextually in an ongoing process.

The Magna Carta
The Universal Declaration of Human Rights
The Humanist Manifesto I and II
The Declaration of Independence
The African National Congress Charter
The Bill of Rights
The Communist Manifesto
The Geneva Conventions of the International Red Cross
The Emancipation Proclamation
Declaration of Sentiments and Resolutions
The Monroe Doctrine
The Dadaist Manifesto

The Bauhaus Manifesto
Manifesto of Surrealism
The United Nations Charter
The Tao Te Ching
The Cyborg Manifesto
The SCUM Manifesto
The Greenpeace Declaration
The Bhagavad-Gita
The Hebrew Scriptures
The Talmud
The Hindu Scriptures
The Nicene Creed
The Koran
The Olympic Charter
The Christian Scriptures
The Gnostic Scriptures
The 95 Theses of Martin Luther
The Documents of Vatican II
The Feminine Mystique

These political, aesthetic, social and theological manifestos reflect philosophies that motivate or once motivated groups of people to organize their lives and work around a common theme. Educators sometimes do the same thing by promulgating national reports or scholarly proposals. Groups of scholars, national commissions or panels of certified experts often come together to investigate educational issues. These commissions generally include governors, university presidents, authors, college professors and school administrators. Some commissions even include classroom teachers and parents, and in rare instances students are invited to participate.

We examine the political implications of the composition of boards and commissions in Chapter 8; however, at this point we invite you to reflect on the messages that documents produced by groups like these convey to other educators. Specifically, compare and contrast the following excerpts from recently published collaborative documents appraising American education quite differently.

EDUCATIONAL DECLARATIONS

A Nation at Risk

A Nation at Risk, the 1983 national report on the state of education in America commissioned by the Reagan administration, uses militaristic images to portray the United States under siege by foreign economic powers and international intellectual invaders. The early 1980s brought a resurgence of a conservative philosophy that blamed liberalism, the counterculture of the 1960s, federal government intrusion and a decline in traditional Christian values at home and in the public schools for American economic and social decay. While countercultural educators and critical theorists vociferously challenged the dominance of the neoconservative educational philosophy in the 1980s, this document ushered in a tidal wave of similar proposals over the next decade for reforming schools so that the United States could regain worldwide economic and political dominance. As you read the following excerpt from *A Nation at Risk* consider this cultural and political context in the United States in the 1980s.

> *Our nation is at risk. Our once unchallenged preeminence in commerce, industry, science and technological innovation is being overtaken by competitors throughout the world. . . . We report to the American people that while we can take justifiable pride in what our schools and colleges have historically accomplished and contributed to the United States and the well-being of its people, the educational foundations of our society are presently being eroded by a rising tide of mediocrity that threatens our very future as a Nation and a people. . . . If an unfriendly foreign power had attempted to impose on America the mediocre educational performance that exists today, we might well have viewed it as an act of war. As it stands, we have allowed this to happen to ourselves. We have even squandered the gains in student achievement made in the wake of the Sputnik challenge. . . . We have, in effect, been committing an act of unthinkable, unilateral educational disarmament. (1983, p. 1)*

This excerpt from *A Nation at Risk* contains allusions to the 1950s, a period in American history when the cold war was at its height and schools were called on to rise to the challenge of the Soviet Communist military threat. When the Soviet Union launched the first space orbiter, Sputnik, in 1957, Americans reacted in shock and fear. A call to improve mathematics and science education reverberated throughout political institutions with the hope that a new generation of engineers and scientists could ensure United States domination in the global community. Many educators and scientists grew wealthy developing new math and science books and materials and conducting research funded by generous federal grants. In 1961 newly elected President John F. Kennedy issued his famous call to American citizens "to land a man on the moon by the end of the decade," a challenge that did not go unheeded. With the end of the cold war, American leaders in the 1990s focused on economic dominance in the world marketplace. *A Nation at Risk* set the tone for many—but certainly not all—of the recent educational reform manifestos. In light of the 1998 global economic crisis, it will be interesting to see how new educational manifestos will approach the issue of economic dominance in the twenty-first century.

In the 1980s and 1990s it was assumed that the superior education systems in Asia produced a workforce and social infrastructure responsible for the continent's economic prosperity. That myth has since been undermined by financial collapse. Fiscal facades have fallen. How can the American prosperity of the 1990s be explained if our education system has been "at risk" since 1983? Such contradictions must be evaluated, and authors David Berliner and Bruce Biddle did just that in their 1996 book *The Manufactured Crisis: Myths, Fraud, and the Attacks on the American Public Schools*. We remind you that *A Nation at Risk*—indeed, every educational document—is not a politically or philosophically neutral manifesto.

America 2000 and *Goals 2000*

In *America 2000* and *Goals 2000*, documents commissioned by Presidents George Bush and Bill Clinton, respectively, and produced by political leaders and bureaucrats in the U.S. Department of Education in 1991 and 1993, we find an emphasis on specific measurable goals that advance the interests of those who wrote the documents. Again they emphasize math and science; the arts and humanities are left out of *America 2000* entirely and are only briefly mentioned in *Goals 2000*. In the spirit of *A Nation at Risk*, competition with foreign countries appears to be a major preoccupation in these documents. Their overall tone reflects a need to produce better educational outcomes, largely through measurable standards that are assessed on voluntary national exams and mandated state proficiency tests. Resources and funding for the ambitious programs go unmentioned, except that the goals are called a "strategy" and not a "federal program." Thus the documents advance a philosophy that "honors local control, relies on local initiative, affirms states and localities as the senior partners in paying for education" (*America 2000*, p. 5).

The manifesto goals in 1991 called for the following: all children enter school ready to learn; increase the high school graduation rate to 90 percent; make students demonstrate competence in English, math, science, history and geography in grades four, eight and twelve so that they will be responsible and productive citizens; make students first in the world in science and mathematics; expand literacy to all adults so that they can compete in a global economy and exercise their citizenship; and, finally, create drug-free and safe school environments. In 1993 two additional goals for arts education and parental involvement in schooling were added. Consider these national goals as you reflect on the words and tone of *America 2000*:

> *We will unleash America's creative genius to invent and establish a new Generation of American Schools, one by one, community by community. These will be the best schools in the world—schools that enable their students to reach the national Educational goals, achieve a quantum leap in learning, and help make America all that it should be. . . . [This strategy] enlists communities—aided by the best research and development the nation is capable of—to devise their own plans to break the mold and create one-of-a-kind high-performance schools. It relies on clear, rigorous measures of success. These World Class Standards—for each of the five core subjects—will represent what Americans need to know and be able to do if they are to live and work successfully in today's world. These standards will incorporate both knowledge and skills to ensure that, when they leave school, young Americans are prepared for further study and the work force. (pp. 13–19)*

Do you see here a reiteration of the philosophy of *A Nation at Risk*? Does the manifesto emphasize the core subjects of math, science, reading, English and social studies? Is the creation of standards and testing tied to preparation for higher education, the work force, compliant citizenship, core knowledge and basic skills? Are there glaring omissions in the core subjects and basic skills advanced by this document? We think so. You should read the entire *America 2000* and *Goals 2000* statements and judge for yourself. What was the context of American politics in the 1990s that influenced these educational manifestos, and why have so many educators and citizens accepted the philosophical premise of these documents without question?

Education 2000: A Holistic Perspective

Another philosophy permeates *Education 2000,* a manifesto composed by teachers and university scholars in Vermont. This statement emphasizes entirely different values. In contrast to *America 2000,* it recommends cooperation rather than competition with other countries, sustainable resource use rather than consumption and direct and authentic human interaction rather than bureaucratic arrangements. *Education 2000* is concerned with ecological issues, human growth and cooperative learning environments. The authors contend that the dominant cultural values of consumption, planned obsolescence, consumerism and competition have been destructive of both the health of the ecosystem and human development. As you read the following excerpt, consider this philosophical tone.

> *[Our] purpose is to proclaim an alternative vision of education, one which is a life affirming and democratic response to the challenges of the 1990s and beyond. We value diversity and encourage a wide variety of methods, applications and practices. (Global Alliance, 1991, p. 1)*

Manifestos such as *Education 2000* challenge traditional notions of education that emphasize standards, reason, math, science and measurable outcomes in favor of holistic practices that include spirituality, aesthetics, ecology and critical analysis.

Center for a Postmodern World

Another recent document that promotes holistic practices is the Manifesto of Beliefs, Purposes and Programs produced by the Center for a Postmodern World (1990) in Claremont, California. Humanity must transcend modernity, according to the Center, in ways that include the following:

> *A post-anthropocentric view of living in harmony with nature rather than a separateness from nature that leads to control and exploitation; a post-competitive sense of relationships as cooperative rather than as coercive and individualistic; a post-militaristic belief that conflict can be resolved by the development of the art of peaceful negotiation; a post-patriarchal vision of society in which the age-old religious, social, political and economic subordination of women will be replaced by a social order based on the "feminine" and the "masculine" equally; a post-Eurocentric view that the values and practices of the European tradition will no longer be assumed to be superior to those of other traditions nor forcibly imposed upon others combined with a respect for the wisdom imbedded in all cultures; a post-scientistic belief that while the natural sciences possess one important method of scientific investigation, there are also moral, religious and aesthetic intuitions that contain important truths that must be given a central role in the develop-*

ment of worldviews and public policy; a post-disciplinary concept of research and scholarship with an ecologically interdependent view of the cosmos rather than the mechanistic perspective of a modern engineer controlling the universe; and finally, a post-nationalistic view in which the individualism of nationalism is transcended and replaced by a planetary consciousness that is concerned about the welfare of the earth first and foremost. (1990, p. 1)

The Center for a Postmodern World regards the cosmos as an organism rather than a machine, Earth as a home rather than a functional possession and individuals as interdependent rather than isolated and independent. This introduction to some of the concepts of the manifesto reveals the dramatic paradigmatic shift in thinking that is required to introduce these concepts into education. Therefore, it is not surprising to us that there has been intense resistance to postmodernism. We will discuss postmodern philosophy in more detail in Chapters 2 and 13.

The Paideia Proposal: An Educational Manifesto

The Paideia Proposal was written by twenty-one educational administrators, researchers, and senior lecturers from throughout the nation. Its chairperson was Mortimer Adler (1982), at the time director of philosophical research at the University of Chicago and chair of the board of editors of *Encyclopedia Britannica*. Adler dedicated the proposal to three American educational leaders of the nineteenth and early twentieth centuries: Horace Mann, first superintendent of public instruction in Massachusetts and founder of the "common school" movement in the United States, who actively promoted the Jeffersonian link between democracy and education; John Dewey, philosopher of pragmatism and founder of the first laboratory school at the University of Chicago in 1896, who believed schools must create communities of learners with an emphasis on experience, scientific methods of investigation and democracy in the learning environment; and Robert Hutchins, president of the University of Chicago and in 1936 author of *The Higher Learning in America*, who sought to revive the humanistic ideal of liberal education with an emphasis on a great books curriculum. Mann, Dewey and Hutchins are the thinkers on whose ideas the Paideia Group built its philosophy of the humanities for many students. Following is a synopsis of group's philosophy:

> *We are on the verge of a new era in our national life. The long-needed educational reform for which this country is at last ready will be a turning point toward that new era. [We believe that] there are not unteachable children. There are only schools and teachers and parents who fail to teach them. . . . You ask: What should we do next Monday morning to get started on the Paideia reform of basic schooling? We answer: 1. Be sure that in every school—from grade one to grade twelve—there are three kinds of learning and three kinds of teaching [acquisition of organized knowledge; development of intellectual skills of learning; enlarged understanding of ideas and values]. 2. In all three . . . set standards of accomplishment that challenge both students and teachers to fulfill the high expectations you have for them. 3. Eliminate all nonessentials from the school day . . . or make them extracurriculars. 4. Eliminate from the curriculum all training*

for specific jobs. 5. Study a second language for a sufficient period of time to as-sure competence in its use. 6. Eliminate all electives . . . except the choice of a sec-ond language. 7. Use as much as possible of the school day's time for learning and teaching. 8. Restore homework and home projects in the arts and sciences. . . . 9. Devise appropriate ways of ensuring adequate preschool preparation for those who need it. 10. Institute remedial instruction for those who need it, either indi-vidually or in small groups. (Adler, 1982, pp. 3, 8, 81–82)

The program proposed by the Paideia Group reflects a commitment to a liberal arts education for many American children in a challenging academic en-vironment. We encourage you to read the document and consider the broader implications of the specific details of *The Paideia Proposal.* As you read, con-sider the cultural, ethnic and gender implications of the materials included in the project.

REFORM REPORTS AND PROPOSALS

Educators constantly confront new reports, proposals and manifestos designed to ameliorate perceived problems with schooling and educational institutions. Each reflects a particular philosophical perspective, and because they may be couched in straightforward and commonsense ideas, inflammatory rhetoric, emotionally charged attacks, pseudoreligious language or glitzy media sensationalism, people often overlook or accept unreflectively their philosophical foundations. Because the educational manifestos and reports that affect schools and teachers all espouse unique philosophies, educators should become acquainted with the more tradi-tional philosophies that informed those administrators, scholars, politicians, au-thors, religious leaders and community activists who go on to promulgate ideo-logical documents. We now briefly consider some of the traditional ways that philosophy of education has been studied, presenting this review so you can evalu-ate critically how traditional philosophies have influenced educational reforms, curriculum proposals, political manifestos and religious dogmas like those intro-duced above. We hope this brief introduction stimulates you to investigate these topics further and helps you critically analyze your own emerging philosophy of education.

TRADITIONAL APPROACHES TO PHILOSOPHY OF EDUCATION

Traditional foundations of education texts divide the study of philosophy into three branches: metaphysics, epistemology and axiology (which examines both aesthetics and ethics). Some texts also include the study of logic or ontology. These appar-ently neat divisions, which we will review shortly, reflect the traditional structure of philosophical study of at least the past five centuries, a structure that directly reflects the proposals of Sir Isaac Newton concerning the rational nature of the physical universe and the quest of European thinkers to achieve enlightened societies. How-ever, if we examine the philosophical dialogues of the ancient Greek philosophers, we find them as interested in the structure of matter and the existence of God as they were in ethics and aesthetics. Thus physics and theology—sometimes called "the queen of the sciences"—also enjoy a long tradition in philosophic dialogue.

The diversity of understandings about the nature of philosophy emphasizes an important consideration about contextualization: traditions vary among communities and over time. In education one can hear a call from some quarters for education to go "back to the basics." One finds a nostalgia for a perceived past that is now threatened or has already been lost. Pertinent to our discussion of the "traditional" understandings of philosophy of education is the question "What tradition?" Should we return to eighteenth-century European Enlightenment traditions, go further back to Greek understandings of physics, astronomy, rhetoric and philosophy, or go even further back to Middle Eastern, African or Asian cosmologies? Better to acknowledge the limitations of the word "traditional" as we introduce you to philosophy. Better to review various philosophical categories in order to move beyond the decontextualized nature of many analytic approaches to the study of philosophy of education. We urge you to be alert to the complexity of such apparently simple slogans as "getting back to basics." A book like *The Way We Never Were* by Stephanie Coontz (1992) documents American family life of the past 150 years and shows that the majority of families did not live like the people on the television shows *Leave It to Beaver* or *Father Knows Best*. Images were created that did not match the reality of the majority. As Joe Spangler reminded us in the introduction, for most people the "good old days" were not really all that good.

The love of wisdom and understanding rarely flourishes in a vacuum; it requires rigorous thinking, extensive reading, ongoing dialogue, critical analysis and intuitive reflection. It requires, as well, sensitivity to the nature of language in the construction of knowledge and meaning and the constraints or manipulations language can impose or effect. Resist if you can a facile acceptance of the rhetoric of any philosophy or manifesto simply because the language seduces with trite phrases, religious metaphors, a reminder of social fears or agreeable political biases. With this caution, we now review traditional approaches to the philosophy of education.

Metaphysics

We introduced three branches of philosophy earlier: metaphysics, epistemology and axiology (ethics and aesthetics). Metaphysics addresses questions of reality. Metaphysicians study the condition of being and existing in the world (ontology), as well as the structure of the universe itself (cosmology). They also investigate the nature of first principles and ultimate forces in the universe to answer the question "What is real?"

Epistemology

Epistemology is the study of knowledge and knowing. It is concerned with finding the truth or the meaning of the idea of the truth. Epistemologists want to understand the answer to the question "What is true?" Is truth the same in every circumstance? Are knowledge and truth preordained by a God or gods or nature? Is knowledge inert or is it constructed? In recent years some scholars have questioned whether any absolute truth that we can know with certainty exists. But these scholars are also asking epistemological questions; they are hardly denying the epistemological approach.

Axiology

Axiology asks the questions "What is good?" (ethics) and "What is beautiful?" (aesthetics). Debates about values are currently running rampant in society. We are concerned about family values, community values, basic values, values education, the value of human life, aesthetic values and the like. Axiologists investigate the nature of the good and the beautiful, trying to ascertain what we should value, whose values are most important, what should be valued as "beautiful" art, what is right and what is wrong. We need only consider the debates about funding for the National Endowment of the Arts; reproductive health services; gays in the military; prayer in the classroom; tracking and segregation in schools; sex lives of politicians; substance control; species and wetland protection; and the censorship of books, museum exhibits, music, movies and Internet sites to understand the influence of ethics and aesthetics in our lives and our classrooms (Slattery & Morris, 1999).

SCHOOLS OF PHILOSOPHY

Understanding the context of education requires thoughtful reflection on philosophical questions about truth, beauty, goodness, justice, knowledge, freedom and responsibility. As a result of this reflection several schools of philosophy have developed over the centuries, continuing their development today. Some of the more familiar categories of philosophies, theories and beliefs include idealism, realism, Thomism, pragmatism, existentialism (and its related philosophy of phenomenology), behaviorism, Marxism, feminism and Eastern philosophies.

Idealism

Idealism proposes a metaphysics that sees the world of ideas of the mind as reality. To exist, something must be perceived by the mind. Reality thus appears in the realm of the spiritual or ideas, or one finds true knowledge (epistemology) by "seeing with the mind's eye" and seeing the consistency of ideas. Ethics should reflect the ideal model of the self, and aesthetics reflects the ideals of perfect beauty set forth by the great masters of the arts. The educational philosophy of perennialism exemplifies the application of idealism in schooling. The curriculum is the subject matter of the mind: literature, intellectual history, philosophy and theology as found in the great or sublime books including Shakespeare's plays, Judeo-Christian scriptures, the works of Homer and the Koran. Students are encouraged to imitate those people who have been enshrined as admirable by past authorities. Lectures, discussions and interpretations of great works dominate the teaching style (Ozmon & Craver, 1999). Perennialism, in short, stresses that which is lasting in the search for ideal truth in the hope that students become philosophers who can articulate such truths and build a great society. Plato even wrote about his goal of the "philosopher king," an intellectual who could guide societies in the highest ideals.

Realism

Realism has much in common with idealism, particularly the belief that truth is unchanging. Realists, however, look outward to the physical world, using their senses to discover and affirm truth. Natural law—a belief that absolute laws of nature exist and should govern human behavior—forms the ethics of realism. Beautiful art, therefore, must replicate nature. The educational philosophy of essentialism (not to be confused with *existentialism*) reflects realism. Essentialism mandates lessons that teach basic factual knowledge in reading, writing and mathematics—the so-called three Rs—and science, history and foreign languages. It emphasizes the scientific method of hypothesis, testing and generalization, but it tends to encourage structured learning environments designed to achieve mastery of basic information and skills. Students must obey, comply with authority and learn the rules of conduct and decorum. Realists promote efficient school structures that advance these goals (Ozmon & Craver, 1999). Scientific realism has been one of the most influential philosophies of the past two hundred years—an influence that we critique in detail in Chapter 2.

Thomism

Thomism (and neo-Thomism) dates back to the Dominican Catholic priest Thomas Aquinas in thirteenth-century France. Aquinas combined his philosophical study of Plato and Aristotle with his religious training to help explain Christian faith and the notion of an immortal soul. His followers expanded Aquinas's philosophy and developed a Thomistic metaphysics that sees the world as the realm of reason and of God. Rational acts determine what is good, and creative intuition about what is reasonable determines what is beautiful. Logical reason and revelation guide people to the truth and to God. Teachers are encouraged to include subject matter of both the intellect and the spirit in the curriculum, and particularly in religious doctrines. Thomists tend to drill students in reason, sometimes relying on a catechism for religion and memorization for other subjects. Disciplining the mind and controlling behavior to conform with natural law are, they contend, the proper goals of education. We will review the religious philosophies that influenced early American education in Chapter 4.

Pragmatism

Pragmatism is a uniquely American philosophy associated with William James and John Dewey, among others, and differs markedly from the first three philosophies in that it emphasizes a need for change and adaptation. Its metaphysics pictures a world of experience in which one must test hypotheses to see what works. Truth is based on this experience; morality is determined by society rather than natural law; and beauty changes according to the public taste.

Two educational philosophies are associated with the philosophy of pragmatism: progressivism and reconstructionism. Progressive educators base their subject matter on social experiences. Thus they highly value a social studies curriculum. They ask students to solve practical problems using groups and projects, and everyone's participation is critical. The reconstructionists take this participation one step further by proposing that education reconstruct society by addressing current events and social problems. Believing that education extends beyond the information in books to include outside involvement in the community, reconstructionists promote social activism for change. Ultimately, reconstructionists and many progressive educators believe that the teacher should guide students in projects and activities that will improve society rather than simply teach lessons that conform to the status quo, which is unjust in so many ways.

Existentialism

Existentialism (with the closely related phenomenology that we discuss in detail in Chapter 9) may be a straightforward theory, but because its practitioners make it sound esoteric, many people think it impossible to understand. In addition, there are many varieties of existentialism—from Christian existentialists who find hope in the examination of the present to nihilists who find that the present world is absurd. There are philosophers including Jean-Paul Sartre and Albert Camus who protest traditional formulations of philosophy—even categories like existentialism itself—and emphasize the tragic, sometimes absurd nature of life; other philosophers including Simone de Beauvior and Maxine Greene emphasize the importance of social action to combat the tragedies of the modern world. Literature and the arts become central to this process of understanding and acting. Existentialists believe that existence precedes essence; phenomenologists believe that immediate subjective understandings of events are the source of reality. In other words, we find truth when we examine our present existence rather than some preconceived notion of the essential characteristics of the world and human beings. Existentialists promote human freedom and the need for people to take responsibility for creating goodness and beauty in the world. Nevertheless, ethics and aesthetics are subjective. Each person exercises his or her freedom of choice to discover the truth.

Because existentialists reject any absolute public norm, existentialism as an educational philosophy promotes alternative approaches to teaching and learning. Students have many choices and electives, especially in art, moral philosophy, literature and other studies that encourage them to become inner directed. Students should discover for themselves the best methods for learning, and ultimately develop personal responses. Following the Greek philosopher Socrates, who taught in the marketplace by gathering students around him for discussion in a dialectic process of investigation that often challenged traditional assumptions, students are encouraged to enter dialogue and to ask probing questions.

Marxism

Like existentialism, Marxism is a difficult philosophical position to describe briefly because there are so many "Marxisms" with conflicting interpretations. Often in Western societies the mere mention of the name Karl Marx evokes intense negative reaction and precludes productive discussion of Marxist educational philosophies. Marxist analysis is not equivalent to describing the social and political system of China or the former Soviet Union; it involves primarily the protest against the bourgeois—having to do with the conventional, selfish, materialistic capitalist class—society produced with the advent of industrialization. In this context Marx argued that social and political phenomena have their genesis in the material (economic) aspects of everyday life. His notion of dialectic materialism asserted that institutions must be studied in their historical contexts to trace the ways that economic production has shaped them. This material base determines the class structure of a society, which, in turn, affects all aspects of everyday life, especially the division of classes into those who own the factories and businesses (the means of production) and those who have only their labor to offer (the workers). When workers become politically conscious of their exploitation they will transform into revolutionaries who will work to change the unfair socioeconomic reality. Schooling and education within the class-divided society, Marx argued, is a farce because schools only serve to further the interests of the dominant class. Pedagogical activity in such a climate is an act of terror against the workers and their children, he reasoned. Once the revolution succeeded, then schooling could begin to raise consciousness and serve the needs of the working class. Such schools, as envisioned by Marx, would combine productive labor with academic learning and physical education for the purpose of producing well-rounded and fully developed human beings.

Behaviorism

Behaviorists believe that behavior is fundamental to understanding mental phenomenan, and thus behaviorism might best be described as a psychological theory rather than a philosophy. Behaviorism has had a tremendous impact on both psychology and philosophy. Scientific behaviorism is associated with J. B. Watson and B. F. Skinner, who searched for independent variables (stimuli) of which behavior (reactions) were a function. Thus, environmental conditions play an important—some behaviorists would say exclusive—role in determining mental activities and physical responses. Schools can teach students by reinforcing positive stimuli and modify student behavior by withholding the reinforcing stimuli. To demonstrate how all human behavior—including cognition and intelligence—can be shaped by the process of selective reinforcement and extinction of responses by prolonged disassociation from an old stimuli was the ultimate goal of behaviorism. We introduce scientific behaviorism here because it exerted such an immense influence on educational theories, testing and assessment practices, classroom management and organizational practices in schools in the twentieth century. However, by the end of the century cognitive theories and constructivism had replaced theories of behaviorism as the dominant ways of thinking about teaching and learning. Behaviorism is much more complex than this brief introduction—including philosophical behaviorism, which explores the meaning of mental expression. We will return to behaviorism and constructivism throughout the book, especially when we look at the social construction of reality and constructivist views of teaching and learning in Chapter 2 and behaviorist-technologist models of teacher education in Chapter 3.

Feminism

Feminists challenge traditional philosophies because they fail to examine seriously women's interests, issues and identities and because they fail to recognize women's ways of being, knowing and acting (Belenky, Clinchy, Goldberger, & Tarule, 1986; Gilligan, 1982; Miller, 1990; Doll, 1995). For example, the eighteenth-century French philosopher Jean-Jacques Rousseau (1712–1778) wrote a book about the education of young men, *Emile* (Rousseau, 1979), in which males are to be allowed to guide their own education so that they will grow to be free, responsible and loving adults but Emile's female counterpart, Sophie, must please men, rear her young, and live a life that is "pleasant and charming at all times" (cited in Okin, 1979, p. 136). Noddings explains that "Rousseau recommended an education for boys that would, so far as possible, preserve their natural freedom and goodness and, at the same time, make them into solid, independent citizens. For girls, Rousseau recommended an education for chastity, docility and subservience. You can see how this fits an essentialist theory. If women are, by nature, intellectually inferior and dependent on men, then their education should be designed to help them make the most of their nonintellectual gifts" (1995, p. 181).

Following the lead of early feminist Mary Wollstonecraft and twentieth-century philosopher Simone de Beauvoir in her important book *The Second Sex,* many feminists argue against essentialism—the belief that women are essentially and naturally docile, subservient, vain, frivolous and less intelligent than men. Wollstonecraft argued that education and socialization had made women dependent and docile, but that, given the chance, women could prove themselves just as morally and intellectually capable as men (see Noddings, 1995, pp. 182–183).

An important concept that feminist philosophers articulate—and one that permeates this book—is a critique of the traditional metaphysics of dualism (dividing reality into separate parts). We join feminist philosophers in faulting traditional metaphysics for splitting the self from the other, the mind from the body and personal identity into separate categories of memories and physical characteristics. This is especially damaging when "masculinity" is identified with rationality and "femininity" with emotionality, and women are then assumed to be less human and less intelligent than men. Feminists would prefer to stress the ways that all people possess rationality and emotionality. They also believe that individuals penetrate each other's lives through empathy, with the mind and body working together in harmony. As we will see in Chapter 2, feminist philosophers join postmodernists in the critique of the assumed objectivity of positivist science. While some feminists prefer to emphasize the problems associated with gender stereotyping and bias, others focus on the subjugation and oppression of women and the ways in which social forces shape women's consciousness. In Chapter 9 we will review various forms of feminist research, and in Chapter 11 we will examine the interrelationship among race, class and gender in schools and in the larger society.

Eastern Philosophies

Some have assumed—either overtly or by omission—that philosophy is limited to the contributions of European and North American thinkers. Such an ethnocentric attitude contributes to the narrow-minded bigotry that divides peoples and fosters oppression and violence. It is true, as we have seen, that Western philosophy—with roots in ancient Greece—dramatically shapes the worldview of Western societies in Europe and North America. However, it is important to note that Eastern philosophies have also influenced Western social, political and religious ideas—and vice versa. For example, there is growing interest in yoga, New Age spirituality and Buddhism in the West, and growing interest in naturalism, postmodernism, progressivism and the philosophy of John Dewey in the East. We should remember that Judaism, Christianity and Islam all have their origins in Eastern cultural settings. Abraham and Sarah migrated with their family from the Tigris and Euphrates valley to a new home in present-day Israel. Many scholars and theologians remind us that it is impossible to understand the Judeo-Christian and Muslim religious traditions outside of Eastern cultural and geographical roots. We must study Eastern philosophy as seriously as we study Western philosophy. Of course, we make a huge assumption here that modern students and citizens study any philosophy at all!

One important dimension of the Eastern philosophical tradition is the emphasis not only on knowing but also on teaching others. Buddha, Confucius, Jesus and Mohammed were all teachers. The Sumarian goddess Inanna, the Hindu goddess Saraswathi and the Vedic goddess Maya-Shakti-Devi all inspire teaching and learning. Inanna is a goddess who undergoes death and resurrection and teaches ways of being that necessitate sacrifice, humility and reunification. Saraswathi is the goddess of wisdom who is always shown with a book in one of her hands; Hindu children are taught to pray to her for the gift of education and success in school (Viruru, 1998). Devi (the Indian word for *woman*) is the teacher of the Vedic gods themselves concerning the ultimate ground and source of their own powers and being (Campbell, 1988). Since these prophets, teachers, gods and goddesses from Eastern cultures inspire the religious and social mythology of many cultures, maybe you, as a teacher, will be inspired to examine Eastern philosophy more closely. We encourage you to do so.

Many prominent Eastern philosophies can be traced to China, Japan, India and the Middle East. While each of these cultures contributes unique perspectives, it is common in Eastern philosophy to focus on the inner life rather than an outer experience. In fact, philosophy in the Eastern tradition is more a way of life rather than a subject to be studied. Intuition, inner peace, tranquility, attitudinal development and, in some cases, mysticism are all emphasized—with religion and philosophy more intimately intertwined than in Western philosophy. For example,

Taoism (which means *way* or *path*) is an influential Chinese philosophy that reflects on the movement of the universe and the way of harmony. In the fifth century B.C.E.—the same era as Socrates, Aristotle, Plato and the pinnacle of Greek philosophy—Lao-Tzu set down such teachings in the *Tao Te Ching,* which guides individuals in the development of their inner life so they can meet the challenge of any difficulty in life. Many New Age spirituality movements teach that the ebb and flow of the universe should inspire us to seek a rhythm and balance in our lives. This sense of harmony is found in the popular belief in the yin and yang of all life experiences, where opposites exist in balance with each other.

PHILOSOPHIES IN CONTEXT

We could review many other philosophies and theories, and we could examine the preceding nine in much greater detail. But we wanted to present only a brief introduction at this time and encourage you to explore these theories in relation to your own developing philosophy. As mentioned in the introduction, we call our philosophy critical constructive postmodernism, a position that will be described in detail throughout this book. While we find some merit in each of the philosophies above, we do not subscribe to any one exclusively. In fact, we critique each of these philosophies for its shortcomings. For example, Western, masculine and white worldviews tend to dominate most traditional philosophical discussions. While we include voices of Eastern, female and diverse ethnic thinkers here and throughout this book, we are aware that we can never do enough to redress the overwhelming cultural bias of the dominant patriarchal, Eurocentric philosophical perspectives. However, we are also positively influenced by some elements of each of the traditional philosophies. We encourage you to look carefully at all philosophies for strengths and shortcomings.

The philosophies reviewed above mean little outside the context of an individual's learning process. It is important that you reflect on philosophy in the context of your life as a student, spouse or lover, musician, church parishioner, worker, family member, ethnic community member, athlete, sorority, fraternity or club member, volunteer and so forth. Recognize also that you have emerging, shifting and conflicting cultural, political, occupational, social, gendered, sexual, racial and religious identities. We are all complex and interesting people. Once you begin to reflect within your own context, you will find reading more about these philosophies helpful and meaningful. Like the existentialists, you must subjectively determine which philosophies inform your life and career. One never masters philosophy; it is a lifelong journey of coming to understand one's self, one's relationships and one's world.

Textbooks and professors too often present traditional philosophy of education in a way students find inaccessible. While we presented our summaries in short, clear sentences, the specialized language and dense jargon of many philosophical discourses often seem difficult and obtuse, lacking in passion and praxis, incompatible with both reflection and action beyond their verbalizing. They seem to discourage *phronesis,* a personal practical knowledge that fosters social competence, and *sophia,* a depth of understanding and insight that fosters wisdom. In addition, the pedagogical styles and methodologies of philosophy professors can be pompous, contrived and impersonal. As a result, education students sometimes conclude that philosophy is removed from both their lived experience and their classroom practice. But philosophy is still too relevant to be banished by the pompous and opaque. We must reestablish its context.

School districts often promulgate philosophies and mission statements their teachers, parents, students and personnel find irrelevant or inadequate to meet the needs of their school context. Committees sometimes revise the school district philosophies, only to discover that the actual classroom concerns and problems have gone unstated and unaddressed. As a result, many educational philosophies, like seasonal decorations or ornaments, collect dust until the administrators take them off the shelf in time for accreditation or evaluation. Somehow a dusty philosophy statement magically justifies the existence and value of a school's or a district's educational programs. One day you may be asked to participate in a school philosophy committee. What contributions could you make to this process? What is the purpose of writing a philosophy or a mission statement for a district or school? As you proceed through this chapter, consider how you might serve as an agent of change in this process.

PHILOSOPHY MISUSED OR MISUNDERSTOOD

Many disturbing, even horrifying practices have been justified in the name of philosophy and ideology. We need only explore the education systems in Hitler's Germany, Stalin's Russia, and Mao's China to find obvious examples (Pinar, Reynolds, Slattery, & Taubman, 1995). Philosophy and ideology have also encouraged abuses in American education as well: segregation and tracking (Fine, 1998; Oakes, 1985); racism (Stannard, 1992; Castenell & Pinar, 1993); corporate manipulation (Shea, Kahane, & Sola, 1989; Spring, 1990); gender research bias (Gilligan, 1982); patriarchal structures (Lerner, 1986; Pagano, 1990; Grumet, 1988b); savage economic inequalities and injustices (Kozol, 1991); religious proselytizing (Provenzo, 1990); social control (Franklin, 1986, 1988); and political conflict of interest and indoctrination (Apple, 1979; Giroux & McLaren, 1989, 1997; Spring, 1993). You can begin to see philosophy of education as far more powerfully influential than just a neutral bystander in schooling debates and cultural controversies. Should philosophy statements address controversial issues like the ones we just listed? We think they should address our sociocultural context. The fact that we rarely even discuss these issues, much less include them in an educational philosophy statement, is a lamentable situation.

An additional problem with traditional philosophy statements is that philosophy is often regarded as an academic distraction in programs preparing future teachers and researchers in the social sciences. As Elliot Eisner observed, "Philosophy is nagging, it cajoles students into asking questions about basic assumptions, it generates doubts and uncertainties, and, it is said, it keeps people from getting their work done" (1991, p. 4). Eisner suggested that the central concepts in the social sciences are themselves philosophical in nature: testing, validity, truth, fact, theory, assessment, objectivity, structure. As we saw earlier, these are not just practical problems in need of solutions; they are also metaphysical, epistemological and axiological questions. Education in contemporary society incorporates the scholarship of many disciplines to address Eisner's concerns and to revive investigation into the vital issues of the meaning of human life, knowledge, schooling, justice, democracy, compassion and ecology.

THE CLIMATE FOR PHILOSOPHICAL REFLECTION IN EDUCATION

The contentious climate surrounding philosophical reflection in schooling relates directly to the broader social discontent; political polarization; global economic upheaval; declining availability of material resources; and debates about multiculturalism, traditional values and fundamentalist religious precepts. Educators too often ignore these strong "external" factors, instead focusing exclusively on academic programs, instructional materials, innovative technology, sociological data, measurable outcomes and disciplinary structures. But we must understand the pivotal role of the philosophy behind political, cultural and religious resistance and pressure in schooling if we want to improve education. While social and political discontent have always accompanied educational reform—from the common school debates of the 1840s (Newman, 1997) through the progressive education programs of the early twentieth century (Spring, 1994) to the social reconstruction proposals of the 1930s (Kliebard, 1986) and the post-Sputnik curricular programs of the late 1950s (Schubert, 1986)—these influences in the current educational climate complicate and even defeat reflection and understanding. Let us examine some of the reasons for this phenomenon.

Media Influences

The media provides instant if superficial reports of schooling practices, often reducing complex issues to thirty-second sound bites and judging broad instructional strategies on isolated applications (or misapplications) in a single setting. Sensationalism always competes with thoughtful introspection and dialogue. Generalizations always provide simple solutions for complex problems. Consider, for example, the massacre in Littleton, Colorado in 1999. As with all other tragic events on school campuses in recent years, "experts" were immediately interviewed on television for analysis. Without any contextual reflection, these experts made absolute judgments about the relationships of the students; the cultural climate of the community; the influence of guns, television, religion and video games, the marital status of the gunman's parents; the economic condition of the school district; and the like. All of this is done without any knowledge of the community or the individuals involved. Speculation and empty rhetoric replace dialogue and introspection. Contextual reflection suffers in such a climate.

Inflammatory Rhetoric

Philosophical and theological reflection too often yield to inflammatory rhetoric and apocalyptic threats that force more timid educators out of the public discourse. As a result, trivial jargon replaces reasoned and prophetic speech. In an editorial the *New York Times* characterized this phenomenon as "rhetorical tiptoeing" (Honan, 1994). Discussing college presidents, William Honan wrote:

> *A generation ago, James B. Conant of Harvard, Clark Kerr of the University of California, Robert M. Hutchins of the University of Chicago and a great many other college and university presidents cut striking figures on the public stage. They called for the reform of American education, proposed safeguards for American democracy, sought to diffuse the Cold War, urged moral standards for scientific research and addressed other important issues of the time. Today almost no university president has spoken out significantly . . . on issues high on the national agenda. (1994, p. E5)*

Honan went on to suggest that the watchwords atop the ivory tower are silence and self-preservation. Administrators want to avoid offending potential donors, boards of trustees, or the local political and religious communities. This self-protective silence and fear pervade our entire society and discourage constructive discussions of social and educational issues. Teachers, too, avoid contention. Controversies in the schools over the curriculum, discipline methods, testing and assessment, historical interpretation, sexuality and AIDS education, race, religion and prayer, values, politics and the like force teachers to shrink from publically discussing the compelling social issues of our times.

Those who choose to reflectively address difficult social, economic, religious, historical and political issues—in short, the foundations of education—may find their job security, promotion, popularity and status in the community threatened. However, reflective and prophetic voices of the past serve as an inspiration to such teachers today. We think of Socrates in the fifth century B.C.E., accused of corrupting the youth of Athens because he raised questions about traditional religious beliefs and social practices. His style of questioning in a dialectical method as he walked the streets with his students today is known as the Socratic method. We think of Deitrich Bonhoeffer in Nazi Germany, who spoke out against Hitler from the pulpit of his Lutheran church. He wrote eloquently about the sacrifices of reflective teaching in *The Cost of Discipleship*. Socrates and Bonhoeffer were both executed for their beliefs and teachings. We think of Oscar Romero, the Catholic bishop of El Salvador in the 1980s and Martin Luther King, Jr., the leader of the civil rights movement in the United States in the 1960s, both of whom were outspoken critics of social injustice and both of whom were assassinated. We think of bold women like Rosa Parks, a black American worker who refused to give up her bus seat in an effort to stop racist practices in the south, and Dorothy Day, a white American journalist who often wrote that prophetic teachers must comfort the afflicted and afflict the comfortable. While we could profile many others, our goal is to challenge you to recognize that reflective teachers can make a profound difference in the world. Despite the risks involved, we encourage you to embrace the reflective philosophical stance. While not all of us are destined to affect the world as Socrates or Rosa Parks did, the opportunity to affect change in our local context is tremendous.

Moral and Spiritual Decline

Another striking feature of American society in the 1990s complicates attempts to understand the philosophical foundations of education: cultural amnesia, which leads to moral and spiritual bankruptcy. Personal greed, senseless violence and calculated revenge appear to increase as communities languish for lack of concern and commitment. While it is wise to resist romanticizing the past, democratic ideals and community cohesiveness have been notably strong at various times in various cultures. But many sociologists currently are observing the emergence of a conscienceless individual; scholars on both the political left and right lament the loss of virtues (Noddings, 1984, 1992; Goodlad, Soder & Sirotnik, 1990; Finn, 1991; Bennett, 1994). The human spirit seems to be deadened in what Christopher Lasch (1984) called "the minimal self," Walker Percy (1954, 1971) called "malaise" and David Ray Griffin (1988a) called "disenchantment." In such a climate the schooling process faces a challenge that demands a different kind of response, one that must ultimately incorporate and engage the philosophical, political, socioeconomic and theological contexts of resistance and pressure if it is to exert an impact. This response will require inquiries beyond media sensationalism and the culture of self-protective silence—an engagement with the philosophical dimensions of the moral, cultural, political and spiritual elements of human learning must emerge. If schools hope to help improve society and resist injustice, educators must enter contemporary social debates and move beyond the "transmission of knowledge" model that currently dominates schooling. Rather than isolate pieces of memorized information readily available at the touch of a computer key, students need to navigate the maze of conflicting ideologies and understand the complexity of living in our postmodern society. Students must be able, in short, to look around themselves and contextualize.

POLITICAL AND RELIGIOUS INFLUENCES ON EDUCATION

Our highly charged conservative political-religious atmosphere has polarized communities and terrorized educators. A close association between reactionary political conservatives and fundamentalist religious groups characterizes this atmosphere. A strong antagonism to these alliances and resistance to all theological sensibilities characterize the political left. Local school board campaigns, letters to the editor, church newsletters and national media reports all carry the abundant accusations and threats that result.

Students are becoming more and more aware of this confrontational milieu, a trend we urge you to examine closely as you develop your philosophy of education. Perhaps typical of the current political-religious tension, the following exchange in a newspaper forum begins with one writer lamenting the growing pressure of the religious right to enact laws affecting education:

> *In this land of ours, we take pride in saying that we have freedom of religion. However, when religious organizations get into the business of making laws, I believe it is time to establish the concept that we in America should also have "Freedom from Religion"! Make no mistake, these are dangerous waters. (Ruiz, 1994)*

A response the following week attacked this position and named the educational programs presumably responsible for the antireligion philosophy:

> *While "Religious Right Bigots" are being assailed, the religious left zealots are preaching their religion of immorality, situation ethics, outcomes-based education, sex education without moral values, school based clinics promoting birth control and abortion, euthanasia, child rights, and on and on. They want freedom from religion from the religious right while they claim a constitutional right to spout their religion. Make no mistake, these are dangerous waters! (Martin, 1994)*

These two letters fairly represent the daily barrage of opinions in which religion, political ideology, school curricula, social programs and school change get lumped together in a stew of attacks and counterattacks filled with ad hominem arguments directed at the person rather than the issue, as well as broad generalizations and apocalyptic warnings based on narrow interpretations of single passages from religious texts or political manifestos often taken out of context. As many critical educational theorists have observed, merely sorting out the arguments and clarifying the rhetoric has become a monumental task (Taxel, 1993).

Educators who ignore this political-religious debate—whether out of naivete or neglect—invite the conflict and community paralysis to intensify (Marzano, 1993). Those who propose school reform, curricular change and innovative practices must expect political, cultural and religious interest groups to attempt to attack those programs they oppose and promote the changes they favor, often from a reactionary position within a narrow ideological perspective. Make no mistake, educational wars are raging: a holy war on the right to save the soul of a supposedly Judeo-Christian nation now wallowing in a quagmire of sin and idolatry, and an ideological battle on the left to preserve all the personal freedom and each democratic right of every individual citizen in a supposedly intransigent political environment.

Innovative school reform and progressive curricular change in that climate can be difficult, as anyone ever caught in the middle of such a battle will affirm (Marzano, 1993). Many teachers and administrators reluctantly or inadvertently drawn into these wars find themselves exhausted and demoralized. Some have changed professions; others have lost their jobs. Many other battle-weary educators are left wary of the school change process. We need a ceasefire with mediation and a new philosophical vision before an entire generation of teachers retreats into the security of mediocrity and anonymity, thus reducing schooling to the most mundane instructional practices using the least controversial textbooks. Preservice education students are wise to understand this situation early. Any discussion of the social foundations of education must take this context as the starting point for understanding philosophy, and then such other areas as sociology, history, anthropology and the curriculum.

Professional educators generally do not desire mediocrity, but self-preservation often compels superintendents, teachers and administrators to avoid controversial programs and practices, even if they consider these changes beneficial. Reform efforts go for naught if teachers misunderstand, underestimate or ignore the political, cultural and religious forces that generate mediocrity and thrive on fear.

RESPONDING TO POLITICAL AND RELIGIOUS PRESSURES

Do we mean that all educators, students, parents and board members must become engaged in philosophical, political, sociological and theological studies? Yes, absolutely! Legislators, officials in state departments of education, school administrators, consultants, publishers, school boards and supervisors can no longer simply promulgate mandates in politically isolated, value-neutral, culturally hegemonic, theologically censored cocoons. The practice of delegating a school's social foundations and curricular reforms to "certified experts" without any contextual community participation and ignoring the interests of all those involved in the educational system is problematic and counterproductive. Past approaches to dealing with these problems include scientific management, behavioral objectives, accountability programs, mastery curriculum plans and similar rational approaches to school change and educational improvement (we discuss these strategies thoroughly in Chapter 2). These approaches, however, are liable to be ineffective in the future, whether we call the contemporary cultural condition postmodern, existential, millennial, secular humanistic, Christian national, nihilistic, fundamental, poststructural or any of the other currently popular names for the sociocultural condition of the early twenty-first century. Each of these adjectives reflects a unique philosophical perspective that can have an impact on teachers. Reading about these philosophies and discussing them can add a useful dimension to your career.

Our language here would probably alarm extremists of any political persuasion. Nonetheless, we contend that the social foundations of education must transcend the fleeting and parochial debates of all extremes. Like John Dewey (1938) in *Experience and Education*, we believe that "either/or" dichotomies are destructive. Educational change can be successful only in an environment that transforms polarized ideologies into an integrated vision respecting multiple interests and philosophies. As Philosopher Alfred North Whitehead wrote, "The harmony of the whole is bound up with the preservation of the individual significance of detail" (1993, p. 264).

Harmony in the schooling process requires a similar vision; respect for and preservation of each unique contribution to the whole education structure leads to an inclusive life-affirming school culture. Dialogue and understanding between those who hold diverse positions remains essential, even though entering this debate and suggesting a way to quell the conflagration can be dangerous. Mediators, visionaries, prophets and arbitrators risk virulent attacks from all sides. Buddha, Elijah, Mohammed, Jesus, Soren Kierkegaard, Mary Mcleod Bethune, Gandhi, Mother Theresa and Martin Luther King, Jr., are just a few examples. We recognize the risk in trying to reconceptualize philosophy in an autobiographical context. While no perfect solution exists, we can imagine a milieu in which innovative, progressive, contextual and ethical schooling practices become possible and then influential. We raise this topic and enter into this debate with you for five compelling reasons: (1) to avert global confrontations, (2) to avoid simplistic approaches to complex problems, (3) to resist closed-minded schooling proposals, (4) to keep from marginalizing students, and (5) to reduce frustration and burnout among teachers.

Global Confrontations

The slaughter, starvation, terrorism and political repression in recent years in Haiti, Somalia, Northern Ireland, Congo, North Korea, Algeria, Rwanda and the former Yugoslavia are hardly aberrations. In 1994, then United Nations Secretary-General Boutros Boutros-Ghali expressed his frustration at the inaction of the world community in Rwanda: "We used to be involved in a classic civil war or international war. Suddenly we have something new, which is the failed state. No more government. Yugoslavia, Somalia, Rwanda: no more government" (1994, p. 37).

Ethnic violence and the breakdown of government structures foreshadow seething hatred ready to explode and spread. Racial, political and religious hatred, intolerance and persecution pervade the global community, including America. The Los Angeles riots following the Rodney King verdict, the murder of several doctors and employees at reproductive and abortion clinics, the resurgence of hate groups, the bombings of New York's World Trade Center and the Murrah Federal Building in Oklahoma City and the hatred and venomous bigotry expressed by too many prominent political and religious leaders all constitute troubling symptoms. Hatred runs deep in the United States; it may even be ingrained in our national character—and may contribute to the rash of shootings on school campuses. It was also tragically demonstrated in the racially motivated killing of James Byrd in the east Texas town of Jasper. In the summer of 1998 Byrd was kidnapped by three white supremists, tied to the back of a pickup and dragged around town. His bloody and dismembered body parts were found over several miles. The deep intolerance and hatred in America reared its ugly head in Laramie, Wyoming, in the fall of 1998 when Matthew Sheppard, a 21-year-old gay student at the University of Wyoming, was kidnapped, beaten, burned, tied to a wooden fence post outside town and left to die by two young men who reportedly had made antigay remarks, and in Navato, California, in 1999 when Adam Colton, a gay high school senior, was ambushed in the school parking lot, beaten unconscious and branded with the word "fag" on his stomach. These are not isolated examples; they are part of a pattern of intolerance, injustice and hatred.

Ironically, hatred seems most pronounced in some religiously affiliated organizations. The increasing injustice, terrorism, racism, homophobia, sexism and repression demand that educators investigate the relationship between issues of ethics, culture and education and search for insights into the appropriate role of the social foundations of education in such a context.

Simplistic Approaches to Complex Problems

Various ethnic, religious and political extremists actively recruit support from and capture the hearts and minds of frustrated citizens. Uncritical allegiance to charismatic figures such as David Duke, Khallid Muhammad, Vladimir Geronowski, G. Gordan Liddy, Jimmy Swaggart, Rush Limbaugh, the Ayatollah Khomeini, Rabbi Meir Kahane and David Koresch has become an increasingly worrisome trend. With educational institutions plagued by violence, drug abuse, racial polarization, fiscal bankruptcy, bureaucratic overregulation, academic malaise and, as Jonathan Kozol (1991) so eloquently documented, savage inequalities, it comes as no surprise that charismatic extremists appeal to people desperate for both villains to blame and simple solutions to complex problems. To resist mindless simplicity we must recognize the larger philosophical explanations for this trend and the impact it has on education, otherwise our efforts to improve schooling lose contact with the growing global social turmoil at the beginning of the twenty-first century. School change and social change are inseparable. Like George S. Counts, a reconstructionist educator in the early part of the twentieth century, we must understand that schools should strive to build a better society for all people in their diversity of contexts.

Closed-Minded Proposals

Educational reforms proposed since the publication of *A Nation at Risk* (1983) often draw on pious language and patriotic fervor to give the conservative agenda the appearance of a divine mandate or a manifest destiny. This pseudoreligious philosophy closes discussion rather than initiates dialogue. In response, reform proposals from the political left often reject all theological and spiritual reflection and reduce social change to politically rigid philosophies that also reduce the potential for dialogue. The stalemate between the two extremes became apparent in the 1990s, as exemplified by the political gridlock in the United States government, the paralysis of the United Nations in the face of genocide and starvation in the global community and the bureaucratic and economic strangulation of school systems. The application of philosophy can loosen this gridlock. Extremism frightens many educators from the contextualization of education, reducing opportunities for school improvement and personal growth. In the context of political, cultural and religious turmoil, innovative educational changes often remain controversial and ineffective as teachers and administrators stay trapped in the grid-lock. A contextual vision of the social and cultural foundations of education—as difficult and intensive as it may be to articulate—is our challenge and promise. We enter into this difficult territory with you to confront the silence and fear inherent in our current social foundations discussions.

Marginalization of Students

In classrooms across the United States we continue to find marginalized children. The rewards go to the popular, athletic, wealthy and compliant students who conform to dominant social and cultural patterns. Intimidation, bullying and abuse of students who do not conform is far too pervasive. Consider that we professors still hear reports from undergraduate women that their school counselors advised them to take computer, business and education courses so that they "will have a job to fall back on as a secretary or teacher when [they] get married." We continue to see program reduction, scheduling conflicts and underfunding in the arts and humanities while the popular athletic programs and the administration enjoy favorable treatment and ample funding. Of course, we do recognize that there are also inequities in funding for some athletics—particularly in so-called "minor" sports and women's sports—and important administrative programs as well.

These are but a few examples of systemic curricular injustice in the schools. On the individual level, many students find themselves ostracized and ridiculed because of their physical, social, ethnic, linguistic, sexual or religious beliefs, features, preferences or orientations. Unconscionable injustice, prejudice and marginalization arising out of narrow philosophical positions and hatred occur regularly in our schools and our society. Education goes for naught if teachers and administrators ignore the outrages at hand in favor of sanitized reviews of sociology, anthropology, history or the curriculum. As we have seen, the current political, cultural and religious climates in the United States foster silence and repression. Teaching is a prophetic enterprise, and when inequality, abuse and injustice go unaddressed, schooling loses its meaning and its inherent power to affect change. In this text we refuse to allow this intolerable condition to continue unquestioned. Our philosophy of education forces us to engage this injustice directly, and we hope you will too. Consider the following letter from the parent of a student who committed suicide after years of teasing and torment at school:

> *Dear Educators; On Jan. 2, 1997, my 14 year old gay son, Robbie Kirkland, committed suicide after a four year struggle to accept and find peace with his homosexuality. Our family loved, accepted and supported him, but we could not protect him from the rejection and harassment he encountered at school. Robbie knew too well society's prejudice toward homosexuals. Since his death I have spoken out in an effort to bring sensitivity, awareness and tolerance for gay youth. Therefore, I am urging educators to reach out to gay students that continue to suffer in silence from the many acts of homophobia which permeate our schools. From an early age, gay students—and heterosexual students who are perceived as*

gay—are often teased and harassed by their peers and even by some teachers and principals because they are perceived as different. As early as first grade, Robbie was teased and harassed because he was not athletic and had a slight lisp. Most of the teasing and physical attacks occurred out of the teacher's view. Many of these acts of aggression were subtle, but persistent. Over time name calling, pushes and general exclusion leave children feeling ashamed, insecure and alone. Victims of harassment rarely disclose these acts to others. By the time Robbie knew he was gay at age 10, he was already aware of the hatred associated with being gay. His schoolmates used the words faggot, queer, gay and homo as the primary means for insulting and attacking one another. I ask educators to reach out to gay students, as well as all students from a variety of diverse backgrounds, by being guardians, advocates and allies for them. Educators need to notice when a student seems upset, uncomfortable or scared and offer private conversation and public support. Schools should have clear harassment policies familiar to teachers and students for all of those marginalized in the schools, including gay and lesbian teachers who need to be protected. Their presence can send a message of hope for gay youth. It is too late for my beloved son, but not too late for other youth at risk of assaults, harassment, isolation, alienation and suicide. Thank you for any effort that you can make on behalf of gay youth and marginalized students. You may never know the eventual impact of your actions. You may save a life. Sincerely, Leslie Sadasivan. (March 19, 1998, Strongsville, Ohio)

Robbie's mother expresses the sentiments of all those who are harassed and teased in schools. We urge you to find the courage to not only support marginalized students and teachers in schools, but also to work against any injustices present in your community. The lives and well-being of your students may literally depend on your actions, and tragic consequences could result from your silence.

Frustration and Burnout

Educators, parents, students and community members sincerely intending to improve schooling often become caught in the tangles of the political, cultural and religious philosophies we have described. While they may enter the school change process with energy, enthusiasm, talent and resources, the intense divisiveness in the school community may force them to retreat in disgust. Supervisors and teachers may hesitate to engage in innovative practices and wait for support for change at a grassroots level. But growing cynicism discourages cooperation and poisons the process. Social foundations of education should provide support for these allies by addressing contextual realities that affect their work in our schools.

Meanwhile, one scans in vain the rhetoric in contemporary textbooks for commitment to a philosophical vision rooted in social justice, autobiographical narrative, personal virtue, community solidarity, democratic values and theological sensitivity. The five problems just identified are so overwhelming that the authors and professors and their students—even those engaged in progressive school improvement—all limit their focus to practical, parochial, immediate or measurable solutions. We consider this a tragic mistake.

THE NEED FOR A LARGER VISION

A broad global vision, however, can lessen a fear of progressive innovation and change. A few scholarly educational writers including David Purpel (1989), William Doll (1993), Nel Noddings (1984, 1992, 1995), James Macdonald (1974, 1981, 1988), Donald Oliver and Kathleen Gershman (1989), William Pinar (1988, 1995), Maxine Greene (1978, 1988, 1995), Ron Miller (1993), and Dwayne Huebner (1988) have proposed a moral vision for education that supports progressive school change and innovative practices. We present our own perspective on the debilitating effects of political, cultural and religious resistance and pressure on the schooling process here in the spirit of the emerging vision of these and other scholars. In our postmodern global society we urgently need a democratic, progressive and ethical vision (in the broadest senses of these terms) that helps educators understand the foundations of education and improve the schooling process.

SCHOOL CHANGE AND SOCIAL CHANGE

A vision of the indissolubility of school change and social change is not a new concept. Nevertheless, educational programs, proposals and standards routinely avoid the broader social and cultural contexts. A broader vision of education situated in a social, cultural, political and theological context enables educators to escape the gridlock in the current debates about outcome-based education, whole language and phonics instruction, multiculturalism and assimilation, cultural literacy and critical literacy, authentic assessment and standardized testing, classroom grouping practices, nongraded elementary schools, instructional materials for AIDS and human sexuality education and abstinence-only programs, the basic core curriculum and electives, a standardized canon and a flexible curriculum and other issues we will address in Chapter 10. All educators should understand that curricular programs alone—no matter how well developed or pedagogically sound—cannot address the needs of all segments of the school community. No ideal program, liberal or conservative, fits all classrooms and all students. Therefore, education must shift its focus from ideologically rigid programming and conformity to the sociocultural context that influences so dramatically the spirit and consciousness of those struggling to survive and flourish and amidst the trauma and marginalization of contemporary education. As Alfred North Whitehead recognized, the harmony of the whole will be secure only if we achieve the preservation of the individual. We can no longer tolerate the marginalization and dehumanization of anyone, most assuredly not our students.

UNDERSTANDING THE SOCIOCULTURAL DEBATES

While educators have yet to accept universally that contextual understandings of the curriculum must be integral to an understanding of schooling, an emerging body of literature and research supports that view. The five recommendations we will review below flow from the preceding philosophical reflection, and we intend for them to encourage discussion and dialogue that move the social foundations debates to a more sensitive, productive and ethically defensible level. These recommendations do not tell you what to do or believe. Rather, they challenge you to reflect on the current dilemma and the possibilities for understanding schooling contextually. These five recommendations represent, in fact, the core of our philosophy statement. We hope you continue to keep notes in your journal as you develop your own philosophy of education.

Aesthetic Sensibilities

We must create affirming and inclusionary rather than exclusionary and destructive aesthetic sensibilities in our schools and classrooms. This responsibility derives from a willingness to take risks and examine other points of view rather than Pavlovian responses to old information that are rarely reevaluated, let alone reinformed by contemporary research and philosophy. We must include a variety of literature and social studies in the curriculum that reflects our multicultural communities and global societies. Educators must become sensitive and responsive to an eclectic variety of cultural, political, religious and social perspectives. This work entails a major risk best met with life-affirming community support.

Accountability to People, Not Tests

We must change our methods of testing and assessing. Our accountability must shift from standards to people. Many teachers already intuitively understand this; however, mastery curriculum plans, teacher-proof curriculum materials, proficiency tests and accountability programs often force teachers to focus on standards first. We must learn to trust students and invest them with more responsibility.

One of the authors learned this lesson dramatically early in his teaching career. He was using portfolios as a part of an assignment for a language arts class. The guidelines were specific and rigid, including the length, style and structure of each writing assignment. During daily classroom writing sessions one student "John," often resisted, became belligerent, or would put his head on his desk after only a few minutes of writing. One day when our colleague instructed the students to write "a one-page essay" on the reading assignment for the day, he noticed that John scribbled one sentence in his journal and then lowered his head. When he encouraged John to complete the assignment, John said he was finished.

Our colleague pointed out that the assignment called for one complete page. John replied that he had written all he could say on the topic. Losing his patience, our colleague told John to open his portfolio and read what he had written for his journal entry for the day. Frustration gave way to amazement as John read one of the most insightful reflections our colleague had ever heard. John had accomplished more in one sentence than many other students had accomplished in "one complete page" following the rigid instruction. Standards, you see, do not necessarily fit or accommodate every student. Our colleague's pedagogy began to change once he understood that students come before arbitrary standards.

Education Is a Process

It follows from this realization that students and their context must be the focus of schooling and that education is a process rather than a product. Education is less a condition that we "impose" or "transmit" or "receive" than an experience—a process of uncovering, discovering, questioning, valuing, and consequently living a changed life. It is a phenomenological experience of knowing with our entire bodies, not just with a separate and disembodied intellect. We are not simply "rational animals" as some of the traditional philosophies hold. Education is the process of learning; it is not a finished product. The moment we think our learning is complete, we are "finished" as educators. Learning is an ongoing process, and we must create schools and classrooms that reflect that.

Diversity and Multiculturalism Lead to Empathy

Teachers must understand and empathize with a diverse range of people and personalities. Too often nowadays people isolate themselves within their own social, political, church or ethnic enclaves, creating "cultural ghettos" where frustration, fear, prejudice and ignorance flourish. Educators must consciously step out of their own comfort zones to meet and accommodate other people, ideas and beliefs. Like the Ulster Project, which gathers together Protestant and Catholic Northern Ireland teenagers in nonthreatening U.S. communities for a summer of friendship and learning, teachers and students should experience many cultures in a nonconfrontational context. We could, for example, attend religious services in a tradition totally different from our own theological beliefs—Buddhist, Orthodox Christian, Pantheist, Unitarian, Wiccan, Catholic, Voodoo, Protestant, Muslim, Hindu or Jewish—and enter into a sincere relationship with a person of that belief, or for that matter a confirmed atheist or agnostic. In the process, we should learn and affirm without proselytizing or debating. Rather than convert or judge, we should seek to listen, learn, care, discuss, appreciate and befriend. We might also seek to befriend persons from minority or excluded groups in the community who are ostracized or feared—maybe a gay or lesbian, a physically challenged individual, a single mother receiving public assistance, a homeless family, a prisoner, a racially mixed couple, a child with learning or behavior problems, a socialist or a fundamentalist.

When possible, educators should visit the homes and gathering places of students from various socioeconomic backgrounds. We once spent a weekend as a part of a discussion group in the New Orleans Desire Housing Project. Several teachers came together with single parents living in poverty in a crime-infested, densely populated neighborhood. Getting to know real people with specific concerns, fears and hopes proved both informative and transformative. African American author Toni Morrison has observed that there really is no such thing as "the other" because "the other" is really "the self." When we get to know people who are "different," we enlarge our own self-understanding; we heal divisions one friendship at a time. True educators seek to enlarge their vision and understanding, a process that begins as we enter the philosophical dialogue.

Traditional Responses of Western Philosophy

Rather than accepting differences and affirming diversity, Western culture traditionally takes one of two other approaches to dealing with otherness. First, it tends to divide all of reality into opposites: black or white, male or female, straight or gay, body or soul, Democrat or Republican, gifted or remedial, teacher or student, Catholic or Protestant, capitalist or socialist, Christian or Jew, liberal or conservative and so on ad nauseam, with each opposite fighting the other for supremacy. The pole with the power dominates, subjugates, enslaves, castigates and generally seeks either to destroy the opposite pole or to force it to conform to the now-dominant values and culture in a process of assimilation. This philosophical perspective, deeply ingrained in the Western consciousness, has contributed to the emergence of such moral catastrophes as the Crusades, the Inquisitions, Salem witch burnings, McCarthyism, Nazism and the Holocaust, enslavement, genocide, ethnic cleansing, the Trail of Tears, gay bashing, Japanese-American imprisonment, "comfort women" of World War II—the list is endless. This way of thinking is played out daily in schools as various groups vie for prestige, power, resources, influence or control: "jocks" versus "geeks"; major sports versus minor sports; men's sports versus women's sports; teachers versus students; administration versus faculty and students; popular kids versus "nerds"; gifted versus remedial; rich versus poor. Of course, society and schools do not have to be reduced to bifurcations and divisions, as we will explore shortly.

Second, Western culture often deals with oppositional perspectives dialectically, with each extreme of the bifurcated pole presenting its values and perspectives, one as a "thesis" and the other as the "antithesis." Through the use of the philosophical dialectic of logic, reason, dialogue and compromise the community then arrives at a "synthesis." This synthesis becomes the new thesis to which one can present a new antithesis. Reasonable people can then exist in harmony in a "melting pot" community. Unfortunately, this process erases diversity and perpetuates injustice as individuals are assimilated into synthetic conformity and surrender their unique heritages.

Both of these traditional Western philosophical solutions to diversity and conflict—namely, annihilation or assimilation—have produced horrific injustice. But in contemporary postmodern society a promising new approach appears to be emerging: an openness to diverse perspectives and elimination of the need to destroy or synthesize people of different races, cultures, linguistic patterns, abilities, sexual orientations or religions or who espouse different beliefs or philosophies. Rather, the acceptance and affirmation of differences becomes a goal (Nieto, 1996). Meanwhile, schools and society must find a way to affirm all people in their diversity and differences, and this promising approach informs the emphasis on context in our discussion of the social foundations of education.

A CONTEXTUAL PHILOSOPHY

At this point you might well wonder how what you have read so far could help you understand our schools and classrooms. These reflections point to the start of a philosophical understanding that can stimulate your thinking and energize a commitment to action. No perfect plan or solution exists for every teacher—even though many school districts now impose "mastery plans" that force uniformity on their educators. You may face a conflict of conscience when your autobiographical philosophy and the mandates of the school administration differ. How will you handle these situations? Will you attack? remain silent and acquiesce? begin a dialectical debate? stand firm on your principles? look for possibilities for compromise in each context? What are the issues on which you will not compromise and why? Attention to your philosophical perspective now can prepare you later to recognize and deal with these situations when they arise.

In any situation it is wise to be calm and reflect as you decide what to do. In effect, you must know who you are and what you believe—what your autobiographical philosophy is—before you can be sure of what to do. Devote some time to reading about the controversial issues of our day, then meditate, ponder, discuss and reflect with an open and inquisitive mind. Become comfortable with eclecticism, ambiguity and diversity. Remember, educators avoid indoctrination or proselytizing; our mission is to open minds, stimulate discourse and build just and sustainable societies. We do this best when we expose our students to the wealth of possibilities in the world of philosophy, arts, theology, humanities and sciences; we do it best when we nurture all students without favoritism or prejudice. How will we know when we have become effective teachers and administrators? We must first explore our own life histories and then encourage students to do the same—even if they come to reject our standards and values.

These suggestions can initiate a philosophical response to the sociocultural wars that tear at our schools and our nation. At any rate, we must begin to work harmoniously, and a holistic context for understanding the philosophy of education guides our approach to the social foundations of education.

THREE QUESTIONS IN CONTEXT

Three important questions can illuminate the meaning underlying the many arguments over the current nature of schooling. These questions at first may seem a long way from education, but your responses to them will help establish a context for your philosophy of education and for understanding the educational philosophies of the administrators, politicians, parents and fellow teachers you will meet.

The Predominance of Good or Evil

Our first question: "Are humans fundamentally good or fundamentally evil?" The essential disposition of human nature has been discussed and debated down through the centuries in a wide variety of cultural and religious contexts. As we saw earlier, some philosophies contend that a "natural law" governs human behavior; others believe humans must enjoy subjective freedom and responsibility. Are humans capable of making good decisions? Is human nature predetermined by natural laws? Your own response will establish a context for making decisions about the rewards and punishments in your classroom, the distribution of resources in your school and your participation in school activities. Do you believe that students are basically good or innately evil? Are all students worth teaching, or are some beyond hope? Should limited resources be spent on all children, especially handicapped children, or should the gifted and average students receive the bulk of the funds? Should the focus of prisons be rehabilitation or punishment—in particular, is there any reason to rehabilitate a murderer, or is it better to execute all those on death row? Obviously there are various shades of responses to each of these questions, but our philosophy of human nature strongly influences the way we respond to these and similar questions.

This question will also influence your interpretation of history and anthropology when we address these issues in Chapters 3, 4 and 5. Jean-Jacques Rousseau believed that children are born good but that society corrupts them, the theme of his novel *Emile* (Rousseau, 1979). Earlier, during the Protestant Reformation, Martin Luther accepted the longstanding Christian position that humans are born in sin and depravity. Some contemporary theologians such as Matthew Fox argue for more emphasis on "original blessedness" rather than on "original sinfulness." In short, a personal answer to this apparently simple question can strongly influence the way we treat our students and colleagues.

With our own students, we often read two novels and compare and contrast the different points of view of the authors: *The Lord of the Flies* by William Golding and *Nip the Buds, Shoot the Kids* by Kenzaburo Oe. In the first novel a group of prep school students is lost on a tropical island following a plane crash. Their attempts to form a democratic society disintegrate into violence and murder. In the second novel a group of reformatory students is isolated in a valley in Japan in the midst of a plague. These children form a democratic and loving community to sustain themselves. In the Golding novel the savage boys are saved from themselves by adults. In the Oe novel the students are beaten and broken by adults who return to the valley. Which author best describes human nature? Could both be correct? Why do most high school students read the William Golding novel but not the Kenzeburo Oe novel? (We will consider this question in Chapter 10.) Reading both of these novels is one way to reflect on this important philosophical question, which eludes a simple or singular answer.

The Problem of Diversity and Ambiguity

Our second question focuses on the issue of diversity. Those in search of a personal philosophy of education must ask whether any one political system, economic system, ethnic background, racial heritage, interpretation of history or literature, sexual preference, competitive sport, aesthetic style or career choice is superior to all others. For a practical example, should teachers tell students that Columbus was a hero who discovered the New World and brought Christianity and civilization to the Americas and the savages who lived there, or should they call Columbus a villain welcomed by the Caribbean people when he became disoriented at sea who then plundered and betrayed those same native people and infected them with deadly European diseases? In short, should Columbus be canonized a saint, as some in the Catholic church have proposed, or condemned as an evil marauder, as some revisionist historians have insisted?

We once met a student who had studied in England as part of a student exchange program. Back in the United States, she remained incensed that her British history textbook portrayed the American Revolution as a lawless uprising inspired by a bunch of thugs. As you discuss the American Revolution or any other global conflict with your students, who will you portray as the villains? Robert McNamara, secretary of state for presidents Kennedy and Johnson during the Vietnam War, later wrote a book to apologize for having deceived the American people in which he called the war a tragic mistake (1995). Antiwar demonstrators twenty-five years earlier had insisted that the war was wrong and immoral, and now McNamara confessed that he had betrayed the American people. These few examples point to the difficulty of determining the absolute truth—even if there were only one true side to every story.

The world has seen far too many tragedies result from a belief that one person, race, religion, culture, sacred book, historical interpretation or manifesto is universally true and beyond reproach: Hitler's belief in the superiority of the Aryan race over Jews, Gypsies, the disabled and homosexuals; the righteous inquisitions of the Catholic church; Senator Joseph McCarthy's anti-Communist hearings in the 1950s; the preferences accorded male athletes and male sports in our schools and colleges and professional arenas; the enslavement of minority peoples throughout history are but a few examples.

The Need to Make Decisions and Choices

Our third question concerns making appropriate decisions about the school curriculum, careers, relationships, religions and so forth. Many people consider some decisions inherently better than others. We contend, by contrast, that the subjective experiences of individuals in different contexts preclude predetermined solutions. The following story illustrates the problem we face when making decisions about schooling.

An undergraduate in a prelaw program at a prestigious university used an elective during his senior year to join the chorus. He had always enjoyed music, sang in the church choir in elementary school and strummed a guitar in high school. He had always wanted to sing, but the demands of a rigorous program of study and family pressures to focus on his legal career had kept him from exploring his interest formally. His father insisted that grades remain a priority to ensure his admission to the best law school after graduation. His father resembled the drama student's father in the movie *Dead Poets Society,* ruling his son's life and career with an iron fist.

The choir director discovered that this student had an outstanding voice. Shortly thereafter, a traveling musical ensemble visiting campus invited him to audition. He agreed, and at the beginning of the spring semester received word that he had been accepted as a member of the troupe for the following school year. He would have the opportunity to travel the world performing. With years of rigorous study behind him and a high grade point average, he thought it time he did something personally meaningful and socially significant with his life, at least for the one year after graduation before starting law school.

Elated by his new prospects, he rushed home to tell his parents the good news. Some twenty-five years later, our friend is still bitter about his father's response: His father threatened to withdraw all financial support and close out a trust fund if his son dared squander a year on such a "ridiculous" enterprise. His father considered singing a distraction that would remove his son from the real world of law and finance. To be sure, our friend is a wealthy and successful tax attorney, but he still laments the fact that he failed to pursue his dream of traveling the world for a year singing with that musical ensemble.

CONCLUSION

As we end this chapter, we hope we have left you with lots of questions and uncertainties. Philosophy can be troublesome. It raises profound issues that scholars, politicians, scientists, theologians, teachers and artists investigate and debate constantly. A devotion to philosophy requires an ongoing process of discovery, revision, deconstruction, recreation and reconceptualization. As you develop your own philosophy of education, we urge you both to consider the wisdom in the ideas discussed in this chapter, and by all means to reflect on the value of your own autobiographical context. The philosophical context of education will exert a powerful impact on your life as an educator. As we continue to discuss philosophy in the next two chapters, we will move toward developing a critical approach to understanding knowledge and meaning. Beginning in Chapter 3 we will connect this critical philosophy to the teaching and learning environment you will enter as an educator.

The Connection between Philosophy and Teaching

INTRODUCTION

We have outlined the nature of philosophy and its relation to education, as well as our perspective on the role of a personal philosophy of education; we now examine dominant versions of philosophy and education in the United States and our responses to them. Over the last century, education here and in most other nations has been influenced by all of the philosophical traditions we discussed in Chapter 1. None, however, has had quite the impact of scientific realism. If realism teaches that we can find an unchanging truth in the physical world, then scientific realism is the highest expression of that realism. Realist scientific research seeks to uncover the actual character of the world—that is, the laws that dictate the relationship between events and objects. Scientific realism holds that natural laws, ideas and information exist whether or not humans know them. Thus, to know truth is to *discover* it, to uncover knowledge that already exists. In this chapter we hope to convince you that such a philosophical stance, whether held consciously or unconsciously, has shaped not only American education but our individual identities and worldviews as well. We believe that the pervasiveness, the wide-ranging influence of this philosophy, has negatively affected education, so we propose alternative philosophies to scientific realism throughout this book.

SCIENTIFIC REALISM AND THE COMING OF MODERNITY

The European love affair with scientific realism began five centuries ago, when philosophers and scientists began to understand that medieval ways of seeing the world no longer answered the complex problems of the time. When bubonic plague, the Black Death, swept across Europe in the fourteenth century, killing one of every four people, rulers found themselves powerless to control it. Every traditional medieval response— prayer, mysticism, scapegoating and magic—failed.

When a society cannot understand—let alone solve—a challenge to its very existence, its conception of reality collapses or a new guiding vision rushes forward. Under the threat of the Black Death, Western society began to develop a new way of seeing the world that would lead directly to scientific realism. The Black Death ushered in the period historians refer to as modernity or the era of scientific revolution. Science helped Western society understand and control somewhat better the outside environment, the world of matter and energy (Wingo, 1974; Bohm & Peat, 1987; Leshan & Margenau, 1982).

The modernist science emerging in the 1600s and 1700s rested on the separation of the knower and the known, a cardinal tenet of the Cartesian-Newtonian (referring to René Descartes and Sir Isaac Newton) way of organizing the world. Descartes's analytical method of reasoning, often termed "reductionism," asserted that one can appreciate complex phenomena best by reducing them to their constituent parts and then piecing the elements back together according to causal laws (Mahoney & Lyddon, 1988). This analysis took place within Descartes's separation of the mind and matter. This "Cartesian dualism" divided human experience into two distinct realms: (1) an internal world of sensation and (2) an objective world composed of natural phenomena. As we saw in Chapter 1, pragmatism, feminist philosophy and Eastern philosophy all challenge this notion of dualisms.

Drawing on this dualism, scientists subsequently asserted that one could uncover the laws of physical and social systems objectively; meanwhile, the systems operated apart from human perception, with no connection to the act of perceiving. Descartes theorized, in other words, that the internal and the natural worlds were forever separate and the one could never be shown to be a form of the other (Lavine, 1984; Lowe, 1982; Kincheloe, 1991). We understand now but could hardly have understood then that despite all the benefits that modernist scientific methods could offer, this rigorous separation of mind and matter would bring profound and unfortunate consequences. Our ability to confront problems such as disease definitely improved as our power to control the "outside world" advanced. At the same time, however, we accomplished little in the attempt to comprehend our own consciousness, our "inner experience" (Leshan & Margenau, 1982). Scientific realism either ignored or rejected any phenomenon that human beings failed to experience directly through the senses. In schools and classrooms today we continue to devalue intuition, insight, autobiographical reflection and inner experience and emphasize instead objective lessons, measurable outcomes and test scores. This is the continuing legacy of Cartesian dualism.

The Cartesian-Newtonian philosophy established a context for the emergence of both scientific realism and a shift in consciousness about the human community. Some call this movement to a modern worldview a paradigm shift. We know about at least two paradigm shifts in human history: first, the move from isolated nomadic communities of hunters and gatherers to feudal societies with city-states and agrarian support systems; and second, the move from tribal and feudal societies to a capitalist industry-based economy relying on scientific technology, unregulated resource consumption, social progress, unrestrained economic growth and rational thought. The first, called the premodern period or the neolithic revolution, dates from about 1,000 B.C.E. to about 1450 C.E. The second, called the modern period or the era of the scientific and industrial revolution, dates from about 1450 C.E. to about 1960 C.E. (some would say it continues into the present).

The premodern neolithic period is featured by slow-changing concepts of time rooted in mythology, religion and aristocratic cultures. The modern scientific and industrial period features linear concepts of time that produce mass culture and a dependence on technology. Some scholars contend that another major paradigm shift from the modern period to the emerging postmodern era began around 1960 (W. Doll, 1993; Griffin, 1988a, 1988b; Slattery, 1995a). We discuss this postmodern shift here and in Chapter 13, but we return now to our focus on the scientific realism of the modern period.

Modernity emerged gradually in the fourteenth and fifteenth centuries as societal leaders tried to come to terms with plagues, new discoveries by Copernicus, Galileo and other scientists and a major population shift to cities. Modern trends like these continue: Consider AIDS, the Hubble telescope and exploding populations in our megacities. Even though a postmodern era appears to be emerging, we live in a time when people cling to the desperate hope that modern scientific realism can answer the perplexing problems we face. The Cartesian-Newtonian compass pointed the way to modernity with its emphasis on centralization, linear progress, concentration, objectivity, accumulation, efficiency and speed. Bigger became better as the dualistic way of seeing reinforced a male-controlled, expansionist sociopolitical order grounded in a desire for power and conquest. Such a worldview often served to dehumanize those who sought control, and such routine dehumanization invited free-rein science and technology to dominate and transform the world.

As most of us learned in elementary and high school, many considered this transformation miraculous. Commerce increased, inventions and discoveries proliferated, nationalism grew and European civilization expanded and rapidly colonized what were considered "less enlightened and transformed" realms. Rationality became the deity to replace premodern superstition and organized religion. Around this new god the credo of modernity developed: The world is rational, capable of being controlled and wholly knowable. Further, we can describe all phenomena—the smallest atom or the solar system, dreams or engines, learning or gunpowder, electricity or forms of government—within the boundaries of this encompassing rationality. When applied to politics and government, for example, scientific rationalism led to the most progressive aspects of modernism: freedom, justice and equality. The French and American revolutions of the eighteenth century dramatically signaled the emergence of this political philosophy in the minds and hearts of ordinary people.

Education in the modern era has, of course, emphasized the positive political, scientific and technological advances of this age of science and rationalism. But as we mentioned earlier, our commitment to scientific realism has also produced devastating consequences: colonization, racism, environmental degradation, poverty and unemployment, a devaluation of the spiritual and mythological, and much more. We intend to expose here the negative consequences of the modern philosophy on the human psyche, global cultures, the environment and, of course, education while still acknowledging the many positive contributions modernity has made. We hope to contribute to the emergence of the postmodern worldview, especially in education, and to confront the persistent abuses of modernity.

Both the emphasis of scientific realism on reason and the attempts by eighteenth- and nineteenth-century philosophers to produce forms of objective scientific inquiry led to efforts to organize everyday life rationally. This movement, called the Enlightenment, cast reason against barbaric behavior and the absence of civilization. The enemies of enlightenment include emotions, animal instincts, intuition, mysticism and premodern philosophies. The Enlightenment set science against religion, magic and superstition, a tension that invited Western culture to consider itself new, different, superior and the very benchmark of civilization. As the paragon of civilization, Western modernist culture found itself free to lust after absolutes and to speak with qualification and with certainty. Twentieth-century French philosopher Michel Foucault spoke of modernism as a way of relating to reality, a way of thinking and feeling that grants a sense of cultural belonging. Modernism is the force that has helped Europeans, Americans and other Western cultures understand their relationship to the cosmos (Smart, 1992; Lather, 1991; Hanam, 1990).

The failure of our history classes to show how modernism has shaped our views of self, intelligence and education suggests the larger failure of modernism itself to explore human beings and the human consciousness. This scientific realist philosophical context presented history, like other disciplines of knowledge, as a preexisting body of knowledge for students to memorize as truth. Social studies courses rarely discuss or analyze the many ways in which history can be interpreted or that history is a subjective human construction. From our perspective, one of the major benefits of studying history is the inherent invitation to measure one's own life and social order against the past. How did we come to hold the religious, political and philosophical beliefs that ground us and connect us to (or disconnect us from) other people and the world around us? This chapter asks that question. We challenge you to examine your life in light of it, and to reflect on how assumptions of modernism, rationalism and scientific realism shape your view of what a teacher does. We begin by discussing the epistemology of positivism.

POSITIVISM: MODERNISM'S EPISTEMOLOGY

Students often treat *epistemology* as a frightening word with few practical applications. But it is neither frightening nor impractical. Recall from Chapter 1 that epistemology is the branch of philosophy that studies knowledge. It asks questions such as: What constitutes knowledge? How do we know if something is true? What is the difference between a fact and an opinion? Can knowledge evolve and change or is it static and immutable? The epistemology that informs modernism is usually called *positivism*. Few philosophical orientations have exerted as much influence on everyday life as positivism. At the same time, few philosophical orientations have been so little understood. But once we understand the nature of positivism we can understand how modernism has affected our view of ourselves and education.

Nineteenth-century French philosopher August Comte popularized the notion of positivism. He argued that human thought had evolved through three stages: the theological stage, where truth rested on God's revelation; the metaphysical stage, where truth derived from abstract reasoning and argument; and the positivistic stage, where truth arises from scientifically produced knowledge. Comte sought to discredit the legitimacy of nonscientific thinking that failed to take "sense knowledge" (knowledge obtained through the senses and empirically verifiable) into account (Knellner, 1984; Smith, 1983). He saw no difference between the ways knowledge should be produced in the physical sciences and in the human sciences, and he believed one should study sociology just like biology. Society, like nature, Comte argued, is nothing more than a body of neutral facts governed by immutable laws. Therefore, social actions should proceed with lawlike predictability (Held, 1980). In a context such as Comte's, education would also be governed by unchanging laws; the role of the educator is to uncover these laws and then act in accordance with them. For example, educational laws would include universal statements regarding how students learn and how they should be taught. The positivist educator, in other words, sees only one correct way to teach, and scientific study can reveal these methods if we search for them diligently.

To begin our analysis of modernism and the ways it has shaped our view of self, society and education, we turn here to the ten characteristics of positivism.

1. *All knowledge is scientific knowledge.* First, positivism insists that only scientifically produced information should be regarded as authentic human knowledge. Scientific knowledge can be verified and proven. It is knowledge about which we are positive—hence the name "positivism." When Newton formulated the theory of gravity, he told us that the apple *always* falls to the ground and that what goes up must come down. No exceptions to these scientific generalizations exist. Scientific knowledge is not merely one form of knowledge, the positivists maintain, for knowledge can *only* be produced by science. Positivists hold nonscience in disdain, and they dismiss ways of knowing through religion, metaphysics and intuition as unverifiable nonsense. This might help us to understand why indigenous and native people were thought by European colonizers to be ignorant savages.

The positivist view of the world exerts a dramatic impact on all of us, teachers in particular. If expert-produced scientific knowledge constitutes the only valuable information about education, then schooling should be organized so that experts and administrators simply tell teachers how to perform their jobs. In this situation experts do all of the thinking, and teachers merely execute plans. Any thought about the purposes of education and the daily work of the classroom remain separate. The positive context denies teachers their skills (some call this "deskilling"), and the teaching act and classroom practice are torn apart. Once deskilled, teachers are provided with teacher-proof materials and must simply implement lessons prepared in advance by textbook companies, computer programs or state and district supervisors. The teacher then functions as a proctor in an ACT, SAT or GRE testing session by reading instructions, distributing materials, regulating time, monitoring for cheating and answering questions.

Teacherproof curriculum materials assume that teachers are incapable of making instructional decisions and must be guided through their daily work. Examples of teacherproof materials include "scripted" lessons that teachers actually read to their classes.

> *The teacher says, "OK class, take out your spelling books and turn to page 23. Do not proceed until all books are on desk and open to the appropriate page." Then the teacher says to a selected student: "Read the first word on the list, Jessica."*

Unfortunately, this scenario is becoming all too familiar. But efforts continue to secure or restore teacher empowerment in democratic workplaces where they are viewed as self-directed and reflective professionals rather than monitors. The political implications of teacherproof materials and the logic behind them disaffects those of us who value democracy; thus we challenge this first premise of positivism, that all knowledge is scientific.

2. *All scientific knowledge is empirically verifiable.* Second, positivism assumes that when we use the phrase "scientific knowledge" we are referring to knowledge that can be verified empirically (through the senses). What the eye sees, what the ear hears, what we can count, what we can express mathematically—these things constitute empirical knowledge. But we contend that many aspects of education resist empirical validation. These invisible factors might include ways of seeing or sets of assumptions. They might include a student's feelings of hurt or humiliation or the self-esteem of an abused child—such human dynamics do not lend themselves to quantification or empirical verification. Indeed, the existence of positivism itself as a force that shapes what we "see" cannot be empirically verified. In other words, positivism cannot study its own assumptions because they are not empirically verifiable.

When we meet educational knowledge that uses such an epistemological base exclusively, we find it limited in what it can tell us about schooling and the learning process. Indeed, when teacher education students learn from materials produced by such a positivist science, they tend to find that the most important aspects of education are left out or distorted. To become the best possible teacher, one should understand the epistemological dynamics of knowledge production. Knowledge about the world, and about the educational cosmos in particular, is never neutral. It is always based on an entire set of values and assumptions about the nature of the world and the people who live in it. These epistemological dynamics shape beliefs about the purposes of education.

3. *One must use the same methods to study the physical world as one uses to study the social and educational worlds.* Third, serious problems result when one applies physical science methods to the study of education. A key aspect of positivistic research in the physical sciences involves the attempt to predict and control natural phenomena. When applied in education, physical science methods then apply social knowledge as a tool to control human beings. Thus, students come to be viewed, understood, used and controlled just like any other *thing*. Positivism loses

sight of the idea that the objects of social research, humans, possess a special complexity that sets them apart from other objects of study.

Positivist social-educational scientists fail to understand that the physical scientists they emulate impose their observations on the objects under observation. Physical scientists do not have to consider the consciousness of their objects of study or their history and sociocultural contexts. Neither need they consider their own consciousness and assumptions. This makes research on humans different from the study of, say, rocks or field mice. If we fail to understand this difference, we miss the very elements that make us human, that shape us or restrict our freedom.

Here rests one of the key points in our discussion of modernism in general and positivism in particular: Modernism and its positivist epistemology lead to a devaluation of human beings and a depersonalization of our institutions. People become just more variables in a larger social equation; our sacredness as spiritual beings disappears. Think of how degraded we feel when we are being processed by large institutions—insurance companies, welfare agencies, university business offices, the court system—that see us as just a social security number or case five on the docket. Impersonal positivism promotes this kind of treatment.

4. *If knowledge exists, it exists in some definite, measurable quantity.* Fourth, positivism teaches that we can express knowledge in mathematical terms. If something exists, positivists argue, we can measure how *much* of it exists. Indeed, we can express the generalizations, principles and theories derived from positivistic data in mathematical language (Beed, 1991; Garrison, 1989). Positivists define systematic observation that produces valid knowledge in terms of mathematical experiments. In this context researchers look for mathematical relations between variables. If such mathematical relations emerge, they generalize the relationships to produce a universal law.

Many of us who call for democratic education and democratic research methods, however, find ourselves uncomfortable with the positivist assumptions that "to be is to be measurable" and that human endeavor can be expressed in mathematical terms. Much of what education researchers want to study does not lend itself to measurability or even direct observation. To address this problem positivists developed what they call "reduction sentences," which are characteristics that summarize statements in a way that makes them more observable and measurable. A hard-to-measure concept such as hunger becomes "20 percent loss of original body weight" for a mature man or woman. Since weight is a measurable concept, hunger can be expressed in terms of weight. Behavioral psychologists who operate within a positivistic context label such reduction sentences "operational or working definitions." Thus, we develop operational definitions for concepts such as intelligence (what one scores on an IQ test) or productivity (output by workers per hour). Indeed, positivists argue, even concepts such as love or creativity can be operationally defined and measured.

These operational definitions may or may not help us understand the phenomena under investigation. But such an orientation often focuses our attention on merely the symptoms of larger issues or ideas—that is, on the consequences rather than the causes. Thus a belief in the measurability of everything actually distorts our understanding of reality, because it hides the assumptions often made in the production of knowledge. For example, what mental characteristics do questions on an IQ (intelligence quotient) test really address? short-term memory? the ability to store and call up a wide range of factual data? Certainly IQ tests cannot measure an ability to see connections between ostensibly unrelated concepts or the skill to apply such understandings to the identification and solution of problems. IQ tests deemphasize such difficult-to-measure but important abilities, while easy-to-measure but trivial abilities gain center stage. Education is thus undermined, reduced to memorization, computation and busywork with little purpose or connection to the passions and complexities of human beings. In such a context education becomes a mindless game, the trivial pursuit of abstract and inert information.

5. *Nature is uniform and whatever is studied remains consistent in its existence and behavior.* Fifth, positivists assume that the objects they study will remain constant. They believe in an underlying natural order in the way both the physical and the social worlds behave. These regularities, or social laws, positivists argue, are best expressed through quantitative analysis using propositional language and mathematics. The goal for educational research within this tradition, therefore, is to develop theories that regularize human expression and make it predictable.

We believe, by contrast, that human beings are much less regular and predictable than the positivists portray them to be. As humans exhibit their irregularities and unpredictabilities—their diversity—we nonpositivists make the case that men and women defy positivist attempts to reduce their behavior to measurable quantities. Teachers and students, for example, are hardly uniform, predictable and consistent in their personalities, actions, psychology and responses. Contrary to positivist opinions, humans are not machines whose behavior can be easily broken down into separate parts. Thank goodness researchers cannot yet provide full and final explanations of the human dynamic.

6. *The factors that cause things to happen are limited and knowable, and in empirical studies these factors can be controlled.* Sixth, positivists believe that variables can be isolated and studied independently to determine specific causes for individual events. Following Newton's laws of the physical universe, they believe that for every action there is an opposite and equal reaction, and that these actions and reactions can be identified and measured. Positivists refuse to acknowledge the complexity of the world, especially the world of human beings. The world, they believe, is neat and tidy, and the noise and confusion foisted on it by the "humanness of human beings" makes positivists edgy. Research would be so much easier if researchers and the researched could only avoid this untidy world and the imprecise medium of verbal language.

Positivists dream of a spick-and-span social science in which all researchers are identical, unbiased, infallible measuring instruments. Modernist positivism accepts a cause-and-effect linearity that works like a machine. For example, when the human body breaks down, doctors may reliably identify one certain factor immediately contributing to the illness. But in reality, the causes are always multiple. Some are environmental, some psychological, some physical. Diet, stress, chemicals, exercise, emotions, heredity and viruses all affect the health of the human body, and these multiple causes rarely function in a simple, easily traced manner. Life processes, like social processes, are rarely neat and tidy; we must view them in the context that shapes them if we want to make sense of the way they operate.

As we think about the positivistic assumption that causative factors are limited and knowable, imagine the way we study classroom management or, as some call it, discipline. Hundreds of researchers have studied classroom discipline in the last thirty years. In addition to problems of sample size and the relationship between what gets defined as good discipline and desirable educational achievements, the control of variables in discipline research presents several other special difficulties. Literally thousands of unmentioned factors can significantly influence what happens in any classroom (Fiske & Schweder, 1986; Barrow, 1984). One student may respond to a specific teacher's discipline one way—not because of the discipline itself, but because he or she is accustomed to a certain type of discipline at home. For example, a student raised in a permissive home may interpret a subtle, mildly coercive, noncorporal disciplinary act quite differently from a student raised in a strict home where punishment is physical. To the first student the discipline is understandable and consistent with prior experience; to the second student it reveals the teacher's weakness.

Another student reacts differently to the subtle, mildly coercive discipline because of the nature of his or her relationship with the teacher. One student, whose parents are long-time acquaintances of the teacher, may know the teacher as a trusted friend. When confronted with corrective action of any kind, this student may feel uncomfortable because he or she is unaccustomed to conflict in his or her relationship with the teacher. What appears to the observer to be a mild admonishment provides a great deal of embarrassment to the student. Another student is affected by the presence of an outside observer and reacts in a way that is inconsistent with prior behavior. Still another student's behavior may be triggered by Tourette's syndrome or some other physical condition that may or may not be diagnosed or known to the teacher. A researcher can hardly account for all the possible variables that may affect what is being observed (Barrow, 1984). Veteran teachers recognize this. When a supervisor or observer enters the classroom, the atmosphere changes dramatically. Students who are usually well behaved and participate actively may suddenly become disrespectful or inattentive.

So the various facets of a student's or a teacher's nature, of every individual's background, of every context and of all the interrelationships and combinations of factors may be each or in conjunction the key elements in explaining what happens in a classroom. This is sometimes called "chaos theory" or "complexity theory." These crucial elements elude positivist researchers. In this context, an education that provides you with five scientifically validated "surefire methods" to discipline students no matter who they are is probably worthless. Unless the methods are contextualized by attention to the teacher's philosophical assumptions, the purposes of education he or she embraces, and the ethnic, class, socioeconomic, religious, cultural, racial and gender backgrounds of the students, such methods generally will lead you astray. In fact, they often can keep you from connecting with students in a way that motivates, validates and inspires them.

7. *Certainty is possible, and when we produce enough research we will understand reality well enough to forgo further research.* Seventh, the goal of positivist social science research involves the quest for sure answers to human questions, and

such a quest implies a definite end point. But because we cannot control all variables, as we just saw—because the factors that cause variable behaviors are unlimited—the quest for positivist certainty is futile and quixotic. If we learn anything definite from positivist science, it is that our ideas about the world change with new revelations and that they will continue to change, probably for all time. The chance of arriving at some juncture in human history where research becomes unnecessary because we all understand the nature of reality is slight.

Better, then, to abandon the quest for absolutes that focuses our attention on the trivial—on only those things we can easily measure. One of the reasons history tests often emphasize dates, people, places and battles is that teachers find it easy to measure whether students have "learned" this kind of information. They find it much harder to evaluate an essay test, with its potential ambiguity and complexity. In fact, the quest for absolute certainty in testing and evaluation encourages the lowest form of thinking (rote memorization) and dismisses higher-level thinking (analysis, interpretation, contextualization and application).

For these and many other reasons, educators often view with skepticism the certainty with which positivists make "valid" arguments. We are generally inclined to take a more humble and limited perspective. Indeed, it seems safe to predict that educational researchers will never determine the five best ways to teach algebra, the five steps to teaching excellence or the eight steps to teacher popularity. There are as many good ways to teach as there are good teachers, and some of them conflict. What we do successfully in one context may fail in another. The best teachers adjust lessons and adapt to changing classroom environments.

Discuss this concept with an experienced teacher in a departmentalized school who teaches five periods of a single subject every day, and he or she will tell you that even though the lesson plans may be identical, each period proceeds differently. The teacher may gain an insight in the first period that is applicable in the next four periods. A student in the second period may ask a question that alters the structure of the lesson. Students in each class ask different questions, have different personalities, have unique learning styles and learning needs and respond differently because of the time of day, weather conditions, events in the school schedule and so forth. A uniform lesson plan for all five sections of the class may be possible, but because of the complexity teachers cannot control, uniform lessons are not. In fact, even if teachers could control every lesson, such control would hinder learning. The best teachers are comfortable with the variety of literary interpretations, mathematical proofs and historical analyses in every subject area.

8. *Facts and values can be kept separate, and objectivity is always possible.* Eighth, unlike positivists, we do not consider scientific research a value-free activity. The popular image of science reflects the belief that the only parameters that limit a scientist's activities are intellect and curiosity. This belief is misleading because values and power dynamics continually shape research. If educational researchers operate in a college of education dominated, for example, by positivist assumptions about the nature of research, they might lose such career benefits as tenure if they attempt to conduct research that deviates from the rules of positivist methods. More important, because financial grants from government and private foundations often determine the type of research that takes place, funded inquiries

typically reflect the values and interests of funding agencies. A brief survey of accepted and rejected grants will illuminate the political values that drive knowledge production in education and elsewhere.

Nevertheless, positivist researchers continue to insist that researchers suppress their value judgments, convictions, beliefs and opinions (Beed, 1991). They insist that empirical inquiry should remain value free and objective and that values are tainted because they are subjective. Thus, the proclamations issued from the positivist pulpit project the illusion of political and moral neutrality. Accordingly, the wizard must be exposed, and the epistemological rules that dictate exactly what we can and cannot count as facts must be uncovered (Garrison, 1989).

The implicit rules that actually guide our generation of education facts almost always reflect specific worldviews, values, religious and political perspectives and definitions of intelligence. Research can never really be nonpartisan, for we have to choose the rules that guide our research. Particular rules focus our attention on certain aspects of education and deflect it from others. Positivism, for example, focuses our attention on education as a technical act. When we measure certain aspects of education to determine how well school systems or particular schools or particular teachers are doing, we cannot separate this question from the political issue of what schools *should* be doing. Therefore, if positivist research can establish the criteria by way of research instruments that measure how well we are doing, it has also established what we should be doing. Positivism thus becomes a political instrument of social control, even while its adherents proclaim their neutrality, their disinterestedness and their disdain for mixing politics and education (Bowers, 1982).

For example, if researchers describe students' readiness for work as the ability to follow orders, respect authority and function as team players, the schools with good evaluations teach these skills. The "objective" process of defining work readiness conceals some very specific values: From a variety of ways to define work readiness, the researchers chose the definition closest to their political and economic beliefs. They want to prepare a society of compliant workers who obey orders without raising questions or challenging authority. Having made a value-driven choice, the researchers are no longer political innocents.

The same holds true for the teacher who gives a multiple-choice test. The test appears to be an objective, value-free instrument of evaluation, but closer examination reveals a set of hidden value assumptions. In constructing the test the teacher had already chosen the textbook on which the test material was based, a value choice that prioritized one book over several others. The teacher also considered particular material from the book more important than other material, a value choice of some facts over others. The teacher chose a multiple-choice format over other formats, a value choice that advanced certain forms of learning (fact memorization) over others (for example, analysis, interpretation and application in an essay or a series of short written answers). Such value choices are inherent in teaching and living. Although we can hardly avoid them, we should understand that we are making them. This awareness is a key goal of the democratic form of education and a cardinal aspect of higher-order thinking.

9. *There is one true reality, and the purpose of education is to convey that reality to students.* Ninth, positivists generally contend that one best way to accomplish a

task exists somewhere. For example, given one undisputed best way (best method) to teach, the purpose of the positivist teacher of education is to pass that method along to students. Educational science grounded in positivist research assumes that the laws of society and the knowledge of human existence are verified and immutable and ought to be inserted directly into the minds of children. Operating on this assumption, educational "engineers" devise curricula and organizational strategies for schools as if no ambiguities or uncertainties in the social and educational worlds exist. In such a context scientific and mathematical knowledge achieves the status of the absolute and sacred, and science and math inevitably receive the highest priority in both the school curriculum and national education documents such as *Goals 2000*.

Moreover, contemporary culture teaches us to revere science and the scientific method and, interestingly enough, to accept its primacy on faith, which is to say, unscientifically. The authoritarian voice of positivist science silences our language of intuition, aesthetics, spirituality, and insight. The view of science that regards the aesthetic and subjective as soft, effeminate, impressionistic and nonscientific devalues such language. Cowed by the authority of positivist science we accede to its demands and allow it to define teachers as mere practitioners (Aronowitz, 1983; Koller, 1981; Eisner, 1984).

In his studies of the street-corner culture in Toronto's Jane-Finch Corridor, Peter McLaren found students from lower socioeconomic classes questioning the school's view of them as passive recipients of sacred and official facts. The teachers less frequently questioned their own passive position in relation to the expert producers of knowledge (McLaren, 1989). When positivists control knowledge and student-teacher evaluations, we find the range of behaviors considered to be good teaching considerably narrowed. Many supervisors find it easy to label creative lessons that fail to follow the "one best method" unsatisfactory. Thus, teachers earn rewards less for their reasonable notions of competence and creativity and more for their adherence to a prescribed format. Like workers on a factory assembly line, teachers in positivist school systems become rule followers with little influence over how the rules are made. They become the executors of managerial strategies for keeping students on the task. Even among the best teachers, the passion for creativity and engagement slowly erodes as positivistic science becomes ever more deeply entrenched in our schools and society. Blind faith in positivism may be one of the great tragedies of our era. But along with many critical researchers and postmodern scholars, we are trying to reverse its philosophical dominance.

10. *Teachers become "information deliverers," not knowledge-producing professionals or empowered cultural workers.* Tenth, in such a positivist context we wonder why society should bother with teacher education programs. If teachers are merely information deliverers, we need hire only those with the abilities to read the scripted teacherproof material and intimidate and control students. In such a context the idea of a scholarly teacher with interpretive and analytical abilities becomes irrelevant. School is simply a memory game in which the more creative teachers make memorization palatable by creating contests and mnemonic devices

designed to ease rote learning. Only a desire to compete or to please their teachers or parents can motivate students in such an educational purgatory. Education has no intrinsic value, no connection to the lived world of human beings.

As we conclude our analysis and critique of positivism, we want to reiterate a point made in the introduction: We do not reject the contributions of modern science, mathematics and philosophy in improving our world. Important advancements have been made in medicine, communication, democracy and astronomy in the modern era that we embrace. In fact, we will sometimes use statistics to help support an important point. Additionally, the new sciences of the twentieth century, such as chaos theory, complexity theory, fiber bundle theory, string theory, the uncertainty principle and quantum physics, move beyond the Newtonian and positivistic worldview. We are more comfortable with the new sciences, but we note their negative features as well. We do not propose an antiscience romanticism that seeks a return to premodern times. Some people have gone to the extreme of rejecting all science and reason in favor of a return to superstition and religion. Neither do we accept a positivist scientific worldview that sees everything as predictable, measurable, controllable and wholly knowable. Our postmodern approach to science will become clear as we continue our analysis.

WHAT IS A PARADIGM AND HOW DOES IT AFFECT TEACHING?

Our description and critique of modernism, positivism and scientific realism's dominant influence in Western societies heralds a larger change that has been occurring over the last three decades. Many observers have referred to this change as a "paradigm shift." A paradigm is a constellation of concepts, values and techniques that a scientific community or dominant culture uses to make sense of itself and its world. As frameworks of understanding, paradigms guide the ways we produce knowledge. Until Thomas Kuhn described his notion of paradigmatic change in 1962, most scholars believed that as scientific knowledge slowly accumulated, theories about the ways the physical and social worlds operate would gradually become more sophisticated and accurate. Kuhn (1970) and others undermined this view, maintaining that major conceptual change never comes as a result of a steady and orderly series of discoveries. Rather, conceptual change is abrupt and traumatic. Einstein's early twentieth-century challenge to the dominant paradigm in physics presents one example of a traumatic paradigmatic change. The universality of Newtonian physics collapsed as theories of relativity and quantum mechanics suddenly portrayed a far more complex physical universe. We would never view the world again in the same way.

Such a paradigm shift, we believe, is occurring in education now. When our models of making sense of the world no longer seem consistent, we can begin to expect a paradigm shift. In our critique of positivism we noted that the positivist way of viewing education no longer answers the compelling questions of students and their teachers. If we are right, the new education paradigm will shape your life as a teacher. The following paragraphs discuss the nature of the paradigm shift in education, the new values that guide it and its implications for teachers and learners. In the most general sense, the shift from the modernist paradigm to a new paradigm involves five basic characteristics:

1. Modernist positivism focuses on the parts (for example, test scores, seating arrangements, discipline plans, lesson plans, administrative strategies and so forth) to eventually understand the whole (human beings in context, the cultural climate of the school, historical events, social issues and so forth). The new paradigm reverses this relationship: We understand the parts only in the context of the whole.

2. Modernist positivism focuses on the identification of such never-changing structures as knowledge as timeless truth, social laws and a fixed-core curriculum. The new paradigm sees every structure as dynamic and constantly interacting with changing processes. Thus, the curriculum is less a fixed course of study or predetermined lesson plans than a context-specific process changing with the evolving needs of society and individuals. The journey is just as important as the destination.

3. Modernist positivism claims to produce an objective science untainted by human values (for example, the curriculum is value free, disinterested, merely the delineation of knowledge we have discovered). The new paradigm makes no claim to objectivity, because it celebrates human ways of knowing that are logical but also intuitive, emotional and empathetic. Such an approach to knowledge production (epistemology) is often referred to as *constructivism* in that the world is "constructed" or brought forth in the process of knowing. Learning becomes not as much an act of memorizing previously discovered information as an act of creating knowledge and ordering our own experiences to achieve deeper understanding.

4. Modernist positivism uses the architectural metaphor of a building to talk about knowledge, and scientific information is characterized as the "basic building block" of matter. Positivist science educators speak of DNA as determining "the structure" of life, not just one of many aspects of living systems. The new paradigm uses the metaphor of a network with all aspects interconnected. For example, the science curriculum is never taught in isolation but in concert with philosophical, political, economic and theological knowledge. It is merely one part that influences and is influenced by the larger universal network.

5. Modernist positivism regards what it produces as the truth (for example, the theory of evolution is true, the law of supply and demand in economics is true). In the new paradigm the interconnectedness of the parts makes explaining the world more difficult. The characteristics of one entity relate to the characteristics of the other entities and since we can never understand and appreciate all of the possible relationships between the parts, we never uncover the whole story. Thus, we offer only approximate

explanations. (The examples of teaching methods we offer in this book are not *truths* about teaching. While they may indeed work in some situations, they may not work at all in others.)

REFUSING TO PLAY THE GAME: PAIN, PASSION AND NEW PARADIGMS

The attempt to collect and comprehend the implications of the paradigm shift is still in its early stages. As a society we remain confused about what it means. Much of the gridlock in America's educational and political lives reflects this attempt to deal with the ramifications of a paradigm shift that few as yet recognize, let alone acknowledge. Unfortunately, in the public conversation about the future of our society and our planet, the issues we raise here seldom receive attention, even though they permeate every problem on the public agenda. One of our many current purposes as authors and educators is to provide the words educators can use to name these issues and then discuss them in the public arena and the educational sphere. The right words, however, are hard to find. In fact, we have yet to agree on a name for what we describe as the new paradigm. Some use the term "postmodern" as a shorthand label; others speak of "constructivism." Because labels tend to produce conceptual problems, disagreement generally accompanies their use. When we discuss the names for the new paradigm, we strive for a clarity that we hope helps you avoid confusion without diminishing the complexity of the issues involved.

To continue this discussion, we draw on several of the philosophical positions outlined in Chapter 1. The new paradigm takes strength from a combination of ancient, new and even modernist ideas. In arguing for its acceptance we by no means advocate a total break from all that has preceded it. Ancient wisdom of indigenous people from around the world, the undeniably great contributions of modernist science, modernist political notions of justice and liberty and, of course, the insights currently emerging from our understanding of the interconnectedness of all "living" and "nonliving" things—all of these shape our eclectic view of the new paradigm. In this context we draw on a variety of the philosophies: idealism for its emphasis on the great ideas produced by people from various civilizations; pragmatism's progressivism and social reconstructionism for their emphasis on the need for consistent change and adaptation, for curricula based on social experience and for the promotion of social activism in the community; and existentialism for its emphasis on human choice, responsibility and freedom.

To state a current commonly held opinion simply, schools have done a bad job of making education meaningful for students. Teachers too often present predigested information to passive recipients. Such a positivist arrangement spreads indifference among students and keeps them from taking responsibility for their own education. As education separates itself from the living and classes break up into arbitrary and abstract "subjects," teaching becomes like banking—a process of depositing data into inert vaults, with no interest accruing. An evaluation format expressed in report card grades forces incremental withdrawals in a quick competitive frenzy. Students learn to play a meaningless, nonsensical game to help them succeed. We all know the game. It is a sort of charade, suggesting that no one really cares about intellectual goals in the classroom or the school. Learning in schools where the purposes of education are undiscussed and undebated becomes an aimless burden, a series of hoops to be jumped through, a credentialing function—in short, a waste of time. Most students intuitively understand this. When we separate our passion from our intellect, when we dismiss serious issues, they know or at least sense it.

At this time when we need to learn to think, to analyze what we feel and to confront the pain of the fragmented, depressed and violent nature of the late twentieth century, we still play games in school. Children and adolescents perform poorly under these circumstances. We discuss these dynamics thoroughly in Chapters 9 and 10; until then consider these ten statistics of contemporary childhood:

One million students drop out of school each year.

Nearly 1.5 million teenage women become pregnant each year.

Between one-fifth and three-quarters of U.S. children live below the poverty line.

On any given night, at least 100,000 homeless children sleep in shelters or on the streets.

Every year, more than five thousand young people take their own lives.

More than 2.2 million cases of child abuse and neglect were reported in 1991.

Fifteen percent of the graduates of urban high schools read at a sixth-grade or lower level.

Almost 10 million children have no regular medical care.

About 20 million children under age 17 have never seen a dentist.

An estimated 3 million grade and high school children have a serious drinking problem (Obiakor, 1992, p. 3).

Beyond these grim social dynamics one senses a powerful boredom among schoolchildren, along with a general anger and malaise in the larger society. Many psychologists practicing from the viewpoint of the new paradigm maintain that contemporary life takes its toll on the human psyche in economically developed industrial nations, particularly among children. These observers suggest that the human mind may be better adapted to life in less "advanced" survival-centered societies. Various people once labeled "primitive" by Europeans lived in a state of harmony with nature, spending perhaps ten to fifteen hours a week finding food.

While they lacked the luxuries of the contemporary Western world, they never craved such luxuries. After securing food, shelter and clothing, these indigenous peoples had time for rituals, reflection, community events and leisure. Although we must avoid the temptation to romanticize these people (they experienced serious illnesses and dangerous conflict and generally died young), they seemed able to escape boredom and malaise.

With its scientific gadgetry and technological wonders, modernist civilization promotes a regulated, intransigent pattern of existence that represses creative impulses. Neither school nor work in our society offers many avenues for creative endeavor. Perhaps the most important difference between traditional and modernist cultures appears in the daily lives of children. In traditional societies children spent the day with their parents and other community members participating in the activities of the group or clan. Constantly engaged, these young people learned throughout each day. By contrast, contemporary children find themselves removed from everyday commerce, sitting by themselves or in disconnected and bored bunches that countenance psychological difficulties and pathological behavior.

By presenting this comparison between modern and traditional peoples, we do not mean to urge that you throw away your microwave oven and return to hunting and foraging. Rather, an examination of indigenous life-styles raises questions to ask of our own lives, institutions and children. We may need to rethink childhood, the purposes of school and the material values that comfort us so much (Cannella, 1996). Perhaps we should strive more to live interesting and meaningful lives rather than affluent and comfortable lives.

WHAT'S PASSION GOT TO DO WITH IT?

As we watch alienated children and adolescents arrive at school with vacant stares only to be met by teachers anesthetized by the education game, we are compelled to present "what could be" within the dynamics of the new paradigm. To confront the current pathology we draw on our human passion and challenge you to do the same. We seek out the company of passionate teachers and students angered by the sadness and pain of contemporary education. Moved by global concerns, yet dedicated to the needs of individual students, passionate teachers keep boredom in the hall. When we bring our passion and inquisitiveness into the classroom, we banish the education game. Our sense of purpose protects us from the epidemic of alienation and cynicism. Understanding teaching in its various contexts, we connect our jobs to the passion that moved us to become teachers in the first place.

Our positivist colleagues sometimes chide us for being impractical. Teachers, they say, need practical guidance to deal with the problems they face. Nothing, we reply, is more practical than a passion to change students' lives. Passion and the commitment it produces are more than just personal traits that some people have and others do not; they can be taught to and experienced by teachers, who can in turn teach them to students. Indeed, passionate men and women have already influenced our lives. But we refer here to a passion informed by new possibilities for human consciousness and higher orders of thinking. An empty, uninformed passion is superficial, all dressed up with no place to go. Informed passion takes sustenance from ideas about social justice, democracy, cosmology, human possibility and the still unexplored depths of education and students. When passion about students joins a passion for knowledge production and ideas, anything is possible, and this "anything" becomes more visible when we add a passion for meaning-making in school.

To leave the cynical education game behind, we must be equipped to demonstrate what education means in the lives of students. Passionate teachers, in our view, must become meaning-makers, or hermeneuticists. The word *hermeneutics* comes from Hermes, the winged messenger of the Greek gods, who interpreted their decisions to other gods and mortals. Hermes both clarified and scrambled these messages, illustrating the complexity and subjectivity of meaning in the world. Thus hermeneutics now refers to the art and process of interpretation, of meaning-making in human affairs. In our view, this hermeneutic or meaning-making function is the passionate teacher's role. As hermeneuticists, teachers connect prose and passion as they initiate students into the life of the mind. Using their meaning-making abilities, passionate teachers work to awaken and enliven themselves and their students, alerting them to their senses and connecting them to various dimensions of the world.

Accordingly, we must practice "aliveness" and "wide-awakenness" and become sensitive to what our senses reveal (Greene, 1978). In this practice we begin to see what had been invisible, whether concrete physical phenomena or abstract social injustice. This mindfulness focuses our attention on the present by immersing us in the living process. It is especially important in this electronic age of hyperreality, with its constant bombardment of stimuli, to focus our consciousness so we can see order in the chaos. Something emerges from the new paradigm that nourishes hope in the midst of despair.

One of us asks education students to visit a public school after the first day of class and record what they see. These assignments are set aside until late in the term, when the students are asked to return to the school and compare a second set of observations with the first. Students come back to class excited by what their senses can perceive after several weeks of college-level meaning-making.

Another assignment requires students to keep notebooks with them throughout the semester to record their observations in all their college classes, without necessarily naming the professors or course titles. The students must then reflect on their reactions and their classmates' reactions—both positive and negative—to various learning strategies and teaching styles. Students are also asked to write short essays about their own classroom experiences as elementary and secondary students.

All of these assignments direct students toward the habit of reflection that may take a lifetime to understand fully. We consistently notice, however, that their excitement for teaching and passion for learning begin to extend to everyone around them. The "spiritual dynamics" we referred to in Chapter 1 apply directly to the connection between prose and passion and meaning-making. Spirituality intensifies aliveness and delineates the purpose of living. Thus, this idea of passionate teaching connects spiritual concepts of aliveness to the psychological realm of heightened perception, the philosophical realm of meaning-making, and the political realm of justice. Passion and expanded consciousness mean little if they overlook a politics of empowerment tuned responsively to the sufferings of the poor and marginalized and their perceptions of reality.

To be frank, we intend here to help you establish a democratic vision on which to ground your philosophy of education. While we obviously hold perspectives and opinions we openly express, you must finally develop your own vision and philosophy, as we encourage you to do. In this process you may find the ideas we have discussed compelling; perhaps not. We are certainly committed to the justice-related aspects of our social vision, an issue so complex that educators often retreat to the safer, more technical and practical questions. As they ignore questions of justice and the pathologies of racism, sexism, homophobia, environmental degradation, economic injustice, religious intolerance and class bias that surround them, teachers and educational leaders leave morality to fend for itself among our children. The new paradigm we envision takes democratic values and social justice seriously and requires a commitment in the everyday practices of those individuals and communities that ascribe to it. Not to overstate the importance of these paradigmatic dynamics, the survival of the human race may be at stake. As we engage you in questions of meaning-making in the new paradigm, we ask both the *why* and the *how* questions about education and teaching practice. The old paradigm ignored these questions, and learning to teach in the new postmodern paradigm may be more difficult than it appeared years ago to modernist educators (Bohm & Edwards, 1991; Fried, 1995; Capra, Steindl-Rast & Matus, 1991; Darder, 1991). We urge you to pursue the difficult task of learning to contextualize teaching. Although engaging in a new paradigm entails risks, rewards await those who help shape a just, compassionate, spiritual and environmentally sustainable community.

Finding Purpose and Making Meaning

Daunting as it may seem, we must learn to reconnect philosophy and science, emotion and reason, understanding and application, why and how. As we said in Chapter 1, education is a holistic experience that brings all the dimensions of life together. Good teaching contextualizes rather than fragments. In the new paradigm philosophy directs the purposes we embrace, the meaning we make and our classroom practice. In the old paradigm teacher education and educational reform too often focused on procedures, rather than purpose. Questions of purpose disappeared in this divided view to the point at which a crisis of meaning began to develop. In the old paradigm the nature of the associations between objects in the world became peripheral. In the new paradigm their properties are established more by their relationships to other things than by their intrinsic characteristics (Wheatley, 1994). This new way of seeing the world defines individuals by their relationships to others and the world in general. Indeed, we become persons by developing more and more complex interrelationships; in fact, the development of these connections becomes a basic purpose of education. Human beings cannot, therefore, separate meaning and purpose from making connections with other people and the natural world, from becoming so aware of our context that we and it, or "I and Thou" as Martin Buber said, become inseparable.

These ecological concerns with interconnectedness and meaning hold practical implications for classroom teaching. We talk often in teacher education about the role of content (subject matter) in relation to teaching methodology. Teacher educators often accuse their colleagues in the other academic disciplines of ignoring methodology in their love of content; historians, chemists, physicists and English professors accuse teacher educators of ignoring content in their love of methodology. Yet both groups miss the point, that one cannot separate the two dynamics. Indeed, the new paradigm forces us to reconsider the nature of content. Without the learning context, academic content holds no significance—it gains meaning only in light of its context as it is viewed in relation to (1) human knowing (how was the knowledge produced?), (2) issues of research (what did the researchers who produced it assume?), (3) comparison to other information (what does it tell us about previous interpretations in the field?), (4) synthesis (what insights emerge when this information is connected to or viewed in light of other data?), and (5) application (what are the benefits to be derived from applying our understanding of this information in differing contexts?). These questions should infuse a teacher's analysis of the content of a course. In the simplest sense, if teachers fail to connect subject matter to the context that gives it meaning, students will justifiably find it boring and irrelevant to their lives. Thus, the disconnectedness and meaninglessness referred to earlier are perpetuated.

If you are like us, you probably forgot much of what you were taught in school soon after you were tested on it. Most of us who were educated in traditional schools grounded in the old paradigm had to consume content with little or no context, to the point where we never wanted to consider the subject again. One of the authors remembers walking into freshman botany class excited to learn about the trees and plants in the surrounding mountains of southern Appalachia. How disappointed he was that the class never went outside, never even looked out the window at the beautiful trees surrounding the botany building. He grew to dread the class, with its endless classification systems and all the Latin names. He tried in vain to memorize the names for the detailed tests and escaped the class with a D and a need to forget its content.

Similarly, consider the words of a teacher describing his experience with college biology classes:

I just graduated from college with my degree in biology education. After a long struggle through five years of studying, I figured it was time for a break. I planned a week's vacation with some high school buddies in the great outdoors. I was excited about camping, fishing, canoeing, and also eager to share—perhaps a bit cocky about sharing—all the biological knowledge I had gained in college. We set up camp on top of a hill overlooking the lake. I was ready to field questions from my buddies. The guys promptly nicknamed me "Mr. Nature"! The group consisted of three business majors and two friends who had not attended college. When questions came up during the week, I became frustrated by not knowing all of the answers. What was going on here? Was my education failing me? Ironically, the two friends who did not attend college were able to answer most of the questions. Not only did they have answers, but they were good answers! The questions they answered were those everybody wanted to know. Sure, I could talk about photosynthesis and describe the steps and many complex chemicals involved, but that quickly bored everyone. I could spew out facts and figures and throw in some buzz words, but many questions I wanted to answer, I couldn't. I didn't know how. I never had the experience or thought about nature in this immediate way. How could this be? I was the educated one. I had just spent five years learning about biology and nature. I had a piece of paper certifying me as smart. How did these other guys know so much? They didn't go to college. Where did all of their knowledge come from? I quickly realized that they spent a lot of time outdoors. They went camping and fishing with their father, grandfather, and an "old-timer" friend. They explained how each of them would tell stories around the campfire. Grandpa and the "old-timer" would tell stories passed down from their fathers and grandfathers. They would answer questions based on their experiences in nature. I realized that these two guys knew so much about the outdoors and I didn't know as much as I thought I did. There were questions and answers that my college books and teachers did not cover and never encouraged me to think about. I was missing the experience of nature while studying biology! (Matt Ricci, 1996)

Matt is a young teacher with outstanding biology credentials but little understanding of nature. He is the product of a positivist and modernist educational system, the kind of system the new paradigm challenges.

In the old paradigm meaning disappeared as information turned into factoids, bits and pieces of data removed from context. We learn to think like this, in fragments, removed from the context that gives thought meaning through its connection to the big picture. Schools ignore these connections; rarely do teachers and administrators talk about human problems and their interconnectedness. We speak, for example, of adolescent suicide as a vexing problem and hold workshops to prepare teachers to identify those students who fit "the profile" of the potential suicide. But that is where the process and compassion stop. Rarely do we connect the increase in adolescent suicide to the larger context of late-twentieth-century life, with its economic problems, social pressures, hierarchical popular culture, homophobia, racism and loss of cohesion and coherence. When it is viewed within this larger context, suicide is understandable at a new level of sophistication. Immediately we are confronted with the decontextualized inadequacy of all those earnest workshops. Once we begin to contextualize youth suicide, our ability to develop viable responses improves dramatically. In the case of suicide—or any other problem—the more ways we contextualize the issue, as we did in Chapter 1 with the story about Robbie Kirkland, the better we understand it and the more likely it becomes that we will find effective solutions.

AN EXAMPLE: THE SIEGE OF VICKSBURG PLACED IN CONTEXT

Another example of decontextualization and the fascination with short-term answers appears in the social studies curriculum. Like Matt Ricci, one of the authors always felt disconnected from his American history classes. Many students continue to report almost inevitable boredom in history classes. The following story offers a clue as to why:

> As a child, I often visited my grandmother's home in Shreveport, Louisiana, where an unusual family tradition got passed down to each new generation. The children would gather around to listen to stories about the Civil War while my grandmother would rub the side of her head and repeat, "The damn Yankees shot Aunt Dora!" She told her story with passion, and even though I did not understand all of the implications of the Civil War, I grew up hating the elusive but evil "damn Yankees" who had shot my aunt. Dora Navra had been the eight-year-old daughter of my great-great-great-great grandparents, Abraham Navra and Ellen Kinney, who settled in Vicksburg, Mississippi, in the 1840s. During the siege of Vicksburg in the summer of 1863, Dora was hit in the head by shrapnel from a canon fired by Union soldiers as she ran back into town after hiding in a cave on the outskirts. Dora had been sent to look for the local doctor to attend her infant brother Samuel who was ill. Dora survived her wound, but Samuel died.
>
> Ever since, members of my family have systematically remembered the federal soldiers who surrounded Vicksburg in 1863 and inflicted misery on its citizens and on our family. I cannot remember studying the Civil War in any detail in elementary school, high school, or college, even though my transcripts indicate that I have credit for several courses in American history. Not once do I remember studying anything about the siege of Vicksburg, and no teacher ever encouraged me to share our family oral tradition. In fact, I doubt I ever made any connection between my unusual family tradition and the study of American history.
>
> Even as a college graduate, I could not have placed the date of the siege of Vicksburg on a timeline, named the generals or analyzed the reasons for the strategic importance of Vicksburg in the war or the event in American history, despite that fact that I excelled in high school history courses and graduated with honors from a traditional liberal arts college. What went wrong? I successfully completed a traditional core curriculum and apparently memorized all of the assigned facts about the Civil War, but I failed to retain any of this information.
>
> But years later when I took up genealogy as a hobby I finally made the connection between my family history and American history. During my years of formal schooling, why had social studies and my family traditions failed to intersect? I am convinced that never having been encouraged to make connections between

the past and the present, between my relatives who were shot by Union soldiers and my life as a student studying the Civil War, explains my ignorance of Civil War history and American history generally. These dimensions—an acknowledgment of the value of these connections—never appeared in the classical curriculum in my formal schooling in the 1950s and 1960s, which kept me from associating the dreary Civil War rote memorization and my exciting family context in relation to the siege of Vicksburg.

The first time I took my children to Vicksburg, I retold the family history and visited all of the historical landmarks and family grave sites. We made tomb rubbings and copies of microfilmed newspaper articles about our ancestors in the public library. I even took a picture with the three children rubbing their "injured" heads at the grave of Aunt Dora. Everywhere we went in Vicksburg we thought about Aunt Dora and her family. We explored the history of the siege of Vicksburg from the perspective of our family, including a visit to the location of the old Navra home. In short, we experienced history in an autobiographical context. The children wanted to buy books and read about the siege as we toured every museum in town. We planned future visits to trim and decorate the family burial plot and erect a historical marker. The climax of the Vicksburg trip occurred while we visited the old courthouse museum, an elegant Greek revival antebellum stone building that houses many Civil War era artifacts. As we moved from room to room, my nine-year-old daughter Katie ran ahead. Suddenly, I heard her shout in the next room, and I rushed to catch up. Katie was standing in awe before a glass case, and she could hardly contain her excitement. She had discovered a display of mannequins with clothing the citizens of Vicksburg wore in the 1800s. Katie proudly shouted out the inscription on the case for the whole museum to hear: "This dress was a gift to Ellen Kinney Navra on her wedding day. The shawl was worn by her daughter, Dora Navra." History came alive before Katie's eyes as she gazed at the shawl. The siege of Vicksburg became her story, always to be remembered because she felt its immediacy and relevance. Katie now tells this story to her fourth grade classmates, who are fascinated by the Civil War and want to visit Vicksburg. (Slattery, 1995a)

This story may seem a bit vague and difficult to understand for those just starting to understand postmodern and constructivist discourses. But the challenge is to examine critically our own stories in context. We challenge students to *enter* history rather than simply observe it from a distance. Teachers must begin their historical studies by entering into the process themselves. Jonathan Kozol proposed exactly this participatory view of history for social studies classrooms, and he attacked schooling that is neither transformative nor a participant in history.

School teaches history in the same way that it teaches syntax, grammar, and word-preference: in terms that guarantee our prior exile from its passion and its transformation. It lifts up children from the present, denies them powerful access to the future, and robs them of all ethical repossession of the past. History is, as the sarcastic student says, an X-rated film. The trouble is that everyone we know, love,

touch, hold, dream to be, or ever might become, has first to be told: I cannot enter.
(1975, p. 83)

History is more than a series of events to be memorized; it is also an opportunity to inform the present and provide access to the future. Kozol challenges teachers to adopt a transformative pedagogy to recover a sense of participating in history education. Education, he explains, must be understood from this participatory, even autobiographical perspective. Historical events lack meaning outside the context of individual educators engaged in the exploration and excavation of the relevance of the events and the people, famous, infamous and anonymous, who have acted in history.

MAKING MEANING: THE PRODUCTION AND "PROBLEMATIZATION" OF KNOWLEDGE

A key difference between education in the old and new paradigms is that the old model emphasizes the *discovery* of knowledge whereas the new emphasizes the *invention* and *construction* of knowledge (Henderson & Hawthorne, 1995). Thus, teachers can become scholars who both contextualize and produce knowledge, all the while sharing their abilities with their students. The classroom begins to resemble a "think tank" or "creative studio," an environment that produces important knowledge with value outside and beyond. Under modernist positivism teachers had to say, "Give me the truth and I will pass it along to students in the most efficient way possible." In the new paradigm teachers will assert their freedom from being all-knowing experts. Such teachers often say, "Please support me as my students and I explore the world of mathematics, sociology or literature." Teachers in the new paradigm refuse to accept without question the validity of perennialism and the Western canon (the great books and ideas, usually written by influential white males, usually taught in the traditional Western curriculum)—or any textbook, canon or curriculum guide, for that matter—as they seek knowledge from many cultures and traditions. Indeed, they become restless operating within a state-mandated framework. They seek to recontextualize questions asked traditionally about schooling and knowledge production in general. While they respect earlier insights and revere the genius of past eras, they display their veneration by continuing to question the work of their intellectual ancestors and by seeking to uncover literature and ideas that have been banished, condemned, neglected or deemed heretical in previous eras.

In this same spirit, your personal context and understanding may lead you to revise and expand many of the ideas we present here. You may also come to new insights that lead you to reevaluate positions you have held for years. Traditional authorities find such questions dangerous because their power, money and influence could be jeopardized by new ideas. We find such questioning refreshing and important.

Teachers from the new paradigm seek new ways of conceptualizing the world. Thus, in the spirit of the Brazilian educator Paulo Freire, they "problematize" the information that confronts them by asking penetrating questions and by challenging simple answers to complex issues. Along with such educators as Henry Giroux, Peter McLaren, Joanne Pagano, Deborah Britzman, Donaldo Macedo and William Pinar, Freire recommends that any paradigm shift be viewed in a critical or socially transformative way. We discuss this "critical education" in more detail later, but we can say for now that such a position maintains that knowledge always reflects larger power relationships in society. This means that those with social, economic, religious and political clout have more say, for example, about what the schools consider official and validated knowledge than those without influence.

Critical teachers understand this tendency and account for it in the way they work to "problematize" classroom information. Problematization in this critical new paradigm involves asking questions such as: Where did the knowledge come from? Who benefits from the acceptance of this knowledge? An ability to recognize these power-related dynamics makes up much of what Freire has called "critical consciousness." Such a way of seeing moves individuals to reconceptualize their world in a way that leads to transformative action, social change and the construction of a just, compassionate and ecologically sustainable community.

Teachers operating in the new paradigm who embrace these critical goals work to help students develop an awareness of themselves as social agents. Such a teaching goal requires that teachers and students contextualize what happens in the classroom in relation to power and social justice issues, as well as their actual experiences. Thus, when students read a section of a science textbook that praises the virtues of nuclear power without references to environmental problems or allusions to Three Mile Island, Chernobyl or nuclear waste storage and contamination, critical teachers insist that power questions be asked. Who benefits by such a description of nuclear power? Who is harmed by this incomplete description? Where are hazardous waste storage facilities located? These are central questions in such a context. Critical scholars, for example, would raise questions about environmental racism where poor and marginalized minorities are forced by economic and political structures to live in polluted and dangerous neighborhoods adjacent to factories and power plants.

This particular question constitutes the major theme of this book: How do we construct contexts that promote critical growth in our classrooms? We will examine activities and methodologies that teachers have used to encourage student reflection on the cultural values that shape personal views of the world and one's place in it. Understanding how our consciousness is constructed provides insight into both who we are and how the world works. Critical teachers welcome such questions.

PUSHING THE COGNITIVE ENVELOPE

Jet pilots who test new models often speak of "pushing the envelope" in referring to their attempts to take a jet higher or faster than anyone has before. The new paradigm encourages teachers to push the cognitive envelope and to place their faith in human potential and the capacity of human consciousness and to expand the prospect of continuing discovery. This is the atmosphere we want to create in our schools among administrators, teachers and students. We all want coming generations to live in a better world than ours with its violence, pain, intolerance, inequality and suffering. We have no certain map for this journey, but we do have some questions that might move us in the right direction.

We embrace a new paradigm in an effort to create a new kind of intelligence. A look at our schools tells us that a large part of what goes on there engages only the lowest forms of human thinking: rote memorization and short-term memory skills. Recall the evaluation methods your elementary, middle and high school (even college) adopted. Is it fair to say that in most cases factual memory was the type of thinking required? How often were you asked to engage in higher-order thinking that required you to interpret information, to transfer cognitive skills developed in one domain to another, to produce knowledge; to invent, create, work for a just solution to a local issue; or to apply your skills to real-life problems?

We need to develop forms of intelligence that transcend mere recall and are carefully tied to the hermeneutic realm of meaning making and living. Meaning-making engages thinkers with the deepest experiences that human beings encounter. Uncertainty naturally accompanies these experiences; once we take the risk and start the hermeneutic process, we don't really know where the path will lead. When we turn over big rocks, we risk surprises. What comes crawling out may challenge the status quo. But we confront our deepest experiences and un-mapped territories as we develop research, interpretive and analytical skills. We also develop an ability to produce and work with knowledge.

Unlike modernist positivism, cognition in the new paradigm embraces both the rational and the intuitive. Moving beyond an exclusive reliance on rational forms of compartmentalizing and categorizing, thinking in the new paradigm embraces both analysis and synthesis, both linear and nonlinear insights. It cultivates an intuitive ability to perceive the whole, the larger context in which an event takes place (Hauser, 1991; Capra, Steindl-Rast & Matus, 1991). Even in scientific research and knowledge production, the new paradigm values the intuitive, the experiential, the poetic and the metaphoric. When we teach our graduate or undergraduate students about research, we discuss with them literary works that inspire each of us. We also make the point that poets, novelists and artists should, as producers of knowledge and interpreters of the world, serve as models for researchers. Their poetic and metaphoric "eyes" may tell us more about the phenomenon under consideration than all the professional insights of historians, mathematicians and ethnographers combined. Even though these researchers closely follow the methodological guidelines, their language tends to be insufficiently rich to exceed a shallow level of description.

Poetic insight and the metaphoric eye can help us pass beyond the low orders of thinking that now dominate many classrooms. Modernist positivism has dismissed metaphoric forms of thinking from the seventeenth century until the present. Sir Francis Bacon, a central contributor to the development of the scientific method, warned his contemporaries to beware "the deceit of the poetic," and viewpoints such as his have led to a modernist dysfunctionality, a disharmony between the intellect and the emotions. The separation of intellect and emotions has precipitated a cognitive difficulty, a psychic impoverishment that has led to social, political, pedagogical and psychological fragmentation. Indeed, many of the problems that face our schools, society and young people at the beginning of the twenty-first century stem from this "cognitive illness."

When positivism fails to account for the role of emotions and feelings in higher-order thinking, it overlooks a major feature of human cognition. Emotions give us the motivation to think, reason and devote hours to solving the complex problems we confront. When we feel emotions, we ask where they come from and what causes them. Emotional "senses" connect with our logical perceptions to provide us information about our world. Thus, emotions and intellect stay in constant contact, seeking to learn from and harmonize with one another. Positivist ways of thinking interrupt this constructive interaction, undermining in the process the cognitive possibilities particular to our species (Bohm & Edwards, 1991). They negate poetic insight and blind our metaphoric eye. They deny the contributions of women, indigenous people, artists and others who may have a different way of knowing the world and explaining reality.

When these insights into cognition in the new paradigm connect with critical concerns about power and justice, teachers and students find their educational experiences enhanced. New forms of consciousness push the cognitive envelope. We begin to understand the political processes that shape accepted knowledge and the dynamics hidden within what we think of as the neutral medium of language. For example, students can begin to understand power dynamics in the school setting. From a discursive perspective (discursive practices involve the tacit rules that define what can and cannot be said, who speaks and who must listen and whose constructions of reality are valid and scientific and whose are unlearned and unimportant), students often see themselves as outsiders in the school community. The farther they fall away from the dominant culture (white, Anglo-Saxon, Protestant, male, heterosexual, English speaking and middle class), the more excluded they feel. A graduate student recently told us about growing up as the only Jewish student in a Christian community. When the school began to prepare the Christmas program in early October every year, he was sent to empty classrooms to wash the boards. He began to wonder what was wrong with him and his religion.

His subconscious response was the inevitable result of the marginalization that schools often impose on minority children, even when they struggle to conform to the dominant values of teachers and society and most assuredly when they rebel against the injustice of social structures. In such a context, teachers could provide a valuable consciousness-expanding and empowering act by introducing students to a study of the school's own discursive practices. Such a study might encourage students to compare the language they use at home and in their peer group to the language the school expects of them. Which language practices are acceptable in school and which are not? Why? Do some school districts—as did one, in the much-discussed decision by the Oakland School Board in California in 1997 to use Ebonics to enhance the teaching of standard English—encourage many linguistic forms? Such methods encourage self-reflection and an awareness of power at the level of discourse, abilities one can transfer to a variety of situations both inside and outside the school (Harred, 1991; Hindman, 1992).

Rethinking Authority

We hold a hopeful vision of empowered teachers who determine the conditions of their own work, have learned to rethink the possibilities of human cognition, make decisions about what occurs in their schools and have organized to protect their academic and professional interests. At the same time these teachers have gained unprecedented power to help shape their own professional practice and school purpose, and they share their new power with their students.

Democratic changes like these may seem frightening. Demanding power is frightening enough for teachers, but then relinquishing some of it to students is close to unthinkable. But the new educational paradigm will almost certainly undermine the hierarchy of expertise. In modernist positivism, experts with backgrounds in empirical research provide teachers with validated teaching strategies and official information. The good teacher in this paradigm passes the official data along to students using the "proper methodology." In the new paradigm the role of expert must be repositioned; teachers and students themselves must become inquisitive learners, empowering one another by their ability to produce knowledge and challenge the knowledge the old paradigm produced. As the role of expert is reshaped, so too does the nature of authority. The form of authority the new paradigm promotes draws on a variety of theological traditions in its assertions that the greatest among us must become the servant of all. Such a position is politically dangerous in its subversive assumption that authority should be shared with newly empowered citizens (Sholle & Denski, 1994).

In the new paradigm authority is no longer the power to dictate as it was in the traditional context; rather, authority becomes a grounding for knowing and acting. Genuine authority emerges etymologically in "authorship." Far too many people in bureaucratic and educational settings exercise authority even though they have no grounding in it. The difference between the leader who possesses the authority provided by knowing and acting experience and the pro forma leader is the difference between *genuine* authority and *authoritarian* authority. Contrary to the opinions of those who protect the status quo, those of us who speak of resisting authority rebel against the authoritarian, not the genuine. Those who wield authority in the new paradigm must be both sensitive to power dynamics and prepared to ask questions about democracy and justice even while exercising their authority. They must also be responsible for the use of their power.

Accordingly, teachers must examine themselves as authority figures in light of these new paradigm dynamics. To move beyond authoritarianism, teachers in the new paradigm use their authorship to empower their students. These teachers help students develop authority by engaging them in the quest for a basis for knowing and acting. In this context, power is used not to dominate and control but to influence and empower others. A teacher's power in the new model encourages analysis and meaning-making so that students can teach themselves and those around them (Capra, Steindl-Rast & Matus, 1991).

Because so many of us in schools and other institutions have grown wary of authoritarian leaders, some advocates of the new paradigm in education urge us to relinquish our authority as teachers altogether and abandon our claim to the authoritative role of the traditional teacher. We find this extreme position both impractical and duplicitous, for teachers remain endowed by their institutional role with the power to assign grades, formulate activities and look after the safety and best interests of their students. This authority need not be authoritarian; teachers can use their authority to facilitate their students' attempts to assume more power in the creation of texts and the production of knowledge. A teacher's authority in the new paradigm can support the oppositional behavior of students, to support minority viewpoints and make sure they receive serious attention and to consider student perspectives in the larger negotiations over what constitutes knowledge. Although we advocate a democratic power-sharing education we do not mean that we can automatically create a completely egalitarian classroom. Artfully subverted, antiauthoritarian, collaborative teaching strategies can be just as authoritarian and coercive as the traditional methodologies (Metzger & Bryant, 1993).

In many so-called democratic classrooms teachers engage in a variety of directive roles: formulating questions and activities for students, serving as interpersonal facilitators, supervising tasks, interpreting students' creative work, acting as spokespeople for the educational community in open discourse and evaluating. Even though teachers may no longer dispense isolated facts and stand in front of the class while the students sit in assigned seats, they remain authority figures and power wielders. Because the decentralized classroom encourages student-based activities in which students reveal their more personal and private aspects, their teachers may gain greater power to manipulate them than they had in a traditional lecture-oriented classroom (Hinchey, 1998).

Consider, for example, the reflective teaching practice of student journal keeping—a practice that is generally popular in democratic classrooms. When they are asked (often required) to share their journals with the teacher to promote dialogue and insight, students sometimes feel compelled to confess their shortcomings or submit themselves to the teacher as therapist. Power may not take its stark form, as in the days of corporal punishment or physical detention, but it is exercised nonetheless. In moving away from the abuses of the old paradigm we must be careful to avoid creating new abuses in their stead. With this awareness we can begin to democratize the journal experience, making it a constitutive (building) experience rather than a confessional activity. A democratic teacher might use journal writing as a constitutive experience to help students consider what it means to be a good teacher in a particular context. Such a situation might reduce the pressure for students to confess and to tell teachers what they think the teachers want to hear. More generally, it might minimize the hidden authoritarianism of the "student-centered" classroom (Harred, 1991; Gore, 1993).

RECONCEPTUALIZING CURRICULUM DEVELOPMENT AND TEACHING METHODS IN THE NEW PARADIGM

Modernist positivism disempowers teachers, making them information deliverers and servants of knowledge, foisting on them curricula produced elsewhere. We envision teachers under the new paradigm taking charge of whole courses of study and drawing on conceptions of what is both truly important and truly useful in the lives of the students they teach. System guidelines will, of course, remain and teachers will continue to follow subject delineations of, say, state departments of education. But teachers will take more responsibility for interpreting how such guidelines fit into their classroom contexts. This interpretation may revolve around what a teacher decides *not* to cover. For example, a detailed examination of the novels of James Joyce with analyses of his life, writing style, literary innovations and criticism of his work might provide students with more insight into the purposes and benefits of literary studies than a cursory, fragmented, fact-oriented survey of twentieth-century novelists. Higher orders of cognitive activity would replace modernist fact gathering and push the cognitive envelope. In no way do we want to suggest that subject matter is unimportant. Content is so important that we should study it in sufficient detail to allow students to make meaning around it. We need to understand the conditions of its production and validation, who benefits from it, who does not and how it relates to other information. Such conceptual understanding rarely forms during a superficial survey of a discipline's subject matter.

Empowered teachers work together to thwart supervisors' efforts to evaluate them on the basis of how much content they cover during the school year. Such expectations reflect modernist positivism's obsession with quantification and measurability. As supervisors speak of how Mr. Jones covered only sixty percent of the required subject matter, one hears few questions about how students made use of the data or even how long they remembered it. Advocates of "less but deeper" and more analytic coverage of content understand that force-feeding students massive amounts of data dulls their interest in a subject and their appreciation of the material. A student's relationship to the survey course that focuses on coverage quantity resembles the position of a contestant preparing for an appearance on *Jeopardy!* The breadth without depth form of learning pays dividends on *Jeopardy!* but has little usefulness in other circumstances. As we learn to make meaning, to search for connections between subject matter and student-produced knowledge and to relate our students' worlds to the lived reality of schools, our methods of teaching and curriculum design begin to change.

As we limit our curriculum coverage and free ourselves from modernist positivism's role of teacher as assembly line worker, we monitor student interest and follow it, engaging and extending it along the way. One fourth-grade science teacher found that the district curriculum guide had given him two weeks to study water. The guide delineated a variety of "water facts" for students to memorize, a few innocuous activities and a battery of multiple-choice tests. One day while the children were playing outside during recess, the teacher noticed a group of children gathered on the banks of a small stream that ran through the schoolyard. One of the students found a crawfish, which excited the students gathered around. Noting their enthusiasm, the teacher began to think of ways of connecting the mandated water studies to the little stream.

The teacher discussed his idea with the class, eliciting their ideas on what they could find out about the stream. Where does it come from? Where does it go? What's in it? The class became a research team divided into groups studying particular questions. They interviewed local meteorologists, geographers, Sierra Club members, biologists and county historians—some so interesting they were invited to class. The students took notes and made audiotapes of their interviews and class presentations. At the end of the second week, the students were still so excited by the project that the teacher extended it another week. During that week the students suggested that they compile their research into a small book. Parents volunteered to type, typeset and reproduce the book. Several copies were placed in the public and school libraries around the county. The students in the class were invited to appear on local radio shows to discuss the history of the stream, some of the pollution problems that plagued it and possible ways to clean it up.

Such a teaching strategy created a far more engaging and insightful lesson on water than those contained in the curriculum guide. While not every topic can be covered in such an inventive and thorough way, scores of methods help teachers move beyond decontextualized factual memorization. In a middle school world history class, for example, instead of a cursory overview of decontextualized facts about a variety of world civilizations, teachers could focus on only one or two cultures. Teams of students could be assigned one question to research and answer for the class. A few examples of the many possible might include (1) Would you call this civilization great? Why or why not? (2) How would being a child in this culture differ from your own childhood? (3) Did justice exist in this society? Who had power and who did not? (4) In what ways did people earn a living? (5) What were their cities and towns like? What would it have been like to live in these places? (6) What technological, linguistic or philosophical contributions did this culture make that we still use today? How has this civilization shaped our lives at the end of the twentieth century? (7) Under what conditions did this culture fall from power?

At the same time they are answering these questions, students might assign the teacher a question he or she could research. As fellow researcher, the teacher could model strategies of inquiry and investigation, helping students in their search for data. One of our colleagues offered this relevant anecdote:

Early in my college teaching career, I taught a history of ancient education class to a group of teachers working on their master's degrees. As we studied the educational histories of the early civilizations of Mesopotamia and Egypt, I pushed them to connect their understandings of the civilizations' educational dynamics to their knowledge of their culture, religion, economics and politics. In addition, I asked them to uncover the purposes and methods of education in those ancient societies and compare them to the purposes and methods employed by their own high, middle, and elementary schools. The students were paralyzed by an assignment that required detailed reading, historical interpretation, and cross-cultural comparisons of educational purposes and methods in contexts where such delineations were not explicitly identified. They informed me of their anxieties in the class meeting following the assignment. In all of their school lives they had never been asked to engage in such an exercise and didn't know where to start. I sensed that innovative pedagogy was required, and I scrambled for ways to help these frightened students without sacrificing the intellectual experience the assigned analysis would provide. I was struck with an idea as I listened to my students describe the short-term memory tests that had dominated their academic lives. Given what we have already studied, I told them, devise a question for me to answer that requires some of the skills and information I have emphasized in class. I will research the question, answer it for you, describe the process I used to collect my information and describe for you my thought processes (the hermeneutics) of how I interpreted the data and formulated my answer. For the rest of the class, the students discussed among themselves the nature of the question they would assign. They struggled, asked for help, and after a couple hours gave me my assignment. Still worried and a little surprised by my offer, they handed me this question: "Compare the educational expressions of ancient Mesopotamian and Egyptian civilizations and the cultural dynamics that surround these expressions. Explain concisely how social and cultural attitudes and political factors affected education in the two civilizations." They smiled as I read the assignment: They had given me a dose of my own medicine. I spent hours in the library the next week, ferreting out the slight data on the subject. Completing my answer the night before class, I stayed up late rereading it and revising it. In a separate notebook I made notes on every step of the process, from the library searches, to the note taking, to the interpretive process, to the writing and revising of the final draft. When the class began, my students were full of curiosity about what I had done. I passed out the essay and asked a student to read it aloud. Although I interrupted periodically to show how and where I had obtained specific information and on what basis I had offered particular interpretations, the whole class focused on the meta-analysis for some ninety minutes. I still have copies of my answer in my files. Here is how it starts:

When beginning a study of education in the ancient civilizations of Egypt and Mesopotamia, historians often focus on the emergence of proto-literacy in the late fourth millennium, B.C.E. This proto-literacy began in both civilizations as a form of picture writing. Because writing was pictorial and symbols were numerous, learning to write became a detailed and tedious task in both

Egypt and Mesopotamia. Trained professionals were needed and this led to the formation of institutions best described as schools. Thus the foundation of education in these cultures rests on the development of writing.

In both Egypt and Mesopotamia, as is the case in most civilizations, educational expression reflected larger social and cultural dynamics. Both civilizations experienced early creative flourishes—Egypt in the Old Kingdom and to an extent in the Middle Kingdom, and Mesopotamia in the days of the early Sumerian civilization. Much of this creativity emerged from a vibrant oral tradition. Once the leaders of the societies sensed the need to preserve their creative literature, the age of creativity had ended. The age of scribal education had begun. Examining both societies, historians have generally agreed that scribal culture both reflected and hastened the death of much creative expression. The scribal culture reflected social instability in Egypt—disorder resulting from social disruptions occasioned by the invasion of the Hyksos. In Mesopotamia, outside invasions and fears of the increasing use of the vernacular caused leaders to employ scribes in the protection of the written language and the social position of the leaders and the scribes themselves. Written language and scribal culture were closely connected to the preservation of the political status quo. By its very nature scribal culture initiated a decline in learning and dynamic socio-educational expression. Its emphasis on the protection of the ancient writings as well as narrowly defined practical and vocational needs for writers tended to stifle both creative expression and philosophical speculation. While Mesopotamian culture was noted for its commercial and vocational orientation, even Egyptian scribal culture emphasized the crudely practical as military and political expansionism increased the need for clerks in a growing political bureaucracy in the Empire. Thus, scribal students faced demands of obedience and strict compliance to authority. Much evidence exists in both cultures of the pervasive use of corporal punishment to ensure such subservience. Indeed, those who entered the community of scribes did not view themselves as creative agents or knowledge producers. They were clerks who did only the bidding of their bureaucratic superiors.

From here I went on to make a series of connections between education and various cultural expressions in ancient Egyptian and Mesopotamian society. Students were amazed at the amount of work I had invested in the task, and genuinely appreciated the effort I made to help them develop the research and interpretive skills they needed for their projects. The class came together and worked to develop interpretive skills and a knowledge of educational history in the two ancient civilizations. Though the history of education in ancient civilizations may not at first strike one as the most intrinsically engaging or applicable topic for teachers to study, almost every student in that class came away from it with a greater knowledge of the social role of education in ancient Egypt and Mesopotamia and with (1) a more sophisticated understanding of the social role of education in all societies; (2) a better understanding of how historical knowledge is produced; (3) new insights into the act of interpretation and meaning making in scholarly pursuits; (4) experience in the meta-analysis of writing at a micro-, sentence-by-sentence, analytical level; (5) a model for conducting secondary historical research that focuses on comparative analysis of other societies including influences on the present and (6) an appreciation for the work of scholars and the specific functions involved in the pursuit of a life of the mind.

Such outcomes are, unfortunately, the less typical results of current schooling. But they are clearly within reach. (Kincheloe, 1991)

We suggest that as prospective teachers you reflect on these scholarly abilities and begin to shape your own education in light of them. Have you been taught to do these things already? If not, where might you go to learn them? How can you make use of such abilities in the subjects and at the grade levels you plan to teach? Relax if you do not yet possess these abilities; few students do. But an awareness of them will, we hope, move you to embark on the lifelong journey of acquiring them. In your first year of teaching you may not be ready to use them, but again, that is all right. The point is that you should slowly begin to integrate research and analytic skills into your curriculum and teaching methodologies over an extended time. Learning about teaching and thinking, many say, has only just begun at certification.

Generating Curricular Themes and Defeating the Lockstep Curriculum

The positivist way of operating assumes that some genius somewhere determined what information should be covered by all students at a certain age. From this viewpoint the curriculum is coordinated so that all students cover the same material in lockstep. In this schooling arrangement the subject matter never changes and the teacher does little more than pass it along to students and test them to see how much of it they retain.

New paradigm teaching refuses to accept the lockstep curriculum, with its attendant boredom and low-level thinking. We believe that students should study their world, learning in the process who they are and what has shaped them. Once they have learned to analyze data, conduct research, make meaning and love the life of the mind, they can begin to specialize in areas of particular interest. The trick, however, is to wean students from the popular media culture and engage them in the excitement of learning itself, the thrill of research and the passion of political commitment to issues of justice. If we had one goal for an eighth-grade math teacher, for example, it would be to imbue his or her students with a love of math, a desire to find more and more uses for math in their lives and a passion to know more about the subject. Any curriculum development or methodology in the new paradigm should bring these goals to the forefront.

Paulo Freire (1970) and Ira Shor (1992) have discussed curriculum development in this context, employing the concept of a "generative theme," which is a topic taken from students' lives that is controversial enough to move them to investigate it. Generative themes work well to elicit the excitement and passion we want to see in our students. They are drenched in emotion and meaning because they play on the fears, anxieties, hopes and dreams of both students and their teachers. Generative themes arise at the point where the students' personal lives collide with the larger society. A great deal of similarity appears between Freire's generative theme and John Dewey's (1916) pragmatism or progressive education. In the early decades of the twentieth century Dewey advised teachers to construct lessons around the life experiences of students. Only by starting with these experiences, Dewey argued, can we ever reach higher forms of knowledge and learning. Starting with student experience and developing generative themes that emerge from it, teachers can induce students to question their experiences and to explore the points where those experiences intersect with larger social issues.

Starting, for example, with generative themes taken from students' famous boredom with politics, one could build an entire high school American government course. As students explain their contempt for electoral politics and cite its inherent corruption and reliance on compromise, the teacher might ask them to provide specific examples. Typically, student arguments in contexts such as this are more intuitive than factual. The teacher who recognizes this can build a unit around the generative theme of student intuition about the corruption of government. Perhaps specifying the unit around the question of how a bill becomes law in the U.S. government at the end of the twentieth century, the teacher can help students organize their research projects. Some students might study the traditional ways such a question is answered in a high school government class: the bill originates in a congressional committee and then is voted on by the House of Representatives, at which time it is placed on the Senate docket. If the Senate passes it, it proceeds to the president, who either signs it into law or vetoes it, and so forth. What is wrong with this description? the teacher can ask. What is being left out?

At this point, students recognize that their cynicism rests on the fact that even though money—legal bribery—plays a major role in the generation of legislation, it is rarely discussed either in school or by the media. They sense that their anger stems from hypocrisy—the contradiction between what we say and what we do in the political sphere. So then, how does money actually shape American government? the students begin to ask. In their research they discover that groups with money—typically corporations and industries—hire "experts" to provide validated scientific information about issues that directly affect their financial interests. The information thus produced is then carried by well-paid lobbyists, some of them former members of congress, to targeted legislators who serve on particular congressional committees. In corporate circles, the students discover, knowledge production has become a growth industry.

Meanwhile, individual citizens concerned that a certain corporate goal—say, a license to dump toxic chemicals—will undermine the quality of their community's life find themselves overwhelmed by the corporation's hired experts, who generate data that serves the corporate interest—say, the benign effects of toxic chemicals. Even though the citizen may have information on the negative impact of the corporate policy, the validated economic and scientific information the experts generate is the data that matters. When this "information politics" combines with the loyalty that legislators naturally feel for those monied groups who help finance their campaigns, the power of economic wealth in politics increases.

In the course of their research the students begin to specify the ways in which corporate knowledge production and campaign financing move congressional committees to pass some bills on to the floor of Congress while suppressing others. Mobilized by their newfound knowledge, students develop a how-a-bill-becomes-law curriculum to replace the misleadingly superficial one taught in most public high schools. Cynical students who were once disdainful of political action are mobilized around an insightful generative theme and emerge as politically active civics educators. Learning and teaching in the new paradigm can be powerful. They can even change lives.

3 Engaging Students in Philosophical Reflection

ENGAGING STUDENTS IN CLASSROOM ACTIVITIES

Teaching prospective teachers how to teach may be the most difficult pedagogical task a university assumes. But too often it is assumed to be a mere technical act with little connection to philosophical purposes, politics, racial or gender questions or epistemological perceptions of what constitutes knowledge. Many of the methods textbooks we read reduce teaching methods to step-by-step recipes removed from any consideration of what we try to accomplish beyond the mechanical transfer of data from teacher to student.

Remember that our overall goal is to contextualize teaching—to connect philosophical issues with what we do in a classroom. Few teacher education texts connect philosophy and teaching methods because it is hard to do. Methods teachers who connect strategies with issues of context and purpose perform a difficult feat and should receive a reward for their ingenuity and skill. How do they accomplish this difficult work? As usual, no one such formula exists for synthesizing purpose and method. But our observations and experience suggest that the process starts with a clear statement of purpose. Our purpose, then, is to create a classroom in which students produce knowledge about themselves and the world; to repeat, the type of knowledge we hope to produce involves questions of power and justice and ecological sustainability. We invite students and teachers to ask how power has helped shape our consciousness, and how the knowledge that results advances the larger attempt to create a just and fair social order. Understanding these purposes, we start the task of creating a classroom with an atmosphere conducive to the pursuit of these goals.

If we want students to become knowledge producers who understand the construction of their own consciousness, they must feel secure in the classrooms where they work. Safety in these classrooms means that teachers and students must have the freedom to fail and the right to make mistakes and then to learn from these mistakes. In modernist-positivist classrooms students often become nervous right-answer volunteers; they are humiliated by their mistakes and adopt defensive postures to protect themselves in this threatening humiliation.

Experimentation and risk taking are far beyond reach in those classes in which students can do only what the teacher tells them—no more, no less. We recently discussed Albert Einstein's misery as a young student (Kincheloe, Steinberg & Tippins, 1999). The questions Einstein addressed to his teachers fell outside the realm of the acceptable in his strict German schools. His questions alone constituted disruptive behavior and his teachers concluded that he had no place in the school. One teacher believed that young Einstein's mere presence undermined the other students' respect for his teaching. These are not the safe classrooms we are trying to construct.

In the safe classes we envision, students produce TV news programs for the school. Every class takes responsibility for a morning *Today in School* program for a week or two over closed-circuit television. Students operate the cameras, serve as anchors, produce videos on school stories or incidents in the local community, conduct interviews, write skits and so forth. In these schools students learn to conduct historical research by examining library collections or courthouse files on a particular citizen from the community's past. Learning as much as they can from the records and from living family members, students take on the character of the residents and tell other students and community groups about them by role playing (Whitford & Gaus, 1995).

Teachers in these schools still lecture—not every day perhaps, but whenever appropriate. Used sparingly, lectures can be inspirational teaching methods when they are conceptual and not simply a recitation of factual data, and when they are interpretive, model forms of hermeneutic meaning making that invite discussion, disagreement and student responses. A lecture in a safe classroom is never authoritarian, and students may respond to it in a variety of ways. In fact, the new paradigm suggests that student responses to lectures can become creative activities, as students use artistic materials to describe their conceptual, emotional and personal reactions to a lecture. Developing ways of engaging students that reflect our philosophical purposes is a central task for the teacher in the new paradigm.

Teaching Methods and the Role of Corporate Power

If we want to create safe classrooms in which teachers and students have the right to question existing knowledge and produce new knowledge, we must prepare you, who are planning to teach, for the problems you will face. One of your most frustrating problems will revolve around your discovery that power can shape and even dominate your life and your school. Social theorists continue to debate the nature of power and the ways it works. We can usefully avoid the more theoretical discussions, but we can say that power is a basic reality of human existence, present in all human relationships, including those of lovers, business partners, basketball teams, teachers and students, college faculties, courts, government bodies and so on.

Our concern with power as it affects philosophy and teaching methods centers on its ability to dominate. Domination arises when different individuals and groups (women, African Americans, Latino/as, the physically challenged, non-English speaking, the poor) find themselves in unequal power relationships. Domination appears in these unequal associations, as it taps what is known as "extractive power"—the acquired ability by power wielders (corporate leaders, political bosses, media systems owners, superintendents, landlords) to exploit and benefit from the work of those with less power.

Teachers in the new paradigm should recognize these unjust relationships and be able to trace the ways they affect their students, the school curriculum and their professional freedom to produce knowledge in their classes. Many of the problems innovative teachers face involve the tendency of the scholastically powerful to maintain the world in general and schools in particular as they currently exist.

Powerful groups have rarely enjoyed as much ability to dominate as they do at the beginning of the twenty-first century. The already awesome power and increasing ability to dominate reside both in government and in what we commonly call "the market"—corporations, businesses, industries, in short, all revenue-generating enterprises. In fact, the coercive power of the market is far more insidious, hidden and elusive than that of the government. The very elusiveness of private power keeps progressive elements from confronting it, for most citizens are unaware of its existence and its modus operandi. The market refuses to stay in its place, as corporate power spills over into the realms of culture, politics and education (Brosio, 1994). This spillover complicates the efforts of those who treasure social justice to protect a fragile American democracy. While individuals retain the freedom to vote, they must suffer coercion in their economic lives. Many progressives argue that without a public understanding of the way economic wealth concentrates political power, democracy will not survive, but to repeat, advocates of democracy must contend with the invisible political impact of power. Indeed, the greatest challenge democracy now faces is to expose the forces that attack it from within (Wirth, 1983; Brosio, 1985).

Through their control of vast resources, American corporations have become a fourth branch of government—a superior branch more than a co-equal branch, really, for corporations can avoid the checks and balances that restrict legislative, executive and judicial institutions. The drive for privatization, a hallmark of national politics in the 1980s, has shifted more and more power into the hands of corporations. As corporate taxes fell in the name of trickle-down economics, power accrued to business and industry in the name of corporate freedom and the free hand of the marketplace. With corporate leaders making more of the nation's economic and political decisions, proponents of a just democracy protest that those who exercise the most power over the daily lives of Americans are elected by no one and have no obligation to act in the public interest. These realizations may not be entirely new. Alexis de Tocqueville, the French statesman who visited

America in the 1830s, wrote extensively about the impact of industrialization. Understanding the tendency of power to follow wealth, de Tocqueville warned that industrial development might lead to the creation of a new aristocracy. This so-called "economic royalty," he concluded, is incompatible with democratic equality (de Tocqueville, 1840; Bellah et al., 1991).

Since the beginnings of industrialization, in the first half of the 1800s, corporations have continually increased their influence in American life. Not content to control the workforce and the process and distribution of production, early twentieth-century corporate leaders sought new techniques to help them control consumer demand. The second decade of the 1900s witnessed the birth of marketing, as the wiles of advertising made cars, clothes, cigarettes and processed foods objects of desire. The contrivances of credit buying and annual model updates and the psychology of packaging coincided with the development of advertising and market research to produce forms of social regulation unimagined in the nineteenth century. With the development of radio and television the possibility for even newer forms of social control increased exponentially. Such innovations in market research as Neilsen canvasses of TV viewership patterns, citizen surveillance and strategies of manipulation place even greater power in the hands of corporate leaders (Webster, 1985, 1986).

This scientific management of political life has reshaped the way Americans live their lives. Particular social sentiments (for example, the belief that wealthy people have worked harder than poor people and thus deserve their fortunes) promoted by corporate leaders mesh with dominant ideologies (ways of making sense and meaning of the world) cultivated by the media, religious institutions and the schools. This concept of ideology plays an important role in our attempt to analyze how power shapes the nature of education and the self-concepts of our students (Harvey, 1989; Aronowitz, 1992). Peter McLaren maintains that the public often thinks of ideology as simply the typical "isms"—communism, socialism, anarchism, nihilism or existentialism. It is much more, he says, and is far more influential than these few formal systems of belief. Ideology is a way of viewing the world men and women "tend to accept as natural and as common sense" (1994, pp. 184–185). Such ways of seeing result from the pervasive influence of power in everyday life. The customs, beliefs and values power helps formulate produce perverted understandings of people's places in the social, economic and educational worlds. Most people come docilely to accept their lowly position in the hierarchy as right and just. The inequitable relations of power and privilege that place them in these positions remain hidden by ideology. One of the authors has seen such an ideology at work in the lives of students:

Randy is a brilliant junior high student from East Texas raised in a home where his father has a garage fix-it shop in which he repairs everything from lawn mowers to automobiles. Randy has watched his father work for as long as he can remember. By the time Randy was six, his father saw that his son possessed mechanical talent. In fact, Randy could take motors apart and put them back together perfectly. Randy's father had finished only the fifth grade and his wife died when Randy was a baby. Randy is not sure whether his father can actually read; there are no books, magazines, or even newspapers in his home. Though he has unusual talents, Randy has always been poor as a student. In a home without reading materials and little awareness of the importance of words, Randy was always behind other students, especially those with parents who attended college. Performing poorly on language-based standardized tests, Randy was inevitably placed on a low-ability track and was told that he was not college material. Randy has always wanted to become a mechanical engineer, but the ideology that presents standardized intelligence tests as infallible measurements of ability also presented his dream as ridiculous. Finding its roots in modernist positivism, this dominant school ideology—in collaboration with power structures in the educational bureaucracy—convinced Randy that it is "common sense" to forget about mechanical engineering. Upper-middle-class students in Randy's junior high rarely have to overcome similar impediments; they grow up in homes with written materials and a linguistic consciousness. Contrary to the ideology of the tests, these upper-middle-class students are not by nature more intelligent than Randy. Indeed, few of them will ever equal his ability to work with machines and motors. Yet schools dominated by middle- and upper-middle-class values do not value Randy's abilities.

Unless teachers like you intervene, thousands of Randys will lose their dreams and aspirations to class-based, modernist positivist views of what constitutes ability. If we want to avoid such wasteful oppression, we will have to rethink the purposes of our schools, reconceptualize the arrangement of our classrooms, and develop new teaching methods.

These changes become particularly compelling when we consider the impact of ideology and power on women. Consider this story of a forty-year-old female student in one of our graduate classes, a successful high school science teacher pursuing a master's degree in curriculum and instruction who had once hoped to become a medical doctor:

When Joan met with her college counselor during freshman registration, he laughed at her career choice. She had been advised by her high school counselor in the 1960s to "take typing, business, and practical courses" so she could "get a job as a teacher or secretary to supplement her husband's income when she gets married." Joan was unaware at the time that her high school curriculum offered choices. So when she arrived at college and decided to enter the premedical program, the university advisor pointed out that she had only taken one science course, no language courses, and only algebra I in high school, and she was therefore ineligible for premed. He advised Joan to enter education, and while she is a wonderful science teacher today, Joan told her graduate education class that she still regrets not pursuing a medical career. She is particularly resentful, she said, because she chose not to marry and "does not desire to provide a second income for a husband."

The most disturbing part of this story to us is the reaction of our undergraduate freshmen year after year. Every semester at least two or three young women respond to this story by reporting that their high school counselors told them exactly the same thing—in the 1990s.

At least a few—perhaps quite a few—high school counselors still believe that young women should prepare themselves for careers in business or teaching to supplement their future husbands' incomes, and thus divert these women away from careers in math and science. Maybe even some follow the philosophy of Rousseau, presented in Chapter 1, assuming that women are intellectually inferior to men or should spend their lives serving the needs of men. Maybe some believe that women should be subservient to men. Is this possible? How else could we explain the continued disenfranchisement of young women in education in the twenty-first century? It is a tragic commentary that the aspirations of today's Randys and Joans could be dashed by an oppressive, unjust but dominant ideology.

Sometimes ideologies become so deeply ingrained in cultural and social thought that otherwise well-intentioned people are unaware they are perpetuating injustice. One reason for exposing unjust ideologies is to prevent ignorance from excusing the advising that victimized Randy and Joan and students like them. We call subconscious or unconscious cultural and social responses *sedimented perceptors*. A sedimented perceptor is a sort of natural subconscious reflex or reaction that nevertheless manages to perpetuate an ideology of injustice or stereotyping. A white friend has lived his entire life in all white communities, is active in his church and professes himself to be strongly antiracist. But during a recent move to a new state, our friend noticed a young, muscular, bare-chested black man mowing the yard next door. Noticing that his own new yard was overgrown, our friend approached the young man and asked, "How much do you charge for a lawn?" The young man replied, "Nothing. I live here."

Despite his studied antiracism and religious beliefs, our friend responded to a sedimented perceptor still common in our society. It never occurred to him that a bare-chested muscular black man might live in the neighborhood, so he assumed the man must be hired labor. The same principal is at work when we ask someone else to speak for a blind person, assuming that a blind individual cannot think, or put a child in a slow reading group because she or he has a southern accent, a lisp, a bad attitude or poor parents. Teachers too often rely on sedimented perceptors to label, track, limit and stereotype their students. We must constantly challenge these sedimented perceptors in ourselves and others so we can confront injustice. Sometimes, of course, injustice is overt and conscious. But whether conscious or inadvertent, injustice presents us as educators with one of our most important duties: to support and empower all of our students by eradicating ideologies that diminish the personhood and aspirations of both students and teachers. We can think of no more important duty for you to reflect on during your teacher preparation program.

RESISTING DOMINATION AND PROMOTING JUSTICE IN THE CLASSROOM

Once we understand the dynamics of power and domination and their impact on schools and the lives of our students, we can hardly walk into a classroom with the same consciousness we once had. As we said in Chapter 1, we want to challenge embedded assumptions, entrenched biases and sedimented perceptions in school, the media and society at large. We make no bones about it: We resent and resist an unjust status quo and the pain it brings to the lives of our poor and marginalized students. Though we realize the controversy it could cause, we feel we ought to do more than simply describe the justice and power inequality in our schools and society; if change is to come, we must identify those specific decisions that cause injustice.

These lessons can hardly start too soon. Early childhood educator Monica Miller Marsh (1992) teaches an antibias curriculum in kindergarten and begins the year with a unit she calls "Getting Acquainted." Before school begins, Marsh plans activities that help children learn more about themselves and their peers including body tracing and painting to help her students learn about race and racial differences. As a preliminary activity, she initiates a discussion of skin color, eye color and hair texture. In introducing the terms "melanin" and "pigment" Marsh explains that some people have more of these than do others. To the children this makes sense; they see nothing unnatural or uncomfortable about these discussions.

The children chose partners to trace their bodies on a large sheet of butcher paper, and as they cut out their tracings they closely examine their partner's skin color so they can mix paints that accurately correspond to their skin tones. As they work, the children engage in extended conversations about who has more melanin and pigment, and their responses to skin color differences become open and comfortable.

Marsh has reported noticing expressions by her students that confirm positive effects. Patrick, an African American child, drew a picture in his journal that he then used to make a valentine for his mother. He drew his blue and black shirt and black pants and, with great pride, colored his skin a bold brown. Now aware of different skin colors and their biological causes, the students had taken a small but important step toward understanding racism and discrimination. Marsh's approach serves education well as we consider the social aspects of teaching in the new paradigm: We cannot start too early making children feel comfortable about issues of race and justice. In order to break down barriers, we must first learn to talk about these important and controversial subjects. Race shapes the lives of all people—black, Native American, white, Asian, Latino, Latina, mixed race. The sooner we learn how this racial shaping happens, the sooner we can work for a world committed to social justice.

At the same time that we reflect on racial justice, we must also examine issues of gender and class justice. Many analysts suggest that modernist positivism enunciates two central themes: (1) realist scientism as developed in the seventeenth century by Descartes, Newton and Bacon (discussed in Chapter 2); and (2) a patriarchal value system derived from much older belief systems and behavior patterns. The two themes are now intertwined almost to the point of inseparability. For example, only in the last couple of decades have women begun to address the patriarchal control of science and scientific employment (McGinty, 1999).

Another example of the inseparability of realistic scientism and patriarchy appears in the writings of Sir Francis Bacon in the seventeenth century. Nature, Bacon maintained, is a woman, and the job of the scientist is "to torture her secrets out of her." On at least a rhetorical level Bacon saw the scientist as a rapist, a manipulator rather than a producer of insight and wisdom. Such forcefulness and disposition for conquest has always been a central feature of masculinity, and not coincidentally the power of science in Western culture (Capra, Steindl-Rast & Matus, 1991). In the new paradigm we begin to question such macho dynamics and rethink our understanding of gender.

Over the last couple of decades women educators have written extensively about the form an education grounded on gender justice might take, and activities that expose our gender assumptions now appear more commonly in American schools. Still, unfortunately, such educational expressions are not yet the norm. Teachers who prize gender equity often ask their students to list men and women they admire as beautiful. The chosen women tend to cluster around a white, blonde, tall, young and thin ideal; admiration centers primarily on appearance. The chosen men tend to be actors or athletes and include a more diverse cross-section of ages, ethnicities and physical types. A dominant impulse noted in this activity is that women on the lists are admired for their physical appearance, while the men are admired for their accomplishments (Weiler, 1988; Yeo, 1997).

In a similar conceptual context Michelle Maher (1992) described the complex ways that patriarchy shapes the experiences and identity formation of young women. Studying the formation of self among sixth-grade girls, Maher found that while they were male identified and oriented toward pleasing boys and willing to compete with one another for attention from boys, they trust each other more than they trust boys. This complex social dynamic demands the attention of educators. We need curricula that expose male validation as a basis for feminine identity and move students to place gender relations within a more just and democratic context. How can girls in the current context break away from the patriarchal tendency to privilege "males as the measure" or maleness as the benchmark of normality?

Maher also described her use of an analysis of gender-related video to promote an understanding of gender justice. Focusing on a series of commercials touting milk's nutritional value, students deconstructed the unstated gender assumptions in the ads. In the first commercial a young male in a football uniform shows the audience a videotape of himself as a younger boy being physically pushed into a school locker by a group of larger, stronger classmates. Motivated by the incident to drink milk, the boy plays a later tape of himself. Now he stands strong, tall and proud, as attractive girls gather around him. He never looks at the girls but stares into the camera, his chin raised in self-confidence. He is a model male, successful now because he is strong, a failure before because he was weak. The message is clear: Boys, drink your milk so you can grow up to be strong and macho and attract lots of women.

Maher plays another milk ad structured the same way as the first, only with a girl. Her "before milk" tape depicts a scene at a school dance where she was unable to attract a partner. She stands alone on the gym floor wearing no makeup and a collared shirt buttoned to the top. Not surprisingly, she begins to drink milk and plays the tape of her "new self." She is wearing heavy makeup and a low-cut sexy dress, and is surrounded by adoring men. She looks at the men to her right and then to her left; she then tells viewers she wants to see the clip again and proceeds to rewind it and play it over. She likes the way men look her up and down. Their objectification of her is proof of her "womanly success." Both her early inferiority and later success are defined in relation to males. By contrast, the football player enjoyed success because he became physically strong and could, therefore, attract women. Both commercials are male-centered in that they value male over female attention. Both depict and depend upon the inequalities of patriarchy—that is, they perpetuate the domination of women by men. Using "found materials" like these, teachers can raise student awareness of issues of justice and how they play out in everyday circumstances.

TRACKING AND QUESTIONS OF JUSTICE

While the classroom is a central venue for addressing questions of justice, one can tease many education and justice-related issues out of the structure of schooling itself. For years modernist positivist educational experts contended that homogeneous or ability grouping (tracking) served the best interests of teachers and students since it made the schooling more efficient. They gave little thought to the emotions of those students treated early as failures and relegated to the lower tracks. Given positivist perspectives on intelligence that equate low IQ scores and low ability and refuse to take social and cultural contexts into account, students from culturally different and economically poor backgrounds were labeled "dumb," when often they were actually quite capable. Without a commitment to justice and an awareness of the subtle ways oppression operates, positivist educators—educational psychologists in particular—ignored the impact of students' lived worlds on their perceptions and performances.

When we study youngsters who have been labeled "unintelligent" by positivist standardized tests and follow them to their jobs, we find their level of measured intelligence making little difference in the quality of their performance. Following a modernist educational science that separates individuals from their lived context, many school leaders have convinced students that race and class-based divisions of students that disproportionately relegate the poor and nonwhite to low ability groups are biologically sound, natural and necessary to the smooth operation of the school (DeYoung, 1989).

After years of arguing that tracking helped teachers dispense standardized information in lockstep to students of similar ability, the more democratic educators began to expose the unexamined assumptions behind this argument. For example, Jeannie Oakes (1985) delineated these four *false* assumptions used to justify tracking in American schools: (1) students learn better when they are tracked with students they match academically; (2) poor students develop better self-esteem when segregated from students with more academic ability; (3) the process used to assess students' abilities and place them in groups accurately and fairly portrays their aptitudes; and (4) segregated ability grouping makes it easier for teachers to manage and teach the students.

Oakes presented overwhelming and compelling evidence to refute these assumptions and the segregation and curricular fragmentation that accompany them. Consider that tracking has harmed most students because it profoundly reduces the achievement level of lower-track students without improving that of upper-track students. View the film *Off Track* by Michelle Fine (1998) and see a New Jersey high school freshman social studies and literature class in action. Students from all abilities and backgrounds are grouped together, and all succeed and thrive as a result of the interactions. Note also the high level of teacher expectations of success for all students. This is not an isolated example.

The utter dismissal of the questions of justice implicit in tracking is as intellectually reprehensible as the premise. Grouping strategies accept that low-ability students are suitable only for specific but simple tasks, while real education ought to be reserved for the academically talented. The student trained for a vocation is deemed incapable of grasping theory, making connections between abstract concepts and concrete practice, or understanding holistic relationships. The trained student employs rule-of-thumb procedures, while educated students invoke theory as they solve problems and reflect on the process (Feinberg & Horowitz, 1990). We need not worry about educating these "dullards"; positivist wisdom has decreed that they cannot be educated.

Several years ago one of the authors was teaching in a small Louisiana college and observing several student teachers each semester.

One day I observed one of my student teachers and her cooperating teacher in a third-grade class engaging twenty-six students in group reading activities. The class had been divided into two groups based on ability. The talented group sat on the floor around the cooperating teacher in the front of the classroom taking turns reading a story out loud. The teacher smiled and the children giggled comfortably and interacted with each other and the teacher. My student teacher had been assigned the low group, and she worked with them on a written workbook activity. They sat in desks at the back of the room far from the empty desks of the talented students. I watched the low students struggle silently for thirty minutes with their workbook assignment. When the gleeful expressions of the talented group became particularly loud, the low students stared at them, expressionless, for a few moments. My student teacher would admonish them to get back to their workbook and they would reluctantly refocus their attention. The physical arrangement of the classroom, the different moods and demeanors of the students in the different groups, and the divergent interaction strategies of the two teachers presented a real-life dramatization of the pathological effects of ability grouping. If nothing else, students in the talented group were active and happy, while those in the low were lifeless and sad. But there's more. All thirteen of the talented students were white; all thirteen of the low children were black. I had gotten myself into difficulty before by pointing out the unjust circumstances I encountered on my student teaching rounds. But difficulty or not, I had to call attention to the patent injustice in this situation. I took the student teacher aside and asked her to describe what had just occurred. She mentioned the two different lesson plans and the individualized nature of the activities, but she never mentioned the alienat-

ing gaps between the two groups or the racial dynamics of the ability grouping. I asked some leading questions, trying to help her identify the racial segregation and the implicit messages it conveyed to all the students in the classroom: What might strike outside observers upon entering the class? What social codes did the grouping arrangements transfer to the students? What aspect of the situation might raise questions of justice or fairness? She began to get nervous, and I rushed too quickly to the point. As I described the racial and emotional dynamics of the lessons, she became visibly disturbed and angry. "I don't see color," she told me. "Children are children and that's all there is to it." I was late for my next observation. I excused myself and told her we would continue the conversation when I returned next week, but when I walked into the classroom a week later I was met by an angry cooperating teacher and a "hurt" student teacher. "I am ready to go to your dean about this matter," the cooperating teacher told me. "Sherry was devastated by your charges of racism and I'm here to tell you that I will not stand for someone from the college coming out here and stirring up trouble." While tears ran down Sherry's face, I listened to the cooperating teacher explain how she had no choice but to group the children this way: "Their test scores demanded such an arrangement." A lot of people had witnessed this classroom, she concluded, and I was the only one who saw any trouble with it.

Obviously educational issues can be sensitive and dangerous, and one must approach them with care and interpersonal sensitivity. But questions of justice often take a back seat to what some educators consider practical concerns, and these concerns too often blind them to the best interests of their students. While our colleague's observations evoked hurt and anger, by raising these issues with teachers, student teachers and preservice teachers like yourself we will, in the long run, encourage reflection and change in the unjust tracking structures that exist in many educational settings.

How might a teacher or school system provide an alternative structure that simultaneously provides individualized tutoring, cooperative learning groups and enrichment projects? Is there a way to meet the needs of all children without relying on tracking? Actually there are many ways. One more example involving another colleague will illustrate this point.

When I was an elementary school principal in the 1980s, I organized a resource learning center in the K–3 wing of our building. The resource center was equipped with science labs, computers, remedial math and reading materials, enrichment books and projects, maps and individual tutorial centers. Staffed by a certified teacher and an assistant, the resource lab was in a classroom easily accessible to all K–3 students and teachers. The teachers drew up a rotating schedule so that all the children could visit the lab. The mix of students varied with each visit. Students would go to the lab for tutoring, independent reading, creative computer assignments, science projects or whatever they required on a regular basis throughout the week. Students looked forward to the special activities planned in the resource lab. Sometimes they worked alone and sometimes in groups, but every child had a chance every week to work at each station in the resource center. In other words, all students could participate in projects often reserved for just the "gifted" or "talented" or "remedial" students. The schedule also gave all students the chance for individualized tutoring. Some needed special help following an extended absence; others required reading or math drills. In any event, the most important feature of the resource lab was that a wide variety of students gathered there on a rotating basis in different small group arrangements, thus avoiding many of the problems associated with tracking.

PROTECTING THE CULTURALLY MARGINALIZED

Poor, gay and lesbian, physically challenged, nonathletic, students of color, overweight, shy and non-English speaking students—among many others—often find themselves silenced and marginalized in the school culture, and it can be hard for talented, popular, athletic, handsome, heterosexual, white middle-class students to understand this reality. Viewing the situation from the protected vantage point of the dominant culture, the latter may be unable to empathize with the problems of those who have been labeled "different." When one lives in the mainstream, one is less likely to notice the ways outsiders are silenced by enforced conformity to unfamiliar norms and discourses.

While all students can be silenced to some degree by authoritarian classroom arrangements that dictate the topics studied, the structure of lessons and the arguments used to support various positions, those with different cultural experiences can find themselves both silenced and discredited in school activities. This discrediting follows from the assumption that an unfamiliarity with school practices constitutes low ability. If they lack an understanding of the discourses, problems, culture and values marginalized students bring to school, teachers and administrators may fail to appreciate the frustration and anger school incites in such students (Gomez, 1992; Metzger & Bryant, 1993).

Antonia Darder described one middle-aged African American college student who felt this anger and frustration. In a journal she kept for one of her classes the student explained how she had suppressed her anger over her school experiences for decades because she wanted to avoid trouble with white people. Though she remained silent for the first six weeks of the term, a class discussion in which white students expressed their resentment about being held accountable for the past racism of others pushed her to the brink. Hearing the white students agree that racism is more a phenomenon of the past than the present, the student responded, "Things may look better to you because you're white and middle class, but maybe you should come to my neighborhood in Watts. Things there are still a mess" (1991, p. 145).

Having been silenced for so many years, the student through her statement pointed herself toward a new empowerment and the dawn of her new public voice in the company of white people. Reflecting on the conversation, the woman later wrote that she felt good expressing her resentment and anger. Looking back at her school and work lives, she realized that she had always worn two faces: one around other African Americans and another around white people. Like millions of other

African Americans at work and school, she play-acted to survive in white-dominated institutions. Teachers in the new paradigm understand the cultural dynamics at work in situations like these and make sure their classrooms and schools remain safe places that support rather than silence authentic voices.

But we also urge you to resist the thought that such support is easy. When the races (classes, religions, sexual orientations, physical abilities, or genders) of teachers and students differ, conflicts on a variety of levels can develop, as one of our colleagues reported:

> *I remember vividly the anger evoked by a high school teacher from an upper-middle-class background who made fun of the poor community I had grown up in. After this ridicule, any attempt he made to teach me was futile. My only response was to make him pay for his class condescension. I don't think we can ever resolve race, class and gender conflicts that arise in a society so deeply divided around these categories.*

What we can do, however, is recognize our own views and the ways our positions shape our relations with individuals from different locations in the social web. The power relations that result from these personal intersections are central to a professional understanding of why students perform the way they do in the classroom. Sociological insight like this constitutes an important piece of the knowledge teachers should bring to the classroom.

When teachers begin to understand cultural and political dynamics they can search for ways to reshape their classrooms in response. They appreciate the fact that cultural outsiders face tremendous threats to the development of positive self-images. With school relations undermining cultural confidence and the mass media conveying images and messages that promote white dominance, children marginalized by race or socioeconomic class need all the help their teachers can give them. Some teachers respond by building programs around the besieged self-concepts of marginalized children. Instead of focusing exclusively, for example, on correct spelling, punctuation and grammar, such teachers help students learn ways to communicate with those particular groups to whom they have something to say. Because they communicate with real audiences, the students find themselves motivated to learn.

The major goal in such projects, however, involves increasing the students' awareness of the forces that shape them. They come to understand the cultural contradictions that thwart their goals—that their home culture is different from the school's culture, for example. Such an understanding helps them describe differences in language, definitions of intelligence and views of success between their home and school lives. The skills prized in their neighborhoods—negotiating with street gangs, taking care of younger brothers and sisters, cooking—are irrelevant in schools. But writing teachers can encourage students to record these stories in anthologies and then share their writing with parents from different social backgrounds, with college teacher education programs or with more privileged students. This earned attention increases the confidence of the student authors and helps their audiences understand the forces that shape marginalized individuals, undermine their efforts and subvert their attempts to progress in school (Hale, 1992; Gomez, 1992).

STUDENTS TAKING ACTION

Self-awareness and a consciousness of the forces that shape the way we interact with the world help define what it means to be educated. Whether it be a writing exercise or a science lesson, some insight into this construction of self always appears in our lessons (Mullin, 1994). This construction of self also guides our efforts to remove students from the role of knowledge consumers and nervous right-answer volunteers, while inviting them to make personal meaning in the context of the curriculum they encounter. As we connect our own passion to our students' desires, we understand that little of any real importance happens in classrooms until consciousness intersects with lived experience.

Once this intersection takes place, we can put school knowledge to use in some activity that is significant in the world outside school: teaching younger students who need special help, cleaning up a public space, writing for a public audience, organizing to promote certain legislation, staging a public debate on a controversial issue and so forth. Real-life activity like this contextualizes school skills in a way that helps students appreciate their utility. As Robert Fried (1995) observed, students who use what they have learned in geometry to design and build a playground for a local preschool come to understand both what they do and do not know about the subject. In instances like these we want students to connect thought and action, to put them in life situations that induce them to move back and forth between abstract conceptual understanding and the environmental changes it implies.

Students need not succeed for positive growth to occur. The relevant dynamic is engagement reflection, self-understanding and the student's realization that he or she can assert a presence in the world (Pruyn, 1994). Many teachers who understand such pedagogical concepts encourage their students to attend to news programs and current events (Smith, 1999).

One class we observed discovered from their news monitoring that a local plant was about to close. The students then found that the factory had a good production record, the corporate owners were financially sound, and the managers had received substantial raises over the last few years. Why, they asked in class, was the factory closing? How would the workers be affected? How would the local community be affected? As the questions increased in number, the teacher urged the students to build a research project around them. Excited and motivated, they went to work. They contacted by e-mail a variety of knowledgeable sources and collected reams of information about the activities and plans of the company. Shutting down the local factory, they found, was part of a larger plan to move all of the company's U.S. operations to Mexico and Southeast Asia, where wages and environmental standards are low. After cutting operating costs and worker benefits the corporation would then be able to raise managerial salaries and increase its investments in other industries.

The students' anger grew when they found that the company would be released from paying millions of dollars in U.S. taxes by the advantages American firms operating outside the United States enjoy. Supported by the wealth of information they had gathered, the students designed a multimedia presentation for various audiences. They traveled after school to retirement homes, union meetings, church groups, and chambers of commerce. They also designed a presentation for the Internet, which was read by Net surfers in other towns afflicted with the same problems. Local television and radio stations and newspapers interviewed the students and ran stories on their work.

The students lost the battle, however, and the company shut down the plant and moved away. Yet no one took the loss as a mark of the project's failure. The students had won great victories despite their seeming defeat. They had learned how to research, how to be activist citizens, how power operates, how to gain publicity for a just cause, the relationship between school and world and the solidarity that results from working together. A project such as this shows what can happen in schools that welcome passion.

CLASSROOM MANAGEMENT: CONNECTEDNESS AND A SENSE OF BELONGING VERSUS FEAR

Almost every teacher education student we have ever taught has expressed apprehension about classroom management. In this anxiety, educational consultants find a gold mine. Armed with bags of tricks and long lists of techniques, the experts typically view classroom management (or discipline) in isolation from an educational purpose, a philosophy of teaching, the social context, the backgrounds of the students and the curriculum. In practice teachers find that the techniques may work with some children in some contexts but are irrelevant in others. Given our concern with contextualization, it should hardly come as a surprise that our view of classroom management centers on its role in the larger conceptual matrix of education we have developed. Beginning with some ecological concerns with interconnectedness and "belongingness," we can create a context for addressing classroom management. This sense of belongingness underlies our understanding of classroom management. People involved with a reality greater than themselves—and who see the organization, classroom or group as connected to that larger reality—are usually the most productive, helpful and cooperative members of the group. Teachers who can connect their students' passion and desire with a larger reality have fewer classroom management problems.

As teachers we see belongingness as inseparable from the scholarly acts in which we and our students engage. Indeed, much of our work in the foundations of education involves the search for ways in which we all belong to one another. Inseparable from this belongingness is the spiritual and intellectual quest to find the relationships that connect all the areas of our lives. Although we ostensibly address discipline here, we can hardly view the topic outside the context of the philosophical dynamics we use to make sense of ourselves and the world: classroom management for what purpose? What do people mean when they use the term "discipline"? Such terms generally have little to do with belongingness, connectedness or meaning making and more to do with personal surrender and a mindless obedience. One of our colleagues tells a story that illustrates this point nicely.

A few years ago, I walked into a middle school in South Carolina and saw in the front entrance a huge cartoon strip an art teacher had drawn. It showed two boys talking to one another. The first boy said to his friend, "I've discovered how to get along well in school." His friend asked, "How's that?" The first boy replied, "You listen to what the teacher says to do and then you just do it." The message seemed clear to me: Obedience, not thoughtfulness and belongingness, is the goal of schooling and classroom management. This Nike "Just-Do-It" theory of obedience might work in a totalitarian state like Stalin's Russia or Duvalier's Haiti, but not for a democratic society. I immediately recognized that American school as a small totalitarian state.

In the new paradigm, classroom management takes democracy seriously and insists that students participate in deciding how a classroom operates. If we commit to the concept of belongingness, we have no choice but to let students help us determine the ways the classroom reflects their self-images and concerns. The alienation we and our students feel in public schools exists in direct proportion to an absence of belongingness. Our goal as classroom managers is to find ways to endow our students with a sense of limitless belonging. In fact, this sense of belonging is a prerequisite to the development of any democratic institution.

In this holistic context of belongingness, connectedness and democracy we can begin to consider the behavior problems that often plague contemporary schools and what we can do about them. We resist any temptation to provide struggling teachers with five sure-fire strategies for controlling students. Instead, we look holistically to the curriculum and pedagogy and at how well students and their teachers themselves understand their purposes. We examine the larger dynamics of the school in general and the classroom in particular, closely observing the interactions between teachers and students (Do teachers "talk down" to students?), the nature of the assignments teachers devise for students (Can they be fairly described as "busy work"?), and the "affect" of teachers (Do they show passion in their teaching?).

Operating in the new paradigm, we look for signs of a teacher manipulating students. Many of the behavior management techniques of the old paradigm were overtly manipulative, and the students generally knew it. Manipulation techniques rarely work permanently. Even when they do achieve short-term student responses, their long-term consequences tend to be detrimental (Capra, Steindl-Rast & Matus, 1991; Fried, 1995). Our goal is to understand students so as to meet their needs and connect them to the goals of the classroom. As Chapter 12 will explain in far more detail, teachers in the new paradigm must understand youth culture and the ways it intersects with the idiosyncrasies of individual students. By acquainting ourselves with these cultural dynamics and using this knowledge to establish connections we can begin to learn the complex process of managing classrooms democratically.

REPOSITIONING CLASSROOM MANAGEMENT BY DEVELOPING THE INTERPERSONAL CURRICULUM

Allow us to reconceptualize what is typically referred to as the curriculum of classroom management—namely, the interpersonal curriculum. This curriculum teaches both teachers and students the values of respect, democracy, tolerance for diverse groups who may not themselves be tolerant, fairness, humane treatment of one another and "de-egofication." In the interpersonal curriculum we learn to disagree and deal with conflict skills that altogether too many otherwise educated people lack. Teachers in the new paradigm realize that conflict in the classroom is inevitable and they accept that inevitability. In fact, a central feature of our view of classroom management is teaching ourselves and our students how to disagree.

This task takes us to Howard Gardner's (1983) work on personal intelligence—one aspect of his theory of multiple intelligences. "Personal intelligence" involves both the *intrapersonal* ability to understand and "get in touch with" ambiguous and highly diverse forms of feelings and the *interpersonal* ability to analyze and make distinctions among the moods, epistemologies, motivations, self-interests and intentions of other people. We discuss personal intelligence more thoroughly in Chapter 12, but for purposes of this discussion of classroom management and the interpersonal curriculum, the concept is invaluable, which is why we get a bit ahead of ourselves here. The interpersonal curriculum is an attempt to increase our personal intelligence in ways that lead to smoothly operating classrooms and harmonious relationships between human beings.

As Robert Fried (1995) pointed out, interpersonally intelligent teachers exhibit a variety of insights that contribute to a well-run classroom, seven of which conclude this chapter:

1. *Recognition of troubled students.* Interpersonally intelligent teachers recognize students who bring out-of-school problems to the classroom. Every day thousands of students walk into classrooms having been abused at home or in their communities. These students find it nearly impossible to contain their inner turmoil. Interpersonally intelligent teachers recognize such situations and adjust their treatment of these students accordingly. The adjustment may involve help from guidance or administrative personnel on one level and personal support and counseling on another. Engaging these students is rarely easy and teachers need to build community networks to help console and work with them.

2. *Identification of student cliques that intimidate and disturb other students.* Regardless of their locations, most schools must cope with cliques. Interpersonally intelligent teachers study the social patterns of the school and learn both to anticipate potential problems and to recognize their causes. The insight will not put an end to this divisive activity, but it can spread understandings and strategies for addressing particular classroom problems. As Robert Fried suggested, teachers cannot solve these problems alone, but they can build support groups consisting of staff members, parents, students and community members.

3. *Recognition of an ineffective curriculum.* A teacher who studies the school the way an anthropologist studies a culture becomes attuned to the interpersonal dynamics of the classroom. Armed with this insight, the teacher can tell when students are bored with or not engaged by the course of study. Recently two teachers from a rural district in central Pennsylvania described for us the boredom they detected in their students. It emerged that these students take six years of grammar, from seventh to twelfth

grades. Understanding the relation between boredom and behavior, inter-personally aware teachers might venture to reconceptualize the curriculum.

4. *Appreciation of the need both to respect students and to expect respect from them.* Interpersonally intelligent teachers understand that students—and people in general—live up (or down) to what is expected of them. We have all watched (no doubt with embarrassment) certain teachers suffer through each day with little respect from their students. Typically these teachers display little respect for their students. One of the authors served on a school evaluation team some years ago and noticed a teacher stop a student in the hall after the final bell had rung: "Just what in hell do you think you are doing in the hall after the bell?" the teacher screamed at the student. The student was obviously offended by such disrespectful behav-ior and reacted appropriately: "I'm walking the hell to the office," he re-torted. At that point the teacher grabbed the student by the collar and pulled him into his room. "Nobody talks that way to me," the teacher said. Then he called the principal's office and asked an assistant principal to come to his classroom. "These kids," the teacher announced as if the student were somewhere else, "they don't respect anyone. I don't let 'em get away with it. I teach them to respect me." When the assistant princi-pal arrived and asked what happened, the student produced a note from his teacher that excused him to go to the office to check out. His mother was ill and his family needed him at home. No apology came from the teacher, and the student received a week of detention for his behavior. Angry to the point of tears by this unjust punishment, the student stomped indignantly out of the room. Notice that the teacher's lack of re-spect for students had led him to *create* "discipline problems." We have watched scenes like this play themselves out time and again in schools where teachers fail to respect the basic humanity of their students. Such teachers set themselves up for misery and failure.

5. *Recognition of the difference between one-on-one student relationships and interactions with students in groups.* Many teachers who develop successful person-to-person rapport with individual students feel betrayed when stu-dents interact with them differently in groups. To maintain a democratic classroom environment teachers must learn to empathize with the intense pressure peers can exert on students. In many student cultures displaying too much interest in school may attract ridicule and even ostracization. Until teachers can establish a justification for their teaching that allays such antiacademic reactions they must be attentive to intrapersonal dy-namics. They must learn to avoid being hurt by inconsistent student be-havior, a difficult task that often takes years to accomplish.

6. *Perception of the need to acknowledge one's own mistakes as a teacher and to tolerate mistakes by students.* Creating a safe environment where mistakes are treated as both inevitable and potentially instructive is a central task for an interpersonally intelligent and democratic teacher. These teachers make their classrooms embarrassment-proof safe places. One teacher we know writes the word "safe" in giant letters on the blackboard during the

first few days of class to emphasize that the classroom is a humane, protected and secure place. When we move beyond a modernist-positivist epistemology that focuses on correct answers, we can begin to attend to the process of thinking, knowledge production and meaning making. In this context we explode the culture of nervous right-answer volunteers created by positivism, and we can allow mistakes to play themselves out in a natural low key.

7. *An awareness that the key to classroom management is engaging and enjoyable learning.* As a fundamental human need, joy is a necessary ingredient in any learning formula. It also happens to be basic to successful human interaction. Contrary to common belief, no contradiction exists between fun and serious scholarship. You can probably remember a few middle school, high school, undergraduate or graduate classes in which spontaneous laughter often mixed with the assignments at hand. Have you ever regretted "wasting time" for fun? In fact, it has probably paid dividends. From both an interpersonal and a new paradigmatic perspective, one of the most important goals for any teacher at any level is filling students with a love for the subject being taught. Better that students leave class with a love of the subject than with specific factual knowledge; love for the subject is difficult to acquire whereas factual knowledge can be gained when the need arises. Moreover, contrary to what many casual observers contend, play is a component of schooling. Once we overcome our biases against the "immaturity" of play we can incorporate its principles into our professional and personal lives. Three of these play principles are the following: (a) "The rules" are intended less to repress freedom than to defeat authoritarianism and promote fairness. (b) The structure of play is dynamic in its relation to the interaction of the players—by necessity this interaction is grounded on their equality. (c) The activity is always viewed as an autonomous expression of self, as the players generally take care not to subordinate imagination to predetermined outcomes. Notice that in play exhaustion is not deadening since the activity refreshes the senses and celebrates the person. We might usefully view interpersonally intelligent teaching and classroom management as a form of play in which teachers and students work together for shared purposes (Fried, 1995; Marcuse, 1955; Aronowitz, 1973). Teaching can be a joy and can provide welcome benefits to teachers and students alike if we can work through the great fear of classroom management.

CONCLUSION

In this chapter we have taken you on a journey through many complex facets of philosophy, scientific realism, modernity, the construction of meaning, cognition, ideology, curriculum and classroom management. We have provided examples of connecting these issues to teaching and learning. We have repeated our philosophy several times and will repeat it again and often: We believe that schooling must serve the purpose of improving society, creating environmental sustainability, addressing injustice and creating spaces in which students and teachers are nurtured and empowered. We think these worthy goals for teacher education students, and we encourage you to develop your philosophy of education in light of them. The modern, rational scientific schooling models tend to ignore the important social, economic, political, theological and cultural issues. We invite you to resist the traditional approach to schooling, which has been overly bureaucratic, authoritarian, regulating, biased on many levels and disconnected from the lives of students. We encourage you to be leaders of a reconceptualized view of teaching, learning and philosophy in education, a view this chapter has introduced.

Part 2

Historical Context
How Did We Get Here?

4

The Ambiguities and Contradictions in Early American Schooling

INTRODUCTION

We have looked at democratic teaching, the new education paradigm and the connection between philosophy and teaching; we now turn back to examine the historical context of American schooling over the last three centuries. This analysis reveals that many of the issues addressed in Chapters 1 and 2 arose long ago. Education in America has, in fact, often been the subject of and a venue for social and philosophical conflict. The American public school system may be the one governmental unit most Americans believe they know intimately. They are simultaneously correct and mistaken in this belief.

To begin with, most of us have been going to school for more than twelve years, learning "reading, writing and arithmetic" among a host of other subjects that make up public education's societal mission. We are also bombarded by books, magazines, television shows, news accounts and movies, all portraying the lives of our children in school. Depending on what we see and then conclude, public schools are either caring and safe educative institutions or sites of conflict in which differing viewpoints, attitudes and appearances become grounds for contention. Worse, the media sometimes portrays schools as sites of unspeakable menace, malice and violence, threatening children, school personnel and even the broader society. Regardless of these images and stories and the multiple meanings behind such projections, you should understand that what we "know" about public education tends to be an uncertain mix of cultural mythology and personal experience, knowledge that can be bent and warped by continually shifting political winds.

Historically U.S. public schools have had the responsibility for educating children to become competent and responsible citizens within the larger political context of a democratic republic (Lugg, 1996a). But as you know, school is also the site where history, politics and a great deal of mythology intersect and swirl about, shaping how children view themselves, their peers, their communities and their country. Even as our students become educated in various academic subjects, they also learn "acceptable" behaviors (that is, what constitutes moral action) and exactly who their teachers and society value. Yet at the same time, students learn what actions are unacceptable and who acts immorally. This very process of "valuing" marks the public school as contested ground and makes both teaching and learning intrinsically political acts. In determining who to value and who to consider "deviant," one makes a political decision that reflects the biases embedded in society (Lugg, 1996a; Edelman, 1974, 1988).

This valuing process—the naming of the legitimate citizens and, by extension, the legitimate children—is hardly a recent development in public education. The current cultural mythology holds that a golden age of American public schooling once flourished, in which well-behaved and enthusiastic children learned from uniformly competent and caring teachers to embrace a shared vision of Western civilization. According to the myth, at a time in the not-too-distant past everyone learned his or her (until recently, mostly his) social/cultural/religious/political place, and the schools efficiently transferred these honored understandings to receptive children. Discussions of the purposes and ideals to be taught by public schools were supposedly marked by civility, rationality and consensus, all parties to the decisions embracing an enlightened "Judeo-Christian" heritage.

The historical record, of course, reveals a far different story of American public education, a story of an ongoing contest between education for social regulation and education for emancipation. This continuing tension helps explain why Americans have had a long and stormy love-hate relationship with their public schools, at least since the introduction of the "common school" (the original name for public schools) in the early nineteenth century. Today's teachers should realize that public schools have *never* been politically neutral. While they may not work in an established political "war zone," public school teachers should know that the history of schooling reveals heated debates over curriculum and over policies that continue to shape our classrooms.

Although many educators and social critics may recoil in horror, conflict is not necessarily a bad thing. Disagreement can be healthy in a republic that has been pursuing various ideas of democratic citizenship since its inception. With public schools representing the lowest level of the official public debate, larger political issues are destined to intrude on the context of schooling. Accordingly, if we had no conflicts in public schooling—if the larger sociopolitical environment were static without debates over who qualifies as a citizen and what citizenship means—we would have little practical need to reform our schools (Cuber, 1989).

We find public education reform (and the conflict it invariably invites) a central theme of American educational historiography, or the writing of educational history. Additionally, throughout much of their existence American public schools have been viewed as both educative institutions and instruments for social salvation (Perkinson, 1991). Schools were, and are, meant to educate children, correct a myriad of social ills and possibly "build a new social order" (Counts, 1978). This ideal may be problematic, for as with citizenship we define social pathology historically along the lines of political ideology, and we tend to single out various minority populations for "special treatment" (Edelman, 1974, 1988).

Given the enormous complexity of the issues that accompany public schooling, you should begin to consider how to challenge, deconstruct or debunk much of the current mythology. In this chapter we set about the business of contextualizing and interpreting the early "American school" in an iconoclastic (idol-smashing) fashion. We present brief examinations of schooling in the seventeenth and eighteenth centuries and explore the antecedents to the nineteenth-century common school, the charity schools. Throughout our discussion we will continually note and explore the tension between education for social control and education for emancipation, and what both of these ideas may have meant in their respective historical contexts.

THE PURITANS AND THEOLOGICALLY GROUNDED SCHOOLING

The roots of contemporary American public education lie with the Puritans in seventeenth-century New England. The Puritans were a forbiddingly austere Protestant sect originating in England during the late sixteenth and early seventeenth centuries. As Protestant reformers indebted to the development of the printing press, they focused their theology on living "God's law"—that is, following Biblical injunctions—as opposed to ecclesiastical (church) edicts. Puritans exemplified a rigid, if not downright dour, code of personal conduct. They were urged to reject "idle recreations and vain display" and exhibit instead a sober and "obedient godliness" (Ahlstrom, 1972, p. 129). Twentieth-century social pundit H. L. Mencken once pointedly observed that Puritanism was "that haunting fear that somehow, somewhere, someone was happy" (Karier, 1986, p. 15).

An important precept of Puritan theology stressed salvation through hard work. God would reward those who worked hard and remained thrifty and morally diligent. The Puritans viewed prosperity as a sign of God's favor for the prosperous person (Karier, 1986). This impression led to what we now know as the "Protestant work ethic." Another aspect of Puritan theology was the "doctrine of the predestination." Briefly stated, it maintained that an omniscient God already knew who would be among the "elect," and thus "saved" from eternal damnation so individuals could do nothing on their own to achieve salvation. The Puritans believed themselves to be among God's elect and treated those who differed with their faith as damned (Rippa, 1992).

In the enormous political and religious turbulence following Martin Luther's Reformation, the Puritans were prickly participants in England's various attempts to achieve a Christian orthodoxy. By the 1620s their political fortunes had so diminished and religious persecution had so intensified that they saw immigration to the "New World" as an irresistible prospect. Charles I granted the Puritans a charter in 1629, and in 1630 nearly one thousand of them sailed from England to establish a colony in New England. They arrived at Massachusetts Bay and founded a "Bible Commonwealth" that would last until 1684, when their original charter was revoked.

The Puritan colonists came to New England doubting they would ever return to England. But they had no intention of becoming "American," and considered themselves loyal English subjects, despite their theological differences. But unlike their Pilgrim predecessors, a small band of settlers who merely wished to be left alone, the Puritans zealously set about building a new society. Led by John Winthrop, they established a "City on the Hill," which they expected to be a shining example of Christian piety for the rest of the world (Spring, 1994; Rippa, 1992). Church and state—if not indeed the same thing—were inextricably linked in early colonial Massachusetts, with Puritan theology guiding daily life and much of the political decision making. Winthrop, in particular, was hostile to any notion of democracy and called it "the meanest and worst form of Government" (Rippa, 1992, p. 37). Accordingly, only male church members, freemen and property holders could vote.

The ability to know the word of God (that is, the ability to read the Protestant Bible) was critically important to each member of the colony if it was to endure. In Puritan theology (as in the theology of other Protestant sects), a person's salvation depended on an ability to read the Bible and, in turn, to know God. With few ministers sailing from England to serve them, the colonists established Harvard College in 1636 specifically to train clergymen and, by extension, other community leaders. This intense theological concern eventually encouraged the establishment of publicly supported reading and writing schools. Social and educational goals in America's first educational institutions, as in most cases since, were inseparable.

In keeping with their religious tenets, the Puritans strictly delineated the social roles of their men, women and children. Since Man had been created in the image of God, men occupied the top of the social hierarchy and took responsibility for all political, economic and religious decisions. Women remained the property of their families and, once married, their husbands. They were without legal rights and could not own property, enter into contracts or sue. Children were subordinate to all adults and were at the bottom of the hierarchy. In fact, by Puritan law, failing to honor one's parents was punishable by death:

> *If any Childe or Children above sixteen years old, and of competent Understanding, shall curse or Smite their Natural Father or Mother, he or they shall be put to Death, unless it can be sufficiently testified that the Parents have been very Unchristianly negligent in the Education of such Children. (Spring, 1994, p. 25)*

Today this may seem an extremely harsh punishment, but remember that the colonial family was a self-sufficient economic unit. It valued children for the work they could contribute to the survival of the family and the household. Colonial-era children were treated rather like miniature adults, and they spent much of their childhood copying and obeying adults and engaging in "incessant work" (Rippa, 1992, p. 24). Consequently, the Puritans saw rebellion as poor behavior and even dangerous to the entire family.

Early Puritan education revolved around home and church, with parents, ministers and employers providing instruction. Still, far too many children reached adulthood unable to read or write, a deficiency interpreted as threatening the very existence of the "Bible Commonwealth." The Massachusetts Law of 1642, reflecting the social order of the time, ordered that all male children be taught to read, and it imposed fines on those adults who failed to "give proper instruction" (Cubberley, 1919, p. 17). Further, if children were not provided an education, they could be removed from their parents' homes or masters' employ.

In 1647 Massachusetts established a system of early education under what later became known as the "Old Deluder Satan Act." The legislation stated that the purpose of establishing schools was to protect men from Satan, "one chief point of the old deluder, Satan, [being] to keep men from a knowledge of the Scriptures." (Cubberley, 1919, p. 17). The law required that communities with at least fifty households appoint a teacher. Those communities with more than 100 households were ordered to establish a Latin grammar school providing classical instruction, to train young men for later attendance at Harvard College. Yet the establishment of the actual schools lagged behind the legislation, for it took time for each community to secure both the resources and the schoolmaster (Elsbree, 1939).

The basic town, or *petty* school provided rudimentary instruction in reading, writing and mathematics for poor boys. They were taught to read using a "hornbook," a piece of parchment with a thin piece of wood located at the top, with the alphabet and Bible verses inscribed on it. Girls, if they were educated at all (and this was a point of great contention from the start), were instructed with very young boys at *dame* schools (Tyack & Hansot, 1990). Boys of the middle and upper classes, those who typically attended the dame schools, later went on to Latin grammar schools.

Given the tightly prescribed gender roles of the era, teachers at the grammar schools were exclusively male. The rigorous education of the grammar school focused mainly on Latin grammar, conversation and composition, but the students also had to study Greek and Hebrew. Note that those who received this instruction were being schooled (or educated) for leadership roles. By studying the wisdom of the ancients, young men would learn what was wise and just, for they were expected to be both the religious and political leaders of their communities.

Reflecting Puritan sensibilities, instruction in all schools was both religious and highly authoritarian, with an emphasis on text memorization and obedience and deference to one's elders. The *New England Primer* (1687) served as the basic reading text for many schools and provides a good deal of evidence of the nature of Puritan schooling. The following verse, which the students had to memorize, reveals just how authoritarian instruction in the Bible Commonwealth was:

I will fear GOD, and honor the KING.
I will honor my Father and Mother.
I will obey my Superiors
I will submit to my Elders.
I will love my Friends.
I will hate no Man.

I will forgive my Enemies, and pray to God for them.
I will as much as in me lies keep all God's Holy Commandments.
I will learn my Catechism.
I will keep the Lord's Day Holy.
I will reverence God's Sanctuary.
For our GOD is a consuming Fire. (Rippa, 1969, pp. 51–52)

In keeping with the theological concept of original sin (the belief that humanity is intrinsically evil thanks to Adam and Eve's transgression), the Puritans viewed children as inherently sinful and, from birth, sorely in need of guidance and redirection. The Puritans saw children, in short, as "depraved, unregenerate and damned" (Allison, 1995, p. 9). The schooling they received could, therefore, be physically brutal, with the whipping post employed as an important pedagogical tool in hopes of beating the "old deluder" Satan out of the children (Karier, 1986; Cubberly, 1919). Children were constantly reminded of the various penalties (both heavenly and earthly) awaiting their misbehavior. Thus, early colonial schooling reflected the Puritan need for social control, for the Puritans felt that their collective salvation and the colony's long-term economic viability would be jeopardized by any "waywardness" in their children.

Even though Puritan theology was part of a dissenting religious tradition, the slightest obviations were quickly punished in colonial Massachusetts (Hudson, 1981), which considered the tolerance of other religions a sin (Elsbree, 1939). The early schools began during a time of great internal dissent, which Puritan theology (or at least the "theocrats") simply could not accommodate. Starting in 1634, various members of the colony fled or were banished for espousing various theological heresies. The most celebrated cases involved Roger Williams and Anne Hutchinson. Williams fled in 1636 and established the religiously tolerant secular state of Rhode Island. He would later refer disparagingly to Massachusetts as "Godland" (Barber, 1992, p. 56). Anne Hutchinson was exiled in 1637 and also found her way to Rhode Island (Ahlstrom, 1972; Hudson, 1981). To the intense annoyance of the Puritan clerics, Massachusetts' merchants, viewing the imposition of biblical restrictions as unduly restrictive on commerce, had backed Hutchinson's attacks on the clergy (Ahlstrom, 1972). No wonder, then, that the Puritan leaders saw their schools as a vehicle for maintaining an existing social and religious order under increasing attack.

Ironically, the rising literacy rate in combination with the Puritans' own tradition of dissent helped loosen their theological stranglehold. The widening availability of printed material, the increasing numbers of those who could read it and the growing numbers of immigrants combined to intensify the very dissent the Puritans considered heretical. Particularly vexing were the attempts by the Quakers (more accurately, the Society of Friends) to bring their variation of Christianity to Massachusetts. The Quakers first arrived in Boston Harbor in 1656 in the persons of Mary Fisher and Ann Austin. The Puritans received them with hostility. According to religious historian Sydney Ahlstrom:

The women were kept on the ship while their belongings were searched and more than one hundred books were confiscated. Although there was as yet no law against Quakers in Massachusetts, the two were hurried off to jail, stripped of all their clothing, and inspected for tokens of witchcraft. (1972, p. 178)

The threat of variant theologies inspired a spate of legal restrictions and fines. Anyone transporting a Quaker into the colony was subject to a £100 fine. Colonists found in possession of a Quaker book were fined £5. But the worst penalties were meted out to the Quaker proselytizers. Massachusetts enacted a law providing that any professed Quaker "coming into the jurisdiction would be arrested, whipped and transported out of the colony without conversing with any person" (Ahlstrom, 1972, p. 178). By the late 1650s and early 1660s the Puritans were hanging people in the name of religious orthodoxy.

A growing population of non-Puritans, coupled with the vicious persecution of Quakers, alarmed the English and eventually sealed the political fate of the Bible Commonwealth. King Charles II intervened in 1662, ordering Massachusetts to turn over Quaker "lawbreakers" for trial in England. The Puritans refrained from sending Quakers to England and the hangings ceased, although floggings continued. English displeasure with Puritan political practices increased, and in 1684 the Puritans' royal charter was revoked. The colony was rechartered in 1691, but this time it "had a royal governor and a franchise based on property rather than church membership" (Ahlstrom, 1972, p. 161). Religious tolerance was imposed on a still reluctant Massachusetts, ending the persecution of non-Puritans. The Bible Commonwealth had lasted just less than sixty years.

As we hope you see by now, the Puritan experiment with the theological state can provide useful insights for today's educators. The familiar political rhetoric excoriating the "evils" of contemporary public schools invokes the wisdom of "our Puritan founders," saintly and pious people who fled England to escape religious persecution and secure freedom. Their experiment receives a noble if not a sacred twist; the rhetoric cites Puritans' commitment to and faith in God made manifest in the establishment of their conservative schools. "If only," think the latter-day critics, "today's 'educrats' would be so enlightened, faith and reason would both be restored to our schools and our society. Our Judeo-Christian heritage would be respected and cherished."

Alas, mythology makes for poor educational policy and worse practice, though it can enliven political debate. The Puritans were a pious people deeply committed to their faith, acutely aware of the flames of hell awaiting those who strayed from God's word. They faced almost insurmountable challenges in the cold and inhospitable New World from which they carved their Bible Commonwealth.

But the Puritans were just as intolerant of the religious differences of their "fellow Christians" as those who had previously persecuted *them*. The early Massachusetts Bay Colony was marked by great theological and political discord, coupled with troubling economic instability. With the expulsions of the various "heretics" beginning in the mid-1630s it quickly became apparent just how fragile the Puritans' political-theological structure was.

In this theocratic context schools were a way of maintaining—imposing, if need be—the Bible Commonwealth at a time when internal divisions threatened to tear it apart. The schools the Puritans established were sort of public and sort of private, highly undemocratic, and often brutal. The primitive curriculum focused on social control to preserve the Puritans' personal sense of spiritual salvation. The system differentiated along class and gender lines, excluding many from receiving the education needed for leadership. Viewed through Puritan eyes, the schools of the "Bible Commonwealth" and their pedagogical practices were intrinsically moral. But any present-day return to that form of schooling would produce investigations by various child protection and civil rights agencies (Demos, 1986).

For all the emphasis on social and religious regulation, the early Puritan schools inadvertently helped stretch the fabric of Massachusetts society by increasing literacy among its population. While children and adults learned to read various religious texts, once they could read their interests took them to other material and then to other ideas. To repeat the irony, the Puritans' own dissenting theological tradition coupled with their commitment to literacy helped to undermine the very social control they sought to impose. Their authority would further erode following the Salem witchcraft trials and the killing of women, children and some men in the name of religion. Yet, the schools the Puritans established survived long after their society itself.

COLONIAL EDUCATION OUTSIDE NEW ENGLAND

While colonial New England established the rudiments of a "system of education," schooling took place in other parts of what eventually became the United States. Mass education remained only a slight concern of the British Crown's for-profit agricultural enterprise in Virginia (Spring, 1994). Several attempts to establish reading and writing schools for white children there produced little enthusiasm. Reflecting the direct political influence of England, the Virginia colonists considered education an individual concern rather than a civil or religious matter (Rippa, 1992). Those who wished to have their children educated did so at their own expense, usually hiring private tutors. In fact, education was a luxury only the affluent could afford. Additionally, educating "other" children was thought to be a dangerous undertaking, for it might rouse the rabble. As Virginia's Governor Berkeley declared in 1671,

> *I thank God we have no free schools nor printing; and I hope we shall not have these for a hundred years. For learning has brought disobedience and heresy and sects into the world; and printing has divulged them and libels against the government. God keep us from both. (Beard and Beard, 1930, p. 185)*

Despite Berkeley's thunder, by 1689 Virginia had six reading and writing schools, still a pittance compared with Massachusetts's twenty-three (Cremin, 1970). Note the interesting paradox embedded within colonial education. If "mass" education in New England was structured toward social regulation, social control in Virginia was fostered by denying the majority of the population an opportunity to learn.

Other colonies took educational approaches somewhere between Massachusetts's zeal and Virginia's trepidation. Both Pennsylvania and New York followed policies of education for cultural Anglicization (making people British). Thanks to its Quaker foundations Pennsylvania became a haven for those fleeing religious persecution, and a wide variety of private schools sprang up there, not all of them English-speaking. A massive influx of German immigrants had sought relief from religious persecution, and their arrival provoked a good deal of consternation among Anglo-Pennsylvanians, who grumbled that Pennsylvania was fast becoming a German colony. Spearheaded by Benjamin Franklin, Pennsylvania attempted in 1753 to establish charity schools in the hopes of more speedily assimilating (that is to say, regulating) German children. Thanks to the schools' blatant anti-German flavor, however, the effort failed by 1764 (Spring, 1994).

The educational situation in New York differed from that in both Massachusetts and Pennsylvania in that New York (New York City in particular) had originally been New Netherlands, a Dutch colony. Prior to the English conquest of New Netherlands in 1664 the basic reading and writing schools were maintained jointly by the Dutch West Indies Company, the city and the local government, with the latter in charge of administration. After defeating the Dutch, the English maintained the arrangement of local control and pursued a policy similar to that in Virginia.

As the colonial era drew to a close, three distinct forms of basic education were available for white children. The first was the basic reading and writing school in evidence throughout the colonies but concentrated primarily in New England. The second was the education provided by a private tutor, concentrated in the South. The third was the Latin grammar school, which provided a classical education for both Northern and Southern aristocracy. A degree of cultural and religious tension shaped educational practices in each type of schooling, particularly in Massachusetts and Pennsylvania. Education served to effect social regulation, but it also became an unintended means for emancipation—a hidden passage in the social control structure.

Before concluding this section, we want to point out who is missing in the various colonial education plans. First, while women received training to some extent, notably as school mistresses, their attendance was limited to the reading and writing schools. Toward the midpoint of the eighteenth century, literate women became popular as teachers, principally because they were cheap to hire (Tyack & Hansot, 1990). For the most part, however, formal schooling for girls remained a low priority.

Second, most accounts of early America make scant mention of what, if any, educational opportunities were available to nonwhites. In the South, because of the institution of slavery, Africans' and African Americans' educational options were typically limited to what their owners provided and the obligatory Sunday Christian service (Woodson, 1919). By the early eighteenth century a few schools in the South provided a rudimentary education for African Americans. These were established by the Society for the Propagation of the Gospel in Foreign Parts, in hopes of converting the "heathen" (see Woodson, 1919; Button & Provenzo, 1989).

Likewise, in the Far West the Spanish established a system of "mission schools" and relocated Native Americans to those areas. Native American males might also receive a "white education" in Virginia, but they rarely found it helpful. In fact, when the young men returned to their tribes they were seen as *bad runners, ignorant of every means of living in the woods, unable to bear either cold or hunger, know neither how to build a cabin, take a deer, or kill an enemy, speak our languages imperfectly, are neither fit for warriors, hunters, nor counselors; they are totally good for nothing. (Best, 1962, p. 16)*

We find little information regarding the formal educational experiences of people of color and indigenous peoples during the pre–1700 colonial era. Frankly, this past has gone largely uncharted because of a lack of interest among white scholars. Discoveries await those interested in connecting past practices, events and individual lives with present-day "democratic" education in the United States. In assessing whether schools educate for emancipation or social regulation, remember that educational exclusion is a powerful form of social regulation.

THE EMERGENCE OF A MODERN EDUCATION

As the American colonial population grew and expanded into the various "Indian territories," the need for some type of institutionalized schooling became more pressing. Their basic survival assured (though some early colonies literally died out, one vanished without a trace), communities looked to broaden both their economic bases and social diversions. Life in colonial America began to assume a more cosmopolitan air, although it continued to be very much shaped by agriculture and the ever-expanding frontier. With the growing availability of printed material, literacy began to serve and define the well-being of the better-off segments of communities. People started to associate some sort of training in the elements of knowledge with building the "good society."

In stark contrast to its seventeenth-century antecedents, a new intellectual force took hold that reshaped both government and educational policy and practice. Puritan education had been medieval in its outlook, with children schooled to be resistant to the deluder Satan. Thanks to the scientific works of Sir Isaac Newton, René Descartes and Francis Bacon, who set forth mathematical and scientific principles governing existence, nature was seen as orderly and predictable instead of capricious and harsh (Karier, 1986; Rippa, 1992). If all things started with the "Almighty Creator," as many of the "enlightened" philosophers who were rational deists still believed, God was more of a celestial watchmaker than an omniscient, omnipotent entity. Accordingly, the workings of a creator were made manifest through the laws of nature, not through individual and identifiable "acts of God."

As we saw in Chapter 2, reason, free inquiry and the emerging empirical sciences began to displace Christian theology as the provider of "truth" in the modernist world created by scientific revolution. Instead of the word of an occasionally vengeful God providing social guidance, the observed workings of nature or "natural law" unencumbered by theological baggage would sooner or later reveal what was true and just. Since God no longer participated actively in the process, it was humanity's responsibility to build a just society (Becker, 1932; Karier, 1986). The existing sociopolitical structures governing daily life underwent a reconsideration according to the new knowledge. One could view humanity more optimistically since it could no longer be assumed to be inherently evil and tainted with original sin. Some of the more radical thinkers of the time, such as Jean-Jacques Rousseau (see Chapter 1), even claimed that human nature was intrinsically good, a truly revolutionary thought. As Rousseau observed, "God makes all things good; man meddles with them and they become evil" (Rippa, 1992, p. 48).

This intellectual development had immediate political applications. First and foremost, this Age of Reason (the Enlightenment) undermined to some degree the political influence of organized religion. Additionally, instead of subjecting political dissidents, heretics, criminals and the mentally ill to exile, torture or execution in the hopes of driving various "devils" from the social deviant, individuals were to be disciplined and occasionally punished through various government institutions: the prison, the asylum or the school (Foucault, 1979). Indeed, a key feature of the emerging modernist social order involved the development of new means of regulating people without physical force. Regrettably, we must examine schooling in the context of this regulatory impulse.

Eighteenth-century American schooling was diverse in form and function, reflecting the needs, religious inclinations, ethnic composition and cultural biases of a given region, with the Enlightenment providing the strongest intellectual influence. Reflecting more and more philosopher John Locke's belief that each child was a "blank slate" *(tabula rasa)* to be inscribed with knowledge and wisdom, as opposed to inherently sinful, schools were to educate children in the ways of reason and order. While Christian belief remained an important element of a reasonable life and was included as a part of moral instruction, it yielded to the growing intellectual appeal of science and mathematics. The notion of schooling children for social regulation was not displaced but was reconfigured following the tenets of reason and natural law, and by the growing presence of the state.

EDUCATIONAL PROPOSALS IN THE EARLY REPUBLIC

Some historians believe that the American Revolution represented the full flower of the Enlightenment, with triumphant revolutionary heroes devising a democratic republic based on liberty and reason, and the state and church relegated to separate spheres. Revolutionary America was, indeed, a dynamic place, with various competing ideas of what the "nation" should be swirling about. By 1787 a federal constitution was in place, and by 1791 ten amendments, known as the Bill of Rights, had been appended. Under the Tenth Amendment education was a right reserved to the administration of the states. It would not become a pressing federal priority until the twentieth century.

Educational historians tend to focus on two proposals developed in the period preceding and during the Revolutionary War. The ideals reflected in the proposals suggest the ongoing dilemmas surrounding the purposes of contemporary "public education." The most insightful and comprehensive ideas that emerged regarding public education were proposed by Benjamin Franklin and Thomas Jefferson. In Franklin's *Proposals Relating to the Education of Youth in Pennsylvania* (1749), schools (academies) were conceived as quasi-vocational institutions that facilitated social mobility. Jefferson contributed his ideas in *A Bill for the More General Diffusion of Knowledge* (1779), thirty years later. Written in the midst of the Revolutionary War, Jefferson's proposal ranged from the establishment of reading and writing schools to the public funding of the College of William and Mary. Both proposals reflect the influence of the Enlightenment on the nature of education. However, we must also remember that Franklin's and Jefferson's proposals—despite their appeals to reason and enlightenment—were based on classed, gendered and racialized prejudices reflected in the two men's educational philosophies and in their political and personal lives.

Prior to the Enlightenment educational institutions had been either perfunctory, like the petty school, or elaborately classical, like the Latin grammar schools. Thanks to the Enlightenment, knowledge was seen as a good in and of itself unrestricted to the service of religious belief. This idea gained further intellectual and political influence in 1662 when Oxford and Cambridge Universities officially forbad non-Anglican students from attending. In the wake of this religious bar, *dissenting academies* sprung up throughout England to promote a more "scientific" curriculum committed to free inquiry. Perhaps the most radical academic innovation was instruction conducted in English rather than Latin, until then the traditional language of instruction. Academies gained popularity among the growing British middle class and population of non-Anglicans. Some educational historians have referred to the academies as "people's colleges," for they provided individuals with access to an education that would otherwise have been denied them. However, these few academies by no means provided for social emancipation or the end to classed, gendered, religious or racialized prejudices of the time. Even as the concept of academies moved across the Atlantic, the colonies continued to struggle with the contradictions between the democratic philosophy and a democratic society.

Franklin drew on both this educational legacy and his own life experiences as a Latin grammar student and apprentice when, in 1749, he proposed that an academy be established in Pennsylvania. His proposal began with a lament: "It has long been regretted as a Misfortune to the Youth of this Province, that we have no Academy in which they might receive the Accomplishments of a regular Education" (Best, 1962, pp. 126–127). Franklin then set forth his ideal curriculum for the academy, combining "the most useful and most ornamental" aspects of knowledge to prepare students for the professions. The useful aspects of an education included those learned in apprenticeships and through reading. The ornamental elements consisted of various social skills including debating.

In the typically American spirit of "getting ahead" rooted in the Protestant "work ethic," the academy education would facilitate the economic mobility of its students. In addition, Franklin's academy was to be a secular institution, with history rather than religion providing the important lessons. Through the careful study of history students would learn "morality, oratory, geography, politics, philosophy, human affairs, agriculture, technology, science and invention" (Spring, 1994, p. 23). As Franklin explained:

*the general natural Tendency of Reading good History, must be to fix in the
Minds of Youth deep impressions of the Beauty and Usefulness of Virtue of all
Kinds, Publick Spirit, fortitude, etc. (Best, 1962, p. 142)*

We should point out that although Franklin used the term "youth" in his proposal
he meant boys, for the education in his academy included an apprenticeship only
young males could pursue. On the whole, however, Franklin's ideas represented a
distinct break from the traditional Latin grammar school, especially with the addition of modern languages to the curriculum. Franklin had only scorn for the inclusion of ancient languages in a curriculum, calling them "the quackery of literature" (Best, 1962, p. 15). In Franklin's eyes, the learning that counted most was
that which would make a boy both employable and socially proper. Since Greek
and Latin were not the languages of colonial American commerce (English,
French, Spanish and German were), Franklin viewed them as scholastic irritants.

You will hardly be surprised to learn that Franklin, who was originally from
Boston, blended Enlightenment ideals with Puritan notions of hard work in his
educational proposal. Schools were to facilitate the "able" to move into the better
classes of society. An historic irony: When Franklin's proposals were finally
adopted, they led to the founding of the University of Pennsylvania, a classical institution, not an academy. Instead of teaching for social mobility, the institution
was dedicated to the business of confirming the status of the already privileged
(Rippa, 1992; Cremin, 1970).

Thomas Jefferson's conception of a state-provided education was far more
comprehensive than Franklin's. In 1779 Jefferson proposed *A Bill for the More
General Diffusion of Knowledge* to the Virginia legislature. His bill envisioned a
three-tiered system of public education that would prepare a "natural aristocracy"
for political leadership and a basic education for the "common man." All white
children would be sent to reading and writing schools for three years. The top
male students would then be sent on to Latin grammar schools. At the conclusion
of grammar school, the best students would proceed to the College of William
and Mary. All education would be provided at public expense.

Jefferson expected his three-tiered educational scheme to produce leaders for
both the Commonwealth of Virginia and the new republic. In Jefferson's words,
"Twenty of the best geniuses would be raked from the rubbish annually" (Spring,
1994, p. 39). Jefferson's intent was quite different from that of Franklin's academy, which was designed to train boys for a world of commerce. In Jefferson's
view education served two purposes: to cultivate a "natural aristocracy" of leadership free from religious orthodoxy and to perpetuate an enlightened citizenry that
would keep the nation free from political tyranny (Beard & Beard, 1930).

Jefferson also differed from Franklin in viewing skeptically the general populace as democratic ruler. Franklin had embraced education for the middle classes as
a means of "getting ahead" in a dynamic society. While espousing the power of
liberty, Jefferson took a more pessimistic view. If the ordinary folk were not
trained in matters of reason, mob rule might prevail. The free use of reason would
defeat tyranny. This sense of distrust infused Jefferson's proposal. Like Franklin,

Jefferson was a child of the Enlightenment and deeply committed to free inquiry, a commitment reflected in his curriculum, which was designed to be free from religious indoctrinations. Schools were to "diffuse knowledge, inculcate virtue (including patriotism), and cultivate learning" (Cremin, 1988, p. 85). More specifically, students in local schools were to be taught the basics: reading, writing and arithmetic. All "free" boys and girls were to receive a free education for three years (Krug, 1966). This education would, however, avoid study of the Bible. Jefferson believed that children were too immature in their reasoning to be exposed to religious indoctrination, and that such instruction could actually be harmful:

> *Instead . . . of putting the Bible and Testament into the hands of the children at an age when their judgments are not sufficiently matured for religious inquiries, their memories may here be stored with the most useful facts from Grecian, Roman, European and American history. (Spring, 1994, p. 39)*

As in Franklin's proposal, history, not religion, was to be the central focus for a Jeffersonian moral education. Experience had convinced Jefferson that state-supported religious orthodoxy too easily became tyranny. Following Enlightenment sensibilities, he considered history the best instrument for helping people defend their liberties, for it would facilitate reason. As he stated, "History, by apprising them of the past, will enable them to judge of the future; it will avail them of the experience of other times and other nations; it will qualify them as judges of the actions and designs of men; it will enable them to know ambition under every disguise it may assume; and knowing it, to defeat its views" (Ulich, 1954, pp. 465–466).

Jefferson had devised a comprehensive and bold plan to provide all white Virginians with a rudimentary education at state expense. But his proposal never passed the Virginia legislature; it was defeated in 1779 and again in 1817. For as conservative as the proposal appears to twentieth-century eyes, it was far too radical to be implemented in the early Virginia Commonwealth. Given Virginia's tradition of tutors and private education, a tax-supported system of public education was too large a sociological leap for legislators to attempt. As with Franklin's, Jefferson's ideals were ultimately realized in a much different fashion, by the founding of the University of Virginia (Spring, 1994).

We note some irony in the educational legacies of Jefferson and Franklin. Generally their proposals represented a move from highly authoritarian and explicit notions of "education for social regulation" to more enlightened ideals of human progress (Becker, 1932; Reisner, 1930). If their proposals did not promote emancipatory education in our critical postmodern sense, they still inform current debates over the purposes of public education. Franklin viewed public education as a means for achieving social mobility. Jefferson wanted a public education to school the general populace in reason, while also cultivating an intellectual elite. But both would have included regulatory aspects to enforce stability while allowing for the emancipation of only the hardiest of poor white males.

Many of today's debates on the educational mission follow the principles Jefferson and Franklin embodied: Should schools focus on providing vocational training to prepare students for economic realities or should they prepare future leaders, selecting and sorting only the most worthy by dint of their intellectual merit? Should schools attempt to do a little of both? or neither? Does either proposal promote emancipation or do both enforce social regulation? Perhaps the most critical question is what *are* the purposes of public schooling in a democratic society? These issues remain unresolved, but all educators must address them to understand their own roles in the profession.

Philosophical quandaries aside, in contrast to Franklin's and Jefferson's defeated proposals, nineteenth-century schools gained a certain amount of popularity and a degree of public funding. Reflecting the Enlightenment ideal of progress, *charity schools* became increasingly popular throughout the eighteenth century as a means of redeeming the poor from their fate. We find here, rather than in the plans of Franklin and Jefferson, the strongest foundation for American public education, a common school.

CHARITY SCHOOLS

Thanks to their enduring faith in the Protestant work ethic, early nineteenth-century Americans tended to view the poor as moral reprobates, deserving their fate as punishment for some hidden intrinsic sin (Nasaw, 1979). In a land with social, economic and political opportunities unknown in Europe, poverty became a sort of moral dilemma. Many Americans concluded that it could only be the result of sloth. America was, after all, the land of the "self-made man." As essayist Gore Vidal has observed,

> *given a rich empty continent for vigorous Europeans to exploit (the Indians were simply a disagreeable part of the emptiness, like chiggers), any man of gumption could make himself a good living. With extra hard work, any man could make himself a fortune, proving that he was a better man than the rest. (1993, pp. 906–907)*

During the late eighteenth and early nineteenth centuries, however, as the new nation grew and the industrial revolution took hold, worrisome signs suggested that all was not well in many American households. By the 1790s already New York City had slums. Many local trades- and craftspeople were being displaced by mechanical innovations and cheaply hired journeymen willing to relocate to gain employment (Nasaw, 1979). Others were leaving the stagnant agrarian economy to pursue their economic luck in the growing metropolitan areas. Still others saw their prospects limited by religious and ethnic bigotry. Increasing numbers of Roman Catholic immigrants found the American shores less than welcoming. In a land of supposedly overwhelming abundance, the growing numbers of paupers seemed a blight on the American social landscape.

It was also a time of general decline in church membership. The Christian (specifically Protestant) religious fervor aroused by the "Great Awakening" between 1740 and 1777 had faded with the passing of a half century. Americans seemed far more interested in building a new nation and their own livelihoods than in the "Kingdom of God." By 1817, an urban missionary in New York City was shocked to discover not only that the poor failed to attend church, but also that fewer than half the households in the city owned a Bible (Nasaw, 1979). The idea that the poor were both morally corrupt and physically threatening quickly gained currency.

Poor adults were viewed as irredeemable, but their offspring might still be saved from a life of crime and prostitution. Early American philanthropic societies set about establishing social institutions to save these children from their parents and themselves. Viewed through nineteenth-century eyes, poor children were in desperate need of a social regulation their parents were either unwilling to or incapable of providing. As social historian David Nasaw notes, "Poor children were adjudged as *a priori* ill-raised, ill-mannered and undisciplined" (1979, p. 11). Some sort of charity or free schooling was seen as one remedy; juvenile reformatories were another.

Charity schools spread rapidly throughout the Northeast during the 1790s and early 1800s as a social tool for eliminating crime and poverty from the American landscape. Not only were poor whites schooled, but in Philadelphia (1770), New York (1787) and Baltimore (1792) separate charity schools were established for freed blacks (Kaestle, 1983). In general, however, most African Americans and Native Americans were excluded from schooling in the North, Midwest and West. In the South, educating African Americans was outlawed under penalty of heavy fines for white teachers and fines, whippings and possibly death for black teachers (Nasaw, 1979). While charity schools went about the work of social regulation, only poor whites were deemed worthy of such regulation. Nonwhites had already passed beyond social redemption. However, those Native Americans who were sent to religious boarding schools in the west and northwest endured forced assimilation and cultural annhiliation in a perverse attempt to redeem and civilize them.

In 1805 New York City formed a "Free School Society" for the training of poor boys under the guidance of Thomas Eddy and John Murray, Jr., both wealthy Quakers (Ravitch, 1974; Nasaw, 1979). The membership of the society included a who's who of the New York economic elite, all apparently disturbed by the growing numbers of indigent urban children. One major complication in their plans for massive moral reform was the daunting task of schooling so many children with limited funds. How could so many poor boys be properly trained in the ways of industriousness, obedience and thrift with so little available money?

The solution to this problem came from England. Joseph Lancaster had designed a rigidly hierarchical system of education that could accommodate up to a thousand students in a single classroom. Lancaster envisioned the process of education as a machine, then broke it down into discrete components. Each boy had a number, which was hung on the wall. If he was "present," each boy would stand under his number to facilitate roll call. Students then marched to and from their various lessons and activities. They sat in straight rows, facing the front of the room. The teacher ascended a platform to oversee his charges (Ravitch, 1974; Nasaw, 1979). He was aided by older students, called monitors, who carried out almost all of the actual instruction. They were unpaid workers who discharged their duties by conveying the lessons to rows upon rows of students and enforcing classroom discipline and order. Submission to authority was the key to making the whole system work, with specific punishments for disobedience (Ravitch, 1974).

Much of the learning consisted of rote memorization. Boys repeated for the monitors the alphabet, spelling words and mathematical computations. To save the expense of so many slates, the youngest boys were taught the alphabet by letters drawn in sand. To maintain the system while promoting achievement, both monitors and students were ranked by daily performance. Those who excelled moved closer to the platform while those who did not fell to the back of the classroom (Ravitch, 1974; Nasaw, 1979; Spring, 1994).

The trustees of the New York Free School Society saw the Lancasterian system as the answer to their prayers. As educational historian Diane Ravitch observed, "It was a fully packaged system that was known to work; and . . . it was cheap" (1974, p. 12). Enormous numbers of poor boys could be efficiently educated and properly modeled in the ways of discipline, obedience and thrift. The society's president, De Witt Clinton, proclaimed in 1809:

> *When I perceive that many boys in our school have been taught to read and write in two months, who did not before know the alphabet, and that even one has accomplished it in three weeks—when I view all the bearings and tendencies of this system—when I contemplate the habits of order which it forms, the spirit of emulation which it excites, the rapid improvement which it produces, the purity of morals which it inculcates—when I behold the extraordinary union of celerity in instruction and economy of expense—and when I perceive one great assembly of a thousand children, under the eye of a single teacher, marching, with unexampled rapidity and with perfect discipline, to the goal of knowledge, I confess I recognize in Lancaster the benefactor of the human race. I consider his system as creating a new era in education, as a blessing sent down from heaven to redeem the poor and distressed of this world from the power and dominion of ignorance. (Cubberley, 1919, pp. 94–95)*

The Lancasterian system achieved similar popularity throughout the Northeast and eventually found its way to Georgia, Cincinnati, Louisville and Detroit. In 1822 the Pennsylvania state legislature mandated that this system be employed in publicly funded schools. Mexico required Lancasterian schools in the Mexican state of Texas in 1829.

Like the Puritan town schools, charity schools enforced student discipline rigidly and sometimes brutally. In both instances, children were viewed as morally suspect. Yet there was a difference. The Puritans' view of children had been ultimately a theological determination, while the charity school proponents' notion of "sin" was much more an economic and political assessment. Perhaps because of the Quakerism or the society's founders Thomas Eddy and John Murray, Jr., the New York Free School Society explicitly discouraged corporal punishment and even devised a ticket system of fines for infractions. But other schools and school personnel were not so reticent and based much of their pedagogical practices on humiliation and shame (Allison, 1995).

The charity schools also promoted a moral education deeply rooted in Protestantism. In New York, however, many of the poor children were Roman Catholics. Their church and their parents considered a "charitable" education promoting social regulation and a narrow cultural and religious assimilation reprehensible. In 1829, American Catholic bishops declared:

Since it is evident that very many of the young, the children of Catholic parents, especially the poor, have been exposed and are still exposed in many places of this Province, to great danger of the loss of faith or the corruption of morals, on account of the lack of such teachers as could safely be entrusted with so great an office, we think it absolutely necessary that schools should be established in which the young can be taught the principles of faith and morals, while being instructed in letters. (Hassard, 1866, p. 228)

The Catholic bishops continued to discuss this concern at the Councils of Baltimore in the 1840s and 1850s. As a result, Catholic parishes were urged to establish their own parochial school system rather than send Catholic children to the public common schools. The Catholic bishops feared that the attempts to assimilate immigrants into a common melting-pot culture of Protestant Christianity would deny Catholic children the freedom of religious expression, a fear that was not totally unsubstantiated—and, we might add, a continuing fear of many religious minorities in contemporary American culture. Catholics, particularly poor immigrants from countries such as Ireland, were viewed with suspicion and hatred. They were called "papists" (followers of the Pope in Rome); the Protestant majority assumed that these papists would undermine the emerging American democracy. Thus, a common school with a common religion and a common politics was judged best to assimilate immigrant children. (We will return to this discussion in more detail in Chapter 5.) This fear and hatred of Catholics runs deep in American history, and it was even evident in the 1960 presidential campaign when John F. Kennedy, the eventual winner and the first Roman Catholic U.S. president, had to defend himself against accusations of un-American loyalty to the Pope. Partly because of religious intolerance in the United States and partly due to religious zeal among bishops and Catholic families, Catholic schools proliferated between 1860 and 1960, becoming the largest nonpublic school system in the United States.

Meanwhile, in the charity schools evidence mounted that the poor students were resisting their "treatment." These charity schools conferred a heavy social stigma: "free" schooling was only for the morally suspect. They also followed an explicit commitment to the social control desired by their wealthy patrons (Ravitch, 1974). The poor resented such regulation and the petty humiliations that went with it. Some schools even required parents to take a "pauper's oath," a public declaration that they were unfit to instruct their children, before the children would be admitted. The New York Free School Society took pains to rename itself Public School Society in 1826, but increasing numbers of children stayed away nonetheless.

Yet the general political popularity of charity schools fueled discussions of offering schooling to all children. The belief that schools were a panacea, or cure-all, for social ills arose during the early years of the republic, and it has been a recurring theme in American public education ever since (Perkinson, 1991). But the pundits of the day worried that the schools might actually widen the class differences between the poor and everyone else. The calls for a truly public system of education, a basic education provided at public expense for all children (at least, all white children) grew. While social regulation and control have always been goals of the American public school system, by the 1830s and 1840s most observers agreed that schools had to be coupled with at least the appearance of bestowing emancipatory knowledge to retain the loyalty of their charges.

TEACHERS IN THE EARLY REPUBLIC

By this time you are probably wondering what it was like to be a teacher during the early republic. Contemporary commentators tell us that today's teachers are far less competent and dedicated than their predecessors. Like the idealized schools and children of times past, there was a once a supposed "golden age" of teaching. But as we shall see, much of this is myth. The historical record—what there is of it—is as contradictory as it is enlightening. For example, in 1939 educational historian Willard Elsbree made the following observation:

> *The colonial schoolmaster is unclassifiable. He was a God-fearing clergyman, he was an unmitigated rogue; he was amply paid, he was accorded a bare pittance; he made teaching a life career, he used it merely as a steppingstone; he was a classical scholar, he was all but illiterate; he was licensed by a bishop or colonial governor, he was certified only by his own pretensions; he was a cultured gentleman, he was a crude-mannered yokel, he ranked with the cream of society, he was regarded as a menial. In short, he was neither a type nor a personality, but a statistical distribution represented by a skewed curve. (Elsbree, 1939, p. 123)*

The very early teachers were, for the most part, "white and male, largely middle-class and young" (Rury, 1989, p. 10). Again, you should remember that public education, as such, did not exist in colonial America, with the notable exception of New England, and even there education was more of a haphazard matter. The towns in New England that maintained schools were typically short of funds, and therefore limited the length of the school year to a mere four- to six-week period. This meant that colonial schoolkeeping was more of an income supplement than a profession, with the schoolmasters holding such jobs as surveyor and innkeeper in addition to teaching (Preston, 1982). Nor did the profession appeal to men who had families to support. According to educational historian John Rury,

> *men do not seem to have thought of teaching as a legitimate career option. Rather, teaching appears to have been a way to sustain oneself in the absence of other opportunities, or a stepping stone to other more lucrative or higher-status careers, such as law or medicine. Because it consisted of men with relatively high levels of education, however, teaching probably drew men from middle- and upper-class backgrounds in colonial America. Its inability to hold many of these individuals, however, was testimony to the low esteem given education in British North America, and to the contradictory quality of teaching as an educated profession in American life. (1989, p. 14)*

Meanwhile, the South clung to a tutorial system of education, with affluent parents securing instruction for boys and occasionally girls. But again, tutors were poorly paid and tended to be single men.

With the gradual expansion of schooling and the rise in the educational level of the general population, opportunities for teaching grew for both men and women. The clearest example is in the development of the New England dame school. As David Tyack and Elizabeth Hansot note, the dame schools originally offered "child-tending," which evolved into quasi-public institutions "as towns began to pay 'goodwives' to teach poor children" (1990, p. 18). Much of the women's work involved nothing more than glorified babysitting, keeping children out from under their parents' feet and out of harm's way.

By the early 1700s teaching had become a "job" open to both men and women. Yet settled gender roles definitely shaped the nascent profession. Owing to their future potential maternity, women were deemed the proper teachers for the very young children, while men with their superior intellects (as eighteenth-century sensibilities assumed) were the better teachers for the older, typically male students. Hiring women also became popular because they "cost less" than men, which greatly reduced the expense of schooling young children. But up until the 1830s teaching remained largely in the male domain.

One issue that plagued many an early school was its teachers' lack of character. Teachers were expected to be pious Christian men and to set an example of morality for their young students. As with today's teachers, colonial school teachers were bound by "morality clauses," and were obligated under contract to uphold community standards of good character. Many areas in colonial America advertised for specific aspects of "good character." For example, one 1772 advertiser sought

> *A Sober diligent Schoolmaster capable of teaching* READING, WRITING, ARITH-METICK, *and the* Latin TONGUE. *The School is quite new, has a convenient Lodging room over it, is situated in a cheap Neighborhood, and its Income estimated at between sixty and eighty Pound a Year. Any Person qualified as above, and well recommended, will be put into immediate Possession of the School, on applying to the Minister of Charles Parish, York County [Georgia]. (Sedlak, 1989, p. 259)*

But the actual job and social skills early teachers presented often diverged quite a bit from those desired by their employers, partly because of the prevailing social policy of awarding "teaching positions to individuals who were incapable of succeeding financially in the competitive economy" (Sedlak, 1989, p. 260). Another influence was a certain societal split regarding teachers present even in the colonial era. While teaching was a "call" to the educated and moral, it was also a job that almost any roughly educated person "could do." Needless to say, the quality of the teachers varied widely.

In particular, drunkenness and financial shenanigans seemed to be the undoing of more than a few teachers (Elsbree, 1939; Allison, 1995). Here, for instance, is the account of the deportment and fate of one Georgia school master in 1749:

> *The Rev^d Mr. Zouberbuhler and the Inhabitants of this Town having made repeated Complaints to this Board, that Mr. Peter Joubert Schoolmaster had for*

some Time past neglected to give proper Attendance to his Scholars, and likewise that He has been of late so much addicted to Drinking, that He gives great offense to the Inhabitants, and what is more pernicious sets a bad Example of their Children. The Board being too sensible of this Complaint, and with concern finding that their repeated Admonitions have not been duly regarded They are now obliged to discharge him. (Elsbree, 1939, p. 19)

Teachers in the North seemed similarly vexed. One schoolmaster described his temporary replacement in 1720:

Here is one Edward Fitzgerald who, during the time I was absent in England which was about twelve months, kept school in this town [West Chester, New York]. [T]hat you may not be in the dark as to this man's true character I give them this acct. which if desired shall be sufficiently testified: He is much given to drink and don't attend the Church. (Elsbree, 1939, pp. 18–19)

These bits of recorded evidence do not convict every colonial-era teacher of being a drunken sot, but many were. Teaching was not a job that typically called "the best and the brightest" early American men. If men did teach, it was only for a brief time on the way toward a better-paying position (Rury, 1989; Allison, 1995). Ironically, the more unfit tended to remain the longest.

The inconsistencies among teachers themselves, coupled with the need to regulate their charges, meant that the early teachers were subject to a good deal of social regulation. Their lives were conducted in the fishbowl of local public opinion and few were willing to make teaching a lifetime career (Clifford, 1989; Allison, 1995). But as schooling expanded in the newly declared United States, teacher shortages became increasingly acute. Who would be suitable for training the youth of the new republic? The answer was as obvious as it was at first disturbing: women. After the revolution the idea of "republican motherhood" achieved great popularity. Postrevolutionary America expected every girl to wed and bear children, for children (and their labor) would help build the new country. Since a child's initial education began in the home, the argument that women should be educated to raise their sons properly for the duties of democracy gained credence, along with the idea that daughters should be trained for the duties of motherhood. Deprived of the vote and elected office—and in many instances the property of their fathers or husbands or eldest brothers—women were not, in any operational sense, citizens of the United States. Yet their participation in nation building was viewed as crucial to the survival of the republic (Solomon, 1985; Allison, 1995).

Proponents of women's education argued for both educating girls and allowing women to teach. They based their arguments largely on conservative precepts. Education would make girls and women more marriageable and better mothers. Their moral superiority made women better teachers for the very young. Given the tightly prescribed social mores of the time, women were also easier to regulate, especially as teachers.

Schooling girls and female teachers was hardly seen at the time as social emancipation, but rather as a means of imposing social regulation efficiently and gently. Girls and women had little access to anything beyond the most rudimentary education, and they were excluded from the rapidly proliferating universities. Yet more publicly funded academies began to accept women. Additionally, a few private schools began to specialize in the education of women, including Emma Willard's Female Seminary in Troy, New York, established in 1821 (Solomon, 1985). With more women becoming educated, and women's work generally undervalued, female teachers became an affordable option for many early schools. It would be a mistake, however, to assume that women entered the teaching profession in droves before the 1830s. While they began to acquire a better education, it would take the expansion of the common school movement, complete with its need for inexpensive labor, to entice women through the schoolhouse door in large numbers.

Amid a gradual expansion of educational opportunities for white Americans, the African American experience was, of course, quite different. In the North, a number of cities established segregated schools for black children, but they tended to be inferior to those whites attended (Tyack, 1974). This was particularly the case in Boston, which devised a tax-supported system of public education in 1789 (Spring, 1994). For thirty years African American parents challenged the quality of the Boston schools and the attitudes of white teachers, for they had little say in the operation of their schools, which were also woefully underfunded (Perkins, 1989). This despite the fact that African American parents, like other Boston residents, paid their full share of school taxes. The situation went unresolved until 1855, when the governor signed a law barring discrimination in schooling based on either religion or race (Spring, 1994; Tyack, 1974).

Professional teaching opportunities generally eluded African Americans until after the Civil War, when they arose principally in segregated northern schools (Rury, 1989). Blacks were barred by law from both learning to read and teaching in much of the South. As early as 1740, South Carolina banned the practice of teaching slaves to read, fearing that education would incite revolts. Enforcing illiteracy was one way the state maintained a caste system designed to portray African Americans as "subhumans" deserving of their enslavement (Allison, 1995).

A number of clandestine schools in the South, however, operated solely to teach African American children in defiance of the law (Woodson, 1919). According to historian Linda M. Perkins, "One school was conducted openly prior to 1819 by Julian Froumountaine, and then made secret after the 1830s. Another was operated by a Miss Dea Veaux for more than 25 years without the knowledge of whites" (1989, p. 345).

Others taught more informally, holding classes after midnight in slave quarters, barns or wherever secure spaces could be found (Davis, 1981). Regardless of the setting, teachers risked their lives to pass along any information they could. According to educational historian James Anderson, "A slave by the name of Scipio was put to death for teaching a slave child how to read and spell, and the child was severely beaten to make him 'forget what he had learned'" (1988, p. 17). This clandestine education certainly aimed at achieving emancipation, literally for the coming day of liberation. Nevertheless, not until the conclusion of the Civil War did opportunities for African American teachers simultaneously expand in the North and contract in the South (Perkins, 1989).

In general, the early schoolmasters mirrored citizenship eligibility in the new republic: white males with property or the ability to secure some tangible wealth.

Like their students, the schoolmasters underwent a great deal of public scrutiny and social regulation. In some instances, schoolmasters earned a certain degree of respect. But given the typical shortness of the school year and the low wages, more often than not teaching was at best a transitory job, a means of securing a better position later. For the most part, as we have seen, only the economically and socially incompetent remained in the classroom for long. Perhaps the strongest cultural legacy from this era regarding what a "teacher was like" is Washington Irving's portrayal of the bumbling schoolmaster Ichabod Crane in *The Legend of Sleepy Hollow*. A classic of American literature, the novel's perennial popularity speaks volumes about how we long have viewed our teachers.

THE CONTRADICTORY ENTERPRISE OF AMERICAN EDUCATION

Our examination of early American schooling reveals the sociopolitical contradictions embedded within the enterprise. From the Puritan town schools, to the founding of charity schools, to the nascent publicly funded schools education was dedicated to social regulation, a goal realized through a variety of practices. Reflect for a moment on those who received "the treatment," the pedagogical practices used, and those who were excluded and why.

Schooling also offered the contrary (and largely unintended) possibility of social emancipation. As with the Puritans, increased literacy bestowed the ability and opportunity to read material that differed from what was approved for public consumption by "the power structure." These contradictions would become paradoxically both more and less apparent as the campaign for a "common school" spread across the country. As Enlightenment ideals of progress were coupled with Protestant notions of hard work, publicly funded schools were increasingly viewed as the panacea for social ills. As we shall see in Chapter 5, the historic political and social complexities inherent in schooling in an ostensibly "democratic republic" would reveal the paradoxes within the larger American society. Education has threatened to undermine the very political regime that expects it to impose a sense of social order.

Common Schools and Beyond

Education for Social Control versus Education for Democratic Citizenship

INTRODUCTION

Andrew Jackson's 1828 election as president marked the end
one educational era and the beginning of another. Jackson's pre
dency brought to fruition the full-white-manhood-suffrage mo
ment—which is to say, the extension of the vote to nonpropert
white males. This liberal trend, in turn, encouraged efforts to co
duct presidential elections through more "popular" and direct v
ing, instead of allowing the state legislatures to select presiden
electors. Once secured, this adjustment loosened at least a little
political reins the economic elite had hitched to the federal g
ernment at the nation's inception.

Not all Americans welcomed the change. In fact, the 18
presidential election was one of the most rancorous in the hist
of the republic. Jackson's opponents charged him with being
usurper, an adulterer, a gambler, a cock-fighter, a brawler,
drunkard and a murderer." Jackson's supporters called his opp
nent, John Quincy Adams, a "stingy Puritan, an aristocrat w
hated the people, a corruptionist who had bought his own [e
lier] election, and a waster of the people's money on the Wh
House" (Beard & Beard, 1930, p. 552).

Shrewdly capitalizing on the extension of the vote, Jacks
built his presidential campaign around an appeal to "ordina
Americans" and soundly trounced Adams. In stark contrast to
more aristocratic predecessors, Jackson presented himself as
backwoodsman, a hero of the War of 1812, an "Injun fighter" a
a man of the common people who happened to be seeking t
presidency. His election confirmed that change now stirred t
young nation and that a fragmented society still rooted in Briti
norms of economic aristocracy was becoming increasingly "dem
cratic." Jackson's subsequent inauguration, an enormous spect
cle, reinforced the most hopeful dreams and darkest fears of bo

sides (Nasaw, 1979). Margaret Bayard Smith, a longtime Washington resident, described the festivities in a letter to her sister:

> *[W]hat a scene did we witness! The Majesty of the People had disappeared, and a rabble, a mob, of boys, Negroes, women, children scrambling, fighting, romping. What a pity, what a pity! No arrangements had been made, no police officers placed on duty, and the whole house had been inundated by the rabble mob.*
>
> *[I]t was the People's day, and the People's President and the People would rule. God grant that one day or other, the People, do not put down all rule and rulers. I feel, enlightened Freemen as they are, they will be found, as they have been found in all ages and countries where they get the Power in their hands, that of all tyrants, they are the most ferocious, cruel and despotic. The noisy and disorderly rabble in the President's House brought to mind descriptions I had read of the mobs in the Tuileries and at Versailles. I expect to hear the carpets and furniture are ruined, the streets were muddy, and these guests all went thither on foot. The rest of the day, overcome with fatigue, I lay upon the sofa. (Rippa, 1969, pp. 159–160)*

Thus, President Andrew Jackson's inauguration quickened the deepest fear of the American elite: that of the power of the mob. If the United States were to be a government of the people (or at least the white males), the need for an educated citizenry as a bulwark against anarchy had become instantly apparent. Only a properly educated voter could protect the fragile republic.

Moreover, by 1828 the country was also becoming increasingly diverse, with thousands of immigrants arriving annually from Ireland and the middle European countries. This is not unlike the current climate in the United States, except that the immigrants today come from Central America, South America, Asia and the Middle East. Many immigrants of the 1800s were Roman Catholics, and their rituals and services provoked nativist fears of "Romanish control" and a religious "takeover." Anti-Catholic and anti-immigrant backlashes swept the nation, with particularly vicious manifestations in New York, Massachusetts and Pennsylvania. Nativists published deliberately incendiary propaganda, slurring priests, nuns and the Pope. The fear, hatred and demonization of immigrants then as now was deeply ingrained in the American psyche—despite the fact that the poem by Emma Lazarus engraved on the Statue of Liberty proclaims that America welcomes "the teeming masses" of humanity in search of life, liberty and the pursuit of happiness. Religious, ethnic and racial slurs today are often directed at Mexican laborers, Middle Eastern Muslims and Asian merchants. In the 1800s, nativists insinuated that the Roman Catholics' "indulgence of their appetites for stimulating drinks" would be the ruin of the nation (Bennett, 1995, p. 75). With the rising religious and political tensions, many observers assumed that the country would become (to use a current phrase) Balkanized, with various ethnic street gangs waging bloody civil warfare:

> *Natives and Irishmen, Protestants and Catholics, clashed in fistfights and knife fights. They exchanged gunfire. They menaced each other with cannons, ready to be loaded with stacks of shot, powder, nails, chains, "anything" as one observer put it, that could be used to "kill and maim the foe." (Bennett, 1995, p. 56)*

One can hardly exaggerate the political danger the early United States faced, for the legacy of the French Revolution remained all too clear in the people's minds. Social reformers sought an institution that would bind the citizens together, inculcating settled values and opinions of what it meant to be an "American." School seemed the most socially and economically efficient means to this goal. If children from various religious, class and ethnic backgrounds were educated in the same school, tensions might lessen or even disappear (Spring, 1994).

But what would be the mission of this "common school" for the "common man"? Was it to be merely a governmental expansion of charity schools? Would schools emphasize social regulation or emancipation? The result would be a common school that none of the debaters could exactly have foreseen. We can understand the evolution of the common school ideal by examining the campaign of the common school's most articulate and ardent proponent, Horace Mann.

HORACE MANN AND THE CAMPAIGN FOR A "COMMON SCHOOL"

Like other social reformers of the era, Horace Mann (1796–1859), a product of the Enlightenment, was committed to the laws of reason (and reasonable laws) to ensure social salvation. Born on a farm near Franklin, Massachusetts, Mann was raised by rigid Calvinists. He abandoned doctrinaire Christianity, however, when his twelve-year-old brother drowned while swimming on the Sabbath (a violation of Calvinistic theological teachings), and the family minister, the Reverend Nathaniel Emmons, used the funeral to warn the assembled youngsters about dying unconverted, embellishing his warning with depictions of the torments of hell (Spring, 1994; Rippa, 1992). Mann reacted by rejecting Calvinism for a more humanistic and optimistic philosophy, even though he retained a Calvinist sense of "moral absolutism" and faith in the merits of hard work (Tyack & Hansot, 1982). As he observed in an 1836 letter, "My nature revolts at the idea of belonging to a universe in which there is to be never-ending anguish. . . . [W]hile we are on earth, the burden of our duties is toward man" (Spring, 1994, p. 66).

Though largely self-educated, Mann gained admittance to Brown University, from which he graduated with honors in 1819. He was admitted to the bar in 1823, and quickly involved himself with the Whigs (a predecessor of the Republican Party). Soon he was serving as president of the Massachusetts state senate. The Whig philosophy stressed positive liberalism: the idea that active government intervention could secure and maintain a just society. Government could and should play a role in "maintaining the economy, regulating morality, and ensuring political and social order" (Spring, 1994, p. 78). More specifically, the Whigs supported restrictions on alcohol and gambling and sought to establish state hospitals for the insane, but disagreed on the abolishment of slavery (Nasaw, 1979; Bennett, 1995). Like their Puritan antecedents, they believed that citizens left to their own vices or devices would gravitate toward anarchy. As historians David Tyack and Elizabeth Hansot observe, Whigs "believed it a virtue to mind other people's business" (1982, p. 56).

Whigs also believed that publicly funded schools could help ensure social stability and that the state had a right to cultivate an educated citizenry. They fought frequent political battles with the more libertarian-minded Democrats for passage of educational legislation and the enabling taxes. Like many current-day libertarians who advocate live-and-let-live, laissez-faire government, Jacksonian-era Democrats saw state-controlled public schools as a usurpation of local control, governmental meddling in local affairs. Such a governmental presence, coupled with the imposition of property taxes to fund the schools, threatened individual liberty and could possibly lead to centralized tyranny (Spring, 1994). The debates in the various state legislatures over a common system of education became both heated and divisive.

In 1837 the Massachusetts legislature appointed Mann its first secretary of the state board of education, a post he held until 1848. Mann went quickly to work, crusading for common schools (Nasaw, 1979). With only a small budget to aid his efforts, Mann attracted support through the sheer force of his personality and a compelling series of annual reports. In fact, educators now consider his campaign for the common school a sort of one-man religious crusade. Mann may have rejected Calvinism, but he definitely believed in the redemption of society through a system of public schools (Perkinson, 1991). In pursuing his quest he traveled more than five hundred miles, much of it on horseback, visiting local schools and reassuring communities that the state sought only to stimulate local efforts, not replace them (Tyack & Hansot, 1982).

Nevertheless, a financial panic that swept across the country in 1837 increased American fears of "mob rule." Unemployment escalated as workers were laid off in massive numbers for the first time in American history. The overwhelming economic distress exacerbated the violence between Protestant and Roman Catholic street gangs, and it swept through the cities of the Northeast. Mann had witnessed one bloody uprising in Boston and blamed the violence on the lack of general education. In the spirit of the Enlightenment he prescribed reason:

> *The mobs, the riots, the burnings, the lynchings, perpetrated by the men of the present day, are perpetrated because of their vicious and defective education. We see and feel the ravages of their tiger passions now, when they are full grown; but it was years ago when they were whelped and suckled. And so too, if we are derelict in our duty in this matter, our children in their turn will suffer. If we permit the vulture's eggs to be hatched, it will then be too late to take care of the lambs. (Karier, 1986, p. 60)*

Mann's widely promulgated belief that a common school could build social stability resonated with many Americans. According to Mann's vision, the schools would train children in the ways of industry and thrift, and through intensive social interaction children would learn to respect each other. Mann believed that only a common school, where children of all backgrounds could be educated side by side, could lay the foundation for social stability. He saw such schools as the panacea for society's ills (Perkinson, 1991).

To be sure, strong conservative elements informed Horace Mann's educational vision. He believed, for example, in molding children into proper Americans. "Men are cast-iron," he wrote, "but children are wax. Strength expended upon the latter may be effectual, which would make no impression upon the former" (Spring, 1994, p. 67). One crucial element of this molding was "moral education," which included the use of the King James version of the Bible. The "common school" would be a Christian institution, for many nineteenth-century Americans equated morality with Protestant Christianity. Yet, in deference to constitutional (and more importantly, political) dictates, the public school would also be nondenominational, and certainly neither Catholic nor non-Christian. Bible verses would be read, supposedly without doctrinal bias.

This reliance upon the Bible infuriated Catholics and some of the more orthodox Protestants, who perceived Mann's vague and generalized Protestantism as a ploy to gain Protestant political support for the publicly funded schools without alienating any specific Protestant denomination. His was a direct appeal to a "nativism" growing in the country and beginning to dominate the Whig party (Bennett, 1995). The overtly Protestant nature of the public schools was also a means of regulating the growing numbers of Catholic children, ensuring that those who attended the common schools would be exposed to the common tenets of the Protestant faiths (Tyack & Hansot, 1982; Karier, 1986).

As yet another means of ensuring that the common schools would regulate their charges, Mann insisted that no "controversial" subjects be studied. He worried that any political, social or economic controversy explored within the schoolhouse would eventually undermine political support for the schools themselves (Karier, 1986; Spring, 1994). So by design, the common school offered a bland curriculum, children absorbed watered-down subject matter in the name of preserving political (and financial) support for their schools and teachers could not freely explore "contemporary issues."

This "common" education gained support from many industrial interests, who paid a significant portion of the early taxes. They recognized the common school as an efficient means of maintaining a skilled and docile labor pool, soon the very buttress of capitalism (Tyack & Hansot, 1982). School taxes became a sort of property insurance, a way of preserving the power of corporate capital (Nasaw, 1979). Immigrants would be educated and assimilated, and radical (that is to say, "foreign") ideas regarding the rights of labor would be extinguished. A common school would ensure that children were properly prepared for the needs of industry. Efforts to understand the origins of state-supported public education in America cannot succeed without a thorough appreciation of these industrial needs, and to discuss the impact of economic forces on American schooling we must now backtrack a bit.

Before the Industrial Revolution, which began in the United States in the 1820s, nineteen of every twenty Americans lived and worked on a farm. A nation populated by rural dwellers needed practical agricultural knowledge to make a living; reading and writing could be taught in the home after work. After the 1820s with the beginnings of the Industrial Revolution, many Americans—especially the new urban dwellers—began to sense that the country was changing. At first Massachusetts was influenced by the socioeconomic effects of industrialization more than any other state, and the economic changes there would create the context for Mann's great idea: the first state-supported compulsory school system in America.

Industrialists found it difficult to adapt agrarian males to the demands of unskilled factory work. Consequently, New England mill owners hired women, children and the inmates of charitable institutions as laborers. When Irish Catholics began to emigrate in larger numbers, industrialists hired them to replace American-born workers. They soon then saw the value in developing "proper" industrial attitudes among both the immigrants and future generations of Americans. This realization led them naturally to consider the role of schools in "attitude adjustment." Thus the industrialists' support of public education did not reflect a concern for either an empowered, educated citizenry or the economic welfare of American citizens; it reflected their economic self-interest—specifically, a pool of workers with attitudes conducive to industrial productivity.

As we said, education professionals should understand this point so as to appreciate the fact that schools pursue more than just academic goals. All educational decisions are also political decisions, since they concern questions of power and its distribution among different interest groups. Americans often have difficulty understanding the dynamics of political questions. Too often we restrict the adjective "political" to the sphere of political parties, candidates and elections, and we thereby miss the power-related aspects of politics. As a result, we could miss the significance of the political dimensions of Horace Mann's common school crusade and its relevance for contemporary educators. Engaging questions of power with the understanding that power elites possess inordinate influence in the shaping of school policy can help educators appreciate how schools work, as well as their personal roles in the larger, sociopolitically driven educational process.

Mann worked hard to "sell" the public schools to his Massachusetts contemporaries. In his conversations with powerful industrialists and business leaders in his home state, he addressed their fear of social disharmony. Made anxious by the growing dissatisfaction of workers with the tedium, danger, long hours and low pay of industrial jobs, factory owners sought ways to ensure social stability and order. When Mann talked of schools producing a "common core of values," the industrialists inferred that such values would support and promote industrial development. The common schools, Mann said, would turn out factory workers who were docile, easily administered and likely to avoid strikes and working-class violence. Schooling would reduce the poor people's hostility toward the wealthy. These implications were music to the ears of industrial leaders, far more concerned as they were with orderly and docile workers than with well-educated and inventive workers—particularly those workers already discussing "working men's associations" designed to protect their interests against the power of factory owners. One finds a fear of worker organization or revolt perpetually preoccupying the minds of factory owners.

An important question arises in this context: Where in a mid-nineteenth-century Massachusetts textile mill would a worker need to exercise creativity or employ a refined ability to analyze and interpret? As far as the owners were concerned, such traits could lead only to labor trouble. As with most educational reform initiatives, the political dimension of the common school movement involved its alliance with monied interests. Although Mann's vision of public schooling went far beyond providing malleable workers, the movement would never have succeeded had the commercial banking and manufacturing interests not believed that schools would yield long-term financial benefits. The key element in the political coalition that brought universal, compulsory, state-supported education to America was the expectation among the power elite that public schools would inculcate a core of values that would prepare students to accept the inherent indignities of industrial life.

By the time Horace Mann resigned his post in 1848, common schooling was thriving in Massachusetts and throughout most of the rest of the country. Numerous state legislators pursued a system of common schooling with a missionary zeal, inspired by Mann's rhetorical acumen. In his last annual report, Mann described the virtues of a free school system:

> *It knows no distinction of rich and poor, of bond and free, or between those who, in the imperfect light of this world, are seeking, through different avenues, to reach the gate of heaven. Without money and without price, it throws open its doors, and spreads the table of its bounty, for all the children of the state. Like the sun, it shines, not only upon the good, but upon the evil, that they may become good; and, like the rain, its blessings descend, not only upon the just, but upon the unjust, that their injustice may depart from them and be known no more. (Rippa, 1969, p. 204)*

Such rhetoric, no doubt sincere, compels the educational historian to fix the socioeconomic context. Only the nonindustrialized South resisted Mann's system of public education; it would take Reconstruction and the promise of industrial development for such a system to gain acceptance there.

Despite their political and economic aims, the academic education the common schools provided probably exceeded what the charity schools offered. While the children of the economic aristocracy stayed away, many middle-class and lower-class white children received basic instruction in the three Rs. Access to schooling, especially in the growing Eastern urban centers, remained problematic, with many people excluded by law (African Americans) or ethnic groups by local practice (Irish Americans). But for many white Protestant Americans of the early nineteenth century, a common school education offered a clear path out of grinding poverty (Lugg & Lugg, 1996).

Nevertheless, with urbanization underway, the United States remained largely a rural nation, and the educational system reflected this demography. The school year was brief, with academic terms tied to the needs of the agrarian economy. The "one-room" school buildings themselves tended to be small and typically in bad repair. Students as young as six and as old as twenty-one learned their reading, writing, arithmetic and a smattering of American history together. As with the earlier charity schools, common school pedagogical practices placed emphasis on proper deportment. While few of the schools were overtly Lancasterian, they maintained a strong flavor of regimentation and brutality. According to one common school teacher, "Whipping was the universal mode of discipline" (Lugg & Lugg, 1996, p. 37). Factory workers accustomed to such physical regulation would, ideally, be less rebellious than undisciplined employees.

While the degree and type of social regulation varied among local schools, standardized textbooks helped ensure a uniform public education. Books like *The English Reader,* Cobb's *Speller* and *The American Manual* were typical (and remorselessly bland) curricular fare. But the crucial textbooks for building "republic citizens" were the *McGuffey Readers,* and no examination of early American education is complete without a discussion of this, the most familiar textbook series in U.S. history. The books were a fabulous publishing success, selling some 122 million copies between 1836 and 1920 (Perkinson, 1991). Each reader contained lessons designed to impart "moral behavior" (Spring, 1994). While a few of the stories described the proper social roles for girls (by and large, models of chastity and charity), most of the morality tales focused on appropriate behavior for boys and young men.

In particular, the *McGuffey Readers* legitimized the growing discrepancies between rich and poor Americans by portraying the rich as moral stewards for the poor. The McGuffey stories reinforced the Puritan notion that God rewards hard work with wealth; hence, a vast personal fortune provided a compelling sign of moral virtue. The books carefully avoided stigmatizing the poor as inherently sinful. In fact, being poor could be "character building," and poor boys were often portrayed as facing and overcoming great moral crises. For example, one poor protagonist "often sees naughty boys in the streets, who fight, and steal, and do many bad things; and he hears them swear, and call names, and tell lies; but he does not like to be with them, for fear they should make him as bad as they are; and lest anybody who sees him with them, should think that he too is naughty" (Spring, 1994, p. 125).

Thus, the McGuffey lessons stressed the need for the social regulation of the poor and the moral worthiness of the rich. The books taught children to accept their stations in life without ill will toward their betters. In short, the *McGuffey Readers* promoted social stability over social emancipation. They assumed the morality of the emerging industrial capitalist order, and framed any challenges to this assumption as disloyal and un-American.

For a country born of revolution and marked ever after by vicious sectarian violence, the *McGuffey Readers* provided soothing and conservative political lessons. They presented homey, heartwarming tales often based on wishful thinking. They provided a surrealistic contrast to the actual lives of many of the children who read them. But the *McGuffey Readers* were nevertheless a far cry from the "gloomy moralizing of the Puritan texts" (French, 1964, p. 74). Their sunny outlook ensured their popularity well into the early twentieth century. In fact, some contemporary private religious schools still use the *McGuffey Readers.*

FROM SCHOOLMASTER TO SCHOOLMARM: THE ROLE OF GENDER IN THE NEW PROFESSION

With the rise of the common school came one profound social change: the feminization of public school teachers. More and more local districts hired female teachers. In 1840 only 30 percent of teachers were women; by 1920 that figure had risen to 85 percent, and it remains near 70 percent in 1998 (Newman, 1998). One of the reasons for this phenomenon was that wages for women were lower than for men, but there were other reasons to hire women. Thanks to their thoroughly inculcated passive social roles, American women were seen as appropriate instructors of young children. The Boston board of education reported in 1841:

> *It is gratifying to observe that a change is rapidly taking place, both in public sentiment and action, in regard to the employment of female teachers. The number of male teachers, in all the summer and winter schools, for the last year, was thirty-three less than for the year preceding, while the number of females was one hundred and three more. That females are incomparably better teachers for young children than males, cannot admit of a doubt. Their manners are more mild and gentle, and hence more in consonance with the tenderness of childhood. They are endowed by nature with stronger parental impulses, and this makes the society of children delightful, and turns duty into pleasure. Their minds are less withdrawn from their employment, but [welcome] the active scenes of life; and they are less intent and scheming for future honors or emoluments. As a class, they never look forward, as young men almost invariably do, to a period of legal emancipation from parental control, when they are to break away from the domestic circle and go abroad into the world, to build up a fortune for themselves; and hence, the sphere of hope and of effort is narrower, and the whole forces of mind are more readily concentrated upon present duties.*
>
> *They are also of purer morals. In the most common and notorious vices of the age, profanity, intemperance, fraud, etc., there are twenty men to one woman; and although as life advances, the comparison grows more and more unfavorable to the male sex, yet the beginnings of vice are early, even when their developments are late; on this account, therefore, females are infinitely more fit than males to be the guides and exemplars of young children. (Elsbree, 1939, p. 201)*

The increasing predominance of female teachers reflected an even broader sociological change in society's impressions of appropriate roles for both men and women. With the emergence of "republican motherhood," a general increase in female literacy, coupled with gradually more enlightened teaching philosophies, women became acknowledged as the natural educators of the very young. Teaching was seen as a logical extension of women's "motherly duties." Since a common school education provided only the barest rudiments of an education (as cheaply as possible), women seemed to be the best teachers. In an institution dedicated to ensuring social stability through the regulation of children, what better strategy than to confer the teaching duties on those similarly regulated?

Yet school teaching also offered many women an opportunity to pursue a respectable profession (Solomon, 1985; Clifford, 1989). Unlike nursing, which pressed women of questionable virtue into service in times of calamity, teaching was a socially acceptable means of achieving greater economic stability and independence. One nineteenth-century school teacher, Miriam Davis Colt, noted:

> *As I reviewed my father's circumstances, I knew that I must make my own way in life—go out and take care of myself; so the height of my aspirations were to attain the position of school teacher, and I hoped that some day I should have a pair of*

scissors hanging at my side, fastened with a large scissor hook to my sink apron strings—have a green silk calash bonnet, and green ribbon to hold it over my face, and walk to and from school with a score or more of little urchins calling me school-ma'am; this would constitute my beau ideal of attainment and honor (Clifford, 1989, p. 302).

Nevertheless, the early schoolmarms faced many paradoxes. With teaching fast becoming a "female" profession, women still received low wages, even though their salaries typically comprised the largest portion of a school district's budget. By employing women who commanded low wages school districts could stretch scarce resources and, in many instances, extend the school year. As the following table shows, women who taught in the early common schools received far less pay than their male counterparts:

Average Weekly Salaries of Teachers, 1841–1861

	Rural		Urban	
Year	Men	Women	Men	Women
1841	$4.15	$2.51	$11.93	$4.44
1846	$4.03	$2.53	$11.53	$4.18
1851	$4.43	$2.95	$14.10	$4.87
1856	$6.07	$3.85	$16.76	$6.10
1861	$6.30	$4.05	$18.07	$6.91

(Source: Butts & Cremin, 1953, p. 284.)

Moreover, female teachers often had to adopt the awkward practice of "boarding around." With their wages so low, their communities were expected to house and feed them. Families would take turns housing the schoolmarm, yet another way communities could economize on public education. Accordingly, female teachers often found themselves lodged in the homes of their students. As one early common school teacher noted, "there were many disagreeable things about this system":

Sometimes I had to go into very crude family life, even into places where the entire habit of domestic economy, eating, sleeping, spinning, and weaving, would be carried out in one room. If one person wished to go to bed early the rest of the household considerately "looked up the chimney." I have been in some places where there was so little room that I had to have two children sleep with me. There was absolutely no recognition of the necessity for hygienic conditions. The beds were usually in recesses called bed-sinks, and trundle beds were under the beds. There was no way to air these bed-sinks, and there was never any thought of airing the bedding. A notable house-keeper was one who made the beds the minute people were out of them. (Lugg & Lugg, 1996, p. 10)

Besides their economic appeal, a certain moral appeal accompanied female teachers. Nineteenth-century America viewed women as intrinsically more virtuous than men, thanks to their more or less predestined roles as mothers and nurturers (Tyack & Hansot, 1982). But certain contradictory caveats attached to this general expectation. To maintain their proper moral standing, female teachers were expected to remain single (Allison, 1995). Not until twentieth-century

Freudian psychology cast "spinsterhood" into moral doubt did the idea of teachers marrying become acceptable. In short, female teachers in the common school era, like some American vestal virgins, dedicated their lives to the moral purity of the republic and their young charges (Spring, 1994). Once married, female teachers were expected to resign their posts unless a dire need for their services remained. Reflecting the gender bias of the times, men escaped this expectation. In fact, the practice of dismissing married female public school teachers would continue until the mid-twentieth century, with inequities in pay continuing on into the 1970s—some would say, up to the present. So the history of American teachers from the common schools to the present is in many ways women's history—the story of millions of women who worked very hard under harsh conditions and with minimal compensation. And despite the important contribution of women like Ella Flagg Young, the first female superintendent of schools who strongly influenced the work of many educators (notably John Dewey), most leadership roles remained in the control of men.

By the turn of the century teachers began to organize to protect their interests and improve their economic security. Margaret Haley and Catherine Goggin, among others, were instrumental in organizing teachers. In 1916, when the American Federation of Teachers (AFT) was founded, the empowerment of teachers was closely tied to feminist issues of voting rights and salary equality. Women held leadership roles and insisted that their struggle to make teachers' voices heard was part of a larger struggle for women's rights in society. However, by 1957, when the National Education Association (NEA) was founded (originally as the National Teachers Association), a few administrators, mostly male, controlled teachers, mostly female. In such a patriarchal climate, some women developed liberating ways of teaching children in the larger society outside the common school system. Elizabeth Peabody created "conversations" with actual people in classroom settings to promote self-knowledge, creativity and community. Like Italian Maria Montessori (1870–1952), who was developing an early childhood curriculum at about the same time, Peabody and Alcott were interested in the development of initiative and self-reliance in children. Their restiveness in the face of routinization in common schools, false relations among human beings, blind conformity and social injustices led Peabody, Alcott and others to find various modes of defiance to challenge the social order. As we will see in Chapter 6, these initiatives by nineteenth- and early twentieth-century women also had an impact on labor and economic issues.

Some women successfully resisted nineteenth-century views of their gender and challenged economic and social class inequities. Social worker Jane Addams (1860–1935) figures prominently in these efforts. Addams was a white woman of privilege who became committed to pluralism in America as a result of her experience caring for children. In 1889 she founded Hull House in Chicago as a center of education, recreation and social programs for immigrants, poor people and women from privileged families. She wanted all people to have contact in the hope that they would develop friendships, mutual respect and understanding in the community. This is similar to our philosophy of mutual respect, presented in the Introduction and Chapter 1. Addams's program was called the "settlement house movement," and she hoped that these houses would serve as models for the common schools and for other social service agencies in America.

> *Public school teachers, subordinated as they were in the solidifying educational bureaucracies, seldom spoke the language of resistence or transcendence. It is well to remember the courageous ones who dared to go south after the Civil War in the freedmen's schools. Not only did they suffer persecution for their efforts; they often fought for their own human rights against male missionary administrators and even against the missionary concept itself. It is well to remember, too, the transformation of the missionary impulse into settlement houses and social work by women like Jane Addams and Lillian Wald. Committing themselves to support systems and adult education for newcomers to the country and the neighborhood poor, they supported union organization with the explicitly political awareness of what they were about in a class-ridden society. They were able to develop . . . the critical empathy needed for enabling the "other" to find his or her way. (Greene, 1986, 161–162)*

Jane Addams's commitment to pluralism and justice continues to inspire educators today; some even contend that Addams was an early forerunner of multicultural education philosophies.

DEVELOPMENT OF THE NORMAL SCHOOLS

As in the colonial era, antebellum teaching qualifications were minimal, with literacy the most basic requirement. States did not license teachers; instead, local districts typically subjected prospective teachers to competency examinations. But the country had neither a teacher training system nor any certification requirements.

> *Up through the mid-nineteenth century, recruiting and hiring teachers was entirely a private, negotiated procedure which occurred between someone with authority to employ and pay a teacher, and someone willing to accept whatever instructional—and maintenance—responsibilities that were wanted. (Sedlak, 1989, p. 258)*

With the expansion of the common school and the feminization of teaching came a gradual demand for better teachers. Most American women were barred from attending most private and many public universities and many other postsecondary institutions. In fact, teachers generally presented little beyond what we would now consider an elementary education. Additionally, only a few schools (or female seminaries) provided postsecondary education for women, but they were few and scattered. Many early teachers, then, came to the classroom poorly prepared. One 1837 report complained that Massachusetts teachers were "exceedingly incompetent in many respects" (Herbst, 1989, p. 217). Thus, it became apparent that states (and in some cases, cities) had to intervene to ensure that teachers were prepared adequately for their responsibilities. In 1838 the Massachusetts legislature took action, establishing four publicly funded teacher training institutes called "normal schools" (from the French *école normale,* so called because they would conform to the model or norm). The first female normal school, located in Lexington, Massachusetts, opened its doors in 1839. Two coeducational schools and another women-only school opened shortly thereafter.

The training the early normal schools provided prepared teachers for work at the elementary level. Normal schools were hardly academic institutions; they focused principally on the vocational (Allison, 1995). They provided a hurried education, cramming many subjects into a one-year program. For example, the first principal of the normal school at Lexington, Cyrus Peirce, found himself teaching ten subjects in a single term while supervising up to thirty pupils, developing the school's curriculum and serving as the building janitor (Elsbree, 1939). As rudimentary as its training may have been, however, the normal school idea caught on and spread beyond Massachusetts to New York, Pennsylvania and the Midwest. By the conclusion of the Civil War, a normal school education had become the accepted route for those who wanted a career in teaching. The training program expanded to two years, as states developed increasingly stringent certification requirements. As Willard Elsbree (1939) observes, "[f]rom the standpoint of teachers, the creating of normal schools was by far the most significant contribution of the period from 1836 to 1860" (1939, p. 153).

RECONSTRUCTION, REDEMPTION AND THE RETURN OF WHITE SUPREMACY

The political and moral dilemmas slavery presented, compounded by the tensions between states' rights and the power of the federal government to determine domestic policy, played themselves out on the bloody battlefields of the Civil War. For the first time in modern history, huge armies employed "trench warfare," while the newly developed art of photography recorded the awful carnage and the vilest of conditions as the war raged for four long years.

With the conclusion of the war came a time for political and economic rebuilding and national expansion. Officially sanctioned slavery ended, and the South lay "physically, economically and politically" smashed (Butts & Cremin, 1953, p. 295). But for all of the violence and bitterness the strife engendered, the defeated Confederacy endured little vengeance. Historian Stephan Thernstrom notes:

> *The only significant bloodshed after Appomattox was caused not by the winners but by the losers—Southern whites who banded together in the Ku Klux Klan and similar organizations to topple the recently established Republican regimes through systematic terrorist raids (1984, p. 358).*

The era immediately following the war became known as the Reconstruction, as the South tried to rebuild without the benefit of slavery. In 1867 the South was divided into five military districts, with the U.S. Army ensuring a measure of "Yankee control." With the passage of the Reconstruction Amendments (the Thirteenth, Fourteenth and Fifteenth) to the U.S. Constitution, southern African Americans gained the rights of citizenship. Further, Congress took pains to limit the vote to 627,000 white Southerners, while enfranchising a black electorate of some 700,000 voters (Woodward, 1966).

Thanks to additional federal legislation, African Americans also gained, to some extent, access to publicly funded education. Before the war, the South offered no system of public education for either whites or blacks, and as W. E. B. DuBois noted, "Public education for all at public expense was, in the South, a Negro idea" (cited in Anderson, 1988, p. 6). Additionally, many Southern states legally barred blacks from learning how to read and write, with whippings and even executions the penalties for disobedience.

With Reconstruction came the Freedmen's Bureau, a federal agency that oversaw, among other social policies, the establishment of schools for African Americans. Thus, a system of common schools was finally established in the South. But with the exception of the New Orleans public schools, which integrated in 1877 but eventually resegregated, public education in the South remained, from its inception, segregated. Not only did the states there operate separate schools for whites and blacks, South Carolina even established a third set of separate schools, for mixed-race "mulattos."

With Reconstruction, both black and white teachers from the North streamed south, inspired by a sense of mission. In fact, this mission often stemmed from a religious calling, as "missionary societies" accounted for thousands of the southbound teachers, who initially conceived of education as social emancipation for African American children (Anderson, 1988). Later, though, it focused on social regulation. Nevertheless, for a brief period educational opportunities virtually exploded for both African American and poor white children. For example, in South Carolina only 8 percent of school-aged black children and 12 percent of white children were enrolled in school in 1868; by 1875, however, enrollments had increased to 41 percent and 50 percent, respectively (Thernstrom, 1984, p. 374).

The new education for African Americans marked a radical departure from the sparse schooling provided them before the Civil War and was rooted in the courageous efforts by formerly enslaved people to establish their own schools during the war, well before the Freedman's Bureau and other agencies supported them. The schooling that emerged reflected the desire of formerly enslaved people to be self-sufficient and independent of white control. For example, one early lesson that examined the interweaving legacies of whiteness and capital:

> "Now children you don't think white people are any better than you because they have straight hair and white faces, do you?"
>
> "No, sir."
>
> "No, they are no better, but they are different. They possess great power, they formed this great government, they control this vast country. . . . Now, what makes them different from you?"
>
> "Money!" (a unanimous shout).
>
> "Yes, but what enabled them to obtain it? How did they get their money?"
>
> "Got it off us, stole it off we all." (Anderson, 1988, pp. 18–19).

The new politics of publicly funded education infuriated many white South-erners, especially the old aristocracy or planter class. As one grumbled, "Every lit-tle Negro in the county is now going to school and the public pays for it. This is a hell of a fix but we can't help it." (Anderson, 1988, p. 17).

But schooling could be a mixed blessing for African American children. They faced a dearth of black teachers, thanks to the discriminatory hiring practices of the private agencies in the North who sent teachers south. Additionally, many white teachers were neither respectful of nor sensitive to the needs of black stu-dents. By the close of the 1860s, only one-third of the teaching force in the South was African American. Consequently, a fair number of southern black parents made enormous financial sacrifices and sent their children to private schools to have their children educated by black teachers. White southerners viewed both black and white teachers from the North with a good measure of suspicion and, at times, outright hostility. More than a few teachers were run out of town, some-times after being tarred and feathered. Others lived in constant terror. As Edmo-nia Highgate, a white woman who was sent south, related such fear in a letter:

> *There has been much opposition to the school. Twice I have been shot at in my room. My night school scholars have been shot but not killed. A week ago an aged freedman just across the way was shot so badly as to break his arm and leg. The rebels here threatened to burn down the school and house in which I board yet they have not materially harmed us. The nearest military protection is 200 miles dis-tant at New Orleans. (Loewen, 1995, p. 187)*

What white southerners most resented were the immense social changes wrought by the Reconstruction, and the northern teachers symbolized those changes. As educational historian Linda Perkins explains, "Many white Southern-ers feared that Northern white missionaries and educated Blacks had unacceptably raised the political, economic and social aspirations of local Blacks" (1989, p. 350). The revision of educational policies, among other social policies, promoted the political emergence of African Americans into mainstream southern culture, however briefly. An incipient "black middle class," comprised of educators, minis-ters, businessmen, and political leaders appeared—all of this profound social change took place in less than twenty years.

But the fact that the Reconstruction-era schools remained segregated suggests the continuing power of white supremacy, in both the South and the North. In fact, the North (and northern congressmen) supported Reconstruction partly to reduce the changes of a massive northern migration of freed African Americans. They reasoned that if social conditions became tolerable for African Americans in the South, northern whites might avoid confronting their own racism.

Reconstruction ended with the political compromise of 1877, which enabled Rutherford B. Hayes to enter the White House. The election of 1876 had been hotly contested, and its result remained in doubt in early 1877. Hayes needed southern electoral votes (that is to say white votes) to win the presidency. But those votes would come at a price: the understanding that Hayes would end Re-construction. Hayes accepted the deal and received his votes; after he took office, the few remaining federal troops withdrew from the South. The compromise of

1877 gave white southerners the political leverage to "redeem" their political power and reestablish a caste system based on race. Reconstruction had ended; the terror known as "Redemption" was about to commence.

With Reconstruction over, African Americans began to lose their educational, political and economic gains in a gradual process that took decades of increasingly stringent laws (known as "Jim Crow" laws for segregation) establishing segregated restaurants, railroad cars, waiting rooms, theaters and other public facilities. A good deal of thuggery and even murder abetted these policies. Civil rights protections vanished as terrorist organizations like the Ku Klux Klan, the White League, and the Red Shirts rode throughout the South targeting prominent or resistant African Americans for lynching and rape. The terror was often brutal and quick. Educator and dentist Bessie Delany recalled her childhood:

> *It wasn't long before we learned the worst news imaginable: Colored folks were being murdered. They were being lynched. We would hear the teachers talking among themselves about some poor Negro just walking down the side of the road, in the wrong place, at the wrong time. These rebby boys would just grab him and hang him from a tree, just for fun. It was like entertainment to those fellas.*
>
> *Papa . . . insisted that my brothers be home by dark and he taught them how to keep out of trouble. You see, sometimes they'd lynch a colored man who objected to being called "uncle," things like that. If a white woman said a colored man had looked at her in a certain way, that was the end of him. The rebby boys would come in the middle of the night, and get him out of his bed and hang him up, in front of his wife and children. Sometimes they'd hang his whole family, or he'd come home and find his woman hung, as punishment for something he supposedly had done. (Delany & Delany, 1993, p. 109)*

The number of lynchings exploded, complemented by the burning and looting of black-owned businesses. This organized violence served the political purpose of forcing a subservient status on some U.S. citizens because of their race. In Shreveport, Louisiana—a particularly active location for post-Reconstruction violence against African Americans—town leaders and journalists openly boasted of their hatred for and violence against blacks. The Shreveport *Evening Judge* described the lynching of a local black man as "beautiful." All "black brutes" should be dealt with in that way, the paper editorialized. "Before the war," the editor continued, "[blacks] kept their places like other beasts of the field" (Hair, 1969, p. 190).

Another Shreveport newspaper, the *Daily Caucasian*, formulated what came to be known as the "Shreveport Plan" for dealing with African Americans. Based on the belief that blacks were less than fully human, the plan suggested that they should not hold such "easy" positions as boot blacks, waiters, porters, cooks, clerks and teachers. Rather, whites "should be forbidden to employ a colored man . . . in any other manner than at the hardest and most degrading tasks" (Hair, 1969, p. 191).

To compound the terror, the federal judiciary staged an all-out retreat in civil rights enforcement. Starting in the 1870s, a series of Supreme Court decisions upheld the right of the states to limit access to public facilities. In the capstone case in this federal abandonment, *Plessy* v. *Ferguson* (1896), the U.S. Supreme Court ruled that segregated facilities did not violate the equal protection clause of the Fourteenth Amendment, as long as those separate facilities were equal. Reflecting the racism of the time, the Court wrote:

The object of the [Fourteenth] Amendment was undoubtedly to enforce the absolute equality of the two races before the law, but in the nature of things it could not have been intended to abolish distinction based upon color, or to enforce social, as distinguished from political equality, or a commingling of the two races upon terms unsatisfactory to either. Laws permitting, and even requiring their separation in places where they are liable to be brought into contact do not necessarily imply the inferiority of either race to the other, and have been generally, if not universally, recognized as within the competency of the state legislatures in the exercise of their police power. The most common instance of this is connected with the establishment of separate schools for white and colored children. (as cited in Morris, 1989, p. 433)

The segregated public school system established under Reconstruction had originally focused on education for emancipation. Under Redemption it helped legitimize the Supreme Court's racist decision that "separate but equal" facilities were constitutional. Thanks to the *Plessy* decision, public education quickly reconstituted itself as education for social regulation. African Americans were deemed worthy of an "industrial" education to ensure the proper habits of hard work and deference (Spring, 1994; Anderson, 1988), not an education for citizenship or emancipation. The "Redeemers'" position on black education is nicely illustrated by a late-nineteenth-century white Louisianian's comment on a black school he had observed. As long as the schools taught blacks to be respectful of whites, he maintained, he could support black education. After meeting the black children on the way home from school, he stated that it was "uplifting and amusing to see them all pull off their hats and bow" (Hair, 1969, p. 127).

Confirmed in their white supremacy assumptions, many whites hailed the *Plessy* decision as ensuring the preservation of democracy in America, at least for white males. As one southern (and progressive) educator observed:

The more white men recognize sharply their kinship with their fellow whites, and the more democracy in every sense of the term spreads among them, the more the Negro is compelled to "keep his place"—a place that is gradually narrowing in the North as well as in the South. (Woodward, 1974, p. 92)

The Redemption and, more specifically, *Plessy* v. *Ferguson,* spelled disaster for African Americans and public education, and not just in the South. Seventeen states and Washington, D.C., would eventually require that public schools segregate. Four other states made segregated public schools a local option. Although segregated schooling appeared in all regions of the country affecting African Americans, Hispanics, Native Americans and Japanese Americans, the largest inequities between two systems—between black and white public schools—could still be found in the South. For example, by 1907 the average monthly public education expenditure for white children in Mississippi was $5.02 and for African American children it was $1.10. These are *average* figures—in many areas the unequity was far worse. According to educational historian Henry Perkinson, "In some counties of Mississippi . . . as much as $30 to $38 was spent for each white child while expenditures for . . . [black] children ranged from 27 cents to a dollar" (1991, p. 40). The inequitable, immoral legacies of *Plessy* and segregation would remain as American as the Fourth of July and apple pie until the 1950s and 1960s, with the remnants of these legacies lingering well into the 1990s—indeed, even intensifying as the twentieth century closed.

Other major social changes began to shape U.S. public schooling as well. The most astonishing and profound of these new forces were the concurrent and interconnected events of massive immigration, industrialization and urbanization. These three factors eventually transformed the institution from a "common school" to a "factory school." In the continuing contest between education for social regulation and education for emancipation, public education during the late nineteenth and early twentieth centuries was viewed mainly as an instrument for ensuring social control.

THE DEVELOPMENT OF THE AMERICAN "FACTORY" SCHOOL

Following the Civil War, American economic development blossomed, thanks to a pent-up demand for consumer goods and services augmented by an era of unprecedented scientific and technological innovation. A pressing need for labor drew millions to the developing industrial, and increasingly urban areas. The United States underwent rapid social and economic change facilitated by the three aforementioned dynamic and interactive factors: urbanization, industrialization and immigration. These three phenomena exerted a profound influence on both American society and the public schools, and the cultural landscape permanently changed as the United States became an industrial economic power, challenging and eventually transforming the global balance of military and economic power.

Industrialization brought enormous economic growth to U.S. urban centers, attracting both residents from rural America and immigrants from around the world. Factories sprang up practically overnight as new inventions and products met growing consumer demand. This massive influx of people arriving in the cities defined the newly minted word "urbanization." Cities such as New York and Chicago literally exploded with growth. Immigration also transformed the American social landscape. For the first time in the country's history, people other than white Anglos began to dominate numerically in some of the larger urban centers, a demographic change perceived as a threat to the WASP (white Anglo-Saxon Protestant) social order (Tyack, 1974). As educator Ellwood P. Cubberley wrote, with notable prejudice:

> *These Southern and Eastern Europeans were of a very different type from the North and West Europeans who preceded them. Largely illiterate, docile, lacking in initiative, and almost wholly without the Anglo-Saxon conceptions of right- eousness, liberty, law, order, public decency and government, their coming has served to dilute tremendously our national stock and to weaken and corrupt our political life. Settling largely in the cities of the North, the agricultural regions of*

the Middle and the Far West, and the mining districts of the mountain regions, they have created serious problems in housing and living, moral and sanitary conditions, and honest and decent government, while popular education has everywhere been made more difficult by their presence.

The new peoples, and especially those from the South and East of Europe, have come so fast that we have been unable to absorb and assimilate them, and our national life, for the past quarter of a century, has been afflicted with a serious case of racial indigestion. (Cubberley, 1919, p. 338)

One obvious social antidote was the public school, which restructured itself to cope with these three profound social changes. Compulsory education laws, coupled with the dramatic increase in population, swelled school enrollment. Many urban areas developed new schools such as the comprehensive high school and night school to cope with the demand for schooling. Since administrators and teachers (and, in fact, parents) expected that many of the children would soon be at work in factories, schools began to resemble factories, complete with bells to signal the start and end of classes, desks bolted to the floor to maintain straight rows and remorselessly imposed order. Schools were where children (especially immigrant children) would be assimilated or "Americanized" into the social and political melting pot. They would learn English, American history and those Anglo-Saxon cultural norms an industrial society required. It was important that future workers learn to be obedient, orderly, mannerly and docile, for the captains of the new industrial order demanded nothing less from the public schools they supported with their tax dollars.

But immigrant children were not the only individuals in need of industrial regulation. By the 1890s, political patronage and corruption had ravaged the public school systems, especially urban schools (Ravitch, 1974; Spring, 1994). Teaching and administrative jobs were routinely bought and sold, or awarded as part of a political spoils system; school funds mysteriously disappeared; taxes went unpaid or uncollected; decision making was highly decentralized and (thanks to the sheer number of school boards and school board members) could be capricious; and recordkeeping was sporadic at best (Callahan, 1962; Tyack, 1974). School reformers of the era found the local political system at the root of these evils, and many of them concluded that too many uneducated people (that is to say, poor, working-class men) were serving as school board members. Witness one pamphlet from the era:

[A] man's occupation ought to give a strong indication of his qualifications for membership on the school board. Employment as an ordinary laborer or in the lowest class of mill work would naturally lead to the conclusion that such men did not have sufficient education or business training to act as school directors. Objection might also be made to small shopkeepers, clerks, and workmen at many trades, who by lack of educational advantages and business training could not be expected to administer properly the affairs of an educational system requiring special knowledge, and where millions are spent each year. (Thernstrom, 1984, p. 521)

The call went up to "depoliticize" the schools—for example, to adopt smaller, nonelected (or at least nonpartisan) school boards; centralize administrations; and professionalize both teachers and administrators. Then the issue became how to achieve these goals. If democratic governance had become not only ineffective but also downright pathologic, how should large school systems operate? Yet again, business provided the model for public schools to emulate. After all, business and the technology it produced had reshaped American society, seemingly following scientific values. That industrial practices demanded a high degree of social regulation and regimentation further enhanced their appeal to reformers wary of the devious practices of the new Americans.

> *The work of education would have to be put in the hands of professional educators; only then would politics be removed from educational decisions. The school system should be organized as efficiently as a great business. No sensible businessman would turn decision-making over to a board of laymen who knew nothing of the business. For the same reason, education should be left to professional experts. (Ravitch, 1974, p. 130)*

Business values permeated the public schools, especially at the governance level, and many administrators and teachers embraced the reforms, believing that they had been granted "the instruments of scientific progress that would enable them to shape society toward even nobler ends" (Tyack & Hansot, 1982, p. 106). The search was on for "one best system" that could efficiently and fairly educate the massive numbers of children entering U.S. public schools.

Although the standardization of school policies and procedures did provide a measure of educational and administrative coherence, many of the daily mundane practices became quickly distorted by the larger social "cult of efficiency." As in business, all sorts of statistical measurements and cost-benefit analyses were applied to every aspect of public educational practice. In a spectacular example of scientism run amok, Frank Spaulding of Yale University determined the cost-benefit ratio of specific academic courses:

> *[It is clear that] 5.9 pupil-recitations in Greek are of the same value as 23.8 pupil-recitations in French; that 12 pupil-recitations in science are equivalent in value to 19.2 pupil-recitations in English; and that it takes 41.7 pupil-recitations in vocal music to equal the value of 13.9 pupil-recitations in art. (Callahan, 1962, p. 63)*

While cost-benefit analyses of curricula like these could and did provoke a measure of outrage, one lasting legacy from this era is the standardized test and its pervasive power to place students on various curricular "tracks," particularly at the high school level. The social climate of the period (between roughly 1880 and 1920) stressed that education had to be scientific, or at least have an air of science about it. Teachers who completed a four-year course of college, university or normal school study received a bachelor of science in education degree. Would-be school administrators studied the current scientific business principles. That supposedly scientific measurements of children's abilities and performances and of teachers' and administrators' professional competence abounded should hardly be surprising.

Standardized testing and curricular tracking are perhaps the most enduring aspects of the quest to make education a scientific enterprise. But while we can trace the history of standardized testing to the early part of the twentieth century, America's entrance into World War I and the compelling need to select and sort military personnel quickly fueled the development of intelligence tests. The most notable, the Alpha and Beta tests developed during World War I, were used only to classify U.S. recruits (Cremin, 1961; Tyack, 1974). After the war; however, school districts eagerly bought millions of the cheap test booklets, then employed them to select and sort students into the "appropriate" vocational or academic programs. One commentator of the time noted that it was "foolish to educate each child to be President of the United States," stressing that inequalities were natural and schools should "give each layer its own appropriate form of schooling" (Tyack, 1974, p. 129).

The emerging field of educational psychology exploited this demand for scientific measures of aptitude and intelligence as various academics scrambled to design and then market their instruments, and by 1917 schools could choose from well over a hundred different tests (Cremin, 1961; Lugg, 1996). These early tests all claimed to be scientific means of predicting future academic and social performance. But problems with these new "scientific measures" gradually emerged, centering mainly on their cultural, ethnic, racial and gender biases (Shipman, 1994). For example, one promoter, Carl Brigham, examined the results of various intelligence tests and found that "Nordic groups were intellectually superior to Alpine and Mediterranean groups, Alpines were superior to Mediterraneans, and Mediterraneans were superior to Negroes" (Spring, 1993, p. 264). By ascribing intellectual and academic merit (or lack thereof) to class, racial, religious, gender and ethnic characteristics, the principal value of the early standardized tests lay in their tendencies to reinforce the established social hierarchy (that is, the white Anglo-Saxon Protestant male with money) during a period of social and economic flux. The rhetoric of the era held that the tests could help educate children efficiently in their future economic roles; thus standardized testing and the attendant system of tracking served as instruments of social control in the public schools. Few individuals ever challenged the biases in the tests themselves or noticed who got tracked into what curricula.

African Americans, of course, faced a particularly striking dilemma with the establishment of the factory school. If public education had abandoned its common school ideal of educating children for the responsibilities of republican citizenship, what was the purpose of an education for black children, most of whom faced the prospect of limited and segregated lives? Remember that African Americans remained under legal, political and terrorist attack, thanks mainly to the 1896 *Plessy* decision. In an era of second-class citizenship and curtailed civil rights, what was the best education for African American children? We can best appreciate the heated and painful debates by exploring the tension between the remedies proposed by Booker T. Washington and W. E. B. DuBois.

Washington and DuBois expressed profoundly differing views regarding the optimal education for African American children. Reflecting his own experiences as a former slave, Washington felt that education should focus on an individual's economic utility. Therefore, he stressed industrial (that is, vocational and agrarian) education, so children could learn a useful trade. Washington perceived many advantages in the factory school, especially with the inculcation of industriousness, punctuality and obedience. In respect to the situation southern blacks faced Washington advised: "Make yourself useful to the South; be honest, be thrifty; cultivate the white man's friendliness; above all, educate your children and prepare them for the future" (Perkinson, 1991, p. 49).

Washington believed that once African Americans were economically self-sufficient they would be granted full citizenship. But a number of problems accompanied Washington's vision, perhaps the most compelling being his tendency to accommodate. He accepted segregation and told whites what they wanted to hear. As one editorial writer of the era charged:

> It is a notorious fact, that the utterances of Mr. Washington are nothing more than to make himself rich by assuring the white people of this country that the Negro's place is in the machine shop, at the plow, in the washtub and not in the schools of legal and medical professions; that he has no business to aspire to those places as they are reserved for the proud Caucasian. (Anderson, 1988, p. 65)

Reflecting his own experiences as a scholar and political propagandist, W. E. B. DuBois felt that African American children should be educated for the full rights and responsibilities of citizenship. The industrial education Washington touted was initially anathema to DuBois (although he would later adjust and develop his proposals). Further, according to DuBois's initial vision, the most capable children (or what he called the "talented tenth") should be classically educated in the tradition of the liberal arts for the duties of leadership. DuBois rejected the notion that African Americans must patiently and even cheerfully "earn" their citizenship rights. Civil rights were not something to be earned, they were intrinsic to American citizenship. Consequently, DuBois saw classical education—the education historically accorded leaders—as one weapon in the movement for full citizenship. In 1906 he declared:

> We claim for ourselves every single right that belongs to a freeborn American, political, civil and social; and until we get these rights we will never cease to protest and assail the ears of America. The battle we wage is not for ourselves alone but for all true Americans. It is a fight for ideals, lest this, our common fatherland, false to its founding, become in truth the land of the thief and the home of the Slave—a by-word and a hissing among the nations for its sounding pretensions and pitiful accomplishments. (Lewis, 1993, p. 330)

As historian David Levering Lewis (1993) analyzes the situation, DuBois offered an educational vision of the future, predicated on the foundation of full political rights for African Americans. Nevertheless, Washington's vision would prevail, for it mirrored both the larger trends of industrial education for all children considered to be "other" and the stark and blatant racism of the era.

The imposition of an industrial education on most African Americans in the late nineteenth and early twentieth centuries remains a prominent historical example of school as a means of social regulation rather than emancipation. Recent revisionist scholarship has begun to reveal the distortion in the history of African American education that grew up over the last five or six decades. The mainstream story goes something like this: Benevolent northern philanthropists, typically corporate and industrial magnates, were morally outraged by the vile racism southern whites foisted on southern blacks. In response, the philanthropists sought to help blacks by supporting black public education. Far more realistic and pragmatic than the radical republicans of the Reconstruction era, these philanthropists entered into an alliance with the southern upper classes to protect blacks from lower-class racism. Overwhelmed by the power of the southern white supremacy movement, however, these benevolent corporate leaders compromised their original goals of challenging racism by goodwill, political skill and hard work. Instead, they did what they had to do and accommodated the white supremacists to salvage what they could for the formerly enslaved African Americans.

All these philanthropists could save was public schooling for black students—the institution that might provide the last hope for black social progress. The key feature of this "great compromise" was that black public education would be modeled on the Hampton-Tuskegee style of industrial education (discussed in the following section). By adopting an industrial education model propounded by Samuel C. Armstrong and Booker T. Washington, the corporate magnates saved black education from total destruction. By advocating industrial education they gained the support of white supremacists for universal public schooling for black students.

This standard portrayal concludes with a partial but important victory: the African Americans won the right to a public schooling emphasizing industrial education. Such an interpretation is, of course, simplistic and reductionistic, as it fails to account for power relations, economic motivation, and even traditional views of educational purpose. More specifically, the different sides of the argument remained separated by their conflicting views of the relationship between schooling and the economy. Educational historians often miss this point in overlooking the importance of this relationship.

SCHOOLING AND THE SOCIAL REGULATION OF AFRICAN AMERICANS

Cherishing the business-factory view of education as the principal promulgator of industrial values for immigrants and the poor, white philanthropists and their supporters saw industrial education for African Americans as an important aspect of the larger effort to construct an industrial economy. Those corporate leaders advocating black schooling in the South, like most other corporate leaders in the industrial cities of the era, based their vision on the value of order and efficiency and on schooling as a means of training the lower classes to be orderly and efficient workers. In this context black education emerged as less a magnanimous effort to transform the social position of an oppressed people and more a part of the larger effort to generate more profits for the wealthy few. In other words, industrial education for African Americans represented a new and sophisticated approach to the older goals of socialization and control of potentially dangerous social groups.

The fear of black violence against whites in the tradition of Nat Turner's 1831 Virginia rampage remained close to the white southerner's consciousness, and as the supporters of the experiment in industrial education pleaded their case they found resistance among those southern whites whose wealth and power rested on the perpetuation of a large, illiterate group of subjugated black agricultural workers. The white aristocracy remained hostile to the northern philanthropists' argument for black industrial education as a means to social order and economic development. The wealthy southern planters lived in a preindustrial, premodernist world in which they could achieve social control by simple coercion. From their socioeconomic position, the southern aristocrats saw no need for the trouble and expense of an industrial education that could do little more than inflate the social, political and economic aspirations of their black workers. Indeed, such an education could subvert the traditional social relations they had enjoyed with their black servants and field hands.

At this juncture a more specific analysis of the nature, assumptions, and goals of the Hampton-Tuskegee model of industrial education is in order. In 1867 Samuel C. Armstrong founded a manual training school for blacks and Native Americans at Hampton, Virginia. Armstrong's disciple, Booker T. Washington, opened a similar institution in 1881 at Tuskegee. Both schools promoted manual labor as a key to disciplining the minds and the wills of children of "ignorance, shiftlessness and moral weakness" (Anderson, 1988).

The superintendent of the post–Civil War Freedman's Bureau, Armstrong built his industrial education curriculum for blacks on an assumption of black racial inferiority. He argued that black children could acquire knowledge about as readily as white children; however, he contended that black students did not have the mental facility to assimilate and digest this knowledge. Black children mature more quickly than whites, Armstrong claimed but they fail to keep up with the "mental strength" of white children. Thus, one of the main leaders of the industrial education movement saw the curriculum as special education for "inferior blacks" (Kliebard, 1986; Bullock, 1969; Anderson, 1988).

While Booker T. Washington held racial views different from those of Armstrong, he did agree with Armstrong's vision of an industrial education for African Americans. Washington formed his educational philosophy as a student at Armstrong's Hampton Institute, where he came to see the purpose of black education as helping ex-slaves adjust to subordinate positions in southern society. When Washington used the term "industrial education" he was referring to the inculcation of good work habits and industrial values. Rejecting any academic purposes in black education, Washington established Tuskegee Institute in Alabama in 1881. If students came from farm backgrounds, he wanted to make them better farmers. If they knew something about mechanics, his curriculum helped to make them better mechanics. Hard work, he thought, would "civilize" the freed slaves and their children. Attempts to cultivate political understanding or lessons designed to encourage thinking were alien to Washington's vision of black education. Hard work would inculcate the right moral habits—and that was enough.

It is easy to see how attractive Armstrong and Washington's brand of vocational education appeared to northern corporate leaders. Steel tycoon and philanthropist Andrew Carnegie bestowed the first major endowment on Tuskegee, proclaiming that the U.S. economy demanded black industrial education. Educational historian Joel Spring (1994) concluded that industrialists welcomed the idea of racially segregated industrial education for its promise of cheap labor and antiunion sentiments. As railroad magnate and Tuskegee supporter William H. Baldwin, Jr., maintained, if the South were to prosper economically and compete internationally, it would have to repudiate the high wages demanded by labor unions and rely on cheap black labor.

In fact, so strong was corporate support for the Hampton-Tuskegee model that philanthropists refused to support black education that deviated even slightly from Armstrong and Washington's prototype (Bullock, 1969). For example, in the late 1800s Richard R. Wright, Sr., a respected black educator, served as president of Savannah State, an institution that offered both industrial and academic courses of study. Politically skilled, Wright convinced an all-white Georgia Board of Commissioners to approve the industrial-academic curriculum, but corporate philanthropists would have no part of it. At the mere suggestion of academic learning for blacks the industrialists closed their wallets and withdrew their support. Liberal whites were generally happy to support black schooling as long as their investment promised a return and as long as the schooling reinforced blacks' second-class citizenship. "We want to help Blacks become better cooks, better servants, better washerwomen, better workmen in the field and farm and shop," whites of the day were heard to remark. As long as this goal was understood, many white people willingly underwrote black industrial education (Anderson, 1988; Margo, 1990). In 1899 William H. Baldwin, Jr., advised Africans to lower their expectations and

> *face the music; avoid social questions; leave politics alone; continue to be patient; live moral lives; live simply; learn to work and work intelligently . . . learn that it is a mistake to be educated out of your environment. (Bullock, 1969, p. 102)*

THE PROMISE OF PROGRESSIVE REFORM

By the 1920s the ubiquitousness of the factory school model had erased the myth of a publicly funded school system responsive to all children. While the factory school efficiently selected and sorted massive numbers of students into various educational programs, it also reinforced the powerful prejudices of the time. If the period from the Gilded Age to the end of World War I witnessed immense economic and population growth in the United States, it also saw the intensification of racial, religious and ethnic hatred (Loewen, 1995; Shipman, 1994). For example, one should note that every president from Abraham Lincoln to William Howard Taft took pains to ensure that the federal government employed African Americans. Not until the supposedly progressive administration of Woodrow Wilson (1913–1921) were blacks systematically denied federal government positions. Further, membership in the Ku Klux Klan peaked in the 1920s (and initiated President Warren G. Harding into membership in a White House ceremony!) thanks entirely to its virulently racist, anti-Semitic, anti-Catholic ideology. In this climate of hate, then, it is hardly surprising that ostensibly scientific and businesslike public school practices regulated the lives of millions of children thought to be less than "100 percent American" (Tyack, 1974; Thernstrom, 1984; Shipman, 1994).

Not all educators or social reformers, however, supported these practices. While a general consensus held that education should be a scientifically grounded enterprise, this assumption did not necessarily mean that schools should operate like businesses or factories, with children treated as products to be selected and sorted according to prevailing social prejudices. Others offered different responses to the educational problems wrought by immigration, industrialization and massive urbanization. Many of these social reform efforts reflected a new political ideology, progressivism. As we have seen, the principal response to the many and enormous social changes the United States underwent between 1880 and 1920 was the factory school, which selected and sorted students for their "proper" roles. Yet some educators and social reformers saw both the factory and the factory school as menaces to community and democracy. Union organizer and teacher-activist Margaret Haley observed:

> Two ideals are struggling for supremacy in American life today: one the industrial ideal, dominating through the supremacy of commercialism, which subordinates the worker to the product, and the machine; the other, the ideal of democracy, the ideal of educators, which places humanity above all machines, and demands that all activity shall be the expression of life. (Tyack, 1974, p. 257)

In contrast to the efficiency experts, democratic progressives between 1880 and 1920 believed that government should be an instrument for the greater good of society. Theirs was a significant movement away from the traditional American fear of possible government tyranny; they perceived the power of vast corporations to be a greater threat to life, liberty and the pursuit of happiness. Given their support of direct democracy (reflected by the passage of the Seventeenth amendment, which provides for the direct election of U.S. senators), democratic progressives advocated a strong political role for the public school: It should serve as the cornerstone of both local communities and the larger democratic society. According to educational historian Henry J. Perkinson,

> If the American democracy became truly a democracy, the progressives argued—if the people participated more fully in government itself—then the perennial fears of strong government would disappear. The people could not fear government if they were themselves that government. (1991, p. 184)

It might overstate the historical case to say that democratic progressives wished to educate American children for social liberation, but we can safely conclude that they supported education for social participation, which is not quite the same thing.

Perhaps the most prominent proponent of a democratic progressive education was philosopher John Dewey. Drawing on the teachings of Rousseau, William James and Hegel, Dewey saw education as a scientifically directed, child-centered endeavor. Each child, he thought, had to see the connections between the information presented and questions posed at school, and the larger society beyond. As Perkinson noted, "For Dewey . . . the school was to be the model for the larger society precisely because democracy, participant democracy, is nothing more than people engaging in joint activity to solve their common or shared problems" (1991, p. 186). In the scientific spirit of the times Dewey established a laboratory school at the University of Chicago to put his theories to the acid test of reality. Other institutions of postsecondary education quickly followed his lead, and lab schools sprang up across the nation (Semel & Sadounik, 1999).

Dewey's vision, however, posed two major problems. First, unlike the factory school, which was cheap and efficient to operate, the Deweyian ideal was highly labor intensive and expensive, which estranged the efficiency experts. Additionally, teacher and student assessments were highly complex undertakings. Historically assessment had been warped by political and personal bias, and African American teachers, in particular, resented the capriciousness of the process. The introduction of "scientifically" designed, efficiently administered measures projected at least the appearance of impartiality. Given the ongoing concern surrounding the cost of public education, self-declared progressive educators found themselves at a significant political disadvantage (Wirt & Kirst, 1992).

Second, the political ideals of democratic progressive education were highly controversial. To many administrators, board members and state and federal legislators, broad notions of democracy and equality within an educational program carried more than a whiff of socialism, a position to be rejected out of hand (Perkinson, 1991). While progressive education would receive a momentary boost in the 1930s thanks to the Depression (it was then reformulated as "social reconstructionism"), the larger ideological and military conflict with the Soviet Union between 1917 and 1991 severely limited any political support for its widespread implementation. The last thing political leaders wanted was a publicly funded education aimed at social liberation, when they saw education for social control as promoting national security. Although the democratic progressive education derived from John Dewey's beliefs greatly influenced educational thought, it had only a limited impact on educational practice (Simpson & Jackson, 1997).

Another problematic educational development arose out of the Progressive Era: teacher militancy. Since the 1830s teaching had been predominantly a female profession, with its attendant low wages and disrespect. Many women taught for only a few years, either quitting or being dismissed. But with industrialization, urbanization and better educational opportunities for women, teaching increasingly became a lifelong career option for female city teachers, so long as they remained single (Solomon, 1985; Fraser, 1989; Urban, 1989). By the 1880s teachers had begun agitating for reforms in employment hiring practices, administrative procedures and respectable pensions. As noted in Chapter 4, the emergence of teacher militancy manifested itself notably with the 1897 founding of the Chicago Teachers Federation (CTF), the forerunner to the modern American Federation of Teachers (AFT), by Margaret Haley and Catherine Goggin. Both were Irish Catholic elementary school teachers in the Chicago public school system, and as unmarried career women they faced tremendous economic and political obstacles (Urban, 1982). Through the CTF, Haley and Goggin fought for "higher salaries, pensions, and tenure; opposed administrative centralization of power; and worked to establish teachers' councils" (Tyack, 1974, p. 259). We see here in the founding of the CTF what was essentially a labor union for elementary school teachers— that is, women who saw themselves exploited by male administrators and boards of education, with no job security, no rights to academic freedom and salary scales at half those for men of equivalent rank, training and experience (Cremin, 1988, pp. 238–239).

The CTF denied membership to superintendents and principals, enabling the elementary "schoolmarms" to gain some educational and political leadership (Fraser, 1989). Given the quiescent social values of the time, the CTF's activism threatened a stunning upheaval in the status quo. Haley, in particular, demonstrated a sensitivity to the inferior status of women in American society, and linked the CTF's efforts with both the women's suffrage and labor movements. In a 1902 move that alarmed the more conservative National Education Association (NEA), the CTF affiliated with the Chicago Federation of Labor (CFL) and then actively sought the vote for women.

Margaret Haley also challenged the NEA's male "old guard," dominated at the time by administrators and college professors. She was in an ideal position to do so. In less than three years after its founding, the CTF had more members than the NEA (Button & Provenzo, 1989). At the 1901 NEA convention in Detroit Haley unleashed her considerable rhetorical talents on William T. Harris, the august commissioner of U.S. education. Harris gave a speech in which he praised the benevolent influence of business on public education. Haley responded hotly, noting that those business influences had stifled teacher autonomy and kept salaries stagnant. Apparently, what unfolded next thoroughly shook the staid, complacent delegates:

> *Harris, now crotchety, told the convention, "Pay no attention to what that teacher down there has said, for I take it she is a grade teacher, just out of her school room at the end of school year, worn out, tired and hysterical.*
>
> *It was a mistake to hold NEA meetings at this time of year . . . and if there are any more hysterical outbursts, after this I shall insist that these meetings be held at some other time of the year." Capitalists were the great benefactors of society, he reassured the audience. Nonsense, replied Haley, who had been bringing railroads and utility companies to court for not paying their school taxes: "I know the facts. Mr. Harris, either you do not know or have not stated the facts."*
>
> *As one eyewitness to Harris's performance later remarked, "In the educational system we don't bury the dead. We let them walk around to save funeral expenses." (Tyack & Hansot, 1982, p. 186)*

The CTF won a number of stunning victories, culminating with the hiring of Dewey's disciple and Haley's friend, Ella Flagg Young, as superintendent of Chicago schools in 1909. But then it suffered a string of political setbacks, starting in 1915 with Young's forced resignation. Additionally, a wave of antiunion, anti-Catholic sentiment washed over Chicago—the CTF was heavily Catholic—and by 1916 it was forced to break its alliance with both the Chicago Federation of Labor and the newly established American Federation of Teachers. The CTF suffered yet another devastating loss in 1917, CTF cofounder Catherine Goggin was killed in an accident. In 1918 Haley

> *withdrew from the NEA, in which . . . she had been a prime mover for greater teacher power. Discouraged by the increasing influence and prestige of the busi-*

ness and bureaucratic forces she had been fighting for two decades, she concentrated on preserving gains already won by cultivating alliances with local politicians. (Tyack, 1974, p. 264)

As with the broader labor movement, teacher unionism faced enormous cultural and political setbacks with America's entrance into World War I. Nevertheless, the new teacher militancy had had a lasting impact on public education. By 1920, most states had established pension funds for retired school teachers, the NEA had adopted a policy of electing a female president every other administration and, although still tightly constrained, classroom teachers had a greater voice within the profession. While the "cult of efficiency" continued its reign over classroom practices and procedures, shaping children's education along the lines of social control, teacher activism had at least opened a space where issues of community, democracy and emancipation could be vigorously debated.

This tension between education for social control and education for emancipation would increase during the post–World War II era, with the deepening Cold War and the expansion of the federal government's role in public education. Prior to 1954, the federal government exerted narrowly limited influence over the shape and direction of public education. But such pressing concerns as desegregation and national defense would expand the federal role and increase the debate over that role.

THE COLD WAR AND THE POLITICS OF PUBLIC EDUCATION

Post–World War II public education faced numerous challenges. For example, its answers to such questions as who should be educated and how and what role should the national government play in public education all stirred heated reactions. Moreover, all these issues arose in the social and cultural context of the ongoing Cold War. The conclusion of World War II hardly marked a total end to hostilities, and a scant five years later American troops were sent to Korea. Instead of a "lasting peace," military anxieties refocused on the Soviet Union, the Warsaw Pact, "Red" China, Korea and looming threats of rapacious communism and nuclear annihilation. In addition, with the return of millions of American servicemen the birth rate exploded, and by 1950 the schools welcomed a generation of "baby boomers" with overcrowded classrooms, staff shortages and deteriorating physical plants.

To complicate matters, by 1953 it became apparent that the many and persistent legal challenges to segregation—segregated schooling in particular—would topple the separate-but-equal precedent set down sixty years earlier in *Plessy* v. *Ferguson*. With the realization that public education had become a major national priority, the debates between those advocating education for social control and those who favored education for emancipation intensified (Phi Delta Kappan, 1953).

Perhaps nowhere were the debates more rancorous, verging at times on violence, than in those over race and universal access to school facilities and programs. Then, in 1954, the Supreme Court handed down its decision in the most important court case of the twentieth century, *Brown* v. *Board of Education*, a rare unanimous decision that declared the separate-but-equal doctrine set forth in *Plessy* unconstitutional. In the words of Chief Justice Earl Warren,

> We conclude that in the field of public education the doctrine of "separate but equal" has no place. Separated educational facilities are inherently unequal. Therefore, we hold that the plaintiffs and others similarly situated for whom the actions have been brought are, by reason of the segregation complained of, deprived of the equal protection of the laws guaranteed by the Fourteenth Amendment. (347 U.S. 483, 74 S. Ct. 686, 98 L. Ed. 873 [1954], as discussed in Yudof, Kirp & Levin, 1992, p. 472)

The following year the Court further clarified its *Brown* decision by stating that those public school systems that had been segregated by law must desegregate "with all deliberate speed" (*Brown* v. *Board II*, 349 U.S. 294, 75 S. Ct. 753, 99 L. Ed. 1083 [1955], in Yudof, et al., 1992, p. 478).

The responses to both decisions ranged from joyful to angry. At the time of the decisions seventeen southern states and the District of Columbia were mandating segregated public education. Four other states—New Mexico, Arizona, Kansas and Wyoming—had made public school segregation a local option (see *The Nation's Schools*, July, 1954). Many southern politicians viewed the *Brown* decisions as federal encroachment upon "states' rights" and local control (Hafter & Hoffman, 1973). White segregationists, in particular, felt threatened by the Supreme Court's entrance into a domain that, until *Brown*, had been specifically reserved to the states. Additionally, conservative southerners (and a fair number of northerners) viewed the Supreme Court's decisions to desegregate public education as federal invasions of both the social and political orders and an attack on white supremacy. The implication was clear that African Americans remained incapable of such duties of citizenship as voting; therefore, they had no need of an equal education. Conservative commentator William F. Buckley explained at the time:

> The central question that emerges—and it is not a parliamentary question or a question that is answered by merely consulting a catalogue of the rights of American citizens, born Equal—is whether the White community in the South is entitled to take such measures as are necessary to prevail, politically and culturally, in areas where it does not predominate numerically? The sobering answer is Yes—the White community is so entitled because, for the time being, it is the advanced race.
>
> National Review believes that the South's premises are correct. If the majority wills what is socially atavistic, then to thwart the majority may be, though undemocratic, enlightened. It is more important for any community, anywhere in the world, to affirm and live by civilized standards, than to bow to the demands of the numerical majority. (1957, p. 149)

Besides the massive resistance to implementing *Brown*, the persistent Cold War discouraged efforts to achieve desegregation. In 1957 the Soviet Union successfully launched the first unmanned space vehicle, *Sputnik*, and the U.S. response to this technological marvel combined vitriol and fear, for it appeared that the "commies" had gained a military advantage. To the question "How could such a thing happen?" an inferior public education system provided a ready answer. Schools had been under continuous assault since the early 1950s, for being unpatriotic, for being academically flaccid, for "harboring communists" and for contributing to "the rise in juvenile delinquency" (see Bestor, 1985, p. 121). Many people believed it public education's fault and particularly the fault of the high schools that the Soviets had beaten the United States into space (Rippa, 1992). The attacks on public schools quickly intensified.

The uproar over *Sputnik* also compelled the federal government to involve itself in public education. Throughout the mid–1950s, various efforts to allocate federal funds to public school districts for building construction had been defeated, mainly because the proposed legislation contained language requiring those school districts receiving federal aid to comply with Supreme Court decisions. Congressional representatives, Democrats from the south and Republicans from the north, repeatedly voted against any requirement that segregated public districts desegregate in order to receive federal aid (McCaskill, 1956). But with the launch of *Sputnik,* Congress abandoned its efforts to link dollars with desegregation and appropriated federal funds under the National Defense and Education Act (Perkinson, 1991), which focused primarily on science, mathematics, foreign language instruction, guidance and career counseling and vocational education.

In short, the government saw its school systems as giant selecting and sorting machines and its role as to repair and maintain those machines. The intent of the National Defense legislation: to improve the regulation of the "products" of the public schools. With the launch of *Sputnik* the fragile remnants of the progressive education movement were swept away by the broom of military preparedness.

Ironically, the federal government's initial move into public education laid the groundwork for more profound changes only six years later. The political climate of 1964 differed vastly from that of 1958. While the Cold War lingered—still dominating the social, political and educational landscapes throughout the 1960s, continuing until the collapse of the Berlin Wall and the Soviet Union in the early 1990s—the success of the civil rights movement finally forced the government to address the longstanding issues revolving around racial discrimination (Orfield, 1969). Through the power of demonstrations, marches and direct nonviolent confrontation, the civil rights movement had powerfully shown the glaring inequalities African Americans faced. During the presidency of Lyndon B. Johnson, originally a segregationist Democrat congressman from Texas, Congress passed the Civil Rights Act of 1964, which guaranteed African Americans access to all public facilities (see Caro, 1990). The Act also empowered the Department of Justice to investigate complaints and, if necessary, bring suits against those institutions found to discriminate. Further, under Title VI of the Act, those public schools that segregated by race were to be stripped of federal aid. At the time of the Act's passage, "almost 99 percent of Black students in . . . eleven Southern states remained in segregated schools" (Orfield, 1969, p. 45).

Political Activism and the 1960s

These changes in the 1960s must be seen in the context of the rise of political activism and protest movements: antiwar protests and demonstrations on college campuses that reached a dramatic climax with the shooting deaths of four students by the National Guard on the Kent State University (Ohio) campus on May 4, 1970; gay rights movements that emerged following the Stonewall uprising in New York City in 1969; civil rights demonstrations, boycotts and the dramatic march on Washington, D.C., at which Dr. Martin Luther King, Jr., presented his famous "I Have a Dream" speech; continuing pressure from labor leaders such as Cesar Chavez and feminist leaders such as Betty Friedan for justice and equality; and Native American activism at places like Wounded Knee, South Dakota, site of one of the last major battles between federal troops and Native Americans and now the site of renewed protests. These events and many others sparked intense debates and precipitated change. President Johnson did not simply implement his Great Society in a vacuum; in many ways he was forced by the American people to begin addressing racial, gendered, military and social issues. Some historians contend that Johnson actually thwarted efforts to provide human rights for all Americans with delay tactics and misinformation. The assassinations of John F. Kennedy, Robert F. Kennedy and Martin Luther King, Jr., in a short five-year span in the 1960s rocked the nation, and under the stress of the social climate President Johnson made a dramatic announcement that he would neither seek nor accept the nomination for a second full term as president in 1968. Many contemporary fundamentalists and right-wing political and religious leaders continue to insist that the 1960s represent a bleak and immoral period in American history. We take a different view. The 1960s certainly were a time of upheaval, experimentation and protest—and in retrospect we can see that mistakes were made by many people. However, we view the 1960s as a catalyst for justice and equality in society and a concrete demonstration of the true spirit of democracy. The people spoke with passion and conviction. Some writers claim that the 1960s birthed a germinating postmodern era. We would agree.

The implications of the social and educational changes of the 1960s are seen dramatically following the enactment of Title VI in 1965, when the Elementary and Secondary Education Act (ESEA) was signed into law. ESEA had been conceived as part of President Johnson's "war on poverty" Great Society program. Ostensibly it was designed to "end poverty in our time," but it was also intended to regulate the poor and bring African Americans into the political mainstream, ideally as Democrats (Piven & Cloward, 1993; see also Diamond, 1995). The rhetoric surrounding the legislation embraced the democratic ideal; however, its effect was to enhance better social regulation through the schools and other public agencies. Nevertheless, ESEA provided yet another lever to pry the doors off segregated schools.

This 1965 Elementary and Secondary Education Act provided large new Federal grants under a formula favoring poor Southern school districts. The interaction

of these two laws [ESEA and the 1964 Civil Rights Act] confirmed the worst
fears of Southern leaders and prompted revolutionary change in Southern schools.
(Orfield, 1969, p. 4)

But even with the power of the Civil Rights Act and ESEA, public school desegregation moved at a snail's pace. Many segregated school districts invoked the
"all deliberate speed" language of *Brown II* as an excuse to move with extreme
caution, if at all. Finally, in 1968, the Supreme Court handed down the *Green* decision, which outlawed "freedom of choice" schemes as a legitimate way to desegregate public schools. Such plans had placed the burden of desegregation on
African American children and their parents, and, given the potential power of
racism and actual threats of violence if they chose otherwise, most black parents
chose segregated public education. More important, the Court ruled that segregated public schools must desegregate immediately (*Phi Delta Kappan*, November 1968, p. 151):

> *In determining whether respondent School Board met that command by adopting*
> *its "freedom of choice" plan, it is relevant that this first step did not come until*
> *some 11 years after* Brown I *was decided and 10 years after* Brown II *directed*
> *the making of a "prompt and reasonable start." This deliberate perpetuation of*
> *the unconstitutional dual system can only have compounded the harm of such a*
> *system. Such delays are no longer tolerable, for the "governing constitutional*
> *principles no longer bear the imprint of newly enunciated doctrine." . . . More-*
> *over, a plan that at this late date fails to provide meaningful assurance of*
> *prompt and effective disestablishment of a dual system is also intolerable.* The
> time for more "deliberate speed" has run out. . . . The burden on a school
> board today is to come forward with a plan that promises realistically to work,
> and promises realistically to work *now* [Green v. City School Board, *391 U.S.*
> *430 (1968) emphasis added].*

The Court clarified what it meant the following year in its decision in *Alexander*,
when it ruled that public school desegregation "must begin at once" (Yudof, Kirp
& Levin, 1992).

Thus, in the 1950s and 1960s the Supreme Court set the stage for massive
public school desegregation. Public school districts that practiced *de jure* (by law)
segregation had lost their final legal battle. But even these reasonable steps toward
a more democratic society and public education triggered a strong political backlash. Additionally, national disillusionment with Johnson-era domestic and foreign
policies began to take hold. Three years of domestic racial unrest, rioting in urban
areas, campus protests, additional civil rights campaigns and the escalation of the
Vietnam War had left increasing numbers of Americans looking for political solutions beyond those offered by the Democratic party and the liberal establishment
(Lugg, 1996a). Republican party strategist Kevin Phillips compiled a massive
analysis of the demographic and voter trends at the time and came to the following conclusion:

The principal force which broke up the Democratic (New Deal) coalition is the Negro socio-economic revolution and the liberal Democratic ideological inability to cope with it. Democratic "Great Society" programs aligned that party with many Negro demands, but the party was unable to defuse the racial tension sundering the nation. The South, the West and the Catholic sidewalks of New York were the focal points of conservative opposition to the welfare liberalism of the federal government; however, the general opposition which deposed the Democratic Party came in large part from prospering Democrats who objected to Washington dissipating their tax dollars on programs which did them no good. The Democratic Party fell victim to the ideological impetus of a liberalism which had carried it beyond programs taxing the few for the benefit of the many (the New Deal) to programs taxing the many on behalf of the few (the Great Society). (1969, p. 37)

Phillips's analysis suggested that "the new popular majority is white and conservative" (p. 31). What this meant in raw political terms was that the Republican party could ignore the black vote and, still win (Lugg, 1996a). This political reality led to the formation of what became known as the "southern strategy," actively courting conservative white voters and thereby antagonizing African Americans.

The 1968 presidential campaign proved particularly rancorous, with Republican candidate Richard Nixon directly and indirectly attacking the policies of desegregation. On the campaign trail he declared, "Our schools are for education, not integration" (Thernstrom, 1984, p. 736) and "There has been too much of a tendency for both our courts and our federal agencies to use the whole program of school integration for purposes which have little to do with education and which do not serve a useful purpose" (King, 1991, p. 143). Many Americans responded to this message and Nixon defeated Democratic contender (and Johnson's vice president) Hubert Humphrey, though by a mere half-million votes.

Safely in office, Nixon settled on a long-term strategy of restraining the civil rights gains. The late 1960s and early 1970s featured immense changes in public education, particularly in the South. Bolstered by the highly controversial *Swann* (1971) and *Keyes* (1973) decisions, Supreme Court desegregation now included mandatory busing for Hispanic students and northern schools (Yudof, Kirp & Levin, 1992). Instead of attacking desegregation directly, which would have been politically and socially disastrous, the Nixon administration embarked on a strategy of restructuring along more conservative lines the federal judiciary, which had endured accusations of "judicial activism" since 1954 (Lugg, 1996a). By 1974, the Supreme Court had been reconstructed to the administration's liking, especially when it handed down the *Miliken* decision forbidding the imposition of desegregation plans on suburban schools.

Concurrently, the Office of Education (forerunner of the U.S. Department of Education) began to promote public school career education. Schools were told to do a better job of selecting and sorting students for their future roles, the traditional social regulation approach to public education. By the time Nixon resigned in 1974 (for crimes committed during the Watergate scandal), the era of civil rights expansion had ended.

Public education remained on the national agenda, however, and again became a presidential campaign issue in 1976 when Jimmy Carter, both a former governor of Georgia and a former school board member, ran against Nixon's successor, Gerald R. Ford. Carter received the endorsement of the National Education Association, the largest teachers' union and at that time the nation's second largest union. It marked the first time the NEA had endorsed a presidential candidate, and Carter owed its backing to his stated intent to establish a cabinet-level Department of Education. First as a professional organization and later as a union, the NEA had lobbied since before World War I for a federal Department of Education. Whether the NEA's support actually tipped the 1976 election in Carter's favor remains a matter of conjecture, but it certainly helped (Cooper, 1988). When President Carter indeed raised education to the cabinet level in May 1980, he promoted his decision as a cost-saving measure, ending or reducing duplication of activities by the various federal agencies; however, the move at last fulfilled Carter's 1976 campaign promise to the NEA (Toch, 1991; Berube, 1991).

While Jimmy Carter's educational legacy proved more conservative than many observers had expected from an "education president," his successor left an unambiguous stamp of conservative ideology on the nation's schools. As a presidential candidate, Ronald Reagan promised to eliminate the Department of Education, considering it an unnecessary public expense and a sign that the federal government had intruded into concerns that should be left to the states. Reagan's opposition to the new department complemented his southern strategy, the Nixonian policy of appealing to white conservatives in the south. But his opposition also complemented his ideological suspicion of the broader welfare state. In general, Reagan invoked the rubric of free market enterprise as the panacea for America's social and economic ills, and after his election in 1980 his administration restructured its social policy, including public education, in conformity with these policy preferences (Lugg, 1996a).

Predictably, the early Reagan administration attempted to dismantle the Department of Education, but met solid resistance not only from Democrats in Congress, but also from Republicans. Instead, the administration focused on fiscally retrenching the department while simultaneously transforming it into a mouthpiece for such controversial policies as organized and vocal school prayer, public and private school choice and schooling vouchers. Further, officials in the department and the administration itself issued blistering attacks on public education in general and on the two teachers unions, the NEA and the AFT, in particular.

The Reagan administration also followed an active anti–civil rights agenda, with the Department of Justice's Civil Rights Division enforcing a sort of counter-revolution. By focusing on intent instead of effect and on individuals instead of groups, Justice turned longstanding institutional practices that adversely affected protected groups into legally protected behaviors. Justice Department officials declared that its civil rights division would ensure equal student outcomes between segregated public schools, while overlooking the inconvenient fact that the schools were in fact segregated. In short, the Reagan administration favored the long-discredited separate-but-equal doctrine established in *Plessy* v. *Ferguson*, and generally ignored the line of Supreme Court decisions since 1954 (Lugg, 1996a).

Ironically, however, Ronald Reagan's best-publicized educational achievement was the book-length report, *A Nation at Risk,* issued by the National Commission on Excellence in Education (NCEE) in 1983. As we saw in Chapter 1, the report provided a scathing critique of the public education system, charging that American schools had become bastions of academic mediocrity and concluding that the U.S. schools were so inept that they endangered the nation's economic future. With its dire predictions of looming economic Armageddon, *A Nation at Risk* riveted the country's attention on public education. At the time of the report's release the country had just begun to emerge from one of the most devastating economic recessions of the twentieth century (Phillips, 1990; Coontz, 1992). In the industrial sector high-paying blue-collar jobs were disappearing, and in the Midwest the family farm had vanished. Small and medium-sized banks that had made agricultural loans, in turn, were failing. Increasing numbers of Americans accepted chronic economic instability as a dismal fact of life. A prestigious report from a blue-ribbon commission finding the distress to be "public education's fault" met a receptive audience (Lugg, 1996a).

A Nation at Risk triggered a massive wave of state-level reform initiatives, all aimed at repairing public education, with the final goal of restoring economic competitiveness. But the Reagan administration seemed indifferent to the actual content of the report, and given his notorious disengagement one doubts that Reagan himself ever read it. Originally the administration had opposed the formation of the NCEE, and its famous report contained none of the White House's policy preferences (school prayer, choice and vouchers). Nevertheless, the administration used the spectacle of the presidential campaign during the summer of 1983 to shape the educational reform preferences of the voters: educational excellence via tuition tax credits, school vouchers and school prayer. *A Nation at Risk* now legitimized the Reagan (and later Bush) administration's view of public school reform as a means to strengthen social control. By 1984, policy discussions regarding educational equity had become both past and passé (Lugg, 1996a).

Stretching between 1945 and 1991, the Cold War's legacy to U.S. public education was the legitimation of pedagogical practices oriented strongly toward a social control enforced by the federal government: a remarkable transformation and expansion of the federal role in just four decades. Prior to the Cold War, in educational policy the U.S. government had deliberately deferred to the states under the guidance of the Tenth Amendment. Only with the perceived threats of the Soviet Union's weaponry accumulation and space triumphs and continued social unrest (notably, the Civil Rights Movement) did the federal government finally step in, supplying resources in the name of preserving the integrity of the nation through greater social control. Although federal fiscal involvement diminished during the early 1980s as resources shifted to support a vast military buildup, the Reagan administration maintained a highly visible federal presence through the skillful use of public relations strategies (Lugg, 1996a; Verstegen, 1990). Conservative Republicans dusted, repainted and then applied many of the business-inspired educational practices from the turn of the century to individual schoolrooms, pupils, teachers and administrators.

Yet in spite of this atavism, the idea of education for emancipation remained alive—witness the varied and growing civil rights activism and some progressive Supreme Court decisions and congressional legislation. Additionally, even with various assaults by the executive and legislative branches on civil rights protections and educational opportunity, many Americans resisted the widely promulgated policy of directing public schooling at economic excellence and military preparedness. Not that academic rigor had lost allegiance—on the contrary, it has always been crucial to improving the lives of all children. But in many of the Cold War–era debates over the purposes of public schooling, the symbol of academic excellence became a "Trojan horse," carrying repressive pedagogical practices and political dogmas into the public school. People of various ideological stripes vigorously denounced such tactics and advocated a more progressive public education (Apple, 1988; Kincheloe, 1993; and Best, 1993, provide just a small sample.) Unfortunately, these calls for educational equity and excellence have gone largely unheeded.

EDUCATION IN A POST–COLD WAR, POSTINDUSTRIAL, POSTMODERN SOCIETY

With the fracture of the Soviet Union in 1991 the United States faced the prospect of international peace and security after nearly fifty years of hostility and the continuing threat of nuclear annihilation. Hopes rose for greater social contentment as people assumed that the country's priorities and energies would shift to domestic needs. Politicians mentioned the "peace dividends" awaiting ordinary citizens, many of whom had suffered significant declines in their standards of living. The painful deindustrialization the United States experienced throughout the 1980s forced wrenching changes, particularly among blue-collar workers in the cities of the Northeast, the Midwest, and the old Great Lakes rust belt. Federal abandonment of urban areas exacerbated this decline, and social services collapsed as corporations and industry left the cities. By the 1990s many of the older cities had become "underserviced, violence-ridden, crack-infested, homeless-burdened, bankruptcy-skirting slum ghettos" (Caraley, 1992, p. 1).

Given the history of militarism in American culture, pressing social needs like these are easily ignored as public policy refocuses on war's proxy: economic competitiveness. The market metaphor has gained increasing salience with the collapse of the Soviet Union. Many social commentators trumpeted their impression that capitalism had somehow "beaten" communism—an idea that is critiqued by those who see the end of the Cold War as more a result of implosion from within communist states. Then gazing upon the festering social conditions at home, particularly the growing number of children living in poverty, they assessed the causes and found a panacea: They determined that the United States should concentrate on competing vigorously on the global economic battlefield. What would cure America's social ills was still more capitalism in the form of free and unregulated markets, the advantage going to those who already enjoyed wealth.

But as we have seen, not all social pundits, or mainstream economists for that matter, embrace this vision of the United States as a free market utopia. As economist Julianne Malveaux notes,

Free markets are like wolves. Without regard to issues of consequence and distribution, markets run prices down, just as without regard to injury, predatory wolves run their victims down, chew them up, and spit them out. (1994, p. 147)

Nevertheless, a post–Cold War policy consensus seems to coalesce around the direction of public education: Public schools should develop students the way corporations develop products for the consumer market. The assumption is that if only the United States could develop and refine its "human capital," it could remain economically triumphant in the global marketplace (Lugg & Dentith, 1996). The logical extension of this premise is that if the United States cannot be first in the world academically, it cannot be first in the world economically. Public education, in short, is now framed in terms of products, outcomes and standardized test scores. Accordingly, one hears various schemes for strengthening the link between schools and workplaces such that policymakers now appear to embrace an updated version of the old factory school, the better to select and sort students for their future careers (Becker, 1993; Reich, 1991).

One component of new factory schools could be "schools of choice." School choice proponents would provide students with vouchers to pay for the schooling they—or more likely their parents—chose. Both public and private schools would compete for the most academically able or suitable students. Those schools that prepared students for the market inefficiently (as defined by standardized test scores) would succumb to "natural selection" (Chubb & Moe, 1990). In fact, the constant threat of being unable to compete economically is the dissonant leitmotif of current U.S. educational policy discussions, and it drowns out any talk of "educational equity." Still, such talk occurs; it is vigorous and it has a history. Many others besides the free-market prophets (teachers, administrators, academics, policymakers) remain concerned with how public education relates to the traditional American value of democracy. "Democracy" retains its radical inference that citizens are not subjects of the government but are *themselves* the government. If government is, to quote Abraham Lincoln, "of the people, by the people, and for the people," the question becomes Just exactly who are "the people"? From this brief introductory exploration of U.S. educational history we know that the term can be fluid and can shift, expanding at times (as in the 1960s), contracting at others (as during the "Redemption").

Public schooling is, of course, closely associated with this question of "the people." If the common school ideal of the 1830s and 1840s was fragile and full of contradictions, it did complement the almost universal impression that public schools can bind the nation together, inculcating shared values and shared ideals of what it means to be an "American." In a post–Cold War, postindustrial, postmodern era, the term "American" has become "Americans." We have far more than just one way to be a citizen (no longer must one be a WASP heterosexual male with property), and we have many ways to educate our children for participatory democratic citizenship. While the focus of much of the current educational policymaking favors education for social control as the one best system, the idea that public education can lead to social emancipation remains influential.

Meanwhile, teachers should remember that U.S. public education has hardly ever been politically neutral, and it has yet to enjoy a golden age. What educators can expect is that discussions surrounding "fixing schools"—and "fixing" students and teachers—will continue and will often be rancorous. Moreover, the various plans of the day will alternate between the political aims of education for social control and the altruistic idea of education for emancipation. Each educator must examine and analyze each reform proposal and pedagogical practice to ascertain both its intent and its possible impact. Teachers must continually be aware of their own conceptions of "the people" and the way these impressions can affect how they treat our children.

PART 3

Economic Context

*Power, Work and
Schooling*

Labor and Economics in a Democratic Society

INTRODUCTION

This chapter contextualizes and analyzes the nature of work, labor and economics and the ethical dimensions of work in a democratic society. We ask, for example, what constitutes good work, socially beneficial work, tedious work, fulfilling work, democratic work. Such questions underlie the foundations of education, with its focus on the social, political, philosophical and economic connections between schooling and culture. These are the questions our book, in general, asks about schooling; this chapter focuses them on work. In the process of analyzing issues related to economics, we develop a democratic image of a just future grounded on a vision of good work. We urge, as well, that America develop an ethical basis on which it constructs its social, educational and—contrary to prevailing sentiments—economic institutions (Simon, Dippo & Schenke, 1991; Dewey, 1908).

WORKPLACE DEMOCRACY

We all separate the concept of work from the idea of a job on the basis of our ethical understandings. We view a job as simply a way of making a living; work involves a sense of purpose and fulfillment. In a job we produce items for consumption; work produces value in our lives. We reflect our purposes in our work, whereas we repress our aspirations in a job (Wirth, 1983). As our work becomes in turn democratic, we in turn begin to speculate more on how it might deny human possibility (Kincheloe, 1999). In this process, more questions about workplace democracy accumulate.

In the consequent negotiations over workplace democracy observers can ascertain how seriously the parties consider the ethic of democracy. The democratic workplace assures workers more participation in the day-to-day activities of a worksite, and one barometer for the success of such participation is the workers' ability to discern the work's results. The critical democratic workplace demands more from management than homage to notions such as Total Quality Management (TQM) or quality circles—business buzzwords alluding vaguely to labor-management cooperation and efficient productivity. For the workplace to become genuinely democratized it must foster an arrangement that guarantees that the voices of workers will be heard while shielding them from capricious management prerogatives. Absent this arrangement, employees lack the freedom to speak their minds for fear of reprisal (Block, 1990).

Workplace democracy also requires that workers assume significant power in the operation of a plant or corporation—power that helps protect them from the special dangers the unstable contemporary corporate landscape presents. For example, in recent years the idea of shareholder democracy, with its diffusion of ownership, has failed to subdue the power of corporate management. In fact, managerial abuses have multiplied as corporate leaders grant each other golden parachutes and extravagant executive compensation packages. In this context of greed, corporate raiders ride into town promising to clean up executive abuses and, in the name of reform, take over the company. But they soon forsake the language of reform, and the evidence at hand shows that corporate raids generally worsen the economic lives of corporations. Most important for workers, these takeovers disrupt their lives and can cancel any pending democratic expectations that shared power in the corporation could reduce managerial overcompensation while granting the workers influence over the corporation's response to a takeover bid. These increasingly prevalent conditions become more compelling in the effort to establish workplace democracies in the technocratic latter years of the twentieth century (Block, 1990; Kincheloe, 1998).

GOOD WORK AND THE STRUGGLE FOR WORKER DIGNITY

If schools and workplaces expect to contribute to the reinvention of democracy and challenge the antidemocratic tendencies of the contemporary era they must carefully define and pursue good work. The following are nine characteristics good work might include.

The Principle of Self-Direction: Good Work as a Labor of Risk

The principle of self-direction reflects the idea that workers ultimately ought to be their own bosses. Workers operating under this principle would be free from the humiliation of supervision that implies suspicion and resembles surveillance. Using a traditional concept of craft, work that is self-directed becomes a "labor of risk" in that workers take responsibility for their own success or failure. Good work depends on the judgment and skill of the workers themselves, not on some mass production techniques using or modeled on automatically controlled production methods. Self-directed workers think analytically to identify and solve problems by making use of their skills, knowledge and aesthetic and pragmatic intuition to create products of worth (Richmond, 1986).

The Principle of the Job as Place of Learning: Work as a Research Laboratory

Good work implies conditions that treat workers as human beings rather than hired economic units and thus turn them from passive instruments into active learners. As active learners, workers develop and use their intelligence, ingenuity and capacities and, thus, begin to direct their own fates. Such workers recognize the degrading way they have been treated in the restricted factory, which sensitizes them to the large numbers of their contemporaries employed in positions that preclude their capacity to learn. They express outrage when they find the number of these positions expanding. Advocates of good work understand that growth entails material limits but no boundaries restrict worker learning. Self-directed workers view the workplace as a learning and research laboratory. Good work establishes workers as equal partners in research and development, for their "shop-level" experiences provide unique insights into the production process. In sites that value good work, workers become researchers who produce knowledge about the influences on the work in general and their work in particular (Simon, Dippo, & Schenke, 1991; Wirth, 1983; Block, 1990; Kincheloe, 1998).

The Principle of Work Variety: Freedom from Repetition and Boredom

Repetitive, boring tasks continue to plague workers in both industrial and postindustrial contexts. In the democratic workplace workers encourage variations in the routine that reduce boredom. Workers who are self-directed learners and thus are involved with the analytic mindset of research and reflection rarely find themselves bored. A good workplace invites employees to perform in varied roles, both to relieve monotony and to provide experiences in which they can better understand the interrelationships among the different aspects of the worksite.

The Principle of Workmate Cooperation: Overcoming the Fractured Social Relations of the Workplace

The industrial ethos has unfortunately produced an atmosphere that discourages one worker from helping another; indeed, in a workplace ruled by the competitive impulse one person's loss may well be another person's gain. In a good workplace workers acquire a self-discipline that attunes them to the needs of others. Understanding that good work is collaborative, workers overcome their egocentric tendencies and join others in a common task. Thus, good work transcends the fractured social relations of the scientifically managed workplace, as collaborative workers sit down together, exchange information and discuss the nature and purpose of their work (Rehm, 1989; Wirth, 1983).

The Principle of Individual Work as a Contribution to Social Welfare

When workers employ this principle, they reconceptualize their work so that they envision it as serving the public good. If work has no social benefits it must gain some. Good work encourages questions like these: Do the goods being produced serve human needs? Do they meet the criteria of permanence, healthfulness and artistic and creative integrity? Are the products ecologically harmful? Good work changes the exploitative relations between work and the environment to symbiotic and synergistic interactions. On-the-job self-directed learners are more likely to recognize the socially deleterious effects of production strategies and goals than are alienated "hired hands" (Emery & Thorsrud, 1976; Wirth, 1983; Lyons, 1988).

The Principle of Work as Proof That Self-Workers Are More Than the Sum of Their Behaviors

Since the introduction of scientific management, workers have often been reduced to organisms with behaviors to be molded by expert social engineers—that is, "scientific managers." As the ideal of expertly controlled workers took hold, managers came to see workers as the sum of their behaviors. Good work rejects this view of men and women and insists that workers explore their powers as creative human beings. Such powers include the abilities to make sense of a work environment, to conceive and communicate ideas, to risk confrontation and to rely on dangerous memories in the process of democratic social change (Wirth, 1983). Thus, good work becomes an individual expression of self that redefines both the role of creativity in the workplace and the very meaning of output. Critically reconceptualized, output becomes inseparable from worker creativity and well-being (Block, 1990). Indeed, a critical definition of output would be incomplete unless it included concerns with the intrinsic satisfaction of the work, the economic security of the workers and the role of work in the workers' pursuit of happiness.

Principle of Work as a Democratic Expression: Freedom from the Tyranny of Authoritarian Power

Good work is a democratic act operating in a free and autonomous workplace. It is self-creating and dedicated to critical forms of change. It transforms the self and the world as it preserves democratic ideals. The democratic impulse must, therefore, confront those often-hidden manifestations of power that subvert good work (Brosio, 1985). When managers quash intellectual and moral freedom, freedom of inquiry, freedom of association in or out of the workplace or freedom of religion, democratic workers resist. Because such antidemocratic actions proceed covertly, unrecognized by the public, democratic workers must carefully refine their resistance strategies to expose the insidious nature of power. For example, the antidemocratic workings of power often take place in the ostensibly neutral personnel administration office (Ferguson, 1984). Democratic workers must enjoy the insight and power to expose the alternative meanings in managerial attempts to increase "human efficiency," to develop "proper work habits," to "improve morale" and to "reduce conflict." All of these goals sound sensible and benign, but all implicitly carry particular views of the workplace arrangement and the role of workers. To resist this form of manipulation, democratic workers must be able to analyze situations so that hidden meanings become part of the public conversation about work. As a democratic expression, good work alerts the public to the way those in power can deploy words to mystify employees, confuse the public and preserve unequal power relations.

The Principle of Workers as Participants in the Operation of an Enterprise

Until workers become participants, any talk of workplace cooperation rings hollow. At the end of the twentieth century we find workplaces arranged in ways that exclude workers from participation in their management. Workers still execute directives they had no part in formulating and often do not understand. Meanwhile, this traditional exclusion thwarts the few attempts to create cooperative workplaces characterized by dynamic flexibility (Block, 1990). In the name of both good work and effective and profitable workplaces, workers should develop a concern for their firms. Indeed, democratic notions have both humane benefits and pragmatic advantages. Empirical evidence confirms that when workers participate in the decision-making process, they are motivated to improve the quality of their own work and the profitability of the enterprise. When workers are well informed, convinced that their proposals will be seriously considered and can criticize without fear of reprisal, they become an invaluable force for innovative change (Bluestone & Brown, 1983). Participant workers devise novel ways to train new employees, propose effective management strategies, develop new production techniques, create new workplace arrangements and revise hiring criteria. As participants, workers refuse to sanction disparate economic benefits for management over labor and insist on a more equitable sharing of both gains and burdens. In short, worker participation in the fundamental functions of a business or industry helps define good work.

The Principle That Play Is a Virtue to Be Incorporated into Work

As most teachers realize, play promotes a freedom and fairness conducive to creativity. But the workplace rationality scientific personnel management imposes has created a context inhospitable to play. Indeed, the workplace as we now know it has become the virtual opposite of play. To suggest that good work entails a spirit of play is to advance a dangerous argument from the perspective of workplace management, which generally associates play with fatuous "down time." But Herbert Marcuse saw play as basic to human civilization and maintained that once we overcome our adult-centered biases, play becomes one of the highest expressions of human endeavors and can be productively incorporated into our work.

More specifically, play can extend our notion of good work in three ways: (1) the rules of play tend far more to encourage freedom than to reify authoritarianism, and thus they promote fairness; (2) the structure of play is dynamic in its relation to the interaction of the players, and by necessity this interaction is grounded on the equality of the players; and (3) play activity quickly becomes an autonomous expression of self, as players take care not to subordinate imagination to predetermined outcomes. Thus, in play exhaustion does not deaden, since the activity refreshes the senses and celebrates the person. We can view good work as a form of play when participating workers labor together for shared purposes (Marcuse, 1955; Aronowitz, 1973; Kincheloe, 1995, 1998).

The widespread failure of democracy in the industrial and postindustrial workplaces has led, in part, to the failure of American education. If we want to change the schools, we must analyze the nature of work in America (Lyons, 1988). One of the reasons for the failure of so many school reform proposals involves the neglect of this relationship between school life and work life. Since school leaders feel pressure in a variety of subtle and not-so-subtle ways to turn out more compliant, less thoughtful graduates, they often perceive critically minded, reflective students as potential troublemaking misfits in the workplace.

Henry Levin suggested that moves toward greater worker participation in a more democratic workplace could hold dramatic implications for school reform. He maintained that if new production strategies required more collaborative human interactions and more thoughtful workers, education would have to meet the social demand for students with these skills (Wirth, 1983). Such expectations could, in turn, create a new era of work and school interaction. If we are serious about good work, with its premise of workers as participants, employees would require and soon demand a more stimulating education. The path to school reform, in this formulation, is inseparable from work reform.

In the context democratic work reform creates, employers and corporate leaders must reassess each firm's status as a "democratic citizen" (Bellah et al., 1991). Profit making as the sole purpose of the corporation produces a *"Jaws Meets Wall Street"* horror movie with a perspective that sees corporations as sharks living off the community rather than as human agencies helping to construct and transform our politics and values. Moreover, the idea of a corporate embrace of both democratic and profit goals is not as far-fetched as one might think. Successful corporations have begun to espouse such goals: Anita Roddick's Body Shop (Roddick, 1991), Ben and Jerry's and Patagonia have all proven that profits and democratic principles can comfortably coexist. The president of Volvo argues that businesses in democratic societies must help maintain the public good, protect natural resources and create economic growth, as well as make profits. Corporations, he explains, must not simply provide jobs, they must also provide meaningful employment where people work in dignified settings with opportunities for individual development (Wirth, 1983). Teacher education students can remain usefully alert to the possibility of good work and its connection to the foundations of American society (Wirth, 1983).

POWER AND THE DEVELOPMENT OF THE MODERNIST ECONOMY

Power is a concept most Americans find repugnant, and it is practically invisible in the literature of education. Yet in order to understand how student conceptions of work and education form, we must understand where power lies in our society and how it is exercised.

Whose opinions seem to matter most? Why is it that we so often hear on television the opinions of business and industrial leaders but not the voices of workers? Why does CNN devote several hours a day to *business* news but none to *labor* news? Why does every newspaper in the country carry a business section but no labor section? These questions relate to power and how it works. As a society, we have grown so accustomed to inequitable and dangerous power relations and their demonstrations that we would all find a newspaper section on labor strange. That newspapers and networks dedicate themselves to the service of business seems almost natural, part of a divine American plan.

THE ORGANIZATION OF WORK IN RELATION TO POWER

Consider a simple idea central to this book: We cannot understand the workplace or the school without understanding how power shapes each. To grasp this concept we must understand the goals of management, which often differ dramatically from those of the workforce. Management pursues at least six goals in a capitalist economy: (1) increases in output for the same wage (higher productivity); (2) reduction of worker turnover; (3) decrease in the conflict between labor and management; (4) loyalty from workers; (5) respect for authority among workers; and (6) respect for a work ethic among workers. Managers typically adopt whatever tactics it takes to achieve these goals, which soon enough shape all aspects of the worksite (Simon, Dippo, & Scheneke, 1991; Lamphere, 1985).

Social relations in the workplace often appear to have little to do with the power of management and its attempt to implement its agenda, which is hardly surprising given that critical sociologists often describe how power hides in the shadows of everyday life. How well an individual conforms to the goals of management often determines his or her on-the-job identity. A subservient worker who is more loyal than thoughtful receives more rewards than his or her more assertive colleague, even though that colleague may have the potential for significant accomplishment. Both workers may find their self-esteem undermined by the ways management rewards and punishes them. Yet we cannot view how workers relate to each other and to managers outside the context of power. We see conflicts among workers or between workers and supervisors typically framed as individual disputes or personality conflicts rather than labor-management disputes (Simon et al., 1991). We often overlook the ways power shapes these conflicts. For example, Mary finds herself drawn into a conflicting relationship with Rhonda, her coowner at a hair salon. Neither recognizes that the salon owner encourages competition to ensure higher profit margins. Workers who understand management goals also understand how these goals would subtly create a situation in which Mary and Rhonda see one another as competitors, rather than colleagues with common interests.

Similarly, students, teachers and workers who understand power dynamics come to see how interpersonal problems can be more than simply private matters but are often, in fact, social conflicts that reflect the larger concepts of workplace organization. Power so regulates the conversation about economic policy and the organization of the workplace that it undermines open communication on the subject. To question the absolute legitimacy of the goals of management is to position oneself as antibusiness and even anti-American. One avoids questioning the goal of higher productivity, even if it means imposing greater stress on workers and reducing the quality of their lives (Webster, 1985–86). One must avoid questioning the goal of reducing conflict between workers, even if it means ignoring the needs of workers. One must avoid questioning the goal of instilling respect for the work ethic, even if it means that workers have no right to ask who benefits as a result of this respect. Once workers and educators understand these dimensions of power, social relations and worker identity, the possibility for alternative conceptions of work appears.

These questions of power, social relations and worker/student identity manifest themselves in a variety of ways. Democratic teachers must always be aware of unanticipated expressions of such dynamics. One important locale in which they show up is the media. As a primary place where education occurs at the end of the century, the media's curriculum of power must be understood by teachers. Gender power, for example, can be viewed in a variety of media curricula. In many movies, for instance, women are viewed as causes of family problems, especially those of children. In *Boyz' n the Hood,* for example, director John Singleton drives home the point that boys without fathers fail—mothers cannot raise boys and often push their sons into trouble. Both *Boyz 'n the Hood* and *Jungle Fever,* two brilliantly written, powerful and appealing movies, designate female sexuality as a threat to male (in these movies, black male) heterosexual identity. Indeed, Singleton and Spike Lee are so seductive as moviemakers that women can actually enjoy their own symbolic denigration. Similarly, network news accounts of economic issues such as unemployment also reflect patriarchal structures in their verbal and visual focus on unemployment in the male-dominated industrial sector. Stories on the dramatic increase in layoffs and permanent unemployment in the service sector, predominantly among "female" positions such as secretaries, information processors and government workers, constitute only *1 percent* of TV news stories on such matters (Wallace, 1993; Apple, 1992). It is no secret that TV producers, scholars and researchers in vocational education devote less attention to women than to men (McLaren, 1994). This is an important understanding for democratic teachers.

This patriarchal power context induces some women, especially working-class women, to devalue their own knowledge and abilities. Instead of understanding what they know as a valuable form of knowledge about the world, working-class women have been conditioned to view it as *"just* common sense." When women view their knowledge as affective and not cognitive, as feelings and not thoughts, their subservient role is perpetuated and their power is diminished. Women scholars have argued that such working-class female forms of understanding make it impossible to distinguish emotional from objective/rational thinking. Such a cognitive form, they conclude, is important for women to study and analyze because that can challenge the false dichotomy patriarchy constructs between feminine emotionalism and masculine rationality.

In the economic sphere, this false dichotomy produces lower-status emotional and intuitive feminine caregiving work and higher-status masculine "skilled" labor.

It further perpetuates an unjust system that exempts men from nurturing, service types of work while holding women responsible for such unpaid forms of domestic toil. It is essential for democratic educators to understand these patriarchal dynamics, for it is these forces that work to hide a young woman's abilities from her teachers, her potential employers and, most important, herself (Luttrell, 1993).

THE POWER OF CORPORATIONS: SUBVERTING THE ETHIC OF DEMOCRACY

In late-twentieth-century America, authority and power reside both in government and in what are referred to as the "market-corporations"—businesses and industries. The coercive power of the market is far more insidious and elusive than that of the government, and since most citizens are only vaguely aware of its existence, the very elusiveness of private power undermines the efforts of progressive elements to confront it. The market will not stay in "its place"; corporate power spills over into the realms of culture, politics and education (Brosio, 1994). This spillover, moreover, sabotages all efforts to protect the fragile American democracy of the late twentieth century. While individuals retain the freedom to vote, they must often submit to coercion in their economic lives. Many progressives argue that without a public understanding of how economic wealth supports political power, democracy cannot survive, and that the greatest challenge democracy faces at the end of the millennium is to expose the forces that undermine it (Wirth, 1983; Brosio, 1985).

Because of the vast resources they control, American corporations have, in essence, become a fourth branch of government—and a powerful branch at that, since they can avoid the checks and balances that restrain the legislative, executive and judicial branches (Wirth, 1983). President Reagan's push for privatization, that marked the national politics of the 1980s, placed increasing power in the hands of corporations. As corporate taxes fell in the name of "trickle-down economics"—the theory that enhanced corporate profits would in turn enhance worker salaries—more power shifted to business and industry. Corporate leaders began making more decisions in the economic and political realms, while progressives noticed, in vain, that those who exercised the most power over the daily lives of Americans had been elected by no one and had no obligation to act in the public interest (Giroux, 1993).

These realizations were hardly new. Alexis de Tocqueville, a French statesman traveling America in the 1830s, wrote extensively about the impact of industrialization here. Understanding the tendency of power to follow wealth, de Tocqueville warned that industrial development might lead to the creation of a new aristocracy. This so-called "economic royalty," he concluded, could not coexist with an allegiance to democratic equality, and democracy rather than the wealthy would suffer (Bellah et al., 1991).

Since the beginnings of industrialization in the first half of the 1800s corporations have consistently increased their influence in and power over American life.

Not content to control the workforce and the process and distribution of production, early twentieth-century corporate leaders set out to find techniques for controlling consumer demand. The second decade of the 1900s witnessed the birth of marketing, as prosaic cars, clothes, cigarettes and processed food became transformed into objects of desire. The invention of credit buying, productive annual models and persuasive packaging coincided with the development of advertising and marketing research to produce forms of social regulation unimagined in the nineteenth century. With the development of radio and television the possibility for even newer forms of social control expanded exponentially. Such innovations in market research as systematic TV viewership ratings, citizen surveillance and demographic analysis have placed even greater power in the hands of corporate leaders (Webster, 1985–86). For example, the 1990s brought us belated news of the tendency of the tobacco industry to target teenagers, women and African Americans with its advertising and then manipulate nicotine content to compel their continuing patronage.

This scientific management of our political, social and economic lives has reshaped the way we live. Orthodox social sentiments (for example, the belief that wealthy people have worked harder than poor people and thus deserve their fortunes) mesh with the dominant ideologies—ways of making sense and meaning of the world—the media, religious institutions and schools cultivate, and they exert a profound effect. This concept of ideology is central to any attempt to make sense of how power shapes the nature of work and the self-images of workers (Harvey, 1989; Aronowitz, 1992). Social and educational theorist Peter McLaren observed that the public often thinks of "ideology" as simply "isms": Americanism, communism, socialism, anarchism, existentialism and so forth. But McLaren believes it is far more influential than these formal systems of belief. Ideology is a way of viewing the world that men and women "tend to accept as natural and as common-sensical" (McLaren, 1994, pp. 184–185). In fact, the pervasive influence of power in everyday life produces such ways of seeing. The customs, beliefs and values that power helps formulate produce perverted understandings of people's place in the social and economic worlds, and as a result, people come to accept their lowly positions in the hierarchy as just. Ideology hides the inequitable relations of power and privilege that relegate them to their situations.

In a gender context an ideology of patriarchy helps maintain male-female power relations. Men are often able to oppress and impose their will over women because of the ways this patriarchal ideology helps construct and sustain social structures of male power. Such structures are surrounded by and help support patriarchal practices, in the process shaping and being shaped by human experience. This power process may be described as the interaction of the macro (the social structures of power) and the micro (everyday, lived world experiences). The relationship between the macro and the micro is very complex as everyday practices can be complicit with the interests of patriarchal power structures, or they can challenge them.

The conflicts between a man and a woman in a marriage or in a school faculty cannot be understood outside the macropower of patriarchy exerted through social structures. Democratic teachers understand that analysis of only the specific relationships and the practices involved with them is to focus on the micro level. This limited view moves us to see everyone operating on an equal field of power and privilege. Educators and educational leaders too often ignore these macro-structures and their invisible role in everyday gender relations (Hedley, 1994; Walby, 1989; Holstein & Gubrium, 1994; Fiske, 1993; Wartenberg, 1992). In this context the educational importance of Sylvia Walby's six structures of patri-archy can be appreciated. In no way does she mean to imply that the six structures operate independently of one another; each structure both reinforces and blocks the effects of all others.

1. *Patriarchal household production relations.* Husbands expropriate the household labor of women. In such a context women must learn to read their husbands and adjust themselves to the emotional distance of men. Thus a patriarchal pedagogy is purveyed that teaches women to give up aspirations of self-sufficiency and independence and settle into an emo-tional dependence on men. In such dependence women become protec-tors of men, especially from democratic attempts to delineate the nature of male oppression of women.

2. *Patriarchal relations within paid work.* The most important aspect of this structure involves the exclusion of women from the workplace or their segregation within it. In this context women's work is devaluated and in-evitably undercompensated. Such a process cannot be fully understood, Walby warns us, outside the context of marketplace and racist forces. In the workplace women find themselves corralled into professionally subor-dinate roles that involve nurturing, comforting and operating as sexual objects. The same ideological forces are at work there as in the household context, as women are enculturated to accept their subordinate place in the workplace hierarchy without resistance.

3. *The patriarchal state.* Women are consistently excluded from equal access to governmental influence and power by this patriarchal structure. Not only do women not have a direct presence in the state but, more impor-tantly, they are unable to muster political forces to pressure the state about gender issues. Women are not equally represented in state institu-tions such as courts, the police or the legal system and as a result sensitiv-ity to issues that affect females is not as great as it should be.

4. *Male violence.* The violent behavior of men is not attributable merely to the psychological problems of a few men; rather, it assumes the character of a social structure. Women's knowledge of men's suprisingly common use of violence against women holds serious consequences as they modify their conduct and mobility in fear of its possibility. In the context that shapes male violence men in patriarchal societies possess a sense of entitle-ment to hold power over women. This patriarchal ideology of male privi-lege enculturates men to embrace violence when their entitlement is chal-lenged. Indeed, in this ideological context men learn to challenge the authority of assertive and self-directed women. This male rage at female

self-direction can be viewed as quite clearly related to feminist assertiveness over the past few decades.

5. *Patriarchal sexuality/compulsory heterosexuality.* This structure produces an ideology that induces women to become heterosexual and to seek marriage relationships. Within this context sexuality has traditionally been constructed as an activity centered around male pleasure. Indeed, male sexual desire is inseparable from an effort to master/gain power over the object. Within this sexual domain many argue that sexual liberation has placed women in a position in which they are expected to have heterosexual sex with men. Such male expectations can be configured as a new form of patriarchal power over women. Obviously this issue is quite complex, as sexual liberation offers women many benefits such as freedom from the stigma associated with having illegitimate children and freedom to enjoy premarital sex. The critical point raised in this context is the problematic nature of reductionistic proclamations that sexual liberation is an unequivocal benefit for women.

6. *Patriarchal culture institutions.* Such institutions include religious, educational and media organizations, all of which play a very important role in shaping masculinity and feminity. Every cultural institution has developed patriarchal discourses that are regulatory in their intent. Religious institutions have set a variety of technologies of control to police women's behavior and limit their power. Educational institutions have differentiated between men and women, validating male power by conferring males with more valuable credentials than women. Also, as we have discussed, educational institutions have tended to validate masculine cognitive styles more often than feminine ways of thinking. Media institutions have produced representations of women from a dominant masculinist gaze that positions women as objects of male heterosexual desire (Walby, 1989, 1990; Dubino, 1993; Lewis, 1990; Pagano, 1990; VandeBerg, 1993; Ramsey, 1996; Smith, 1996; Hedley, 1994; Layton, 1994; Hauser, 1992).

One can easily understand how such a powerful patriarchal ideology shapes the educational and job experiences of women.

One can watch another power-driven ideology—this one around the structure of socioeconomic class—work among students in vocational education classes. Much like Randy, the junior high school student from East Texas that we discussed in Chapter 2, Maria has been tracked into vocational education. Maria is a first-language Spanish speaker from Brooklyn whose parents both work at McDonald's earning minimum wage. Despite both parents working full-time (and sometimes overtime), there is never enough money for Maria and her three sisters to make ends meet. Her parents have attempted to get better jobs but neither has a high school degree and their English is not all that good. Thus, Maria gets little parental help with her schoolwork because the parents simply don't have the English skills or much academic experience.

Teachers at Maria's school, knowing that she gets little support at home, speak of her parents' lack of concern for her. Nothing could be further from the truth. Maria's mother and father love her with all their hearts but their efforts have met with frustration. They attempted to take her to an English tutor but they couldn't afford it. Thus, the socioeconomic class dynamics that work to shape their lives and thwart their efforts to help Maria are viewed by some of Maria's teachers as examples of parental neglect. One teacher who believed Maria's parents were disinterested in her education said: "If they don't care then there's nothing I can do to help her; I can't take the place of her parents."

In these typical everyday interactions you can see the structures of socioeconomic class disable students. Maria is a smart girl, blessed with a good heart and the desire to do what she considers the right thing; but her class status, like Randy's, works against her. The knowledge she posseses of life in the streets of Brooklyn pays few dividends in the middle-class culture of school. Knowing about the ideology of class and its effects on millions of students like Maria, you can prevent the Marias and Randys you teach from being swallowed by the blackhole of class ideology.

This ideological influence operates on many levels. Social theorists tell us that knowledge is power and whoever controls knowledge exercises it first and most. Corporations can often hide information or issue misinformation and, in the process, shape the consciousnesses of those who help make social and economic policy. For example, few consumers who eat Perdue chickens know that their prices reflect unfair labor practices. Most Perdue workers receive only minimum wage and no benefits, and many suffer from repetitive-motion illnesses brought on by labor speedups. But because they can manipulate public access to information with their advertising and sophisticated public relations strategies, corporations like Perdue can hide unfair and dangerous practices. In a general way we realize that many firms dump toxic waste into the ecosystem, but because they can suppress this information the public perceives many of these corporations as benign neighbors and even concerned environmentalists. To the degree that business leaders can conceal their sins against workers and the environment, they can manipulate both consumer behavior and voter activity (Pollin & Cockburn, 1991; Boycotts in Action, 1998).

This corporate control of information also affects the everyday lives of workers, as managers hide data on job costing or company profit margins from the rank and file. Such knowledge control keeps workers from entering negotiations on an equal footing (Roditi, 1992). Moreover, as interlocking corporate boards subtly begin to dominate the media they can shape the perspective from which the media present the news. Michael Apple examined a series of network news stories on unemployment and found few of them attempting to explain the rise in unemployment. Most of the reports, like TV news in general, focused on the consequences rather than the causes of everyday events. Any attempt to report conscious efforts by management to control workers would quickly attract charges of media bias. In lieu of any analysis of cause, network reports spoke of tough times for individuals, but economic ups and downs, news people implied, were merely part of a "natural" progression of events that operated outside the control of human beings (Apple, 1992).

Corporate power operates on still more levels. In addition to controlling information, corporations have steadily increased their demands on local governments to create "good business climates." These "climates" typically involve agreements between business and government to lower corporate taxes, provide infrastructure improvements and relocate people living on lands needed for worksites. Business and industry often receive tax "abatements"—tax reductions or exemptions—as incentives to move from one location to another. But what do these agreements do to the tax bases of the local communities and school districts? Some argue that the new payrolls and community enhancement corporations provide affect the revenue lost to schools and social services. But this is a smokescreen. What happens when that beneficent corporation is lured away by the next tax incentive? Schools suffer, jobs disappear and the community is left desolate.

Barry Bluestone described the agreements between the city of Detroit and General Motors that preceded the construction of the "Poletown" Cadillac assembly plant. Having lost two GM production facilities, Detroit was eager to replace lost jobs—like most other cities with high unemployment. GM leaders hinted at a willingness to build a new Cadillac plant in Detroit if the city would make some concessions. GM asked Detriot (1) to grant it two-thirds of a heavily populated square mile of land in the middle of the downtown; (2) to relocate the three thousand people who lived in the area; (3) to raze 160 small businesses in the neighborhood; (4) to demolish the 170-bed hospital and three nursing homes there; (5) to redirect two major highway ramps and move a railroad right of way; (6) to transfer a Jewish cemetery to another location; (7) to clear the area to a depth of ten feet so GM would not have to worry about water, sewer, telephone and gas lines; and (8) to grant it a 50 percent tax reduction for twelve years (Bluestone, 1988).

The costs of the concessions reached a half billion dollars, but the city council approved them unanimously. Ironically, once GM built the plant it was not used for Cadillac production and lay fallow. Even if it goes into full operation the plant will provide only 6,200 jobs for Detroit workers.

With arrogance to match that of GM, International Harvester informed Fort Wayne, Indiana, and Springfield, Ohio, that it planned to shut down a plant in one of those two cities and that the community offering the most concessions would keep its plant. After much analysis and debate Fort Wayne offered International Harvester thirty million dollars in tax breaks, loan guarantees and a series of subsidies. Springfield countered with a thirty-one million dollar offer. Soon thereafter, the company closed its Fort Wayne plant. Never before have corporations possessed so much power and been so willing to impose it.

Vocational and academic programs don't escape the influence of corporate power. School and business partnerships have become increasingly popular in recent years. Because these arrangements have been proclaimed a success by many companies, the mainstream media devote little analysis to them. But when we study the scant research available, we find that schools possess little power in their relationships with firms and that businesses generally exercise veto power over any learning material that portrays companies negatively. Those who have worked to develop national student performance standards report that while many of their colleagues might want to encourage questions on unions and democratic issues in the workplace, businesses withdraw their support the moment these topics arise.

One could even say a conflict of interest has developed, as businesses increasingly demand "ideological purity" (that is, unquestioning support of the ideology of laissez-faire economics) in vocational education programs. At the same time, progressive vocational educators turn in hopeful appeal to the Perkins Act and its requirement that students be schooled in "all aspects" of their trade. Illustrating the power of business and industry once again, most states ignore the intent of the Perkins Act. Recently passed state and federal youth apprenticeship legislation pays little attention to democratic workplace issues. Disinclined to reflect critically on issues of economic justice, many programs simply instruct students to master the appropriate skills and adopt attitudes that meet the needs of business. Hannah Roditi concluded her research on apprentice programs with the observation that the goals of most apprenticeships involve the production of docile workers. Educating worker-citizens acquainted with democratic principles and capable of independent thought, Roditi noted, is just too dangerous (Bluestone, 1988; Roditi, 1992).

CULTIVATING INEQUALITY: THE WIDENING CHASM BETWEEN WORKERS AND MANAGEMENT

Nothing illustrates the power of corporate management better than the reliance of the U.S. economy on a segmented workforce. One need not look far to find that some jobs are defined as information-based management positions, while others are described as low-skill, low-status, low-income assignments. Even more disturbing, a disproportionate and growing percentage of recent jobs fall into the low-wage category (DeYoung, 1989; Block, 1990). As the middle class shrinks, more and more workers confront under and unemployment. In fact, a new economic category has emerged to describe the work experience of thousands of Americans: "contingent employment," work that offers few benefits and no job security. By the end of the 1980s the percentage of full-time workers earning low wages was growing rapidly, and workers without college degrees, the principal constituency of vocational education, found their earnings had declined by 18 percent during the decade. By the early 1990s, the real earnings of male high school graduates had fallen below those of comparable workers in 1963. Moreover, a large percentage of the jobs created in the 1980s were part-time and paid low wages, usually to women balancing homemaking schedules (Coontz, 1992; Block, 1990).

The conservative climate of the 1980s produced policies aimed at cutting government spending on the poor. Welfare spending fell by an average of 30 percent per recipient, and in only a few years the social safety net for economically disadvantaged people unraveled (Ellwood, 1988). By 1990, twelve million Americans received incomes that constituted less than half the amount the federal government specified as living in poverty. This growing economic inequality now strains the American social fabric. To be sure, inequality has always existed in America, but in the 1950s and 1960s, when incomes and wealth were growing, a more equal distribution of wealth attracted little concern. Hope thrived as people assumed each generation would live better than its predecessors. But as the economic health of America faltered in the early 1970s, hope began to crumble and inequality became a serious issue once again. In the 1990s economists reported that the distribution of private wealth surpassed the fiscal inequality Marx documented in the middle of the nineteenth century (Coontz, 1992; Lather, 1991).

From the perspective of America in the 1990s we observed the arrival of technology-based capitalism ("techno-capitalism," as Douglas Kellner (1990) called it). This new economic reality suggests conflicting possibilities: a more democratic social organization, or a more repressive society stratified by class that exacerbates the current fiscal inequality. The early aspects of techno-capitalism supply little on which we can pin progressive hopes. Simultaneous with the rich getting richer (the 1980s and 1990s), the public sector deteriorated, homelessness exploded, permanent unemployment increased, health care systems broke down, the infrastructure (bridges, roads and public works) disintegrated, farm bankruptcies became an agricultural commonplace, bank failures multiplied, the public debt mushroomed and financial scandals proliferated.

Workplace health issues nicely illustrate the current social inequality of workers. The media have devoted thousands of pages and hours to the stress-related health concerns of managers and professionals. Yet they rarely discuss the stress-related problems of blue-collar workers, which are much more serious than white-collar health concerns. Imagine a foundry worker in an automobile assembly plant who endures each day a blazing hot workstation with ambient oil mist in the air. After working there for a few months he begins to notice a degeneration in his health. Reflecting on his situation, he concludes that he will not be paid for the years of life he seems certain to lose. His plight, meanwhile, escapes the attention of newspapers and TV newscasts. This is not a description of some nineteenth-century factory. It accurately represents many factory jobs in the 1990s; moreover, it illustrates a growing inequality between management and labor. Compounding this inequality, recent fiscal demographics confirm a shrinking but ever wealthier upper class, an expanding lower class and a middle class struggling to maintain its economic equilibrium (Kellner, 1989; Ferguson, 1984).

Prophets of the new age of technocracy forecast a technotopia, a great society predicated on technological development. On one level these prophets are correct: technological development always exerts social consequences (Wirth, 1983). Thus, progressive social analysts and vocational educators should ascertain how the social and political implications of new technologies affect both production and the everyday lives of workers. On another level, however, the prophets of technotopia miss the boat. Economists have found that while technological development tends to increase productivity, managers also use it to tighten control over their workers. The modernist science on which technology is based embraces predictability, repeatability and quantifiability as central goals. Accordingly, as science devises new technology it also establishes procedures for its appropriate use, a strategy liable to eliminate the need for human judgment (Pollin & Cockburn, 1991). Absent uncertainty and ambiguity, workers simply follow the rules and leave the incidental thinking to their superiors. While technology can produce countertrends that upgrade the skills demanded of individuals, the deskilling impulse still degrades far too many high-tech workers and almost all low-tech workers.

Arguments over this question of high-tech deskilling raged in economic circles in the late 1990s, but agreement emerged that throughout the late nineteenth and early twentieth centuries large factories intentionally fragmented and deskilled the labor process in order to increase efficiency, control workers and reduce labor costs (Valli, 1988). Few managers either noticed or cared that such policies separated the planning, execution and evaluation of work. Planning and conceptualizing are, after all, the domains of those managers who design the production process; execution is the domain of deskilled workers, who simply follow the plan devised by the experts; evaluation is the domain of management-controlled supervisors, who check to see that the workers actually follow directions. Clearly such a process undermines the dignity of workers, but it also deprives managers of the valuable insight workers might provide during the planning and evaluation phases of production. Apparently no one in management can see this process from the workers' viewpoint. From the perspective of corporate leaders, the goal of control over labor renders a worker's insight insignificant, expendable and even dangerous. Deskilled workers are easier to control when they must depend on those who conceptualize and plan production (DeYoung, 1989; Pincus, 1980; Kincheloe, 1995, 1998).

Indeed, deskilled workers in the twentieth century often come to accept the mindlessness of their work lives. Some workers see their jobs as paid incarceration, like prison, the army or school. We have long associated the word "deskilling" with blue-collar assembly-line work, but the fragmentation and rationalization of work now permeate all aspects of the workplace, and so white-collar positions increasingly show signs of deskilling (Ferguson, 1984); rationalized and fragmented just like assembly-line positions, white-collar decision making is replaced by procedure following and demands for strict conformity to the rules of the organization. Consider the book and movie *The Firm,* in which a young lawyer quickly perceives the unstated rules he must follow and the conformist norms he must adopt if he is to succeed among corporate attorneys.

This penetration of deskilling to new venues hardly ends with the rationalization of white-collar labor; workers can gain technological skills and still undergo deskilling in relation to their access to the logic of workplace management and organization. Operating in a culture of deskilling, vocational schools and "tech prep" programs subconsciously mimic this orientation when they attempt to adapt their students to the demands of the workplace. As they set about adjusting their students to the status quo, vocational educational leaders may argue in response to progressive critics: "We're teaching them survival skills; we want to get them ready for the workplace."

Progressive vocational educators understand the need to help students survive in the workplace, but they reject the idea that survival means an inability or an obdurate refusal to analyze and criticize the sociopolitical assumptions that currently guide work in America. We do not need more of the Homer Simpson types who supervised operations at the Three Mile Island nuclear plant. Ignorant of the over-all planning and conceptualization of the facility, they were lost when unantici-pated breakdowns occurred. Nothing in the manual presented a response to the unexpected.

In light of the disturbing differences in public perspectives toward managerial and worker health, the undermining of worker access to knowledge deskilling im-plies and the resulting degradation of worker dignity, monumental pay differences only add insult to injury. Their pay having actually declined in real dollars since 1973, wage-earning Americans find it difficult to fathom—let alone accept—the salaries of corporate leaders (Coontz, 1992). Imagine hard-working men and women reacting to these unconscionable extravagances: The year Texaco, Inc., entered bankruptcy proceedings and recorded a $4.4 billion loss, its chief execu-tive, James W. Kinnear, received a 14 percent pay raise, making his yearly salary $723,000; in the late 1980s, the median yearly earnings for chief executives passed one million dollars; Lawrence Coss, the CEO of Green Tree Financial, is paid $102.4 million per year; John Grundhofer, CEO of First Bank, $14.9 million; Lawrence Perlman, Ceridian Corporation, $13.8 million (*Pioneer Planet*, 1998); the same two years that Lee Iaococca made $38.4 million, Chrysler profits fell 7 percent Japanese businessmen express frequent amazement at the size of American executive salaries that pay managers more than fifty times the salaries of line work-ers. Japanese executives earn only ten times more than line workers.

To those who contend that such disparate pay simply illustrates the result of the free market in action, the dictates of the law of supply and demand and compensa-tion for the extreme stress managers must endure, progressive critics offer a different assessment. Pointing out that executive salaries show little correlation to perfor-mance—failure is, in fact, rarely penalized—critics emphasize the ethical absurdity of such disparities, which (they say) undermine the basic tenets of American democ-racy. They do, of course, require us in the name of economic justice to provide more and better educational and economic opportunities for our dispossessed vocational students. Contrary to corporate propaganda, which attributes this disparity to fixed economic laws, federal, state and local government policies in cooperation with both academic and vocational educational reforms could, if they chose, help reverse these trends. The contemporary allusions to Total Quality Management fall on cynical ears when managers benefit unjustly from the labor of their workers. Progressive vo-cational educators understand the need for a just workplace with an equitable distri-bution of gains and losses (DeYoung, 1989; McLeod, 1987; Block, 1990).

MYSTIFYING POWER: CONTROL IN THE NAME OF DEMOCRACY

In democratic societies power attains its goals by seeming to promote equality while producing the stratified workforce corporations and employers demand (Livingstone, 1987). Scholars call this process "hegemony," which Peter McLaren defines as the maintenance of control less by the use of actual force than by subtly coercive social practices in churches, government, the mass media, the family and the school that win the consent of individuals. Many citizens, McLaren concluded, are unaware that they give their consent to those in power and, as a result, participate in their own oppression. When schools, for example, teach the individualist ethic (that is, the myth of individual achievement), the dominant culture ensures that economically or racially marginalized students who fail at school will blame themselves. In other words, such students are hegemonized to accept their subordination (McLaren, 1994). When these students find themselves unemployed or in low-paying dead-end jobs, they blame no one but themselves, an attitude that nicely serves the corporate powerbrokers since it blinds workers to the injustice of a system that needs people in low-paying dead-end jobs.

With their power to control information and manipulate public opinion, corporate leaders can convince people that an economic system built on job stratification actually serves their interests. In recent decades such leaders have convinced the public of some strange ideas indeed. For example, corporate-backed politicians convinced a majority of Americans that tax decreases for the richest citizens would "trickle-down" so as to improve the economic lives of the poor. These same politicians convinced many Americans that regulations designed to stop American companies from moving their factories to other countries and leaving hard-working Americans unemployed were superfluous. Then they further convinced many that companies poised for such migration should receive tax breaks.

Many Americans came to believe that weak schooling had caused the American economic disparities in the 1980s and 1990s. The fact that corporate leaders failed to retool their factories or create jobs when higher-skilled employees became necessary was omitted from the story. If large percentages of laborers held jobs that required minimal skills, what did it matter whether they were well educated? Production quality seemed to hold steady when American factories relocated in economically deprived countries with unschooled and illiterate workers. Something about these arguments failed to add up, but few who opposed them gained a voice in U.S. social institutions. Hegemony is complete and triumphant when every day people speak out and vote against their own self-interests (Carlson & Apple, 1998).

Even the most "democratic" discourses of the late twentieth century, Total Quality Management (TQM), Continuous Quality Improvement (CQI) and Quality of Work Life (QWL), serve hegemonic purposes wonderfully. Instead of achieving worker empowerment, these deceptive slogans often lead to elaborately articulated plans designed to manipulate workers into supporting the status quo. Labor unions routinely discover that management uses nominal support of industrial democracy programs to subvert employee-sponsored initiatives. As a result, many unions now urge their members to distinguish between genuine power-sharing plans and subtle attempts at union busting. In an era when public relations and administration science have become well-developed arts, workers should understand that yes can mean no, black can mean white and peace can mean war. Wrapping themselves in the flag of democracy, industrial leaders often set out to reach totalitarian ends (Wirth, 1983).

In this context, school leaders have begun to wrap themselves in that same democratic flag while designing school programs that train students to fill corporate niches. Too often vocational programs work hard to adjust students to their tasks and fail to help them understand the economic realities that keep them from shaping their workplaces (Simon, Dippo, & Scheneke, 1991). Except in sectarian prayers and patriotic recitations, such topics as democracy, public morality and inequality rarely play important roles in American schools or in the practical preparation of their students for work. Historians of education bluntly analyze the historical purpose of vocational schooling in America. John Hillison and William Camp, for example, argue that from the very beginning federally funded vocational education in this country "was designed primarily to serve the needs of industry and secondarily to consider the needs of the individual" (Hillison & Camp, 1985, p. 48).

Sociologists of education are quick to point out that operating in the name of democratic opportunity, academic and vocational schooling effectively sustain the division between technically qualified professionals and managers on the one hand, and low-skill manual labor on the other (Livingstone, 1987). School leaders and their business associates show little inclination to invite lower-level workers from disenfranchised groups into a more democratic, participatory economy. Their real objective is to produce obedient workers content to increase productivity within the boundaries of undemocratic workplaces and subservient roles. We see here why the noncognitive skills of punctuality and rule following attract such disproportionate emphasis in school settings. Docile workers rarely become militant workers who challenge policies and advocate strikes. Corporate ideology permeates the halls and classrooms of American schools, but few individuals comment on or even notice it (Pincus, 1980; Steinberg & Kincheloe, 1997).

When vocational educators undertake to lead their students through a study of democracy in the workplace and the various programs designed to implement it, they must help the students develop ways of distinguishing the genuine from the bogus. Their students should know that all genuine democratic workplace reforms meet these four criteria: (1) workers are participants during all phases of planning and change processes; (2) any alterations in workplace organization must lead to increased worker autonomy; (3) workers, like managers, must share in the economic benefits; and (4) workers must retain the right to pull out of a reform program if they find it contrary to their interests (Wirth, 1983). The time for silence in our schools on questions of genuine democracy in the workplace has long since passed. Schools must now speak out and live up to the democratic principles that provide our country with political guidance and an ethical anchor. To appreciate fully the mystification of democracy and its cooptation by antidemocratic forces, however, we must first understand the development of scientific management—a concept introduced in Chapter 2. It is time now to explore scientific management in relation to democracy and work.

SOPHISTICATING POWER: THE DEVELOPMENT OF SCIENTIFIC MANAGEMENT

The publication of Frederick W. Taylor's *The Principles of Scientific Management* in 1911 changed forever the way managers wield power over workers. Not only did business promptly start to operate on these principles, but also much of American society in general arranged itself into hierarchical strata, with its work broken into parts and its individuals assigned to these parts according to some scientific measurement of their ability (Kolberg & Smith, 1992). Frederick W. Taylor is undoubtedly one of the most important individuals in both American economic history and American social and educational history. Born in 1856 in Philadelphia to wealthy philanthropists, Taylor was educated as a mechanical engineer. The consummate modernist, he worshiped devoutly at the altar of science and reason (Nelson & Watras, 1981). In fact, he believed that scientifically grounded social engineering and rational planning could help create a wonderful new world. Unfortunately, Taylor's abstract images of utopia under actual application became a dystopia as his scientific management degenerated into social engineering and the rationalist regulation of human beings (Lather, 1991).

Scientific management begins with the assumption that workers and other humans are objects to be manipulated in a manner that fits the needs of an organization, and under this assumption managers often forced workers into activities ill suited to their physical or mental well-being (Ferguson, 1984). The history of clerical work provides insight into the effect of scientific management on the nature of work and its impact on workers. In the nineteenth century, some 99 percent of all clerical workers were men and more than one in five American jobs was clerical. In 1850, clerical workers found themselves making more money than 90 percent of all other workers. But as women began to enter the clerical market in the late nineteenth century, the high status of the occupation began to shift and (to be frank about it) decline. No longer was clerical employment viewed as highly skilled and demanding work.

In 1917, William Henry Leffingwell published, *Scientific Office Management*, which introduced efficiency and time management to the clerical office. Typewriters were outfitted with stroke counters to calculate wages for the typists; who were now paid according to the number of strokes they typed each day. Quickly enough, the typists outwitted the managers, devising strategies to increase their daily strokes (for example, they used the space bar rather than the tab key to indent). Of course, such resistance undermined efficiency and slowed production.

Complex systems followed to monitor worker's output and to devise time-saving improvements to increase clerical productivity. Scientific managers obsessed with office layouts tinkered with the placement of water fountains and conveyor belts. Eventually they designed everything so that clerical employees would never have to leave their desks and squander their energy. Managers ignored the mental and physical well-being of workers and the value of visits to the bathroom and water fountain. They refused to understand that the most efficient way to arrange a clerical office is not always the most humane or even the most ostensibly productive way (Simon, Dippo, & Schenke, 1991).

Clerical work is, of course, merely one of many areas in which scientific management changed the nature of everyday labor. Factories, too, felt the dehumanizing impact of rationalistic management. Because scientifically managed factories left employees with so little room for task variation, workers there rarely had the chance to exhibit creativity or intelligence. It soon became apparent that in a scientifically managed workplace, employees could be reliable or unreliable, but never outstanding or excellent (Ferguson, 1984).

By the second decade of the twentieth century the American public, already fascinated with scientific management, began to see it as a panacea for all social ills. Advocates of women's rights attempted to apply the principles of scientific management to the home in order to free women from the daily housework grind. Clerics spoke of applying rational management to church projects to make redemption a more efficient enterprise. Indeed, on a variety of levels scientific management inspired an almost religious sense of wonder, a reverence for its possibilities. To become efficient in the eyes of scientific managers was to achieve salvation. Even as it continued to achieve a high rate of return on investment, efficiency began to assume new powers.

By 1915, efficiency was connected with social relations, social harmony and the suppression of class tensions. Sin was described as personal inefficiency, and personal success was considered the result of efficient programming. One could solve even perennial labor-management problems by applying efficiency. Bring the self-interest of employers and employees into congruency, Taylor argued, by using scientific standards to figure production rates. If one could break down the physical movements a work task requires into basic units of action and measure them by scientific time and motion analysis, one could then designate an absolutely equitable rate of production. Workers would understand that their pay had been determined by scientific measurement, rather than by the whim of greedy managers. By the grace of science, managers could envision a day free from workplace disagreement. Modernism had reached its zenith, and scientific rationality was going to save the world (Nelson & Watras, 1981).

Schools were part of that world, and it did not take long for the prophets of efficiency to focus on education. Just as industrial efficiency experts fit the right worker to the right job, educational efficiency experts would fit the right student to the right curriculum. To Americans in the first decades of the twentieth century the idea of efficiently training the individual in relation to his or her capabilities sounded like common sense. Few scholars foresaw that such an ostensibly innocent premise would require assumptions about the intrinsic abilities of children to perform academically. Educational sociologists would later confirm the intuitions of educators such as John Dewey—namely, that marginalized children placed on lower ability tracks would be condemned to "live down" to their teachers' low expectations. Why should the children of the poor or the nonwhite study algebra, trigonometry, physics, international relations and advanced composition? How would such courses complement their future low-skill, low-wage jobs? Indeed, policies based on scientific efficiency sealed the fates of many thousands of marginalized students. Rather than helping them escape from poverty and bigotry, their schools condemned them to narrow and impoverished lives in the American underclass.

As the result of scientific management, the school came to resemble the factory. Reflecting the modernist tendency toward fragmentation (discussed in Chapter 2), scientific managers applied their task reduction to teaching. Dividing each educational activity into its most basic elements, Taylor apostles W. W. Charters and Franklin Bobbit set out to rationalize the schools. Analyzing, for example, the role of the school secretary, Charters identified twelve basic duties and divided them into 871 specific steps. Young women in secretarial education programs subsequently mastered each step. Soon thereafter, Stephens College for women asked Charters to create a curriculum for the "job" of being a woman. After Identifying 7,300 categories he devised a scientific training program for a course in womanhood. Need we say that his program left no room for evolution in the role of women? What constituted an effective and efficient woman was determined, once and for all, by how society defined femininity.

This scientifically managed, fragmented curriculum of womanhood is not some isolated historical event that is quaintly interesting as an amusing anecdote. Charters's curriculum created long-lasting effects that are built into schools' and workplaces' view of women. In line with many of Charters's assumptions, women's paid work is still constructed around two types of division: (1) a vertical division of labor in which women as an economic group receive lower wages than men, and (2) a horizontal division of labor in which women are concentrated in specific types of work. Women workers are more vertically and horizontally divided in the United States than in any other country in the advanced capitalist world. Many Americans are surprised to learn, for instance, that today women with three years of college earn less than a man who finished only the eighth grade.

In the early decades of industrialization in the nineteenth century, women worked alongside men in vocations as widely diverse as mining, manufacturing and printing. In the first decades of the twentieth century, however, a new form of patriarchy began to arise that associated "heavy" labor in the industrial sector with manliness and male strength. The "gender wisdom" that developed in tandem motivated legislators to pass laws "protecting" women from industrial work and crafts. World War II, of course, interrupted such viewpoints, but the system struggled to reassert itself when the men came home from the war. The cultural debate about women's "proper" place has raged ever since (Apple, 1985; Coontz, 1992; Johnson, 1991; Aronowitz & DiFazio, 1994).

An important thread in this debate has involved the equation of paid work with masculinity. Skill is a male discourse. If women pushed their way into the workplace where a particular skill was performed, then the skill was devalued. Thus, the male attempt to exclude women from the workplace was not simply a matter of men thinking that women were not capable of performing a job skillfully; rather, it was more an attempt to protect their craft's integrity from the devaluation caused by women's involvement with the work skills in question (Aronowitz & DiFazio, 1994). "I think a lot of the men were threatened," women steelworkers reported after encountering extensive male resistance to their presence in the mills, because "here was a woman coming along who said she could do it just as well as they could" (Livingstone & Luxton, 1988, p. 31). In addition, male steelworkers were embarrassed to disclose their shopfloor behavior to women. As one female steelworker put it:

For them it's like having two personalities. Like Jekyll and Hyde sort of thing. . . .
At work they swear, they throw their garbage on the floor. I'm sure they don't do

that at home. . . . They're like kids at work . . . and I could just see them go home and be, you know, straight and narrow, very serious with their wives, and as soon as they get to work it's crazy. . . . Some of them just cannot handle women being in their line of work. (Livingstone & Luxton, 1988, p. 32)

Gender bias in the workplace never operates in some simple manner. It can be understood only as a constellation of social, cultural, economic, political, psychological and ideological forces that intersect at various points in the web of reality. In order to intervene in a democratic manner, critical educators must grasp the complexity of the forces at work and expose the modernist, male-centered assumptions in these interrelated economic and educational contexts.

Straight out of this modernist mind-set came behaviorist psychology, a science of the mind that would profoundly affect teaching for the rest of the twentieth century. Drawing on the intellectual foundations of modernist science and efficiency, John B. Watson reduced human behavior to its most basic expression, stimulus and response. Like Charters's atomization of the curriculum, Watson reduced behavior to the point at which one could study through scientific experimentation. Both curriculum efficiency and behaviorism tended to erase any concern with either larger purposes or ethical consequences while focusing exaggerated attention on the empirically quantifiable—that is, those human actions that lent themselves to measurability. The behaviorists failed to take into account that the trivial may often be easy to quantify while the profound is less so (Nelson & Watras, 1981; Garrison, 1989).

Scientific management finally failed to keep its grand promise, yet it continues to influence work and vocational and academic education. Even though managers came to acknowledge the unnecessary bureaucratization the system imposed—with its army of supervisors, planners and inspectors—they still welcome the control over workers it provides and justifies. Based as it was and is on a disregard for workers, scientific management virtually ensures the development of tension and hostility between workers and managers. Earlier workers heard of Taylor's reference to them as "drays and donkeys." One of his most notorious quotes centered on those men most qualified to shovel pig iron: They were like oxen, he maintained, so dumb that they could do nothing else.

Such comments were hardly conducive to good labor-management relations. But despite numerous denials, the human relations schools of workplace management that developed in the years since Taylor still consider workers objects to be manipulated. In many ways, human relations management is Taylorism after a facelift. Aimed at men and women with more middle-class educational and cultural backgrounds, human relations management depends more on the development of consent than on naked coercion. Yet it still fits our definition of a hegemonic practice, even as it wraps itself in the banner of humane and democratic values. In fact, it is far more effective than direct coercion and thus more dangerous to workers in particular and American democracy in general (Wirth, 1983; Ferguson, 1984; Nelson & Watras, 1981).

THE CONSUMMATION OF THE MODERNIST ECONOMY: THE RISE OF FORDISM

In conjunction with Taylor's scientific management, the business ideas Henry Ford promoted produced the modernist economy. To follow the development of vocational education, we should turn our attention at this point to the evolution of what postmodern scholars call "Fordism." For many nineteenth-century economists the iron law of wages dictated that the wealth of business and industrial managers depended on the poverty of workers. To make a profit one had to procure raw materials cheaply and keep wages as low as possible. Many observers before and since have understood that this strategy produces inevitable conflict between management and labor. Cheap raw materials demand economic imperialism, with the consequent struggles between weak nations and strong nations, while the attempt to keep wages low demands sweat shops, crowded tenements and dangerous working conditions.

Karl Marx expected this situation to precipitate a workers' revolution and the start of a new worker-centered era. Henry Ford offered an alternative. His automobile factories would produce more at reduced costs, which would boost sales. As sales increased so would profits, Ford contended, leading to more prosperity for everyone. Some of the huge profits would go to pay higher wages, which, in turn, would create a larger group of consumers. Marxism would thus be defeated, as workers with free time and a little money in their pockets were unlikely to foment a revolution. Thus, workers and owners struck a Faustian bargain, a deal that would define Fordism: Workers would tolerate the meaningless, boring work of the assembly line in return for consumer rewards. Workers would buy into the system (with a little help from advertising and time payments), working hard with one hand and spending freely with the other (Aronowitz, 1992; Wirth, 1983).

The Fordist era began in 1914, when Henry Ford introduced the five-dollar, eight-hour day at his automobile assembly line in Dearborn, Michigan (Harvey, 1989). The mass-production system used there would not only shape the workplace but also would mold social institutions, vocational education in particular. Drawing on the rationale of modernism, Fordist production procedures became the highest expression of modernism and the lowest expression of worker dignity. Ford's four production principles included (1) product standardization; (2) special-purpose machinery adapted for use on the line; (3) the fragmentation of tasks into their component parts and task assignments modeled on scientific management time-motion principles; and (4) the replacement of static model assembly with flowliness (instead of workers building a static product, the cars flowed past them on a line).

Ford did not originate mass production and the assembly line—examples of these methods date back to the eighteenth century. But he was the first to bring the forms of modern industrial organization together all at once with higher wages for his workers. With all its elements now synthesized this way, the new technology swept across the American landscape like a plague of locusts devouring social traditions. In only a few years Fordist production strategies and their socioeconomic consequences changed America forever (Murray, 1992; Nelson & Watras, 1981).

The one nineteenth-century critique of industrialization Ford declined to address involved the tendency of industrial work to separate itself from the creative spirit of the worker. An inevitable form of existential death accompanies the job when a worker tightens bolts over and over again, day in and day out. Like other forms of modernist fragmentation, Ford's assembly line turned every task into a standard unit measurable in time and number. As workers became integral portions of the line, they became as interchangeable as any other mechanical part. Add scientific management and industrial psychology to the recipe, and you have progressively deskilled workers. Thus Ford brought Taylor's gospel of efficiency into the automobile plant, replacing traditional ideas of fairness with the glitter of efficiency (Nelson & Watras, 1981; Kellner, 1989; Harvey, 1989).

Other industries separated managerial planning and control from worker execution, but the totality of his scheme made Ford's project unique. Ford wanted to create a new type of worker and a new type of man (he did not hire women on the line): not just the productive worker, but also the worker as a consumer. Fordist laborers would live, work and consume in a new society—a modern, rationalized world. Writing in Italy from one of Mussolini's prisons, social theorists Antonio Gramsci recognized Fordism as "a new mode of living and thinking and feeling life" (Harvey, 1989, p. 126). So complete was Ford's system that in 1916, eager for his workers to learn how to consume properly, Ford sent a division of social workers into the homes of his employees to teach them morality, proper family life and the characteristics of rational shopping. In general and in many particulars, Fordism became synonymous with the scientific forms of regulation associated with modernism (Grossberg, 1992).

The phrases "regime of accumulation" and "mode of social political regulation" refer to the consistent, long-term ways products are produced and consumed and the way the population is regulated to support their production and consumption (accumulation) processes. Fordism serves as the perfect example of a regime of accumulation and a mode of sociopolitical regulation. Between 1914 and 1945, however, Fordism faced numerous disruptions in its attempt to function smoothly in both of these roles. Two of the most serious issues involved labor's growing resistance to the devaluation of craft skills in routinized assembly line jobs, and government's reluctance to adopt fiscal policies to mollify labor and divert its attention from an unequal distribution of wealth. Only after World War II were these problems finally addressed so as to ensure the ascendancy of Fordism as a regime of accumulation and mode of sociopolitical regulation. In this capacity, Fordism set the stage for the postwar economic boom, which lasted until 1973. Fueled by strong growth in auto production, shipbuilding, transport equipment, steel, petrochemicals, rubber, electrical goods and construction, the American economy devoured massive supplies of raw materials from noncommunist countries and came to dominate world markets with its consequent products (Harvey, 1989).

Labor's tendency to resist the degradation of work still presented Fordism with a problem. But with the suppression of radical labor movements in the immediate postwar period, Fordism began to devise strategies of labor control. Encouraged by the government, the police launched vicious attacks against unions for supposedly inviting communist infiltration, while the Taft-Hartley Act of 1952 undercut labor's organizing power in the workplace. Though unions retained some collective bargaining power and the benefits of social security and the minimum wage, they kept this influence in return for accepting Fordist production strategies and corporate schemes to boost productivity and tighten worker discipline.

Thus, a grand compromise was hardly a compromise at all. Corporations undertook to assure stable growth in investments, thus guaranteeing productivity and raising living standards. They would accomplish this by committing to technological upgrades, mass capital investments, research and development in production and marketing and the use of economies of scale by way of even greater product standardization. They would extend and sophisticate their use of Taylor's scientific management in order to control production, personnel relations, on-the-job training, product design and even planned obsolescence, a strategy for increasing consumption and accumulating even bigger profits by manufacturing goods that were purposely designed to wear out or break down in a short period of time. Thus it would be necessary for the consumer to throw out the old product and buy a new one.

The so-called grand compromise rested on the faith that if one linked wage increases to increased productivity, profits would increase. Thus, business and labor appeared to become partners in a common economic struggle. Government would serve as the bow-tie referee, were one needed, in theory protecting each institution from the excessive power and the low blows of the other. For example, the traditional exclusion of African Americans from the mainstream labor force began to cause both partners problems. The state forced the inclusion of the excluded into the world of labor and business, even sending the National Guard when necessary to scatter the forces of discrimination. Appearing to serve everyone's best interests, government presented itself as the protector of the egalitarian impulse. Yet in reality, the liberal leaders of these politically motivated interventions soon found themselves subordinate to corporate power. While differences lingered between the major political parties, in the long run they were and are insignificant. Both Republicans and Democrats agreed to the goals and strategies of a now-dominant Fordism, and both have long since ratified a powerful consensus controlling the political and economic fortunes of postwar America to 1973 (Harvey, 1989; Grossberg, 1992).

THE BREAKING POINT: THE DECLINE OF FORDISM

In 1973, practically overnight, the Fordist compromise began to break down, and observers perceived not simply an economic decline but a decline in a way of life as well. As the economic expression of modernism, Fordism symbolized Western civilization; it reflected the modernist faith in progress, technological development and rationality. But these very elements and the arrangements of the Fordist economy began to undermine the supremacy of the American economy (Borgmann, 1992). For schools, for vocational educators and for other institutions grounded in this technocratic rationality, such news was bad. Technique became an end in itself even as human concerns and the goal of empathic understanding were devalued. The decline of Fordism signaled misgiving in the absolute modernist faith in rationality. As American products grew shoddier and shoddier, profits predicated mainly on planned obsolescence rose and students emerged from schools appearing to understand less and less about the world, the evidence of decline mounted (Bellah et al., 1991).

The recession of 1973 destroyed the stable environment for corporate profits Fordism had established, and the transition to a new regime of production and a new mode of social regulation began. Many economists trace the beginning of the end of Fordism to the mid–1960s and the rise of the Western European and Japanese economies, the displacement of American workers achieved by Fordist rationalization and automation strategies, the decline in corporate productivity and profitability and the beginning of an inflationary trend (Harvey, 1989). The ability of Fordism to contain the contradictions of capitalism seemed to weaken during this period as the inflexibility of American economic arrangements became more apparent. Evidenced by long-term, large-scale fixed-capital investments in systems of mass production, this inflexibility thwarted attempts to devise or adjust to the new designs necessary in changing consumer markets. With regard to labor markets and contracts, inflexibility subverted attempts to reform workplaces with new forms of worker deployment. As social security, pension rights and other so-called "entitlements" expanded, a stagnant economy stymied government revenue collection. The only avenue toward flexibility entailed a change in monetary policy that involved printing money at an accelerated rate to keep the economy stable. Thus began the inflationary spiral that abruptly ended the post–World War II boom. All of these specific rigidities depended on a configuration of political power that united acquiescent big labor, big capital and big government in mutual allegiance to a set of narrow vested interests that undermined the productive capacity of the national economy.

Many Americans were excluded from the benefits of Fordism, and as time passed their discontent became increasingly apparent. Only certain sectors of the Fordist economy benefitted from the labor-corporate compromise; those spheres with volatile demand or insufficient investment in mass-production machinery never prospered. Therefore, workers in so-called monopoly sectors remained poor. These excluded workers acquired social tensions that spawned civil unrest and social movements based on deprivations attributable to race, class and gender. The civil rights movement unleashed resentment that often took the form of a revolutionary anger that particularly affected the inner cities. As women increasingly found themselves confined to low-paying jobs, their resentment set the stage for the women's movement. As expectations rose and mobility declined, discontent with Fordist arrangements festered (Murray, 1992; Harvey, 1989).

An oil crisis exacerbated the serious recession of 1973, calling starkly into question the ability of American capitalism to extend the consumer dream to a citizenry primed by high expectations. No longer did even middle-class Americans assume that their economic lives would inevitably improve. The 1970s and 1980s brought attempts at an economic restructuring that might respond to the collapse of Fordism, the first manifestations of an emerging economic paradigm shift. But with evidence of an economic crisis all around it, the American middle class perceived no dramatic economic change until the 1980s. Indeed, even in the mid–1980s, most Americans framed those changes they saw in terms of a moral breakdown: a loss of American economic, political and military hegemony in the world. The "American decline" became a question of will, a renewal of nationalism and military preparedness that could restore American dominance.

This chauvinistic response to decline set the tone for a lot of short-term political, military, educational and economic policy making directly related to current educational reform proposals that were launched with the publication of *A Nation at Risk* in 1983. (We looked at the 1980s reform movement in Chapter 1, and we will return to it in Chapter 10.) Committed to an economic policy slavishly devoted to the "wisdom of the market," conservatives attacked the remnant of the liberal Fordist compromise with its embrace of the "welfare state." Setting about to withdraw the last governmental compensations for the disadvantaged, conservatives redefined "freedom" in economic terms. Freedom, they argued, implies the right to compete and fail; it is more an entrepreneurial liberty than a civil liberty. With the conservatives in power the state abandoned its old Fordist role as referee among competing interests and embraced corporate interests, mainly in profits. Even as conservatives won a series of political victories, many businesses sought desperately to escape the Fordist inflexibility in the workplace (Grossberg, 1992; Murray, 1992; Borgmann, 1992).

All this anxious, restless maneuvering suggests the need to analyze post-Fordism, which we will do in the next chapter. Meanwhile, teachers and students should understand these macroeconomic issues and their impact on work and education if a humane and productive workforce is the goal. Workers, too, must understand their role in the larger economic, social and moral order. Chapter 7 continues this contextualization of work, focusing more attention on the ethical debate over work in late-twentieth-century and emerging twenty-first-century America.

7

Political Debates about Work

SHAPING THE DEBATE OVER WORK ETHICS AND ECONOMIC POLICY: THE RISE OF THE NEW RIGHT

We can best understand the conservative New Right political movement that started to rise in the 1970s as a response to the breakdown in the Fordist compromise between corporations and labor and the concurrent decline in the American economy. The movement unequivocally invoked free enterprise and unregulated capitalism with freedom defined in economic terms: We all have the right to compete and fail. As the conservatives devised their response to a changing world, the leaders of America's multinational corporations struggled to address their changing relations with the world economy, as well as their changing labor constituencies. For example, the rise of service workers, the decline of workers involved in manufacturing and the changing ethnic and gender compositions of the workforce, coupled with the deterioration of profit margins, presented corporations with serious adjustment problems that demanded a comprehensive reconceptualization of the role of the corporation in American politics and culture.

In order to prosper in this new environment, American business leaders resolved to accumulate enough additional political power to operate more freely with fewer government restrictions and lower taxes. The consequent corporate "power play" of the late 1970s and early 1980s included such strategies as the funding of political action committees (PAC), conservative think tanks and national advertising campaigns.

As this corporate strategy took shape, an alliance between New Right political conservatives (often organized around charismatic fundamentalist Protestant leaders such as Jerry Falwell or Pat Robertson) and corporate executives began to come together. New Right fundamentalists staged a Sunday school morality play, depicting "liberals" of the 1960s as the demons whose ungodly permissiveness had initiated America's moral, spiritual, educational and (worst) economic declines. Confident, divinely sanctioned preachers made the Puritan dream (see Chapter 4) fashionable again, as they parroted John Winthrop's famous metaphor of America as a "city on the hill, a shining beacon" of Christian morality for a corrupt Old World. Though the blue-suited moguls found the evangelical crowd a little gauche and a bit too zealous, they nevertheless welcomed its members into a political alliance that would change the social, political and economic faces of America (Grossberg, 1992).

Meanwhile, the economic changes of the 1970s and 1980s devastated some groups while having virtually no impact on others. For example, the per capita income of families whose members were under the age of thirty dropped 27 percent between 1973 and 1986, exactly the same decline experienced by the same demographic group between 1929 and 1932, during the Great Depression. But during the 1973–1986 period, older, more affluent families actually experienced an increase in income. Because the drop occurred gradually over thirteen years and affected individuals with less power and media access, it remained hidden from the public consciousness (Scatamburlo, 1998).

After 1973, worldwide economic changes coupled with the growing power of the New Right began to discourage government spending on public sector needs. But as revenues fell, the U.S. government lowered taxes, producing a situation reminiscent of those in contemporary exploitative societies: private affluence and public squalor. America's urban communities suffered a decrease in funding that produced environmental negligence, unsafe and unsanitary playgrounds, dangerous parks, deteriorated public housing, underfunded public transportation, inadequate social services and public schools that reflected the same decay. Visiting Europeans expressed shock at the absence of publicly funded planning strategies to shape urban development and revitalize inner cities. In the midst of this economic decline, with its accompanying inflation and diminished tax revenues from corporations and the wealthy, the poor (especially the young poor) grew poorer even as their numbers swelled. Finally, the decline brought job disruption, marital stress, disintegration of the family and a consequent increase in single-parent families.

In this context women were once again hit especially hard by the economic dynamics. Because of the decline in working-class wages, women were required to enter the workforce. Thus, there emerged a gender dynamic that saw women working a double shift; their "day shift" at work and their "graveyard shift" at home which has rarely been addressed by political or educational leaders. If men were plagued by such a problem, corporate, government and educational organizations would scramble to solve it. As long as the double shift is a women's problem little action will be taken, because women are expected to take care of domestic tasks *no matter what their circumstances.*

In the political climate of the 1990s, many elected officials have ridiculed the idea that society should provide assistance for women who are both mothers and workers. The most obvious form of assistance, public child care, would provide a wider range of choices to working-class women's increasing participation in the American workplace, but public policy has continued to be based on the assumption that outside-the-family child care should be reserved for children with inade-quate parental care.

American day care is woefully inadequate for the needs of contemporary working mothers. Indeed, federal day care funding has declined by almost 25 percent since the early 1980s, and further cuts are threatened. The dire state of day care offers important insights into the relationship between economic and gender dynamics in America at the end of the twentieth century: (1) despite the women's movement and the national conversation about family values, women and children remain quite powerless; (2) despite the rhetoric of equal opportunity for women and men, political leaders do not want female workers taking employment opportunities away from men; and (3) despite repeated denials as to the existence of a patriarchal power structure, men in positions of power do not want to give up their place in the patriarchal family. Public provision of day care, they fear, would empower women to the degree that the hierarchical relationships of the patriarchal family would be disrupted (Ferguson, 1984; Palmer & Spalter-Roth, 1991; Pascall, 1994; Sidel, 1992).

MARKED CHANGES IN AMERICAN SOCIETY IN RECENT DECADES

After 1973 America changed dramatically; the most disturbing aspect of that change was a radical redistribution of wealth. By the middle of the 1980s, the chasm between the rich and the poor had widened to a point unknown since the Great Depression. Income for the poorest 20 percent of the nation dropped 5.2 percent; at the same time, the wealthiest 20 percent recorded take-home pay increases of 32.5 percent, and the income of the richest 1 percent of Americans increased 87 percent.

Meanwhile, in 1950 U.S. corporations paid 26 percent of all local, state and federal taxes, but by 1990 they paid only 8 percent. If the corporate tax rate had remained steady over the forty years between 1950 and 1990 local, state and federal governments would have received more than thirteen trillion extra dollars. What is most suprising about these figures and the disparity they represent is less that the conservatives accomplished their mission so quickly; rather, one can barely assimilate the fact that most middle-class and low-income Americans accepted it without dissent. The acceptance of this monumental shell game may constitute the greatest hegemonic act ever perpetrated (Coontz, 1992; Bellah et al., 1991; Grossberg, 1992).

With "selective attention" on the economic decline, middle-class Americans failed to perceive a crisis until the 1992 elections—and even then they revealed confusion over the causes and consequences of the problem. Guided by an increasing conservative influence on the production and dissemination of their knowledge, many voting Americans began to frame economic problems in terms of a loss in American military, political and economic leadership (Grossberg, 1992). Americans thought economic regression was caused by a widely advertised "decline of traditional values," and so saw it more as a problem of national "manhood" and international domination than as a problem of economic justice, let alone economic survival.

Stung by the embarrassment of the 1973 oil embargo and the Iranian hostage crisis between 1979 and 1981, many Americans welcomed Ronald Reagan's portrait of the way America used to be. The politics of nostalgia, with its figurative return to *Little House on the Prairie* and *Happy Days,* evoked emotional responses from Americans who believed the nation to be unjustly under siege. What have we done to deserve the Iranian hostage crisis, they asked, unaware and uninformed by the mainstream media of U.S. complicity in attempts to overthrow the Iranian government. (See Joe L. Kincheloe (1989) *Getting Beyond the Facts: Teaching Social Studies in the Late Twentieth Century* for further explanation of this issue.) The key themes Reagan, his vice president, George Bush, and Dan Quayle, later George Bush's vice president, enunciated—going "back to the basics" and an assertive militaristic foreign policy—were supported by many Americans and "blessed" by an acquiescent and uncritical media.

The new conservatives enjoyed unexpected success in dismantling the old FDR New Deal coalition, with its alliance of farmers, union members and urban ethnic voters. After the Fordist prosperity of the 1950s and 1960s, the members of the coalition no longer cared to be identified as allies of the dispossessed. By the 1970s they had aligned their interests with the affluent. By the 1980s and 1990s, transfixed by reactionary glorifications of greed and individualism, they were loath to empathize with the wretchedness of the poor.

As the rich grew blithely richer and the financial plight of children and the underclass continued to worsen, liberal memories of the truly needy faded into images of "welfare mothers" and other low-life "cheats." The right wing had disarmed yet another group that should have been worried by the growing disparity of wealth. By the mid–1980s, in fact, the idea of economic and political inequality raised few eyebrows. The rhetoric of "traditional values" served to condemn all those who fell outside the mainstream (that is, the nonwhite poor, advocates of women's rights, gays and lesbians, single-parent families, migrant and iterrant workers, immigrants and non-English speaking citizens and so forth). With the New Right firmly in power, social and economic policy followed a whole new set of rules.

Those rules typically involved neoclassical economic theory and its familiar allegiance to the freedom of the market. In brief: Anything under free-market conditions that turns a profit is permissible and state regulation invariably impedes economic progress. More specifically, the right-wing rules stipulated (1) the privatization of government service agencies; (2) the reallocation of wealth from poor to rich; and (3) the establishment of a free-market philosophy that promotes individualism, self-help, human resource management and consumerism in lieu of the application of ethical precepts in the public sphere. As market maximizers became paragons of success, the old game of Monopoly reemerged as the prototype for public life. Economics assumed the status of a science able to explain all human questions and all of life's mysteries. One interesting exception to the belief in the unfettered market involves what critics refer to as military "Pentagon socialism." Despite the virtues right-wing government leaders find in privatization and free markets, they continue to underwrite huge and elaborate weapons systems as a way of maintaining jobs, economic health and voting allegiance in local economies (Grossberg, 1992; Bellah et al., 1991).

Despite all the contradictions, free-market politics and the politics of nostalgia have produced a virtual revolution in the American way of seeing the rest of the world. Though Bill Clinton's 1992 victory exposed some of the hypocrisies of the conservative movement, his campaign and presidency illustrated less a reluctance to confront right-wing ideologies than to appropriate them. The conservative deployment of "the decline of family values" smokescreen continues to block any public understanding of the poverty caused by neoclassical economics, and liberal politicians and educators have yet to challenge it. The conservative deployment of the politics of nostalgia has successfully shaped America's impression of a family-oriented past. Asked to describe the traditional family throughout American history, Americans now tend to picture grandparents, parents and children all working together; nurturing mothers protecting children from early exposure to sexuality and adult concerns; virginal couples consummating their marriages; faithful spouses devoting every waking moment to marital and familial responsibilities—in short, *The Waltons*.

These pervasive images are, of course, ludicrous. Children who worked in family enterprises with parents and grandparents had little time for entertainment and recreation. Mothers who worked in such enterprises as the family farm had little time to nurture young Wally and Beaver Cleavers. They often relegated child care to older children and rarely stopped to celebrate baby's first step or worry over report cards. Failing to consult family historians on the accuracy of their romanticized vision, conservatives continue to argue that had these traditional families persisted into the 1990s, America would be free of the social dilemmas now facing it. Moreover, school leaders accept this rhetoric, identifying the cause of the decline in American education as a "parenting deficit" and blaming divorce and unwed motherhood for poverty and inequality. In his 1992 State of the Union speech, President Bush attributed the crisis of the city to "the dissolution of the family." In his 1994 State of the Union address, President Clinton repeated this neat formula. American leaders appear to have accepted the family values argument across the political spectrum so that by the late 1990s, it was beyond debate.

But any serious analysis of poverty and its relation to family status in the 1990s reveals a reality quite different from the mainstream portrayals. If we could magically revive the traditional family, researchers wonder, how many of the social problems America faces would it solve? Their agreed-on conclusion: very few. Throughout American history, family structure crises have typically followed economic and political upheaval, and the family problems of the 1990s are no different. The current crisis follows closely on the economic problems that began in the late 1960s with international market alterations and the destruction of well-paying reliable union jobs. These changes brought suffering to families, and some of them responded in ways that made matters worse. But this much is clear: The economic and social upheavals would have occurred with or without any widespread commitment to family values. The Census Bureau reported in 1991 that the average family that fell below the poverty line when the father left was already in severe economic distress before his departure; in most cases the distress came about when the father lost his job (Coontz, 1992).

This rhetoric of family values holds disturbing implications for the well-being of women in U.S. society at the beginning of the new millennium. As we discuss throughout this book, power creates identity or, as we put it, constructs consciousness. The patriarchal power grounding these conservative portrayals of family values and women's role in the family and society often blame assertive women for the breakdown of the family and other social problems. Because women have been forced by the changing economic realities of the last few decades to leave home and take jobs to support their families, they are blamed in the family values rhetoric for undermining the family.

We will analyze these dynamics in more detail later in this book, but it is important to point out in this discussion of economics and education that female students face unique problems that democratic teachers must address. Due to the conservative family values assumption that women's role involves the *necessity* of marriage and motherhood, female employment or unemployment is not viewed as an important problem, as it is with males. Critical teachers need to analyze the ways economic conditions, conservative family values perspectives and schooling construct relationships between future work and the lives of young women (Arnot, 1992). In the process, they can begin to develop teaching strategies that subvert the disempowered destinies that await many of their female students.

Socioeconomic and educational arrangements based on biological determinism must be exposed as socially rather than genetically constructed; the placement of women in low-status, low-paying roles in the post-Fordist economy is not an aspect of the larger natural order as envisioned by the advocates of family values and neoclassical economics. Educators and policymakers often do not realize that America has a high level of unemployment among specific population groups in the globalized economy. Of course, among such groups there is an inordinately high number of female-headed families. Avoiding the connections between these realities, such professionals fail to discern that the causes of poverty among women are often different than those among men.

Thus, the same remedies, the same educational experiences for women and men will not address these gender-related differences. Gender expectations—such as those of the right-wing family values advocates—will not address these gender-related differences. Gender assumptions define different locations in the cultural terrain, in schooling and in the economic sphere. For example, women's lives are often intimately involved with caring for others. Most people understand that women devote much time to child care, but the effort they devote to taking care of men, aged parents, grandchildren, friends and distant relatives is less frequently acknowledged. As weavers of the fabric that connects us, women have less time and energy to devote to making a living. When their domestic work in housekeeping and child rearing is added to the mix, time for paid work decreases even further. Gender expectations once again intersect with issues of socioeconomic class to produce a context hostile to contemporary women (Sidel, 1992).

When these issues are studied, especially in light of how they interact with the post-Fordist, globalized economic terrain, teachers gain insights relevant to their professional practice. For example, Silicon Valley, located in California's Santa Clara County, is widely recognized for its high-tech microelectronics industry and the economic revolution it catalyzed. The home of the nation's most celebrated computer jocks and financial whiz kids, Silicon Valley hides a labor force that is more heavily stratified by race, class, gender and nationality than any other economic segment in the United States. It doesn't take a genius to realize that the celebrated multimillionaire Silicon Valley executives are almost all white males, whereas the vast majority of low-paid manufacturing workers are minority women. The tendency of Silicon Valley managers to hire minority women—primarily Asian and Latina women—is not limited to Santa Clara County but is typical of high-tech glamour industries around the world.

Thus, race, class and gender hierarchies structure the good for those who are small, poor, foreign and female. Employers argue that women can work for less, even though they possess little if any specific knowledge about their female employees' family circumstances. Post-Fordist microelectronics company managers generally assume that their female workers are married to men who are earning a "livable" salary. In actuality, more than the majority of women employees in the industry are the primary earners in their families (Kincheloe, 1995, 1998).

Karen Hossfeld (1994) has contended that when employers assume women, nonwhites or immigrants accept low-paying work because they are content with it or because they are unprepared for or undeserving of better work, they are in complicity with forces that keep the marginalized in their place. She labeled these managerial assumptions racial, immigrant and gender "logics." In the high-tech microelectronics industry there is no conflict between these logics and "capital logic"—business strategies that contribute to profit maximization while increasing class and gender stratification and the control of labor.

Obviously, white employers' use of racism and sexism to construct an exploitative division of workers is nothing new and is not limited to the microelectronics industry. We can find the same social dynamics in the international textile industry, with its racial and gendered labor hierarchy. In many industries managers justify their use of women from Third World countries in repetitive assembly-line tasks because of such workers' alleged superior hand-eye coordination and patience. White male managers frequently report that the tiny size of many Asian and Mexican women allows them to sit still for hours at a time performing detailed work that would push larger (white) people beyond the limits of sanity. When certain workers were asked to respond to such a comment they argued that one manager preferred to employ small female workers so that he could feel superior and appear more intimidating around the plant (Hossfield, 1994). Critical teachers need to understand the effects of such masculine anxieties on their female students and prepare them to deal with such discrimination.

ADAM SMITH, THE SEQUEL: THE EMERGENCE OF NEOCLASSICAL ECONOMICS

Neoclassical economics, the belief in an unrestricted economy with all its decisions left to the undisturbed functioning of the market, gained great favor in the late 1970s and 1980s. Gradually replacing the contributions of religion, tradition and literature with a common fiscal language raised to the level of morality, neoclassical economics provides the modernist cult of self-interest with a sort of code. In this cult of the free market, economists maintain, one can apply economic analysis not only in determinations whether to increase overhead cost for the fiscal year, but in all other types of decision-making situations as well. So, the message is that marriage is less a matter of love than a matter of supply and demand within the spouse market. Suicide occurs when a remaining lifetime utility falls to zero. In other words, one can understand all human behaviors from an economic vantage point no matter how much altruism, emotion, love or compassion appears to intrude (Bellah et al., 1991). Many political and educational leaders with philosophical roots in this neoclassical tradition attempt to analyze schooling as merely a function of marketplace laws. Campaigning to privatize schools in line with their market philosophy, these leaders undermine the human dimension of the educational act while diminishing the importance of democracy in the public space (Giroux, 1993).

Proceeding from the premise that individuals always act rationally to maximize their self-interest, neoclassicists present a model of a self-regulating market that harmonizes the demands of production, labor and capital. Supply and demand regulate prices in such a way that all human and material resources are used efficiently. The market is all knowing, and as a result, it has the ability to adjust to dramatic changes. Assume, for example, that technological innovation automates a production process to the point that 80 percent of the workers are laid off. Always working to restore equilibrium, the market (according to the neoclassical economists) will provide a solution. As the cost (potential wages) of the displaced labor declines and the profits of the automated industry increase, the enterprising entrepreneur sees an opportunity to rehire the unemployed workers in a firm producing a different product.

But what is wrong with this picture? Unfortunately, the neoclassical model works best when the workers' skill levels remain low. Workplaces that require advanced skills find it difficult to find suitable out-of-work laborers. Specialization complicates a quick adjustment to disruption. But when an industry shrugs off positions, neoclassicists cheerfully assume that its displaced workers will find work quickly because (they also assume) few job-specific skills exist and sales clerks can easily become computer programmers (Block, 1990).

Like other modernist philosophies, neoclassical economics reveals a penchant for decontextualization. When analyzing economic issues, neoclassicists strive first to separate those issues from politics and culture. Just as an educational psychologist who measures an I.Q. ignores the context in which the student has been raised, neoclassical economists deal only with those variables that are internal to the economy. Removed from its social and political context, however, economics also loses a moral context (Nooteboom, 1991).

The prevailing rhetoric of economic battle—the appeal to win the "economic war" with the other nations as exemplified in *A Nation at Risk* (see Chapter 1)—reveals the emptiness of the neoclassical conversation. Its proponents seem unable to grasp the idea that an economic thinker might want to increase prosperity for all human beings and that determining winners and losers misses that point (Chesneaux, 1992). When a rural government chooses to keep the only grocery store open despite its unprofitability, it has, according to the high priests of neoclassicism, violated the prime directive: Thou shalt not interfere with the free function of the market. Forget the fact that local residents would go hungry or have to move. Hunger and cultural disruption are not economic issues.

Some advocates of neoclassical economics take their case even further, contending that an unhindered market in babies would resolve the various problems surrounding unwanted pregnancies, teenage mothers and surrogate mothers. If women could sell their babies on the open market and publicize baby prices the way the commodity markets quote prices for winter wheat futures, the free market would quickly solve the problem. Americans have always seemed shocked and then annoyed hearing the French refer to the U.S. economic system as *le capitalisme sauvage*—"savage capitalism" (Bellah et al., 1991, p. 91). U.S. public school teachers and students cannot speak these taboo words. But silent censorship like this cannot continue in a democratic society that supposedly values freedom of speech and discussions of issues. We must demand the right to examine the problems that plague our economic system and our work lives.

More specifically, educators must demand the right to discuss and debate who benefits from these neoclassical forms of unregulated capitalism. Critics of the free market argue that instead of offering opportunities for all, it lowers an ideological curtain that hides a tendency to bestow the greatest benefits on those who already own the wealth and power (Richmond, 1986). Free market capitalism creates a climate that justifies the view the privileged few have of reality. Market forces and competition appear in this painting of the world as cherubs and angels joyously but silently working to create harmony between supply and demand, wages and prices, goods and services. The free market never worked this way in the nineteenth century, and it does not work this way in the last years of the twentieth century—not with multinational corporations able to sway whole governments and control markets, the government obsession with military spending and the maintenance of the "defense sector" of the economy and the formation of "economic communities" and oil cartels. No local economy is free from those larger influences that undermine free trade and equal competition. The neoclassical market model fails to account for these intervening factors. Despite all appearances to the contrary, neoclassicists operate in a simple universe—a fantasy land that exists only in their imaginations.

Nevertheless, the social foundations of education revolve around these issues, these questions of social, political moral and—to be sure—economic context. The field of economic sociology has become especially important for the purposes as vocational educators. Economic sociologists challenge the socially decontextualized portrait of economics the neoclassicists propound. Arguing that cultural factors continually shape economic activity, these scholars provide example after example of the influence of noneconomic "background factors" in economic affairs. The type of work deemed appropriate for different social groups, for instance, is more than just an "economic issue." Because of particular social assumptions, black men in the early twentieth century worked as train porters. The free market did not dictate that reality. Women were assigned to low-status clerical jobs near the end of the nineteenth century, replacing men whose status as clerks had been quite high. Again, the market did not dictate this development. How do individuals weigh the value of more money against that of more leisure? What factors determine the decision of a graduate student to pursue or not a doctorate instead of stopping with a master's degree? Obviously economic factors are not the only "variables" at work in these situations (Block, 1990).

The folly of reductionist economic explanations of daily affairs should by now be obvious. A man wants to buy a book on the relationship between education and the economy at a corporate-owned chain bookstore. He picks up a copy of Richard Brosio's *The Radical Democratic Critique of Capitalist Education* for $39.95. A salesman notices his choice and says, "Why Brosio for forty dollars? We have a special on books on economics and education."

The buyer responds, "But I wanted a book that questions everyday assumptions about economics and schooling."

The salesman picks up a new edition of neoclassicist Milton Freidman's *Free to Choose*: "But, sir, this one is our red, white and blue light special. It's a hot value at only $9.99. You'll save thirty dollars. Come look at our other economics and education volumes. They're conveniently arranged by cost."

Another customer interrupts the salesman: "I'd like a book on postmodern architecture in the eleven-dollar range."

Economic considerations hardly dictate all consumption decisions. This facetious bookstore example illustrates our larger point: We cannot ignore the social and moral context of economic affairs. This larger point becomes particularly compelling when we discover that neoclassicists view labor markets as just like any other commodity market. The fact that human beings with feelings and emotional concerns dwell in the labor market is irrelevant. The neoclassicist mind-set quickly dismisses human factors. The people themselves are not "inputs" in the process of production, but rather one or more of their skills. What matters about human beings in the free market is not their sacred spirit but their capacity to do work. Notice that the central concern of educators is that our students lose their humanity and become reduced to merely more factors in the production process (Block, 1990).

AUTOMATION AND THE FUTURE OF GOOD WORK

As we meld our analysis of good and bad work with our understanding of the dehumanization and decontextualization of neoclassical economics we can begin to imagine work in the future. The debate about the impact of technology and automation is multifaceted and still unsettled and ambiguous. But when we examine the debate in light of our ethical and democratic concerns, we provide educators with considerable insight. One paramount question emerges in the study of high-tech automated jobs, and the future of work: Will the emerging economy contribute to the authoritarian control of workers or will it empower workers to participate and use their creativity and intelligence in their daily work lives? Too often we hear high technology and automation sold to industrial and corporate leaders as a way of lessening labor costs and reducing their reliance on skilled workers. At the same time, new technologies and automation tend to guarantee production quality and increase industrial flexibility (flexibility involves the capacity to change quickly from one product line to another or to produce a diverse array of products without interruption) (Copa & Tebbenhoff, 1990, Block, 1990).

Refusing to invest in workplace innovations in the 1960s and 1970s when the generation known as the "baby boomers" began to reach the labor market, American firms fell behind other industrialized nations in the quantity and quality of their production. By the 1980s, report after report called for immediate workplace reforms and the development of sophisticated technologies and workers with the skills to match. The authors of these reports realized that only empowered high-skill workers could, under these suddenly different conditions, improve a firm's productivity and the quality of its products. As an organization undergoes the workplace reorganization technological change requires, few onlookers know for sure how to reconceptualize the labor process. In these situations, empowered workers can play a central role in redefining the organization of work and production. Few managers, after all, possess the everyday practical knowledge that comes of dealing with the microproblems that plague the work process (DeYoung, 1989; Roditi, 1992; Block, 1990).

Analysts understand that technological development and its accompanying automation have slowed the growth of jobs in both manufacturing and service and information (Harris, 1981). But other than this understanding, economists, labor researchers and business people agree on little else. One of the most basic disagreements concerns the general nature of the economic future before us. As we discussed in Chapter 6, the twentieth-century economy, the Fordist era, relied on a famous compromise: workers tolerating repetitive factory jobs in return for consumer rewards.

With its mass production, inflexible technologies (mainly the assembly line), standardized work routines, economies of scale (larger factories that produce more products can produce each product for less money than smaller firms producing only a few products) and the accompanying cultivation of a market for standardized products, Fordism produced great national wealth. But as it began to decline in the 1970s with the oil crisis and the rise of foreign manufacturing, scholars argued whether a new economic era had dawned. Is there, in short, such a thing as post-Fordism? The question remains difficult to answer because evidence of Fordist and anti-Fordist production patterns coexist in contemporary society. Before we explore this question any further, however, we need a quick delineation of the five characteristics of post-Fordism perceived so far.

1. Post-Fordism implies a decline in consumer interests in mass-produced products replaced by growing interest in specialized items. Consumers become progressively more interested in quality and more willing to pay for it.
2. The demand for specialized products implies a need for shorter production runs. Thus, in a post-Fordist economy, smaller plants with flexibility replace large factories producing uniform products.
3. New technologies make possible then profitable new forms of flexible production. Post-Fordist factories employ computerized machinery programmed to produce a variety of items.

4. Post-Fordist workers deploy more skills than their Fordist predecessors. To deal with the sophisticated technologies, workers must operate both with greater sophistication and greater autonomy. Thus a new, more progressive workplace appears.
5. The diversity in the post-Fordist workplace is mirrored in the society as a whole. Post-Fordist workers demand more differentiated products, lifestyles and social activities (Ritzer, 1993).

But where are we now? The economic world at the beginning of the twenty-first century seems an amalgam of Fordist and post-Fordist dynamics, and as we said earlier, the impact of technological innovation and automation has so far been paradoxical. Some employers use the same technology in quite different ways; some of those ways empower workers, others deskill them. Therefore, it is difficult to generalize about the nature of the era. Employers who want to automate their factories can reduce labor costs by eliminating repetitive tasks, but a conflict often arises between reducing a reliance on skilled workers and trying to improve quality and increase flexibility. Without diverse skills, workers will find coping with unusual machine problems difficult, a limitation liable to undermine quality improvement.

The need for quality and flexibility should, therefore, encourage corporate leaders to seek workers with higher skills. For example, the complexity of the mechanical and repair operations all around us now requires highly skilled workers. Although some deskilling might be possible in auto mechanics, maintenance mechanics and office-machine services with the development of diagnostic machinery, someone needs to know enough to fix the machinery when the diagnoses or the diagnostic machines fail (Block, 1990).

At the same time, however, elements of Fordism live on unaffected by these post-Fordist trends. In his 1993 book, *The McDonaldization of Society,* George Ritzer traced the persistent Fordist trends. "McDonaldization," Ritzer wrote, is "the process by which the principles of the fast-food restaurant are coming to dominate more and more sectors of American society as well as of the rest of the world" (p. 155). The process is perfectly compatible with the homogeneous products, rigid technologies, standardized work routines, deskilling and quantification of workers and customers we associate with Fordism. At the same time that post-Fordist production processes expand in America, McDonaldization moves out from the restaurant business into education, the workplace, travel, vacationing, dieting, politics, TV evangelism and the family. In the contemporary American economy there are two expanding forces, McDonaldization and post-Fordism, moving concurrently but apparently in opposite directions (Ritzer, 1993). No one said understanding the social and economic contexts of the foundations of education would be easy!

While one finds many progressive impulses within post-Fordist workplaces— notably their emphasis on highly skilled and flexible workers—the jobs there figure to occupy no more than 30 percent of the workforce by the early twenty-first century. The U.S. Labor Department found the growth in high-skill jobs stagnating in the middle 1990s; at the same time, it predicted steady job growth in fast-food restaurants, small retail stores and service establishments. Other studies at the Bureau of Labor Statistics have found many college graduates settling for less than

high-skill jobs: As the creation of high-skill jobs stagnated 568,000 college graduates began work as sales clerks; 475,000 as secretaries and typists; and 125,000 as
bartenders, waiters and waitresses (Weisman, 1991, p. 14).

Another continuation, if not expansion, of the Fordist trend involves the rationalization and deskilling of professional jobs. Stanley Aronowitz (1992) calls
this the "proletarianization of professionalism" (p. 229). The term "proletariat"
refers to the lowest class of citizens in a community. Thus, "proletarianization"
conjures up the debasement of what were once high-skill positions in a way that
strips the dignity of skill from professional practitioners. The medical profession
might seem to be the last to experience rationalization and deskilling, but the past
decade witnessed the trend even in medicine. Physicians increasingly find themselves under the external control of managers and bureaucrats in insurance or
health maintenance organizations (HMOs) outside their profession. These controls seek a predictability that removes the mystery and passion from a doctor's
everyday life. In such situations doctors abandon their personal medical judgment
in determining a procedure; rules, regulations, financial constraints or the demands of technology make the decisions for them. Notice how this rationalization
proletarianizes and deprofessionalizes the work of physicians. In other words,
medical doctors surrender the power to control their own profession to the ration-
alizing structures of modernism. Even high-status professions feel the deskilling
pressures exerted by developing technologies (Aronowitz, 1992; Ritzer, 1993). In
the late 1990s in New York and California, the unionization of medical doctors
began—unthinkable only a few years ago. We spoke with a medical doctor in New
York who told us that he favored unionization—despite his membership in the
Republican party—because he did not want medicine "to become like teaching."
In other words, he could foresee lower wages and a loss of autonomy for physicians if the deprofessionalization trends continued unabated.

Developments of the last twenty-five years challenge the assumption that service and information jobs require higher skills than industrial jobs. When service
and information workers see their work divided into deskilled separate tasks, they
understand that it has been debased. Good service work has devolved into industrial
services. Simple, uninteresting, repetitive tasks performed in an office amount to the
same bad work as simple, uninteresting, repetitive tasks performed in a factory.
Moreover, bad work in the services can have dramatic consequences, as alienated
nurses and hospital workers, for example, have been known to tease, torture and
even kill their patients. The low pay service and information jobs offer reflects this
bad work; in fact, a majority of these jobs fall within the low-level wage segment of
the labor market. Indeed, nowadays white-collar work may not be better paid, more
prestigious or require more intellect than blue-collar work (Harris, 1981).

As the old stereotypes about white- and blue-collar work crumble, the matter
becomes further complicated in the upskilling taking place in the blue-collar labor
market. Many labor analysts notice a marked difference between the automation
of 1950s and the automation of the 1990s. In the 1950s, machines introduced
into industry entailed major investments and contributed mainly rigid functions to
Fordist forms of mass production. The automation of the 1990s generally has involved computer innovations that accommodate changes in the production

process. Such flexibility nicely matches automation and brief, small-batch production. When industries become computer-automated they can achieve highly flexible, continuous-process production, which allows them to transform raw materials into finished products without any human ever touching the product. Workers in such situations become involved in the supervision and maintenance of production equipment rather than in the physical transformation of raw materials. Thus demand for labor lessens, and the role of labor changes.

Industrial workers in newly automated plants find themselves in new roles with new demands. For example, they find their skill depth reduced and their skill breadth expanded ("skill depth" refers to the time it takes to master a specific task; "skill breadth" refers to the diverse types of understandings and skills workers need to perform effectively). New technologies that promote flexibility reduce skill depth because workers no longer work directly with production; the hands-on knowledge they have accumulated over time becomes useless. Their skill breadth expands as jobs become interdependent with one job marked by a variety of assignments. Because of the nature of the machinery and the demands of continuous-process production, errors become increasingly expensive. In such a workplace, one small employee error can ruin the entire product run, with automatic equipment turning out thousands of flawed products before anybody sees it. The workers who attend these machines must understand the nature of the process in great specificity and detail; thus, their work demands upskilling.

When workers must oversee numerically controlled machines—computer-driven machinery programmed to operate either individually or in groups—they may experience long and frustrating periods of inactivity before they do anything at all. Even though skill demands may be high, the work is typically boring and unsatisfying. Those who work with numerically controlled equipment often ask for computer programming work in an attempt to ease the boredom. In fact, a few companies encourage their operators to do their own programming, a "pastime" that significantly increases their skill breadth. Currently, however, only about one in five machine operators has been taught to program; until the majority of numerically controlled machine operators gain this skill, we can expect to see these workers suffering from boredom and alienation. In similar situations in Japanese industry, machine operators make continual programming alterations and are expected to write new computer programs for all aspects of the workplace. Japanese analysts refer to these workers as "highly skilled engineers with multifunctional responsibilities." Moreover, Japanese firms devote three times more attention to upgrading employee skills than do American companies.

The introduction of robotics into the workplace also affects the nature of work dramatically. As robotics substantially decreases the need for workers, it increases the skill levels of the remaining laborers. As with numerically controlled machines, workers must learn to repair and maintain the robots. Accordingly, most of the jobs created in robot-driven industries figure to require highly skilled workers and most of the new positions will require at least two years of higher education. Like workers in charge of numerically controlled machines, workers in charge of robotics experience long periods of inactivity and boredom despite their skills. As employers, unions and vocational educators strive to establish good work, they must remember that a high-tech workplace carries no guarantee that highly skilled work will be interesting. High skills are often matched by more stress and increased boredom (Block, 1990).

To those who would predict the future of work, automation and technological development present numerous and dramatic challenges. Educators committed to the principles of good work and economic justice must understand the complexities and ambiguities inherent in the emerging workplace. The competing workplace values embodied in Fordism and post-Fordism complicate all general pronouncements, and the competing trends within post-Fordism add to the ambiguity. The ideal of good work serves as a beacon as we navigate troubled waters on our way to a calm and bright future. Without ethical guidance, we could lose our way and forget that we achieve productivity growth and rising GNPs in a human context. Our students deserve an education that addresses these ethical questions and equips them with a philosophical, historical and sociological understanding of education.

THE BUCK STOPS OVER THERE: RESHAPING THE WORKPLACE

No matter what future economic projections indicate, the current message from American business is perfectly clear: American productivity has fallen because American workers offer inadequate skills. Millions of Americans accept this declaration and build their political lives around the assumption of worker incompetence, yet it does not reflect the perspective of those outside the small circle of power. It seems clear that the major business decisions of recent decades have served the interests of the nation far less well than any alleged worker incompetence. Failing to recognize the need to reshape the workplace so as to empower workers, managers have perpetuated bad work with its low skill expectations and top-down administration. Such managerial methods dramatically lower incentives; combined with a reluctance to embrace long-term global views of markets, they account by themselves for foundering American business (DeYoung; Goodlad, 1992; Kolberg & Smith, 1992).

Businesses have ignored the calls for workplace democracy, the calls to form worker councils that might help implement plans for workplace reorganization, and the calls for a commitment to high-skill jobs. In general, American firms refuse to admit that they could better use the talents and skills their workers already possess. *America's Choice: High Skills or Low Wages,* a 1990 report prepared by the Commission on Skills of the American Workforce, found that only one in twenty U.S. firms had attempted to reorganize work to place a premium on high worker skills. A study by Towers Perrin and the Hudson Institute, also in 1990, indicated that only 13 percent of U.S. firms had ever tried self-managed work groups. Most companies (86 percent) refuse to teach academic skills at work, and a majority of managers admit that what they really want is a low-skill, obedient workforce that accepts hierarchical organization. At the dawn of a new century, most business leaders still consider frontline workers incapable of playing a role in making firms more profitable. Despite the post-Fordist trend toward high-tech skill upgrades, low-skill jobs continue to proliferate, a fact that democratic educators cannot accept (Kolberg & Smith, 1992; Roditi, 1992; DeYoung, 1989; Weisman, 1991; Block, 1990).

In this debate over the future of the workplace, one can easily hear the voice of the neoclassical economists. Neoclassicists contend that the available skills determine the nature of the labor market—that is, the types of jobs avaliable and the way the workplace is arranged. In this context, these economists argue that better jobs result from simply increasing educational opportunities. Rejecting this formula, Barry Bluestone argued that low wages and bad work result from entrapment in bad jobs. Provided an opportunity to work in high-wage jobs, most of these workers would succeed. In a large percentage of cases, Bluestone concluded, workers in low-skill jobs can perform well even without years of extra education, massive infusions of job training or indoctrination into some new "industrial discipline" program (DeYoung, 1989).

Despite the insights of economists such as Bluestone, the neoclassicist position still dominates the debate over the school's relationship to the economy. The folk wisdom of the 1990s tells us that bad work results from ill-trained employees whose incompetence undermines America's ability to compete internationally. High-skill jobs, the tale continues, become available only when the schools produce highly skilled laborers. Ever since the National Commission on Excellence in Education published its jeremiad *A Nation at Risk* in 1983, the neoclassicist argument that we needed educational improvements to maintain our slim competitive edge in world markets has been the accepted dogma (Weisman, 1991).

Critics counter that a more realistic assessment positions schools as a convenient target for corporate leaders who have mismanaged the economy in much the same way they did in the 1920s and 1930s. Just as educational scholars began to see how corporate America had undermined and withdrawn educational and economic opportunity for the disadvantaged, the critics continue, corporate leaders attacked the schools—a diversionary tactic of the highest and most cynical order (DeYoung, 1989).

The corporate attack on schools obviously ignored the way cultural factors influence the performances of marginalized students. Focusing instead on a supposed lack of rigor and discipline, the corporate rhetoric suggested that if academic standards were raised, the national economy would prosper. If SAT scores went up, they concluded, we could expect higher productivity and a stronger economy; if they went down, the reverse would occur.

The problem with this portrayal is that the National Commission on Excellence in Education and other advocates of the orthodoxy offer no proof. Little if any evidence suggests that schools alone can solve the riddles of international trade and economic development. They offer selective evidence for the failure of our public schools but no real proof of a connection between academic failure and economic decline. For example, can the schools be blamed for the decision of U.S. automobile manufacturers to continue producing cars with low gas mileage until they lost their domination of the car market? Did poor teaching keep American industry from automating until European and Asian manufacturers had acquired a large share of the world market? Should schools assume the sole blame for economic problems like these (Goodlad, 1992; Spring, 1984; Weisman, 1991)? Likewise, should schools and teachers be given the credit for the strong American economy in the late 1990s while Asian markets collapsed—despite low test scores by American students compared to Asian competitors? Do we dare conclude that low SAT scores fueled the economic prosperity of wealthy Americans and U.S. corporations in 1998? Again, we concluded that there is not a simple and direct correspondance between test scores and economic conditions. The economic context is much more complex.

Absent a direct relationship between the failure of schooling and economic development, the educational reform movement of the 1980s and 1990s must have been misguided. By absolving corporate and industrial leaders of responsibility, the advocates of orthodoxy have established U.S. schools as scapegoats for private sector mismanagement. The time has come to redesign educational reform with advice from educators, labor unions and advocates of a progressive view of good work sharing influence with business and industry.

Everyone, of course, welcomes enlightened school reform. The crucial point, however, is that business, labor and education must all change if we expect to address American economic, educational and social problems seriously. Moreover, friends of good work cannot allow powerful groups to paint an unrealistic portrait of the respective roles of schools and business in the shaping of American economic life. Few issues illustrate the way power shapes public conversations and public policies better than the current attempt to blame schools for our broad, multifaceted socioeconomic problems. With their campaigns financed by corporate interests, many politicians project the illusion of aggressive action against economic decline by advocating educational reform; invariably they ignore workplace reorganization. Thus, their cozy financial relationships with the powerful corporate lobbies remain undisturbed and the status quo is preserved, a status quo marked by too much bad work (Weisman, 1991).

DEVELOPING EDUCATION THAT CHALLENGES BAD WORK

Throughout this book we introduce you to the sociological, historical and philosophical factors that either undermine or support attempts to create a democratic pedagogy. By understanding the modernist context that gave us scientific management and bad work we can start to make sense of the problems, the successes and the roles education plays in both schooling and the larger society. In the modernist, scientifically managed organization, the driving tripartite dogma is managing, organizing and controlling. Human resources—that is, workers—are treated as components of a physical system (Senge, 1990). Accordingly, dehumanization can take place to the degree that a worker's well-being can safely be ignored (Wirth, 1983). Operating under such precepts, corporate power brokers look to the schools to perform this specific function: to prepare children for an unchanging world in which passivity and unquestioning acceptance of the scientifically managed workplace is necessary (Nelson & Watras, 1981).

John Dewey and his progressive colleague Boyd Bode specifically rejected the general scientific management mind-set and its perspective on the role of schooling. Bode, for example, wrote in 1927 that scientific management missed the point when its proponents contended that progress came from doing the same things more efficiently. Progress, Bode wrote, came from creating a new vision. More than seventy years later, we still see the personnel management descendants of Taylor and his efficiency corps deferring Bode's vision.

Dewey argued that scientific management undermines social imagination and even thinking itself. Workers would have understood what Dewey was saying if they had enjoyed access to his writing. They experienced, as have their descendants, the banishment of thought and creativity from their daily work. We think of our friend Don who is a retired disabled worker from an automobile manufacturing plant in Michigan. Don is a jovial man in his late forties with two teenage children. He began working on the assembly line after high school. Don read and studied Christian scriptures in his spare time and became a deacon in his church at age thirty. Over the years he taught himself three foreign languages, including Japanese so that he could attend an automobile seminar in Japan. Don plays the piano and loves all kinds of music. Over the years Don has coached many sports teams for his two sons. In short, Don is a typical and friendly middle class American. However, when he talks to us about his experiences in automobile manufacturing, he becomes livid and incensed. First, he reports that managers constantly watched him and pressured him to work faster. Even his bathroom breaks were timed. As he got older it became increasingly difficult to perform the heavy labor, especially when he began to develop muscle spasms. Second, he complains about the monotonous routine that allowed for little creativity or communication with fellow workers on the line. And finally, he becomes most enraged when he talks about management practices of relocating employees and redistributing job assignments. As a Deacon in his church, Don often ministered to the families of coworkers. He baptized their babies, married their children, buried their parents. Whenever management noticed that the employees were fraternizing or socializing, even for religious reasons, people would mysteriously be reassigned to a different shift or a different task. In one particularly offensive move, Don reports that the company built a new facility in the same community and divided the workers in half. He described this process as "divide and conquer," a management tool to diffuse collaboration and solidarity. Today, Don's disability is more emotional than physical. Yes, he has arthritis that slowed his work. But the emotional scars of psychological pressure to perform beyond his physical capacity and the years of manipulation of relationships exacted a heavy toll. Don visits regularly with a psychiatrist and a medical doctor, but he does not collect disability pay. The company forced him into early retirement at reduced benefits. We see too many bitter and broken workers like Don, and many of them in schools as well. Teachers face the same problems described by Don. They are disconnected from coworkers and isolated in their classrooms. Teachers lack the opportunity to influence their work environment since most decisions are made by administrators, school boards or state legislators. They also face intense pressure to produce high test scores and disciplined (i.e., quiet and complaint) classrooms in environments that are often unsafe or overcrowded where basic materials and supplies are inadequate. Even their bathroom breaks are regulated.

The memory of how American workers have been underutilized and marginalized can help current educators in the struggle for good work, and more specifically in the effort to shift responsibility for planning and executing work to the place where work is actually performed (Wirth, 1983). In such a struggle educators, guided by their vision of good work, can discover the hidden abilities and the creative potential their students possess (Alvesson & Willmott, 1992). At the same time, they make visible the possibilities for alternatives democratic workplaces create.

THE DEMOCRATIC POST-FORDIST WORKPLACE AND THE DEBATE OVER THE CHANGING PURPOSE OF EDUCATION

As the context now shaped by technology and the politics of the corporation becomes clearer, the need for an alternative vision of a democratic post-Fordist workplace and a progressive democratic education also presents itself. Only by constructing an evolving idea of good work can Americans begin to reclaim the power to rebuild a humane public domain. The democratic precepts of good work and a critical form of teaching provide the bases for our perspective and the criteria for our judgment. As always, we take democracy seriously.

The neoclassical view of the "workplace of the future" is a happy and cooperative place free from unions or worker organization. This Disneyesque view both holds out false hope and places the workers (especially the peripheral workers) in great jeopardy. Any workplace arrangement that ignores the power of technology and the politics of the corporation in a post-Fordist or a Fordist economy undermines the interests of students and workers. Thus, even if democratic educators turn out thoughtful, creative and highly skilled workers, good jobs for them will remain elusive until those workers understand the dynamics of workplace power. Any democratic economic movement must provide working people with a more equitable share of corporate and business profits. Worksites must become safer, less authoritarian and more hospitable spaces, with workers playing major roles in their everyday administration. In such places, jobs can be evaluated not only for their material rewards but also for the opportunities they provide for people to develop their knowledge and skills (Carnevale, 1992; Bluestone & Harrison, 1982; Simon, Dippo & Schenke, 1991).

In a democratic post-Fordist workplace, skilled workers are rewarded for acquiring knowledge and skills related to the functioning of the larger operation. The degree to which an industry is democratic depends on what percentage of its workers are included in these high-skill, high-compensation dynamics (Grossberg, 1992). When we view skills, performance and initiative as *social events*, a new type of thinking begins to transform the workplace and our understanding of cognition. In *Toil and Trouble: Good Work, Smart Workers, and the Integration of Academic and Vocational Education*, Kincheloe analyzed this new form of worker cognition and called it "post-formal thinking" (Kincheloe & Steinberg, 1993). Such thinking entails an ability to understand the origins and contexts of systems, while at the same time identifying patterns that characterize by first refining new forms of analysis. Democratic post-Fordist businesses and industries become post-formal learning organizations marked by a generative form of learning that catalyzes the ability to create (Senge, 1990).

The democratic post-Fordist learning organization cultivates employees' abilities to identify and solve problems. Acting on the information and insight workers provide, post-Fordist learning organizations come to regard their skills and knowledge as the most important dynamic in the production of wealth. Frederick Taylor's unyielding dictates of one person at the top of the organizational hierarchy discerning what to do and then making sure everyone else does it becomes obsolete. When learning takes place at all levels, a firm can develop a shared vision of its purpose. However, such an enterprise requires that management take the workers' knowledge of design and production matters into account. When managers take the workers seriously, they soon appreciate the value of worker autonomy. Deskilling steps aside for "multiskilling," as leaders recognize the underutilization of the workers' insights as a major organizational mistake.

A sacred view of work now develops that perceives the achievement of material affluence as merely one of many organizational goals. Individual learning and development and other "intrinsic" benefits become increasingly important in the democratic post-Fordist workplace (Block, 1990; Senge, 1990; Kolberg & Smith, 1992; Rumberger, 1984).

THE CONTINUING DEBATE: *TRAINING* FOR WORK VERSUS *EDUCATION* FOR WORK

Since the late nineteenth century a debate has raged between advocates of work preparation as a form of technical training and advocates of work preparation as a form of democratic education. Unfortunately the debate remains unsettled as America moves into an era of changing economic arrangements. The training argument, led by the progeny of David Snedden, has changed somewhat in light of a need for more flexible post-Fordist workers; while the means of production have advanced technologically, however, the purpose of work training remains faithful to a perceived need to regulate workers so that they can be fitted to the needs of the workplace (Copa & Tebbenhoff, 1990). Still dedicated to the attempt to train students for entry-level employment, training proponents rarely express interest in the goals of higher-order thinking or creativity. Trapped in the modernist mindset that fragments skills into a neat series of subskills, trainers ignore the production of meaning (Brosio, 1994; Block, 1995).

A teacher who believes that "a creative mind is a flawed mind" finds little value in studying the social foundations of education. Nevertheless, throughout the history of American education, we have focused more on teaching obedience and compliance than on nurturing craft orientations and analytical abilities. Whereas work training values imitation, a democratic education values inventiveness; whereas work training seeks technical proficiency, a democratic education seeks intelligence. As John Dewey argued at the beginning of the twentieth century, work education does not simply teach skills; such an education also involves inquiring into which values are worthwhile and should be pursued.

Only in the context Dewey promulgated can we develop a democratic education that encourages and nurtures the potential of every student. As students come to understand the nature and conditions of work, they gain the ability to shape their own personal agendas. In the process, they learn to protect themselves from the corporate public relations specialists who all too often induce them to act against their own best interests. Teachers who understand the economic context in which schools operate can begin to fight the battle to enlist schools in the larger struggle to rescue the faltering American democracy (DeVore, 1983; Marshak, 1993; Lakes, 1985; Nelson & Watras, 1981; Rehm, 1989; Steinberg & Kincheloe, 1997).

Empowering Teachers

INTRODUCTION

At the end of the twentieth century American teachers find themselves in a society increasingly marked by disempowerment—that is, a society increasingly shaped by powerful interest groups. In this context knowledge has become an important source of influence, as groups gain the capacity to dominate others by dictating what constitutes valid knowledge. Experts in various fields pronounce upon everything from "healthy" child-rearing practices and "proper" family values to the nature of social deviance and acceptable sexual behavior. Widespread acquiescence in this trend disempowers individuals, since it forces them to defer to and rely on the advice of experts with increasing frequency. Such a social setting compels educators to pursue strategies of empowerment more than ever. Always mindful of teachers' potential to change lives, we must guard against the forces of oppression: modernist positivism and the tyranny of its experts, wielders of economic power with their self-centered educational agendas, and political leaders indebted to their wealthy patrons who, as we have seen, fear a well-financed independent educational system.

In this contemporary era, teachers are disempowered less by the threat of force and violence than by our consent to domination. As Antonio Gramsci (1971), an Italian social theorist, observed as a prisoner in a fascist prison decades ago, this domination based on the consent of the citizens is called *hegemony*. The organization of consent is a complex task that takes place in everyday life. Powerful groups win public consent by way of a pedagogical or educational process, a form of learning that takes place at the cultural level and transforms people's conceptions of the world so as to bring them into conformity with elite interests. For example, when the public becomes persuaded that current U.S. schools and teachers are weaker than those of a romanticized past, one can build the case that education should return to a nineteenth-century–style drill, memorize and recite methodology. Such rote-based schooling serves the power elites in that it removes students from the world outside the school. Focusing on the repetition of what teachers tell them, students become less likely to learn the critical thinking skills democratic citizenship requires. Without knowledge of the way the world actually works or the skills of citizenship, students are more liable to accede to the demands of the status quo—they are, in short, more liable to become disempowered. Still, with the intervention of only one critical teacher and relying on the volition of students themselves, we can challenge the injustice of the status quo.

CONTEXTUALIZING THE DECLINE OF PERSONAL AUTHORITY

The American public senses that a process of disempowerment has taken hold in the last third of the twentieth century. It understands the weakening of the democratic notion that social institutions should revolve around the ethical idea that, regardless of social position, every human being counts. Whether in the workplace, a government agency or the school, Americans are uncomfortable with the narrow and increasingly exclusive ways such institutions are organized. In the declining post-Fordist economy, and noting the anger of the American public on the increase, organizational leaders began to speak the language of empowerment and develop programs that promised democratized institutions. For example, managers initiated cynical quality of working life (QWL) programs meant to give the impression that workers are invited to become full participants in management decision making. In his book *Empty Promises: Quality of Working Life Programs and the Labor Movement* Donald M. Wells (1987) exposed the true interests of QWL programs: Given the economic threats from such emerging industrial giants as Japan, American industry had to find new ways to remain competitive. Management realized that the goal demanded massive investment. To protect their profit margins (and their own exorbitant salaries) managers grew desperate to increase productivity and had to squeeze their workers harder than ever. Thus, they concluded that they needed more control over workers and more power over the conceptualization of how workers do their jobs. It was not enough to *make* workers obey; through QWL programs management became hegemonic—that is, it induced workers to *want* to obey.

Engaged in programs that seemed to grant them decision-making power in the workplace, workers came to trust the pronouncements of business owners. Through QWL managers hoped to produce enthusiastic workers who would unleash those creative capacities managerial control had traditionally crushed. Granted more autonomy to make small, inconsequential decisions on shop floors, workers would become less inclined to demand more voice in the larger production decisions. Workers imbued with a sense of self-direction would be less liable to press collective bargaining demands. In the early 1980s executives at General Motors circulated a confidential memo encouraging plant managers to use QWL programs to convince workers that their demands threatened the health of the company. In short, workers were being induced to accept an empowerment plan that would undermine their best interests while appearing to involve them in a more democratic workplace.

One can learn important lessons here. Workers, teachers and citizens in general must become aware of the ways managers can use democratic and empowerment rhetoric to secure undemocratic, nonparticipatory ends. If, for example, one wants to address worker alienation seriously, one must grant employees genuine influence over the control of the workplace. Workers must be true partners in the formulation of policies of personnel selection and training, product design, the use of new technologies and the scheduling of production. Empowerment for educators entails similar goals as teachers attempt to control the educational workplace.

THE PSEUDOEMPOWERMENT OF TEACHERS

In the positivist-grounded quest for enhanced measurable educational productivity, teachers' work has increasingly became controlled from above. Public perceptions of teacher incompetence, like public perceptions of worker incompetence, justify those educational managers who are engaged in an increasing teacher deskilling process. Teacher education has often neglected those traditional teacher skills that include a knowledge of academic subject matter, an understanding of a variety of child development theories, an appreciation of the social context in which education takes place, an acquaintance with the relationship between educational purpose and the needs of a democratic society and an overview of the social goals education has historically been expected to accomplish. Colleges of education often emphasize the technique of teaching, focusing on the inculcation of the "best method" for delivering a body of predetermined facts and the familiarization of teachers with the "proper format" for lesson plans, which enhances supervision efficiency and thus invites stricter accountability. Just as the technicalization of the workplace deskilled workers by making them appendages to their machines, teacher deskilling ties teachers to prepackaged curricular materials and the teacher-proof materials we discussed in Chapter 2 and will explore in more detail in Chapter 10. Traditional teacher skills seem unnecessary in this situation, for all the conception and planning goes on far away from the school and the unique students it accommodates. Thus, teachers relinquish control of the teaching act, and teaching becomes disconnected, alienating work.

For a moment, compare the world of teaching and its workplace to a so-called "Third World"—developing nations—culture with hierarchical power structures, scarce resources, traditional values and teachers as the disenfranchised peasants (Oldroyd, 1985). If we accept this comparison, the work of Paulo Freire (1970) becomes relevant to our attempt to make teaching good work. Like the developing nation's peasantry, teachers are preoccupied with daily survival; time for reflection and analysis becomes elusive and even irrelevant, given the crisis-management atmosphere and the immediate attention survival demands. In such a climate, those who suggest that more time and resources be delegated to reflective and growth-inducing pursuits are impractical, meddlesome and devoid of common sense. Thus the status quo is perpetuated, the endless cycle of underdevelopment rolls on, and its peasant culture with its low morale merely "reacts" to daily emergencies. Visualize the modern teacher as the plate juggler on a television variety show, frantically running from plate to plate, keeping each one spinning atop a stick, unable to pause long enough to reflect on the purpose of the enterprise. Time to reflect might be dangerous: Why juggle plates in the first place? Current academic analysts tend to avoid such basic questions, researchers prepare their research for other researchers, and the teacher is a separate species, to be studied objectively.

In the sphere of higher education, total quality management (TQM) recently became the "empowerment technique" administrators use to appear to increase the autonomy and self-direction of educators. To read the TQM literature is to immerse oneself in images of humane administration based on collaboration and power sharing. Yet on closer examination, one senses a troubling emphasis on conformity and consensus that borders on the tyrannical. "Quality" becomes a synonym for a lack of variation among practitioners. Those who reject the viewpoint of the majority are not "team players." Assumed within the TQM mind-set is that educational institutions are culturally homogeneous and that everyone agrees on an objective set of values that shape schools and the knowledge they transmit; little room exists here for the production or questioning of knowledge. Assuming for itself the mantle of neutrality and objectivity, TQM ignores the new paradigm's call to reconsider such concepts. Using familiar traditonal measures of excellence, TQM rewards teaching and leadership styles that conform to positivist models of knowledge production. The empowerment derived from TQM models depends on a practitioner willing to surrender to the values and mind-sets of those in leadership positions (Bensimon, 1994).

Even as administrators mouth the TQM language of empowerment, autonomy and self-direction, state boards of education and local school districts impose policy after restrictive policy. Shielded from public scrutiny by the centralized control emanating from official state and local agencies, "reform measures" specify what to teach and how to teach it, as well as what constitutes student and teacher competence. With such specification, teaching becomes more technical and less autonomous—in short, more deskilled. Such hierarchical domination can occur only when we assume teachers to be expendable laborers or members of a craft culture rather than a profession. The logic of such reform posits that we must replace the undervalued intuitive knowledge of these "teachers as craftspeople" with research-based algorithmic teaching strategies (Porter, 1988; Elliot, 1989). One of the many flaws in the logic of this hierarchical reform involves the genesis of the so-called "research-based knowledge," often verified by a snapshot of the complex, highly contextualized classroom. Positivist researchers observe for brief periods and administer simplistic or arcane tests to measure student progress. The focus is far too limited, the observation much too short, and the results ignore context but purport to explain the dynamics of the classroom and go on to prescribe generalizable procedures for effective teaching.

Thus, schools and teachers fall prey to the positivistic syndrome of overmanagement. School leaders fail to see educational problems as teachers do and thereby foster policies far removed from the daily world of teaching and learning. Such policies are notoriously insensitive to the reasons teachers underachieve and withdraw from student engagement. Typical of such a situation is the implementation of the infamous time-on-task research in American schools. Empirical research showed, not surprisingly, that when the time students spend on a particular subject increases, their standardized test scores on that subject also increase. Accordingly, principals and supervisors seek to control teacher work time to ensure that they teach directly to specific objectives. Not surprisingly, they excluded teachers from the process of negotiating the policy implications. The teachers' perspectives on the loss of classroom autonomy, the loss of their freedom to assess the level of student understanding and the need to adjust the pace of instruction were irrelevant in policy making. Overmanagement separated educational policy and the lived world of the classroom (McCutcheon, 1981).

Thus are teachers manipulated and infantilized by positivist notions of management. They find themselves socialized into school cultures too often interested in neither their students nor democratic principles. In these cultures "belongingness" becomes irrelevant, as teachers find themselves silenced. In such a context disempowered teaching methods develop around concepts of top-down management, assumptions of neutral knowledge and fragmented conceptions of educational evaluation. Just how these assumptions infected American schools is a fascinating aspect of educational history in the last half of the twentieth century. As we trace it below you should begin to understand the institutionalization of teacher disempowerment better; armed with an understanding of the forces that have shaped disempowerment, we will all be better equipped to restore dignity to the teaching profession.

Unanticipated Disempowerment: Well-Intentioned Legislation and Positivist Evaluation

In the mid–1960s public sentiment generally supported social and educational reforms designed to fight the poverty that had existed in America for so long. Under the leadership of President Lyndon Johnson, the Great Society initiative delegated funds to a variety of social programs. Before Congress would appropriate funds for educational programs for economically disadvantaged students, however, its members demanded a rigid system of accountability. The resulting system reflected many of the assumptions of modernist positivism, and it continues to exert a major influence on educational policy and the role of teachers. Reflecting systems analysis and cost-benefit analysis techniques used by the Pentagon and the military, the evaluation methods imposed a scientific realist view of knowledge characterized by fragmentation and decontextualization. We can hold responsible Senator Robert Kennedy for the accountability features that accompanied the new education programs designed to reduce the social disadvantages of the poor (compensatory programs). Kennedy demanded a scientific system of reporting the effects of the new programs. Economically disadvantaged parents, especially poor black parents, he argued, deserved access to the statistics on how their children were doing. He reasoned that these statistics (in the form of standardized test scores) would hold school officials accountable to their constituents. Though his well-intentioned purpose was to help economically poor students and their parents become informed participants in the educational process, Kennedy's plan was flawed by a positivist overemphasis on test scores.

This positivist sabotage of a well-intentioned program supplies a useful lesson on the failure of the modernist paradigm. The sabotage began in August 1965, when President Johnson introduced the planning, programming and budgeting system (PPBS) throughout the federal bureaucracy. In response, the Department of Health, Education and Welfare (HEW) established a new office, the assistant secretary for program evaluation, and then filled it with William Gorham, who had helped implement PPBS in the Department of Defense. With his assistants Alice Rivlin (who would later take Gorham's place) and Robert Grosse, Gorham attempted to develop goals that could be stated, measured and evaluated in cost-benefit terms. Gorham, Rivlin and Grosse were not particularly interested in Senator Kennedy's attempt to make the schools responsive to local parents. Rather, they viewed the evaluation problem as a research effort to identify *efficient* approaches to educating disadvantaged children (House, 1978). When Congress passed the Elementary and Secondary Education Act (ESEA), with all of its accountability provisions, in 1964 Gorham, Rivlin and Grosse saw Title I, which emerged from it, as a "natural experiment" for identifying the most effective teaching methods. These "best methods" would be passed on to teachers and administrators so that resources could be allocated efficiently. They would remedy teachers' ignorance of "what works"; scientific research would provide the positive knowledge needed to improve teaching.

But problems emerged. Even though the systems analysts had been able to require an evaluation stipulation for all subsequent social and educational legislation, they found educators poorly equipped to provide the uniform data to complete the cost-benefit analysis procedures necessary to determine which programs worked efficiently. Programs, the systems analysts argued, would have to be arranged in a way that would facilitate evaluation. In response, state after state adopted reform movements that incorporated positivistic systems analysis-based assumptions about educational evaluation, knowledge and research.

Alice Rivlin soon emerged as the dominant theoretician and spokesperson for the systems analysts. In 1971 she enunciated her assumptions about social and educational research in *Systematic Thinking for Social Action*. Before any policy-producing research can take place, Rivlin argued, educational experts must identify the objectives of education. Such a pronouncement resembles the accountant's advice on how to become a millionaire who pays no taxes: First, get a million dollars. The deep differences over educational goals that were dividing the public and educators went ignored with Rivlin guided by the assumption that the social consensus over what schools should do would allow educational experts to dictate educational objectives. "I believe there is a wide measure of agreement in the nation . . . about desirable directions of change," Rivlin wrote (pp. 46–47). Differences between the right, the middle, and the left over social and educational policies remain extraneous to the objectives of such policies. Rivlin and her systems analyst colleagues ignored a world in which different groups compete for power and resources. They saw the educational interests of rich and poor, management and labor, black and white, men and women as basically the same. The historical and contextual natures of social scientific knowledge passed beyond Alice Rivlin's understanding (Rivlin, 1971).

The important goals of education are both easily identified, and can be measured, Rivlin claimed. Standardized test scores accurately reflect reading proficiency, mathematical competencies and acquired knowledge in various other subjects. Thus, she reasoned, one should "focus on these measurable outcomes" and how best to produce them. Goals are already determined, she argued, so we should turn our attention to the identification of the most efficient methods of improving our scores. When faced with the failure in 1968 and 1969 of her early evaluation studies to detect a cause-and-effect relationship between educational policies and test score improvement, Rivlin clung to her attempt to identify efficient methods. The problem, she argued, was that social services and education were not organized to answer properly questions of methodological efficiency. That, she concluded, would have to change (House, 1978).

Indeed, the goals of evaluation did begin to change. Once evaluations had been designed to measure the success of programs; now the programs were designed to ensure the success of the evaluations. In the process, Rivlin called for more government control over all aspects of the programs, design through evaluation. Teachers, she reasoned, possessed too little expertise to produce efficient and effective products. Ignorance of productive techniques and methodologies explained the difficulty of delivering a good education. Experts were charged with the task of establishing a "production function"—that is, the identification of a functional relationship between resources employed and results produced. "Stable relationships," Rivlin wrote, "exist between these outcomes and the 'inputs' to the educational process: different types of teachers, facilities, equipment, curriculum and teaching methods" (1971, p. 70). Just as the engineer sought regular relationships between inputs and outputs, Rivlin's social researcher would seek similar associations in the world of education. The knowledge of education produced would be certain because it would be verifiable.

Note Alice Rivlin's use of physical scientific and manufacturing analogies. She viewed educational methods and children in the same way she viewed raw materials in manufacturing. The analyst would arrange the methods and the children in various combinations, trying to ascertain the grouping that provided the best output. The best output in the manufacturing process was the product; in education it was the test score. The Pentagon origins of these systems analysis methods remained in the expression heard frequently in HEW during the late 1960s: "We want the biggest bang for the buck" (Rivlin, 1971). What was good for missile systems and manufacturing was also good for social services and education. Immersed in the positivist view of knowledge the "Pentagon boys" followed, Rivlin found it difficult to understand the mind of the educator. Some of the educators she met were "frightened by words like 'input' and 'output production function.'" School people simply did not understand the necessity of good recordkeeping, she complained, and without that it is impossible to make sense of standardized test results. Rivlin's efforts to institute national standardized testing met with "illogical" resistance. "National testing," she reported in frustration, "is a bugaboo of school people." She appealed to "common sense." Surely we can measure our success in a logical way, Rivlin wrote. We can take into account changes in test scores, drop-out rates, attitudes and so forth and use our data to determine connections between success and the methods employed. "It seemed logical," Rivlin recollected, and most people agreed.

Rivlin applied herself to studying the Title I programs, but the data the schools submitted to federal evaluators proved to be too scanty and imprecise. It was not merely that the nature of the programs resisted evaluation but, as Ernest House (1978) argued, the *world* was not organized properly to yield convenient information about production functions. It was too complex, too messy to allow for precise identification of cause-and-effect relationships; it was too ambiguous, too contradictory to allow for positive knowledge. Such realities, however, hardly deterred Rivlin. The problem, she argued, was not with their paradigm, not with the foundations on which her research and evaluation rested. Rather, the problem was with the design of the Title I programs. Even with more rigorous evaluation methods, Rivlin maintained, experts would still face gaps that would limit what they could learn about the programs. To yield useful evaluation data the programs would have to be designed more scientifically. As it was, she saw no experimental design and no control groups. School people, Rivlin continued, made "no attempt to define promising methods or approaches and try them out in enough places to test their operation under different conditions." School people would have to learn the techniques of the physical scientific laboratory (1971, pp. 83–84).

Rivlin saw no alternative to designing social and educational programs as laboratory experiments; that was the only way to gather the information necessary to improve the effectiveness of social and educational service. The physical science approach would work, she thought. All one had to do was delineate the treatment precisely and then control all extraneous influences. The knowledge Rivlin hoped to produce would enable social scientists to duplicate conditions and reproduce results. Thus, educational events could be predicted and controlled in the way positivist science demanded. Control would be centralized in the hands of federal bureaucratic agencies. Educational laboratory experiments (Rivlin called them "systematic innovations") would not happen spontaneously. An experimental strategy would take careful planning, research-based organization and adequate funding formulae devised by a cadre of federal experts. Worshipping at the shrine of the expert, Rivlin wanted empirically trained bureaucrats to design curricula, teacher training methods and teacher recruitment policies. The voices of individual teachers would be silenced. The implementation of these policies obviously required decision-making centralization, and Rivlin believed that America was achieving that goal in the last half of the twentieth century. State governments were attaining more and more control over local schools and big-city school systems were sufficiently centralized to carry out systematic innovation on a major scale. It would take little prodding, Rivlin wrote, to encourage a success-oriented school superintendent to engage in systematic innovation, but once provided with the "best new ideas in curriculum and approaches," he or she would "map out a plan for trying the most promising ideas in a systematic way in his or her own system. . . . Why does it not happen this way?" Rivlin wondered (1971, pp. 92–93).

Alice Rivlin admitted that such centralization could result in bureaucratic red tape and rigidity. But there were ways to avoid these problems. Accountability procedures must not focus on compliance with inputs—for example, teaching methods, curricular arrangements and detailed guidelines. Rather, evaluators must focus their research on outputs—for example, standardized test scores, drop-out rates and school attendance statistics. Federal grant monies could be used to reward those systems that improved and increased measurable outcomes. School leaders could be rewarded just like plant managers in large corporations whose promotions depend on sales and profits.

Rivlin's faith in positivistic research methods and conceptions of knowledge has had profound implications for all concerned with democratic teaching. Educational experts from the systems analyst school seek to impose research-based techniques on teachers in place of the knowledge of teaching that derives from experience, apprenticeship and the study of educational purpose. Such context-stripped research-based knowledge can hardly replace professional knowledge. Much of this professional knowledge is subtle and tacit rather than object and overt, and one can acquire it only after years of practice. From Alice Rivlin's positivistic perspective, such experiential knowledge is dangerous and misguided in that it diverts the teacher's attention from the validated generalizations produced by strict adherence to the rules of empirical and statistical research methods. But if teachers based their practice on the basis of validated generalizations about educational practice only, they would be paralyzed. That is not how human beings function. Teaching is like speaking; if a speaker were to rely on positivist research-produced generalizations about the rules of quality speaking he or she would be mute. Improvisation and the spontaneous insights and ideas that characterize the work of good teachers would disappear from this modernist positivist context. Teacher empowerment and self-direction would be defeated by such measures.

The centralization of decision-making power in the hands of educational experts reduces teachers to mere executors of the expert's conceptualization of the teaching act. Rivlin and her colleagues expressed little embarrassment over the autocratic, controlling features of their social science. Systems analyst Charles Schultze, who was later head of the Council of Economic Advisors in the Carter administration, wrote of the need to control local administrators and practitioners in order to secure their allegiance to the goals the experts set. Fidelity to the objectives of control would be guaranteed by including a set of incentives for those who complied and penalties for those who resisted.

Educator Arthur Wirth (1983) was uncomfortable with such control-oriented views of knowledge production and people processing. The positivist scientific tradition is inadequate for producing knowledge about education and human affairs, he argued. It treats human problems as if they can be solved by only "the one right way" a rigorous application of physical science techniques provides. When positivism and its view of knowledge veer off toward an inquiry into human life, the main interest becomes the identification of the natural laws of human behavior. Once he or she identifies these laws, the positivist uses them to predict and control. The result of Alice Rivlin's research orientation, Wirth reasoned, is to translate life and the world into a mathematical form. Can you sense something about human life deeply violated by such an outlook?

Henry Giroux (1988, 1992) and Michael Apple (1979, 1985, 1999) picked up where Wirth left off. Arguing that knowledge must be constantly challenged, redefined and negotiated by all participants in social and educational settings, teachers are counseled to resist the domination of the education experts. In order to resist, teachers (and their students) must gain the ability to analyze the truth the experts claim and to uncover the genesis of the knowledge that becomes official. To be critical, teachers must analyze how knowledge conceals or distorts the social, political and economic status quo.

Teachers in the critical new paradigm need to understand these dynamics to control their own professional lives and to gain and maintain psychological freedom from those entrenched forces with the means to produce and validate knowledge. Stanley Aronowitz and Henry Giroux (1985) adduced educator Chester Finn as an example of a political leader who employed positivist definitions to produce "uncontestable" knowledge about teaching and schooling. Finn (1982) argued that educators must use testing as a method to ensure quality in teaching. "Hesitant to pass judgment on lifestyles, cultures and forms of behavior," Finn wrote, "we have invited relativism into the curriculum and pedagogy" (p. 32). He demanded a set of absolute standards, which broke the ground for objective measurement. Finn echoed in the educational community the visions of Rivlin and Schultze: Let the experts determine the definition of quality and the goals of schooling.

As you know, the cult of the expert is alive and well as teachers continue to search for their voice in the educational workplace. Teaching practice remains for the moment commodified, prepackaged and mass distributed. Teachers, in turn, are expected to take the prepackaged knowledge of the various subjects and dish it out to passive students. If receptive, the students will become "culturally literate" and "vocationally competent."

JOHN DEWEY, EDUCATIONAL KNOWLEDGE AND TEACHER EMPOWERMENT

The educational results of applying positivist views of knowledge often prove unfortunate. Aronowitz and Giroux (1985) charged that Finn and his ilk had renounced the critical intents of knowledge acquisition and of education in general. This critical intent involves an understanding of who we are and the forces that have shaped us. It concerns the ability to *connect* the formal knowledge of schooling with the ever-changing conditions under which everyday life takes place. This ability to connect is central to the critical intent of education. The evaluation techniques Alice Rivlin's experimental programs required can hardly measure the student's or the teacher's ability to make these connections. The only knowledge they can measure are fragments of unrelated data, which by themselves grant us little insight into the nature of reality. To compare educational techniques efficiently, curricula must be standardized and focused on the measurable. By definition, the critical intent of knowledge acquisition cannot be included—it is much too imprecise and subject to individual variation. Rivlin and Finn treat as irrelevant the wisdom of John Dewey and his speculations on the nature of school knowledge. Consider a few of Dewey's speculations on school knowledge and their incompatibility with the fragmentation, context-stripping and personal disempowerment characteristic of the positivist position.

Long before the clichés became fashionable, Dewey (1859–1952) expressed impatience with what school reformers of the 1970s, 1980s and 1990s would call "knowledge of the basics," "knowledge that informs cultural literacy" or "the essential knowledge of the Western tradition." Of course, proponents of this knowledge refer to it as neutral and objective. Ideas about essential knowledge are hardly new; educators in Dewey's day made the same arguments. In 1916 Dewey wrote that in these essentialist conceptions knowledge is external to students—a body of facts they might store in a warehouse. They render study a process whereby one draws on what is in storage. Such a perspective misses an important point: The educational function of knowledge is to make one particular experience applicable to other life experiences. Dewey then distinguished between knowledge and habit. His distinction is important, for Dewey's description of habit sharpens our understanding of the type of knowledge taught in schools managed under the modernist positivist paradigm.

When learners form a habit, they gain the ability to use an experience so that they can take effective action whenever they face a similar situation. Habit formation has value, Dewey argued, for everyone faces similar situations in the process of living. A child who learns to solve long-division problems will certainly face such problems again and again. But habit is not enough; it makes no allowance for changing conditions or for novelty. An individual who learns a habit is unprepared for change and thus is vulnerable to confusion when faced with a previously unencountered problem. The habituated skill of the mechanic deserts him, Dewey wrote, when something unexpected occurs in the running of the machine. On the other hand, the person who *understands* the machine is the one who is empowered—that is, who knows what he or she is about. This mechanic understands the conditions that allow a certain habit to work and can initiate action that adapts the habit to new conditions. Notice that the type of teaching and the type of schools that engender this kind of thought are far different from the positivist schools that treat all knowledge as empirically measurable.

Dewey provided another example of the difference between habit and his definition of empowering knowledge. A so-called "primitive" group of humans watch a flaming comet streak across the sky. Frightened by the spectacle, they react to it as they react to other events that threaten their security: They try to scare it away as if it were a wild animal. They scream, beat gongs and brandish weapons. To people who understand astronomy and the contextualization it provides, the sighting of the comet and the actions of the group seem bizarre. From our astronomical vantage point, we recognize that the primitive observers revert to a cognitive habit that exhibits its limited ability to make meaning. We do not act the same way since we see the comet not as an isolated event but as part of a process. We see its connections with the astronomical system and, based on our *knowledge,* respond to its *connections* and not simply to its immediate occurrence. Knowledge based on connections, then, empowers us by providing a context in which we can consider a new experience.

To Dewey the *content* of knowledge is what has happened—that is, what is considered finished and settled. But the *reference* of knowledge, he argued, is the future. Knowledge in the Deweyan sense provides the means of understanding what is happening in the present and what can be done about it. This aspect of Dewey's theory of knowledge informs Aronowitz and Giroux's (1991) notion of the critical intent of education. It is, in their words, "the ability to connect contemporary experience to the received information that others have gained through their generalized experience" (p. 9).

The positivist "basics" proponents and the systems analysts intent on precisely measuring the "output" of education continue to misunderstand the inexact and ever-changing nature of knowledge based on connections. Many educational thinkers, Dewey contended, deny the future reference of knowledge. These thinkers regard knowledge as an entity complete in itself. Dewey's Hegelian background, with its emphasis on the dialectic (the belief that all concepts are part of an interactive context that must be understood to make sense of the concept) helped move his view of knowledge beyond the "knowledge in isolation" format. The dialectic notion of process was always present in his view of the nature of knowledge. Far ahead of his time in 1916, from Dewey's perspective knowledge could never be viewed outside the context of its origin and its relationship to other information. We only have to call to mind what passes in our schools as acquisition of knowledge, Dewey wrote, to understand how it lacks any meaningful connection with the experiences of students. A person is reasonable, he concluded, in the degree to which he or she sees an event not as something isolated "but in its connection with the common experience of mankind" (pp. 342–343). Alice Rivlin, the systems analysts, Chester Finn and the advocates of the essential knowledge of the Western tradition have consistently failed to understand this important precept. As a result, generations of teachers and students continue to be disempowered and disconnected from the world around them.

THE CULTURE OF PASSIVITY: TEACHER EDUCATION AS INSTITUTIONALIZED DISEMPOWERMENT

In the context of our discussion of teacher empowerment and disempowerment return for a moment to the historical themes we discussed in Chapters 4 and 5. The modernist dynamics of regulation and disempowerment permeate America's educational past, and regulatory features have shaped the education of teachers in profound ways that often make teachers more controllable than intellectually perceptive. We have seen that concerns with the development of a rational and controlled social order influenced the common school crusade of the 1840s and the subsequent development of public schools and normal schools for teacher training in the rest of the nineteenth century. Still, modernism's greatest assault on the institution of schooling came with the infusion of hyperrational management strategies into conceptions of pedagogy around the turn of the twentieth century. The scientific management principles developed by efficiency expert Frederick W. Taylor led to a complete reordering and then a calcification of the power relations between administrators, teachers and students. When behavioral psychology joined the pedagogical recipe, teachers began to be seen more and more as entities to be controlled and manipulated. In the spirit of the times psychologist Edward Thorndike announced that the human mind is an exacting instrument given to precise measurement. However, teachers, he said, are incapable of measurements; therefore, the formulation of instructional strategies and curriculum development should be left to experienced psychologists. As Popkewitz (1987) noted, it is hardly surprising that the behaviorists soon won the battle for the soul of the school, shaping its climate with their control over instructional design.

Though subsequent decades have witnessed an evolving sophistication in their strategies, the forces of efficiency, productivity and scientific management unleashed by Taylor and Thorndike helped shape twentieth-century education and teachers have been trained to follow an efficiency model taken directly from their work. In other words, most teachers have internalized as common sense a professional approach that breaks the complex task of teaching into a series of simple steps that even unskilled laborers can perform—that is, they have been deskilled. As Taylor put it to one of his workers, "[You're] not supposed to think; there are other people paid for thinking around here" (Wirth, 1983, p. 12). Taylor's system eliminates the need for a worker's judgment. It thus rationalized the deskilling of teaching and separated the conception of the pedagogical act from its execution. Teachers had no need to learn the intricacies of subject matter, nor did they need to understand the sociohistorical context in which the knowledge to be taught had been produced. All they had to do was identify the subject matter to be transferred to the learner, break it into components, present it and test their students on it. It was a strategy as right as rain and so commonsensical it defied any need for justification.

A brief examination of the teacher manuals that accompany reading textbooks documents the progressive deskilling of teachers. In the 1920s small manuals offered only brief professional discussions and bibliographies for students. The pamphlets emphasized the teaching of reading. Fifty years later the manuals had added scores of pages that included complete scripts (about four pages per day) specifying exactly what teachers were to say, where to stand as they said it and how to test and evaluate their students after they finished saying it. The manuals of the 1970s were less concerned with the teaching of reading than with teaching the specific skills required by standardized tests (Popkewitz, 1987).

You should be able to see clearly what has happened here. The scientific management of teaching, with its accompanying deskilling and disempowerment, has initiated a vicious circle of harm to the profession. As teachers became deskilled they lost more and more autonomy. As they grew accustomed to the loss of autonomy, they were perceived to be incapable of self-direction. While in no way romanticizing the conditions under which nineteenth- and early twentieth-century teachers worked, we can see contemporary teachers subjected to forms of control unimagined by older teachers.

Moreover, teacher education often enculturates teachers into their deskilled role. Prospective teachers learn to be supervised in courses that teach them to write meticulous behavioral objectives and lesson plans in an "accepted" format. At first expecting an academic culture of possibility, teachers find themselves in workplaces that impose both teaching objectives and testing procedures. As a result they enjoy little influence over what to teach, how to teach it or how to judge the outcome. Such a system insults a teacher's dignity, since it assumes that teachers are too ignorant or too lazy to assume these responsibilities. They become the cogs in a machine of expertise—just as Thorndike envisioned it—taking orders from experts conversant with the language of efficiency and scientific management. In such a system, some teachers do indeed grow lazy and apathetic. But should we be surprised, when they have grown up passively in a bureaucratic system that discourages initiative? Critical and responsible teachers too often find themselves treated as pariahs, outsiders who risk banishment with their "bad attitudes" and their reluctance to become "team players" (Kamii, 1981).

In forming the suspicion of autonomous, freethinking educational professionals, a positivist functionalist social theory views schooling as serving a society responsible for the transmission of culture so as to protect the system's equilibrium—in other words, so as to uphold the status quo. Despite protests issued in the language of democracy promising important decision-making roles for teachers, they continue to take roles as spectators, receiving the directives of their superiors (Britzman, 1991). Students, meanwhile, continue to suffer from their contact with teachers whose intellect and autonomy go unrespected. Students who struggle earnestly to learn within the current educational framework suffer special frustration because they so often need a nurturing teacher with a creative approach to learning to release them from a cycle of failure. In the schools modernist positivist reformers envision, however, these students find only constrained teachers with little control over the curriculum, discouraged from taking creative approaches and chained to the conventional instruction standardized tests demand. Unfortunately, students in need of special attention slip through the cracks of the system uneducated. Indeed, most students find school to be more a sorting and labeling machine and less a vehicle for intellectual and personal growth (Bullough & Gitlin, 1991; Benson, Glasberg, & Griffith, 1998).

THE BEHAVIORIST-TECHNOLOGIST MODEL OF TEACHER EDUCATION

Over the last four decades behavioristic teacher education has become one of the most influential doctrines in U.S. colleges of education. Before the work of Edward L. Thorndike at the turn of the twentieth century, most people assumed psychology to be concerned with the structure and functions of the mind. Under the influence of modernist positivism, however, psychologists began to consider behavior their rightful subject matter. Given positivism's rules of evidence, the observability and measurability of behavior rapidly became psychology's central concern. The mind cannot be observed or even defined, many behaviorists argued. In fact, they said, it may not even exist (Wingo, 1974). So embedded did behaviorism become in American institutions that state legislatures began to mandate teacher education programs reliant upon behaviorist assumptions (see Chapter 1). Even though much of the behaviorist view of human psychology has been discredited in academic circles, behavioristic professional programs continue to dominate both public schools and teacher education (Garrison, 1988; Pumroy, 1984). Representing possibly the height of modernism's hyperrationality, behavioral teacher training traces its roots back to Thorndike and Taylor but found its modern expression in the work of Ralph Tyler in the late 1940s.

Tyler (who we will discuss in more detail in Chapter 10), saw education as a process of modifying behavior patterns. To accomplish this objective, Tyler maintained, teachers had both to specify the behaviors to be changed (and express the changes as behavioral objectives) and to develop a scientific approach to determine if the objective had been attained. In the process, learning became simply a technical problem of management. Break knowledge into discrete parts so you can accurately measure a learner's progress. Use standardized materials that carefully specify objectives and delineate exactly the knowledge to be memorized. Train the teacher to oversee the process. In effect, the procedure removes the teacher as an active agent in the educational process. The curriculum guides, the standardized materials determine the action of the class, not the teacher (Bowers & Flinders, 1990; Britzman, 1991, Slattery, 1995a).

Robert Bullough and Andrew Gitlin (1991) discerned six effects of behavioristic teacher training. First, they noted, it creates a technical ethos and then a constructed view of teacher thinking, which reduces the intellectual act of teaching to a mere technique. Teachers become rule followers, guidebook readers discouraged from engaging in interpretive acts. Second, it creates a radical individualism that pits teacher education students against one another in competition for grades, praise from supervisors, instructional resources and ideas and, of course, positions in the schools. Most important, this individualist ethic masks the common interests of teachers and obscures the need for their collective action in the struggle for educational change. Third, the resulting teacher reliance on experts leads to disparate power and status relations that invariably position teachers on the bottom rung of the status ladder.

Fourth, a banking view of teaching and learning develops that positions the teacher as a banker storing and dispensing knowledge with the students as customers taking out loans of facts to apply on tests. Fifth, teachers act as consumers rather than producers of knowledge. Accordingly, the life histories and experiences teacher education students bring to their studies and then to their teaching become irrelevant. They simply revert to shapeless blobs of clay waiting to be molded into teachers. Sixth, an exaggeration in the importance of measurable schoolwork takes place. The spotlight shines only on explicit, observable forms of knowledge. Such an emphasis matches the view of teaching as a managerial act; it trivializes learning and it transforms the student from spirit to product, an entity to be shaped and packaged to meet the demands of future employers.

Within the behaviorist-technologist model of teacher education, such alien ideas as Henry Giroux's vision of "teachers as intellectuals" befuddle and annoy the technologist professors of education. An emphasis in the behavioral tradition hardly leads to the production of scholarly, reflective practitioners; rather, its raison d'être revolves around technical competence and mastery of the predefined skills. This emphasis on training for technical competence leads to conformity. Experience is monosemic (open to one interpretation only), and the task of the neophyte is to adapt to existing institutions by imitating the behaviors of those serving within them. This culture of conformity naturally produces hostility toward those who are in some way different. Social relations become defensive and devoid of honest criticism, as specialists trained for specific tasks perform narrowly defined jobs: counselors advise; janitors clean; administrators discipline; math teachers teach math; reading teachers teach reading (Lesko, 1989). Fences go up, and "No Trespassing" signs abound.

Nothing illustrates the perversity of technical forms of teacher education as clearly as the defining of good teaching in such contexts. Simply put, a teacher is good if he or she produces students who on average answer correctly more questions than expected on multiple-choice standardized achievement tests, based on their performances on the pretest. Under such conditions the technologist evaluator will proclaim that students in the effective teacher's class have *learned* more than expected. Such a definition *demands* that teachers use methods of direct instruction, assumes nothing problematic about the knowledge the tests cover and covertly imposes, in the name of neutrality, a particular vision of educational purpose—a purpose that assumes schools exist to transmit information and culture without comment. The proper way to accomplish this task, it concludes, is to fragment the knowledge of that culture into components one can insert into student consciousness (Ashburn, 1987; Jones & Cooper, 1987).

THE CRUDE PRACTICALITY OF TEACHER DISEMPOWERMENT

A crude practicality characterizes technically oriented teacher education programs. Course work that fails to impart "how-to" information is deemed impractical, superfluous or too theoretical. Schools-as-they-are are taken as the norm, and the role of teacher education is simply to fit the neophytes to them. Questions about the nature and purpose of schooling, the connection between school and society, the relationship between power and teaching, schools as social organizations, what is worth teaching or the nature of school knowledge usually go unasked. Rarely considered are the implicit meanings of such commonly used terms as "educational excellence" and "quality education." On interrogation, for example, we often find terms conveying definite class and race dimensions, and poor or minority-dominated schools are rarely deemed "excellent." Without such forms of analysis, young teachers too often learn simply to follow orders, to accept without question a predetermined body of information and transfer it to students via a battery of approved strategies (Ross, 1988; Britzman, 1991; Greene, 1986).

More disturbing yet, many teacher education programs maintain a virtual silence on the influence of the sociocultural patterns that shape teachers' thinking. Because the Cartesian-Newtonian lens of the old paradigm focuses only on the explicit level of school life, that which one can observe and measure, the less obvious cultural dimensions go ignored (Bowers & Flinders, 1990). Worse, some technical educators vocally reject the importance of studying the cultural dynamics of education. For example, Daniel Duke (1979) argued that cultural contextualization is more than just superfluous to the education of teachers, it is actually dangerous. When we attempt to explain social behavior in terms of cultural influences, he contended, we depersonalize blame. Those who value culturally grounded analyses allow individual students guilty of misbehavior to escape responsibility for their actions. Duke thought that educational professionalism would be better protected by dismissing context and recognizing the supremacy of individualism.

Duke's position resembles those students who argue that we avoid any study of racism because "it will just make blacks angry." (One student recently told a foundations of education class that "black people just can't handle such knowledge of *past* injustices. It would cause a riot.") Along with Duke, students like these would remove race as an acceptable curricular topic. But such a naive view ignores the ways individual identity is structured. The cultural forces of race, class, socioeconomic status, gender and geographic place form our subjectivities; such factors are beyond our power to reverse because they construct boundaries and possibilities in our various relations. They help shape the kind of friends we have, the work we do and the mates we choose. Our interactions with our families, churches, peer groups, workplaces and, of course, schools help shape our identities. Moreover, as Aronowitz and Giroux (1991) pointed out, as if these forces were not enough, our involvement with changing technologies, the mass media and the popular culture they help produce constructs our consciousness. Embedded within the naive notion of individualism is an historical amnesia. Duke's individuals, for example, have no connections with the past; they live in a freeze-frame present. In this conception, the school is lifted out of history. What exists always has been; school must not be seen as an evolving institution that grows and falters through the years. We have no way of understanding the motivations of individuals or the purposes of school. We are incapable of self-analysis, for we have no grounding that empowers us to see where we originated. In the same way, we can hardly commence a critical analysis of school purpose, for we have no idea why schools do what they do. This is the rationale and the condition under which much of teacher education now takes place.

Peter McLaren (1991) extended this theme, arguing that since teacher education has been mired in the language of efficiency and the logic of management techniques and accountability schemes, we should have expected cultural questions to be ignored. Technically oriented teacher education programs cannot be bothered to study the power dimensions of tracking students into college-bound or vocationally bound curricula. The college-bound track enjoys higher status and teaches more abstract and symbolic knowledge than the vocational track. A white middle-class student from an affluent home has less trouble with this material than a minority student from an economically disadvantaged home because in the affluent home this material occurs in the language and social dimensions of everyday life. When prospective teachers fail to study these cultural contextual aspects of schooling, they go on to blame the victims of power inequities for their own failings. Without empathy, the vicious cycle of economic disadvantage and educational disenfranchisement continues uninterrupted; without empathy, these students are banished from the school community and stripped of any sense of belonging. Not encouraged to avoid any study of these dynamics, teachers emerging from the crude practicality of behaviorist-technicist teacher education programs lack access to the social world of marginalized students. These teachers are still further disempowered.

We often find missing in the literature written for teacher education students thoughtful discussions of teacher education. Yet what better way to create reflective and empowered teacher education students than engaging them in analyses of the programs that teach them to be teachers? We hope you will become a student of your own education. Ask yourself now, what values permeate your program? What assumptions go unstated and unquestioned? Is the purpose of the program to empower you or just to train you? Questions like these can liberate students from behaviorist-technicist models of teacher education saturated with experiences rewarding individualistic, competitive and decontextualized modes of thinking and behaving.

Prospective teachers find few opportunities to challenge the status quo in schools. Given the way educators generally conduct research, the "knowledge base" they produce tends to perpetuate that "which is" (Zeuli & Bachmann, 1986; Floden & Klinzing, 1990). As long as teacher educators consider the survival of their students a cardinal goal and believe that teachers learn to teach best by serving in apprentice like positions, little substantive change will occur. Apprenticeships induce neophytes to model the master teacher, rendering the study of teaching less essential than "correct performance" based on the master teacher's opinion and local standards. The conformity that results leads to uniformity of thought, a mechanistic approach to the profession, and an inability to intervene critically in the world of school practice (Cruickshank, 1987; Britzman, 1991).

Students often enter a college of education with a set of conservative expectations and predispositions. They want to become teachers like those they have known, and they expect to teach students just like the ones who were their friends. More often than students in other fields, they attend colleges close to their homes and hope to teach in their home states. Accordingly, their acculturation into the profession requires little break with their past and their childhood values. In short, teacher education students tend to avoid alternative ways of seeing; they often show little interest in finding new lenses through which to conceptualize knowledge and pedagogy. Instead they walk into their classes searching for information delivery recipes and classroom discipline approaches. Questions of purpose, context and power are alien and irrelevant. What, they ask, does such information have to do with teaching (Zeuli & Bachmann, 1986)?

At least moderately successful in high school, prospective teachers cling to the conventional educational practices that worked for them. Thus, they often feel that schools are all right as they are; with a few practice attempts out in the field and a few strategies to achieve discipline, everything will be fine. The culture of passivity works at all levels: It certainly worked for the prospective teachers when they were elementary and secondary students; there is no reason to believe that listening well and following directions literally will fail now.

Meanwhile, skepticism, interpretation and intellectual flexibility rest at the core of what university faculty members call "essential cognitive acts." Technicist-oriented teacher educators tend not to appreciate these traditional academic values. Indeed, teacher educators who work closest with schools and student and practicing teachers often find themselves isolated from the more traditional culture of higher education. Theirs is often a terrain of eight-to-five, punch in–punch out, time-clock hours, with little professional reading, lots of ideological naiveté, limited interpretative practice and minimal analysis of the professional world. The logic of these familiar working conditions diverts one from interpretive thought. A sort of undertow builds in such an environment—an unseen tendency to surrender to the given and to view existing institutional arrangements as objective realities. Without the catalysts of interpretation and an intellectually active analytic community, the pronouncements tend to "speak for themselves." Without an analytic view of the everyday institutional requirements and activities, one's thought becomes fragmented and conceptual syntheses are blocked. Indeed, one's relationship to knowledge is severed. As a result, one's role as a participant in social and institutional life goes unexamined and one's power to anticipate the consequences of social actions is erased (Zeuli & Bachmann, 1986; Greene, 1988; Britzman, 1991).

Jesse Goodman (1986) studied the effects of this modernist teacher education culture on student teachers. He found that even those who began practice teaching with beliefs in a teacher's responsibility to help shape the curriculum, the advisability of emphasizing the interpretation of social content over fragmented skills, the value of curricular integration, the obligation to use learning activities to promote critical thinking and the sanctity of creativity—even they found themselves far more concerned with technicist school objectives by the end of their practice work. Karen, one of the students Goodman observed created an original progressive unit on occupations at the beginning of her student teaching. But after a few weeks of immersion in the schools, she discarded the unit. Almost all of her lessons, Goodman reported, came point-by-point from the teachers' guides. Karen became more and more concerned with using the textbooks effectively—indeed, this concern became far more important to her conception of good teaching than the ability to make curricular and instructional decisions. Her interest in teacher power disappeared as she worked to win the approval of her supervisor, her practicing teachers and the other school personnel.

TEACHING AS A TRADE: THE DANGERS OF DISEMPOWERMENT IN EVERYDAY SCHOOL LIFE

As it did with Karen in just one semester, daily school life takes its toll on anyone's effort to make teaching a professional, practical, caring and scholarly activity. Behaviorist-technologist teacher education lurks in the everyday routine of teaching. One becomes reluctant or unable to see beyond it, to imagine what could be or to push the envelope of teacher thinking. Teaching conceived in the critical new paradigm seeks to understand and then transcend the disempowerment inherent in everyday school life. The entire structure of school experience, thus, is open to analysis. Bill Ayers (1992) empathized with the deadening routines teachers must face in the name of order and passivity. After pledging allegiance to the flag, lining students up to go to the bathroom, dealing with interruptions by the intercom and the bells and attending to the obsession with classroom management, few teachers have the emotional strength left to analyze issues of justice and larger educational goals. When reminded that attention to these larger questions of purpose could bring down the wrath of peers and administrators, many teachers naturally choose disempowerment and apathy. As Ayers noted, there is safety in conformity: No one does get in trouble for assigning worksheets, tolerating injustice or speaking disparagingly of poor students' families. One does get in trouble when one challenges commonsense convention, when one respects students, when one names and protests injustice. Behaviors-technicist teacher education refuses to address these existential teaching dilemmas.

Hundreds of experienced teachers have dismissed our efforts to move beyond the prevailing disempowerment. "It sounds good or looks good on paper," they say, "but ideas like yours will never work in practice." We disagree, though we understand their cynicism. They have yet to be exposed to the ideas of paradigms, postmodernism and critical theory. They were first victimized by and then got used to years of educational theory and reforms that come and go like clothing fads. One year district school leaders place all their faith in outcomes-based education; the next year they tout cooperative learning; three years later they present workshops on total quality management. How can teachers help but grow cynical when they have never been consulted about these top-down reforms? But one can and should learn from such reform folly. In speaking of issues of critical empowerment we seek to go beyond just a few adjustments to schooling and teacher education to rethink the entire enterprise—to reformulate the role of teachers in a way that makes them pragmatic scholars and decision-making professionals. We want to help teachers become students of the everyday world of schools—we refuse simply to adjust them to it.

As we have seen, however, *adjustment* continues to be the goal of many teacher education programs. Indeed, the implicit message of technicist teacher education, the positivistic research that often grounds it and the state reform movements that share the same epistemological assumptions is that teachers should do what they are told and be careful not to think about themselves. You can see how this caution might turn to apathy as teachers lose interest in the creative aspects of teaching that attracted them to the profession in the first place. Teachers' thinking tends to be strongly influenced by the top-down flow and the "teacherproof" curricula that assume incompetence on the lower levels. Rewarded in their training for passive acceptance of expert-generated knowledge, prospective teachers gain little experience in contextually grounded interpretive thinking about the purpose of teaching in a democratic society. Management science has been designed to control human beings and has aligned them with visions of institutional efficiency and standardization. Teacher education often contributes to this management orientation by conveying the impression that the laws of social and educational life are settled and unambiguous (Glickman, 1985; Baldwin, 1987; Popkewitz, 1981).

In this context, consider Madeline Hunter's (1982) popular teaching and supervision model, used in thousands of teaching education programs and school districts. Hunter's model assumes a predetermined prescribed version of teaching based on "seven essential steps." Guided by Hunter, teachers follow these specific (and measurable) steps in every lesson, regardless of the subject matter. The supervisor's evaluation is simplified, standardized and streamlined as administrators come to define good teaching as that which conforms to Hunter's model. Accountability is ensured, Hunter and the technicists argue, as teachers come to understand what is expected of them so they can perform appropriately.

The range of appropriate teaching behaviors narrows under Hunter's model. Supervisors and teacher educators concur that innovative lessons that fail to follow the model must be evaluated as unsatisfactory. Thus, rewards for teaching are based less on reasoned notions of competence and creativity than on adherence to format—that is, compliance. Teacher education in this context becomes a conformity mill, an assembly line, a mere adjustment procedure in which novices on the Hunter channel are fine tuned. Like workers in Frederick W. Taylor's scientifically managed factories, teachers in the technicist system Madeline Hunter advocates are stripped of their role in the conceptualization of the teaching act. Teachers become the executors of managerial plans. The moral and ethical dimensions, not to mention the cognitive and conceptual aspects of the teaching act, are submerged in a pool of standardization and conventionalism (Garman & Hazi, 1988).

When thinking and cognition are taught in behaviorist-technicist teacher education programs, they are rarely presented in the context of the everyday reality of the classroom or civic life in contemporary America. Cognitive theories are merely one more part of the irrelevant memory work students must "master," as they are typically presented one after another without any attempt to assess them or relate them critically to actual classroom practice. Such information is presented at a low cognitive level, as students commit to memory whatever someone says B. F. Skinner, Kurt Lewin, Sigmund Freud or Jean Piaget said. Inspired perhaps by emotional attachments, particular students accept certain cognitive theories. Many of these theories are useless and have little to do with the everyday life of teachers. Consistent with the technicist assumptions about neutrality and objectivity, many education professors believe that students should learn a little about every major cognitive theory so they can make their own choices. Such an approach is in many ways an abrogation of pedagogical responsibility, since it ignores each theory's significance, its explanatory power, its paradigmatic and epistemological dimensions and its relationship to teacher self-direction and empowerment. If teachers were empowered to understand the relationships between Piagetian constructivism and, say, Skinnerian behaviorism from pedagogical, epistemological and political perspectives, they would resist the simple-minded imposition of lesson plan *formats,* behavioral objective writing or bulletin board decorating that dominate their pre-service and in-service teacher education (Kamii, 1981).

THE MYSTERY OF CRITICAL THINKING: EMPOWERMENT THROUGH CONTEXTUALIZATION

Most people involved with teacher education pay lip service to the need for teachers to be "critical thinkers," but few understand just what critical thinking entails. As with many education buzzwords (popular but only vaguely understood jargon), the meaning of the phrase "critical thinking" got lost somewhere along the way. Accordingly, we will now frame a more specific description of critical thinking that draws on women's and indigenous people's ways of knowing, on critical theory and on the connectedness of the new paradigm (see Kincheloe & Steinberg, 1993; Slattery, 1995a; Kincheloe, 1995; Semali & Kincheloe, 1999). We base our description on the idea that the straightest route to teacher empowerment follows teachers' ability to expand cognitive awareness (as we argued in Chapter 2), and to develop new, more sophisticated notions of critical thinking. One point is obvious: Teachers must learn to expand their own cognitive horizons before they can teach students to do so. We call this form of critical thinking "postformal thinking" because we think it exceeds Jean Piaget's highest order of thinking, formal cognition. A practitioner's ways of knowing and thinking are unique, quite different from the technical, scientific ways of knowing and thinking associated with the old paradigm's ideas of professional expertise. Professional expertise of this variety, Donald Schön (1983, 1991) argued, is an uncertain enterprise because it confronts constantly changing, unique and unstable conditions. Teachers never see the same classroom twice because teaching conditions change every day. The students who responded to a set of pedagogical strategies yesterday may ignore them today. Schön's practitioners relinquish the certainty that accompanies professional expertise conceived of as the repetitive administration of techniques to similar types of problems. In our postformal reconceptualization of practitioner thinking, the ability of practitioners to develop research strategies that explore the genesis and efficacy of comfortable assumptions and implicit objectives becomes extremely important.

In education, postformal teachers become teachers-as-researchers who question the nature of their own thinking as they attempt to teach higher-order thinking. What are the limits of human ways of knowing? Where do we begin conceptualizing postformal modes of teacher thinking that lead to a universal perspective and to empowerment? Drawing on our critical new paradigm of meaning making, look for ways of knowing and levels of cognition that extend beyond Piagetian formalism. Adults do not reach a final cognitive equilibrium beyond which no new levels of thought can emerge; there must be modes of thinking that transcend the formal operational ability to reach abstract conclusions, understand cause-and-effect relationships and employ the traditional scientific method to explain reality. As Arlin (1975) suggested, we already know too much to define formality as the zenith of human cognitive ability.

Modernist psychological models of cognition fail to address the issue of critical empowerment: the ability to disengage oneself from the tacit assumptions of discursive practices and power relations in order to exert more conscious control over one's everyday life. The rational, accurate thinking that emerges from modernism's one-truth epistemology produces both a congregation of timid rule followers and a mediocre level of education unrelated to any ethical effort to use our ability to reason constructively. What technicist efforts there are to cultivate higher order or critical thinking among teachers usually necessitates removing prospective practitioners from their lived worlds in order to control "the variables of the situation." As a result, thinking becomes sequestered in laboratory settings that suppress passion and authentic feelings of love, hate, fear and commitment. Cartesian-Newtonian models of the rational process are always culturally neutral, always removed from the body and its passions. These modernist models assume that practitioners can be removed from their embeddedness in a physical context without affecting cognition (Hultgren, 1987; Bobbitt, 1987; Bowers & Flinders, 1990; Kincheloe, Steinberg, & Villaverde, 1999).

This modernist positivist decontextualization naturally leads to student and teacher disempowerment. Whether we teach high school math, elementary language arts or teacher education, the approach is the same: break down the information to be learned into discrete, easily memorized parts. Cognitive theories, grammar rules, vocabulary, math computation skills and the "causes" of the Civil War can all be "learned" this way. As long as we treat the curriculum as a technical specification with unassailable facts to be learned, with standardized test improvement the instructional goal, with little effort granted to connect school and life, with no debate over the role of learning in a democratic society, we can be assured that modernist science has proven we know how to teach (Jones & Cooper, 1987). Consider, for example, the way modernist positivist science has taught us to teach reading. Mastery learning programs break reading skills into such subskills as beginning consonant sounds, vowel sounds, ending consonant sounds, consonant blends and vowel diagrams. Teachers learn to teach these in a structured, sequential way until students pass the mastery test of each subskill. Again, the commonsensical, linear methodology seems to satisfy everyone's demands. On deeper examination, however, problems materialize—even, in fact, on the superficial level where these programs are assessed (Kincheloe, Steinberg, & Hinchey, 1999).

Researchers have found that in the first few years of the program, reading skill scores among early elementary students actually increase. Yet by the time the children reach the sixth grade, their reading levels have actually decreased and they begin to curtail their reading. Although the students scored high on achievement tests, the examinations measured only what early grade teachers had taught them, the subskills. Reading or language arts classes centered mainly on subskill worksheets or dittos, and little actual reading took place. The students had learned the fragmented curriculum well. They had mastered the isolated subskills and reflected that mastery on the standardized tests. Even so, they were not reading for knowledge, enjoyment or meaning—in fact, they were not even reading! The reading program had committed a fatal modernist error: It had assumed that the parts add up to the whole. As with most human endeavors, the whole was far greater than the sum of its parts (Fosnot, 1988; Shannon, 1989; Grumet, 1988; Block, 1995).

To move beyond such limited ways of seeing and teaching and the disempowerment they invite, we focus our teacher education students on the idea of contextualization in our theory of postformal thinking. Postformal contextualization includes the acceptance that knowledge can never be complete in and of itself. When one abstracts, one takes something out of its context. Abstracting is necessary in everyday life because we have too much information for our minds to understand it all in detail. If we cannot abstract an object of thought, we will lose it in a larger pattern. While postformal thinkers are certainly capable of abstraction, at the same time they keep in sight the conceptual field, the context that provides separate entities with meaning (Raizen & Colvin, 1991). For example, modernist schooling has typically concentrated on teaching students the "what" of school subjects. Life and job experience have traditionally taught us "how" and "why." We learn data (the "what") best in the context of the "how" and the "why." Thus, we might best acquire academic knowledge in a vocational context, perhaps through an apprenticeship, a work-study job or a practicum.

Ideally, however, we would reflect on and recontextualize such learning in a natural setting away from the practice site and in light of the larger issues of cognition, application, social relations and justice. If we desire deeper levels of understanding, then we must appreciate the contexts in which such understanding fits. A math teacher operating in relation to this concept could introduce students to the life and professional situations in which they might use trigonometry. With these contextual understandings in mind we begin to see that a novice is one who possesses no specific knowledge of a particular teaching or work setting even though he or she may come to the situation with everyday knowledge and academic information. These "greenhorns" become seasoned veterans only after they gain familiarity with specific social, political, symbolic, encoded and technical types of school or workplace dynamics—that is, the *context* of their situation.

AWAKENINGS: THE POSSIBILITY OF EMPOWERMENT

The birth of modernity established a tradition of protesting the application of modernist science to education. This tradition of dissent, which found early expression in the writings of Jean-Jacques Rousseau, embraces a romantic form of maturationism. "Romantic maturationists" argue that the most important duty of education is the innate development of the child. The child is the center of the educational universe and his or her cognitive, social and emotional development are simply a process of biological programming. In his 1762 autobiographical novel *Emile*, Rousseau compared the child to a flower, implying that children are innately good and need only a gentle, nurturing environment to reach their full potential. Arnold Gesell extended Rousseau's metaphor by numerous observations and subsequent delineations of developmental stages. His work, in effect, warned educators to avoid tampering with the child's divinely ordained maturation process. When romantic maturationists planned curricula and instruction they heeded Gesell's warning, and teaching became a process of assessing the development levels of children and planning the appropriate activities for them (Fosnot, 1988; Zigler & Finn-Stevenson, 1987).

Though their attempt to confront the power of modernist science was noble, the romantic maturationists were doomed to failure. Teaching collapsed into endless attempts to match assessments and activities. Usually trained in early childhood programs and in the "free schools" of another era, the teachers assumed the role of therapist or unobtrusive guide, trying to help students achieve personal growth. After teachers constructed the environment they withdrew, allowing play activities and experience to foster learning naturally. Teachers were not the deskilled laborers of the efficient technicist schools, but little need arose for any higher-order practitioner thinking (Ashburn, 1987; Fosnot, 1988).

In recent years, however, educational thinkers have begun to realize the need for both teachers and students to transcend the rote-based, fragmented thinking modernist schools impose. Many of the attempts to foster such cognition—referred to as "critical thinking"—became entangled within a modernist logic in which thinking was hyperrationalized and reduced to a set of micrological skills that promote a form of procedural knowledge. In its reductionism this "uncritical critical thinking" removed the political and ethical dimensions of thought. Students and teachers were discouraged from confronting why they tended to think as they did about themselves, the world around them and their relationship to that world. In other words, these uncritical critical thinkers gained little insight into the forces that had shaped them—that is, their consciousness construction. In addition, viewing cognition as a process taking place in a vacuum, the critical thinking movement remained oblivious of the consequences of thinking. Thinking in a new way always requires a personal transformation; indeed, if enough people think in new ways, social transformation is inevitable. But this social and personal change was unimportant to uncritical critical thinking (modernist critical thinking) advocates.

Unable to transcend the boundaries of formal thinking, these proponents of modernist critical thinking reduced cognition to microskills—in essence teaching a fragmented version of scientific thinking (the highest expression of Piaget's formality). They taught students to differentiate, to group, to identify common properties, to label, to categorize, to distinguish relevant information from the irrelevant, to relate points, to infer and to justify—usually in isolation from any larger conceptual problem. Such an approach to critical thinking often obscured more than it exposed by hiding its hyperrationality behind its scientific appearance. Once again wellintentioned, the movement never recognized critical thinking as more than a cognitive skill to be mastered. It remained the province of the gifted, only and its proponents failed to orient teacher education toward teaching critical thinking in the context of reflective practice. Modernist critical thinking always saw higher-order thinking as a process separate from the school environment. Its proponents never saw the critical emancipating dimensions of thinking that are inseparable from the democratic way students, teachers and administrators should interact with one another (Hultgren, 1987; Grimmett, Erickson, MacKinnon & Tiecken, 1990).

What, then, constitutes "critical thinking"? New paradigm critical thinking moves toward emancipation with a ubiquitous sense of self-awareness. Moving in an emancipatory direction implies a concern for the development of a liberated mind, a critical consciousness and a free society. A critically thinking teacher is alert to the construction of the consciousness and the ways that social and institutional forces work to undermine the autonomy of professionals (Ashburn, 1987; Hultgren, 1987). Drawing on the critical new paradigm, emancipatory thinking sets the self "in question." It reexamines self-images, inherited dogmas and absolute beliefs, and teachers begin to see themselves in relation to the world around them, perceiving the school as a piece in a larger mosaic. As the boundary between feeling and logic begins to fade from the cognitive map—a map redrawn by cartographers from the critical paradigm—teachers begin to see an inseparable relationship between thinking and acting (Weil, 1998).

In short, an awakening from the modernist-positivist dark ages is under way. Educators have begun to realize that teacher education and teacher thinking lead to specific ideological consequences. We cannot think about thinking without considering the power dimensions of the act—that is, the em*power*ment of higher orders of thinking. Thinking in an emancipatory manner necessarily involves empowered actions—activities undertaken in the best interests of students, community members and other teachers, and conduct enabling those affected to apply their own intelligence and ethics. Thus, the move to new paradigm critical thinking requires one to transcend the impression that thinking is merely a cognitive psychological activity. This transcendence may be the key to understanding the static flatness of modernist critical thinking. As both a psychological and a social activity, teacher thinking is now understandable as "in process," perpetually in a state of construction. For example, teachers cannot think about the curriculum as separate from a social context. If they do, the apparent political innocence of a body of agreed-on knowledge being systematically passed on to students by an ever-evolving but always neutral instructional process deceives them.

We now know too much to be seduced by the sirens of apparent political neutrality. As a deliberate process, the curriculum is always a formal transmission of particular aspects of the culture's knowledge. Do we teach women's and African American history in eleventh-grade social studies? Do we read Toni Morrison and Alice Walker in twelfth-grade literature? These are sociopolitical questions—that is, they involve power. (We will explore this concept further in Chapter 10). Thinking affects social practice; it is never detached. How we think about teaching either changes or maintains the status quo. Descriptions of the world do not rest, they do not retreat to a sociological easy chair. They remain part of the world's commerce; as they define it, they change it. Thinking is always a major strategy in the cultural battle. Accordingly, we can never sequester conceptual matters in the psychological domain. Cognition in a critical paradigmatic context becomes sociocognition (Codd, 1984; Harris, 1984; Hultgren, 1987). Thus, empowered teachers in the new paradigm connect their critical thinking to specific actions. What form might these empowered actions take? What might schools with empowered teachers look like?

ELEVEN TASKS FOR EMPOWERED TEACHERS

Responsibility naturally accompanies empowerment, and a teacher who employs critical thinking faces the eleven pleasant tasks we describe in this section.

1. *Empowered teachers understand the purposes of education and work to reform schools so they accomplish such purposes. Call it "trickle-up reform."* Any serious educational reform that stands a chance of working will be led by teachers who understand precisely why they seek change. They will know how reforms will affect their students and the type of learning in which they will engage. At the beginning, at least, the "why" questions will be more important than the "how" questions; however, all these questions will ultimately become inseparable. Empowered teachers will build these new schools on the basis of their moral commitments and will use these commitments to avoid the gimmickry and entrepreneurship that often pass for educational reform. Unlike piecemeal reforms, an educational reformation led by empowered teachers will possess a large and cohesive philosophical, political and moral vision of educational change (Darling-Hammond, 1995; Pruyn, 1994). Indeed, empowered teachers themselves take the initiative for change rather than wait for a principal or administrator to initiate action.

In fact, as teachers take the reins of reform, leadership is redefined. In this context, new paradigm reform becomes less trickle-down change than trickle-up revolution (Ayers, 1992). The teachers themselves—not politicians or educational experts—own this trickle-up revolution. The revolution empowered teachers lead will rely far less on the new technology, national standards, teacher accountability or new schedules and timetables; instead, it will come from actions taken as a result of a considered understanding of educational purpose.

The revolution will, of course, attract opposition; the important question for teachers is how they will handle their antagonists (Fried, 1995; Lieberman, 1995).

Few principals, supervisors or superintendents have been educated in a manner that acquaints them with larger educational purposes. Too much of the professional education of school leaders is technical, focusing on management and supervision. Empowered teachers will keep administrators from usurping their power by mystifying them with phony "power-sharing" programs wrapped in the language of inclusion and democracy. A classroom teacher recently observed that his school's reform agenda "allowed" teachers to take part in decision making. His first decision in the new participatory plan was selecting the color to paint the teachers' lounge. His choice was between blue and mauve. This is not the kind of trickle-up reform we have in mind.

2. *Empowered teachers appreciate the centrality of knowledge production in their pedagogy: The collision of student-teacher experiences with information derived from the disciplines produces knowledge in the classroom.* In the new critical paradigm teachers are scholars who (as we emphasized in Chapter 1) engage in rigorous thinking, extensive reading, ongoing dialogue, thorough analysis and intuitive reflection. Most of the current teaching and educational reform efforts adopt the assumption that knowledge is an external body of information independent of human beings, and the teacher's role is to insert this knowledge into the minds of students. This "knowledge" is a body of isolated facts to be committed to memory by generally apathetic students. Evaluation procedures that emphasize the retention of isolated bits and pieces of data strengthen this view of knowledge. Conceptual thinking vanishes as schooling trivializes learning. Students are evaluated on the lowest level of human thinking, the ability to memorize. Thinking skills involving the ability to ask unique questions, to see connections between concepts or to apply conceptual understandings lose importance. Empowered teachers focus on using these thinking skills to guide the interaction between them and their students and the content of the disciplines. In this process both students and teachers reinterpret their own lives and uncover new insights and talents. Unless students and teachers can incorporate school information into their own lives to produce new knowledge, schooling will remain but a routine rite of passage into adulthood.

If empowered teachers cannot engage empowered students in the production of knowledge, educating thoughtful, knowledgeable teachers serves no purpose. Why bother with a college degree if teachers simply deliver information? Why interest teacher education students in the rules of knowledge production, the values implicit in certain kinds of information or questions of social context and power? The "genius" of great thinkers lies less in their ability to retain the information they encounter, than in their ability to produce new knowledge. When schools operate at a critical level and the collision of student experience with the information of the disciplines produces knowledge, traditional knowledge is not necessarily tossed on the garbage heap of history. We may indeed reexamine what constitutes traditional knowledge, the traditional canon, but at the same time we must recognize value in the knowledge others have produced. The salient point here is that we interrogate this knowledge and consider it in light of new contexts and questions. This analysis is an important step in the creation of new knowledge because it precludes the simple concrete-level "mastery" of secondhand data and the disempowerment it leaves in its wake.

3. *Empowered teachers make use of that knowledge and those understandings that have heretofore been devalued and excluded: subjugated and indigenous knowledge.* Schools have traditionally used white, Anglo-Saxon, middle-class, Judeo-Christian, heterosexual, able-bodied, English speaking male norms to identify what it means to be educated. Schools present the belief systems, definitions of citizenship, views of success and histories of members of this group as privileged while they devalue the perspectives and histories of other groups. In the new paradigm, empowered teachers incorporate into the curriculum the cultural knowledge *all* students bring to school. Everyone profits from these understandings: Students from the dominant culture gain insights into the struggles of those different from themselves—invaluable knowledge in a society that values harmony based on understanding—and students from the subordinate cultures gain an appreciation of their heritage—an appreciation that becomes a source of self-respect and a basis for family and community solidarity. As we come to value excluded understandings, we include voices in the school that grant us new perspectives on the world. For example, a foot soldier's perspective on war, a grandmother's perspective on women's history, a union member's perspective on labor-management relations, a child of same-sex parents' vision of family values, a migrant family's perspective on the American landscape and labor market, a freedom marcher's view on race relations all provide the bottom-up rather than the top-down perspective. This inclusion raises new questions and creates new ways of relating to information (Books, 1998).

In such a context as this, empowered teachers draw on liberation theology's notion of "subjugated knowledge." With its roots deep in the Latin American struggle against poverty and exploitation, liberation theology morally situates our attempt to rethink the epistemological assumptions on which we rest our view of education. Liberation theology makes no apology for its identification with the perspective of those who are excluded and subjugated. Proclaiming their solidarity with the poor and marginalized, liberation theologians work alongside such people to expose the oppressive and unethical aspects of the social order. Hearing the voices of the subjugated, we begin to see schooling from the perspective of those it has failed. On the basis of this subjugated knowledge, or this "dangerous memory," we can formulate an approach to teaching that reveals at whose expense the dominant culture maintains its structure. Then we can design strategies for overcoming this oppression. At the same time, we can produce knowledge forms that challenge injustice (Semali & Kincheloe, 1999).

Because subjugated knowledge is produced often within a culture in subjugation, it reflects a "double knowledge," an understanding of both the subjugated culture and the ways of the oppressor culture. W. E. B. DuBois called this double knowledge the gift of second sight. This second sight constitutes the type of subjugated knowledge that can revolutionize education. A critical understanding of education uses gender or racial diversity as DuBois conceptualized it: as a means of rethinking the basic assumptions, concepts and theories of a discipline. In this context of empowerment working-class women's subjugated knowledge forms part of the conceptual base on which education, cultural institutions and work are transformed (West, 1993; Zinn & Dill, 1994).

Writing about the rural Kentucky of her youth, bell hooks discusses the African American woman's perspective toward work. "Work makes life sweet," her elders told her; pride can be taken in a job done well. Subjugated notions of work permeate hooks's memories:

> *My Aunt Margaret took in ironing. Folks brought her clothes from miles around because she was such an expert. That was in the days when using starch was common and she knew how to do an excellent job. Watching her iron with skill and grace was like watching a ballerina dance. Like all the other black girls raised in the fifties that i knew, it was clear to me that i would be a working woman. Even though our mother stayed home, raising her seven children, we saw her constantly at work, washing, ironing, cleaning, and cooking (she is an incredible cook). And she never allowed her six girls to imagine we would not be working women. No, she let us know that we would work and be proud to work. (hooks, 1992, p. 41)*

A work philosophy that stressed commitment to any job was an important coping device for African Americans stuck in a racist society. That viewpoint is similar to the Buddhist perspective that teaches that any work becomes sacred when it is undertaken with dignity and care. When such an ethic is connected to what black women often referred to as "motherwit," work becomes not only sacred but something that allowed one to display her intelligence (hooks, 1992; Luttrell, 1993). Such intelligence was essential when working for white people, with their predisposition to believe the worst about black people—lying, cheating, stealing and so on. These forms of black women's knowledge not only become valuable lessons for students and teachers, they can form the value base on which resistance to back work and elitist education can be constructed.

Women's subordinate position in education, like African Americans' subordinate location in the social hierarchy, has necessitated the development of these subjugated knowledges as survival skills. In an era in which poverty has been feminized, women must draw on such knowledge to help them understand the race, class and gender power dynamics that lead to exploitation and control. This insight into the workings of patriarchy allows women to fight male domination on a variety of levels. A critical education is part of this fight, as it exposes these power relations. In this context, it helps young women devise skills and analytical abilities that aid them in their struggle to participate equally in schooling. In an era of misogyny, where women's attempts to achieve justice earn them the labels of "aggressive bitches" and "femi-Nazis," women's self-sufficiency becomes a serious issue. Statistics show that a large percentage of women will be forced to lead independent lives, despite what may be their personal preferences.

In addition to exposing patriarchal power relations, women's subjugated knowledge provided an alternative to patriarchy's hierarchical and bureaucratic conception of education. Women's subjugated knowledge often cultivates the understanding that the struggle for social justice is as much a matter of emotion as factual data, related as much to human empathy and connectedness as to analysis. Often those who struggled for justice in the past were men who did not appreciate the power of such *feelings* and who, as a result, failed to link their social analyses to the domain of the visceral. Women's subjugated knowledge operating at this affective level provides an antihierarchical orientation that sutures the fissure between private and public life. Connection with others is a primary feature of most women's lives, as their self-assessments often revolve around questions of responsibility and the care of others.

This notion of women's networking presents valuable possibilities for schooling, with hundreds of examples of women's educational and labor networks around the world. For example, Microsyster is a network of women computer technicians, workplace technicians and clerical workers based in London. The Women's International Information and Communication Services is a source for names and addresses of scores of groups that are involved with the various aspects concerning women and their relation to education, work and technology. Teachers and students need to link up with these organizations in their struggle for a democratic education, good work and gender justice (West, 1993; Lamphere, 1985; Hacker, 1989).

Another mode of expressing this idea of subjugated ways of seeing engages the emerging interest in indigenous knowledge, knowledge generated and transmitted over time by those who live and work in a particular locality and must cope with their physical and social environments. Developed from the experience of individuals and passed down from generation to generation, such knowledge provides educators with valuable perspectives they can use to rethink identities and practices (Semali & Kincheloe, 1999).

While teachers are hardly an oppressed or indigenous group in the way Peruvian peasants or Native Americans are, they have been marginalized as professionals and knowledge producers. In our critical new paradigm, therefore, teachers can recover their own subjugated knowledge, which has been devalued by modernist, positivist educational experts. Empowered teachers form networks sharing ideas, studying issues and providing support for one another. These networks produce knowledge around issues of critical reform and the recognition of the oppression the experts exert. As teachers discard the programs, manuals, taxonomies and prepackaged materials, they begin to produce their own context-specific resources. Thus, they come to the point where they respect each others' work as scholars and find recognition for it beyond their own ranks. Teachers recognized as knowledge producers are better prepared to encourage and draw on the knowledge students bring with them to school. Children's names often provide the starting point for history and geography lessons, or a crime committed in the local community can generate knowledge and understanding of the local legal system. In a classroom managed by empowered teachers who produce knowledge, almost anything is possible (Hauser, 1991; Weiler, 1988; Ayers, 1992).

4. *Empowered teachers model and teach postformal thinking.* Critical teachers in the new paradigm set out to produce self-conscious students aware of how they

have come to think as they do and aware of the theories of thinking in general. These students learn about what constitutes postformal thinking as a beginning stage in their attempt to achieve such knowledge. Students who think about thinking this way start to see how their own assumptions are formed. They seek both to solve problems and to discover how problems originate. In this way they move beyond the limitations of "common sense" as they begin to see beyond the expected. An example of what we call a "postformal thinker" Albert Einstein could see beyond the expected, understand how his thinking about physics came to be shaped and then look beyond the official perspectives. In doing so he recognized relationships between such ostensibly unrelated entities as electromagnetism and gravity. In these previously undiscovered relationships he found keys to unlock the mysteries of the physical universe. Similarly, empowered teachers want their students to gain an awareness of how thinking is shaped, an awareness that allows them to move further. To reach such goals, teachers must first learn to think about their own thinking. Only then can they transfer such awareness to their students (Kincheloe, Steinberg, & Tippins, 1999).

Postformal thinking takes up questions of meaning, self-awareness and the nature and function of the social context. Such concerns move a postformal thinker beyond formalist concerns with proper scientific procedure and the *certainty* it should produce. Postformalism grapples with purpose, devoting attention to issues of human dignity, freedom, power, authority, domination and social responsibility. As one of its main features, postformal thinking expands the boundaries of what one may casually label "sophisticated thinking." When we begin to expand these boundaries, we find that those excluded from the community of the intelligent seem to cluster around exclusions based on race (the nonwhite), language (non–English speakers), class (the poor), gender (the feminine and homosexual) and religion (nonmainline Christian).

Recall that the modernist conception of intelligence promotes an exclusionary system based on the premise that some people are inherently more intelligent than others (Case, 1985; Klahr & Wallace, 1976; Murray & Hernstein, 1995). Modernists think of intelligence and creativity as fixed and innate, while at the same time finding these mysterious qualities in only the privileged few. The modernist definition of intelligence stresses biological fixities altered only by surgical means. Such an essentialism presents us with a psychology of hopelessness that locks all people into rigid categories that follow them throughout life (Bozik, 1987; Lawler, 1975; Maher & Rathbone, 1986). But since postformal thinking emphasizes the production of one's own knowledge, it should be noted in any discussion of the characteristics of postformality that few boundaries exist to limit what may be considered postformal thinking. Postformal thinking and postformal teaching become whatever a student or a teacher can produce in the realm of new understandings and knowledge within the confines of a democratic pedagogy and critical ethics.

Including the idea of a *contextualization* (we discussed it earlier, along with its understanding that knowledge can never stand alone or be complete in and of itself), postformal thinking includes three basic features.

a. *Etymology* (the origin of validated knowledge)—the exploration of those forces that produce what the culture validates as knowledge. Those who think etymologically pay close attention to the sources of their intuitions and "gut feelings." Rarely do we form such feelings independently, for most thoughts and feelings are collective in origin (Bohm & Edwards, 1991; Senge, 1990). Consider, for example, that language itself is entirely collective. We may think that we generate our assumptions by ourselves, but typically we draw them from a reservoir of culturally approved assumptions. The concept of "thinking for oneself" must be reconsidered in light of this information; indeed, without an awareness and understanding of etymology, people are incapable of understanding why they hold particular opinions or specific values. A lack of these appreciations seriously inhibits reflection and analysis. It is hardly an exaggeration to say that a capacity for critical thought is grounded in the postformal concern with etymology.

b. *Pattern*—the understanding of the connecting patterns and relationships that support the lived world. Two of us recently spent a harrowing night in a small bathroom with three of our children and three dogs seeking shelter from a hurricane, and came to realize the power of that cyclonic weather pattern. Picking up energy from the warm ocean waters, hurricanes develop a rotation that accelerates to generate incredible energy. High- and low-pressure centers developing in differing locations become part of the hurricane system as they interact with prevailing wind patterns to direct the path of the storm. Each component of the pattern influences the others in a way difficult to view. One can comprehend the system of a hurricane only by thinking of it as a totality, not as a collection of independent, discrete parts.

Educational systems also follow invisible patterns with interlocking activities. Situated in the middle of these patterns, teachers can find them difficult to identify. Modernist science and education have typically focused on separate elements of the patterns, often overlooking the system itself. As a result, serious problems go unsolved while mainstream "experts" concentrate on specific events. "American worker productivity falls again," Tom Brokaw tells us his *Nightly News* audience, fragmenting our understanding of long-term deskilling patterns in the workplace and causing us to fight the wrong battles in our haste to restore our productivity. Indeed, no matter how educated individuals become, if they cannot escape the confine of formal thinking they will remain entangled in unseen patterns (Senge, 1990).

c. *Process*—the cultivation of new ways of interpreting the world that make sense of both ourselves and contemporary society. With its Cartesian-Newtonian logic and scientific reductionism, modernist civilization stifles human creativity. All human beings can aspire to creative thinking processes, but acculturation and especially their education cost many of them this capacity. Many analysts argue (as we did in Chapter 2) that prehistoric peoples lived a more creative existence than we do now—a shock to our modern sensibilities. They both devised tools and useful objects and created ornamental and spiritual articles. Unlike many teachers and students, they avoided mechanical routines. For prehistoric humans, every day was different, new and potentially interesting and exciting. The postformal idea of process attempts to recapture that excitement and interest by devising new ways to perceive the world. The postformal process attempts to rethink thinking so as to reposition men and women as active producers, rather than passive receivers of knowledge. These postformal abilities can help ground the process of empowerment in a way that prepares us for critical action.

5. *Empowered teachers cooperate with school and community and facilitate cooperation between them.* Empowered teachers understand that a school must see itself as part of the community that surrounds it. Schools shaped in the critical new paradigm must connect with and draw on all constituencies within the community, not just the dominant few. As a school takes its place as part of the community it coordinates educational activities within it. In this context, teachers and students become students of their communities, aware of the myriad educational resources every community offers. Teachers and students come to view the community as a minilaboratory for democratic participants. All communities experience their successes and failures, and students and teachers should explore and learn from them. The community's history is extremely important to a democratic school, which can explore it for its own value and for its connections to the history of the state, the nation and the world. The community becomes in microcosm the lens through which students can analyze world events and their effects. Understanding the place we come from and the ways it has shaped our consciousness promotes both education per se and its applicability.

Our understanding of cooperation between empowered teachers, communities and schools, however, excludes public relations (PR) image building within the community. You should already be able to sense the difference between PR strategies and authentic teacher-community-school collaboration. Authentic involvement may consist of parent-student writing sessions, in which parents come into classrooms, write along with their children and then engage in discussions about their writing. Community cooperation in the form of open forums about race or gender relations are essential to a well-informed group of parents. Parents and community members should feel both that they are welcome in the schools and that they play an important part in the schooling process. In our experience, mentor programs encourage authentic community involvement. Using parents as classroom speakers can also integrate community and school. Parents are more valuable as partners in the learning experience than as committee member peanut vendors for the fall fund-raiser. Critical democratic schools offer much more than just back-to-school nights.

6. *Empowered teachers build learning networks between schools and communities that make use of recent developments and innovations in communications technologies.* Computers with Internet connections and e-mail capabilities provide new dimensions of interaction between and among teachers, students, schools and communities. Everyone can benefit from the proliferation of information access and instant interactive communication between educators, businesspeople, legal professionals, government workers and so on. In cyberspace traditional assumptions about the role of schools disintegrate and the implications for curriculum and instruction increase. To take advantage of these infinite possibilities, however, we must move beyond the simplistic notions of computer instruction that dominate

modernist schools. Using computers to process information is but a baby step along the road toward a larger understanding of educational technology. Such an understanding involves, of course, both the practical use of technical tools and the questions of how they affect our epistemologies—that is, our attempts to make meaning. Empowered teachers engage students in the analysis of what technology enables us to do and what it keeps us from doing. Such new technologies as computers more than simply add a new dimension to the world; they are also ecological in the way they modify existing relationships and ways of being (Postman, 1995). Thus, they change interrelationships among teachers, schools and communities—sometimes in ways we never expected. For example, we suggest in Chapter 12 that technology has created such dramatic changes in cultural relationships that it forced us to adjust our mid–twentieth-century ideas of childhood almost overnight. Because children now enjoy access to all the adult secrets, the curtain that once separated adulthood from childhood hangs in shreds. A change like this forever alters educational relationships among teachers, students, schools and communities.

   7. Empowered teachers become researchers and teach their students sophisticated methods of inquiry. If schools are to teach students to think above and beyond a concrete, rote-based level, they must encourage one of the most important activities that teaches thinking: research. The creation of knowledge to which we repeatedly refer often depends on our ability to engage teachers and students in research. Teachers as researchers are better able to control their own professional lives and they better understand their students' past and present life histories, their concerns, their strengths and their weaknesses. Such understanding enhances their ability to motivate, appreciate and evaluate students. As researchers, teachers gain the objectivity and skill to question their own practices, question their own assumptions and understand their own situations contextually. Anyone who can engage in these activities has moved on to high-order conceptual analysis. Using their research-driven powers of analysis, teachers can develop curricula for their schools by researching problems and sharing their findings with other teachers during in-service meetings and team-planning sessions. They can also bring dignity and intelligence to their self-evaluation procedures. We will explore this concept in detail in the next chapter.

   Students-as-researchers similarly become empowered as they learn fieldwork skills: observing, interviewing, photographing, videotaping, note-taking and life history collecting. In the process, they learn and polish the traditional skills we value in the curriculum: reading, writing, arithmetic, listening, interpreting and thinking. Students learn to uncover the forces that shape their everyday lives: their place in the social hierarchy of their peer groups, their romantic relationships, their vocational aspirations, their relationships with teachers. Teacher and student researchers work together exploring one another's life histories. In this process they share stories of everyday life, their hopes, their fears, their joys and their sadnesses. They explore one another's dreams and the factors that have interfered with those dreams. Together student and teacher researchers construct interpretations of the various events and their relationships to the community with its larger social and cultural influences. In addition to the basic academic skills, students as researchers learn to derive meaning from themselves and the world around them. Research is a necessary step toward the goal of empowerment (Kincheloe, 1991).

8. *Empowered teachers encourage schools to support their continued learning.* School leaders and the community must endeavor to make teaching good work—a profession in which teachers receive support for their efforts to raise their knowledge of students, subject matter, the community and pedagogy to new levels. Schools must accept psychological theory, socioeconomic context, and the political outcomes of learning as information worth knowing. Schools must avoid at all costs the teacher deskilling authoritarian (top-down) management strategies, standardized test-driven curricula and prepackaged (teacherproof) curriculum materials. In many classrooms teachers have little time for anything more than daily survival. Time for further learning, reflection and analysis remains elusive given the low esteem in which teachers are held, the crisis-management atmosphere and the immediate attention survival requires. In such a climate, those who suggest devoting more time and resources to reflective and growth-inducing pursuits are viewed as impractical dreamers. Thus the status quo is perpetuated, and the deskilling cycle rolls on, lowering morale. If schools are to be reformed, this cycle must be broken. Teachers must be treated with the respect due them; they must be supported in their attempts at professional improvement.

Remembering how John Dewey described his school as a community of learners, we can describe the critical school of the new paradigm as an organization designed primarily for learning (Wirth, 1983). Such an arrangement draws on natural human proclivities: All of us are learners who enjoy learning together. We enjoy being part of a team with larger purposes, a group in which individual strengths complement one another and individual weaknesses are overcome. In these fleeting moments of solidarity, men and women accomplish great things because such synergistic interaction makes us all smarter, higher-order thinkers. Through our dialogue we discover insights not normally attainable individually as we tease out those patterns that impede our attempts to derive insight.

Postformal teachers possess the ability to promote this type of knowledge production. Just as such thinkers push the cognitive envelope, they also recreate schools in a way previously unimagined. We are passionate about this recreation process, and we can hardly wait to witness its effects.

9. *Empowered teachers recognize the inability of modernist-positivist teaching methods to explain the current world of schooling.* With the precedent-shattering work of Albert Einstein and the formulation of quantum theory, Newtonian physics became only tangentially relevant, mainly in subatomic contexts. Newtonian terms could not explain the quantum dimension, an irrational land of mystery where objects instantly transformed themselves from particles to waves and matter walked through two doors at once. Similarly, the "Newtonian world" of education no longer exists. We live in a media-propelled landscape markedly different from the world of one-room schoolhouses and quilting bees. Late twentieth-century education and the society that shapes it are far removed from the culture that gave us teacher education and the methods for studying education still in use. Students now confront a world of computers, sound bytes and sophisticated manipulative strategies aimed at controlling the minds of consumers and voters.

Much of the research conducted on education fails to account for the ways information access and media technologies affect our students and teachers. To capture these effects we need to adopt new research methods developed to study media effects. Moving beyond surface appearances, educational researchers and empowered teachers uncover the hidden effects of contemporary technologies. Employing techniques borrowed from anthropology, film studies, literary criticism and history we decipher the subliminal codes and detect the intended and unintended effects of computers, television, video games, advertising, earphone stereo systems and other contemporary influences. With the new technologies surrounding us, we must be open to new ways of doing what educators have traditionally done. Our vision of educational reform compels us to suggest that educational changes undertaken to confront contemporary social and cultural realities take advantage of recent research advances. Such advances reveal that modernist science has failed to specify and respond to what teachers see and hear every day. When the sciences try to generalize from everyday methods and particular anecdotes as rationales for dictating universal official teaching strategies and theories, the context-specific nature of the particular classroom thwarts the effort (Fried, 1995). The ecological balance of a particular teaching context is delicate—you cannot transplant a cactus into a rainforest.

10. *Empowered teachers invent new and appropriate modes of assessment.* When Albert Einstein came to the United States after winning the Nobel Prize in physics, he was already regarded as the smartest man on Earth. As he disembarked onto the New York pier, a swarm of reporters met him. One of them shouted:

"Dr. Einstein, what is the speed of sound?"
"I don't know," Einstein replied.
The baffled journalist responded, "But you're the smartest man in the world. Why don't you know?"
"I don't need to know," Einstein told the reporter. "If I need the information, I can look it up." (Kincheloe, Steinberg, & Tippins, 1992, pp. 226–227)

The reporter's question reflects the naïve modernist views of intelligence, educational purpose and assessment: intelligence involves the mind's capacity to store information, educational purpose concerns the ability to cram information into the mind and assessment involves seeing how well we accomplish the cramming. As we move toward postformal definitions of intelligence and critical democratic schooling purposes, empowered teachers must develop assessment models that correspond to these changes. Modernist positivists argue that objective standardized tests are the only "fair" way of evaluating students. Under this assumption, standardized test proponents maintain that teachers need to specify precisely what students must know and then check to see whether they know it. Meanwhile, administrators need to specify precisely what teachers need to do and then check to see whether they do it. Modernist positivists assume that we already know what it is students need to learn and teachers need to do; there is, they contend, no call for debate about such issues—case closed. Thus, in such a positivist context students and teachers must be shaped to meet the characteristics of the evaluation—

squished, stuffed and pushed into a bordered category that displays ranks and percentages.

A new paradigmatic elastic approach to teaching that features divergent thinking, question asking, research, the production of knowledge and improvisational teaching hardly negates one's ability to assess student work. In fact, the students in critical democratic classrooms have a voice in their own assessment. When students and teachers together design assessment methods, students enter into a democratic partnership that gives them possession of their own educational expectations. Assessment is not an isolated process designed to alienate the student from knowledge; it is—or should be—an extension of the learning process. The only way to measure qualities and talents is to let students express what they know, not what they do not know. In this situation, measurement takes on a less quantitative, more contextualized character. How, for example, might empowered critical teachers have assessed Albert Einstein's work to circumvent short-answer, rote-based, decontextualized questions about bits and pieces of his knowledge— for example, What is the speed of sound? Einstein might have written a book on his theory of relativity. Would that book demonstrate his understanding of physics as well as his answers on a standardized multiple-choice test would? Obviously, yes, it would. The knowledge needed to ground and contextualize a new theory of physics would illustrate far more sophisticated understandings than random answers to a series of questions. In fact, one of us assigned writing a book as the assessment exercise in a graduate class. Students had to obtain a publishing contract, and write and edit a book on whiteness and education, the class topic. Their ability to accomplish such an assignment revealed much more about the quality of their understanding than the results from a battery of objective tests formulated by the Educational Testing Service's most respected experts. Empowered teachers can develop numerous creative, challenging and insightful evaluation strategies once they consider assessment in this context.

11. *Empowered teachers recognize how power shapes them, their students and the everyday schooling context.* Power operates in schools to muzzle the very people it claims to liberate. In modernist schools teachers never learn how curriculum knowledge is produced. In modernist teacher education, college students rarely ask which social voices are represented in the curriculum and which are excluded. Modernist reform proposals view teaching as a narrow practice, a technique with little if anything to do with knowledge production or the analysis of ethics or justice issues. How does schooling contribute to the production of our identities, our self-concepts, our ability to function in the world? Does it matter that we come from rich or poor homes, white or nonwhite homes? These questions go unrecognized as questions about power—indeed, they are rarely recognized at all. The idea that education is a social practice operating within a society characterized by unequal power relations generally eludes the public discourse about schooling. In an education that moves beyond the old modernist paradigm—one that is grounded in a critical social vision—these questions of power stand out. As schools confront the subtle forms of racism, sexism, homophobia, religious intolerance and class bias that keep the disempowered weak, we begin to understand the emancipatory force of postformal thinking—the sociocognitive orientation

that attunes us to questions of power and the insidious ways it shows itself in our schools.

Critically empowered teachers act on the basis of their passion for justice and egalitarian relationships among human beings. In the contemporary world, with its technologically guided explosion of corporate agendas and media images, this passion has become a requirement for confronting those forces that undermine social justice in education. Beginning with our passion, we learn to decipher the power codes, the repressive ways ideological interests invade not only the schools but the popular culture as well. Our critical concern with reading the world as text emerges at this point, impressing us with its ability to expose the invisible workings of contemporary power. Teachers concerned with the preservation of democracy must possess these deconstructive abilities if we are to help children understand where they stand in the web of sociopolitical reality. If schooling is to empower its students rather than muzzle them, we have our work as proponents of an empowering democracy cut out for us.

PART
4

Teaching Context
Teachers as Reflective Thinkers, Curriculum Leaders and Action Researchers

Teachers as Researchers

INTRODUCTION

John Dewey understood the relationship between teaching as empowered democratic work and teacher as researcher. In *The Sources of a Science of Education* (1929) Dewey argued that one of a teacher's most important responsibilities was to inquire into and investigate educational problems. Writing of the "teacher as investigator," Dewey saw teachers as the most important determinants of the success or failure of the school; in fact, he saw no other way to produce viable educational research. Not only, Dewey thought, did these investigations lead to knowledge about the school, they also led to good teaching. Indeed, the benefit of teacher research seventy years later continues to be good teaching, defined both as effective ways of conveying information and as understanding the significance of ideas and their effect on humans (McCutcheon, 1981; Duckworth, 1987; Semel & Sadovnik, 1999; Simpson & Jackson, 1997).

Certainly, one of the surest ways to apply teacher research to the pursuit of good teaching involves, quite simply, listening to students. This "research on students" is a central tenet of good teaching, with teachers detailing their observations and their reactions to their students. These observations can then be contextualized by considering the social environment in which both student and teacher consciousness forms and education takes place. As teachers come to understand how both their students and they themselves construct understandings of the educational process, they can move themselves into unknown territory, out onto new frontiers of thinking. In this way teacher research revolutionizes traditional conceptions of staff development, making it a democratic, teacher-directed activity rather than a manifestation of the hierarchicalized imposition of the modernist workplace. It promotes empowered teachers by assuming that teachers are knowledgeable and entitled to make decisions about their profession (Wood, 1988).

SHARPENING OBSERVATIONAL SKILLS

In many ways this conception of teacher research is just a commonsense explanation of what good teachers already do. By making it a central point in the conversation about good teaching, however, we can extend the value of the concept. When Patricia Wood (1988) began her work with teacher research, she thought she had already incorporated the basic elements of the action research model: planning, acting, observing and reflecting. But by focusing her attention on the process, she sharpened her observation skills and began to reflect in a more textured, conscious manner. A "textured reflection" on one's teaching requires a thorough understanding of one's own practices, especially the ambiguities, contradictions and tensions implicit in them. When the teacher as researcher joins other teachers as researchers and a college faculty interested in these ambiguities, contradictions and tensions, a dynamic process begins. This process is the basis of educational change, of critical pedagogy, of a new democratic paradigm (Elliot, 1989; Torney-Purta, 1985).

Teacher education that neglects these aspects of teacher research misses the point—which is to say, the distinct demands of the teaching workplace, the implications educational theory holds for democracy and the ambiguity in a practitioner's ways of knowing. Jean Piaget (1973) recommended that teacher educators acquaint teachers with the nature of research as quickly as possible. The idea of teacher research, Piaget believed, cannot be separated from any other component of teacher education. The act of research engages teachers in the dynamics of the educational process, as it brings to consciousness the creative tension between social and educational theory and classroom practice. What exactly does this creative tension mean? Among other things, it involves a form of thinking that moves into a postformal realm of *problem discovering*. It transcends the Piagetian formal stage of *problem solving*. As a researcher, a teacher travels into a realm of analysis that forces him or her to weigh the associations among (1) social vision and its concern with the nature of justice, (2) educational purpose and its concern with the effects of how we define education, and (3) how we as educational leaders conduct our professional lives. A teacher education that introduces this three-dimensional association cannot be simplistically technicist, and it cannot help connecting theory and practice. Moreover, it has to view teachers as self-directed agents, sophisticated thinkers and active researchers in ever-changing, often ambiguous contexts. It encourages teachers to construct their own views of their practice; it encourages them to question the constructs of others and to avoid acting in response to the officially certified knowledge base. It encourages teachers to discover along the path toward harmony the asymmetries and contradictions between critical conceptions of justice and the untidy world of learners and schools.

Modernist forms of teacher education—with their emphasis on universal methods, behavioral management and predetermined objectives—have paid little attention to the connection between researching and teaching. About the only time modernist colleges of education ever teach research methodology is in graduate courses, where students are encouraged more to lead or supervise than simply to teach. Even there, graduate students learn empirical quantitative research with its experimental designs and statistical analyses—not the type of research that lends itself to everyday applicability in the life of a teacher. The type of research we describe here has teacher empowerment as its primary purpose. This quest for empowerment (we discussed it thoroughly in Chapter 8) involves teachers in the process of developing skills that help them reflect constructively on their teaching. The teacher research we propose may not formulate theories of education generalizable to schools around the world. Rather, our conception of critical teacher research is designed to make teaching more reflective and more responsive to social and historical contexts. Teachers as researchers gain the skill to interrogate their own practices, question their own assumptions and understand contextually their own situations (Carr & Kemmis, 1986).

In short, we envision teacher education programs that encourage future professionals to critically analyze the impact of teaching styles, methodologies and practices in local contexts. This orientation will require more early contact with classrooms, students and teachers; personal reflection and ethnographic investigation; and sophisticated communication and interpersonal skills. As you can see, the teacher as researcher must do more than implement predetermined goals, objectives and methods; he or she must be an active participant in the construction of each learning environment.

THE RISE OF ACTION RESEARCH

The term "action research" has been prominent in the conversation about teacher research since the 1940s. In the decades since, the concept has sometimes been applied, notably in Great Britain and Australia, and drawing on several academic traditions, action research has been praised as an important innovation in social inquiry. Kurt Lewin (1946), a researcher in the field of social psychology, did the most to popularize the term, and he used the method in a variety of contexts, including industry and American Indian affairs. Following World War II, Stephen Corey at Teachers College in New York led the action research movement in education. Corey believed that if teachers applied the results of their own inquiries to instructional practices, they could reform curriculum practice. Corey found considerable enthusiasm for his movement, but in the late 1950s action research became the target of serious criticism and it started to decline in popularity. That decline appears to have been precipitated by the positivist separation of science and practice that the cult of the expert produced. As policymakers came to rely more and more on expert educational research and developmental laboratories, the curriculum and pedagogical practices were dictated from the top down. Thus, the production of research separated from the world of the teacher (McKernan, 1988).

In the 1970s action research enjoyed a recovery, and by the 1980s it had aligned itself with the attempt to redefine teacher professionalism. Its revival paralleled the emergence of the new critical paradigm, with its skepticism of the positivist view of knowledge. Such a view, critical analysts had begun to realize, emphasized prespecified measurable learning outcomes and degraded the role of teacher as an empowered, self-directed professional. Teachers began to question the usefulness of positivism's abstract generalizations in the concrete and ambiguous situations they confronted daily. The teachers and analysts who advocated the teacher-as-researcher movement began to reformulate the whole idea of educational research, which, they maintained, is as different from empirical research as teacher knowledge is different from traditional scientific knowledge (Elliott, 1989a). An appropriate teacher action can hardly be preordained by an education deity; it is a matter of personal judgment in a particular situation. "Generalization" carries a different meaning for the teacher-researcher than it does for the empirical researcher. Constantly confronting one unique situation after another, the teacher-researcher would be guilty of a crude and impractical reductionism if he or she claimed to have sorted out positivistic cause-and-effect relationships in the classroom (Elliott, 1989a; Lincoln & Guba, 1985).

As an example of the way that this positivistic cause-and-effect relationship affects a classroom, consider the case of the fourth-grade teacher who was having a particularly difficult time with one student. The boy frequently blurted out inappropriate, vulgar words, embarrassing both the teacher and his classmates. He would often interrupt the class with his twitches, snorts and sudden outbursts. He would drum his pencil on his desk and distract the rest of the class. Nearly defeated by these constant interruptions, the teacher met with the principal, called the boy's parents, implemented assertive discipline techniques, talked to the student after class and, as the year progressed, punished the student at recess almost every day. Nothing seemed to work. The school had few resources, no counselors and an overworked administrative staff.

Finally the teacher contacted a consultant at the local university and asked her to observe the classroom. On her initial visit, the consultant discussed the concept of teacher as researcher and proposed that together they could "investigate" the situation. After several days of observation and conversation, the consultant invited a school psychologist from a neighboring district to join them. When the school psychologist observed the classroom, he suggested that the student might have the medical condition known as Tourette's syndrome (recall our reference to Tourette's syndrome in the Introduction). With the permission of the boy's parents and the principal, they consulted a medical doctor who confirmed that the boy had Tourette's and required a very different approach to his outbursts than assertive discipline or recess punishment.

While distressed to learn of the condition, the teacher was relieved to have a better understanding of the young man's behavioral problems. This situation exemplifies the complexity of the classroom and the human context. No simple cause-and-effect relationship can explain every event in the classroom. You cannot simply apply a behavior management plan to all students and expect successful results. Teachers as researchers must constantly explore the complexity and be open to multiple—often unexpected—solutions to their problems. Applying traditional behavior management techniques to a student with Tourette's syndrome, or any other handicapping condition, is both ineffective and unjust. Teachers must constantly apply action research methods in their own classrooms and look for alternative, humane solutions when concerns arise.

While exposing the inapplicability of positivist generalizations is an important component of teacher-directed action research, the benefits move beyond epistemological issues involving knowledge acquisition and information processing. Teachers acquainted with the dynamics of action research are better equipped to attend to their students, to understand their unique situations, and to listen to their needs. Teachers who listen to their students and elicit their opinions and perspectives enjoy a variety of benefits. Students who can express thoughts and ideas they previously suppressed for fear of censure or retribution experience a form of catharsis that leads to a healthier teacher-student relationship, improved communication and mutual understanding. In effect the student is confirmed, his or her experiences are validated and he or she feels a greater sense of self-worth resulting from the teacher's attention and interest. This attention encourages students to organize their previously unsystematized thoughts so that the teacher can understand them. Thus, they employ an element of interpretation: a hermeneutical act relatively easy to elicit from students because it connects with their lived worlds (Reinharz, 1979; Shor, 1992; Gallagher, 1992; Slattery, 1995a).

Some action researchers refer to student interviewing as "debriefing." They ask their students questions that encourage them to recollect and reconstruct their experiences. From this information, teachers can draw valuable conclusions and make dependable decisions about how to improve their courses and develop the curriculum in ways that are responsive to their students' needs. We find altogether too few examples in the curriculum research literature that use students' perceptions of what they have learned and what it meant to them. Instead of asking students what they have learned, instrumentally rational researchers settle for empirical observations of student classroom behavior or students' responses to standardized tests or highly structured survey instruments. Daniel Duke lists seven debriefing questions teachers might use for student interviews:

> *What did you learn in the class?*
>
> *You just told me what you learned. What do you think learning is?*
>
> *Now that you've defined learning, is there anything you learned in class that you didn't mention in question one?*
>
> *What do you know as a result of taking the class that you didn't know before taking it?*
>
> *What can you do as a result of taking the class that you couldn't do before taking it?*
>
> *What one point did the teacher emphasize the most during the course?*
>
> *You tell me that you can reduce what you learned in an entire course to a few minutes. Is that all you learned in the course? (1977, p. 674)*

Thus, teacher research becomes a valuable teaching tool. As they reconstruct their own experiences by answering Duke's debriefing questions, students take responsibility for organizing, interpreting and making sense of their academic lives.

The Brazilian philosopher-educator Paulo Freire (1972) focuses our attempts as critical action researchers to involve our students in our research. When we act on Freire's conception of inquiry, teacher research becomes a powerful teaching tool and learning experience for students. Freire specified no traditionally defined objects of his educational research; rather, he insisted on involving the people he studied as partners in the process. He immersed himself in their ways of thinking and levels of perception, encouraging them all along to begin thinking about their own thinking. This method of critical research, which involves the study and criticism of the research process itself, is also a pedagogical process. Everyone involved, not just the researcher, joins in the process of investigation, examination, criticism and reinvestigation. Everyone learns to see more critically, to think on a higher level and to recognize the subtle and overt forces that shape their lives.

Critical action researchers can put Freire's methods to work in their classrooms. In the process of conducting their own research they can teach students the research techniques they have learned. They can encourage their students to use such fieldwork skills as observing, interviewing, picture-taking, videotaping, tape recording, note-taking and life history collecting. In the process, students learn and practice the traditional classroom skills: reading, writing, computing, speaking, listening, interpreting and thinking. One excellent example of student research is the Foxfire Project, developed in Georgia a quarter century ago, in which students developed research skills by collecting local folklore.

Another example of field-based action research is the African American studies oral history project in one Louisiana high school. A local antebellum plantation museum and the teacher collaborated on the course, and the students gathered stories, artifacts and genealogies in the community and brought them to class. Together the teacher, the museum staff and the students began to reconstruct the history of the local African American community, with an eye toward designing displays for the museum. Southern museums often minimize or exclude information about the enslaved Africans who lived and worked on the plantations, and this oral history project sought to redress decades of historical oversight. While some local people found this project controversial, it captured the attention of the national media and researchers. Far from inert information about the past, history became active, important and compelling ideas about the present (Weaver, Slattery, & Daspit, 1998).

As teachers conduct this type of research, Freire believed, the researchers (be they teachers or students) educate and are educated along with their students. When we return to the research site to put the results of our inquiry into practice, we not only educate and are educated, but we also research once again. Thus, the teacher-research process continues without end. When we implement the plans that emerge from the research, we change the consciousnesses of both our students and ourselves—a change that initiates a new set of questions and a new phase of research. In the plantation history example, new insights and information gathered by the students dramatically changed the museum and the local community. First, the museum expanded its collection beyond the artifacts of white European settlers. Second, the community was forced to discuss and reconstruct its own racist history and analyze the lingering impact of slavery. Third, students had the opportunity to research local history, with an eye toward validating silenced voices and neglected information (Carson & Sumara, 1997).

As you might expect, Freire's critical democratic concept of research confutes the instrumental rationality of positivist researchers. His invitation to the examined to participate in the formulation, criticism and reformulation of the research directly challenges the positivist cult of the expert with boilerplate solutions to every problem. Suddenly alternate solutions, marginalized voices, hidden memories and challenging ideas enter into the educational process. At the same time, action research provides critical educational researchers with a sense of direction, an orientation that transforms our idea of research from mere data gathering into a consciousness-raising, transformative pedagogical act.

Notice that central to this emancipatory action research is an appreciation for and a mobilization of the student's perception of schooling. Before Freire's approach can work, teachers must understand what happens in the minds of their students. Critical analysts following Freire seek to uncover the social construction of consciousness by focusing on their students' motives, values and emotions. Operating within this critical context, the teacher-researcher studies students as if they were texts to be read. The teacher-researcher approaches them with an active imagination and a willingness to view them as socially constructed beings (Grady & Wells, 1985–86).

When teachers approach action research from this perspective they usually uncover some interesting information. In a British action research project, for example, teachers used student diaries, interviews, dialogues and shadowing (following their pupils as they pursued their school routines) to discover a preoccupation with what came to be labeled a "second-order curriculum." This curriculum included matters of student dress, conformity to school rules, strategies of coping with boredom and failure and methods of assuming their respective roles in the social pecking order. Teacher-researchers found that much of this second-order curriculum contradicted the stated aims of the school to respect the individuality of students, encourage sophisticated thinking and engender positive self-concepts. The students themselves learned that the daily lessons (the intentional curriculum) operated on a set of assumptions quite different from the assumptions that guided their out-of-class teacher interactions. Teachers often miss or misinterpret the hostility this inconsistency produces. An action-research project that values the perceptions of students can explicate their emotions and allow a teacher to address them, however (Oldroyd, 1985).

THE "CRITICAL" IN CRITICAL ACTION RESEARCH: THE TEACHER'S INQUIRY AND THE STRUGGLE FOR DEMOCRACY

Both a cognitive and a political act, research teaches us to think more deeply and at a more complex level as part of the broader process of empowerment. Accordingly, we can appropriate the action-research movement as a major part of our campaign to transcend modernist assumptions about the teaching profession. Critical teachers as researchers who understand the philosophical, historical and sociological contexts of schooling and who acquaint themselves with a panoply of research skills are equipped to operate as empowered, self-directed professionals. Action research that can be termed "critical" meets five requirements:

1. Critical action research is always designed and pursued in relation to practice; in fact, it exists to improve practice.
2. Critical action research rejects positivist notions of rationality, objectivity and truth and assumes that research issues and methods are always political.
3. The critical action researcher is aware of his or her own value commitments, the value commitments of others and the values promoted by the dominant culture. In other words, one of the main concerns of critical action research is the exposure of the relationship between individual values and practice.
4. Critical action research requires an awareness of the social construction of the professional consciousness.
5. Critical action researchers attempt to uncover those aspects of the dominant social order that undermine efforts to pursue emancipatory goals.

With these five criteria in mind, you can see that critical action research is the consummate democratic act: It allows teachers to determine the conditions of their own work. It facilitates their attempts to organize themselves into communities of scholars dedicated to emancipatory experiences for their students. When teachers unite with students and community members to ask serious questions about what is taught, how it is taught and what the goals of the school may be, critical self-reflection is promoted and group decision making is achieved (Carr & Kemmis, 1986; Aronowitz & Giroux, 1985).

For example, when students, community members and teachers set out together to discover where in the community students can learn in ways that combine vocational skills with personal empowerment and the cultivation of postformal thinking, a democratic dialogue results. In the course of this dialogue, democratic imperatives are strengthened and social imaginations are enriched by the analytical conversation. Students, community members and teachers all have to consider their respective roles in the selection process, while at the same time engaging in a dialogue about the goals of schooling and the nature of thinking. Wise teachers engaged in such a process could elicit from adult workers in the community self-examinations centered on which aspects of their jobs require postformal thinking. Induced to examine their own assumptions in relation to their applicability to the selection of sights, community members might make major contributions to the cultivation of postformal thinking among students. The democratic ties and the cognitive advances this simple example of action research could engender suggest the power of the form.

More than a catalyst for postformal thinking and democratic action, critical action research is an antidote to the perception of teachers as low-level routinized workers. Research and theory building lie outside a teacher's domain in the modernist paradigm. Experts take care of such concerns; teachers stick to their prescribed tasks. Such modernist hierarchical elitism precludes teacher-directed research and democratization of the workplace since it reinforces authoritarian status distinctions that demean the role of teachers and perpetuate public perceptions of their incompetence (Altrichter & Posch, 1989). Critical action research is incompatible with the modernist notion of "vanguardism," the idea that institutions change only when small groups of leaders force their will on the workers, leading them on to greater efficiency or productivity. This undemocratic idea discourages teacher-led movements that reject the top-down orientation that has guided the educational reforms of recent decades (Agger, 1991; Floden & Klinzing, 1990).

Critical orientations to research and reform tend to reverse the usual flow of communications in the teaching workplace. Teachers speak with a more authoritative voice to their supervisors, and modernist pedagogies that reduce teaching to the technical act of imparting information certified by experts yield to skeptical inquiry. When critical action researchers develop a hermeneutic to guide their research design, select research methods, interpret their research and act on the basis of their research, their way of constructing their professional self-identity changes forever. Unable to claim scientific neutrality, critical action research can hardly avoid challenging the undemocratic, scientifically managed modernist workplace of teaching. Teachers as critical researchers feel compelled to reclaim knowledge and their schools and to expose the political and cognitive consequences of modernist and technicist forms of school management and teaching. Action research can exert considerable influence in the struggle to salvage the dignity of teaching from the ravages of narrow accountability (Bogdan & Biklen, 1982; Longstreet, 1982; Torney-Purta, 1985; Oldroyd & Tiller, 1987; Kroath, 1989).

As action researchers challenge techno-teaching and procedural thinking, they seek unity with critical democratic groups outside the school. Using their research skills to identify subjugated knowledge in the local community, teachers as researchers become cultural workers eager to unite with small and often oppressed groups who come to think of cognition as a political activity. For example, once women (hardly a small group!) come to understand that their intuitive ways of thinking have been socially devalued and can connect their personal stories to this larger concept, they become allies in the critical postmodern project to reconceptualize the purpose of our schools. Understanding that any insecurity about their own intellectual abilities tends to originate with the politically validated male-centered discourse on cognition, women become empowered to redefine themselves and the prevailing perceptions of what constitutes sophisticated thinking. Critical action researchers seek solidarity with these types of individuals. Teachers find that their connections with such groups provide two-way benefits: First, they awaken the dormant curiosities and insights in individuals connected to subjugated knowledges. Second, the awakened individuals induce teachers to ask questions of their own previously unconsidered practices. A public democratic dialogue like this leads to dramatic social and cognitive change.

RETHINKING ASSUMPTIONS AS A POLITICAL ACT

We return here to explore John Dewey's (1916) early assertion that the type of research he imagined challenges the technicist search for control and certainty. Our vision of critical action research shares Dewey's understanding in that it undermines the positivist comfort with taken-for-granted assumptions. In a dominant culture that devalues reflection among its teacher professionals, action research becomes an *oppositional activity,* pushing professionals in a variety of fields to reconsider their assumptions (Greene, 1988). Peter McLaren (1992) argued that new paradigmatic forms of inquiry claim a truth that implies an awareness of the metaphors that guide their meaning. Such research forms do not assume knowledge to be something to discover. Rather, information produced by such inquiry, McLaren contended, is a self-conscious social text produced by a variety of mutually informing contexts. All of us who were educated in modernist schools from the 1940s through the 1980s have trouble at first understanding such a concept. In addition, the oppositional notion of critical action research may sit uneasily with those teacher education students whose main concerns revolve around fitting into the schools in which they plan to student teach or establish a career. So what *did* McLaren mean? Well, knowledge in the new paradigm research he supports is "constructed" or "invented," not found or discovered; it is self-conscious in that researchers are aware of their own contribution to what emerges as knowledge; it is a social text in that all knowledge is open to different readings just like a book or any other "text" is open to various interpretations and understandings; it is produced by its relation to a variety of settings—for example, its historical, socioeconomic, class, gender, racial, religious and educational environments. If we fail to view knowledge as a part of a larger set of processes connected to these contexts, we can hardly understand its importance or its relation to ourselves, our students and our pedagogy.

If teacher-researchers as critical agents encourage epistemological analysis and professional self-reflection on the nature of the construction of their consciousness, then they necessarily adopt a political role. Indeed, technicists complain that these roles politicize the schools. Their contention that schools should remain politically neutral reflects a popular naiveté that neglects to identify dominant definitions of neutrality as problematic (or, in fact, political). They fail to realize or acknowledge that the role of the teacher as a neutral transmitter of prearranged facts is politicized. If schools seek to achieve teacher and student empowerment, they must reconsider the idea of what constitutes politicization. Along with many other critical theorists, we refuse to accept the concept of political neutrality. (In Chapter 10 we discuss the concept of the "null curriculum.") In fact, even the topics we do neglect or decline to cover and the issues we avoid—in the name of neutrality—establish political and social values. When we fail to discuss the Puritans' Christianity, Walt Whitman's homosexuality or Henry David Thoreau's idiosyncratic tax protests, we make a political judgment about the value of specific information and ideas.

When we use the term "political"—contrary to popular assumptions—we do not refer to elections and government. We use the term to address the concept of power, particularly the way power is distributed among definable social groups and types of individuals. All educational acts involve power. Who has access to school is a question that has been answered in many different ways throughout American educational history. African Americans, Latinos, migrant workers, immigrants, the poor, women—all have been denied access to schooling in general or to good schools or influential school programs in particular. We see here power-related issues, with some students gaining greater access to knowledge than others.

Another educational power issue centers on what gets taught in U.S. schools—that is, what knowledge should be included in the curriculum. Do we teach about the great deeds of women? Do we study African or African American literature? Do we analyze the art of Latino/as? Do we examine the epistemologies of indigenous peoples around the world and interpret the lessons they might teach the so-called "developed world"? Do we explore the teachings of various world religions and philosophies? These are political issues because they involve power dynamics related to whose tradition and whose heritage are considered worthy, or "of worth." Students who find their cultural heritage dismissed in school experience disempowerment and damage to their self-esteem. This impact discourages their efforts to achieve success and seize the opportunities education can provide.

We must bring political understandings like these into the light of analysis. Teacher-researchers must specify the power dynamics that inform the "texts" of curriculum, disciplinary policies, school communications, teacher contracts and so forth. Confront these issues and battle with texts as a form of research, or so Paulo Freire and Ira Shor (1987) exhorted teachers. Resist the demand of the official curriculum for deference to official interpretations and the "rules of schools," they argued as part of their larger vision. A surrender to certified textual readings is hardly an act of political neutrality. In their refusal to accept the authority of texts and the dictates of the official curriculum, critical action researchers come to see themselves and their students as knowledge producers. This partnership can be difficult for teachers and students to accept, for most of their public school and university experiences contradict the concept. Research, as defined for them, constitutes finding and assimilating information already produced by experts (Apple, 1999).

Many college students welcome the passive student role by the time they enter teacher education programs. They find themselves required only to finish their assignments on time and pass exams that call on their low-level cognitive ability to memorize factual data. For those influenced by such instruction, knowledge is received—that is, it consists of isolated bits and pieces to be collected and then returned to instructors on tests. Knowledge is something "out there" to be discovered with the application of recommended procedures. Imagine students' cognitive and epistemological discomfort when confronted with the need to become action researchers, actual producers of knowledge. Before we can immerse these students in such research activity, they must be made conversant with the cognitive, political and epistemological issues that surround critical teacher research.

But once they recognize these issues and experience action research, their professional lives change forever. As knowledge producers, these teachers and incipient teachers begin to construct curricula around the student experience, promoting their students' understanding of the social, economic and cultural forces that affect them. Students learn ethnographic, semiotic, phenomenological and historiographical forms of inquiry, and in the process learn to study and identify the ideological forces that shape their lives. They start to explore their place in the social hierarchy of their peer group, their romantic relationships, their vocational aspirations, their relationships with teachers and their definitions of success.

Meanwhile, their teachers' understanding of why and how critical action research serves as an oppositional activity deepens as they step back from their conditioned view of the world. In the process they uncover the constructing forces: the linguistic codes, cultural signs, power-driven representations and embedded ideologies. Here they are, learning to research, to teach and to think, all at once. Critical teachers as researchers produce knowledge—that is, they remake their professional lives and rename their worlds (Adler, 1991; Slaughter, 1989; Schön, 1983, 1987, 1991).

THE CASE FOR QUALITATIVE RESEARCH METHODS

The type of research methods action researchers use are qualitative rather than quantitative. We have no problem with quantitative methods of research in education, as long as a researcher uses them to analyze questions that involve frequency or statistical relationships—and many educational questions fall in this domain. Too often, however, researchers rely on quantitative methods to count aspects of human and educational events better *understood* than *counted* (Pinar et al., 1995), and these *applications* strike us as inappropriate, not the quantitative methods themselves. The information social and educational researchers collect may include observed behavior, documents and artifacts. But one ought not separate these source materials from the meanings past, present and future human beings grant them. The qualitative dimension of research attempts to incorporate an appreciation of these human meanings. As qualitative researchers concentrate on the meanings participants give events, they gain more understanding than a list of descriptions or a table of statistics can give them.

When, by contrast, a positivist researcher focuses an inquiry exclusively on a quantitative dimension, he or she tends to narrow that research to those aspects that lend themselves to numerical expression. Instead of focusing on a student's attitude toward learning or his or her creativity, the educational research tends to focus on achievement—typically an operationally defined "achievement" based on standardized tests (Popkewitz, 1981). The data such a process produces is hardly the knowledge teachers find useful in making pedagogical decisions. Teachers need contextual understandings that illuminate a student's consciousness, his or her motivations, pain and dreams.

We realize you may not be acquainted with the technical aspects of research, quantitative or qualitative. The subject and its attendant issues are often absent at the undergraduate or even the master's level. But these issues should be part of your education—indeed, we believe that teaching people to conduct research should be at the core of a college education, especially teacher education. Preliminarily, then, we outline five important dimensions of qualitative research as an introduction to further levels of understanding action research:

1. *Concern with context* (this dimension of qualitative research inspired the title of this book, *Contextualizing Teaching*). "Context stripping" has become a regrettable feature of modernist-positivist science such that scientific methods that fail to avoid this stripping routinely distort the reality they claim to portray. Human experience takes shape in particular con-

texts and cannot be understood if removed from those contexts. Accordingly, qualitative researchers attempt to be as naturalistic as possible, meaning that they avoid constructing or modifying contexts. Research must take place in the normal, everyday context of the people or communities being researched. Ethnography (the research methodology anthropologists use), for example, is a nearly ideal form of qualitative research since it studies events as they evolve in natural settings.

2. *Holistic view of experience.* Qualitative research focuses on all aspects of an experience. As they explore human situations, qualitative researchers must attend to the variety of factors that shape them. In their quests for holism they address those underlying complexities of school experience quantitative researchers—who concentrate on statistics—so often overlook. The connections between experiences that provide their significance in human affairs are essential features of holistic qualitative research.

3. *Methods of inquiry must be appropriate to aims of inquiry.* Questions about particular topics compel certain research strategies. Thus, for example, we would avoid statistical analyses in an investigation of a handicapped child's psychological discomfort in the company of insensitive peers. This does not mean that qualitative researchers never borrow or share different methods; in fact, they are typically eclectic and diverse. But they will be consistent with the dimensions of the question they try to answer. Instead of intervening in experience by removing it from its natural setting or by structuring the "important" aspects of the experience quantitatively, qualitative researchers look for social and cultural patterns of experience, relationships among various occurrences or the significance of specific events as they influence specific human purposes.

4. *Concern with human experience as it is lived or felt.* This concern with human consciousness is an essential aspect of qualitative research. Qualitative thinking engages the affective and sympathetic dimensions of human activity, which of course border on the aesthetic dimension. Thus, qualitative research attempts to describe human experience in a manner that respects the human actors who feel it or live it. Ethnography as a mode of qualitative research succeeds to the degree that it enables one to understand what goes on in a society or a social circumstance, as well as in the participants. The readers of successful ethnography should sense that if they found themselves in the school described there they would understand the forces that moved the principal, for example, to act in a certain way. As Eliot Eisner, professor of art and education at Stanford University, observed, "There's an aesthetic dimension to everything. Every school environment, every setting you create to spend time in, enhances or diminishes the quality of life. Whether you are teaching science or art, the challenge is to make it beautiful" (address to ASCD, Spring, 1990).

5. *Interest in using the knowledge produced to make judgments.* The "appraising aspect" of qualitative research helps one to describe the essential qualities of events, to interpret the meanings and relationships among those events and to appraise the significance of the events in the larger picture

of social and educational concerns. In making these types of judgments qualitative researchers are explicit about the social values and human interests on which they base their appraisals. Without this explicit delineation, qualitative research falls prey to the same oversights it finds in much quantitative research. Such characteristics may make it seem that we produce our qualitative action research for the consumption of others. While insight into one's daily context and the successes and failures of one's own professional practice may be the primary concern of qualitative action research, we see no reason why such inquiry should be kept from other teachers, curriculum committees, parents and community members.

Thus, teacher researchers open a new world of educational practice when they use qualitative inquiry to examine the lived world of pedagogy. After involving ourselves in action research, do we possess new and better ways of appraising educational events? Are we better able to conceptualize educational questions in general and questions about our practice in particular? Can we transcend the empty rhetoric and the clichés that often dominate education talk (for example, "We're here for the children"; "We believe in quality education for everyone"; "Our school system seeks to provide educational excellence")? Does our qualitative teacher research equip us, in the spirit of anticipatory accommodation, to transfer and apply insights from one context to another? The purposes of qualitative research are multidimensional. In fact, the inquiry attempts to engender understanding on three levels simultaneously: the issue being researched, the research process itself and the researcher. When we frame our qualitative research in the epistemology of the new paradigm it becomes transformative in the sense that it seeks to change for the better the issue being researched, the research process and the researcher (Donmoyer, 1987; Reinharz, 1979).

By adopting techniques that help us to see from new perspectives what schools are like and why they have come to be that way, action researchers heighten their consciousness of themselves as players on the educational stage, take themselves less for granted and view themselves as objects of study. As teachers observe and evaluate themselves, they ask such questions as Who do I call on in class? Who do I criticize? From whom do I withhold criticism? Where do I stand or sit when I'm teaching? How do I arrange my room? Do I need desks? Do I encourage student involvement in classroom decisions? Do I respond differently to the misbehavior of different students? Do I hold class outdoors or in the community?

Such a perspective gives teachers a sense of critical distance—that is, ironically, a closeness to students marked by an awareness of who they are; what their concerns, interests, experiences and socioeconomic backgrounds are; and how diverse their forms of intelligence are. It also provides a metaphorical distance that allows them to step back and watch how their own backgrounds influence their daily lives at school, their self-definitions, the perceptions other teachers have of them and their educational success (Bogdan & Biklen, 1982).

At this point we will introduce you to a few qualitative research methodologies we hope encourage you to study in more detail ways of performing qualitative research that, in turn, helps you address the questions just listed.

PHENOMENOLOGY, THE STUDY OF CONSCIOUSNESS AND PERCEPTION

Phenomenologists consider consciousness an essential aspect of humanness, and they recommend that one study it if one seeks insight into the affairs of human beings. But phenomenologists warn that the study of consciousness is limited by two important factors: (1) unlike the concrete elements of nature, consciousness is not an object and (2) some aspects of consciousness resist the traditional empirical methods of science. Ever fascinated with the content of elusive consciousness, phenomenologists skip over the empirical question of what is or is not real. They simply begin with the nature of consciousness—whatever that nature might be—as significant data to be studied. Phenomenology calls into question all presuppositions about the nature of its own activity, the object being investigated, and the method appropriate to this kind of inquiry (Husserl, 1970). Accordingly, phenomonologists argue that consciousness is intentional, meaning that it is directed toward a specific object. In other words, consciousness is consciousness *of something*. It requires an object. Thus, phenomenologists consider it absurd to divide reality (or the research process) into subjects (researchers) and objects (the researched). The two cannot be separated, and any attempt to do so distorts reality (Stewart & Mickunas, 1974).

We can see, then, that phenomenologists attempt to grasp the meanings that others ascribe to their own lived worlds. This form of understanding involves putting oneself in place of others and attempting to recreate in oneself their feelings. It is easy to see the impact phenomenology might have on other modes of research. When researchers ask less about the absolute meaning of a work of art or a classroom environment or a student essay and more about its meaning for a certain individual or a group, they move research in new directions. The qualitative knowledge that emerges when researchers ask about and attempt to interpret the meanings that particular individuals attribute to particular events provides new understandings of and unique perspectives on social activities and those who participate in them. The human realm of meaning making becomes accessible in a way empirical researchers rarely imagine, as scholars interrogate the conventions, forms and codes of everyday social life (Smith, 1983; Donmoyer, 1985; Soltis, 1984; Noblit, 1999). The understanding of the way individuals construe their world and their place in it phenomenology produces leads in turn to intersubjective knowledge (understandings of a social vein shared by a group of individuals), then on to new dimensions of seeing social experience. In educational inquiry such ways of seeing help researchers understand how teachers and students give meaning to their lived worlds in light of social and cultural forms they reflect and help produce. Indeed, such forms of inquiry produce understanding of the often hidden and always ambiguous process by which education initiates us into our culture (Kincheloe, 1991; Soltis, 1984).

Phenomenology provides a qualitative alternative to the epistemology of positivism. It also provides a starting point for a teacher-researcher attempting to move beyond the traditions that too often dictate the curriculum, perpetuate teacher deskilling and turn schools into stressful workplaces. Secure in our understanding of the epistemological aspects of paradigmatic change, phenomenological insights can help us connect our philosophy with our teaching. No longer do we see the role of teacher as an agent of administrative policy; no longer do we see research as a part of a process of explaining, controlling and predicting. Phenomenology teaches that we cannot understand an educational act without understanding the context within which teachers, students and administrators make sense of their thoughts, feelings and actions. Phenomenology teaches us to abandon such positivist deductive devices as prior hypothesis formation, which hampers researchers by directing their attention toward measurable but often trivial factors.

As with qualitative research in general, so in phenomenology, the focus of our study emerges as the inquiry progresses. We focus on the perceptions individuals possess, seeking the insiders' perspectives. Of course, at the critical level we also search for the various ways larger social forces construct this perspective. To the critical phenomenologist, the most influential and important reality is human perception, a reality more important than any so-called objective reality because people act on what they perceive, and perceptions have consequences, they move events, they shape lives. Consider how these ideas affect the research act in educational settings. While the positivist researcher seeks objective, factual, verifiable portrayals of reality, phenomenologically oriented action researchers seek to understand the participants' comprehension of what is happening and how such perceptions influence their lives. Because they hold such different goals, research data produced by the two approaches present quite different perspectives on the world and the school (Fetterman, 1988).

We find the phenomenological perspective almost poetic in its aesthetic, emotional and metaphorical descriptions of the world. But this dynamic appears nonsensical to positivists, with their demands for strict rationality. Teacher-researchers who employ phenomenology in their classrooms enter into a practice of thoughtfulness: they heed what is around them, attempting to comprehend what it means for themselves and their students to be alive. Such teachers use this perspective both to understand their immediate worlds and to connect them to the curriculum. A phenomenological curriculum attends to questions of consciousness and feeling in relation to traditional disciplinary knowledge, as well as the knowledge produced in the classroom. Phenomenological educator Max van Manen (1984) listed four tentative steps for beginning research: (1) choosing a topic (a phenomenon) that emotionally and intellectually touches the researcher and connects him or her with the world; (2) investigating the chosen phenomenon as it is lived, felt, and experienced; (3) identifying the central themes or structures that characterize the phenomenon; and (4) describing the phenomenon, injecting the lived experience with new meaning. Using these steps, or variants of them, teachers attune themselves to the joy, pain, humor and metaphors of their students and other teachers—in other words, the "here and now" of school situations (Pinar, Reynolds, Slattery & Taubman, 1995).

A short example of phenomenological education analysis may increase your understanding of the approach. Max van Manen maintained that educational research on students must move beyond diagnostic evaluations of what a student possesses or lacks. A much deeper form of description is necessary. Here is van Manen's phenomenological description of a student named Travers:

Travers is a bright student and a formidable debater. He cannot do wrong in the eyes of the debating club coach, since he is the star of his school-team. The social studies teacher, too, is aware of Travers' eloquence. In class discussion, when historical or contemporary issues are discussed, Travers seems to derive great joy from attacking any possible issue and trying to effect a clash of views with whoever has uttered an opinion. On the one hand, the social studies teacher has to admire Travers' oratorical skills. Travers' class involvement often contributes to an animated atmosphere and lively discussions. You can always call on Travers for a well-articulated argument no matter what the issue is. He will debate the affirmative as strenuously and as persuasively as the negative. He always argues the other side. The teacher and all the kids in class have come to know Travers. Frequently, when he challenges something that the teacher or one of the students says, they just smile and pass over it: "There you go again, Travers!"

On the other hand, the teacher wonders about Travers' real commitments. While Travers is always ready to start up a debate, he is curiously indifferent about his personal commitment to any cause, no matter what its social or human relevance. Rather, he seems to enjoy debating for the sake of debating and for the sense of victory it provides him. He mockingly calls himself "amoral, above all morals, as long as I am having a good time!" But the teacher wonders, Is Travers with his love for argument just a kid who is seeking attention? Does he have a need constantly to prove himself superior? Or is he already so cynical about life that he cannot believe in anything? Today, the teacher is surprised because one of the students, Ronene, hits exactly at this point. There is a discussion in class about "the morality of euthanasia," and she stops Travers in mid-sentence and asks, "But what do you really believe, Travers? How am I supposed to respect a person who seems to shift his position so easily from one day to the next?"

Of course, Travers is ready with an answer, "We are not discussing the respectability of my person, but rather the soundness of my point of view." Ronene shakes her head and mutters something like, "What a jerk." Now the teacher steps in. She says, "Let's stop the debate here and let each of us individually write a short essay on the topic under discussion. Understand, you are not arguing for or against any particular point of view; rather, you are to clarify how you would personally answer the question of the meaning of death by euthanasia as a human phenomenon. You are to address neither another person nor a particular policy, but rather the meaning of euthanasia as it would be relevant for you if it were to affect your own parents or someone for whom you care deeply." (1991, pp. 93–94).

Notice the sensitivity of the phenomenological account to the dynamics of the life story and the attention to Travers's consciousness. In this fine example of action research the teacher explores Travers's consciousness, then acts on her understanding of it.

Another excellent example is recounted by Professor Joe Norris of the University of Alberta in Canada:

Marcel had a short fuse. Often he would be found in the hall or near the principal's office for blowing up over the most trivial of things. Although he got along with his peers, they, with their own sense of humor, enjoyed seeing Marcel explode. On one occasion Marcel came to class quite irritated and as soon as he sat down the person behind him nudged him playfully. That was enough for Marcel, and he immediately stood up and began to pick up his desk to throw it. Although current trends in educational discipline recommend de-escalation as a classroom management strategy, I have found in extreme situations like this, the oil fighting metaphor is an appropriate one. I make an explosion strong enough to put out the fire. Then, and only then, can I start fixing the well. Using my strong male voice, I yelled loudly and firmly, "Out!" It worked, and Marcel went to the hall. Once I got the class settled, I went to talk to Marcel. I planned to proceed with my forceful approach, but as I entered the hall, Marcel cowered. I was immediately struck by the humor of our situation, and I broke into laughter. Marcel followed suit. He, I believe, recognized that I was not laughing "at" him but at the bizarreness of the drama which we found ourselves playing. I smiled and said, "Get back in." But a remarkable thing had happened. Unknowingly at the time, Marcel and I found that we had discovered a way to defuse the bomb. Whenever I noticed Marcel getting a little hot under the collar, I would smile and he would chuckle. My smile helped Marcel step outside of his skin, take a look at himself and balance his anger with humor. The technique, of course, is contextual. It won't work all the time and with all people. It wasn't a planned approach based upon some grandiose classroom management theory. It was based upon an authentic response in a phenomenological context which was responded to genuinely. Marcel and I had, after "working" together for approximately five months, found out a way of "being" together. Not to my surprise, he also seemed more attentive in my class since our shared moment of laughter. (Norris, 1998, personal communication)

ETHNOGRAPHY, THE CULTURAL PERSPECTIVE

The phenomenological concern with the human perception of lived worlds nicely complements the growth of ethnography as a qualitative research method and its application to educational research over recent decades. Ethnography is often described as the most basic form of social research. It is like anthropology, except that the researcher studies living people and communities in their everyday context. While ethnographers disagree over the relative importance of their various purposes, they all are attempting to gain knowledge about a particular culture, to identify patterns of social interaction and to develop holistic interpretations of societies and social institutions. Thus, ethnography in education attempts to adduce an understanding of the nature of schools and other educational agencies in these ways, and ethnographers there seek to explain the social processes that "move" educational events. Ethnography makes explicit the assumptions one takes for granted as a member of a culture. The culture could be as broad as Japanese society or as narrow as the upper-middle-class student culture of George Washington High School. The critical ethnographer of education seeks to describe the concrete experiences of everyday school and educational life and the social patterns and the deep structures that construct it. One of the most basic tools of the critical teacher-researcher involves the research orientation derived from the combined phenomenological-ethnographic tradition (Hammersley & Atkinson, 1983).

Ethnography associates situations with a larger cultural context. Teacher researchers, for example, might analyze classrooms, gymnasiums, playgrounds, bathrooms or parking lots in relation to the larger culture of the community surrounding the school. Teachers as ethnographers look at their classrooms and schools as cultural systems. For example, teachers can discover much about student classroom behavior by observing and investigating playground socialization, lunchroom seating arrangements or after-school activities. The entire context of student life impinges on the academic milieu of the classroom.

From a critical ethnographic perspective, culture involves a set of understandings and actions that when analyzed reveal the tacit assumptions behind social situations that seem natural (Lesko, 1989). For a long time modernists viewed ethnography from a perspective that valued neutral techniques thought to provide objective accounts of what researchers witnessed in the field. But, as you now know, the critical new paradigm ethnographies emphasize researcher self-reflection that helps ethnographers understand the angle from which the researchers view students or the community that surrounds the school. In such a context, teacher ethnographers must construct their perceptions of educational culture anew in ways that challenge what appears natural and open to question what appears obvious (Kincheloe & McLaren, 1994; 1999). The insights into the hidden cultural rules of the school that result can be surprising and even profound, and acting on an understanding of such cultural dynamics can revolutionize schools.

SEMIOTICS, OR DECIPHERING CODES AND SIGNS

Semiotics is the study of codes and signs we humans adopt so as to help us derive meaning from our surroundings. Action researchers in education can use semiotic methods to gain insights into deep structures that shape classroom events. Indeed, classrooms are diamond mines for semiotic study, for they abound in codes and signs and conventions that require keen observation and persistent analysis to be understood. The way teachers, students and administrators dress; the language students use when speaking to teachers as compared to in conversations with classmates; the graffiti in the restrooms; the systems of rules that govern social behavior; the memos administrators send to parents; the tone of the local conversation about school athletics—these are only a few of the many practices and pageants a teacher-semiotician could study. Critical researchers who can see the profound in the mundane begin to move beyond traditional questions of teaching into uncharted territory—that is, into questions of who we are becoming as a result of our educational experiences (Whitson, 1991; Britzman, 1991).

The beauty of semiotics is that it automatically turns the given into an object of thought and critical focus. Semiotics naturally resists the shallowness, the one-dimensionality of the quantitative analysis of lived experience; instead, it searches for ways of seeing that describe the invisible empty spaces of the picture. From this perspective, a gifted and talented program might, for example, involve far more than a set of enrichment activities for the students who have scored high on a standardized test. Levels of obscured assumptions begin to jump out of the shadows when one focuses the light of grounded critique on such programs—assumptions unseen even by those who make them. Thus, semiotic research moves from the glorification of the novel to the analysis of the assumed. Semiotics helps language transcend its basic role as information conduit. Semiotic analysts consider the relationship between speaker and listener or writer and reader to be based on constant interpretation in the context of the codes all participants bring to the act of communication. Thus we face the realization that communication becomes less a matter of extracting meaning from communiqués and more a matter of constituting meaning based on the cultural context, values and social identities of those involved (Greene, 1988; Britzman, 1991; Bowers & Flinders, 1990; Manning & Cullum-Swan, 1994).

When researchers turn such interpretive strategies on their own practices, they engage in a "semiotic of introspection." As they analyze their actions with attention to ritual, metaphor and questioning strategies, they begin to uncover the hidden dimensions of their belief structures, their familiar cognitive strategies, their assumptions about students and their attitudes toward a teacher's "proper" deportment (Courteney, 1988). No longer can knowledge producers hide in the shelter of positivist objectivism, which shields the self from the deeply personal issues that infuse all educational acts. Semiotic researchers cannot view themselves as "transhistorical beings" (people unaffected by the forces of history and culture); rather, they understand their places in the web from which they see reality. Contextualized in this way, the values and the belief structures that remain shrouded in the comfortable familiarity of consciousness suddenly stand out, as though dyed by the ink of semiotics. The historical contextualization of self depends on the insight of difference, as we finally begin to see ourselves clearly when we are placed against an unfamiliar social backdrop of values and unfamiliar ways of perceiving (Scholes, 1982; Hodge & Kress, 1988; Kellner, 1991).

CURRERE: THE EDUCATIONAL EXPERIENCE OF THE INDIVIDUAL

Critical action research can follow these phenomenological, ethnographic and semiotic themes and thus help educators understand educational experiences better. Much of this effort focuses on apprehending the nature of the interior experience of the individual, especially within a broadly defined educational context. This interior experience is essential to social understanding in that (1) it is affected by the external (social) world, and (2) it provides the basis for the understandings and actions that help shape the external (social) world. This reflexive purpose illustrates the importance of interior experience to educational research. It is the habitat of what we call human consciousness and the territory where meaning is produced. It is also the headquarters for a body of connections between human beings and their lived worlds. To understand the rich complexity of political and social forces, researchers must first understand interior experience (Willis, 1977).

Understanding interior experience requires a heightened individual awareness. Phenomenological pioneer Edmund Husserl (1970) delineated methodologies designed to produce an understanding of the structure of consciousness and therefore the way meaning is attained. This method, which he called "bracketing," involves consciously setting aside everyday accepted assumptions about one's immediate perceptions (Chamberlin, 1974). Once this bracketing of assumptions takes place, the individual examines and makes explicit all the meanings tacitly grounded within these immediate perceptions. In this way, awareness increases as previously hidden assumptions appear. The individual thus finds him- or herself more in touch with the subconscious values, fears and associations that direct his or her actions. Continuing analyses of these factors may uncover their origins, thus contributing to greater self-understanding and self-knowledge.

As we discuss the importance of self-knowledge in this action research context, we want to avoid the appearance of advocating an inert, narcissistic self-absorption. Teachers and students need to cultivate a form of self-knowledge that, once acquired, invites them to turn their focus outward to a more complex and textured understanding of others. Thus, the critical qualitative methods of such research offer a new dimension of understanding. Here is where William Pinar (1994) enters the qualitative conversation. Pinar appropriated this phenomenological concern with consciousness and self-knowledge and fused it with autobiographical methodology, psychoanalysis and aesthetics. He calls his approach *currere*, and he uses it to investigate the nature of individual experience.

Derived from the Latin root of the word *curriculum, currere* returns us to the *Lebenswelt* (the lived world of human consciousness) and its relationship with educational experience. Pinar concluded that in educational research, meaning typically derives from the analysis of the relationship between signs and experience. Taking his cue from Maxine Greene (1975), Pinar contended that the quest for an understanding of experience compels researchers to tap their own consciousness so that they can transcend "common sense." In other words, we must go beyond what we take for granted. As researchers we must ask such questions as What is involved in moving beyond the commonsense world? How does one start the process? What possible benefits are to be derived? Are there examples of other individuals who have accomplished such a transcendence, and what did they gain? and How do such attempts affect what we know in education? Questions such as these help us approach the *Lebenswelt*.

Pinar suggested that as we engage in this phenomenological bracketing of experience in our own lives, we become better prepared as researchers to recognize aspects of consciousness as they appear to us in educational contexts. The liberation that results includes a freedom from modes of perception that reflect cultural conditioning. We must loosen our identification with these aspects of consciousness to gain some distance from them. From this new vantage point we can observe those psychic realms formed by conditioning and unconscious adherence to social convention. Critical theorists would associate this process with the demystification of the ideological construction of consciousness (Pinar, 1975). Once we start to address and apply *currere,* Pinar believes, we will uncover a great diversity of formats and sources. The educational *Lebenswelt* comes in a variety of packages: one package may contain historical information, another the insights of free association, another the contemplations of specific literary passages and another still ostensibly insignificant slices of school life. Both cognitive and intuitive insights (or a creative synthesis of the two) will inform our perception of *currere.*

At first the information derived from the attempts to apply *currere* may remain within one's own consciousness. Eventually, however, our examinations will uncover aspects of a collective or transpersonal realm of educational experience. In other words, once we transcend the unique details of an individual's biography we may unlock the doors to secret rooms where structures of human experience hide from view. Such structures may, as phenomenologists have anticipated (for example, Merleau-Ponty, 1962), appear diversified when viewed at the level of individual personality but then appear homogeneous when analyzed at their root level. The understanding of these structures and their relationship to the sociopolitical world, and thus their impact on the world of education, may be one of the most beneficial outcomes of *currere.* Think about what *currere* addresses: the realm of private experience. When action researchers in education use it, they open a whole new realm of educational insight. To put it simply, *currere* uncovers the ways academic studies affect the consciousnesses of students. In a contemporary electronic setting, teacher-researchers may use a cultural *currere* to understand the effects of television, video games, popular music, the whole "cultural curriculum" on student consciousness. In short, thanks to *currere,* a whole new realm of experience is open for inspection.

HISTORIOGRAPHY, OR THE RELATIONSHIP BETWEEN PAST AND PRESENT

The research method historians typically rely on, a basic form of qualitative research, often goes underused among other qualitative researchers. But applied in a critical action research context, historiography has much to offer the teacher as researcher.

Historiography provides both an understanding of the relationships between the past and the present and a research orientation that leads to an understanding of more traditional ideas of educational research. Moreover, a critical historiography provides a convenient starting point for an exploration of consciousness construction and the forces that shape the lived world of our students and ourselves. With a few adjustments in the traditional approaches, educational researchers from a critical new paradigmatic background can use historiography as another form of action research. On a microlevel we can use its methodologies to trace the life histories of our students and the historical forces that shaped the school. On the macrolevel we can focus on the concept of memory and on how it relates to the connections between past and present (Popular Memory Group, 1982).

Unlike history, memory has a verb form—to remember. Because the past lives in the present—and certainly in the minds of those who inhabit the present—memory plays an important role in the struggle for self-production, for consciousness construction. When professional historians or teacher researchers approach memory, they engage in a political act. How we remember matters because it informs our existence in the present, our view of the purpose of schooling, our vision of what constitutes good teaching and our vision of the future (Frisch, 1981).

What does it mean for a teacher-researcher to remember student life histories, the school's history or more general educational histories? What can educational action researchers do with historical memories to make them active and alive rather than quaint, interesting curiosities? A vital resource in political life, in social action or in education, memory counters the oppressive presentism of late twentieth-century life by helping us make sense of the nature and changeability of our current conditions. Teachers, administrators, community leaders and students all use memory to gain self-consciousness about the origins of their own commonsense beliefs, derived as they are from their ideological, social and cultural contexts. In fact, this self-consciousness applies to both individuals and institutions. The collective memory of educators, for example, contributes to an understanding of a shared social reality that underlies our perception of purpose. In other words, it matters if teachers forget John Dewey, the origins of public schooling in industrial societies or the historical justifications for vocational education. Memory matters so much because the association between memory and history became fractured in the late twentieth century (Popular Memory Group, 1982). How and why were curricula originally developed? How and why did schools assume their current forms? Teachers, administrators and the public often have no idea; we all suffer from social amnesia (Weaver, Slattery & Daspit, 1998).

Armed with "dangerous memories" of human suffering, social injustice and unequal power relations, critical teacher researchers in the new paradigm connect past and present. Such teachers study history for more than just its own sake; they study the past because it continues to live, undetected, in the present. Action historical researchers seek out the connections between the everyday academic and social lives of students and their historical moment. Thus, when subjected to historical analysis, mundane classroom activity can become a valuable source of insight.

We can see student language in a new light as a manifestation of history. The process of reading, for example, occurs within an historical context: it is a social construction open to critical analysis. As a social construction, it designates the reader as the "locus of integration" in the sense that students synthesize their own cultural meanings with the author's meanings to produce their personal interpretations of texts. Teacher-researchers can use their historical understanding to begin analyzing their students' readings, in the process gaining valuable insight into their students' consciousnesses—their cultural histories, their fears and dreams and the forces that shape them. Such understandings provide critical teacher-researchers with useful insights into how students from, say, dominated or dominating cultures bring their experiences, desires, voices and ghosts to the reading act.

Thus, the teacher-researcher's historical grounding provides a revolutionary perspective on what happens in the classroom. Traditionally, school personnel and researchers examine only how students receive knowledge: how much they retain, how good their memories are, whether they "master" European history. Armed with an historically grounded critical perspective, teacher-researchers can begin to see how students produce knowledge. They can examine how students bring their own socially constructed meanings into the learning situation; they can explore the interaction between student life histories and school knowledge. Thus, critical action researchers take seriously the historical experiences of their students. When they appreciate this history, education can no longer abet cultural conquest or "intellectual colonialism." It becomes instead an agency that rescues the valuable insights, cultural uniqueness, and subjugated knowledge of subordinate groups.

Once teacher-researchers use student histories and subjugated knowledge to emancipate their students, their pedagogy is forever transformed. They begin to build their curricula around student experience, encouraging their students to understand the social, economic and cultural forms that influence their lived worlds. Students then learn to expose the ideology embedded in their everyday lives—that is, their places in the social hierarchy of their peer groups, their romantic relationships, their vocational aspirations, their relationships with teachers.

Michelle Gibbs Russell (1983) explained the use of memory and student histories for grasping how ideology can shape the lived worlds of students and teachers. Teacher-researchers collect memories by inviting students to exchange stories of everyday life—for example, how a student got a funny name, how a student's clothes got ripped, why some students are always late. As life historians, these teachers also elicit descriptions of the dreams students hold for the future and the specific influences that interfere with those dreams. Russell encouraged the critical teacher to list these dreams on the board, as well as the impediments to their realization. Then the teacher would ask the students to generalize from these concrete specifics. While the histories speak for themselves, they also reveal the ideological forces that covertly shape history and our lives. Thus, interpreting for oneself and one's students information about their lives becomes a critical aspect of action research. In the process of constructing these interpretations, historically grounded teacher-researchers can use their understanding of the community to connect students—especially students from subjugated cultures—to the traditions of that community.

In our discussion here of the role of history and the use of historical methods in teacher research, we draw on the People's History Movement, which developed gradually over the past three decades. People's history, like critical action research, rests on Antonio Gramsci's (1988) proposition that nonintellectuals do not exist. Nobody is incapable, People's History advocates argue, of influencing the construction of his or her own history or the history of the community. When applied to education, People's History focuses action researchers on

1. the historical experience of consciousness construction of the student, other teachers and the action researchers themselves;
2. the student's understanding of his or her own school experience and the forces that shaped it;
3. the effort to blur the boundaries of professional and amateur educational history to subvert the cult of the expert, as action researchers construct their own educational histories of groups, communities, schools and individuals; and
4. the attempt to understand the role of schooling and such informal agencies of education as media, religion, advertising and so forth in consciousness (or popular memory) formation.

This type of useful history in many ways resembles Paulo Freire's literacy work in that it can achieve intellectual and political empowerment. Social history, like Freire's pedagogy, lets people know that they can make their own histories in both meanings of the phrase (Green, 1984). In a Deweyan and Freirean sense, "doing" people's history may have as much empowering political significance as the findings. Critical teacher-researchers can uncover pedagogies from people's history that teach their students to teach themselves, and teach them to view themselves as participants in the social, political and educational worlds of which they are a part. This historical work can also teach people that the social, political, economic and educational institutions that influence their lives have themselves been formed by historical forces and human choices (Benson, Brier & Rosenzweig, 1986). The purposes modern schools serve are hardly ubiquitous and eternal. The values the modern media promote are hardly constant. The definition of a "good student" commonly accepted in contemporary schools hardly encompasses all of what could constitute a good student. The application of People's History can challenge the tyranny of the present (Simon, 1992; McLaren, 1995; Loewen, 1995; Zinn, 1997).

Historically grounded educational action researchers extend the hope of social change as they redefine the idea of professionalism among historians. Dedicated to the exploration of the effect of the past on the present and the duty of historians to share their research with the public in a way that speaks to its needs and experiences, critical teacher historians certainly take on unfamiliar challenges. Not the least of their objectives involves connecting the school and community around the identification of their common historical shaping forces. As an example, historically grounded action researchers might inform community members of the original justification for the local vocational programs, who promoted them and whose interests their adoption served. Such an historical investigation could galvanize a community into evaluating the effects of vocational programs. Students themselves could marshal political action on behalf of those adversely affected by such programs. Teacher research with results like these takes seriously Harvey Kaye's (1989) contention that history must be made ever more public; it must become a part of the popular media and the everyday lives of citizens in democratic societies.

Additional examples of historically grounded teacher research can promote an understanding of the aims of critical teaching. Historically grounded action researchers will find few more appropriate and promising venues than African American communities and the students who come of age in them. Employing students and community members as coresearchers, Dominic Candeloro (1973) described an African American people's history project with serious implications for action research in the new educational paradigm. Candeloro began his research with a two-hour interview of a local black leader who provided a general historical overview of the black community in Lima, Ohio, and a list of social themes that promised additional insight.

From that brief interview Candeloro constructed a battery of questions designed to elicit data on black participation in politics, religion, the union movement and education. Then he assembled a list of resource people who contributed special insights into particular aspects of Lima's black history. The resource people both contributed valuable oral historical accounts and alerted Candeloro's researchers to numerous forgotten documents and other sources of information. Candeloro reported that the project increased a general awareness of the origins of the problems in the African American community and how the past influenced current realities in Lima. Not only did Candeloro himself gain practical insight into the research process, but his students were introduced to the methods and purposes of inquiry and the ways research contributes to cognitive development. For Candeloro and his students, research became a form of critical pedagogy and a way of applying the act of learning.

Similarly, Thad Sitton (1981) documented methods of incorporating African American history into school settings. The school, Sitton concluded, is an ideal place to locate public history projects. Teachers have access to the school's technical resources (typewriters, computers, tape recorders, VCRs, photographic equipment and so on), which are invaluable in historically oriented action research. Sitton modeled his Lockhart, Texas, black history project on the student oral history and folklore work of Foxfire in Georgia. Drawing power from ethnic pride and a sense of place, the Foxfire projects developed unique insights into the techniques of people's history and have initiated hundreds of school research and publishing projects around North America since the early 1970s. Operating originally in the rural South, Foxfire exposed the effects of Anglo domination on socioeconomic life—consequences that included the eradication or suppression of raw documentary materials that might be used to construct an understanding of the historical context from which African American students emerge. But granted access to a microphone or a video recorder, black adults and students began to tell their valuable stories—and instantly recreated the missing historical sources. The act of preserving this oral history can be the first step in an emancipatory journey. As social studies teachers and black studies scholars have argued for nearly thirty years, and as John Dewey maintained long before that, the community is a laboratory in which students can study data, draw conclusions, make decisions and think about the future of their neighborhoods, schools and cities (Hayden, 1986).

FEMINIST RESEARCH AND THE BENEFITS OF PASSION, EMOTION AND CONNECTEDNESS

Feminist scholarship may provide the best current illustration of how researchers can tap their own consciousnesses to transcend positivist-imposed "commonsense" definitions of reality. Feminist scholarship is, almost by definition, a phenomenologically informed enterprise, finding its origin in the bracketing of everyday experiences as they relate to gender assumptions. It begins with a search for self-knowledge and eventuates in a broader knowledge of the interior experiences and the exterior social forces that shape the consciousnesses of others. Feminist research can thus serve the critical functions of liberating both men and women from socially determined ways of living that reflect cultural conditioning and giving teacher researchers a metaperspective (a view from another angle) on the way gender expectations shape the inner self. In the 1990s, feminist research defined the center of the critical new paradigm. Aware of tacit value assumptions of modernist science and the political power it exerts under the banner of objectivity, feminist researchers declined to acquiesce in its authority. Instead, feminist researchers subverted the positivist principle of a neutral, hierarchical and estranged interaction between researcher and researched (see, for example, Fee, 1982; Mies, 1982; Olesen, 1994; Hekman, 1990; Flax, 1990; Ferguson, 1993; Collins, 1990; Clough, 1992; Butler, 1990).

Meanwhile, note here that no single unchallenged articulation of feminist theory yet exists. Liberal feminists focus on gender stereotyping and bias; radical feminists argue that the subjugation of women is the most compelling form of oppression. The form of feminist theory we use is often called "critical postmodern feminism," although we call it "critical new paradigm feminism." As feminists focus on and affirm that which is absent or peripheral in modernist ways of seeing, they ground their critique in lived reality, in the material world (Kipnis, 1988; Jaggar, 1983). As critical new paradigm feminists challenge modernist patriarchal exclusions, they analyze the connections between an unjust class structure and the oppression of women (Weiler, 1988; Rosneau, 1992). Often, they contend, male dominators of women adopt class structure as a metaphor and refer to the "feminization" of poverty and the growth in the number of "homeless women" in recent years. To combat such a mind-set, we need an analysis of the implications critical new paradigm feminism holds for action research in education.

Grounding their critical theory and research in everyday practice, feminist researchers extend our appreciation of the effort to connect emotion and reason, knower and known. For example, Renate Duelli Klein (1982) described an action research project involving battered women. The researchers refused to view the researched (the battered women) as objects of research but instead saw them as sisters, students, teachers and mirrors of themselves. The researchers approached their project from the viewpoint that the battered women were coresearchers; as such, the researchers and the researched compared their own experiences as women and negotiated the findings of the project so as to extend the experiences of each group. Such innovative and productive strategies as these place critical educators at a distinct advantage. As researcher and researched interact, they can connect new insights into the interactions of teachers and students, teachers and teachers, teachers and administrators and education professors and teachers to their cognitive, pedagogical and affective levels.

Because it offered such benefits, feminist analysis moved quickly to the center of the critical research stage. Announcing its marriage to and transformation by feminist insight, critical theory has now moved beyond the paradigm of inquiry in which the concept of social class is privileged and exalted as the master concept in the trinity of race, class and gender. A critical theory reconceptualized by a new paradigm, feminism promotes a politics of difference that refuses to pathologize or exoticize the Other, those who are different from the mainstream. Such a stance seems likely to revitalize communities; marginalized groups in thrall to a condescending modernist-positivist gaze can edge closer to the borders of respect.

Kathleen Weiler's 1988 book, *Women Teaching for Change: Gender, Class, and Power,* provides a good example of critical research framed by feminist theory. Weiler shows not only how feminist theory can extend critical research, but also how we can reconceptualize the idea of emancipation in light of a feminist epistemology (Morrow, 1991; Young, 1990; Lugones, 1987). Emancipation run through the feminist filter loses the turgid finality one achieves by applying the "correct theory." It becomes instead a contingent state, ever flowing with changing contexts and new insights, and constantly washing and exposing forms of oppression and regulation.

Madeline Grumet (1988) extended our current understanding of the feminist attempt to transcend modernist-positivist logic-centeredness by connecting the languages of the body and of feeling with inquiry. Modernist social science, she argued, is caught in a male-dominated snare of abstraction. Grumet sought new methods of inquiry capable of drawing the body and feeling into the public conversation about education. Making use of such qualitative methodologies as history, theater, autobiography and phenomenology, she confronted androcentric abstraction with the uncertainty, specificity and contradiction of the private, corporeal and feminine. From the perspective of the guardians of the Cartesian tradition such epistemological confrontations amount to treason. After adopting such ideas, inquiry can no longer claim to be a coldly rational process. As feeling, empathy and the body enter into the research process, when the distinction between knower and known blurs, and as truth seeking invites the naïve knowers to play active roles, passion informs the inquiry. In such a context critical action researchers see themselves as both passionate scholars and passionate teachers who connect themselves emotionally to those students they seek to understand. You can see here, we submit, a sort of pedagogical ideal.

Here, also, is the point at which feminist theory shakes the foundation of the modernist Cartesian-Newtonian tradition. Modernist researchers often weed out personalities, denying intuitions and inner voices in the process of producing re-stricted and objectlike interpretations of socioeducational events. By the tradi-tional definitions, these objectlike interpretations are certain and scientific; femi-nist self-grounded inquiries are inferior, merely impressionistic, and "journalistic" (Reinharz, 1979, 1992). Rejecting the restrictive authority and certainty of sci-ence, feminist researchers contend that its so-called objectivity is little more than an excuse for evading social and ethical responsibility, for ideological passivity and for the privileged sociopolitical position of the scientific researcher. They further argue that modernist false objectivity demands the separation of thought and feel-ing and the devaluation of any perspective maintained with emotional conviction. With feeling safely designated as an inferior form of human consciousness, those who rely solely on logic can justify any repression of research tainted by emotions or feeling. Feminist theorists point out that men have traditionally used this thought-feeling dichotomy to oppress women. In intimate heterosexual relation-ships, if a man can present his position as the rational viewpoint and the woman's position as an emotional perspective, he has won the argument. His is the voice worth hearing.

Drawing on feminist analysis, critical action researchers have learned that in-quiry can and should be informed by our "humanness" and that humans serve nicely as research instruments. From this perspective, the inquiry begins with re-searchers scanning their own experience. Since educational researchers are human beings studying other human beings, they are already privy to the inner world of experience. Utilizing their own empathetic understandings, they can watch educa-tional phenomena from within—that is, they can know directly. In the spirit of cur-rere, the private becomes public. As consumers of the research, we get closer to the private experiences of students, teachers and administrators and the effect of those experiences on the public domain, and we gain access to the private experience of the researcher and the effect of that experience on the public descriptions he or she presents of the observed phenomena (Reinharz, 1979, 1992). Thus, not only do we learn about the educational world that surrounds us, we also gain new insights into the private world within us—the world of our constructed consciousness.

No longer can critical teacher-researchers allow science to blind the knower and restrict what science can "see" in the world of education. But revealing what can be learned from the everyday, feminist scholars have opened a whole new area of inquiry and potential insight. They have found information in the silences and gaps behind the places where traditional scholars had found only "what was there." To initiate an inquiry focused only on method and technique instead of on value assumptions is irrational in the sense that it separates the way men and women obtain knowledge and make judgments. Flannery O'Connor once ob-served that "judgment is implicit in seeing"—that is, constructing judgments is never an isolated process. When one tries to isolate it, one trivializes the act of judgment to the point that the insights one derives are bland and even inconse-quential (Westkott, 1982). The work of Donna Haraway (1991, 1997), Evelyn Fox Keller (1984) and Sandra Harding (1986) has been especially helpful in ex-posing the silent values that drive modernist research. When this powerful feminist critique is deployed within the methodological traditions of phenomenology, ethnography, semiotics, *currere* and historiography the acts of researching and teaching are forever transformed.

Philosopher of science Sandra Harding (1986) provided a fine example of these critical research concerns in the context of gender and biological research. Using her understanding of socially constituted gender-related influences on the consciousness of biological researchers, Harding sought to demystify androcentrism (male-centeredness) in biology and produce new knowledge out of critical paradigmatic concerns. In her analysis of previous attempts to explain human evolution in terms of the strides men made in hunting societies, Harding adduced an interesting gender bias. Assuming that sex-role distinctions (hierarchical sex-role distinctions at that) exist across all cultures, biological researchers had traditionally argued that man-the-hunter developed tools as aids to hunting. This exclusive masculine use of tools led to bipedalism and upright posture, which led to more effective hunting techniques characterized by a division of labor among the hunters. The researchers interpreted this hunting behavior as the evolutionary origin of male bonding in modern society and as a justification for why males might want to bar women from their economic activities—including the pursuit of science.

This traditional extended hypothesis portrays men as the agents who precipitated the evolutionary break from prehuman cultures and took the giant evolutionary leap into more advanced human culture. The traditional biological accounts of the activities of women in modern societies presents them as basically the same as the feminine activities in prehuman groups. Aware of the unexamined androcentric mind-set of traditional biological scholarship, and eager to expose its assumptions, feminist scholars posed an alternative woman-the-gatherer hypothesis of human evolution. Where men had invented stone tools, women invented tools made of sticks and reeds. Since women gathered crops in the early societies, they also developed tools to defend against predators that threatened them in the woods and fields. Thus, one could argue that woman-the-gatherer produced the tools that encouraged the social organization that propelled humans into a new evolutionary epoch.

The point of this gynecentric (woman-centered) story of the origins of human cultural evolution is not to prove its superiority over the androcentric interpretation. Harding specifically pointed out that it is equally impossible to prove either story—that is exactly the point. If one cannot be proved over the other, to what can we attribute the preference for the androcentric theory? The origins of the interpretation come not from any data but from the assumptions of the researchers who formulated it. It was socially construed, emerging from unexamined commonsense assumptions of male superiority. The theory was based arbitrarily on a restrictive understanding of human possibilities. In biology, for sure, but no doubt in all other sciences too, intrapersonal and interpersonal knowledge are treated as irrelevant. Sandra Harding alerted us to the value of such knowledge forms even in a science as empirically based as biology. We see there androcentrism tacitly informing the research as it dictates the selection of what might be considered a scientific problem, the important concepts and theories of the discipline, the acceptable research methods and the interpretations of the resultant research.

SYNTHESIZING THE CRITICAL RESEARCH TECHNIQUES: GETTING BELOW THE SURFACE AND BEHIND THE CURTAIN

Sandra Harding's work illustrates for qualitatively oriented critical action researchers the need to transcend appearances and use the tools of phenomenology, ethnography, *currere,* historiography and semiotics to uncover the ideological constructions and tacit assumptions that still drive educational research. In the context of the new paradigm we learn that little is as it appears to be. When critical action researchers search for deep structures, which are there to be uncovered in any classroom, we discover a world of personal meaning socially constructed by a variety of forces that often has little to do with the intended meaning of the official curriculum or those who present it. With this understanding, the teacher-researcher focuses on the world of the learner's consciousness, on its uniqueness, on the forces that have helped construct it and on the ways the learner may become aware of how it was constructed. This realm of personal experience (Pinar's *currere*) may be the least explored aspect of school life. Standardized testing and traditional quizzes cannot assess it; it cannot be measured in any positivist sense.

   To understand this hidden realm, teacher-researchers can rely on the phenomenological, ethnographic, semiotic, historiographic and feminist synthesis, ask questions; make observations; and analyze the codes contained in what they hear and see. Such research might begin with the following questions: What was going on in your mind during the lesson? Do you see any relation between the lesson and your life outside school? If you could have taught the lesson, how would you have set it up? What were some of the daydreams that ran though your mind during the lesson? Can you imagine a way that you might ever use what you learned here in your everyday life? The researcher might proceed with a semiotic reading of the codes embedded in the answers. What signs and codes consistently turn up, and what did they mean? Did conspicuous patterned silences recur in the student responses, and what do they suggest?

   Rosalie Wax (1971) provided early insight into the way educational action researchers might use our qualitative research synthesis. Examining education on a Native American reservation, Wax used her personal experience as a foundation for analyzing the personal experiences and perceptions of the students there and some of the forces that shaped them. As she and her colleagues rushed to get to teacher meetings on time, they discovered on a personal level—a level perceivable only by a "human research instrument"—why reservation teachers and students experienced unique difficulties. Though they got out of bed at 6 A.M., then washed and groomed themselves vigorously, Wax and her colleagues could never get themselves to look presentable in a middle-class way. Prairie dust covered their clothes and toilet articles every day; they had no closets to protect their clothes, no irons, no clean water, no hot water for shaving, no mirrors and so forth. Wax reported that the attempt to maintain a middle-class appearance exhausted them. From this conscious empathy, rather than with questionnaires or even interviews, the ethnographers developed an emotional understanding of why people who attend school on reservations do not look like middle-class students. It became apparent to them that teachers who had never lived without conveniences, residing in homes off the reservation or in on-reservation teacher housing equipped with such middle-class accouterments, lacked the experiential background to appreciate why the Native American students and their parents looked the way they did. Teachers often say Indian students and parents are careless and dirty. Wax and her colleagues saw on a phenomenological level the anxiety among those Native American mothers whose children insisted that they dress them so as to win the approval of their teachers.

Other examples of qualitative research abound, and they illustrate how the phenomenological, ethnographic, historiographic, semiotic and feminist tradition "expands the research envelope" traditional researchers accept. One of the best examples of such research is Peter McLaren's (1986, 1994, 1999) booklength critical ethnography of a Catholic school in downtown Toronto, *Schooling as a Ritual Performance: Toward a Political Economy of Educational Symbols and Gestures.* McLaren employed phenomenology, ethnography and semiotics to analyze schooling as a ritualistic system. In the course of his inquiry, McLaren viewed school culture from an angle that revealed new ways of seeing the race, class and gender-based struggle to control school knowledge. For example, students resisted the school's attempt to marginalize their street culture and street knowledge. The visceral knowing, the body knowledge and the rhythms and gestures of street culture differed greatly from formal classroom knowledge with its fragmented data ("factoids") and its suppression of the body and the emotions. McLaren watched students enlist their street semiotics in their clandestine attempts to challenge the "bland redundancy" of the school.

McLaren focused his attention on the class clown, analyzing the codes and symbols that individual used to subvert authority and the larger significance of the struggle between clown and school. The clown deconstructed the familiar, revealing the boredom, tenuousness and arbitrariness of the prevailing rules. The clown proved to be much more than simply a buffoon; he became a knowledge-producer, a teacher who walked the thin line between street-corner and dominant cultures. McLaren saw him as a semiotician, exposing the cultural codes on which the daily life of the classroom rested. The clown, McLaren concluded, conveyed through his actions that the codes of the school were tenuous and negotiable.

As a subversive agent, the clown undermined the authoritarian hold the dominant codes had on the students. As an ethnographer, McLaren attempted to move beyond simply an emic perspective (the viewpoint of the natives, in this case the students and the teachers), instead attempting to assume an etic perspective (the perspective of the outsider) as well. Analyzing the two perspectives separately and in relation to one another, McLaren examined actor subjectivity vis-à-vis social and economic structural conditions influencing the students' and teachers' consciousnesses. Thus McLaren, acting well within the boundaries of our idea of critical research methodologies, used critical new paradigmatic understandings to direct his qualitative role as knowledge producer. In the process, he revealed hidden relationships between formal classroom and the students' oppositional codes and the larger socioeconomic structure.

A teacher-researcher exploring classrooms from such angles can develop strategies for resisting the tendency for classrooms to become repositories of dominant knowledge that anesthetizes our souls, severs our connections to our consciousness and ignores the meaningfulness of students' lived experiences. Critical teacher-researchers, perhaps following McLaren's qualitative experience, begin to act on their research and the unique ways of seeing it provides. The one-dimensional view of the classroom teachers receive in their preprofessional and inservice training is transformed by their acquaintance with critical action research. Once a black-and-white Kansas, the classroom becomes a Technicolor Oz, a lively, symbolic arena in which the dominant culture, school administrators, teachers and students struggle over how the classroom is to be read and which cultural meanings will be legitimized. A synthesis of critical research techniques can provide teachers with insights that help them construct a new relationship with the world and the people around them.

In this chapter we reviewed many approaches to action research that you, as a teacher, may use in your classroom. Phenomenology, ethnography, semiotics, *currere,* historiography and feminism all contribute positively to teacher and student empowerment in the process of improving education. We hope you will explore these research processes and methodologies in more detail in your preservice educational experience and, most important, apply them often throughout your career.

Curriculum Issues and Debates

Introduction

In this chapter we discuss various definitions of curriculum and instruction, the implications these definitions hold for teachers and students, examples of curricular programs and practices you will meet in your career and controversies surrounding the day-to-day implementation of curriculum and instruction strategies in the social context of contemporary American education. We also offer our reflections on the national debates about curriculum, as well as stories of individual teachers struggling daily to create stimulating and meaningful instructional programs for their students.

You will discover that both the definitions of curriculum and the purposes of instruction are controversial issues. As a preservice education student you may have the impression that curriculum and instruction are simply the subjects and materials teachers present to students in classrooms. While different school districts prescribe different textbooks, activities, tests and resources, the general impression is that the differences in books, instructional styles of teachers and school district curriculum guides are merely local idiosyncrasies while what the schools teach remains basically the same. Some believe, for example, that algebra, literature, science, geography and history are specific bodies of information that are identical everywhere, and that instruction always has the same purpose: imparting this knowledge to students. The evaluation of the curriculum that follows becomes, then, an objective test score or grade that measures how much of the knowledge students retain. Thus curriculum, instruction and evaluation have often been presumed to be uncontested concepts with universal application.

This traditional understanding of curriculum and instruction strongly influenced U.S. education throughout the nineteenth century. Nevertheless, this transmission of information model is only one conception of curriculum, instruction and evaluation. Other definitions, various programs and new understandings of curriculum and instruction have emerged in recent years and are being explored in many school districts and universities in the United States, Canada and internationally. This chapter discusses many of these emerging understandings of curriculum and points you toward several references for future study.

A CONTEMPORARY VISION OF CURRICULUM

Among the many emerging concepts of curriculum, some educators now suggest that a curriculum includes all of a student's experiences in school, at home, in the community and through the media. Other definitions suggest that the curriculum is a process of understanding the self in relation to the world, not simply the concrete information students must memorize or master. Contemporary scholars analogize instruction to a personal journey, with the teacher as travel guide, advisor, author, wise mentor or philosopher more concerned with the growth, maturity and empowerment of each student than with the information each student regurgitates on standardized tests. In this conception, evaluation becomes an authentic expression of each student's unique understanding and application of learning in a journal, portfolio or project. These reconceptualized visions of curriculum, instruction and evaluation enjoy popularity in some school districts, and some teachers now implement practices based on this philosophy. These practices are also controversial, however, and many other school districts resist or reject them.

As a teacher you will be confronted with both traditional and reconceptualized understandings of curriculum and instruction in the schools where you teach. You will often be required to choose instructional strategies, teaching materials, grading practices, textbook series, evaluation methods and other curriculum tools and strategies for your classroom or, as a member of a curriculum committee, your entire district. Although this chapter will help you understand the traditional and reconceptualized paradigms of curriculum and instruction, you should know that we strongly support the contemporary view of curriculum, instruction and evaluation just outlined.

We recommend an inclusive, contextual and autobiographical model for teaching, learning and assessment because we believe that the context of education can no longer be minimized, as traditional programs have done. We support the reconceptualized definition of curriculum and instruction that values all of the experiences teachers and students bring to bear on institutional schooling: classroom activities, extracurricular clubs and teams, cocurricular events, family experiences, peer group initiations and political perspectives, as well as the unintended outcomes of schooling practices that affect the psychology, ethics, spirituality, intuitive sensitivities, creativity and relationships of everyone in schools.

In short, our "holistic model" values the social and cultural contexts of the schooling process. We believe that students are more than mere receptors of inert information, and teachers more than mere functionaries who rely on prepackaged and rote instructional practices to dispense this information. Teachers and students are complex, dynamic and creative individuals who must be encouraged to explore the meanings of history, mathematics, science, literature, geography, sports, arts, politics, religion and all dimensions of human investigation using their unique talents while engaged in a community of learners on a journey of discovery toward wisdom.

Our vision moves beyond a static and universal application of knowledge with predetermined outcomes and prepackaged methodologies to a dynamic and contextual process of teaching and learning. T. S. Eliot critiqued the rational obsessions of the modern world—and, by implication, modern schooling—when he asked in his poem "Choruses from the Rock" the following provocative questions:

> *The endless cycle of idea and action,*
> *Endless invention, endless experiment,*
> *Brings knowledge of motion, but not of stillness;*
> *Knowledge of speech, but not of silence;*
> *Knowledge of words, and ignorance of the Word.*
> *All our knowledge brings us nearer to our ignorance . . .*
> *Where is the life we have lost in living?*
> *Where is the wisdom we have lost in knowledge?*
> *Where is the knowledge we have lost in information? (1971, p.96)*

Eliot's poem succinctly synopsizes our vision of curriculum, instruction and evaluation. Education is about communities committed to justice, democracy, compassion and ecological sustainability. These communities constantly ask questions, initiate dialogue and seek wisdom. The answers and solutions are not predetermined; knowledge is more than just information transmission. Like T. S. Eliot, we have noticed that this wisdom has been lost in modern schooling and wonder how it might return. We search for a way to reinvigorate education with a reconceptualized vision of the curriculum.

FIVE DEFINITIONS OF CURRICULUM

Understanding the reasons for the commitment of modern schooling to transmission of information models of curriculum and instruction requires an awareness of the conflicting definitions of curriculum itself. As you read the five following definitions, remember that U.S. schooling practices reflect ideological beliefs about society and culture and philosophical understandings of politics and education. Ponder these definitions and imagine how your classroom might look and feel if it were guided by each of these definitions.

Curriculum as Subject Matter

Some view the curriculum as the essential knowledge contained in the academic subjects taught in schools and included in the great books of literature, science, mathematics, philosophy and the humanities. This definition of curriculum assumes that what is taught by teachers and studied in books is identical to what students learn. This definition fails to address these epistemological questions: What is "essential" knowledge? Does knowledge change? If so, should subjects also change? Who decides what knowledge is "essential" and will be included in the curriculum?

Curriculum for Social Adaptation

This definition of curriculum focuses on the short-term needs of individuals and society. Subjects under study are those most useful for securing employment or addressing immediate community problems in the labor force, in economics, in society and so forth. Schools are encouraged to accommodate themselves to society as it exists rather than change society. Thus the curriculum should turn out a well-trained workforce. This definition ignores such questions as these: What is "useful" knowledge or "gainful" employment? If we focus only on short-term needs, technical preparation and job skills, what happens to long-term vision, intellectual development and individual creativity? Is living in the world simply a matter of functional expediency, or should other aesthetic, spiritual, psychological and political issues guide curriculum and schooling for the long-term benefit of individuals and society?

Curriculum as Planned Activities

This definition emphasizes the responsibility of the school district for planning the learning and ensuring that students retain what is taught. It raises the question of the significance of the planned activities: How do we know that the planned curriculum is the best curriculum? Who decides what to include and exclude among the planned activities? Can teachers really exclude from the curriculum the unplanned questions, events and ideas that emerge in the classroom? Should the school district restrict the learning activities? If so, precisely how does it decide what to include and exclude?

The Curriculum Includes All Student Experiences Related to Schooling

This definition includes everything students learn under the guidance of the school, planned or not. Personal questions, extracurricular activities, spiritual experiences, team sporting events, creative insights, library research, peer-group interaction, ethnic heritage and playground relationships—all of these provide important learning sources. Some contend that this definition provides no basis for differentiating between positive and negative experiences, and that it makes the responsibility of the school too broad. Some questions we must ask are: What are the limits, if any, to the areas of learning to be covered in the curriculum? With limited resources and overcrowded learning environments, how can schools manage a curriculum under such a broad definition? What is the difference between "planned activities" and "experiences," and which should the school direct? How can schools distinguish between positive and negative experiences?

The Curriculum Includes All Student Experiences in the Course of Living

This definition expands the curriculum to include all experiences, both in and out of school. Learning is not restricted to the school, but one can integrate all one's experiences and activities into a unified learning process. Some question how the schools can plan any instruction at all if every experience counts as legitimate knowledge. On the other hand, some teachers purposely plan activities in the context of these life experiences to enhance formal instruction. This definition requires that we explore the relationship between individual lives and schooling activities. Who or what decides or guides the course of individual lives? What is the relationship between life experiences and schooling experiences? Are all experiences equally valid in the teaching and learning process? How can the issues of confidentiality, privacy and individual rights be protected under such a broad definition of curriculum?

CURRICULUM AND INSTRUCTION

Curriculum and instruction are the heart and soul of schooling. You will find your career intimately bound up with books, academic resources, instructional materials, analyses of students' learning styles and classroom practices, curriculum committees, student research projects, testing and evaluation procedures, extracurricular activities, students' personal questions, the life experiences of colleagues and students and the special academic needs of your students. We consider it essential to explore the definitions of curriculum and instruction to help you to deal with the many classroom challenges ahead. This investigation will help you become what Donald Schön calls "the reflective practitioner."

Schön (1983, 1987, 1991) challenged professionals to examine their purpose and function in society. In effect, he insisted that we cannot separate the thinking about the meaning of our profession from the practice of our profession. (In Chapter 1 we presented the similar concept that theory cannot be separated from practice, which explains the applicability of a contextual understanding of schooling, and in Chapter 9 we discussed teachers as researchers who are empowered by reflection in action.) More particularly, Schön encouraged educators to overcome the distracting and tiring effects of bureaucracy, disconnectedness and inertia by promoting learning through experience. Schön's recommendations are reminiscent of the philosophy of John Dewey, introduced in Chapters 1 and 8. Dewey called for democratic participation, investigations that rely on the scientific method and learning through experience in schools.

JOHN DEWEY'S CONTINUING RELEVANCE

John Dewey (1859–1952), the American philosopher and educator who viewed education as a process of social activity related to democracy, experience and active learning, has been mentioned throughout this book. We have pointed out that he sought to establish a continuity between the student's world of experiences and a curriculum that arises out of and develops the student's experience. Dewey realized that this experience naturally stimulates motivation and interest. Critics of Dewey still challenge this observation, contending that adults have an important (some even say exclusive) role in transmitting the American culture. In addition, critics insist that students must apply themselves to learning basic information before they can develop interests and motivation. The debates between those who encourage experience as the basis of learning and those who insist that effort and knowledge precede interest continues today.

We agree with Dewey that student experience is an essential element of the learning process. In fact, by ignoring the living context of each student, schooling creates an atmosphere of drudgery and boredom. Such an atmosphere saps the desire for learning. How can the curriculum reignite the passion for learning? Is it possible for students to study and learn scientific, mathematic, literary and historical concepts and artistic, creative, physical and mental skills in an environment in which experience is the primary focus? Consider the following example.

Freshman Studies Example

Most universities require a course, variously called "freshman orientation" or "freshman studies," for all freshmen as an introduction to college. Colleges typically design these courses to provide incoming students with information about college life, campus activities, the library, study skills and so on. Some such courses also include an introduction to college-level reading and writing. You probably took a similar course as part of your required college curriculum. Colleges and universities have struggled for years to create meaningful freshman orientation courses, usually with mixed results and sometimes with little success. Undergraduates often complain that these courses waste time or are irrelevant to their college education. An experimental freshman seminar at a midwestern university set out to address these objections.

A colleague of ours teaches a freshman seminar entitled "Autobiography and the Whole Person: Get a Life." In 1996 professors at this university were asked to add one section of the freshman seminar to their teaching load. With minimal requirements—only that they include some quality reading and writing assignments—twenty professors designed their own courses, selected their own titles and compiled their own readings and activities assignments. The course titles, syllabuses and reading lists were advertised in advance, and the freshmen could select the course that most interested them.

Some sections read Shakespeare, others read Zen and still others studied Latin American women novelists. Some professors organized visits to museums and plays; others created art shows and produced segments of plays. Students in some courses wrote research papers about novels; others composed poetry or journals.

Our friend's syllabus included a novel by Ernest Gaines, the Broadway musical *Pippin*, dream analysis related to the work of Carl Jung, an art museum visit to study Jackson Pollock and Georgia O'Keeffe and autobiographical journals. The overall success of the experimental program related more to the freedom of each professor to create a syllabus related to her or his areas of interest and experience than to a standardized curriculum. The success also depended on students' selecting a section of the course that best connected to their interests and experiences.

While some might find fault with the diversity and flexibility of this course as it was taught, most participating professors found that beginning with topics of interest rather than mandated methodologies and assignments made it far stronger and more enjoyable than the usual freshman orientation course. In other words, a dynamic educational experience emerged.

The professors also discovered that, freed from absolute concepts of knowledge and reality, students tend to question and then understand inherited traditions and values. This understanding, in turn, leads to invention, discovery and innovation. Students can then use knowledge as an instrument for solving problems in their postmodern world. Contrived methodologies and predetermined information deaden this spirit of inquiry. The freshman seminar experiment provided an opportunity for both professors and students to explore reading, writing, visual art, music and the self reflectively and experientially. In short, it provided a contextual introduction to the college learning environment the students could understand and appreciate (Cary, 1999).

On a trip with students to the Cleveland Museum of Art, one of us participated in an individual discovery project in which we discussed the importance of phenomenological experiences while the class lingered in front of a Jackson Pollock painting for nearly an hour. The students were told the story about my own encounter with Pollock at about their age, a story that created the context for the learning experience. The response of one student, in particular, we will relate shortly. First, though, here is that story.

My journey to understand and appreciate art contextually and experientially began in the Metropolitan Museum of Art in New York City during a high school senior trip. Our teacher took us there to view a retrospective exhibit of the history of art from medieval times through abstract-expressionism. I walked hurriedly through the art of the ages with my high school friends, eager to reach the end and order pizza for lunch. As we entered the final gallery, a huge canvas covering an entire wall startled us. It was filled with swirls of color, particles of glass and dirt, random drippings and splashes from paint brushes and buckets. We all laughed at the mess, and we wondered aloud why it would be included in a major art exhibit. As I reached the turnstile to leave, a magnetic pull from the painting caused me to freeze. I had to go back and investigate this strange painting. My teacher agreed to let me stay and rejoin the group after lunch.

I stood alone before Jackson Pollock's Autumn Rhythm. *The intensity of the emotions struck a chord. I sensed the pain of the artist's struggles and suffering, which resonated with my own turmoils. Pollock's frustration with social structures matched my own indignation over the Vietnam War and racism. I sensed Pollock's inner battles and connected them to my own life. My father's alcoholism crossed my mind, and later I learned that Pollock also fought this disease. I did not "know" Jackson Pollock's work at the time, but I felt his emotions in* Autumn Rhythm.

Hundreds of people must have come and gone while I lingered in the room, but time stood still for me. I am not a painter; I have never studied art formally. Yet I became united with Jackson Pollock through his painting. When I left to catch up with my friends, I decided to keep my mysterious experience in front of Autumn Rhythm *to myself.*

Jackson Pollock continues to influence my life and education. I experienced a phenomenological moment of revelation and personal understanding that, like the beauty and intensity of nature in autumn, shapes my life. Studying the technical details of the abstract-expressionist style or reading a biography of Pollock could never have replaced that empathic experience in the Metropolitan Museum of Art. But after my encounter with Autumn Rhythm *I devoured every book available about Pollock and his art. I visit museums regularly to find new Pollock paintings, reflect on the changes in my life since first seeing* Autumn Rhythm *and discover new experiences of art and artists to inspire and instruct me. All of which explains why I included Jackson Pollock on my freshman seminar syllabus. While I am hardly a professor of art, my personal experiences of art provide a rich resource that invariably find their way into my successful teaching.*

THE IMPORTANCE OF EXPERIENCE

The story about *Autumn Rhythm* and Jackson Pollock illustrates the educational importance of experience. Knowledge is rarely ordered logically and waiting to be discovered; rather, it is constructed in random and spontaneous experiences. As Suzuki, Fromm and DeMartino observed, "The intellect may raise all kinds of questions—and it is perfectly right for it to do so—but to expect a final answer from the intellect is asking too much of it, for this is not in the nature of intellection. The answer lies deeply buried under the bedrock of our being" (1960, pp. 48–49). *Autumn Rhythm* provided no answers for the intellect, but it did touch the bedrock of one individual's being and initiated a search for meaning and understanding, not only about art history, abstract-expressionism and Jackson Pollock, but also and most significantly about the purpose of life, the reasons for suffering, the tragedy of alcoholism and the relationship between inner confusion and turmoil. The visit to the Metropolitan Museum of Art was more than a scheduled lesson, it was a border crossing, a seminal moment, an empathic event—an authentic curricular experience—that initiated a journey into the realm of contemporary art and postmodern living. This experience created a context within which the future study of art has been enjoyable, vitalizing and educational.

THE IMPLICATIONS OF NARRATIVE

Experiences of transformative pedagogy such as this challenge the educational community to reevaluate the traditional understanding of the learning environment and the teaching process. Even such a traditionalist educator as Mortimer Adler could write, "Our concern with education must go beyond schooling. . . . Education is a lifelong process of which schooling is only a small part. . . . Schooling should open the doors to the world of learning" (1982, pp. 9–11).

Perhaps John Dewey provided the most thoughtful analysis of aesthetics in education in *Art as Experience*. Dewey (1934b) wrote about the significance of the arts and concluded: "In the end, works of art are the only media of complete and unhindered communication between man and man that can occur in a world full of gulfs and walls that limit community of experience" (1934b, p. 105).

Education philosopher Maxine Greene (1978, 1995) referred to an attention to those alternatives that provide hope as "wide-awakenness." She argued for a strong emphasis on arts and humanities to promote this wide-awakenness and self-understanding that can emerge from synthetic moments like the one in the Met. Greene turned to Henry David Thoreau for inspiration: "Thoreau writes passionately about throwing off sleep. He talks about how few people are awake enough for a poetic or divine life. He asserts that to be awake is to be alive" (1978, p. 162).

David Orr also turned to Thoreau for understanding: "Thoreau did not research Walden Pond; rather, he went to live 'deliberately'" (1992, p. 125). Thus, *Walden* became a mosaic of philosophy, poetry, natural history, geology, folklore, archeology, economics, politics and education for Thoreau, and in this sense aesthetics leads to wholeness. As Orr explained, "Thoreau's subject matter was Thoreau; his goal, wholeness; his tool, Walden Pond; and his methodology, simplification" (p. 125). This is the antithesis of the modern curriculum that artificially separates subject matter, isolates and analyzes discrete parts and obfuscates simple beauty. Orr concluded:

> *Aside from its merits as literature or philosophy,* Walden *is an antidote to the idea that education is a passive, indoor activity occurring between the ages of six and twenty-one. In contrast to the tendencies to segregate disciplines, and to segregate intellect from its surroundings,* Walden *is a model of the possible unity between personhood, pedagogy, and place. For Thoreau, Walden was more than his location. It was a laboratory for observation and experimentation; a library of data about geology, history, flora, fauna; a source of inspiration and renewal; and a testing ground for the man.* Walden *is no monologue, it is a dialogue between a man and a place. In a sense,* Walden *wrote Thoreau. His genius, I think, was to allow himself to be shaped by his place, to allow it to speak with his voice. (pp. 125–126)*

We see here the reconceptualized vision of curriculum we recommended earlier: the inspiration of nature and poetry; the unity of self, pedagogy and place; becomings through encounters with places; encouragement for the voice of self-expression.

THE FRESHMAN SEMINAR STUDENTS RESPOND

This understanding of curriculum and experience, rooted in John Dewey's philosophy, guided our colleague's freshman seminar visit to an art museum. Following a review of many styles of art and a discussion of Dewey's philosophy of art, the students went out alone into the Cleveland Museum of Art for an hour of reflection and with instructions to encounter some work of art themselves, a phenomenological exercise that had a profound impact on one student.

The class later gathered in a coffeehouse near the museum and for several hours described their experiences. One student reported his encounter with a huge Anselm Keefer canvas. He thought about his own life as he followed the image of two railroad tracks to the vanishing point at the center of the painting. He said he felt uneasy, almost frightened, and when he read the adjacent discussion of Keefer's concerns with World War II, the Holocaust and modern ecological destruction, his uneasy feelings became more concrete. "I almost felt," he said, "as though I were present at the Holocaust." The student also reported that he had always suspected his immigrant grandparents were hiding something from him about his heritage. The Keefer painting touched a nerve, and he was now eager to explore his genealogy and reflect on his identity. Later he indeed discovered that his "Christian" grandparents were really Jewish exiles who converted out of fear of death. Thus the freshman seminar has given opportunities both to learn about reading, writing art and music and to associate learning with lived lives. In short, we can reinvigorate schooling with a passion for exploring the fine arts, science, mathematics, literature and all dimensions of learning from a contextual perspective, and learn about life in the process.

SYNTHETIC MOMENTS AND THE CURRICULUM

While the past informs and conditions the present, every moment also contains possibilities for change and new directions. The aesthetic experience can inspire new personal realizations, as for the student described above or one author's experience in the Metropolitan Museum of Art in New York. An aesthetic approach to curriculum ensures that consequential learning will occur because the life experiences of the student become intimately bound up in the learning process. As Dewey explained in *Art as Experience*:

> *A work of art, no matter how old or classic, is actually not just potentially, a work of art only when it lives in some individual experience. A piece of parchment, of marble, of canvas, it remains self-identical throughout the ages. But as a work of art it is re-created every time it is aesthetically experienced. . . . The Parthenon, or*

whatever, is universal because it can continue to inspire new personal realiza-
tions in experience (1934b, pp. 108–109).

This aesthetic encounter with art as a recreation that continues to inspire, en-
lighten, inform and teach is exactly the kind of experience teachers must nurture
and direct. No universal curriculum or inert knowledge awaits memorization.
There is only a process of contextualizing the experiences of students and teachers
in order to create and recreate understanding and knowledge in each encounter
with art, music, literature, history and science. Pablo Picasso described artistic creation in a similar way:

> *A picture is not thought out and settled beforehand. While it is being done it*
> *changes as one's thoughts change. And when it is finished it still goes on changing*
> *according to the state of mind of whoever is looking at it. A picture lives a life like*
> *a living creature, undergoing the changes imposed on us by our life from day to*
> *day. This is natural enough, as the picture lives only through the person who is*
> *looking at it. (1971, p. 268)*

Picasso and Dewey each described one of the important phenomenological
dimensions of the reconceptualized curriculum we are proposing: Events find
their meaning in subjective encounters where knowledge is constructed and reconstructed in every new situation. In this sense, a work of art exists only in the
encounter. Locked in a darkened vault, a painting is simply an aggregate of materials. Art, like curriculum, is the process of becoming and recreating in each new
situation. Experiences require descriptions in the curriculum so that each student
and teacher can understand and create the world. The purpose is not just to describe phenomena or memorize information—say, an artist or a painting—but to
understand what lies behind them, their *being* or ontology.

As you can see, a phenomenological understanding of curriculum (as we explained in Chapter 9) replaces the modern obsession with standardized literature
and fine arts interpretations (particularly and ironically, in humanities departments), predetermined methodologies, dictated writing, painting and researching
styles and universal explanations of reality applied to knowledge acquisition.

Experientially based learning, by contrast, leads to the creation of landscapes of
learning and synthetic moments of self-understanding, which supports our case for
reconceptualized curriculum and instruction. In fact, aesthetic experiences like those
just described may ultimately be the only justification for our teaching, or even of
our very existence. As Friedrich Nietzsche wrote in *The Birth of Tragedy,* "We have
our highest dignity in our significance as works of art—for it is only as an aesthetic
phenomenon that existence and the world are eternally justified" (1968, p. 52).

Understanding the insights of John Dewey and other philosophers of education could make the difference between a career of monotony, drudgery and conflict and or a career of excitement, diversity and engagement. A curriculum can
provide great satisfaction if approached from an informed and reflective stance.
We encourage you to be a reflective teacher who navigates the difficult and sometimes controversial understandings of curriculum, instruction and evaluation in
the institutional context of schooling.

The Value in the Classroom of the Student Experience

Our discussion of the importance of starting curriculum studies with student experience and the context of learning may initially appeal to many preservice teachers. Yet once in school, they often avoid contextualizing teaching. Some blame the bureaucracy. School boards, state departments and administrators often insist on predetermined objectives and goals, along with mandated standardized tests to measure the retention of the information deemed important. The school structure, with its short time blocks and crowded classrooms, limits the freedom of both teachers and students. Financial, transportation and other logistical factors often constrain teachers as well. One of the greatest obstacles to an experientially based curriculum and learning process, however, is the school system's typical reliance on norm-referenced and criterion-referenced testing.

Norm-referenced tests are standardized tests used to compare individual student results with the scores of a norm group. You took many of these tests as a student. The ACT is used for college admission. The CAT, Iowa Basics and other achievement tests are given to elementary students in many districts, annually in some schools and on alternating years in others. These tests are scored in various ways, the most common being percentile, grade-level equivalency and stanine achievement brackets. The general impression is that the percentile score allows parents, teachers and the community to compare their students' results to those of students elsewhere. This approach to testing raises several problems, however.

Norm-Referenced Testing and Curriculum Alignment

First, students are not compared to all of the other students who took the norm-referenced test at the same time. Their scores are compared to the norm group—a control group of students who took the test several months or years earlier. The norm group is a statistical sample of a student population. School districts may choose from various norm groups the testing companies offer. Should a school district compare its students to a sample of the general population, students from northeastern private schools, inner-city public school students or Catholic school students? Who decides on the composition of the norm groups? When a student receives a percentile score, who are the students in the norm group he or she is being compared to? School officials rarely address these questions because the answers could present difficult issues. John Cannell, a West Virginia physician, brought this problem to national attention in 1987. Joseph Newman reported on Cannell's project:

> *Cannell thought that the news sounded a little too good when he heard that, in almost every local school system in his state, the scores of elementary students on the Comprehensive Test of Basic Skills were above the national norm. Since West Virginia, one of the nation's poorest states, ranks low on most other educational indicators, the doctor was surprised. Checking several neighboring states, he found*

that their students, too, were above average. . . . He [later] discovered that state superintendents in every state boasted that their students are above average. In other words, scoring above the norm is the norm (1998, p. 259).

How can everyone score above the norm? Simple. Since some testing companies only renorm tests every few years—that is, they create new sample control groups for comparison purposes—school districts have time to "align" the curriculum. Testing companies renorm tests only now and then because to do so is expensive. Testing companies are businesses; they want to make money and keep their customers satisfied. Testing companies that can provide above-average scores to a given school district are assured of continued business. Such companies have no vested interest in challenging the curriculum alignment process.

"Curriculum alignment" refers to matching the curriculum to the test. In other words, teachers specifically emphasize material students will encounter on the tests. Sometimes this proceeds honestly, as when teachers try to find ways to enhance student learning in preparation for the test. Other times it proceeds dishonestly, as when teachers and students secure copies of material on the test—or simply recall what was on it from the previous year. We remember a local newspaper printing a copy of the answer key to a standardized test the week before the test was to be administered. Even as the issue sold out on the street, the newspaper sent an investigative reporter to uncover the scandal of inadequate test security.

TEST SECURITY

As a teacher you will often have to prepare students for standardized tests and then administer them. Why should test security be a concern? Why would a teacher or administrator steal or cheat or act dishonestly? The reason problems with test security and honesty in the evaluation process arise relates directly to the pressure on educators and students to perform well. Scholarships, college admissions and athletic eligibility—all of these objectives and more put pressure on students to perform well on tests. As a teacher you will face tremendous pressure as well. Some states offer merit pay plans that tie salaries to student performance on standardized tests. Other districts publish the names of the teachers and the average test scores for their students. In such a situation your principles might conflict with your job security, community reputation or financial interest.

Administrators, who often are held personally accountable for the overall success of their schools on standardized and state-mandated tests, face other pressures. Just as a football coach with a poor record may be fired, so do principals face the same kind of pressure, particularly in those school districts where the local papers publish student performance rates. One secondary school principal reported a dilemma he faced in preparing his school "report card," a published list of all high schools in his district with the following information: the average ACT scores of the senior class, the number of expulsions, the number of suspensions, the total dollar amount of scholarships awarded and so forth. The coverage invited the entire community to rate the school's and the principal's success on this report card.

In calculating the average ACT score of the senior class, the principal found a mid-year transfer student on the list. (This is a common occurrence in schools. The "turn-over rate" of students reflects the number of students who drop out or transfer to another school after the beginning of the school year and the number of new students admitted during the year compared to the initial student enrollment. The rate can range from anywhere near 10 percent to as high as 90 percent in some schools. This raises the question of which scores to include on the school report card. Back to our principal.) He was preparing to ask the superintendent not to include this student's ACT score in the class average since she had not yet begun studies at her new school. He planned to argue that her ACT score would not indicate the quality of the faculty and the curriculum at her new school. However, he changed his mind when he saw that the transfer student had already taken the ACT and scored a 32, a score that would raise the senior class average, improve the school report card and make the faculty and principal look better in the public's eyes.

The principal told us this story several years after it happened. He still felt remorse for his dishonesty. He was upset, as well, that he and his counselors had systematically discouraged academically weak students from taking the ACT. Despite the fact that some students could have benefitted from taking the ACT, the counselors and administrators were worried about their jobs, their merit pay and the public perception of their performance on their annual report card. Why, they thought, encourage students who may never attend college to take the test and lower the class average? In Chapter 3, we provided several examples of situations in which students were tracked or limited in their educational opportunities because of political-ideological reasons. Here is yet another example.

Standardized testing, as suggested earlier, is a multi-million-dollar business with high-stakes implications. It should come as no surprise, then, that it is riddled with fraud, dishonesty and deceit. It should also be clear that curriculum alignment is a natural consequence of the emphasis on standardized testing. As many educators understand, the testing "tail" too often wags the curriculum "dog." Some educators resign themselves to standardized testing as inherent in the teaching and learning process, despite the negative impact it has on the curriculum. We resist this attitude. If we are to achieve an experienced-based curriculum, we must reduce the emphasis on standardized testing (Owen, 1999).

CRITERION-REFERENCED TESTING

As if it were not enough that norm-referenced tests now drive the school curriculum, educational bureaucrats, state government officials and religious fundamentalists have collaborated in recent years to sabotage the curriculum with another series of tests. As an outgrowth of the "accountability movement" of the 1980s discussed in Chapters 3 and 8, many school districts now mandate criterion-referenced tests, sometimes called "proficiency tests," "exit exams," "minimum competency exams" or "mastery exams" because they measure how much information a student has "mastered" in each subject area.

These tests generally include multiple-choice recall questions about the factual material in state or district curriculum guides for specific courses. Occasionally, as in Kentucky in the early 1990s, a portfolio is included. Some states include a writing sample; however, a rubric (standard guide for grading) is used by trained examiners to insure conformity. Some states have dropped the writing component because examiners have been idiosyncratic and scores have varied greatly. Help is on the way, however, with new computer programs that can "grade" essay questions!

These tests are supposed to ensure that students know specific basic information about reading, writing, computation and other subjects. The logic appeals to some: Test the students to make sure that they can pass basic reading, writing and math before promoting them to the next grade or allowing them to graduate. Some states even require that students pass these proficiency tests before they receive a driver's license or promotion to the next grade level.

We have many concerns about these tests. First, teachers pressured to ensure that their students pass the criterion-referenced test spend huge amounts of time drilling minimal competency skills. This preoccupation eliminates the possibility of any experience-based approach. Second, memorizing information hardly ensures a long-term memory or even a short-term engagement with the learning process. Third, learning is reduced to memorization rather than critical application, scientific investigation and understanding. Fourth, students who perform poorly on written tests have no other chances for demonstrating learning proficiency. Fifth, as we explained in Part 3, the political implications of allowing educational bureaucrats, state lawmakers and testing companies to determine the content of the "basic curriculum" are complex and frightening.

The proficiency test movement appears to be reducing the curriculum to a small body of inert information disconnected from the contextual experiences of the learning process. Disaffected students lose interest in school and drop out. Teachers who are already under extreme pressure lose their interest in and enthusiasm for academic investigation and experientially based learning. Teaching and learning in an environment like this become an assembly-line function devoid of critical inquiry and investigation.

To move beyond the minimal competency and proficiency testing mentality of modern schooling, teachers must equip themselves with other models and possibilities, which happens to be the goal of this chapter. Before we continue our discussion of reconceptualized visions of curriculum and instruction, however, we will review the traditional concept of curriculum to ensure that you understand the philosophy that drives the modern classroom. Although we promote a contextual experience-based approach to curriculum, instruction and evaluation, we recognize that accountability movements and proficiency test requirements exert a tremendous influence on all teachers, especially beginning teachers concerned about job security, tenure and acceptance in the profession. Accordingly, the following overview of the traditional approaches to curriculum will help you to investigate the reconceptualized curriculum within the current context of schooling.

THE INSTITUTIONAL CONTEXT OF TEACHING AND LEARNING

People generally associate the "school curriculum" with all the lesson plans, books, scope and sequence guides, published materials and learning objectives teachers use for instruction. In this sense "curriculum" is understood as all of the planned learning events the school directs in such subjects as mathematics, reading, language arts, social studies, science, physical education and the arts. The following paragraphs discuss twelve elements of a traditional curriculum and instruction program.

1. *Aims, goals and objectives.* "Aims," "goals" and "objectives" are terms used to describe what education does and how it proceeds. "Aims" are often considered the broadest purposes and "objectives" the most specific and incremental. All three terms describe the direction of teaching and learning. Those long-range goals we seek to accomplish are called "ends" or "end points" by Ralph Tyler (1949) and Hilda Taba (1962). Often both the goals and the objectives of the curriculum are determined by faculty committees, school board requirements, state or district guidelines, testing companies, publishers or a combination of two or more of these.

2. *Behavioral objectives.* Individual teachers are often asked to write specific statements outlining the ends they hope to accomplish with their classroom lessons. These short statements form the basis of a unit of study or a daily lesson plan that guides the teaching and learning process. Also, teachers must often write a series of statements of exactly what the students will do in each class session and match these statements with a district or state curriculum guide on a scope and sequence chart.

3. *Scope and sequence chart.* A scope and sequence chart provides a comprehensive list of the topics to be covered in a particular subject, course of studies or textbook—the scope—with the exact order in which each topic will be taught at each grade level—the sequence. For example, the publisher of an elementary school reading program generally provides a textbook for each student and a teacher's manual with test banks, answer keys, resource material and recommended lessons for the teacher, along with a chart that lists every topic and skill covered in the student textbook series. The chart shows when to introduce each topic or skill in the program and when the students should review and master each skill. The scope and sequence guide is thus an overview of the written curriculum of the school district or state.

4. *Mastery of learning instrument.* After instruction, students complete a test or activity to determine their level of mastery of the material covered in the behavioral objectives. These tests are called mastery of learning instruments.

5. *Subject area discipline.* When we categorize learning into specific bodies of information, we call the categories "subject areas" or "disciplines." We call a branch of knowledge such as mathematics, physics, economics or literature a discipline. Scholars in the various fields of study still argue over what constitutes a discipline and when new knowledge becomes a discipline. Thomas Kuhn (1970) wrote an important early study on the nature of scientific revolution and the reformulation of what constitutes the knowledge of a discipline. Kuhn called a scientific revolution a "paradigm shift." That is a "constellation" of values, beliefs and methodological assumptions, whether implicit or explicit, inscribed in a larger world-view. A paradigm shift is a gradual change that leads to a crisis and eventual dissolution or rupture of a dominant scientific world-view (i.e., the world is flat, the Earth is the center of the universe). Kuhn observes that throughout the history of the sciences there have been paradigm shifts that have led to a discontinuous change provoked by altogether new assumptions and theories. What paradigm shifts do you see occurring as we begin a new century? How are our worldview and cosmology changing as we begin the twenty-first century? For us curriculum has undergone the paradigm shift we describe in this chapter.

6. *Course of study syllabus.* Teachers will often be asked to write a short overview of the philosophy, objectives, evaluation procedures and reading assignments for every class they teach in the curriculum. This overview of the course of study is called a syllabus. In some schools a committee of teachers from the same grade level or department prepares each syllabus.

7. *Textbooks.* The choice of textbooks in the school district always shapes and sometimes dictates the curriculum. The textbook publisher provides a scope and sequence chart and other ancillary materials to assist the teacher in presenting the course of study. Some districts expect their teachers simply to teach the material as outlined in the textbook. Other school districts may allow teachers to select from a variety of trade books, novels, anthologies and textbooks to supplement their approaches to the teaching and learning process. As we have seen, political, religious and financial considerations often outweigh educational concerns in the adoption of textbooks (Apple & Christian-Smith, 1991). Some states, such as Texas, demand that textbooks be aligned with state-approved curricula, there the TEKS (Texas Essential Knowledge and Skills) curriculum. Thus, many publishers offer a special edition of all books with "Texas Edition" emblazoned on the cover. Without such books the publishers would lose sales and profits in Texas. However, that means Texas students are exposed to only the state-approved curriculum.

8. *Ancillaries.* Ancillaries include such supplementary or complementary instructional materials as computer software, audio tapes or CDs, overhead transparencies, artwork, posters, trade books, manipulatives (any hands-on objects such as blocks or cubes or science equipment students use to experience a lesson tactilely), flashcards, videotapes and multimedia disks. Most teachers find these materials in short supply and must purchase them themselves or improvise. Many more classrooms are sterile and impoverished, lacking any stimulating or investigative materials.

9. *Computer-assisted curriculum.* The curriculum is sometimes presented on software that allows students to work independently or in small groups on a personal computer or at computer stations. A variety of encoded material is now available for teachers and students, including CD-ROM databases for research, multimedia stations for creating hypercard stacks for presentations, Internet bulletin boards and interest groups, academic reinforcement games, subject-area exercises and proficiency tests.

10. *Cognitive-domain objectives.* When teachers compose objectives related to the mental and cognitive dimensions of human beings and the learning process we call them "cognitive-domain objectives." Students demonstrate cognitive abilities by applying formulas, writing essays or memorizing data.

11. *Affective-domain objectives.* When the teaching objectives relate to emotional and psychological dimensions of human beings and the learning process we call them "affective-domain objectives." This could include such things as music appreciation, literacy creativity or scientific inquisitiveness.

12. *Psychomotor-domain objectives.* When teaching objectives relate to physical movement and kinesthetic activity in the learning process we call them "psychomotor-domain objectives." This could include physical skills, sports, science experiments using bodily movement or classroom activities that require students to move their bodies.

Notice that all twelve of these elements of the traditional curriculum development model have one thing in common: They are all nouns. For most of the twentieth century educators have defined the curriculum in terms of tangible *things* they can measure and codify. Even the affective domain of learning objectives has been defined in behaviorally observable and measurable terms. Objectivity and precision have preoccupied educators for decades. (Recall from Chapter 2 that the emphasis on scientific measurement, specialization and management in the early twentieth century heavily influenced the emerging conceptualization of schooling. Educators sought respect and acceptance as professionals; thus they imitated the understanding of knowledge prevalent in the academic community.)

Veteran educators confirm that colleges, universities and normal schools (teacher-training institutions) taught the curriculum as a process of writing lesson plans with observable and measurable behavioral objectives in the cognitive, affective or psychomotor domain of learning. All objectives were to begin with the phrase "The student will . . . " followed by a verb such as "write," "recite," "repeat," or "demonstrate" and were to conclude with a measurable activity for testing or assessment. This has been the history of teacher training for curriculum and instruction. The context of the student as a dynamic person, the local community as a vibrant place of learning and the teacher as a unique individual with special talents to be utilized in the formation of lessons—the study of curriculum and instruction never adopted these concepts. In fact, traditional teacher training discounted these contextual elements as legitimate sources of knowledge. Just how did this understanding of curriculum and instruction originate and become so pervasive?

HISTORICAL EXAMPLES OF CURRICULUM

Educators often hear calls for the curriculum to go "back to the basics." Generally speaking, proponents of this concept yearn for the structured, orderly classroom with a focus on reading, writing and computation skills. Some also propose a return to sectarian Christian prayers, traditional "family values" and citizenship lessons in the curriculum. Others insist on specific "value-neutral" materials in the schools so that parents can teach values in the home. Finally, the call for "back to basics" for some also means a return to traditional Greek, Roman and European literature at the heart of the curriculum, with an emphasis on the "great books" and the Greek and Latin languages. We discussed these educational theories in Chapter 1 and referred to them as essentialism and perennialism.

When we examine the historical development of curriculum in schooling, we find that different subjects, books and lessons take prominence at different times in the United States and in other countries. Thus, the call for "back to basics" in the curriculum raises questions not easily answered, despite the fact that those who propose a "traditional" or "basic" curriculum assume consensus on the meaning of this approach.

In Plato's ideal society, individuals received an education that matched their assigned social roles. Early education for children ages six through eighteen included music and gymnastics. But "music" included the areas of letters, reading, writing, choral reading and dancing. Later Plato's students received instruction in the library classics, censored so as to emphasize poems and stories epitomizing obedience to authority, truthfulness, courage and emotional control. Many authorities ascribe to Plato's philosophy today. Former U.S. Secretary of Education William Bennett (1987, 1995) has become an outspoken proponent of classics in the curriculum, and has carefully selected, edited and even revised the stories in his best-selling *Book of Virtues* to reflect the political and moral values he promotes for all American children. Over his loud calls for morality and values, it can be difficult for the casual reader to detect the political manipulation behind Bennett's work.

When we examine two of William Bennett's books, *The James Madison High School* (1987) and *The James Madison Elementary School* (1988), we find an overview of his ideal curriculum for all American students. He outlines both the exact classes he believes all students should take and a description of precisely what should be included in their lesson plans. In high school, for example, Bennett calls for fours years of English, three years of math, two years of a foreign language, three years of social studies, three years of science, two years of physical education, and one semester each of art history and music history. Electives would complete the schedule. This may seem to many a logical plan, but closer examination reveals several problems with Bennett's curriculum.

The four-year English curriculum includes introduction to literature, American literature, British literature and world literature. Here is Bennett's proposal for tenth-grade American literature:

Students read a careful selection of American fiction, drama, and poetry. A good syllabus designed to spotlight that distinctive American achievement in literature might include Franklin, Irving, Hawthorne, Poe, Whitman, Twain, Melville, Dickinson, Faulkner, Wharton, Hemingway, O'Neill, Fitzgerald, Frost, Ralph Ellison, and Robert Penn Warren. Regular writing assignments are made and continued emphasis is placed on clarity, precision, and frequent revision. Students are given increasing experience in classroom speaking. (1987, p. 13)

Bennett outlines the major authors to be included in the American literature curriculum. Why are there only two women on the list? Why only one black? Where are the Hispanics? Where are the voices of Native Americans? Where are the transcendentalists, and why does Bennett exclude the giants Thoreau and Emerson? It happens that the political views of the transcendentalists conflict with the conservative politics of William Bennett. Might this explain the oversight? Contemporary African American authors such as Langston Hughes, Maya Angelou, Ernest Gaines, Toni Morrison and Alice Walker are absent from Bennett's curriculum because he is committed to a view of the classics as a time-honored tradition—a tradition formed by those with the power and influence to create it. Even if this were true, why does Bennett exclude black intellectuals and artists of the Harlem Renaissance? Author Jonathan Kozol often writes about this problem.

Kozol (1967) published his first book, *Death at an Early Age,* as a result of his experiences as a beginning language teacher among disadvantaged African American children in Boston's public schools. Kozol told the story of his frustration with dilapidated facilities, overcrowded classrooms and outdated textbooks. None of the authors William Bennett recommends in American literature reflect the contextual experiences of the students Kozol taught. Moreover, there were not enough books to go around, and the books that were available were damaged and missing pages.

Browsing through a Boston bookstore one day, Kozol caught sight of a collection of poems with a picture of an African American poet on the cover. He purchased the book for his class. He wanted to show the students what a new book looked like, and he also wanted them to see that black poets exist, since none were represented in their textbooks. Kozol found himself fired by the school district for "curricular deviation," having read Langston Hughes's poem that asked "What happens to a dream deferred? Does it shrivel like a raisin in the sun? . . . or does it explode?" Kozol related how one particularly angry young woman who had resisted him throughout the course asked to borrow the book and memorized the poem. The poetry of Langston Hughes transformed the students and Kozol's classroom, but it also disturbed the school authorities, who were afraid of what might happen if poor black children began to read "radical" poetry. Since Hughes's poetry did not appear in the curriculum guide or district syllabus, Kozol was fired. He went on, of course, to write a library of inspiring books about such topics as the lack of education for the children of the homeless and migrant workers, the politics of literacy in the United States and the "savage" economic inequalities of American schooling. The works of Jonathan Kozol remind us that curriculum is hardly a politically neutral activity. William Bennett's curriculum ignores the importance of multicultural literature, the contextual experiences of students and teachers and the political consequences of censoring and editing the curriculum.

Supporters of Bennett's curriculum might respond that he manages to include world literature in the senior year of high school. But take a careful look at the works he recommends:

> *A good syllabus might include a small number of works by authors from classical Greece and Rome (Sophocles and Virgil); a more generous selection from noted authors of Europe and Russia (Dante, Cervantes, Moliere, Balzac, Chekhov, Dostoevsky, Zola, Mann, and Ibsen); and* depending on the instructor's knowledge and interests, *a small number of works from Japan, China, the Near East, Africa, and Latin America. (1986, p. 13, emphasis added)*

Bennett reduces world literature to a limited canon of works from Greece, Rome and Europe; a strong bias toward Western culture is clearly visible. Bennett tosses a bone to *world* literature by including "a small number" of works from all of the Eastern and Southern Hemisphere cultures. His narrow worldview and political ideology permeate—we might say "infect"—his curriculum. It seems a bit naïve to assume teachers who have been exposed to only a classical curriculum have "knowledge and interest" in literature from Japan, China, Africa or Latin America. But Bennett is not naïve. He designed his curriculum to accomplish definite political ends, with the suppression of diversity, human experience and the contextualization of schooling. We should examine closely efforts by William Bennett and others who call for a return to a classical curriculum and expose the damage they would inflict on our students (Courts, 1997).

We can see some of this damage in a second example from *The James Madison High School*. In the introduction Bennett congratulates three states for having attained the ideal curriculum: "These standards [basic academic subjects] were endorsed by President Reagan, and they have since served as an important national goal. Since 1983, nearly all of the 50 states have made progress toward this goal, and three—Florida, Louisiana, and Pennsylvania—have attained it" (p. 2). A colleague of ours who was a principal in Louisiana when he read Bennett's statement recalls his response.

> *I was amazed that my state—a state consistently at the bottom of every educational and economic indicator—was being praised for having attained the ideal curriculum. This was an absurdity that contradicted all my twenty years as a Louisiana educator! I was compelled to investigate the contradiction.*
>
> *I discovered that Bennett based his praise for the Louisiana curriculum on legislation that required the completion of the basic courses he recommended. In particular, Louisiana had recently enacted legislation requiring all students to pass Algebra I in order to graduate high school. But Louisiana schools were in turmoil over this issue. The high school dropout rate—already near 40 percent—began to increase as students found themselves unable to complete the ideal cur-*

riculum. Math teachers met frustration as they attempted to force Algebra I stud-ies on students who were incapable of or unprepared for algebra. Therefore, many teachers simply taught consumer math, business math, computation or other math skills and called the class "Algebra I." It was a frustrating situation for everyone involved, but at least Louisiana now offered the ideal American curriculum.

How did we reach the point at which curriculum issues have become so con-troversial, political and frustrating? The roots of the current curriculum debates can be found in our dependence on an approach to curriculum planning called the "Tylerian Rationale."

THE TYLERIAN RATIONALE

Professor Ralph W. Tyler of the University of Chicago in 1949 published a book entitled *Basic Principles of Curriculum and Instruction* that proposed four ele-ments of curriculum: goals and objectives, lessons and instructional plans, organi-zation of learning experiences and evaluation of lessons. Since labeled the "Tyler-ian Rationale," this formulation has shaped the definition of curriculum for half a century. Ralph Tyler proposed four central questions related to each element of curriculum planning that should guide the curriculum and instruction process:

1. What educational purposes should the school seek to attain (what are its "ends" or goals or objectives)?
2. How can learning experiences be selected that are likely to be useful in at-taining these objectives (lesson plans)?
3. How can meaningful learning experiences be organized for effective in-struction (scope and sequence guides)? and
4. How can the effectiveness of learning experiences be evaluated (tests)?

Preservice teachers usually hear a lot about the four elements of the traditional Tylerian Rationale of curriculum and instruction—possibly more than they would like. Many university education schools continue to emphasize the development of goals and objectives, formal lesson plans, scope and sequence materials and measurable evaluation and testing instruments. They assume that one can deter-mine ends and goals in advance and then implement uniform procedures accord-ing to the lessons teachers and other experts draw up. We call this assumption about goals and objectives "overt," "explicit" or "stated curriculum" (Eisner, 1994) because school districts and educators write and distribute it before imple-menting the lesson or unit to study. The written behavioral objectives state exactly what the students will study and learn in every classroom before the lessons begin.

The explicit curriculum assumes that the stated objectives will be taught and students will memorize, analyze, understand and apply the information presented. Over the past century educators have spent unimaginable amounts of time and en-ergy writing explicit curriculum and instruction materials and lessons. Schools and classrooms overflow with volumes of these materials. In fact, the education library or instructional media center at your university probably swells with samples of textbooks, curriculum guides, teacher manuals and state department curriculum guides with these explicit (or overt) curriculum materials you will be assumed (or expected) to use each day.

We take exception to this definition and understanding of curriculum and instruction, and we will explain shortly why we reject an understanding of curriculum limited to overt behavioral objectives. To start with, it is no longer the universally accepted definition. In fact, the concept of the curriculum is far more complex than the simple overview we have presented thus far. Briefly, we resist defining the goals, objectives and ends of education in advance and outside of the context of each student, teacher, classroom and local community. But we are getting ahead of ourselves. We should first discuss two other important dimensions of curriculum and instruction: the hidden curriculum and the null curriculum.

THE HIDDEN OR UNSTATED CURRICULUM

Many scholars in recent years have challenged the idea that the explicit curriculum is the only important dimension of the schooling process, and they insist that the discrete parcels of information and knowledge schools present for categorization and memorization and recitation are only one small part of the curriculum. In short, they find a "hidden curriculum" behind the explicit curriculum. For example, Apple (1979) suggested that schools and classrooms socialize students to the values that are a part of the culture of the school and society. More specifically, Jackson (1968, 1992) noticed that the current structure of classrooms, with large numbers of students, socializes those students to delay gratification and sharing of their successes because teachers cannot satisfy all the needs of all the children simultaneously. Many of these critics of the explicit curriculum also contend that schools foster compliant behavior rather than cultivate initiative, as they generally claim to do.

The hidden curriculum often works like a subliminal message. Advertisers create subliminal (below the threshold of consciousness) messages to sell their products. Scantily clad women fall from the sky in beer commercials; muscular men promote exercise equipment and cigarettes. Sex, images of presumed beauty or promises of wealth and happiness sell products. Some merchants use subliminal messages to discourage shoplifting. Inaudible voices announce under the soft music that "shoplifters will be prosecuted." Until the practice was banned in the 1960s, movie theaters would insert and flash film frames of popcorn or sodas to lure viewers to the concession stand. These frames flashed by too quickly to register overtly with the viewer; thus they were subliminal or hidden.

Some elements of the curriculum operate in exactly the same way, practices that have gone unchallenged until recently. For example, a high school civics teacher who is committed to the Tylerian Rationale plans a unit on the Bill of Rights. In her lesson plan she introduces the first ten amendments to the Constitution, presents an overview of each amendment, discusses examples of legal cases related to each amendment, shows a film about the history of the Bill of Rights and prepares notes for the students that outline the information in the textbook. She presents a well-prepared lesson in a traditional format.

As the teacher starts the lesson, her thirty students sit quietly in six rows facing the blackboard. In the middle of the introduction on the first day of class, one student raises his hand. The teacher calls on him and he says, "I don't agree with the Bill of Rights. We do not have rights in this country. The government controls everything." This particular bright student has challenged the teacher all year, and frankly, she is sick and tired of his constant interruptions. She responds, "This is not the time for comments. After we study the amendments and understand their purpose, then we can discuss examples."

The persistent student raises his hand again: "Look, you say that we have freedom of expression and freedom of speech in this country. The school newspaper wouldn't print my article last week because they said it was too controversial to interview pregnant girls on campus."

This time the teacher interrupts the student. She is furious that he constantly tries to challenge her, and she is particularly disturbed that he would bring up such a sensitive issue as pregnancy. She raises her voice and scolds him: "You are constantly interrupting the class. Our lesson calls for learning the Bill of Rights today. Put your hand down and write the notes. You will have a test on Friday and a proficiency exam later this year in which you will have to name the first ten amendments and discuss how they protect our freedoms. Now be quiet and get busy!"

This scenario recurs every day. Teachers demand that students learn information using a methodology that contradicts the very premise of the lesson. In this case, the annoying student may memorize the fact that the Bill of Rights guarantees freedom of speech. But he has actually learned that there is no freedom of speech, no opportunity to discuss controversial subjects and no forum for challenging concepts presented in textbooks or lesson plans. Many authors, including Eisner (1994) and Apple (1979), argue that the hidden curriculum is actually more influential in the learning process than the explicit curriculum. That is what students really remember.

We have observed many civics classes like the one just described, and so, no doubt, have you. Conservative critics such as Chester Finn (1991) and books such as *Civitas* (Bahmueller, 1991) recommend more civics in the classroom. They want to be sure students know the facts about American government and history so they will participate in the democratic process. These critics expect more rigorous civics classes to improve our democracy. They cite low voter turnout, voter apathy, a general reluctance to participate and declining trust in the government as reasons for teaching a more rigorous civics program. They also propose a proficiency test to make sure that all students know the facts about the Constitution, the Bill of Rights, the branches of government and American history.

Accustomed to the traditional teaching and learning methodologies, some students may indeed memorize the information for the test, but all of them will continue to learn the reality of American government from the hidden curriculum while the learned critics wonder why American citizens do not vote and remain disaffected. It is not simply because we sometimes fail to teach the facts about government; it is because the hidden curriculum conditions students to distrust their government.

Meanwhile, those who are most vocal about training students with the traditional methodologies actually raise a sort of smokescreen. They want to protect their status quo privilege and train the next generation to accept the values of the culture and government without question. The hidden curriculum is at the very least a subconscious communication of values, ideas and social realities within the schooling community; at worst it is a conscious effort on the part of some teachers, politicians and educational bureaucrats to perpetuate injustice and retain the prevailing social arrangements using the subliminal programming Madison Avenue advertisers employ.

THE NULL CURRICULUM

The "null curriculum" refers to what gets left out of the curriculum—those authors, ideas, topics and issues that go undiscussed. As a teacher you will face decisions in curriculum planning about the inclusion or exclusion of material. As you come to the end of a hectic year, what chapters will you skip? Like William Bennett's world literature curriculum, what authors reflect your own knowledge and interests? How much time will you allocate to each topic, chapter or book? What issues are too controversial to discuss? HIV/AIDS? pregnancy? religion? politics? race? gender? What books are banned? What well-known books are absent from the school library or forbidden outright? For example, some teachers worry that if they discuss the topic of racism, civil rights, the Civil War, the Million Man March, the Ku Klux Klan, reconstruction in the south, genetics, interracial dating at the prom or some other topic remotely related to race parents will complain or a riot will break out in the school. Therefore, many school districts and teachers ignore or gloss over these controversial topics, which is the null curriculum in action.

At one Alabama school in 1994, the principal threatened to cancel the prom when he heard that a black and a white student planned to attend the dance as a couple. One mixed-race student then asked the principal who she could date. The principal reportedly replied that she was a "mistake" and represented the evil consequences of interracial dating. Later in the year the school building burned to the ground and the principal was removed from his position.

This episode suggests, among other things, that attempts to silence people by forbidding discussion of controversial topics and prohibiting freedom of ideas and association can be explosive. Nevertheless, the null curriculum remains pervasive and oppressive. As we saw in Part 3, textbook companies avoid controversial topics in order to appeal to the widest possible audience. Students suffer when they receive incomplete information as a result of the belief that silence protects them from suffering. Jonathan Silin (1995) wrote an insightful book, *Sex, Death, and Children: Our Passion for Ignorance in the Age of AIDS*, in which he documents the devastating consequences of remaining silent in the age of AIDS. The null curriculum hardly protects children; an insistence upon silence handicaps children, and when the suppressed information involves AIDS, it can kill them.

A colleague of ours once supervised a student teacher in a rural Louisiana school district. During our colleague's first visit to the classroom in early February, she observed a lesson on the Bush administration in the social studies class. After discussing the lesson with the student teacher and wondering why they were studying contemporary American history, our colleague asked the supervising teacher about the syllabus. The master teacher explained, "When I first started teaching here twenty years ago during integration, we decided to start the United States history classes at 1900 and move to the present. Then we go back to the early explorers and work our way to the 1840s. We are about half way through the curriculum right now."

The student teacher noticed, of course, that the curriculum omitted the years between 1840 and 1900. She told the teacher that the historian Shelby Foote, who had narrated a PBS series on the Civil War, considered the Civil War period the most significant time in American history because everything before 1860 established the context for the war and everything after the war involved attempts to deal with its consequences. "How could the Civil War be excluded from the curriculum?" she inquired.

The supervising teacher replied that it was too controversial to discuss these issues in the community. Nevertheless, he did tell her he regretted the fact that he could not teach the Civil War: "The Civil War period is my favorite. I have been teaching United States history for twenty years, and I have never been able to cover that period."

It happened that this supervising teacher was the only high school U.S. history teacher in that rural district. Thus, the entire Civil War had been relegated to the null curriculum for all of the citizens of this community for two decades. It also happened that race relations in this rural community were unusually tense. Could one trace those tensions to the null curriculum in the schools? We think so. Like the hidden curriculum, the null curriculum has a greater impact on students than the overt curriculum. The null curriculum and the hidden curriculum affect students forever; whereas students often forget the overt curriculum shortly after they complete their proficiency tests (Goodson, 1997).

RECONCEPTUALIZING TEACHING AND LEARNING

Recent studies of the curriculum challenge traditional Tylerian assumptions and begin to reconceptualize the curriculum. A book by Pinar, Reynolds, Slattery and Taubman (1995) entitled *Understanding Curriculum* proposes that the curriculum is not a scope and sequence chart or a list of objectives but rather a process, a journey toward becoming during which all life experiences are valued for their potential to inform and inspire learning. This process affirms important dimensions of curriculum often overlooked in the traditional model: the relational dimension of learning in communities, the autobiographical stories of teachers and students, subjective interpretations and personal insights, the sociocultural environment of education, multicultural and political concerns and theological dimensions of the learning milieu. Our understanding of curriculum must no longer remain separated into discrete subjects to be studied and memorized. Rather, the curriculum must be an interdisciplinary experience that unites learning with the community in a process of growth for each individual on the journey to becoming a more insightful, just, committed and involved member of the human community. In the reconceptualized curriculum, community involvement is hardly a peripheral issue; the community context is necessary for learning environments to exist.

A RECONCEPTUALIZED LESSON

A graduate student in one of our classes in Ohio who studied the concepts of curriculum presented in this chapter appreciated our perspective, but she could not imagine implementing reconceptualized visions of the curriculum in her school. Her principal demanded daily lesson plans with specific outcomes outlined in the curriculum guide. The district administered proficiency tests in math, reading, science and English. Her tenure and promotion depended on how well her students performed on these tests. Her very pay scale followed a merit system that rewarded compliance with the traditional curriculum program. She resented the environment the system created in her classroom, but she saw no realistic chance to deviate. Further, her students behaved so disruptively and their participation was so sporadic that she doubted they would accept a contextual and experiential curriculum. In short, she considered our curriculum philosophy too idealistic and impractical. For her final course project, however, she explored the possibilities of a student-centered experiential curriculum.

Because her district did not test social studies, and because most teachers skipped the thirty-minute social studies block to spend more time on the "important" subjects, our student decided to experiment with her relatively safe social studies curriculum. She videotaped her lessons for a two-week unit on deserts and then shared the video with us. Instead of writing lesson plans in advance with specific objectives and evaluation requirements, she introduced the lesson with this simple statement: "Today we begin our next unit in social studies. Our topic is deserts." Bored and distracted faces appeared on the video. A few took notes. Most sat silently waiting for instructions. Then she dropped her bombshell: "I don't know very much about deserts. I have never been to a desert. We are going to have to figure out how to learn about deserts together."

Immediately one student raised his hand. "I went to a desert in California last summer." He described his trip enthusiastically, but he struggled to remember the name of the desert. Another student suggested that they look at a map and find its name. The class moved to the map. Another student pointed to Africa and said that her father once went hunting on a safari. "What's a safari?" another student asked. The class consulted the dictionary to find the answer.

Over the next few days, the students decided to divide themselves into groups to investigate deserts. One group selected animals of the deserts. They made a small-scale model of a desert and a safari. Another group made maps of the various deserts of the world. Other groups investigated plant life, human habitation and survival.

The teacher, our graduate student, reported that she had never seen such enthusiasm for a unit of study in her career. Students who formerly presented severe behavior problems emerged as group leaders. Another group of students went to the library every day at recess to find more information about their topics. The maps and models of deserts were displayed in the corridor and caught the attention of other students. Our student was convinced of the power of our reconceptualized curriculum when she completed this experimental project. We suspect that she will find ways to resist a steady dose of the traditional approach to curriculum and instruction in the future.

A Schoolwide Example of Interdisciplinary Curriculum

As an example of this philosophy of curriculum in practice, consider an interdisciplinary curriculum program at an elementary school in Louisiana that incorporates some of the best elements of the emerging understandings of curriculum. This school undertook a museum project to provide educational experiences that draw on and support the entire community: school, university, benefactors, teachers, students, alumni, churches, school and parish boards, students in other schools—even tourists.

The school is located adjacent to the historic property of a prominent cathedral. The grounds include the 450-year-old vice president of the national Live Oak Society (only trees can be members), the town's first cemetery and the former bishop's home. The school grounds are located within a few blocks of the local university. In 1992 the church vacated an office building adjacent to the cathedral, and the school had a chance to use the space. Its faculty decided to dedicate part of the space to a new museum featuring the local history of the school, church, cemetery, oak tree and prominent citizens buried in the cemetery.

With the encouragement and guidance of several teachers, junior high students volunteered to collect artifacts to be displayed in the museum. They also learned to serve as tour guides in the museum, applying lessons from their daily French classes to speak with tourists from Quebec and France. They interviewed relatives of several people buried in the cemetery, including descendants of the founder of the original settlement in 1821, a Civil War general, an American ambassador to France and others. A museum board was formed.

The students and teachers also collaborated with a professional filmmaker to create a videotape for tourists to view as they arrived on the property. At various times during the year the students conducted tours of the property for tourists, Boy Scout and Girl Scout troops and visitors from other schools.

This museum project provided students with leadership opportunities, and it established historical links for future generations. Everyone in the community benefitted from this curricular innovation: Students found themselves immersed in local history. The school and church strengthened their mutual bonds while publicly displaying their common heritage. Teachers and club leaders now enjoy a convenient site for field trips, family outings and discussion sessions, and the school alumni have a visible reminder of their school and community heritage.

The local university also became involved in the creation of the museum, loaning several artifacts from its special library collection. A professor of history and several graduate students in social studies education provided information for the video script.

But how might this special, one-time museum project be a model for total community education? First and most obvious, the inclusive nature of the collaborative enterprise benefitted all the participants. Church, school, university and local citizens all provided materials, information and advice. Second, the students had leadership roles, providing meaningful decision making, making creative suggestions and taking responsibility. Third, focusing attention on the historical roots of the school, community and cemetery provided alumni, grandparents and benefactors a focus for renewing their connections to the community.

EDUCATION AS A LIFE-LONG PROCESS

Education is a life-long process that includes a variety of experiences: formal programs, informal activities, learning exercises, cooperative ventures, informative presentations, spiritual revelations, psychological discoveries and personal relationships. Education transcends singular definitions; it is an ongoing process of becoming that includes the emotional, physical and relational dimensions of life.

Meanwhile, the institutionalization of education as schooling has become a complex phenomenon with a rich but tortuous history that includes both successes and failures. As we have seen, many people have acquired a personal interest and investment in formal schooling. But the ability of schooling to further the educative process while promoting a just and sustainable global community directly relates to the ability of all those education affects to cooperate, share resources, listen with empathy, accept differences, remain open to possibilities and understand history. This vision is essential to the emergence of the holistic curriculum and instruction process we propose. Local projects like the museum curriculum suggest that it can be done.

The cooperative community milieu we just described is too often the exception rather than the rule. We have all seen the divisiveness that exists in so many institutions. Various school departments and programs fight with each other for limited funding or recognition. Boards of education, school committees, administrators and teachers bicker over funding or program implementation. The allocation of facilities and resources often generates distrust and anger. Disagreements about the educational process result in feuds and threats. In other words, the current curriculum reflects in a microcosm the problems of the larger society.

CURRERE

Recall from Chapter 9 that the word "curriculum" derives from the Latin verb *currere,* which means "to run the racecourse." Yet, as we noted earlier, the modern school curriculum has reduced the curriculum to a noun, "the course." We have forgotten that curriculum is an active process; it is not the lesson plan, the scope and sequence chart, the mastery test, the goals and objectives or the textbook. The curriculum is an integrated experience of living the journey toward becoming a whole person—emotionally, physically, psychologically, spiritually and socially. The curriculum never ends; it is always ongoing and tentative.

This simple concept is apparently difficult for many to understand. Ever since the Enlightenment and the development of philosophies that polarized reality, individuals have been busily fragmenting all elements of life. An atmosphere of holistic education offers an opportunity to reconceptualize ("reverse" is the impolite word) this modern obsession with fragmentation and specialization.

The current school curriculum reflects this separatist ideology in many ways. For example, the learning process is artificially divided into school subjects taught without any connection to the other subjects. Math and science get special priority—as we saw in the discussion of the *Goals 2000* document in Chapter 1—and the arts and humanities become the first casualties of budget cuts and scheduling conflicts. Spelling and punctuation become the dominion of language arts specialists. The school schedule and social culture revolve around a few popular or dominant activities such as a sport, a club or a social event.

Thus, severe fragmentation too often characterizes the school curriculum. Despite efforts to integrate the curriculum through team teaching, modular schedules, interdisciplinary units, writing across the curriculum and cooperative programs, education too often remains driven by preplanned goals and objectives, disciplinary units, lectures, memorization and standardized tests. With continued specialization and new standards in every field of study, teachers are actually becoming more isolated from each other and from subjects beyond their areas of specialization.

We have met Algebra I teachers who are uncomfortable discussing math with calculus teachers, much less writing across the curriculum with English teachers. We have heard teachers in the earliest grades request greater departmentalization. Kindergarten programs that focus on child-centered needs are becoming the exception instead of the rule. More tests and proficiency exams intrude on the schooling process every year. Faculty members and students under extreme time pressures feel overwhelmed by the amount of material they have to cover. The traditional school schedule, with numerous bells and short periods, frustrates many teachers.

We contend that much of this pressure arises from the fragmentation we see in the schools. In response, we must break down the barriers that divide math from

English, art from science, physical education from academic education, administration from faculty, school from district, parents from teachers and teachers from students. We must find a way to stop thinking and acting in terms of "us and them," or worse, "us versus them." Only when an integrated vision of living in a just and sustainable community emerges can we reconceptualize the curriculum and instruction.

HISTORICAL PERSPECTIVES

Is history a progressive series of distinctly separate and chronological events on a linear timeline or is it a procession of interrelated occasions with the past and future embedded in the present moment? The first perspective implies a commitment to the objective analysis and categorization of discrete parcels of information that become quantifiable objects of study. From this perspective, an historian attempts to explain events logically according to a narrative of human progress through the centuries.

The second perspective (which we discussed in Chapter 9) implies a commitment to ongoing reinterpretation, the primacy of subjective experience, the interpenetration of meaning and context, the social construction of knowledge and the interdependence of events within a time and a place. In short, we can understand history either as events separated by time and space or as the integral interrelationship of events unified with time and space.

Logical positivists and analytic philosophers generally ascribe to the first perspective, as we noted in Chapter 2. Either these philosophers ignore historical analysis because of the subjectivity inherent in the interconnectedness of contextual realities or they objectify and segment history to control reality so that events conform within the paradigm of modernity. Many contemporary curriculum scholars challenge the assumption that historical interpretation should work to validate the knowledge and values of the dominant modern paradigm. Contemporary curriculum studies celebrate the eclectic, innovative, revisionist, ironic and subjective dimensions of historical interpretation.

Our reconceptualized curriculum development model challenges the traditional approach modern logical positivists take to the study of history as a linear timeline of events. It encourages autobiographical reflection, narrative inquiry, revisionist interpretation and contextual understanding so that we can understand knowledge as reflecting socially constructed human interests, values and actions. Herbert Kliebard explains:

> We often make half-conscious decisions as to what knowledge is most appropriate to include in the curriculum then afterwards devise the plausible-sounding reasons for so deciding. Those half-conscious decisions are tied in many instances to such matters as social class allegiances and to self-interest generally. As such, curriculum history is not so much involved with traditional epistemological questions as with questions closely associated with the sociology of knowledge. The history of the curriculum is, in other words, critically concerned with what is taken to be knowledge in certain times and places rather than what is ultimately true or

valid. . . . A fundamental question embedded in the history of curriculum, then, is not simply one of who went to school and who did not, but the way in which the social machinery may be constructed to differentiate access to certain forms of knowledge. [This difference is] significant not just in a pedagogical sense but in terms of status attainment and social relations, if not social justice. (1992, p. 158)

In effect, the curriculum must seek to understand and inculcate history contextually rather than delineate a coherent analysis of selective events and artifacts. Just as the curriculum is affected by social conditions and values, so can it help reshape or preserve those conditions and values. The relationship between society and the curriculum, in other words, is reciprocal.

Contemporary curriculum discourses assume history to be contextual, multidimensional, ironic, contingent, evolving and personal. Educators can no longer simply "teach" history. Because the autobiographical, local and particular are essential to an understanding of history, teachers must now listen to students and their life stories. As feminist scholars insist, history is not just "his story"—that is, the master narratives of Anglo-Saxon, European, Protestant, heterosexual, male warriors. Rather, "her story" is also integral to history.

This participatory view of history is what Jonathan Kozol proposed for social studies classrooms. Kozol argues against schooling that is not transformative and against schooling that does not participate in history:

School teaches history in the same way that it teaches syntax, grammar, and word-preference: in terms that guarantee our prior exile from its passion and its transformation. It lifts up children from the present, denies them powerful access to the future, and robs them of all ethical repossessions of the past. History is, as the sarcastic student says, an X-rated film. The trouble is that everyone we know, love, touch, hold, dream to be, or ever might become, has first to be told: I cannot enter. (1975, p. 83)

We must, therefore, keep history from becoming a series of events to be memorized, and make it an opportunity to inform the present and provide access to the future. Kozol challenges educators to adopt a transformative pedagogy in order to recover a participative mode in history education.

Another contrast between the modern and our critical constructive postmodern view of the function of the social studies curriculum is portrayed in a familiar classroom poster headed "Occupations to Which Interest in History May Lead." The poster lists archeologist, curator, writer, critic, archivist, anthropologist, librarian and teacher. Nowhere does this list suggest the possible goal of becoming someone who "enters history." The curriculum must challenge both teachers and students to enter into the historical process as participants rather than as observers.

Our schools have recently experienced a flood of textbooks and curriculum materials that promote "critical thinking." We would normally welcome this trend, but close examination of these critical thinking materials reveals that some of them establish boundaries around thinking and actually limit the parameters of knowledge by offering specific interpretations of human history. Luckily some educators go further, encouraging freedom of interpretation from an existential perspective. The resulting conflict centers on the question of whether English and social studies teachers, for example, should encourage or even allow their students to offer subjective interpretations of literature and history, or whether critical thinking should be directed toward a range of legitimate interpretations scholarly authorities have already established. Curriculum historians today insist that theories and narratives simply cannot present politically, theologically, racially, gendered and culturally neutral perspectives. History, like knowledge, is socially and culturally constructed. We are convinced that the curriculum today must include more eclectic and subjective understandings of interpretation and critical thinking, even though traditional Tylerian modernists will denounce us as heretics. For example, *Civitas,* (Bahmueller, 1991), a new national framework for civics education mentioned earlier, issued this warning:

> *Citizenship training, if it means anything at all, means teaching students to think critically, listen with discernment, and communicate with power and precision. If students learn to listen, read, speak, and write more carefully, they will not only be civically empowered, but also they will know how to distinguish between the authentic and the fraudulent in human discourse. . . . Civic education for a new century also must provide students with a core of basic knowledge about social issues and institutions, to allow them to put their understanding of democracy into perspective. (1991, p. xvi)*

Like other conservative calls for cultural literacy, core knowledge and a fact-based curriculum, *Civitas* is concerned with teaching basic information so students can make informed decisions that protect the current political and social arrangements and be socialized into the American political structure. The unstated assumption is that students left to their own interpretations or subjective analyses without authoritative guidance and reason will be unable to participate effectively or appropriately. The modernist approach to science and history contends that knowledge builds on itself in progressive stages. Thus, students must know an objective past before attempting to apply critical thinking in the present. Those with this perspective require us to apply the truth of past scientific discoveries and historical analysis to build new knowledge. This philosophy continues to guide the traditional approaches to the curriculum, which assume that learning takes place in sequential steps and that students must master one set of skills before proceeding to the next level of difficulty. If this assumption were true, we would delay one of the most complex dimensions of human learning, speech and language, until much later in life rather than fool ourselves into thinking that babies can learn to speak.

The contemporary curriculum challenges this outdated concept of time and linear scientific progress. Albert Einstein, who as a young man had major difficulties with formal schooling, provides a case in point. Einstein's vision of the physical universe in his theory of relativity initiated a search for a unified foundation for physics beyond the modern worldview of Newtonian physics. Einstein's theories called into question traditional understandings of time and space and, by extrapolation, the concept of contextfree knowledge accumulation outside of time and space that dominated research and scholarship in the nineteenth century. The postmodern rejection of chronophonism, the modern idea that time is strictly chronological and linear, thus gained credence. Was it personally important for Einstein to challenge the classical physics that dominated the formal schooling of his time? We think it was, and we contend that the conception of curriculum and chronology that pervades modern schooling actually inhibits the creative genius of the Einsteins in our schools today (Kincheloe, Steinberg, & Tipping, 1999).

Students often complain about the boredom they feel in social studies classes, particularly history. In fact, if one discipline in the curriculum exemplifies the failure of the modern behaviorist and analytic approach to education, it is history. Teachers often reduce history to a series of events on a linear timeline to be memorized and evaluated in the context of artificially contrived epochs of sociopolitical or cultural development. The linear model divides time into the past, present and future and, as a result, removes any potential autobiographical connection to the historical events discussed in textbooks or classroom lectures.

In short, the modern curriculum has decontextualized history, and an ahistorical, antihistorical attitude has appeared. Perplexed teachers address this problem by reciting, mantralike, George Santayana's warning that those who do not remember the past are doomed to repeat it. Frustrated students ignore these pleas from their equally frustrated teachers. Then, to compound the problem, national reports condemn educators because students cannot date the American Civil War in the nineteenth century or identify the president responsible for the New Deal. Typical is Chester Finn's complaint in *We Must Take Charge: Our Schools and Our Future* that U.S. students cannot demonstrate routine competency in subject matter areas: "Today we want evidence of learning, not just of teaching. We look at outcomes. Unsatisfactory results were what led the Excellence Commission to exclaim that we were threatened by a 'rising tide of mediocrity'" (1991, p. 3).

The conservative response in the 1980s was a series of reform proposals that raised standards, objectified evaluation and measured predetermined outcomes. The objectives were (1) to ensure that American students could demonstrate some recall of the information the reformers considered essential for cultural literacy, (2) to achieve the socialization of American students, and (3) to reproduce and perpetuate the dominant values of American society.

Teachers often agree that their students remain oblivious of factual information required for progressing through the school system and passing standardized tests, but they throw up their hands in desperation, blaming disengaged parents, boring textbooks, overcrowded classrooms, drugs, television, ineffective elementary classes or any other convenient scapegoat. Nevertheless, social studies teachers continue to use the same teaching and evaluation methods that have dominated curriculum development for a century. Is the problem that educators have yet to master the modern methods? Or is it that the modern methods no longer serve the postmodern era? The latter possibility has become the main focus of contemporary curriculum discourses.

EXPLORING HISTORY CONTEXTUALLY

As we have already insisted, personal narrative both enhances the study of history and makes connections that hold in long-term memory. A recent book provides theoretical support for this postmodern position: *Making Connections: Teaching and the Human Brain* by Renate Nummela Caine and Geoffrey Caine, published in 1991 by the Association for Supervision and Curriculum Development. Donna Jean Carter, president of the association at the time, made the following comment in her introduction to the book:

> *Intuitively, I have known for some time now that many capable youngsters are either so bored with their education or so stressed out by their experiences, that optimum learning cannot take place. I have also seen many students "flower" in a learning environment that builds on their current knowledge base and personal experiences. The authors not only explain why this is so but also show how a reconceptualization of teaching, based on knowledge of brain functioning, can enhance student learning.*
>
> *Teachers must become facilitators of learning, and they must expect students to go beyond the surface knowledge frequently achieved through rote memorization and unconnected content. By integrating the curriculum, we can assist students in their search for deeper meaning and thus enhance the brain's quest for patterning. The implications of this seminal work for teaching, testing, and remediation are far reaching. Repeated practice on isolated skills becomes inappropriate as an option for acquiring knowledge. It becomes obvious that skills and content must be presented in a context that is familiar to the learner. This contextual approach also supports authentic modes of assessment. (in Caine & Caine, 1991, p. v)*

Carter's enunciation of the central theme of the Caineses' book repeats the problems with traditional approaches to curriculum and instruction described in this chapter. We often fail to establish an atmosphere in which students can make connections to their personal historical contexts. Recall the young man in the university freshman seminar: When he returned to school after the first semester break, he reported that he had spoken to his parents about his uneasy feelings at the Anselm Keefer painting in the museum. For the first time, his parents told him that Jewish relatives in Germany had been killed in concentration camps. His immigrant grandparents had rejected their religion and converted to Christianity, and they had decided not to discuss their Jewish heritage. The student's sense of "being there" when he viewed the Keefer painting became all the more poignant and meaningful, and it has led him to study the Holocaust, Germany and World War II. The connection resulted from an experientially based approach to art. This student will continue to learn in the years ahead, as will all others who enjoy similar educational revelations.

Caine and Caine challenged another strongly held traditional belief: One can separate teaching into cognitive, affective and psychomotor domains of learning. Such artificial categorizations may help in the design of research projects, but it can actually distort one's understanding of learning. Caine and Caine also contended that the brain does not separate emotions from cognition, either anatomically or perceptually. Like the freshman seminar student, we must nurture the holistic experiences that lead to meaningful life-long learning.

THE FACULTY PSYCHOLOGY MOVEMENT

In the early nineteenth century an influential movement called "faculty psychology" (or mental discipline) emerged from the findings of many scholarly reports, including *The Yale Report on the Defense of the Classics* in 1828—sometimes considered the beginning of the American curriculum field. The Yale Report expressed two key concepts in faculty psychology: discipline and furniture. The aim of the curriculum, it said, was to expand the capacity of the mind and store it with knowledge. This curriculum philosophy sought to arrange the information the memory gathers as one would arrange furniture in a room. It further proposed that one exercise the muscles of the brain routinely, as one does the other muscles of the body.

In many classrooms today teachers continue to require memorization, believing that memorizing poetry, formulas and spelling lists stimulates brain function. These teachers believe that mental exercises create intelligence and enhance learning. The experience of one of us challenges that belief. Here is our story:

As an elementary school student in the late 1950s and early 1960s, I studied spelling for eight years with teachers who followed the mental discipline philosophy. They assigned weekly lists of words to memorize without any context for relating the words to my other studies or experiences. At the end of each week I took a spelling test. The teacher would say, "Take out a blank sheet of paper and write your name in the top right hand corner of the page. Number your page from one to thirty. You now have ten minutes to write your spelling words in alphabetical order."

I never performed well on these spelling tests, even though my mother tried to help me memorize each word using codes, acronyms and humorous associations. One example that I recall is the word "occupy." As a child I had a wild cat named "CC," for Crazy Cat. My mother taught me to spell "occupy" by memorizing the question, "Oh CC! You pee, why?"

Despite the efforts of my mother and teachers, I never mastered this method of spelling instruction, and I continue to struggle with spelling. Occasionally when reading, I find myself getting frustrated with the spelling techniques my mother and teachers used because I stop on certain words and check for the code or association. For example, I cannot read the word "separate" without looking for "A RAT in sep-A-RAT-e."

While I could always spell a few normally confusing words like "occupy" and "separate" because of their humorous associations, I eventually learned to spell reliably by reading and writing within meaningful contexts. Reading words in the literature and scholarship of my profession, then using these words in my writing, correspondence and communication—this approach finally proved successful.

My son now has the same spelling problems I had at his age. At the end of third grade, he received a final grade of "D" in spelling and high marks in all of his other subjects. When I asked him about his school year, he responded with enthusiasm, "Dad, I had a great year, and all of my grades were fine." I agreed, but I asked for his perspective on the "D" in spelling.

"I can spell very well, Dad," he said. "I just wait a year. In first grade I had trouble with words like 'see' and 'me.' But in second grade I could spell all of the first grade words. After third grade I could spell all of the second grade words. Next year I'll know all of the third grade words." It appears to me that my son is learning to spell in his own context as he needs the words.

The Faculty Psychology Movement holds that the brain is a muscle that needs rote memorization exercises and mental drills to enhance the functioning of the mind, which can then accumulate more information and rearrange the data, as in the spelling examples. But Caine and Caine finally established the foundation for the case against faculty psychology:

A physiological model of memory also calls into question the notion that learning must take place through rote memorization. In addition, by understanding properties of our spatial memory system, educators can understand that teaching behavioral objectives ignores other functions of the brain and other aspects of memory and learning. Indeed, we have come to the conclusion that educators, by being too specific about facts to be remembered and outcomes to be produced, may prohibit students' genuine understanding and transfer of learning. (1991, p. vii)

The Caineses' work demonstrates that learning and teaching involve multifaceted human beings in complex interactions. Contemporary curriculum scholars, alert to this complexity, move beyond narrow definitions and practices. Thus, Caine and Caine support the vision of curriculum that embraces complexity, tolerance of ambiguity, acceptance of uncertainty and authentic, situated assessments. Evaluation becomes contextualized for the individual teaching environment, and evaluators reject formal standardized instruments designed for universal application. These dimensions of curriculum and evaluation are absent from the traditional curriculum, which inhibits students from making the connection between the rote memorization and the subjects being taught—as in the spelling example or the Civil War story related in Chapter 2. Contextualization becomes the cornerstone of the reconceptualized curriculum, where connections promote learning.

This chapter presents a comparison and contrast of traditional and reconceptualized understandings of curriculum and instruction. Our contextual approach to the teaching and learning process depends on educators who accept an experiential curriculum. We have explored philosophies from Plato to John Dewey, we have examined the commentary of contemporary educational spokespersons including William Bennett and Jonathan Kozol and, most important, we have presented examples of teachers and students struggling daily in their classrooms to implement and experience a meaningful and consequential curriculum.

As we said at the beginning of this chapter, curriculum and instruction are the heart and soul of schooling, and traditional methodologies have disheartened students and deadened the spirit of investigation, analysis, reflection and understanding. But our reconceptualized vision of curriculum and instruction can establish a process of learning that inspires students and teachers once again to ask questions, ponder alternatives and act with courage and enthusiasm.

PART 5

Social Context
*Students as Learners in
Contemporary Culture*

The Impacts of Race, Class and Gender on Education

INTRODUCTION: THE NEED FOR SOCIAL MOBILITY

All of our talk of new paradigms, belongingness and passion means little if America fails to deal with its problems of social injustice, prejudice and inequality. By 2010, two of five Americans will not be white; because racial and ethnic minorities are more than twice as likely as whites to live below the poverty line, dramatic consequences for all will no doubt accompany this statistic. In fact, by 2050 half of all Americans will be persons of color or members of traditional ethnic minorities, changing the nature of racial majority and minority configurations. A city such as Houston—with one-third of the population in each of the racial categories Hispanic, white and black—or a metropolitan area such as Los Angeles—with languages and cultures from around the globe—will reflect the norm for most U.S. cities in the twenty-first century. In addition, as the twenty-first century progresses four out of five new workers will be women, nonwhites or recent immigrants. Yet virtually nothing is being done to prepare for these major demographic shifts. As America faces the twenty-first century, the marginalized have few friends and often argue among themselves. White men hear that they are privileged—and relative to other demographic groups, they are. But to working-class or poor white men, the "privileged" label seems a cruel joke, as they teeter on the edge of poverty. In such circumstances, many of them feel threatened when minorities or women gain access to formerly all-white-male jobs and strongholds. Failing to understand mobility issues in a macrosociological context, they blame the latest victims of an unfair system. Thus the possibility of working-class solidarity or a unified challenge to the greedy goes unrealized (Banfield, 1991; Wolfe, 1991; Rubin, 1994).

It has been hard for Americans, and working-class Americans in particular, to grasp the implications of the disintegration of

"Fordism" after 1973. For young people from poor families, it means that the American ideal of universal upward mobility has become an illusion. As Peter McLaren (1986) and Jay MacLeod (1987) point out, the American social ladder is harder to climb than once thought. Young people from the lower half of the class structure feel so burdened by their poverty that any upward aspirations seem a hopeless indulgence. Working-class Americans have, of course, traditionally harbored the hope of "moving up"—if not for themselves then for their children. The hope may always have been greater than the possibility, but the possibility became reality often enough. Poor and immigrant parents dedicated to achieving a better life for their children did the "dirty work" so their sons and daughters could do the "clean work," and the promise of upward mobility shaped American lives and indeed America itself (Rubin, 1994).

But the last quarter of the twentieth century has been unkind to America's young people, and their intractable economic hardship is especially bitter, coming as it does on the heels of the dream of upward mobility and financial security. They enter school on the assumption that they are being prepared for economic prosperity in their adulthood yet in their late twenties many of them still work at their part-time high school jobs. With such dim prospects it is hardly surprising that many men and some women from poor families find gangs appealing. Nothing speaks more directly to the breakdown of the hope of social mobility than the rise of street gangs in our cities and many of our suburbs. America's poor and minority youth now face daunting obstacles to social mobility, but few barriers rise to gang involvement and the quick financial rewards of theft and the drug trade. Having studied and emulated the organized crime networks of the past, contemporary gangs have established efficient markets and turned impressive profits, offering the lure of economic prosperity to young people currently excluded from the legal economy (Gaines, 1990; Rodriguez, 1994; Jankowski, 1991).

THE DREAM BANDITS

In short, many poor and minority students find that the world they have been told to trust no longer works. As they see their impoverished childhoods ending, these students assume adult responsibilities with headlong speed. Looking back they realize that someone has stolen their dreams and replaced them with narrow choices and a diminished sense of self. Youth suicide was hardly even a statistic before 1960; by the 1980s it had become second only to accidents as the leading cause of death among young people. By the 1990s youth suicide was being described as an epidemic. By the time many children enter high school vocational education they are already world weary and drained of any hopeful expectation. They have "heard it all": the phonies peddling their manipulative pseudohope based on everything from televangelism to drugs to schooling. They have acquiesced in the false prophets of education-for-success who shunt them into the low-track classes, and they have figured out the consequences of this deceitful process (Ferguson, 1994; Gaines, 1990; West, 1993).

Economically and racially marginalized students deserve the truth, and as we have seen, all too often the schools fail to provide it. Critical teachers from the new paradigm have to explain the impediments poor and minority students must overcome to succeed academically and vocationally. As educators, we must take the lead in organizing students, workers and other citizens to reshape our schooling to complement our lives as democratic participants. Hope for our young people—especially our poor and minority young people—can be restored only by such a movement. Our campaign to tell the truth will be difficult. Critical teachers will rarely find rewards for the effort, and school and community hierarchies will resist it. Donna Gaines, a sociologist who studies young people, searches for humor in the cold facts and finds irony:

> *So what if it's the end of the world as you know it. You'll find a new place, eventually. Meantime, have you thought about the service sector? I hear they have lovely jobs! Why not put in an application* today. *Meanwhile, even though the world around you is falling to bits gloriously, please say no to drugs and don't forget to use condoms. (1990, p. 167)*

The ascendancy of right-wing political ideologies in the mid–1990s reinforced a general refusal to examine the social context into which poor and minority students are born. It has quieted questions about social justice and the conditions of socioeconomic mobility and posited inequality as the price we pay for freedom. In such a world, economically disadvantaged students enjoy four choices: (1) Despite the long odds, play the game and try to get ahead. Of course, if you are poor you probably lack the dominant cultural capital (the ways of talking and acting that bespeak the middle and upper-middle classes) necessary to achieving social mobility. Management seeks middle-class people to fill mid-level positions; thus, those who begin on the bottom rung of the social ladder receive little consideration. (2) Accept the fate of your parents, work hard at a dead-end job, hope for a better life for your children and seek consolation in religion and family or sex and drugs. The work can, of course, be psychologically and physically painful, and the pain must be addressed one way or another. (3) Join the military. Some young people do learn a skill in the military, but far too many return to the same conditions they left. As one Army veteran told us, "I wanted an adventure where I could learn electronics, radar or airplane mechanics, but I ended up stacking trays in the mess hall." (4) Take the big risk, leave school, run scams, break the law, work for the big payoff. Chances for social and economic mobility for poor and minority students who stay in school are bad enough, but they worsen for dropouts. Poor and minority dropouts experience poorer health and greater chances of going to jail. Yet an important distinction exists between the effects of dropping out of school for white males as opposed to, say, African American females: only three out of twenty white male dropouts will live in poverty, as opposed to almost two out of three black females (McLaren, 1994). Students who choose to live outside the law are often motivated by one simple, obvious fact: Given the choices, crime seems to offer the best opportunity to escape poverty and its hopelessness.

In this bleak context, think again about the recent growth of youth gangs in America. The conventional wisdom asserts that gangs provide those young people beset with identity problems with firm new identities. While this explanation may hold in a few individual cases, however, most youth join gangs simply to improve their living conditions (Jankowski, 1991). Bombarded with images of failure—street derelicts, government-assistance dependents, parents laboring in degrading jobs—young people join gangs as an act of resistance, refusing to let themselves succumb to a hostile, terrifying environment. Middle-class observers often ask why a young person would place him- or herself in physical jeopardy by joining a gang. They fail to realize that urban poor and minority youth feel more of that danger as *non*gang members and join to protect themselves against it. Thus, like others who have organized throughout human history, they come together to reduce their anxiety, fear and suspicion. In fact, these youth follow the advice corporate America expresses in its advertising: "Go for the gusto"; "You can have it all"; "Just do it." They know they may speed to the top or crash to the bottom but, as they tell us, they have nothing to lose if they figure to end up losers anyway. These youngsters tell the same story over and over again: My greatest fear is having to take the dead-end jobs that ruined my parents' lives. Besides, if nothing else, being in a gang provides a temporary postponement of the life such jobs entail. And maybe, as one gang member from Boston put it, "I could hit it big at something we're doing and get the hell out of this place" (Jankowski, 1991, p. 46). A twenty-year-old gang member from Los Angeles told this story:

> *I just joined the T-Men to kick back for awhile. My parents work real hard and they got little for it. I don't really want that kind of job, but that's what it looked like I would have to take. So I said, "Hey, I'll just kick back for a while and let that job wait for me. Hey, I just might make some money from our dealings and really be able to forget these jobs." (1991, p. 46)*

Many gang members reveal painful memories of their parents' vulnerability to the whims of their employers, the drudgery they faced day after day and the defeat they lived with. An eighteen-year-old expressed his feelings:

> *A few years ago I would be pissed at my old man 'cause he didn't do things like save his money and move from the projects. He just seemed to be unwilling to improve himself so that my mother and us kids were better, you know? . . . Later I could see that he didn't have much of a chance, given that he was just a worker. I resented that, not him, but the situation. But you know, after I talked to him, I was more pissed at the way he felt than anything else. He felt like he had no control over the situation; and I said to myself, "I'll do everything I can not to let the fuckers make me feel like that." And I hustle all the time trying to develop projects to get money. (p. 108)*

We, as teachers, should study these stories carefully. Who among us cannot relate to the pain and the "social death" of dead-end work? Social death includes the loss of dignity and the reduced sense of self-worth that accompany routinized work and the despair of a way out. Even those youngsters who live through the gang experience often take dead-end jobs once their resistance wanes. For those who have yet to figure it out, America has a big and growing problem. We cannot without consequence teach and broadcast the myth of social mobility, sell the idea that one's self-worth revolves around the acquisition of expensive consumer items and refuse to address the social and cultural dynamics that keep poor and minority youth as mere sideline observers.

WHERE TO START? DRAWING ON VALUES

Easy answers to the problem of social injustice currently elude us, and we lack neat recipes for addressing its victims: poor and minority children. When teachers enter a room full of such students, they quickly see that these students already have two strikes against them. As you confront the underside of modernist positivism and its educational decontextualization, you might observe its association with the growing inequality in American life. Often asked to observe schools, we have seen curriculum developers ignore the racial and class differences among their students. Besides lowering their expectations for marginalized students, they tend to proceed in standard ways regardless of the social context. When we think of *contextualizing teaching,* we find the question of the impacts of race, class and gender on academic performance and life possibilities at the heart of our perspective. Curriculum and teaching must change in relation to students who have gone without sleep the night before, dodged bullets on the way to school or function as adults at home at the age of nine or ten. Teachers who see themselves as researchers pay attention to such lived-world dynamics. As phenomenologists, they explore the effects of such life histories on the consciousnesses of their students. Critical teachers *listen* to such students; they call on their own educational philosophies and values to help them work productively and compassionately with such students. In other words, they take these students seriously and attempt to understand the complex constellation of forces that shape their lives.

UNDERSTANDING CULTURAL DIFFERENCES

Critical teachers from the new paradigm can most effectively break with positivism by valuing the knowledge and world views of those traditionally excluded from the mainstream. This "valuing of difference" can change our lives and our teaching. Moving beyond the official positivist knowledge, critical teachers make use of the marginal and previously excluded experiences that help us all to see the dominant culture in a new light and provide mainstream white observers with insights into the construction of the ways they have been viewing the poor and racially different.

Critical teachers conscientiously include previously marginalized knowledge (subjugated knowledge). Drawing on, for example, African American novels, Latino/a musical forms, Asian philosophies, gay and lesbian poetry, the environmental insights of indigenous peoples and women's ways of knowing to open other viewpoints on the world, new paradigm teachers expand the consciousnesses of their students. As the students confront this knowledge, those from white mainstream backgrounds in particular begin to see their own points of view as only one among a galaxy of possible worldviews. Engaged with excluded voices, students and teachers expand their epistemological vocabularies, in the process reaching new plateaus of meaning. For example, while teaching on a Sioux reservation one of the authors came to realize that Native American students viewed dreams differently than did those in the mainstream Anglo culture. The Sioux students told how their grandmothers had taught them to attend to and make use of their dreams.

Taking their stories seriously, one can learn traditional Sioux techniques for inducing dreams and then applying them during waking hours. Students induced dreams about their school work by focusing on a particular body of material during the day and before going to bed. Achieving moments of lucidity in their dreams, a conscious awareness that they were dreaming without interrupting the dream, students would focus their dream minds on making new meanings of the academic material. On awakening the successful dreamer would find that insight into connections between the material and other issues had been developed. Deeper levels of understanding resulted, generating great excitement. One might easily employ this little-known technique in one's own teaching, writing and music making.

Consider how this one simple piece of cultural knowledge could be incorporated into a critical classroom. You could build a whole curriculum around the concept, as students and the teacher study the Native American use of dreaming. If the school were near a reservation, Native Americans could visit the classroom and describe their tribal or individual relationship to dreaming. You could ask your students to keep their own dream journals. Several books have been written on dream induction and use. You and your students could practice induced dreaming in conjunction with creative writing: To induce dreaming about stories to write, students should pause several times a day, shut out all distractions, and consciously focus on the story topic and visualize the forms it might take in a dream. Just before going to sleep, they should consider the topic once again.

Several benefits accompany this approach. For example, it opens students to an appreciation of Native American forms of knowledge. The exercise is also an effective motivator, as students get caught up in the excitement of expanding consciousness. Indeed, many students may find themselves excited for the first time by the life of the mind. Also, the exercise can lead to further studies of Native Americans; of the mind; of Jungian psychology; of Jewish, Christian and Muslim dreams in religious scriptures; or of dreaming in history. Moreover, the exercise serves to start the process of incorporating the concept of difference into classes and the students' own lives. "Difference" can be a valuable concept in new paradigm instruction for students from both the dominant culture and from oppressed cultures, as this anecdote shows:

> I remember the first class I taught on the Rosebud Sioux Reservation at Sinte Gleska College—an introduction to American history. Before and during the class, I worked both to develop a curriculum that acquainted my students with what I considered some of the main themes of American history and to illustrate the relation of these themes to American Indian history in general and to Sioux history in particular. After explaining Manifest Destiny, for example, I would illustrate the concept's effect on Native American–U.S. government relations and the Sioux's encounter with General Custer and the massacre at Wounded Knee. I had expected my historical connections to elicit stories from my students, who ranged from their late teens into their eighties. When eighty-year-old Irmalee Yellow Eagle and sixty-five-year-old Albert White Hat began to tell stories about General Custer passed down from their grandparents, the classroom came alive. Stories about relatives who received their names at the Battle of the Little Big Horn, about attempts to practice the traditional religion after the federal gov-

ernment outlawed it, about uncles who had run away from home to avoid being sent back East to Indian boarding schools—they all painted a human face on the important themes of American, Native American and Sioux history. In fact, I found the stories so insightful and fascinating that when Irmalee and Albert began to talk, I took notes. My motive was innocent and simple enough: I wanted to remember the details. But the effect of my note taking was surprisingly powerful in the context of our discussion of cultural difference and subjugated knowledge. After a month, during which my Sioux students took notes on my stories about American history and I took notes on their stories about Sioux history, one student finally asked what I was writing in my notebook. When I told her, murmurs rose in the classroom. One of my elderly students was the first to speak. "Why are you writing down our stories?" Before I could respond, another student said, "You're learning from us, and we're learning from you!" Smiles appeared on their faces. Though it had never occurred to me in so many words, my students felt flattered and validated by my interest in them. As the term progressed, they spoke of my respect for them as peers—a respect, they confided, other white teachers had not always granted. That simple act of taking notes on their stories illustrated for my Sioux students my respect for them and their ways of knowing. As the months passed I found I had gained a reputation as a teacher who refused to condescend to my students, a teacher who declined to see himself as a missionary bringing "civilization and education to the poor Indians." My reputation intact, we could explore together the effects of the American conquest of the Sioux on the shaping of their consciousness—that is to say, phenomenology of their colonization and assumed assimilation. My two years on the reservation were emotional, hopeful, intimate and often painful and sad—but always positive. When I left, the tribe organized a going-away party, and in one of the proudest moments of my life, Rosebud Sioux Tribal Chairman Carl Waln made me a member. As he bestowed my Indian name and tied an eagle feather into my hair, he said, "We appreciate you very much. We especially appreciate the fact that you didn't try to save us." (Kincheloe, 1999)

DIFFERENCE, EPISTEMOLOGICAL CIRCLES AND TIME WARPS

As travelers have discovered, the attempt to understand the cultural schematas of peoples from other ethnicities and countries often leads to a recognition of belief systems and social assumptions in oneself. When an exposure to nonwestern perspectives widens their epistemological circles, students gain understandings of value in a multicultural society. Such understandings may seem simple on the surface. For example, in an America destined to be marked by larger non-Anglo populations, an ability and willingness among different groups to not simply tolerate but to understand and appreciate each other becomes an actual survival skill. The critical postmodern ethic of appreciating and learning from diversity could be essential to the survival of the planet. In the new paradigm's curriculum of difference, students can focus their perspectives on work, leisure, competition, success, individualism or time to learn about cultural differences.

Take time, for example. Modernist societies are trapped in a time warp of speed and efficiency that affects all aspects of our consciousness. Critical new teacher education students who study the effect of time perceptions on teaching and perceptions of intelligence discover that while premodernist cultures concluded that "haste makes waste," modernist cultures believe that speed reflects alertness, power and success. Hurried Mad Hatters late for their important dates, modernist educators speak of "slow" and "fast" students. Some cultures admire pondering, reflecting or musing, but not the modernist West. Our colleague who taught on the Sioux reservation was often reminded of the Native American belief that only a fool provides a quick answer to a question. A wise person, the Sioux believe, takes time to think through a question first. A question asked during a Monday afternoon class might go unanswered until Wednesday afternoon when some student will offer a wise—though long delayed—response.

In a study involving male undergraduates, psychologists found the highest scores on standardized exams produced by those students who placed the highest value on speed. Students from traditional, indigenous and agrarian cultures tend to place a low value on speed—thus, for cultural rather than cognitive reasons, such students tended to score low according to the dominant modes of educational evaluation.

In addition, researchers have discovered a correlation between one's socioeconomic class and one's perception of time. Without the challenge of difference, educators coming of age in a modernist culture find it hard to overcome their cognitive and epistemological unidimensionality. Some sociocultural assumptions such as temporality remain hidden. Educators perceive students who exemplify the modernist values of speed and efficiency as intelligent, and those from the margins of modernity as "slow." Hence they perpetuate the status quo and deny difference and condemn the economically and culturally different to failure. Buoyed by our critical understanding of difference, we can step out of the limited modernist paradigm to view the relationship between time and intelligence from a variety of perspectives. Viewing students from outside the mainstream in new ways, we can uncover forms of intelligence previously overlooked. Emancipated by difference, we critical teachers can learn from each student's uniqueness (Rifkin, 1987; Slattery, 1995b).

The possibility of schools' shedding the cognitive and political blinders of modernism depends on our ability to act on our understanding of difference. A teacher's sensitivity to the transformative possibilities that emerge from the perspectives of those on the outside looking in can change both the school and the world. Serious attention to those with sexual preferences different from our own can change our perspective on how gender role constructs our consciousness. Careful attention to those with racial identities different from our own can deepen our understanding of how our racial identity constructs our consciousness. Listening critically to those from social classes different from our own can enhance our appreciation of how socioeconomic class constructs our consciousness. Engagement with individuals shaped by places different from our own can heighten our awareness of how geographical place constructs our consciousness. Our schools can hardly remain unchanged and the rigid discourse of the current disciplines can hardly resist change when challenged by the power of difference.

The growing pluralism among our students has at last forced Americans to reconsider the nature of a multiracial, multiethnic society. But while some people read the projected twenty-first-century demographics of diversity as a summons to value difference, others, like the self-proclaimed racist David Duke, see it as a call to protect the traditional Western heritage at all costs. In general, Americans have yet to appreciate the significance of the early battles between Allan Bloom and the multiculturists, and William Bennett and the feminists. These are more than simply struggles over the curriculum at Stanford or the curriculum presented by the New York regents. These are the first skirmishes in a larger struggle to define who we are, to determine how we see the world and even how we learn to think. We are in a fight between a modernist tradition of consensus and a new ethic of difference.

Those of us in the new paradigm who value difference and the new vantage point it provides focus our pedagogical imagination on multiple expressions of intelligence, multiple epistemologies, diverse spiritualities, and a variety of ethical systems. Drawing on a multiculturalist education, critical teachers search through premodernist societies for unique and practical ways to avoid the nihilism of modernism and reestablish human solidarity. We can best cure the cognitive disease of modernism by serving a postmodern broth of three taro leaves—a recipe that borrows the democratic and egalitarian impulses of modernism, the communitarian and ecological respect of premodernism, and the self-awareness and appreciation of difference of the critical new paradigm. The broth leads to an awareness of the fact that our consciousness has been historically constructed, and having understood this construction, the critical teacher can reconstruct his or her consciousness in a more emancipatory manner. The pedagogy that results from this reconstruction induces us to step outside our cultural incarceration into a new freedom (Gergen, 1991).

SPECIFYING DIFFERENCE: THE CONCEPTUAL TIES AMONG RACE, CLASS AND GENDER

Race, class and gender are the three categories around which U.S. society now constructs many aspects of human difference. The three categories hardly represent separate and distinct characteristics of human beings, however; rather, they overlap, sometimes conflict and constantly shift their meanings and influences. Thus, issues of difference in relation to race, class and gender are bound to be complex in their manifestation and profound in their effect. Before beginning this analysis of race, class and gender, therefore, we should note that although we present separate discussions of each, that should not imply conceptual isolation. The study of race, class and gender can produce new insights into education and oppression, and as you study this "trinity" and its members' relation to schooling, notice how race and class dynamics often work together to produce a combination one-two punch reinforcing oppression. At other times, racial experience can mitigate the effects of one's class and gender oppression—for example, a lowersocioeconomic class white woman retains a measure of influence. The point is simple: The interactive dynamics of class, race and gender confound attempts to study them as isolated phenomena.

The discourse on difference and oppression has become increasingly difficult in recent years. All of us find at least some distrust and anger in classroom conversations about these topics. Our teacher education students come to us with an acute sense of fairness, a desire to do the right thing. When our discussions turn, as they inevitably do, to issues of race, class, gender, mobility and school performance, this sense of fairness expresses itself in ways consistent with the public conversation and the conventional wisdom. Why should we talk about issues of race, class and gender, they ask. The only fair way to deal with questions of difference is to erase them from our collective consciousness. As beginning teachers, they propose to ignore questions of difference and "treat everyone the same" because they want to avoid any appearance of prejudice.

They express their sincere viewpoints with passion and commitment. The question for us and our colleagues is where to engage this passion and commitment so as to produce a more textured understanding of race, class and gender dynamics and their relationship to schooling. Before beginning this analytical task here, we need to explore in some detail the dynamic relationship among class, gender and race. Strides have been made recently to understand how these dynamics shape our lives, our education and our work. Our own analysis begins with the development of social theoretical explanations of the relationship and then moves to specific analyses of the class, gender and racial dynamics at work in a pedagogical context.

Don't be intimidated by the term "social theory." We have been theorizing about society throughout this book. Just for clarification, all "social theory" refers to is the attempt to explain rather generally why things happen as they do. For example, social theory helps us understand why a man hired for a job advances more quickly than the woman who helped "show him the ropes." It can help us understand why one sees fewer women than men in educational leadership positions (Hacker, 1989). How do these patterns develop? Who benefits from these arrangements? Who loses? Social theory takes up questions like these, which shape our analysis here.

Mainstream Views of Class, Gender and Racial Connections

In general, educators little understand and largely ignore the connections between class, gender and race. Mainstream liberal and conservative educators both have failed to understand the interactions between class, gender and race and have been relatively uninterested in exploring the connections that unite the spheres of politics, culture and the economy with education. This mainstream indifference to such issues accounts for the current lack of emphasis on foundations courses in philosophy, history and sociology in many of our teacher education programs. The indifferent educators and educational leaders take refuge in merely addressing prejudicial attitudes toward women and minorities. From these modernist perspectives, American life emerges in fragmented segments— with education isolated from politics, economics and culture. Like many of our students, conservative and liberal analysts see "unattached individuals" unaffected by their membership in racial, gender or class groupings. Yet critical researchers maintain that such fragmentation distorts our view of how schools and workplaces operate.

When conservative and liberal scholars fail to account for power dynamics in schools, workplaces and the socioeconomic context that shapes them, specific processes of the domination and subordination of students go unexposed. In the place of an exposé, the behavior of irrationally prejudiced men and women becomes the convenient sole cause of unfair treatment. While isolated irrational acts of prejudice certainly occur, they hardly account for all of the oppression of racial, sexual and economic "outsiders." To get to the point at which we can explain the particular processes of subordination, critical educators must understand both the dynamics of class, gender and race and how their intersections in the lived world produce tensions, contradictions and discontinuities in everyday lives (Amott & Matthaei, 1991; McCarthy & Apple, 1988).

In this context Carol Gilligan's (1981) critique of Lawrence Kohlberg's taxonomy of moral reasoning takes one giant step toward explicating the gender biases within mainstream educational theory. Gilligan delineated the male-centered aspects of Kohlberg's description of "high" and "low" levels of moral reasoning, and subsequent analysis has confirmed that gender is just one of the many social categories that shape the ways individuals engage in moral reasoning. When we add race and class (as well as geographic place, national origin, religion, sexual orientation, language, learning differences and other categories) to the social stew, we discover that women from different social locations reason differently. Thus, gender analysis is by itself insufficient; we must examine the way gender interacts with other social categories to form a richer picture of moral reasoning (Stack, 1994). Such examinations can help us understand why different individuals engage with schooling and the workplace in different ways, understanding that can, in turn, help us distinguish between being *different* and being *deficient*—a distinction that can reduce or eliminate some forms of institutional sexism, racism and class bias.

THE INTERRELATEDNESS OF CLASS, GENDER AND RACE: THE PRIVILEGES OF SOME DEPEND ON THE OPPRESSION OF OTHERS

Our argument is simple: We can understand racial, sexual and class forms of oppression only in structural context. In other words, gender bias plays itself out on the terrain of economic and patriarchal macrostructures. An economic macrostructure might include the white male domination of the highest salary brackets. A patriarchal macrostructure might include the small percentage of upper-level corporate managers and school superintendents who are women or, in a domestic context, the spousal abuse many American males perpetuate. Differences in women's lives in general and economic opportunities in particular tend to revolve around power inequalities. For example, African American women, Latinos, Asian American women and Native American women experience gender as one aspect of a larger pattern of unequal social relations. Indeed, how one experiences gender depends on its intersection with other hierarchies of inequality—those other hierarchies in which the privileges of some individuals grow out of the oppression of others. There is, in short, no shared generalizable experience of gender subordination among women (Zinn & Dill, 1994; Zinn, 1994; Amott & Mathaei, 1991).

Accordingly, a critical educator might usefully point out for students specific places where gender, race and class intersect and note that some intersections create privilege. For example, if a woman marries a man from the upper class, gender and class intersect to create privileged opportunities for her. On the other hand, if a woman is Haitian American, forms of racial prejudice may exacerbate how she experiences gender bias. Thus, whether or not they occur through subordination or privilege, class, gender and racial dynamics affect everyone, not just those at the bottom of the status hierarchy. The problem is that those at the top of the class, gender and racial hierarchies often fail to understand the ways the intersections of the various axes affect them. The economic divisions of class can control how society treats race and gender. Though we understand that connections between class, gender and race exist, rarely can we predict the effects of the interactions. Racial and gender hostilities, of course, can subvert class solidarity. Conversely, class solidarity can interrupt gender networks. Working-class women, for example, feel little affinity for the middle- and upper-middle-class feminist movement (Zinn, 1994; Amott, 1993).

Teachers who understand these class, gender and racial dynamics gain a much clearer appreciation of the reasons for the performances of their students. For example, a critical teacher who receives blank stares from Ted when she asks him questions refuses to rush to judgment about his abilities. Understanding that Ted comes from a lower socioeconomic background, with parents who never finished the eighth grade, she may come to appreciate the lack of familiarity with the expectations of school Ted brings to her classroom. Even though he is poor, Ted's whiteness may inhibit him from bonding with the large number of Puerto Rican boys in the classroom. Thus, in addition to his poverty Ted finds himself socially isolated by ethnic conflicts. A critical teacher could use such sociological information to ground ways of understanding and developing activities for Ted that differed substantially from assignments for other students. Helping Ted feel comfortable and secure in the classroom, for example, may be necessary before academic learning is possible. Such contextual understandings by teachers may make the difference in Ted's failing or succeeding in school.

As these class, gender and racial forces interact, sometimes in complementary and sometimes in contradictory ways, the school experience reveals itself less as an uncomplicated reflection of social power and more as exceedingly complex. While general patterns of subjugation occur, they play out in unpredictable ways with particular individuals. Cameron McCarthy and Michael Apple (1988) noticed that schools mediate with rather than impose power on their students. In other words, students from lower socioeconomic backgrounds are not simply and routinely classified and relegated to low-status classes and ultimately to low-status jobs; instead, the forces of class, gender and race create a multilevel playing field on which students gain a sense of their options and to some extent negotiate their academic and vocational possibilities. Class, gender and racial dynamics combine to lay out larger playing fields with more options for some and smaller, more limited fields for others. Under these various combined constraints, students struggle to make sense of and deal with several divisions of the social gridiron where they must tackle fractious social classes, genders and racial and ethnic groups. *Star Trekkies* understand the three-tiered gridiron in terms of Mr. Spock's three-dimensional chessboard, with all three dimensions in play at the same time.

On their 3-D social playing field, young women must deal with gender destinies and socially fixed representations of women. Owing to the social assumption that women are destined for eventual marriage and motherhood, society views female employment as a lesser problem than male employment. Vocational teachers, for example, should examine the ways families and vocational programs construct relationships between future work and the everyday life of young women (Arnot, 1992). In the process, they might begin to formulate interventional strategies to subvert the disempowered destinies that await their female students.

In the instance of young women in vocational education, we should expose social organization based on *biological* determinism as part of the *social* context; the placement of women in low status, low-paid vocational roles simply does not conform to a larger *natural* order. Liberal educators often argue (persuasively) that gender diversity is important and that we should emphasize women's long-term vocational needs in our programs and curricula. Critical educators from the new paradigm see this emphasis as useful but insufficient. We must go beyond merely the recognition and inclusion of difference. We must use the knowledge that women, racially diverse people and poor people produce in their everyday experiences to reshape the most basic concepts and explanations of schooling (Mullings, 1994; Zinn & Dill, 1994).

QUESTIONS OF CLASS: BELL CURVES, DYSGENESIS AND OUR FRIENDS RONNIE AND BRANDON

We recently published a book entitled *Measured Lies: The Bell Curve Examined* (Kincheloe, Steinberg & Gresson, eds., 1996), a study of Richard Herrnstein and Charles Murray's best-selling book on the associations among class, race and intelligence, *The Bell Curve: Intelligence and Class Structure in American Life* (1995), so we know quite a lot about the bias that still permeates our schools and society. Few social debates reveal a class-biased elitism more clearly than the conversation about intelligence in positivist teacher education and educational psychology. The debate becomes particularly elitist and condescending when it raises issues centered on the intelligence and abilities of poor and nonwhite students.

As critical teachers from the new paradigm aware of the intersection of class, gender and race, we urge the academic community to face this elitism and restructure schools in light of its reconsideration. The elitism in *The Bell Curve* becomes downright oppressive, as the authors speak matter of factly about dysgenesis ("devolution," the declining intelligence of the population) and the social havoc poor and nonwhite people have wrought. Adopting an "us-versus-them" social stance,

Herrnstein and Murray completely ignore the ways class and race-based experiences shape the ways of knowing among particular groups. Using modernist-positivist methods of determining "aptitude," schools privilege white middle-class ways of knowing over the alien, "subjugated" understandings. This elitist view of knowing confuses difference with disability and inflicts immeasurable damage on economically and racially marginalized students. Every day, thousands of brilliant students are told that they are stupid. Our friends Ronnie and Brandon nicely illustrate this point.

Ronnie and Brandon are carpenters who completed some renovations on our house a few years ago and became our good friends in the process. They talked often about education, their own in particular. Like many in the trades, they hated school, which had led them to consider themselves academically unworthy. They naturally chose a vocation that seemed far removed from the skills schools teach. Yet in their everyday work they followed sophisticated geometric and algebraic applications, solving unstructured problems with their improvisational math. When we mentioned this sophistication, they found our praise difficult to accept. "This isn't really math—it's not like the math you do in school," Ronnie insisted. But as we explained how their math was in some ways more sophisticated than typical high school math, they listened intently. Focusing on their facility with unstructured problems, as opposed to the structured problems in school, we suggested that they were a lot smarter than they thought.

As we gradually explained critical conceptions of class bias in education and the exclusionary, and the elitism inherent in the educational psychology view of intelligence, they began to understand the socially constructed nature of intelligence and how they had been victimized by the elitist viewpoint. The more we talked, the more excited they got. Initially reluctant to discuss their concerns about the elitism of schooling with college professors who taught teachers, Ronnie and Brandon began to express the anger and resentment they harbored toward formal education.

In subsequent conversations with other men and women in the trades, we have encountered similar anger. Schooling has had little positive effect on their lives. They associate school with embarrassment and hurt feelings, a place where their failures and inadequacies took center stage. "I just kept my mouth shut and hoped the time would pass quickly," Ronnie told us. As long as we continue to demean manual forms of intelligence, students such as Ronnie will suffer irrelevant and humiliating school experiences.

What Ronnie and Brandon intuitively understood was their "place" in the hierarchy of the schools they attended and the wide gaps they found between schooling and everyday life. Even when they studied algebra and geometry, for example, they found little relevance to carpentry. "I had to learn it all over again when I started working," Brandon explained.

The school Brandon and Ronnie attended followed the logic that if students learn a body of general skills, they can transfer and adapt these skills when the need arises on the job. It taught the skills as isolated subtasks and evaluated each student by his or her ability to perform the task successfully when called on. The concept of employing skills in appropriate contexts continues to appear irrelevant in most schools (Raizen, 1989). Brandon and Ronnie were alienated by this de-contextualized drill on fragmented subskills. Drawing on their experiences in class-biased schools, they understood our explanation of the modernist cognitive illness, with its privileging of mind over body and its fragmentation of knowledge in a way that separates schools from the world in which people live and work.

As we write this book about the context in which education takes place and this chapter about the elitism and class bias that shape the education of the poor, we cannot help personalizing these concepts as they relate to Brandon and Ronnie. Indeed, our discussions of philosophy, interconnection and empowerment should help us all influence individual lives and personal experiences, or they are pretty much worthless. What kind of education would have spoken to Brandon and Ronnie and addressed their needs? What curriculum arrangements would have made schooling meaningful in their lives and given them a sense of belonging? What could teachers have done to reduce the pain of the class bias they faced every day? These personal questions emerge naturally from a contextualized understanding of education.

THE OMINOUS SILENCE: AMERICA'S RESISTANCE TO ISSUES OF CLASS

Put bluntly, American educators fail to confront reality when they remain silent about issues of socioeconomic class and education. When they ignore issues of class, these leaders miss the connection between the consequences of schooling and students' socioeconomic backgrounds. In the everyday world of human beings, this scholarly blindness can produce concrete results. Intelligent and creative students such as Ronnie and Brandon become convinced of their intellectual inferiority when experts fail to understand the socioeconomic context in which they have matured. Lacking exposure to, say, an ethic that values education or the language conventions schools adopt, these students are incorrectly and unjustly deemed intellectually inferior. The same mind-set shapes the formulation of such educational reforms as *Goals 2000*—that is, a concern with socioeconomic class and its effects on American schooling is missing. Some reformers worry so much that someone will accuse them of incorporating the concept of "class" in their reform proposals that they invent euphemisms such as "the economically marginal," "disenfranchised students," "disadvantaged students" and "at-risk students" to express the idea (McLaren, 1994; Macedo, 1994). When the term "class" appears, conservatives respond that because America is officially egalitarian, class analysis has no place in public education. Then they accuse the analysts of stirring up trouble, of encouraging class conflict or even of being subversives.

As we have already seen, however, education for the poor has been a class-biased issue throughout American history. As part of a larger effort to discipline an industrial workforce laboring in low-skill, boring jobs, vocational education, for example, exhibited all the trappings of socioeconomic class division. Indeed, had it not been for these inherent social divisions, vocational education would not have existed in the first place. Corporate and business leaders would have been reluctant to support any work education that failed to yield them commercial profit and shore up other dominant power groups. The elite control of local school boards guaranteed that school policy would mirror the interests of these dominant groups.

Class analysis as a tool for making sense of American society has never been more useful than at present, with a massive redistribution of wealth from the poor to the wealthy underway. In 1980, for example, the average business or corporate chief executive officer (CEO) earned 38 times the salary of the average school teacher and 42 times more than the average factory worker. By the end of the decade, the average CEO earned 72 times more than a teacher and 93 times more than a factory worker (DuBois, 1973; West, 1993; Coontz, 1992). In the 1990s the disparity continued to expand.

Where inequality—not to say simple greed—like this flourishes, class analysis is obviously appropriate, even essential. When we analyze the specific dynamics of the polarization of wealth in America in detail, we uncover many new insights into American mobility. Americans have always placed a high value on hard work, and most believe that people who work hard should be rewarded. Indeed, Americans believe that our very society depends on hard work. Most Americans would be surprised to learn, therefore, that those who profit most from the recent redistribution of wealth produce little work at all. Much of the wealth generated in the 1980s and 1990s did not come from inventing a better mousetrap or after long hours of study or overtime labor. Most of the new wealth befell those already enjoying enormous assets, who were able to reap "instant wealth" from rapidly fluctuating return rates on their speculative investments. We find dividends, tax shelters, interest and capital gains at the center of the action—not hard work (Coontz, 1992). Thus the connection between one's class position and one's willingness to work hard appears to be more tenuous than Americans assume. Any attempt to dismiss class as an American issue should be exposed for what it is: an instrumental fiction designed to preserve the status quo by pointing to the presumed laziness and incompetence of the poor as the reasons for their poverty.

FOUR CLASS MYTHS

Consider four class myths perpetuated by the power elites that lay the ideological foundation for dismissal of class in the economic, political and educational lives of America.

1. *The myth of equal opportunity* holds that the schools help democratize America. If one has the ability and the willpower, economic success awaits.
2. *The myth of meritocracy* maintains that to those who succeed in schools and society go the spoils of victory. This myth is often expressed by the old cliché "the cream rises to the top." Herrnstein and Murray, authors of *The Bell Curve*, relied on the myth of meritocracy in arguing that poor people in America tend to be the least intelligent members of the culture.

In this context, conservatives can easily make the argument that biological factors form the infrastructure for class divisions and that poor, black and Hispanic students will never successfully compete with white middle-class students because of qualitative differences in their gene pools.

3. *The myth of equality as conformity* asserts that when democratic progressives advocate social and educational policies designed to achieve the goal of equal access to upward mobility, they envision a communist China-like society characterized by rigorous conformity. You will, of course, recall that advocates of a critical education value individual differences and the right of individuals to challenge the demands of conformity.

4. *The myth of power neutrality* suggests that power arises out of and tends to complement independence. But informal (nonelected) constellations of power always work collectively to maintain their own interests and their activity is hardly neutral, since it strives to maintain existing power relations. Elite groups tend to interact with one another more than with nonelite groups. Clint Allison (1995) pointed out that the various elites belong to the same golf and civic clubs, their wives all tend to serve the Junior Leagues and they generally attend the same social functions. If they do not sit on local school boards, they know someone who does. The point here is that they have "connections"—which is to say, informal access to policy makers. Poor and marginalized women and men lack these connections.

When these four class myths go unexamined and the socioeconomic context ignored, class bias and racism come out of the shadows. Why waste the school's money on students who are inferior? Why attempt to make access to jobs more equitable when particular class and racial groups are doomed never to perform as well as us? Questions like these are asked daily at the highest levels of power in contemporary America, and the mind-sets behind them see nothing wrong with tracking policies that place 90 percent of white students on college prep tracks and relegate the majority of African American and Latino students to the lowest tracks. With this modernist decontextualized way of seeing so prevalent, no wonder almost $300 million of the $981 million appropriated by the Perkins Act in 1991 for disadvantaged students was returned, unspent, to the federal government (NCRVE, 1992). This perspective views unskilled and semiskilled workers as expendable production units—a contingent workforce to be hired and fired at the command of the market. The short-term corporate profits that accrue this way pale in comparison to the long-term effects on the nation and its workers. When middle-aged workers cannot count on permanent jobs, the social compact between them and the nation dissolves. Given these realities, it should come as no shock that our land of opportunity now fosters a greater overall disparity between the rich and the poor than does Japan, Sweden, Australia, the Netherlands, Germany, the United Kingdom, Norway, Canada or France (Rubin, 1994).

During the 1990s, right-wing politicians began to resemble Robin Hoods in reverse, taxing the poor to reward the rich. Republican Party legislation introduced in 1996 proposed to take away 11.4 percent of annual income ($13,325 cut to $11,804) from the poorest 20 percent of American families with children.

Indeed, this poorest fifth would have lost even more income both per family and as a group than the highest 80 percent of American families combined. Moreover, many economists argue that these figures actually underestimate the impact on poor Americans; one should add to the proposed 11.4 percent cuts restrictions on Medicare and Medicaid that would take away another 12 percent of the average poor person's income, as well as further losses from cuts in earned income tax credits traditionally granted to the poor. At the same time, families earning more than $70,000 annually would receive an average tax cut of $1,350 (Whitman, 1995).

A Strange Alchemy: Poor Children in Middle-Class Schools

A strange alchemy occurs when poor students encounter the middle-class dynamics of their schools. The middle-class mind-set views poverty as a badge of failure. One African American child learned this lesson in her first school experiences, as her response to the question What is poverty? shows: "Poverty," she said, "is when you aren't living right." Lessons like this take their psychic toll, ensuring that students from poor backgrounds reject the academic world and its culture as a matter of self-protection. We think here also of a *New York Times* front page story on October 14, 1998, featuring a picture of Wendy, a middle-school student who lives with her family of modest income and attends a typical middle-class public school. Wendy was tormented constantly by her peers, who ridiculed her secondhand clothing, trailer home and crooked teeth. The story reported that one boy demanded the girl's seat on the school bus with the words "Move it, trailer girl!"

School leaders still have trouble understanding that the poor may sometimes be ignorant but are not stupid. Working-class children and lower-class homes ascribe little importance to academic work in the way middle- and upper-middle-class students and their parents do. Working-class and poor students often see academic work as a series of artificial short-term tasks rather than as a project of continuous development with a long-term affect on their lives. Real work, they believe, is something you get paid for once it is done. Without such compensation or long-term justification, these students often display little interest in school, a lack of motivation their teachers tend to interpret as inability or lack of intelligence. Poor performance on standardized achievement tests then scientifically confirms this "inferiority" (Oakes, 1988; Nightingale, 1993; DeYoung, 1989; Woods, 1983).

It happens every day. Educators mistake lower socioeconomic class manners, attitudes and speech for lack of academic ability. Citing their poor students' social discomfort around students from wealthy backgrounds, some teachers place these students in low-ability groups or recommend their placement in vocational education precisely because of their class backgrounds. They should stay with "their own kind." The standard practices of American schooling too often assume a constricted view of the human capacity for development and an exclusive modernist understanding of human diversity (Block, 1995). Intelligence is operationally defined as one's performance on an I.Q. test, rather than as the unique and creative accomplishments one can achieve in a variety of venues and contexts. An understanding of the social context and power relations of the culture at large and the school culture in particular is fundamental to the further understanding of the class dynamics of student performance.

Research on the education of low-status groups in other countries provides some useful insight into the performance of marginalized students in American schools. The Swedes view Finnish people as inferior, and the failure rate of Finnish children in Swedish schools is comparatively high. When Finnish children immigrate to Australia, however, they do well—in fact, just as well as Swedish immigrants. Koreans do poorly in Japanese schools, where they are seen as culturally inferior; in American schools, on the other hand, Korean immigrants are remarkably successful (Zweigenhaft & Domhoff, 1991). Such examples are numerous, and the results follow the same pattern: racial, ethnic and class groups viewed negatively or as inferior in a nation's dominant culture tend to perform poorly in those schools. Critical educators should attend to these lessons on their way to challenging the class bias that hurts their students. Such research helps dispose of the argument that school failure results from the cultural inferiority of the poor or the marginalized. It teaches us that power relations between groups (classes, races, ethnicities, genders and so on) come into play when we study the performances of various students. Without the benefits of these insights, brilliant and creative young people from marginalized backgrounds will continue to be drafted into the vast army of the supposedly inferior and untalented. Such injustice is intolerable in America.

WHEN CLASS MEETS GENDER: THE FEMINIZATION OF POVERTY IN CONTEMPORARY AMERICA

Since the early 1970s the daily lives of millions of women have undergone a remarkable transformation. In a relatively short period, women have entered the workforce in massive numbers: In 1950, about one in three women worked outside the home; by 1990 seven of ten did. Since the early 1970s women have entered such professions as the law, medicine, business, banking, film directing and publishing. During the same period they broke blue-collar taboos to find partial acceptance in the traditionally male provinces of police work, firefighting and, in limited roles, the military.

As women's lives were being transformed, however, socioeconomic changes created a climate of vulnerability working women found unfamiliar and uncomfortable. After the Reagan-Bush victories in the 1980s, social and economic policy changed so as to virtually ensure that poverty rates among women and children would grow. Cuts in such human services as Medicaid and maternal and child health programs suddenly placed poor and minority women in precarious economic situations. All the training and employment programs under the Comprehensive Employment and Training Act (CETA) disappeared; some 80 percent of the Youth Employment Demonstration Projects' funds were cut, and Employment Demonstration Project funds were likewise significantly reduced. The tendency to cut or eliminate programs such as these intensified throughout the 1990s, until more than a decade and a half of budget slashing had touched all poor people. No group has been devastated more than families headed by women, however. Reductions in socioeconomic government programs more than doubled the numbers of working mothers living below the poverty line—numbers that continue to grow (Malveaux, 1992; Sidel, 1992).

In the mid–1990s women reached higher unemployment rates than men, women college graduates earned less than men with eighth-grade educations, minority women made less money than any other demographic grouping of workers, pregnancy was the leading reason for dropping out of high school and 60 percent of women living in poverty had dropped out of high school. Moreover, two-thirds of the women who worked outside the home were the sole or primary source of support for themselves and their families (McLaren, 1994; Sidel, 1992).

Obviously, however, not all women are in imminent danger of falling into poverty: Gender intersects with class in a way that excuses most upper- and upper-middle-class women from such anxieties. These women typically enjoy the financial resources, the cultural capital, the education and the skills to control their own lives even if they find themselves without men. Still, the socioeconomic and political changes in the last third of the twentieth century have left all women considerably more financially fragile than their male counterparts. Far too many are now members of the new poor—women who were not born into poverty but were pushed into it by the social, economic and personal dynamics that shaped their lives. When the globalization of the economy, with its corresponding depletion of good jobs, combines with government budget cuts in education and social programs for the poor, women are the first to feel the pressure. All it takes for them to fall through the widening cracks is a job loss, a divorce, serious illness or an unplanned birth.

This new vulnerability sets into motion a vicious circle of workplace oppression. For example, low-income teenage single mothers who find few economic opportunities even after intensive self-sufficiency and employability training must eventually resign themselves to welfare recipient status. Without social services, adequate child care and the hope of meaningful employment, they have the highest rates of pregnancy, abortion and childbearing in the industrialized world. In fact, U.S. teenagers under age fifteen are five times more likely to get pregnant than youths of the same age in other industrialized countries.

Wealth polarization does, indeed, correlate significantly with high teenage birth rates, and the poverty rate among the children born to teenage mothers is also extremely high. The lack of employment and lifestyle options for poor women causes devastating consequences for both their children and society at large. As Fine (1993) observed, with poverty just a divorce away for millions of women, educators should appreciate the critical importance of career counseling for and financial awareness among high school—age women. Americans, in general, must appreciate the need for a humane environment in which women can work and raise their children. Critical educators appreciate the need for political action to ensure the welfare of these women.

Specifically, women need protective political action that responds to the connection between their role as caretakers of children and the feminization of poverty. Men may impregnate and run, but women then face a twenty-year commitment. They cannot count on a man taking care of them and, as a result, they must prepare for economic self-sufficiency. This traditional faith in men as caretakers has become a cultural dinosaur. Yet social, political and educational institutions still presume and cultivate female dependence, making it difficult for women to transcend their assigned roles. When these cultural realities form the backdrop, as recently, for the intolerable neglect of prenatal and well-baby care, accessible day care and after-school care and a responsive child welfare system, the harsh reality of patriarchal negligence stands revealed. Such a reality obviously undermines the dignity of women and the sacredness of children. When child care becomes a desperate plight for working mothers we can expect to read about cagelike cribs, dog leashes restraining children and all manner of abuse in day care warehouses (Aronowitz & DiFazio, 1994; Sidel, 1992). A coherent, democratic, mother-friendly, child-oriented American family policy has fallen victim to fatuous moralizing about "family values" and "patriarchal irresponsibility." Until we take political action, poor working women will remain victims.

DEFINING THE WORLD IN HIS OWN IMAGE: THE POWER OF PATRIARCHY

Patriarchy refers to the gender arrangement in which men constitute the dominant social group. In a patriarchal society, the male role enjoys higher status than the female role. While "patriarchy" originally meant control by the father, we use the term here in a more expansive sense to denote the power men gain by birthright to define reality and earn the rewards of privilege by dominating subordinates (Balsamo, 1985; Ferguson, 1991). Patriarchal power, as with most other forms of power, interacts along the axes of race and class, and is either weakened or enhanced by the interaction. Patriarchal power's capacity to define reality, for example, becomes more pervasive when it combines with the power of socioeconomic class privilege and the racial privilege of whiteness. The male definition of reality in this privileged context is inseparable from the tenets of Cartesian-Newtonian modernism, which sees the world as constructed of physically, socially and biologically disembodied entities ruled by predictable laws that "men of science" can rationally perceive and deploy. Thus, in this patriarchal cosmos one can view the world objectively with disinterest. In such a context, scientific work is an admired enterprise conveniently suited to controlling those of lower status. Some critics call this activity "bad science"—"bad" in the sense that it places research "purity" and rigor above the needs of people and community problems. These critics urge us to resist the patriarchal ways of seeing and reestablish our connections with one another and the natural world (Ferguson, 1984; Williams, 1992).

The emotional repression and lack of interpersonal connection patriarchy relies on and produces create severe social dysfunctionality, especially in the areas of family, child care, education and women's issues. Practically speaking, men who cannot deal with emotional conflict and the interpersonal dynamics of marriage and family relationships are leaving their wives and families in ever-increasing numbers. These fathers shun the role of the "breadwinner loser" who forfeits his patriarchal power (his "male energy") in domestication, fidelity in marriage, dedication to job and devotion to children. This "domesticated loser" became a reliable subject of male ridicule in post–World War II America: to the beatniks he was square; to *Playboy* readers he was sexually timid; to hippies he was tediously straight. The resultant embrace of the hip male identity in a patriarchal culture of disconnection has devastated family stability and child development. Indeed, in a patriarchal culture, to connect with one's family and to develop a faithful and communicative relationship with one's wife is to lose status among one's fellow men (Kincheloe, 1996).

Accordingly, the male's escape from commitment has become the order of the era. Many of those men who flee their families refuse to assist the wives and children they leave behind, to the point that women now find the lack of child support distressing. When this failure of male commitment combines with women's inability to earn suitable wages, their families, as we have seen, often fall below the poverty line. Even when the courts mandate child support, more than 25 percent of the women never see the money, and less than half ever receive the full judgment. An even more telling statistic reveals the average *annual* child-support payments for white, Hispanic and black women: white women receive $2,180; Hispanic women receive $2,070; and black women receive $1,640 (Sidel, 1992).

Meanwhile, in patriarchal societies like that in the United States, men's claim to the production and validation of knowledge carries more influence than women's. While different classes and racial groups of women hold different perspectives on this social dynamic—white working-class women seem to acquiesce in it more than other groups of women, for example—men's knowledge about work and other activities commands the most deference. We see this power exercised in board meetings, union meetings, shop floor meetings or teachers' meetings, where men interrupt and speak over women or appropriate authority over what women say—for example, "What Cindy meant was that. . . . " The same pattern appears on television when an advertisement promotes a household product. While the ad shows a woman using and enjoying the product ("My hands are softer after washing the dishes"), a male voice-over provides the technical information ("Three out of four dermatologists conclude that new, improved Daylite Liquid . . .") and the trappings of authority. The woman, with her "inferior" affective, subjective knowledge, is seen as a totally inadequate authority figure in a patriarchal society. Bring in the man with the deep voice (Luttrell, 1993; Meissner, 1988).

Network news accounts of such economic issues as unemployment also reflect patriarchal structures in their verbal and visual focus on unemployment in the male-dominated industrial sector. Stories on the dramatic increases in layoffs and permanent unemployment in the service sector—predominantly "female" positions such as secretaries, information processors and government workers—constitute only 1 percent of television news stories on such matters (Wallace, 1992; Apple, 1992). It is hardly a secret that TV producers, scholars and researchers in vocational education devote less attention to women than to men (McLaren, 1994).

Critical educators and researchers alert to this situation are working to change it. They realize that the patriarchal context induces a lot of women, particularly working-class women, to devalue their own knowledge and abilities. Instead of recognizing what they know about the world as valuable, working-class women have been conditioned to call it "just common sense." When women view their knowledge as affective, not cognitive, and as feeling, not thought, they perpetuate their own subservient roles and diminish their power.

Women scholars have argued that such working-class female forms of understanding make it difficult to distinguish emotional from objective and rational thinking. They conclude that women should analyze cognitive forms so as to challenge the false dichotomy patriarchy constructs between feminine emotionalism and masculine rationality. In the economic sphere this false dichotomy demotes emotional and intuitive feminine caregiving work and promotes masculine "skilled labor." It supports an unjust system that exempts men from nurturing, service types of work while holding women responsible for unpaid domestic toil. Critical educators in the new paradigm must understand these patriarchal dynamics, for these forces can hide a young woman's abilities from her teachers, her potential employers and, most importantly, herself (Luttrell, 1993).

Most critical educators are keenly aware of the effects patriarchy exerts on their male and female students. They know that two-thirds of all poor people over age sixty-five are women; that women head four out of five single-parent families and a substantial majority of them are poor; and that one in six wives is beaten by her husband. Incredibly, as Sidel notes, in almost all of these situations, from poverty to abuse and assault, women tend to hold themselves responsible:

> If your life does not fit the middle class, or even better, the upper-middle-class image that appears on TV, something is wrong with you. For, if you are poor in America, you are an outsider and it's your own fault. If you are blind, disabled, or old, there is some excuse; you are one of the worthy poor. But if you are a welfare mother, you must be doing something drastically wrong. (1992, p. 8)

THE "GIRL CURRICULUM": UNDERSTANDING THE IDEOLOGY OF DOMESTICITY AND THE CULTURE OF ROMANCE

Inherent in the patriarchal system, the marginalization of women's abilities is a form of oppression that illustrates the intersection of class and gender as a force. The "ideology of domesticity" and the "culture of romance" refer to women's responsibility for unpaid work at home and their acquisition of status by way of male relationships. In the culture of romance women gain self-esteem to the degree that men "desire" them. Home and family, in this context, become central concerns for working-class female students, and their interest in wage labor tends to remain secondary. This perspective and these expectations set them up for failure in a patriarchal society, in which they find themselves vulnerable to the whims and moods of their male partners. If a man leaves a domestically identified woman as the sole supporter and caretaker of the family, she generally has little experience to draw on in her attempt to earn an income outside the home. This feminization of poverty is hardly a scenario fixed in the late twentieth century. Indeed, this informal "domestic code" has long dictated and still dictates that women's work in the economic marketplace is worth about 60 percent of men's work, arbitrary math that fails to provide single mothers with sufficient resources to support a family (Valli, 1987; Weis, 1988). We recall the story of one of our grandmothers, who in 1942 was a thirty-year-old widow working as a clerk for a financial company while raising two infant children. Her male supervisor was called to duty for World War II, and being the senior member of the staff, she assumed the role of supervisor of the office but remained on a clerk's salary. As she struggled to make ends meet for her children, she asked for a raise to a supervisor's salary but was denied because "the higher salaries are reserved for breadwinners." She desperately tried to explain to the company that she was a widow and the breadwinner for her two small children, only to be told that only men are considered breadwinners. To add insult to injury, when the war ended in 1945 a young man was sent to her office by the company to become the new supervisor. He was unmarried, untrained in finance, and ten years her junior, yet he immediately received the "breadwinner" salary. For the next six months she trained the young man while still performing her supervisory duties, after which she was demoted back to her clerk position. We contend that similar injustices based on class, gender and race still regularly occur, even at the dawn of the twenty-first century.

Lois Weis (1988) found women caught in a double bind: They define themselves around themes of home and family but are forced by economic realities to work outside the home. When the current economy virtually forced married women into the workforce, little change took place in the social dynamics and work responsibilities within the home. Women found themselves bound by a double workday: full shifts in both the home and the office or factory. Recent studies indicate that employed married women perform three hours of housework for every one hour their husbands perform. In addition to their jobs outside the home, employed married women perform an average of five hours of domestic work a day. If a married woman's domestic work were compensated, her family's income would increase by more than 60 percent.

Critical educators recognize the negative impact of the domestic ideology and romance culture on women, working-class women in particular. Thus, they deplore society's refusal to provide special support for women in these circumstances. Many critical educators build gender curricula around these issues, hoping to prepare their female students to address the hostile social dynamics while engaging them in the larger struggle to increase public awareness of the need to redistribute some of the caring functions and lighten the double workdays. Ideally, the critical consciousness that produces this awareness can help the American public employ these caring female qualities to humanize its society, schools and workplaces (Sidel, 1992; Wolff, 1977).

Incidentally, when applied to the reconceptualization of education and other social institutions, this feminine ethic of caring holds great promise. However, it can undermine women's best interests when it is superimposed on the current power relations between women and men. When working-class women operating out of an ethic of caring place their own concerns and needs last, they inadvertently reinforce patriarchal power relations between themselves and their husbands. Indeed, many working-class women can justify their educational pursuits only in terms of their commitment to husbands and families: "I'm doing this for them," they often tell their teachers.

This nurturance ideology, this traditional way of making sense of women's role in the world, reached the level of social obsession in the years immediately following World War II. The ideology of domesticity and the culture of romance expressed themselves on television in June and Ward Cleaver, Alice and Ralph Kramden, Lucy and Ricky Ricardo, and persistent visions of mother in the kitchen and father at work. Late-twentieth-century feminism responded to the emotional toll this view of womanhood exacted on the "loving housewife" of the 1950s and early 1960s. Psychological depression, increasing divorce rates and a general discomfort with family life actually characterized this era of outwardly serene domesticity (Luttrell, 1993; Rubin, 1994). Recall a book we recommended in Chapter 1: *The Way We Never Were: American Families and the Nostalgia Trap* (Coontz, 1992). The author does an excellent job of demonstrating that television images do not reflect the way the majority of Americans lived in the twentieth century. Child labor abuses, alcoholism and drug addiction, absent fathers, malnutrition and dislocation due to employment and environmental factors were rampant. There was no such thing as "the good old days" for African Americans in the segregated south; gays and lesbians living in fear of being discovered and harassed; widows and single mothers trying to raise children alone; migrant, immigrant and poor children living without food, shelter or schooling; physically challenged individuals or children with learning disabilities trying to survive in schools and a society that ignored their special needs; non-English speaking, deaf or autistic children living in a world that refused to communicate with them.

Women caught in the patriarchal trap who fail to understand the underside of the ideology of domesticity and the culture of romance can hardly guard against the social forces that have feminized poverty. Self-sacrifice and passivity, common features of traditional notions of femininity, should come with a surgeon general's warning. Young women who embrace such traditionalism, Michele Fine (1993) reports, are far more liable to incur unwanted pregnancies and child care duties than their more assertive sisters. In her study of girls in a New York City public high school, Fine noticed that a larger number of those who got pregnant were quiet and passive—as opposed to the girls whose dress and manner signaled worldliness and experience. Fine's observation should not be taken to mean that teenage mothers are always one certain type of female; obviously the issue is far more complex. What it does mean is that the traditional feminine attitudes and practices often subvert the economic, social and educational development of young women.

Some of our own students assume that the United States has long passed beyond this ideology of domesticity and culture of romance, that they are relics of the past. But we urge them to focus on the second curriculum, the "girl curriculum," that still operates covertly in American schools. Researchers have found that schools offer more career choices to boys, white upper-middle-class boys in particular, and fewer to girls, lower-class nonwhite girls in particular. Career education booklets typically list four career options for boys for every one they list for girls. Thus, high school career counselors often direct female students to career choices that actually reduce their wage-earning options and lead them toward a life of poverty (Johnson, 1991).

Even in the newer educational programs these gender dynamics still operate. Pulling's (1994) study of fifteen federal school-to-work demonstration programs developed in the 1990s found that three of the programs enrolled no girls and four enrolled three girls or fewer. The types of programs students attended conformed to traditional gender stereotypes: The girls were guided into office, allied health and clerical programs; the boys enrolled in electronics, metal working and automation programs. Critical educators address these gender dynamics in all phases of their curriculum designs, instructional methods and student counseling. Young women who are aware of the patriarchal assumptions embedded in education, home life and the world of work are better prepared to overcome their oppressive effects. Young men who recognize these assumptions can model more just and humane ways of accommodating the aspirations of both women and other men in their social and educational interactions. If we are serious about creating schools and communities where everyone belongs, we must address the social pathologies patriarchal traditions produce.

THE BRIDGE OF WHITENESS: RETHINKING OUR PLACE IN THE WEB OF REALITY

In working with rural teachers a few years ago on concerns of race, class and gender, one of our colleagues observed a fascinating phenomenon. He found white teachers for the most part reluctant to speak frankly about racial matters with African Americans present. In a mixed-race class of thirty, for example, only a handful of white teachers addressed interpersonal dynamics relating to race in their private or professional lives. After class, however, when all the black teachers had left, these white teachers wanted to discuss their perceptions of race in their everyday lives. During this "private time" they told stories of "reverse racism," incompetent black teachers and preferential hiring of blacks and Hispanics. As our colleague Aaron Gresson (1995), put it, these teachers sought to construct a bridge between him and them on the ideological basis of their whiteness, as if the antiracist in-class pedagogy had been irrelevant. These teachers seemed to consider integration a public facade either the school or the discipline required. Once white people were alone, the honest talk could begin. During these conversations the teachers spoke in hushed tones, constantly looking around to make sure they were alone and safely segregated. When they spoke the word "black," they would become even more quiet—sometimes only mouthing, not even whispering the word. It quickly became apparent that two conversations were proceeding about race among many of these white teachers: (1) a public discourse of feigned civility; and (2) a private discourse of racial solidarity based on the perception of whites as victims. Only in the private conversation did the teachers' authentic feelings emerge. In this context we need to examine carefully the nature of racism and its relation to education in contemporary America (Kincheloe, Steinberg, Rodriguez, & Chennault, 1998).

Because of their oppressed historical position in the web of reality, nonwhite people often see whites differently than white people see themselves, and this "subjugated knowledge of whiteness" can promote an understanding of race and education. If critical theory teaches us that self-knowledge—an understanding of those historical and social forces that have shaped us—is useful, then an understanding of the impact of being white is essential for both nonwhite and white people. Defining whiteness simply as the racial identity of individuals who think of themselves as white, the identity can forcefully shape one's personality and view of the world. Because we rarely talk about whiteness the concept is invisible, but its ubiquity and dominance make it a hidden marker of normality. In other words, all people's lives are shaped by race. Yet whiteness confers the power to suppress ethnicity: "Me? No, I'm not ethnic, I'm just white." As a people that are ethnically positioned, we all take part in unequal power relations whether we want to or not. In this context whiteness gets shaped in relation to blackness; both white racism and white antiracism shape white identity (Frankenberg, 1993). The white teachers just described were not acting outside an ethnic-racial identity; they were operating as white ethnics.

The exploration of whiteness in relation to education can be a dangerous topic because everyone has a place in the pageant of racism. A white person can no longer say, "I had nothing to do with racism. That happened a long time ago. Leave me alone!" All white people understand that African Americans have had to endure inequities imposed on them by whites, but they differ in how they make sense of this knowledge. At some level of their consciousness, white people understand that their skin color provides them with certain privileges. For example, while it cannot guarantee success, if nothing else it does protect them from being viewed as black. This is a problematic message for working-class white people in light of their declining financial positions. But even as these people laugh at the idea of white privilege, they denounce affirmative action. If they fully understood and acknowledged their privileges as whites, they would have to question their accomplishments. Psychologically, in relation to their own self-esteem it is better for them to dismiss any notion of white privilege (Hacker, 1992).

The presumption of white supremacy is, of course, endemic to American culture, grounded, as it is, on the historical idea of Manifest Destiny: It was God's will that white Americans control the North American continent from the Atlantic to the Pacific. In their presumed superiority, white people were and are bound by divine commitments to subdue the savages and to civilize them; it was and is the "White Man's Burden." In this superior historical position, American whites often feel victimized when the courts, legislatures and schools fail to support their privilege. In these instances white people often allude to the pain and discrimination their immigrant ancestors suffered. In response to African American, Latino and Native American calls for social and educational justice, they often argue that "nobody helped our grandparents. They made it here in America because they worked hard." The implication, of course, is that black, Hispanic, Native American and other minority peoples do not work hard. In these arguments rarely do white people refer to their ancestors' "trump card": their status as white people. The Irish, for example, initially were not viewed as whites when they arrived in the United States in the middle of the nineteenth century. But as the decades passed they proved their whiteness and achieved economic mobility. As an important part of this "whitening" process, they adopted the racist positions of other white people. This same whitening process recurred among a variety of ethnic groups. Our ethnic place, our location in the social web, makes a tremendous difference in our ability to pursue educational, economic and social success (Kincheloe, et al., 1998).

SPONTANEOUS COMBUSTION: ECONOMIC DECLINE, WHITE PRIVILEGE AND MINORITY RACIAL AWARENESS

Drawing on our earlier discussion of the widening gap between rich and poor, and the core and peripheral workers in the "post-Fordist" economy described in Chapter 6, an examination of the racial dynamics of America at the end of the twentieth century is now in order. The recessions and stagflation in the 1970s intensified a perception of scarcity. At exactly the same time, affirmative action and minority preference hiring policies allowed a few nonwhites to make small but visible intrusions on what had been all-white terrain. The combination of the two social trends was incendiary. Throughout the 1970s and 1980s, the U.S. economy faltered repeatedly; local, state and federal governments continued to cut services; the quality of life of the middle and lower social-economic classes continued to deteriorate; and the passion of the debate over who would get the leftovers accelerated. Indeed, as power concentrated in the hands of the richest, predominately white segments of the society, social discord between everyone else intensified (Rubin, 1994).

One of the most important and influential manifestations of this discord centers on the claim many conservative whites make that racism in America is now a thing of the past, that we live in a "postracist era." America being the land of opportunity, goes this conservative white narrative, and with everyone granted access to material well-being, those who cannot achieve it have no one to blame but themselves. This reencoding of black and Latino inferiority relies on the familiar old social-Darwinist survival-of-the-fittest theory: "Those who whine about discrimination would be better served to shut up and get their lazy butts in gear."

Meanwhile, the mobility enjoyed by a small number of middle-class African Americans in recent years and the high visibility this successful group receives are misinterpreted by many struggling white working-class Americans as evidence of overall African American economic success. Closer examination hardly supports this interpretation; indeed, the slight black middle-class success highlighted fiscal inequality in the African American community, as tens of thousands of black Americans fell into poverty and the underclass. Thus, the very groups victimized by the inequitable distribution of wealth in America—African Americans and working class whites—have so far found little solidarity in their similar plights. Instead they have become political enemies fighting for an ever-shrinking slice of the economic pie (Stafford, 1992; Rubin, 1994; Jones, 1992; Cotton, 1992).

THE RECOVERY OF WHITE SUPREMACY: EMPATHY OR ELSE

The current inequitable economy and the accompanying social discord can be nasty. Educators need hardly be reminded of the racial tensions they witness in their every-day professional lives. Critical educators are alert to the distrust and suspicion interra-cial competition for limited opportunities arouses. With racial interaction currently packed in a pressure cooker, disharmony is bound to erupt. Renewed racism in new forms calls for new understandings and approaches on the part of critical educators. We should avoid confusing the corporate use (the "commodification") of nonwhites and superficial celebrations of diversity in the media with genuine democratic move-ments to decentralize wealth and distribute political power more equitably (Fusco, 1992). Critical educators must point out that these movements have yet to take place in this country. They must warn their students against equating the corporate com-modification of ethnicity—expressed in terms of "Shaq attacks," "Be Like Mike," and "Oprah at 5:00"—with black and others' access to economic mobility. Such misleading images distort both the public conversation about and individual percep-tions of the associations between hard work and schooling and financial success.

Critical educators in the new paradigm must appeal to the best instincts of their students, colleagues and communities—that is, they must call on their com-passion, sense of justice and empathy. African Americans must empathize with working white people and their frustrations over their own lack of mobility and crushed aspirations. At the same time, white Americans must empathize with black, Hispanic, Native American and other Americans and their continuing frus-tration over their inability to realize the American dream. Until this empathy flows back and forth, the possibility of dialogue and unity among Americans victimized by the vicious new forms of racism, sexism and class bias will elude us all. Such em-pathy can lead to dialogue and unity; unity can form the basis of an American prodemocracy movement, an interracial, interethnic struggle for political and eco-nomic justice.

These words may strike you as idealistic—they are; but we urge you to nourish dreams of better days to come. This book, of course, is itself a sort of social dream in that it lays out a sense of possibility for critical educators and their students. This chapter focuses on one of the most abiding impediments to hope: racism, with all its effects and mutating expressions. An awareness of this phenomenon among teachers and students has an importance beyond simply understanding the phe-nomenon of racism itself. Knowing how our consciousness is socially constructed around issues of race (along with issues of class and gender) grants us insight into the way the world works and the way power relations subtly induce us to adopt identities and perspectives that undermine our self-interest and our collective in-terests as a culture and nation. In this context Aaron Gresson's (1995) description of "racial recovery" and its social divisiveness becomes extremely important.

Hegemony, as noted earlier, makes the world seem natural, as if one can ex-plain it with a dominant cultural story. Certain stories become privileged at partic-ular historical junctures because they serve so well to maintain existing power rela-tions. Gresson has noted the emergence over the last couple of decades of a new dominant story: the narrative of the recovery of white supremacy. In many ways this new white story inverts a traditional black story. The new story rejects overt racist assertions of nonwhite inferiority, substituting a narrative of nonwhite privilege. Drawing on what it considers the media's ratification of black and other minority group success, the story contends that in the 1990s the balance shifted and racial minorities gained greater power and opportunities than whites. In short, they gained privilege at the expense of white Americans, especially white males. The story gets told on several levels and in many ways, but always with the same effect: It produces white male anger aimed at African Americans, Latinos, Asians, Native Americans and women. Such anger naturally works to divide poor and working-class people of all races and genders and to preserve the interests of the privileged few who remain the wielders of power.

This new story induces white Americans to see themselves as a people under siege. Sociologists confirm that individuals and groups under threat tend to react by reasserting their power and former social position; they refer to it as the social phenomenon of "status anxiety." This reassertion, of course, can take many forms and exert many degrees of intensity. Manifestations may include modest efforts to reassert one's self-worth by way of private expression of racial disdain or racial superiority. White reassertion may work more on the level of group recovery with the passing of "English only" legislation in such heavily Latino regions as South Florida, California and Arizona. It can lead to battles over "multicultural curricula," as evidenced in recent years throughout the nation (Frankenberg, 1993). More extreme expressions include the dramatic growth of white supremacist organizations in the 1980s and 1990s and the terrorist activity associated with some of them, such as the bombing of the Oklahoma City federal building in April 1995. Most Americans reject this new angry white narrative, yet the perception of whites as victims becomes more and more deeply embedded in the white collective consciousness as the century comes to an end.

CRYPTORACISM: THE CONTEMPORARY SOCIAL PLAGUE

In an era some consider "postracist," when supposedly whites suffer the only form of racism left, all the rules of racial talk in America have changed. The critical analyst's attempt to track mutating neoracism resembles the effort by the Centers for Disease Control (CDC) to track the evolution of the Ebola virus, with new outbreaks and strains popping up in unexpected places. This "Andromeda Strain of racism" can best be described as cryptoracism ("crypto" meaning concealed, secret, invisible), racism that employs thinly veiled code words and phrases to evoke images of white superiority (Nightingale, 1993). Steve Haymes (1995) uncovered the virus and its damage to the public conversation about education concealed in discussions of "illiteracy" and "basic skills," and their *cryptic* identification of blacks and Hispanics with these problems. The subliminal message depicts illiteracy and the lack of basic skills as a black and Latino problem so severe and pervasive that it consumes the educational resources needed for students who could make good use of them (read, white students). Thus, shortages in educational funding for middle- and upper-middle-class white students are not the sins of those communities and political leaders who cut educational funding in general; instead, the deficits are the fault of minority groups. According to the authors of the best-selling book *The Bell Curve,* these funds are wasted because the racial minority and the poor are incapable of profiting from the programs they subsidize (see Herrnstein & Murray, 1994; Kincheloe, Steinberg & Gresson, 1996). The story of white victimization is extended, and more fuel feeds the fire of white anger.

Cryptoracism produces a form of "doublespeak" that not only transforms whites into the victims of racism but also redefines the word itself. Antiracism, in this new discourse, becomes racism. References to the existence of racism and calls for its eradication are redefined by cryptoracists as racist practices—that is, as "playing the race card" or "evoking the tired cries of racial discrimination." So pervasive has this neoracism become that many black, Latino, Asian and Native American workers hesitate to mention racism on the job. They know that merely bringing up issues of race can undermine their chances for advancement (Macedo, 1994). Cryptoracism has even developed a "proper syntax" of racial reference relying on coded phrasing that escapes detection as racism. It is a language of white supremacy that constantly denies its racist undercurrent. As it distances itself from any overt invocation of biological inferiority, cryptoracism aligns itself with four familiar ideas:

1. *A common culture.* Here is the idea that all Americans hold particular, sacred values and understandings, which are really assertions that many nonwhites do not share these values and understandings.
2. *Urban troubles.* U.S. cities definitely present mammoth intractable problems in the late twentieth century. But unstated here is the assertion that because urban demographics have changed so dramatically over the last half-century (minorities now constitute the majority of many urban populations), we can safely blame urban troubles on nonwhite social pathologies.
3. *Family values.* America, it is said, is in decline because of the breakdown of family values. Unsaid but implied in this discourse is a supposed inability among those who are not white, especially African Americans, to lead conventionally moral lives.
4. *The epidemic of drugs and violence.* Something must be done to end the organized attack on American communities mounted by unscrupulous drug dealers. The message encoded here relies on a presumed connection between drugs and racial minorities. Drugs and the violence that attends them are products of the ghetto and of black and Latino gangs.

Notice the ingenious distortions in these four examples of rhetorical codings. The first assertion, that we all share a common culture, assumes a national culture based on consensus—that is, all citizens ascribe to an unchanging homogenous culture characterized by a universally known and accepted core of uniform values. But national cultures, especially the American variety, have never been constructed on this level. As we have been saying throughout this book—especially in the Introduction and in Chapters 1 and 4—there is far more diversity than critics would like to recognize, for to admit that millions of people refuse to be melded into a bland melting pot would be to admit defeat in the effort to assimilate all races, ethnicities, sexualities and religions into one uniform culture. Those who resist assimilation often insist that we must "celebrate diversity."

The second assertion, implicitly blaming racial minorities for urban troubles, misleads. The flight of middle-class residents and corporations from the inner city spawned an economic-political-social crisis for the people without their own mobility who were left behind. The refusal of citizens and politicians to address the problems and needs their flight created accounts for most of the nonwhite hopelessness. Who is really at fault here?

The third assertion, positing the decline of family values, fails to account for the remarkable strength of black and Hispanic family structures throughout American history. Regardless of the historical context, African American and Hispanic families reliably produce resilient men and women equipped to cope with and often transcend violence, poverty and all the other manifestations of their powerlessness.

The fourth assertion, blaming the ubiquity of drugs and violence on nonwhites, ignores the abundant sociological data refuting the myth that inner-city nonwhites are primarily responsible for drug use, drug sales and the accompanying violence. White women are statistically more likely than black women to use and abuse drugs—despite the reality that black female drug users are ten times more likely to be reported than white women users. Almost 80 percent of illegal drug use in America takes place outside the inner city. In fact, the prototypical crack cocaine addict is a white middle-class man between the ages of forty and fifty. At the same time, FBI statistics indicate that while the proportion of African Americans arrested for aggravated assault is three times greater than that for whites, the National Crime Survey, which tabulates and studies victims of assault, has found black and white aggravated assault statistics to be almost identical. In short, cryptoracist codes purposely portray a distorted picture (Rizvi, 1993; Haymes, 1995; Coontz, 1992).

An ambiguous and complex trend, cryptoracism systematically sullies the impressions of blacks, Latinos, Native Americans and others in schools and other social institutions even as it increases the power of the dominant culture. Indeed, its promotion of the recovery of white supremacy serves the interests of our overwhelmingly white corporate and political leaders. The economic and political advantages of white recovery were specifically outlined by political analyst Kevin Phillips in *The New Republican Majority,* published in 1969. Phillips understood the power to be derived from exploiting the developing perception that minority groups were gaining too much of the heretofore white economic pie.

Struggling to retain the profit margins of the 1950s and 1960s, corporate leaders and their political allies deployed the rhetoric of white recovery to gain the electoral cooperation of their natural adversaries, the white laboring class. So strong did the white workers' racial concerns prove to be that they began to support economic and political policies clearly contrary to their own interests. Employing the four cryptoracist codes of the welfare state, drugs, crime in the streets and family values, and adding for good measure allusions to the liberal assault on

Western Judeo-Christian values, conservative and reactionary political candidates began the process of promoting business with lowered corporate taxes, reduced government regulations, lowered wages and increased public expenditures for defense-related enterprises (West, 1993; Amott, 1993).

We can easily trace this conservative political and economic trajectory through the last three decades of the twentieth century. Richard Nixon deployed "busing" (read, upsetting white schooling patterns) as a cryptoracist term as early as 1968. Quickly the Republican Party adopted the language of white male recovery to win white voters away from the labor-identified Democrats. By no means can we absolve the Democratic Party from complicity in the recovery effort, but the Republicans perfected the politics of white recovery using race and gender codes to divert the white workers' attention from the politics of the workplace. With the help of advisors Mike Deaver and Roger Ailes, Ronald Reagan mastered the cryptoracist recovery rhetoric and managed to gain worker support for a no-tax business policy and government grants to corporations.

Lacking Reagan's charm, George Bush resorted to racist visual imagery, using a photograph of rapist Willie Horton in his 1988 campaign ads to link the recovery rhetoric to his persona and agenda. The imagery worked so well that in his 1990 race against a black challenger, North Carolina Republican Senator Jesse Helms used TV ads that referred openly to minorities' taking white working-class jobs—all the while denying any racist intentions. Helms's references had little to do with reality: The job losses in North Carolina had resulted from corporate flight to the Third World, flight made possible by tax incentives passed by the business-friendly Helms and his corporate-financed government colleagues.

The success of such outwardly benign, inwardly poisonous strategies kept raising the racial ante. Racial scapegoating, the politicians noticed, works. How far can we go? the candidates began to ask. How can we convey the codes most effectively? By the early 1990s the American political landscape included far more radical and daring cryptoracists. David Duke, a former Ku Klux Klan and Nazi Party leader, pushed the racist envelope. Nixon, Reagan, Bush and Helms had plowed the ideological and cultural fields to make them more receptive to racist seeds, and in Louisiana's 1991 gubernatorial race Duke received nearly two-thirds of the white working-class vote (Marable, 1992). By the middle of the decade, the rhetoric of white recovery had become an all too familiar element in political campaigns in all regions of the country, and white supremist organizations like Council of Conservative Citizens (CCC) even gained support from Senate majority leader Trent Lott of Mississippi and Georgia congressman Bob Barr in 1998.

CRYPTORACISM AND THE NATURALIZATION OF WHITE SUPREMACY

Because it makes unequal power relations between whites and nonwhites seem as though they could have been no other way, cryptoracism naturalizes the forces that ensure racial inequality. In such a process the historical influences that help shape the present social order—existing racial dynamics in particular—get erased. We defer our hopes for a better social order, and for racial harmony. Cryptoracism becomes an ideology offering to help people make sense of their lives in ways that do not serve their own best interests. For example, whites who accept the attractively packaged doses of white supremacy may then support economic policies that ultimately cut workers' wages while raising the salaries of those in managerial positions. The principal ideological construction achieved over the last three decades has been the power bloc's ability to win consent from working-class whites to the politics of racial recovery.

This hegemonic ideological process is complicated. It requires reception, construction, and reconstruction to help individuals make sense of, deal with and act in their lived worlds. Cryptoracist political depictions of, for example, unqualified minority workers taking white jobs encourages white workers to organize their realities and focus their anger. Conflicting forms of consciousness often arise in this process. Studies indicate that students who sincerely ascribe to multiculturalism and racial justice nevertheless accept (1) patterns of isolation between racially different students, (2) a rhetoric of us (whites) versus them (nonwhites), and (3) the assumption that school values are and should be our (white people's) values. The cryptoracism encoded here has been described as "aversive racism," a liberal form of race consciousness that denies its inclination toward discrimination even as it reveals its low opinion of the racially different.

These reasonable and understandable paradoxes tend to be expressed in a common and recognizable rhetorical style: One asserts one's rejection of racism in a preliminary phrase ("I am not a racist but . . . ") followed by an explicitly racist characterization ("these Cubans are so pushy and arrogant"). An ability to identify the various ways racism manifests itself is, of course, extremely important for educators. At the same time, it is important that educators understand that no matter what guise racism assumes, its structural consequences remain pretty much the same. Its victims are marginalized and excluded (not necessarily legally) and denied equal access to and treatment by institutions.

The message systems schools use can legitimate and reinforce a student's provisional aversive racism. Students' perceptions of who they are and the nature of their social identities are inseparable from these educational message systems (Rizvi, 1993). Therefore, we can understand how education fits into this complex social puzzle. The tracking and social stigmatizing so central to the logic of modernist schooling coincide with and support cryptoracism. Vocational education, for example, is the place reserved for the academically and intellectually inferior. As white students watch the racial minority and handicapped relegated to the vocational space, they notice and then appreciate their "separateness" from this group. Vocational students are the abnormal, those distanced from the norms of middle- and upper-middle-class whiteness. The message is clear: Though the world is populated by different groups, cultures and ethnicities who deserve our lip-service respect, we live separate lives. It is *we,* as white students, who dwell within the boundaries of the norm; our culture constitutes *the* culture; our friends and daily associations come from among those receiving an academic education; we may never use the explicit, but we are the dominant group. This is how the modernist school constructs a consciousness and perpetrates inequality.

CRYPTORACISM AND THE SOCIAL DYNAMICS OF VOCATIONAL EDUCATION: THE HISPANIC-LATINO EXAMPLE

Hispanic and Latino peoples are profoundly and particularly affected by the racist forces we have been discussing. Any examination of the relationship among racism, Hispanics and Latinos and education should start by acknowledging the diversity within the umbrella term "Hispanic-Latino," which includes five principal population groups: Mexican Americans, 63 percent; Puerto Ricans, 12 percent; Central and South Americans, 11 percent; other Hispanics and Latinos, 8 percent; and Cubans, 5 percent.

Hispanics and Latinos now constitute the fastest-growing demographic group in America, and at least one-third of their school-age children can expect to be tracked into vocational education, most of the time without any counseling about the social and educational consequences of their placement. For example, when Hispanics and Latinos find jobs, they make on average 53 cents for every dollar white males earn. Thus, cryptoracist educational practices represented as antiracist, multicultural, and equal-opportunity-oriented victimize Hispanic and Latino students. Though couched in the language of democracy, these practices exclude Hispanic and Latino students from honors and higher-level programs, making them more liable to drop out, more liable to enroll below their grade level and less likely to attend postsecondary programs than any other ethnic and racial group in America. Given the proliferation of these ostensibly helpful "multicultural" programs, Hispanic and Latino students have lost educational ground as measured by such standards as rates of high school graduation over the last three decades (McLaren, 1994; Perez, 1993; Rendon & Nora, 1991).

Few educators would intentionally impede the academic and vocational progress of Hispanic and Latino students. Vocational counselors rarely think, "Oh, here's a Salvadoran; I'll send him to the metal shop." The process is more subtle and complex, but the dynamics of social regulation do come into play. Studies indicate that minority students and their parents generally have little influence over curricular placement. Counselors and teachers take responsibility for these decisions, typically basing their judgments on each student's grades and test scores. Test score analyses rarely take into account the fact that many Hispanic and Latino students adopt English as a second language, and for many of these Hispanic and Latino students who are recent immigrants, testing takes place long before they have a chance to orient themselves to North American life. Decontextualized assessment procedures cannot account for these and other mitigating factors, practically guaranteeing unmediated placement onto low-ability tracks as the result of understandably low test scores.

Thus, Hispanic and Latino students march into vocational education, finding themselves, "before they know it," trained for the low-pay, low-status grunt work minorities traditionally hold. The process goes on year after year as counselors operate within the modernist paradigm, grounding their decisions on such cryptoracist codes as the "cultural deficiencies" of Hispanics and Latinos. Given the situation they face and the routines they must follow, the only realistic form of advice the counselors can offer an Hispanic or Latino student is to lower his or her professional aspirations and choose a track that prepares him or her for roles commensurate with the talents he or she already has or can gain quickly (Oakes, 1985; McLaren, 1994; Banfield, 1991).

In his historical documentation of these unjust educational practices, Clinton Allison (1995) described the reactions of educators to poor, minority and immigrant parents who refused to accept teachers' descriptions of their children's cognitive and academic limitations. Twentieth-century educators often view with annoyance or contempt parents who fail to accept "scientifically validated" assessments of their children's limitations. Educators understand that an important aspect of their professional role is to disabuse poor and minority parents of their "delusional hopes" for upward mobility by way of professional careers for their children.

Critical educator Donaldo Macedo (1994) described his encounter with a vocational guidance counselor upon entering the Boston public schools as a student, with Portuguese as his first language. Though Macedo's interest had nothing to do with the work, the counselor advised him to become a television repairman. Similarly, one of our academic colleagues, a professor of education, was encouraged by his high school guidance counselor to become a piano tuner, a vocation he had absolutely no interest in. We can, therefore, empathize with Macedo and the tens of thousands of Hispanic and Latino students whose counselors draw on encoded perceptions of them as incapable to relegate them to a vocational track. Donna Gaines recorded this all-too-common encounter between a marginalized student and his vocational counselor:

> *"So, Roy, what do you see yourself doing five years from now?" And Roy is thinking What did I do wrong? What does she want me to say? What is going to come down on me now? And then the guidance counselor will say something about Roy's lack of spectacular grades: "Not on any teams or in any clubs, are you, Roy?" And Roy starts feeling stupid and maybe he fiddles with himself nervously, and says the first thing that comes to his head, like how much he enjoys working on his car. Like she shouldn't think he's a total loser. And that's that! He's never really given much thought before now, but today, the future is laid out before him and now Roy's going to vocational high school and he's going to learn about cars. (1990, pp. 145–146)*

Hispanic women and Latinas, of course, face special forms of cryptoracist encodement, as literature and the media depict them as powerless and sometimes pathologic. As subjugated, subservient, loyal daughters, wives and mothers, they are blamed for their own victimization, often portrayed as unresistant to their positions as sex objects and as befrilled consorts with a culturally backward proclivity to excessive praying. Teachers and counselors need to recognize these cryptoracist codes and reformulate their teaching and counseling to address them. Critical educators must help Hispanic women and Latinas learn to confront such ethnic encoding by developing strategies of resistance. The young women and their teachers and counselors must insist that (1) Latinas enjoy access to academic courses; (2) they receive exposure to programs and curricula that teach them about reasonable and attractive career and life options; and (3) they understand the power and ethnic dynamics that threaten to force them into dead-end jobs and stultifying life choices.

Moreover, U.S. schools should connect these racial, ethnic and cultural considerations into integrated academic and vocational curricula, building, when and where needed, centers designed to help all marginalized people cope with the stress, role conflicts, vocational dynamics and cryptoracism contemporary society inevitably forces them to face. These centers might provide such services as child care, apprenticeship placement, math anxiety reduction classes and financial aid and financial planning study groups (Rendon & Nora, 1991).

With the resurgence of racism, class bias and the feminization of poverty, students from marginalized backgrounds have less chance of escaping injustice than in previous decades. Accepting and acting on the ideas we offer here may not make you popular with your peers and may alienate your supervisors. Yet despite the consequences, the ideas are just and humane and worth struggling to present and uphold in schools and communities. What you do with these ideas is up to you. If you are white and upper-middle class, you may find the concepts alien or uncomfortable, in which case it may be helpful for you to explore the construction of your consciousness. Why do you feel uncomfortable with these ideas? How does your discomfort affect the way you see yourself as a future teacher? Where in the web of reality do you stand? We hope you will confront these questions as the result of your encounter with the issues of power, social placement and the purposes of education.

12

Youth Culture

INTRODUCTION: KINDERCULTURE'S PRODUCTION

New times appear to be accelerating childhood, a trend many ed-
cators and parents choose to deny or ignore. We believe that in o-
der to contextualize teaching, we should contextualize the re-
world experiences of our students—"real world" in the sense th-
everything children experience becomes part of and influenc-
their lives. "Everything" naturally includes films, television pr-
grams and advertising, student and youth clubs, church and soc-
groups, sports, comic books, trading cards, computer games, t-
Internet and so forth. We call the pervasive influences in the n-
childhood era "kinderculture." Taking the German word f-
"child," *kinder,* we add "culture" to describe any condition with-
our society that directly affects children and youth, conditions th-
appeal directly to them and some that escape our notice (Steinbe-
& Kincheloe, 1997). Under the kinderculture heading we gro-
many of the people, media events and images that we know infl-
ence our students, and the subsequent contextualization helps -
understand "where they are coming from."

Evidence of the dramatic cultural change in childhood su-
rounds us all, but unfortunately, many of those who study or ca-
for children professionally have yet to recognize this historical w-
tershed. Furthermore, few observers appreciate the fact that t-
current information explosion plays a central role in undermini-
traditional ideas of childhood. In fact, those who shape, direct a-
use the information technology play an exaggerated role in the -
formulation of childhood. Childhood is as much a social and h-
torical artifact as it is a biological and chronological conditio-
Many believe childhood to be a natural phase of maturation. N-
ural or not, one can hardly escape noting that those passi-

through this phase of life experience social, cultural, political and economic forces. Indeed, that which people call "traditional childhood" at the dawn of the twenty-first century is itself only about 150 years old. In the Middle Ages, for example, children participated in the adult world every day, acquiring vocational and social skills early in life. The concept of the child as a particular classification of human being demanding special treatment differing from that accorded adults had not yet been developed.

CHILDHOOD AS A SOCIAL CONSTRUCTION

Thus the idea of childhood appears to be a creation of society and is subject to change whenever major social transformations take place. The emphasis on what we call traditional childhood lasted only from about 1850 to 1950. Protected from the dangers of the adult world, children during this period left the mines and factories for schools. As the prototype of the modern family developed in the late nineteenth century, agreement on the proper parental behavior toward children coalesced around ideas of tenderness and adult accountability for children's welfare. By 1900 many considered that childhood a "birthright"—the perspective that eventually led to a biological rather than a cultural definition of childhood. During this era of the protected child, modern child psychology developed inadvertently from the tacit assumptions of the period. Great child psychologists such as Erik Erikson, Arnold Gesell and Jean Piaget viewed child development as shaped by biological forces.

His brilliance somewhat clouded by his nonhistorical, socially decontextualized scientific approach, Jean Piaget generalized the genetic expression of child behavior he saw in the early twentieth century to all cultures and historical eras—an error with serious consequences for those concerned with children. Considering biological stages of child development fixed and unchangeable, teachers, psychologists, parents and welfare workers who ascribe to Piaget's philosophy still view and judge children along a fictional taxonomy of development. They relegate those children who do not "measure up" to the realm of low and self-fulfilling expectations, and they confuse the racial and economic privileges of those children who "make the grade" with ability (Polakow, 1992; Postman, 1994). In reaction, kinderculture joins the emerging concepts of social theory that question the biological assumptions of "classical" child psychology (Cannella, 1996).

Living in a period of major change and social upheaval, critical observers have just begun to notice changing social and cultural conditions in relation to this view of childhood. Traditional categories of child development appropriated from modernist psychology appear to hold little relevance for raising and educating contemporary children. As childhood itself began to change in the 1950s, 80 percent of all children lived in homes with their two married biological parents (Lipsky & Abrams, 1994). No one has to be told that American families have changed over the last fifty years and that the social transformations have been unsettling. Before the 1980s ended, the number of children who lived with their two biological parents had fallen to a mere 12 percent, and today children of divorced parents are almost three times as likely to suffer emotional and behavioral difficulties as children raised in two-parent homes. Nevertheless, social institutions have been slow to recognize different, nontraditional family configurations and respond to their special needs. Without support, the "postmodern family" of the late twentieth and early twenty-first centuries, with its multitude of working and single mothers and growing numbers of single fathers, same-sex couples with children, blended families, interracial and cross-racial families, faces intractable problems deriving from the feminization of poverty and the vulnerable position of women in both the public and the private sectors (Polakow, 1992).

THE CONTEMPORARY CRISIS OF CHILDHOOD

In short, changing economic realities, coupled with children's access to information about the adult world, have drastically changed childhood. Recent observers of contemporary childhood speak of "childhood lost," "children growing up too fast" and "a child's terror in the isolation of the fragmented home and community." Images of mothers drowning children, babysitters torturing infants, children pushing smaller children out of high-rises, razor blades in Halloween apples—even parents on vacation leaving the children home alone—saturate the contemporary conversation. Popular culture provides haunting images of this crisis of childhood that raise and engage our worst fears. The film *Halloween*, for example, tells on one level a story of the postmodern childhood: fear of isolation. The specific isolation involves separation from both absent parents and a nonexistent community. No one is around to help; even on the once festive Halloween night no children are present. Even in "safe" suburbia, the community has fragmented to the point that it can no longer guarantee the safety of trick-or-treating children (Ferguson, 1994; Paul, 1994). The crisis of contemporary childhood, now signified in many forms, usually includes, at some level, danger faced in solitude.

THE NEW LEARNING SITES: CORPORATIONS AS EDUCATORS

Having acknowledged this crisis of childhood, critical teachers are compelled to examine its causes. While a range of factors has conspired to construct the perils children now face, this chapter focuses on one factor in particular: the corporate production of popular kinderculture and its impact on children. For this pervasive influence we use the term "cultural pedagogy," or the idea that education takes place in a variety of social sites including but hardly limited to the school. Pedagogical sites are those places where someone organizes and deploys power, and they include libraries, television, the movies, newspapers and magazines, toys, advertisements, video games, books, sports and so forth. Our work as education scholars demands that we examine both school and cultural pedagogy to make sense of the entire educational process (Steinberg & Kincheloe, 1997).

Assuming that learning changes one's identity, we see the pedagogical process engaging our desire (our yearning for something beyond ourselves shaped by the social context in which we operate, and our affective investment in that which surrounds us), capturing our imagination and constructing our consciousness. The emergence of cultural studies now helps to examine the cultural practices through which individuals come to understand themselves and the world that surrounds them (Grossberg, 1995; McLaren, 1995). Supported by the insights of cultural studies we can examine the effects of cultural pedagogy with its identity formation and its production and legitimation of knowledge—which is to say, the cultural curriculum.

The organizations that create this cultural curriculum are not educational agencies; rather, they are commercial concerns that operate primarily for individual gain and only secondarily, if at all, for the social good. Cultural pedagogy is structured by commercial dynamics, forces that intrude into all aspects of our own and our children's private lives. Patterns of consumption shaped by corporate advertising turn commercial institutions into the teachers of the new millennium. Corporate cultural pedagogy has "done its homework"; judged on the basis of capitalist goals, its educational forms and strategies are wildly successful. Replacing traditional classroom lectures and seat work with magic kingdoms, animated fantasies, interactive videos, virtual realities, kick-boxing TV heroes, spine-tingling horror books and various other entertainments produced ostensibly for adults but eagerly consumed by children, corporate America has revolutionized childhood. Marketing strategies for children from birth to three years old hope to establish a consumer attitude from the very earliest stages of life. The revolution hardly proceeds in some crassly cynical manner with bureaucratic corporate generals checking off a list of captured institutions. Instead it comes to us in fragments over our television sets, so we and our children can watch it in vivid color. Using fantasy and desire, corporate functionaries create a perspective on culture that melds with business ideologies and free-market values. The worldviews corporate advertisers produce always let children know to some extent that the most exciting things life can provide come from our friends in corporate America. The economics lesson gains power when repeated thousands of times.

We believe it is our parental, civic and professional responsibility to study the corporate curriculum and its social and political effects. Indeed, as parents, citizens and teachers, we must hold corporations accountable for the pedagogical results of their activities—that is, for the "kinderculture" they produce. We must intervene in this cozy association between popular culture and pedagogy shaping our students' identities. In the interest of both our children and the larger society, we must exercise our personal and collective power to challenge and neutralize the many ways corporate power (gained as purchased access to the media) oppresses and dominates us. We must cultivate an awareness of the ways cultural pedagogy operates so we can scold when appropriate and rewrite contaminated texts whenever possible. Kinderculture is primarily a pedagogy of pleasure and, as such, cannot be defeated merely by removing our children from it. We must, instead, devise strategies of resistance proceeding from an understanding of the relationship between pedagogy, knowledge production, identity formation, desire and, of course, the contextualization of teaching.

SITUATING KINDERCULTURE IN CULTURAL STUDIES AND PEDAGOGY

We can clarify and discuss questions about kinderculture and its relationship to cultural pedagogy within the academic field known as cultural studies. Kinderculture resides at the intersection of educational and childhood studies, curriculum theory and cultural studies. Defining cultural studies can raise problems in that its adherents avoid traditional academic disciplinary definitions. Nevertheless, cultural studies includes the effort to produce an interdisciplinary (or "counterdisciplinary") way of studying, interpreting and often evaluating cultural practices in historical, social and theoretical contexts. Refusing to equate "culture" with high culture, cultural studies scholars attempt to examine the diversity of a society's artistic, institutional and communicative expressions and practices. Because it takes up cultural expressions traditional social scientists often ignore, cultural studies is often equated with the study of popular culture. Yet the equation misleads: Although cultural studies addresses popular culture, that is not its exclusive concern. Indeed, the interests of cultural studies scholars are much broader, including in particular the "rules" of academic study itself—for example, the various discursive practices that guide scholarly endeavor and the legitimization of forms of data representation.

Thus, cultural studies promises exciting new ways of studying childhood education, with its emphasis on the discursive dynamics of the field. How do children embody kinderculture? How do the power dynamics embedded in kinderculture produce pleasure and pain in their daily lives? How can critically grounded parents, teachers, child psychologists and childhood professionals in general gain a view of children that accounts for the effect of popular culture on their self-images and world views? What effect does the kinderculture curriculum exert within and outside of schools? Questions such as these open new domains of analysis in childhood studies as they seek out previously marginalized voices and the vantage points they bring to both scholarly and practitioner-based conversation (Grossberg, 1995; Nelson, Treichler & Grossberg, 1992).

While we welcome the benefits of cultural studies of childhood, we are wary of expressions of elitism within the discourse of cultural studies itself, a tendency made more disturbing by the claim by cultural studies to the moral high ground of a politics of inclusivity. Unfortunately, academia traditionally regards the study of children as a low-status exercise; so far, at least, cultural studies has acquiesced in this power-status dynamic and has generally avoided studies of childhood. The cultural studies scholars avoid children as their subjects; kinderculture fills this gap and promotes a new literature in the area.

THE VALUE OF THE CURRICULUM OF POPULAR CULTURE

Studies of traditional forms of kinderculture—fairy tales, for one prominent example—have, of course, granted scholars insights into the hard-to-reach domains of child consciousness. Moreover, the more disturbing and violent the image or the fairy tale, some would argue, the more insight we gain into the "primitive" feelings that shape us in early childhood and guide us toward adulthood. Understanding the connection between kinderculture and childhood desire and feeling points adults toward the *Lebenswelt* (life world) of children and grants them access to childhood perceptions (Paul, 1994).

The study of children's popular culture goes beyond providing insights into childhood consciousness to provide new pictures of culture in general, however. Thus kinderculture inadvertently suggests what is disturbing us in our everyday lives and what irritants chafe our individual and collective subconsciousnesses. As we analyze G.I. Joe, we notice the connection between Joe and changing public perceptions of the role of the military in American society. The Hasbro Corporation changed both its marketing strategies and the physical appearance of G.I. Joe himself in response to the firm's sociological impressions of the public mood. An analysis of something as basic as a toy could provide a clearer insight than traditional sources into the social history of American perceptions of war and diplomatic policy (Axtell, 1996).

In addition, of course, these kindercultural analyses highlight the ideological curriculum such toys deliver to American children. Research into the history of Disney's Huey, Dewey and Louie, Donald Duck's nephews, follows the evolution of the comic strip as it paralleled American political themes. David Kunzle's (1992) study of the progression of Disney's duck family from the 1930s through the Vietnam War showed how the dominant themes in American political history were played out in the comics. Kunzle concluded that Disney propagandizing is hardly surprising given Walt Disney's conservative ideology and the racist aims of the American war efforts. As children and adults laughed through the decades at the selfish antics of Scrooge McDuck and the cleverness, silliness and accomplishments of the three nephew ducks, Disney surreptitiously planted persuasive ideological and philosophical seeds.

POWER, PLEASURE AND KINDERCULTURE

To encourage understandings of kinderculture that lead to democratic pedagogies for childhood at the cultural, familial and educational levels, cultural studies scholars connected to a democratic pedagogy for children repeatedly explain how children's consciousnesses can be galvanized around issues of social justice and egalitarian power relations. Thus, they often focus their analyses on exposing the fingerprints of power left by the corporate producers of kinderculture and their likely effects on the psyches of U.S. children. Appreciating the ambiguity and complexity of power, those committed to a democratic pedagogy challenge manipulative and racist, sexist and class-biased entertainment for children. They are equally opposed to those other manifestations of kinderculture that promote violence and social and psychological pathologies. Children's entertainment, like other social spheres, is a contested public space in which different social, economic and political interests compete for control. Unfortunately, as we have pointed out, overt discussions of power make Americans uncomfortable, and that discomfort allows power wielders to hide behind sanctimony or escape notice altogether while shaping cultural expressions and public policies in their own interests—interests that often conflict with those of less powerful social groups such as children.

Americans tend to be poor students of power. All too often the analyses of power in the literature critical scholars publish are vague beyond use. To clarify, then, when we refer to "power wielders" in America we refer not merely to a social class or category of humans. Applying John Fiske's (1993) use of the term "power bloc," we refer to particular social formations designated by race, class, gender, language, sexuality and ethnicity that enjoy special access to various resources (for example, money, information, cultural capital, the media) that they can use for economic or political gain. Retaining power requires a panoply of strategies aimed at maintaining the status quo and keeping it running with as little friction (social conflict) as possible. Therefore, those individuals and groups that profit most from existing power relations find it advisable to protect them from pests such as academic skeptics. When studying this power bloc, we borrow Fiske's idea that it can be more useful to ask "what it *does* than what it *is*" (1993, p. 11).

Importantly, as we said, the application of the power bloc in the production of kinderculture does not imply a conspiracy of diabolical corporate and political kingpins churning out material to harm our children intentionally. Rather, the idea revolves around alliances of interests that may never include individual relationships between representatives of the interests or organizations in question. In fact, power-bloc alliances are often temporary, coming together around a particular issue but falling apart when the issue fades.

As you can see, power is a complex and ambiguous concept. But because of the power bloc's inherent contradictions, it rarely dominates absolutely. Along the lines of its contradictions may exist points of contestation that open opportunities for democratic change. Larry Grossberg (1995) suggested that because power never gets all it wants, opportunities for challenging its authority arise constantly. In this context we can examine the corporate production of kinderculture, analyzing the ways power both represses the production of democratic artifacts and produces pleasure for children. If power were always a matter of "just saying no" to children's desires, it would gain little authority in their eyes. The power of Disney, Mattel, Hasbro, Warner Brothers and McDonald's is never greater than when it produces pleasure for children. Recent cultural studies of consumption link it to the identify formation of the consumer, meaning that to some degree we are what we consume (Warde, 1994). Status in one's subculture, individual creations of style, knowledge of cultural texts, role in the community of consumers, emulation of fictional characters, and internalization of values promoted by popular cultural expressions all contribute to one's identity. Popular culture provides children with intense emotional experiences often unmatched in any other phase of their lives. It is hardly surprising that such energy and intensity exert powerful influences on self-definition—that is, on the ways children choose to organize their lives.

Obviously, power mixed with desire produces an explosive cocktail; the colonization of desire, however, is not the end of the story. Power permeates both the conscious and the subconscious in a way that evokes desire—to be sure—but also guilt and anxiety. The intensity of the guilt and anxiety a child may experience as a result of his or her brush with power is inseparable from the cultural context in which he or she lives. Desire may take a back seat to the *repression* of desire in the construction of child consciousness and unconsciousness and the production of identity (Donald, 1993). The cocktail's effects may last longer than first assumed, as earlier repression may reveal itself later in bizarre and unpredictable ways. To make this observation about the relationship among power, desire and repression of desire and the way it expresses itself at the psychological level is not to deny human agency or self-direction.

While the power bloc has certainly commodified kinderculture, however, both adults and children can successfully deflect its repressive elements. The role of the critical childhood professional involves helping children develop what John Fiske (1993) called the "affective moments of power evasion." Using their abilities to "reread" Disney films along the fault lines of gender or to reencode Barbie and Ken in a satirical mode, children take their first steps toward self-assertion and power resistance. While such affective moments of power evasion hardly constitute the ultimate expression of resistance, they do provide a space around which teachers can inculcate and students can assimilate more significant forms of critical consciousness and civic action. Kinderculture is not to be changed or censored, merely critically read by the consumers of a socially aware curriculum.

MEDIA AND POPULAR CULTURE LITERACY

The recent information explosion and the media saturation, with its access to private realms of human consciousness, have imposed a sort of social vertigo often called "hyperreality." Hyperreality exaggerates the importance of power wielders in all phases of human experience. Its many signifiers in everything from megabytes to TV advertising diminish our ability either to find meaning or to engender a passion for commitment. With so much power-generated information bombarding their senses, both adults and children lose the faith that they can make sense of anything (Kincheloe, 1995). Thus the existence of hyperreality forces us to rethink our conversation about literacy. As Semali & Pailliotet (1999) recently argued, children who have been educated by popular culture approach literacy from a different angle. Media literacy becomes not some subtle and slight addition to a traditional curriculum but a basic skill necessary to negotiating one's identity, values and well-being in power-soaked hyperreality. Few schools considered—let alone seriously discussed such ideas. Mainstream education has yet to view either media literacy or power as topics for children (or even adults). As Peter McLaren and his colleagues (1995) found, the same educators who reject the study of media literacy or kinderculture are the ones who must cope with its effects.

Jan Jipson and Ursi Reynolds (1997) described their efforts at cultivating a critical media literacy among practicing graduate-level educators. As their course progressed they watched students shift their analysis of the effects of media-based kinderculture from the women and children in "TV land" to themselves, and through themselves to their own children and students. The course motivated Jipson and Reynolds's students to teach their own students ways of analyzing media and the effects of its cultural pedagogy. In particular, the early education teachers in the class came to define one aspect of their educational task as encouraging media literacy among the parents of their students. We consider one point in this context extremely important: As Peter McLaren, Rhonda Hammer, David Sholle and Susan Reilly argue in *Rethinking Media Literacy: A Critical Pedagogy of Representation* (1995), a critical understanding of media culture requires students not simply to develop an ability to interpret media meanings but also to understand the ways they themselves consume and invest in media. Such an attempt encourages both critical thinking and self-analysis, as students begin to realize that they do not necessarily make their everyday decisions freely and rationally. Rather, they are encoded and inscribed by emotional and bodily commitments relating to the production of desire and mood, all of which lead, in Noam Chomsky's famous phrase, to the "manufacture of consent."

DEVIL OR ANGEL? THE COMMERCIAL AND DEMOCRATIC IMPULSES OF TELEVISION

Commercial television in America has always straddled the conflicting demands of commerce and democracy, and any study of kinderculture will find these competing dynamics at work at various levels of the texts under examination. When analysts and consumers begin to understand the cultural authority children's television and other entertainment forms exert, the bifurcated imperatives for the medium begin to take on significance. Television's democratic moments are profound but far too rare. The exposure of Joseph McCarthy's insanity, the evils of racial segregation, the perils of pollution, the most obvious abuses of patriarchy, the inhumane excesses of Vietnam and the criminality of Watergate undoubtedly represent the zenith of TV's democratic impulse. Ironically, the consequence of these successes has been corporate restraints on and government regulation of any attempt to replicate such achievement; witness the Bush Administration's restrictions on the press coverage of the Gulf War so as to prevent "another Vietnam." When such media management combines with TV's tendency to fragment and decontextualize those issues it chooses to broadcast, events are often stripped of their meaning. The emptiness and confusion cognitively impair those children who depend heavily on television for their entertainment and thus for their worldviews (Kellner, 1990). TV's curriculum for today's children has not been crafted by media moguls interested in projecting the principles of democracy. Commercial concerns dictate media kinderculture, and profit margins are too important to waste time on concerns for the well-being of children.

Thus, you will not find society's most influential teachers in schools; nor is the nation's children's policy constructed by elected officials in Washington, D.C. America's corporate producers of kinderculture are the most influential pedagogues and education policymakers. Henry Giroux (1997) found blurred boundaries between entertainment, education and commerce, as Disney imagineers inject their teachings into chidren's dream worlds. Giroux found nothing transparent about children's TV or movies, however, their clear messages delivered directly to America's children with the intent of eliciting particular beliefs and behaviors serving the interests of those who produce the messages. Bifurcated as

TV's imperatives may be, democracy takes a backseat to money-driven logic. Next to those who promote the many "products" of kinderculture, child advocates have only limited access to the airwaves. Those corporations that advertise children's consumer paraphernalia sell a "consumption theology" that, in effect, promises redemption and happiness via the prescribed ritual: consumption. Advertising and pleasure production run on a direct line through the imaginative landscapes of our children, a mindscape children use to define their view of America.

Educators, child professionals and parents should understand that most people are products of the mechanisms of power, a reality that often goes unnoticed in the everyday world. The central contradiction of human consciousness at first confounds its observers: People make culture, yet culture makes people. Meaning emerges at the level of the social, where the interaction and the ways of seeing (ideologies) it produces shape individual consciousness. As a social and ideological phenomenon, consciousness is constructed both by its contact with culture and by an interaction with a view of culture—a view "edited" by ideological refraction.

"Refraction" refers to how the slant of light changes when it passes from one medium to another—for example, from a crystal to a wall. The refracted light we see on the wall differs from the light that originally encountered the crystal; one aspect of the light's "reality" has been displaced. "Ideology" is like the crystal in that it refracts perceptions of the lived world. This is not to say that the light (perceptions of the world) prior to its encounter with the crystal (ideology) is some Godlike pristine light (reality). No transcendental, totalizing view of the light (of reality) exists; we always perceive it from some position in the web of reality. Leaving this metaphor behind, the point is that kinderculture provides a mechanism for ideological refraction. It is a social force producing particular meanings that induce children (and adults) to interpret events within a specific range of possibilities (Steinberg & Kincheloe, 1996; Donald, 1993; Mumby, 1989; Thiele, 1986).

Kinderculture speaks with an authorial voice that can be either candid or covert about its ideological inscription (Lincoln, 1995). Not surprisingly, corporate-produced kinderculture chooses Monty Hall's *Let's Make a Deal* curtain number three. Kinderculture colonizes American consciousness so as to repress conflict and differences. Thus the critical childhood professional should understand ideology, its refraction and its effect on consciousness construction as the conceptual basis for any attempt to expose the pretense of kinderculture as a politically pristine, uncontested sphere of social activity. Just as classroom teaching and the school curriculum are never simply neutral and disinterested transmitters of data, corporate kinderculture follows an agenda.

McDonald's family values ad promotions of the early Reagan years and the company's financial ties to the right wing of the Republican Party suggest both how American politics works and the context within which kinderculture is designed and then displayed. Such an understanding does not require us to deprive our five-year-olds of their Happy Meals. Our understanding of the patriarchal depiction of Kevin's (Macauley Culkin's) mother as a failed caretaker of children in two of the *Home Alone* movies while excusing his equally culpable father for his part in the abandonment grants insight into the way misogyny is transmitted across generations (Kincheloe, 1995). It does not mean we, as gender police, must keep our eight-year-olds from renting the movie. An explanation of what is happening along gender lines and a mutual celebration of Kevin's self-sufficiency might even turn *Home Alone* into a positive critical literacy experience.

Childhood professionals have rarely been students of power, but given the power of kinderculture, they should be now. As students of the power dynamics of children's popular culture, parents and professionals would begin to understand child behavior from a new perspective. Given their power to exploit the private lives of children, the corporate producers of kinderculture constantly destabilize their identities by introducing new products—toys, movies, television shows, video games, fashions, texts—designed to control their desires and consumption patterns. The study of power vis-à-vis children and contemporary kinderculture can provide educators and parents with a conceptual tool for criticizing social, economic and political practices and explaining how they restrict young people's life choices.

The artifacts of culture, from toys to automobiles (if a difference exists there), have always helped us create ourselves and our social affiliations. Our task as "kinderculturalists" is to expose these invisible but influential forces, these micropractices that shape our children's lives. This task is complicated by the fact that those most visible and unquestioned in commonsensical practices operating on children at play tend to be those most saturated with power. An ability to recognize them lends us the wisdom to distinguish between just and unjust kindertexts, between manipulative and liberating corporate activities. Thus empowered, we can piece together the complex and often ambiguous ways corporate actions modify children's behavior, and how advertising and its promotion of childhood hedonism produce an ethic of pleasure and a redefinition of authority. These issues lie at the core of who we are as a people and who we want to become (Kellner, 1992; Wartenberg, 1992; Seiter, 1993; Ball, 1992; Grossberg, 1995; Abercrombie, 1994).

CORPORATE POWER AND KINDERCULTURE

The study of power and kinderculture can produce insights into American politics that may at first seem only incidental. When educators and parents start to explore child activist avenues, they immediately notice the trend to concentrate power into fewer and increasingly corporate hands. Many child advocates and concerned parents then notice that the corporate-dominated power bloc tends to retaliate against those who question the impact of its products. In light of the failure of oppositional institutions to challenge corporate hegemony, corporations enjoy a mostly open invitation to produce almost any kinderculture that promises a profit. Of the thousands of interest organizations or "pressure groups" active in Washington, D.C., most are business or corporate sponsored. Public-interest organizations are outnumbered ten-to-one in formal congressional proceedings on regulatory issues. The antidemocratic implications of this system, with its corporate curriculum designed to adjust public opinion to support business agendas, chill the true democratic citizen (Greider, 1992).

Much of this expansion of corporate power has occurred recently. When pollsters in the 1970s noticed a decline in public confidence in businesses and corporations, corporate leaders jumped into action. To counter public perceptions of them as greedy and indifferent to the public good, corporations diverted hundreds of millions of dollars to public relations advertising designed to promote corporate images and ideologic dispositions. Designed from the start to engineer consent, these legitimation ads focused on treasured common experiences in our lives, families and childhoods, parental events in particular. Among many others, the Ethan Allen Furniture Company adopted the family, childhood and parental triad, attaching its corporate identity to a right-wing notion of traditional family values. The Ethan Allen legitimation ads talked about the rise of juvenile delinquency and its threat to those of "us" who care about "our" children. Our treasured ways of raising our children, the ads warned, are under threat by an unidentified group of individuals who disdain traditional family values and the sanctity of old-fashioned ideals.

Discussions of McDonald's family-values–oriented legitimation ads documented one of the more obvious examples of the corporate colonization of family values and parental and child consciousness (Kincheloe, 1995, 1996). In one particular ad, a young boy and a younger girl stroll along a tree-lined trail in a park. The camera watches them walk away. The small girl runs to catch up with her big brother. Both wear oversized baseball uniforms with "Tigers" spelled across their backs and their baseball caps on backwards. They are "adorable" *American* children. The little sister loves her older brother, who waits for her when she gets too far behind and lets her grab his shirttail for support on the way home. The musical accompaniment sings, "You, you're the one. Your moms and dads and brothers, sisters and sons. We're stronger for each other." McDonald's set out here, of course, to associate its image with the best interests of children and to legitimate itself as a company with a heart, an organization that would remain responsive to the family's best interests. Viewers need not remember the specifics to allow the ad to work as McDonald's intended, to absorb the emotional valence it imprints and to make the positive association between treasured childhood memories and the golden arches.

Corporations and the free enterprise system that protects their right to operate more or less as they see fit bring us these warm, familial moments. True patriots would protect them from those subversives who would regulate them and interfere with all the good they do. The truth is obviously irrelevant in these legitimation ads. In fact, in the early 1980s General Motors ran a multimillion-dollar ad campaign demonstrating—to the great hilarity of the United Auto Workers—the extraordinary amount of influence the line workers exerted in automobile production decisionmaking. As for McDonald's veracity, Kincheloe (1996) unearthed founder Ray Kroc's explicit demands that McDonald's employees keep their family concerns far down the priority list if they hoped to climb Kroc's corporate ladder.

McDonald's corporate culture is hardly unique in the corporate pantheon. Indeed, Goldman (1992) traced the decline of traditional family life and the safe climate for children to corporate development. After the end of World War II corporate America pursued a variety of policies jeopardizing traditional family arrangements, including intensified expectations of employees, the promotion of hedonistic and individualized life-styles, opposition to government aid to families fragmented by economic need and the promotion of consumption patterns designed to pit children against parents and parents against children in the battle to purchase satisfaction. Nevertheless, legitimation ads have worked well enough to protect companies from demonstrating authentic social responsibility.

THE POWER TO REPRESENT: CORPORATE HISTORICAL REVISIONISM

As parents and child advocates become more attentive to those pedagogical locales where child consciousness is shaped, they begin to notice the influence of such giant corporations as Time-Warner, Disney-ABC, Murdoch Communications, Turner Broadcasting and the other conglomerates that control information and entertainment lock, stock and barrel. So powerful are these corporations that they can literally rewrite American history to suit their ideological needs. Because all political positions embraced in the present reflect particular ways of viewing the past, the manipulation of history has a powerful effect. For example, children who study the Disney Frontierland curriculum, with its uncomplicated portrayal of brave and pure Europeans fighting the savage Indians as they follow God's plan of Manifest Destiny, may well become insensitive to serious issues of justice. Boys and girls who learn at the Disney School of Eurocentric Knowledge take part in a political curriculum with serious implications for the formation of their ideological consciousnesses. Jeanne Brady (1997) analyzed the corporate historical revisionism that took place in the marketing of the American Girl Dolls series, with any suggestion of conflict and exploitation repressed so as to keep unquestioning citizens oblivious of struggle and imperialism. Even when the company included an African American doll, Addy, an exslave living during the Civil War, the marketers removed those illustrations of Addy they considered "too graphic and depressing" for children and decreed that slaves should have smiling faces.

In 1995 Disney reinvented Pocahontas. Historical documents present Pocahontas as a twelve-year-old "Indian" girl who befriended early white settlers. The Disney Corporation took an imperial band of British sailors and made them an innocent group of adventurers out to meet new people and visit new lands. The move turned Pocahontas into a mature twenty-year-old "saving the day" for her people and her new friends. Attempting to atone for all its previous sexist and racist stereotypes, the Disney Corporation presented Pocahontas as an athletic, vibrant young woman determined to help both the new "citizens" and her own people. It made no mention of the inconvenient fact that at the age of thirteen Pocahontas left for England, stayed there and married John Rolfe, a great pioneer in the trade of tobacco, and became part of the British aristocracy. Nor does one find Disney mentioning the Indian wars and genocide that took place, wiping out many tribes and pushing others farther west. In one scene Disney has the British and the Indians juxtaposed in a song that echoes the badly beaten Los Angeles motorist Rodney King's plea, "Why can't we just get along?" Acknowledging that each culture has its idiosyncrasies, the song ends in a mutual recognition that diversity must be acknowledged (Steinberg, 1997). (Interestingly enough, the British sailors all have names and distinct faces whereas the natives all look exactly alike and stand in clumps without demonstrating any interaction or making any interpersonal remarks.)

Even as the Disney Corporation tries to atone for its racist depictions, it continues to lack the sensitivity to detail that might free it from the institutional racism and sexism still alive at the studio. Such curricular sanitization hints at America's crisis of democracy in the new millennium, a threat fueled by a reluctance among political leaders and corporations to address the growing divisions between classes, racial polarization, accelerating poverty, an expanding underclass living in hopeless urban ghettos and an exponentially increasing number of poor children.

When we examine the 1980s corporate takeover of TV in this context we see the power of cultural pedagogy more clearly. During the Reagan-Bush era, corporate America seized a golden opportunity to capture the major television networks and use them to advance their own political and economic interests. Stories that might grant children and their parents insight into the greed of the corporate world went unbroadcast. Though television is a public utility required by law to serve the public interest—a service supposedly separate from and critical of the agendas of state and corporate interests—with corporations securely controlling it, television began to exercise its great power to represent the world to and for children and their parents. Where the great military powers could once geographically occupy and economically control vast territories for exploitation, national and international corporations now occupy mindscapes, the realm of consciousness (Kellner, 1990; Fiske, 1993). As the colonizers of the new millennium these organizations profit richly from their occupation of the human psyche, a piracy that puts the plundering of their military antecedents to shame.

Changing Childhood with Kinderculture and Popular Culture

Even as childhood changes, often in response to its contact with kinderculture and other, more adult manifestations of media culture, all audiences of popular culture play important roles in making their own meanings of its texts. In fact, kinderculture and adult popular culture exert specific influences, affecting maps that emerge in the social contexts in which children encounter these cultural expressions. Because today's parents no longer control the cultural experiences of their children, they have lost the role parents once played in shaping their children's values and worldviews.

In the 1920s, with the protected childhood firmly established, children had few experiences that fell outside of either parental supervision or child-produced activities shared with other children. Since the 1950s, corporations rather than parents or children themselves produce most of our children's experiences. Television shows, movies (now on pay-per-view cable), video games and music (with earphones that ensure seclusion from adults) have become the child's private domain. As you examine the corporate curriculums of kinderculture, contrast the traditional ideas of childhood as a time of innocence and adult dependency with the child's current access to popular culture.

THE DILEMMA OF THE POSTMODERN CHILDHOOD

Such a new reality presents adults (parents and teachers, in particular) with a complex dilemma within postmodern childhood. The contemporary child's access to commercial kinderculture and popular culture both motivates that child to become a hedonistic consumer and undermines the innocence, the protected status from the tribulations of adult existence children have experienced since roughly the 1850s. Advocates of traditional family values and corporal discipline for children understand that something has changed and that, for some reason, authority has broken down. We often hear these advocates attribute the breakdown of authority to feminism and its invitation for mothers to pursue careers outside the home and to permissive liberals who oppose corporal punishment and other harsh forms of child control. Adult authority over children has broken down, but not because of feminist mothers or milksop liberals. The electronic media of hyperreality has given children access to the adult world and subverted their consciousness of themselves as dependent. The new self-assured consciousness mixes the poor with such institutions as the traditional family and the authoritarian school, based as they are on a view of children as incapable of making decisions for themselves.

Why have children become so defiant, so difficult to control and so violent in recent decades? Part of the answer is that they see themselves differently than adults see them. Postmodern children are unaccustomed to thinking and operating as little tykes who need permission and approval from adults. Not all children evidence kinderculture and their access to popular culture this way; different children respond differently. The reality remains, however, that adults have lost much of the authority they used to have because they once had information, they "knew things" sheltered children did not know. Yet children now see the world as it is (or at least as corporate information producers depict it). Examples of the effects of children's information access and the new view of themselves it produces abound. In the *Home Alone* movies, mentioned earlier, Macauley Culkin's character, Kevin, constantly confronts and is annoyed by adult assumptions that a ten-year-old is just a child. In the *Problem Child* movies the problem child casts knowing glances at the camera (and his fellow kids-with-adult-knowledge), indicating his adult take on an unfolding situation. Depictions of this real-life dynamic have dominated movies centered on children from the early 1970s to the present (Kincheloe, 1995).

This new access children have to adult knowledge about the world and the changes in the nature of childhood it produces have undermined the conceptual-curricular-managerial assumptions upon which schooling has depended. One could even argue that these cultural changes should force schools to reorganize themselves from the bottom up. The current school curriculum is organized as a continuum of experience developmentally sequenced as if children learned about the world only in school and only in progressive increments. Right-wing efforts to protect and petrify outmoded school organizations and the traditional ideas of childhood that come with them are, in some ways, understandable but ultimately doomed to failure. We cannot protect our children from knowledge of the world hyperreality has presented to them. Such a task would demand a sequestration tantamount to solitary confinement. The task that faces us is daunting but essential: We must develop education, parenting skills and social institutions that address this cultural revolution in a way that teaches our children to make sense of the chaos of information they meet in hyperreality. Engaging this challenge, school becomes less an institution of information delivery and more a hermeneutic site—that is, a place where meaning is made and understanding and interpretation are engendered. The task is difficult but road maps are available.

THE BACKLASH: LOATHING FOR THE WORLDLY CHILD

The worldly postmodern child often appears in popular culture as a "smart-ass." This child can be easy to hate, a theme Joe Kincheloe (1995, 1996) traced in movies about children in recent decades. Children with power are especially threatening to adults, a fear that has manifested itself particularly in horror films since the early 1970s. *The Exorcist,* which presented the evil child Regan as a monster in need of punishment, encouraged an entire school of evil children movies including *The Omen, It's Alive, It Lives Again, Firestarter, Children of the Corn, Halloween* and *The Brood.* The precocious child has always been a threat to what Valerie Polakow (1992) called "the order paradigm," a way of seeing that demands pedagogic adherence to the established developmental sequence and reward for the docile and obedient student. Indeed, something about the child-savant who learns about life "out of sequence" from television and other electronic media does seem to disrupt the established order. Independent and self-sufficient youths with "inappropriate" insight into the adult world constitute the monsters in the evil children movies.

The recent film demonization of children is impressive: The murderer in *Halloween* is six years old; in *Firestarter* the young female protagonist, Charley, uses her power most effectively in destroying those around her; in *The Other* the evil child kills his father and carries around his severed finger; the rebellious students in *The Exorcist* are objects of revulsion who must be controlled at any cost (Paul, 1994).

All these films—these cultural artifacts—express something resembling a fear of knowledgeable children. One important theme in the recent history of childhood thus emerges: parents becoming fearful of the latent monster in all children. The middle-class emphasis on order and equilibrium intensifies in response to these repressed parental fears. The precocious child must be rendered obedient, the body must be regulated, "it's-for-your-own-good" echoes in the land. Parental fears find legal expression in new laws defining new classes of juvenile crime, in calls to lower the age for capital punishment to as young as eleven, in making public juvenile records, in establishing boot camps for young criminals, in outlawing the sale of spray paint to curb graffiti and in eliminating age guidelines in the treatment of youthful offenders (Vogel, 1994). Gang activity is fought by banning bandannas and gang "colors." School boards constantly pass trivial, even silly regulations to address serious social dilemmas. A bandanna does not create a street gang.

Recently published children's books attempt to frighten precocious children who become "too big for their britches" back into both obedience and a new form of dependence. Written to counteract too much child identification with Macauley Culkin's precocious, independent and successful character in *Home Alone,* Molly Mia Stewart's *Ellen Is Home Alone* (1993) paints a gruesome picture for children who stay home alone. Her message is simple and straightforward: Staying home alone is scary; as a child you are incompetent; if you try to act like an adult you will be severely punished; if you resist parental control you may die. Stewart's infantiphobia and the "hellfire pedagogy" she uses to enforce discipline harken back to Puritan minister Jonathan Edwards's imagery of children among those sinners in the hands of an angry God (see Chapter 4), or the conclusion of *The Bad Seed* in which a lightning bolt strikes and kills the precocious Rhoda.

FAMILY VALUES: CODE WORDS FOR CHILD NEGLECT

If you look carefully, you can find hiding behind the right-wing call for a "return to family values" an antifamily, antichild agenda. This antifamily aspect of the family values slogan establishes discouraging obstacles for working-class families— working single mothers in particular—and great suffering in the everyday lives of their children. In the Reagan-Bush revolution of the 1980s and the Gingrich-Dole insurrection of the 1990s, "family values" served as a cover for greed and excess in the former and mean-spirited punishment of the poor in the latter. As a cover for more malevolent goals, "family values" has served the right-wing agenda well. Providing the facade of concern, the slogan helps conservatives convince millions of Americans that new monies for education, antipoverty programs and child care are futile when the real problem is the absence of family values: a complete abstraction. A central but often unasked question should occur at this point: How many families struggling in poverty would be saved if they embraced traditional family values? The answer: very few. To understand the economic problems that plague an alarmingly large proportion of America's children, one must explore a progression of structural changes in the global economy in the 1970s, 1980s and 1990s. These changes have rendered traditional family values and structures characterized by working fathers and homemaking, child-rearing mothers inconsistent with the new economic realities.

The family, Norman Denzin (1987) observed, has been a locale of political and ideological struggles since the late eighteenth century. These struggles recently succeeded in establishing the realization that the all-American nuclear family is no longer the social norm. In fact, as we noted in Chapters 1 and 11, it may *never* have been the familial model most Americans experience (Coontz, 1992). In the present era the nuclear family is a site of submerged hostilities as precocious children wrestle with their parents for adult privileges and material goods. As a result, screenplay writers and movie directors must walk a political tightrope over a canyon of family and child-related issues. The *Home Alone* movies, for example, work hard to camouflage the familial fault lines the plot introduced. The right-wing family-values rhetoric represents one response to the seismic waves erupting from these family battles and from the fear of precocious children. Precocious behavioral problems, the conservative argument goes, arose out of a liberal age of permissiveness. The problems of undisciplined youth, the conservatives maintain, are especially prevalent among the poor and the racial minorities, and the only way to deal with these "sociopaths" is to get tough (Griffin, 1993). With the help of wayward feminists, the rhetoric continues, family values and traditional family structures continue to erode to the point at which jailing youth is the only alternative to chaos. So interpreted, the rhetoric of family values hardly conveys a loving, supportive approach to child advocacy.

The political climate for children has indeed grown hostile with Newt Gingrich's *Boys' Town* solutions and Republican social service cuts in the name of "tough love." Incarceration for criminal children is, of course, directly antithetical to crime prevention, rehabilitation or the reduction of repeat offenses. Juveniles in adult institutions are five times more liable to be sexually assaulted, twice as liable to be battered by institutional employees and 50 percent more liable to be beaten with a weapon than young people in juvenile facilities. Repeat offenses by juveniles in adult institutions are also significantly more frequent (Vogel, 1994). Equally depressing is the discourse of many liberal child-advocacy groups premised on an instrumental view of children requiring that public investments in child welfare demonstrate quantitative cost-benefit outcomes. In this situation, childhood intervention programs endure continual tests of their academic practicality, social appropriateness, crime reduction achievements and effectiveness at decreasing dependency. A person with such a mind-set is generally indifferent to the need for a quality child care system in a nation in which more than half the children under six have working mothers. Often the funds are withheld on the family-values, catch–22 belief that mothers, not child care workers (or husbands), should care for their children at home. Thus, right-wing profamily policies continue to erect obstacles to family welfare that cause increased suffering among children (Polakow, 1992).

The Cold Reality of Violence in Families and among Children

As often as we locate problems within the discourses of family values and child advocacy and deplore the fear and hatred of children we find in the public subconscious, we acknowledge the difficulties of child rearing and the current frustrations of parents and teachers. Child and juvenile crime is a fact of life and continues to escalate in urban, rural and suburban settings. Every other home in America is now a scene of family violence—not typically perpetrated by children—at least once a year. How surprising can child violence figures be when we learn that children in 60 percent of American homes annually confront physical abuse—including sexual abuse, hitting and battering—not to mention random acts of emotional abuse (Denzin, 1987)? Whatever the context, the reality is unavoidable: Children are increasingly involved, passively or actively, in violence. We believe that kinderculture and popular culture in general constitute a contributory social dynamic to violence among young people.

No one has yet been able to establish statistically valid causal connections between media violence and violent behaviors in children; variously worded research questions produce divergent results. From a more qualitative perspective, however, violent kinderculture generally presents violence as the most effective problem-solving method available in the daily lives of children. Competitive pressures push the sponsors of children's television programs and producers of cinematic kinderculture to manufacture ever more violent products that turn increasingly higher profits. Doug Kellner (1996) argued that such pressures are certain to intensify as the number of television channels increases and competition builds. In his research on professional wrestling, Aaron Gresson (1995) found the exhibitions tailor-made for postmodern audiences lusting after the primitive spectacle of brutality and violence. Like other forms of media violence, wrestling glorifies barbarity; indeed, it lays the foundation for a larger aestheticization of violence with blood and sweat sailing through the air to the strains of romantic melodies. Watching children glued to the television while bullets explode torsos and spew brains is a sobering but all-too-common parental experience in hyperreality.

As the video game industry establishes the rules for the development of interactive TV, new forms of aesthetic violence couched in racist and sexist contexts figure to follow and reinforce already-established expectations. In *Video Kids: Making Sense of Nintendo* Eugene Provenzo (1991) traced the escalating violence from the early video games (*Pac-Man* and *Space Invaders*) to those of the mid–1990s (*Double Dragon II* and *Streets of Rage*). To win the latter games, one must immerse oneself in the battle-for-survival virtual cosmos and learn to maim and kill all one's rivals. One establishes a tolerance for aggression, as violence becomes a "natural" amphetamine, a sanctioned entitlement to "get high on death" and kill the boredom of the postmodern childhood. Virtual violence is, of course, an abstract violence that removes brutality from its IRL (in real life) consequences. But some children imitate the actions of interactive characters, even though they understand perfectly well the fantasy behind the games and videos; there is nothing simplistic, linear or cause-and-effect in how children replicate media violence in their lives. Pathologies hidden in a particular subconscious may be triggered and brought to the surface by violent imprints of video games, wrestling, movies or television; other children with the same kindercultural experiences may be relatively unaffected (Provenzo, 1997).

KINDERCULTURE AND QUESTIONS OF JUSTICE

Any analysis of childhood today must attend to inferences about race-, class- and gender-related injustice embedded in the various kinderculture formats and then presented to child audiences. Many poor and minority children find that the world they have been encouraged to trust no longer works. They have seen their dreams stolen, replaced by a hopelessness that narrows their choices and ruins any impression they may have had that their actions can make a difference. World weary by the age of twelve, many children feel overwhelmed by everyday life in hyperreality. Overwhelmed by pressure and devoid of hope, too many children opt for suicide in the land of the free (Ferguson, 1994; Gaines, 1990; West, 1993). Kinderculture generally offers a welcome escape from such harsh realities. No wonder television viewing time is so high among poor and dispossessed children (Steinberg, 1997).

These sobering descriptions of the marginalized child's experience are absent from corporate-produced kinderculture. In a discussion of the *Mighty Morphin Power Rangers,* Peter McLaren and Janet Morris (1996) observed that children's media culture rarely takes into account the perspectives of the poor and racially or ethnically marginalized. In fact, kinderculture usually declines to challenge patriarchal power structures or provide alternative vantage points on the world. The "good *guys*" of kinderculture tend to be white males who fight the good fight for neoimperialist causes. The consumer product advertising that supports television programming for children seems oblivious to the gross economic inequalities it approvingly projects (Seiter, 1993). In the name of a "common culture," kinderculture ignores the experiences of economic inequality and the lived understandings of oppression that too many American children endure. In this manufactured context, questions of differences in children's levels of opportunity and privilege disappear. But note this important distinction: Cultural and racial differences may be represented by television, movie or print producers, but they are almost always dehistoricized and stripped of any depiction of the power differences that cause suffering among marginalized children and their parents (Kincheloe & Steinberg, 1997).

Television heroes typically come equipped with the dominant mainstream cultural values. As white, male, classless (that is to say, middle-class) protagonists, they don their WASP values to vanquish violent villains who often enough are nonwhite or even non-American. Like the Lone Ranger of the past, white heroes frequently tolerate a nonwhite or female "sidekick" to suggest overtly the value of diversity— a strategy that covertly registers the advisability of white male control over a diverse society (Fiske, 1993). Thus, kinderculture sometimes acknowledges the presence of difference; indeed, advertisers and marketers have enthusiastically embraced difference, from Jamaican Barbies to ethnic snack foods. But notice that Mattel's multicultural Barbies and American Girl Doll's Addy constitute a corporate "containment policy"—not of communism this time, but of creeping multiculturalism. We see at work here a niche marketing strategy that uses diversity as a method of reaching beyond standardized mass production's economies of scale. It is, however, a safe, common culture type of diversity that sanitizes and depoliticizes any challenge to the harmony of the status quo.

Racialized Kinderculture

An analysis of commercials aimed at children on cable television and Saturday morning network programs reveals advertising set in a WASP-oriented middle-class reality. The homes used as backdrops for toys are spacious, with generous play areas—suburban utopias. Talent agents report the ad casts tend to meet the "all-American" standard of appearance (that is, they tend to be white). When non-whites appear, they frequently lurk on the periphery (the left third of the screen), leaving the leading and instigating roles to white boys. Black characters in children's commercials often dance and play basketball and display vivaciousness or flaccid ("loose") bodily characteristics, they are not the scholars, the actors to a purpose, the children with secure vocational futures. More than most other child-oriented corporations, McDonald's employs African American children in its ads, but in racially mixed commercials rarely in the lead roles. The slightly out of focus nonwhite children in McDonald's commercials grace the edges of the picture. Below the conscious realization of their viewers, commercials that use nonwhite actors reproduce the racial hierarchies that privilege whites. In one McDonald's ad that links the corporation to traditional family values, the "families like yours" lyrics accompany an immigrant family arriving in America. But by the time the lyrics get to "yours," the scene has shifted to an upper-middle class WASP family. While referencing the great American melting pot, the commercial covertly labels "your" family, the now normalized all-American family, as white and upper-middle class (Seiter, 1993; Goldman, 1992).

Gendered Kinderculture

With all the gender analysis and reconceptualization that have taken place over recent decades, it surprises parents and educators that kinderculture can remain as gender differentiated as it does. While the gender analysis of popular culture advances, compiling important insights into media constructions of gender, kinderculture continues to promote delineated gender roles. Toy advertising for girls has changed little since the 1950s; missing only are references to how well toy stoves provide training for real home cooking and the demands of motherhood. Similarly, toy ads for boys show only minor alterations over the years. The adult male voice-over may be gone, but the close-ups of the toys and the boys' voices making engine and weapon sounds continue. Boys still become one with their toys, while girls, ever the adoring nurses, take care of their dolls.

As Henry Giroux (1997) pointed out, in Disney's animated films girls and women appear within constrictive gender roles. In the 1990s films *The Little Mermaid* and *The Lion King,* the women are subordinate to the men: Ariel, the mermaid, appears to be on a liberating journey against parental domination. But in the end she gives up her independence, trading her fin for legs so she can pursue her fair prince. In *The Lion King,* all the leaders are male recipients of patriarchal entitlement. After King Mufasa dies, the duplicitous Scar becomes the new monarch. The lionesses are powerless, granting Scar the same deference they had accorded Mufasa. The female lions have no agency, no moral sense; they serve merely as backdrops to the action the males initiate and they take part in. Similar gender dynamics characterize *Aladdin* and *Beauty and the Beast.* Recall, as well, that Pocahontas is depicted as repressing her love for John Smith to stay and help her people thrive. In each case the Disney studios show female sacrifices for either the greater familial or cultural good or the male good. For Disney, a woman's destiny is to serve those around her.

At work in these films and innumerable other manifestations of kinderculture is what Linda Christian-Smith and Jean Erdman (1997) call "hegemonic masculinity." Such patriarchal messages obviously hold serious implications for women, but they distort male development as well. Boys are encouraged by various forms of the kinderculture curriculum to assume patriarchal roles that appear to entitle them by birthright to define reality and enjoy the rewards of privilege by dominating subordinates. Such an identity, unfortunately, often requires the young boy to deny his connections with other people. Late twentieth-century American patriarchal culture defines manhood in terms of separation and self-sufficiency: The Clint Eastwood character comes to mind in his man-with-no-name, *High Plains Drifter* movies. Here was a man who was so alone he had no use for a name. Setting the standard for male disconnection, Eastwood's characters hid their feelings from the world. The only strategies for dealing with one's emotions hegemonic masculinity approves are evasion, bravado, boasting, lying and aggression. Attempting to master these strategies, young boys cultivate a "cool and detached" male pose around the time they enter the fifth or sixth grade. In its extreme manifestations, the pose negates public displays of emotion. Obviously crying is forbidden, but even smiling and displays of enthusiasm are discouraged (Nightingale, 1993). We think here of a friend who, at the age of forty, still vividly remembers an event at age five that shaped his view of himself and his masculinity. The day before he was to begin kindergarten, his father burst into his bedroom and confiscated several Barbie dolls from his toy box. Along with his trucks, blocks and soldiers, he had often played with these dolls passed down from his older sisters. His father looked at him sternly and said, "Now that you are going to school you will not play with dolls. No son of mine is going to be a sissy!" At this point the father ripped the heads and limbs off the dolls and threw them away. The violent message was indelibly imprinted in the boy's mind. Parents and teachers reinforce gender role stereotypes that have a lasting impact on youth. For example, how many young men are unprepared or incapable of nurturing a child because they have never been allowed to develop nurturing instincts at home or in school? How many young men grow up to "rip the limbs off" their partners and children?

The repression of emotions and personal detachment hegemonic masculinity teaches boys produces severe social dysfunctionality. Boys who are unable to deal with emotional conflict and the interpersonal dynamics of family and peer relationships grow up to be men who have difficulty loving. They often become the men who leave or abuse their wives and families, an ever-growing modern trend. Such social-psychological issues move the kinderculture gender curriculum to the front burner. They should convince teachers, parents and other citizens to examine McLaren and Morris's disturbing picture of the gender issues at work in *The Mighty Morphin Power Rangers,* with its patriarchal construction of the macho-military warrior prototype for boys. Some *Power Rangers* viewers notice that the show features both male and female characters; unfortunately, the female Rangers are weak characters who constantly rely on males for support. Moreover, Girl

Rangers exchange the feminine ethics of connectedness for the patriarchal macho "kick-butt" competitiveness. In this ethical universe, they occupy low-status positions in the warrior hierarchy and betray such "traditional female tendencies" as boyfriend identification and jealous competition with other girls over love interests. A home or school curriculum that takes kinderculture seriously helps children recognize and analyze these gender issues and their effects on the formation of self-concepts (Hauser & Jipson, 1998).

MISBEHAVING KINDERCULTURE

Popular films and music repeat those themes that appeal most to children and youth, and misbehavior is one of the most popular themes. As they watch *Beavis and Butthead* or *South Park,* children identify with labeling life itself as a state of being that "sucks." Adults tend to avoid these shows; however, they would do well to understand what makes these characters so popular with children and youth. MTV allows teachers as researchers to enter the world our students occupy and value. We do not advocate that anyone become a fan of shows such as *Beavis and Butthead,* but we do advocate becoming fans of our students. Exactly what makes them identify with these two losers? They act stupid and disgusting, yet youngsters seem to "get" their messages.

As parents and teachers, we can decide either to censor shows or to discuss their implications critically. Why do so many children agree that life "sucks," especially privileged middle-class suburban children? What makes their lives so difficult? Discussions and research, with their students taking part, empower both teachers and students with explanations and equip them with more questions.

As with television, the most popular films for youth also depend on the misbehavior theme. When Ferris Bueller took his day off, thousands of students "ditched" school in sympathy. The movie also suggested that the truly important happens *outside* of school. That frightens educators, as the truth so often does. Why do the five students on detention in *The Breakfast Club* discover essential meanings of life in each other? Adults are excluded from the conversation; indeed, much of the students' problems stem from the fact that both parents and teachers spend more time criticizing than communicating. Discussions of films popular with students invite them to help deconstruct a cultural artifact that is important to them. What does the filmmaker touch on that is so evocative? What is it that so many parents and teachers just "don't get"? Debates, deconstruction and discussion addressing kinderculture can open a dialogue between students and teachers, and dialogue leads to empowerment. Students become researchers into their own lived worlds when they bring their own curriculum and opinions into the discussion (Steinberg, 1997; Steinberg & Kincheloe, 1997).

Films allow students and teachers to apply fictional situations to real life. Films about teaching, for instance, can open frank and lively classroom conversations about what good teaching is and what constitutes a good student. What are reasonable expectations? Does school "work"? What would make school work better? What should we expect from students? from teachers? What responsibilities should both students and teachers respect within and outside the school? While film may not always provide apt or useful examples, through entertainment (kinderculture) it can certainly bring adults and students into a joint effort to understand both the film and each other (Dalton, 1999).

Music has always exerted a strong influence on youth. We can all recall turning up the local station in the morning, knowing the words to all the popular songs and spending (depending on our ages) our last dollar on a 45, an album, a tape or a new CD. Music resonates with the deepest human emotions. We can often say or hear in music what we cannot convey or gather in a conversation. Postmodern youth listens to a wide variety of music, much of it frightening, violent and angry. Knowing this music exists, listening to it and engaging in conversation about it invites students to explain why certain sounds and lyrics attract them. Once again, we ask here for no advocacy of "grunge rock" or "gangsta rap." But we do advocate learning what gangsta rap is and how it developed. What causes certain bands to destroy their instruments on stage, to tear at their bodies, to scar themselves, to scream and shout profanities? What causes certain students to bond with these bands and performers? Why does the music reach our youngsters when we adults so often fail?

Answering these questions is far from our goal here. Instead, we suggest that merely discussing them and knowing that strong influences far removed from a planned school curriculum remain very much the curriculum youth actually follows. We consider kinderculture the most influential curriculum of all, and it usually originates outside of the school, entering the school with the students. By becoming students of kinderculture ourselves we can reduce the alienation that youth and children so often infer from adults.

LEARNING TO UNDERSTAND KINDERCULTURE

Society's failure to recognize that power plays an inflated role in the shaping of personal experiences prevents any widespread understanding of the pedagogical power of popular culture in general and kinderculture in particular. Ironically, the relationship is so apparent that it often gets lost in its obviousness (Grossberg, 1995). Power produces images of the world and the people who inhabit it that make meaning for those who receive the images. The films, books, video games and television shows of kinderculture shape the way white children, for example, understand the poor and racially marginalized—and then how they come to recognize their own privilege. Language patterns connect with this production of images to reinforce the power to control the context in which children encounter the world.

Meanwhile, the advent of electronic hyperreality has revolutionized the ways knowledge is produced and the ways children come to learn about the world. To identify and guide the formation of knowledge, parents and educators need to appreciate the nature of this revolution and its role in identity shaping. A simple condemnation of kinderculture from politicians such as Bob Dole and calls for censorship are inadequate; equally ineffective is a policy of benign neglect. Concerned individuals should begin with an attempt to understand these dynamics in all their complexity and ambiguity, then involve themselves in the public conversation about them. In this way, adults can come to appreciate the fact that social confusion and identity disorientation among postmodern children may be reasonable reactions to the incongruity between kinderculture's and schooling's positioning of those children (Daspit & Weaver, 1998).

RETHINKING CHILDHOOD EDUCATION

As we begin to address these issues, the need for a reconceptualization of childhood education presents itself (Cannella, 1996). An enlightened rejection of a child psychology predicated on the adjustment of children to the existing social order compels this reconceptualization. Valerie Polakow (1992) argued that this "adjustment psychology" requires an "order ideology of schooling" predicated on the removal of the child from any experience of conflict. Inherent in this psychological model is an infantilization that denies children the autonomy to make decisions about issues that affect their lives and to negotiate their relationships with conflicting imperatives.

Our rejection of the order ideology does not mean that we embrace anarchy; instead, it means we seek to understand and learn to appreciate even the desires and libidinal impulses that bubble in childhood and reach full expression in adolescence. Kinderculture viewed this way incites neither rebellion nor violence; it pokes and irritates the beast of desire—an affective force present in romantic love, in the bond between parent and child and in our spiritual expressions (Ventura, 1994).

A critical pedagogy of childhood acknowledges and assimilates childhood desire, connecting it when possible to children's efforts to understand the world and themselves. As Paulo Freire (1970) maintained, a critical childhood education welcomes and uses the knowledge and intuitions children bring to school. In hyperreality such a pedagogic principle means that educators are obligated to study kinderculture, its effect on its consumers and its relationship to desire. If we want to know our children, such a pedagogy provides us a direct line into their consciousnesses as well as their perceptions of themselves and the world. What happens when children nurtured by kinderculture encounter the certified knowledge of the school? The answer to such a question leads us to new forms of learning and new insights into the construction of contemporary childhood around which we can restructure our schools and rethink the role of modern parenting (Steinberg, 1997).

13

Educational Futures

Introduction: Leaving Modernism Behind

Just as the world enters a new millenium, American education enters a new era. Educators are uncertain what to call it, but almost everyone agrees that, like the world, education is changing at an accelerating rate. While modernism continues to exert its influence on social and educational practices, a new impulse has developed. Some call it "postmodernism" or "the postmodern condition." What complicates the term, beside its assimilation of the word "modernism," is that postmodernism has yet to replace modernism, instead existing concurrently with it.

Return for a moment to our discussion of modernism in Chapter 2. Understanding the failures of the medieval ways of seeing the world, modernist thinkers sought new methods to understand and control the outside environment. In due time Cartesian science became a foundation for this new impulse, as science set out to make sense of complex phenomena by reducing them to their constituent parts before analyzing them in detail. Following this scientific orientation, an analogous socioeconomic feature of modernism came into being: capitalism, with its insistent faith in the benefits of science and technology, its doctrine of progress, its cult of reason and its logic of organization that would culminate in an authoritarian empirical science and an assembly-line mentality in the twentieth century.

Distinguishing Postmodernism from the Postmodern Condition

Postmodernism, then, has something to do with questioning these modernist tenets, and with the establishment of a new paradigm—that is, a new way of seeing the world. More specifically, postmodernist observers analyze those social assumptions the modernist ethos previously had shielded from view. They admit once inadmissible evidence, derived from new questions asked by previously excluded voices; they challenge hierarchical structures of knowledge and power that promote "experts" above the "masses"; and they seek new ways of knowing that transcend empirically verified facts and "reasonable" linear arguments deployed in a quest for certainty (Calinescu, 1987; Hebdige, 1989; Slattery, 1995; Best & Kellner, 1997).

When postmodernism is based on a critical democratic system of meaning concerned with analyzing knowledge for the purpose of understanding oneself and one's relation to society, naming and then changing social situations that impede the development of egalitarian communities committed to economic and social justice and understanding how worldviews and self-concepts come to be constructed it provides a powerful tool for progressive social and educational change (Kincheloe, 1991, 1993). These issues are complex, however, and we must stick to careful explanations. Our purpose in this chapter goes beyond simply discussing the new paradigm analysis of postmodernism. It also analyzes the postmodern condition—a social impulse currently shaping society and education. To understand the nature of education as it takes place in both schools and cultural sites, we must understand the nature and effects of the postmodern condition.

First of all, be careful to avoid confusing postmodernism as a social critique, a new paradigm and a new way of looking at the world with postmodernism as a social condition ("hyperreality" is a familiar synonym for the "postmodern condition"). To describe the emerging new era we use the postmodern critique (a way of seeing) to isolate the special features of the postmodern social condition. The postmodern critique and the postmodern condition may be closely connected, and in the attempt to distinguish them, many educators get lost in the landscape. French philosopher Jean-Francois Lyotard used "postmodernism" to refer to the general condition of contemporary Western civilization. The "grand narratives of legitimization"—that is, the all-encompassing explanations of history such as the modernist Enlightenment story of the inevitable victory of reason—are no longer believable in the postmodern world. Modernists fail to understand that they no longer tell their stories from an omniscient perspective, but being human, they must now tell human stories from a particular social and historical vantage point. Reason was undermined; it was usurped by those in power who spoke with the authority of a disembodied science unrestrained by self-analysis (Kincheloe, 1993). The postmodern condition arose from a world modernism created and extended by technology; thus the postmodern critique takes us beyond the understandable nihilism and emptiness of the postmodern condition.

Unfortunately, we cannot simplify this discussion of an ambiguous and contradictory concept. We simply cannot view the postmodern condition as a homogeneous historical period. Not all cultural expression in the contemporary era is postmodern (Smart, 1992; Borgmann, 1992). For example, flexible accumulation coexists with mass production of standardized products. Advocates of a postmodern frame of reference always risk overstating the uniqueness and newness of the concept. Although we affirm the existence of a postmodern condition, we can hardly celebrate it without persistent interrogation and thorough analysis.

Our analysis so far tentatively reveals that most dimensions of postmodernism share a reaction against modernist forms. Whereas the postmodern critique refuses to accept modernist elitism and authoritarianism and thus disrupts the stability of what exists, the postmodern condition includes a sort of social vertigo produced by a cultural hyperreality, itself caused by a loss of touch with the traditional impressions of time, community, self and history. New structures of cultural space and time generated by bombarding electronic images from many local, national and international locations almost at once shake our personal sense of place. Electronic transmissions move us in and out of different geographical and cultural locales instantaneously, juxtaposing nonlinear images of the world with homey, folksy, comfortable personalities who steady us in the midst of the chaos they help foment (Gergen, 1991; Aronowitz & Giroux, 1991; Smart, 1992).

Allowing these personalities to become our trusted guides, we make ourselves vulnerable to image and relinquish any desire for self-direction in the overgrown informational jungle of hyperreality. As we enter hyperreality, we relinquish our ties with our close-knit community. Trading community membership for a sense of pseudobelonging in the mediascape, residents of hyperreality receive temporary comfort from the proclamations of community the "personalities" offered by the 6:00 P.M. "eyewitness news." "Bringing the news of your neighbors in the tri-state area home to you" media marketers attempt to soften the edges of hyperreality and medicate the social vertigo. Television does not bring the world into our homes as much as it takes its viewers to a quasifictional place: hyperreality (Luke, 1991).

STUDENTS AND TEACHERS OF THE TWENTY-FIRST CENTURY FACE A NEW WORLD: FRAGMENTATION IN HYPERREALITY

Electronic systems of communication extend the postmodern condition. As the tides of the industrialized societies change, we confront yet another historical watershed that promises to reform both our identities and our interpersonal interactions. The postmodern revolution will have as great a social impact as the Industrial Revolution of the nineteenth century, and the accompanying educational and political conflicts will center on the management of the revolution. Technocrats see a future of harmony in which materially satisfied people inhabit a world of creative accord. Structural changes in our political, economic and educational institutions would be unnecessary in this technocratic world, because such high-tech tools as advanced computers remedy all human ills. Teachers operating much like the technocratic educators of the present will turn out standardized students with acceptable attitudes and rationalist cognitive styles.

This bright "*Jetson*esque" vision pales, however, when we remember that high-tech jobs can be more tedious and deskilling than traditional assembly-line work. Technocratic optimism sours when we remind ourselves that electronic communications (telephones, television, video recorders, CD players, video games and computers) have increased our isolation from one another, locking many of us into private cells. Instead of achieving a close-knit global community, high-tech communications exaggerate the power of dominant elites by granting them more prominence via television, video, CDs and computers, as well as new surveillance techniques. The love of technology (technophilia) is a blind infatuation blocking our view of technology's darker implications.

Holding before them a new spirituality, a strong sense of social justice and a new paradigmatic way of making sense of and producing knowledge, students and teachers must guard against a dystopian future. Our sojourn in hyperreality diminishes our ability to find meaning and sustain commitment. With so many particles of information bombarding our senses, we despair of making sense of anything. If nothing makes sense, what possibly merits commitment? David Byrne and the Talking Heads addressed this condition in their album *Stop Making Sense:* If hyperreal meaninglessness is a natural part of the postmodern condition, then stop trying so hard to deny it; just stop making sense. Raised in hyperreality, our students reflect the emotions (or the lack thereof) that hyperreality engenders. The postmodern pedagogical mission aims at rescuing meaning even as we witness its destruction in the postmodern information landscape (McLaren, 1991a).

ADDRESSING THE CONCENTRATION OF POWER: AN OVERDUE AGENDA

Technology invites power to concentrate in fewer and fewer hands, a tendency that shows little sign of abating in the near future. Spiritually minded critical teachers, meanwhile, understand that the effort to save democracy and achieve a just public education requires them to address the relation between this concentration of power and information technology. As industrialization and technology evolve, power becomes increasingly difficult to identify and trace. Perpetually disguised, power exerts itself so subtly that most of us remain unaware of the insidious oppression at work in our own lives. Of course, this crafted subtlety explains how the right wing achieved such dominance in contemporary life. In hyperreality, power seems to require the coproduction of those who generate electronic information and those who consume it. Those who produce information must seduce the consuming public into collaboration. But the production and dispersion of seductive images required is so expensive that only extremely large corporations can afford it. In this situation, new technologies perpetuate class and racial inequalities and at the same time hide those inequalities more effectively by isolating those with limited access to information from those who produce it. In hyperreality, media consumers refer blandly to a nebulous "they" who control information and in the process exercise some mysterious, unspecified control over their lives (Luke, 1991).

This mysterious control, this exercise of power in hyperreality, can assume a variety of forms. One of the most influential forms is the seducer—another way of saying the *power to educate.* Relying on advertising representations of particular identities, power interests in hyperreality deflect and then absorb the antagonistic and irreconcilable resistance the dominant society attracts. Properly managed, rebellion not only fails to threaten the social order, it can also protect the status quo. Sooner or later, most citizens can style themselves as something of a rebel, perhaps like Jeff Daniels's "Charlie" character in Jonathan Demme's *Something Wild*. A little bit rebel, a little bit yuppie businessman, Charlie's occasional failure to pay his restaurant check poses no real threat to the status quo. Affecting a James Dean persona and joining the Nike Revolution as John Lennon sings the theme song hardly calls for FBI surveillance. As a dominant motif in selling products and services, the quiescent rebel can enlist us all as collaborators (Ashley, 1991; Luke, 1991).

Importantly for education, hyperreality foreshadows the changing location of educational activity. Expect to see school buildings become secondary sites for education; expect the mediascape to be primary. Such a change suggests both progressive and regressive possibilities. On the progressive side, we will have greater access to information via the Internet and other personally accessible information networks. With remarkable ease, we will communicate with like-minded people sharing similar political and social concerns, in the process opening new avenues for democratic political organization. Those of us with the motivation will enjoy new opportunities to produce information, especially information that challenges that which powerful elites with ulterior motives produce. In this progressive context, the prospect of opening new democratic education and information production sites is certainly promising. To reach this goal, however, we must guard against the regressive applications of the new technologies. Achieving the critical education of the future requires that we avoid these already visible tendencies on the hyperreal social and educational landscapes.

Peter McLaren (1991) made the essential point when he observed that postmodern power organizes life along affective or emotional structures as it mobilizes desire, mood and pleasure. Regressive social control in the mediascape depends on the organization of attractive conditions for collaborating with the power wielders. Seduced by the pleasure of the image, individuals see themselves as self-managed entities who are, as we just said, too rebellious to be controlled. Failing to admit to their own seduction, to decipher the collaboration conditions or to appreciate the educational power of the media, they jump headlong one after another over the cliff. Science fiction plays with the idea of people controlled by electronic devices implanted in their brains. The electronic information providers of hyperreality bring science fiction (we should probably say "cognitive science fiction") to life, controlling postmodern men and women less by coercion than by the "freedom" of consumer gratification or life-style choice (Langman, 1991).

THE NEW SCHOOL OF HYPERREALITY: EDUCATING THE SELF, REFORMING IDENTITY

Hyperreality is a world of social saturation where, bombarded by ever-increasing images, people must find their identities and try to direct their changes. The drama of life has appeared so often on television that, for the most part, we know how it goes. As many postmodern analysts have put it, we become pastiches, imitative conglomerations of one another. In such a condition, we approach life with a "flat affect"—that is, with a sense of postmodern ennui. Our emotional bonds slacken as television, computers, VCRs and stereo headphones assault us with routinized sounds and images. Traditionalists circle the cultural wagons and fight off such imagined bogeymen as secular humanists, extreme liberals and utopianists, all the while ignoring the impact the postmodern hyperreality exerts on their hallowed institutions. The nuclear family, for example, has declined in influence not because of "radical feminists" but because electronic communication systems have invaded the home. Particular modes of information put individual family members in constant contact with specific subcultures. While they may be physically at home, they exist emotionally outside it. The construction of their consciousnesses and the formation of their emotional investments take place in a manner far different than most educators assume (Gergen, 1991; Poster, 1989).

As we confront this social saturation of hyperreality we enter into a postmodern consciousness. Although we appear to one another as single, bounded identities, we are socially superabsorbent, hiding beneath our surface mazes of personality fragments. We are all part game show host, evangelist, quarterback, cop, criminal, local news anchor and secret Kellogg's Frosted Flakes addict. All personalities are latent and, given the right stimuli, ready to come alive. Thus, the boundaries of individualism begin to fade like batter's box chalk lines. As they do, we start to see the wisdom in constructivism's idea of the social formation of the individual. Indeed, we even begin to recognize limitations in the middle-class idea of individualism. In the name of individualism, we take a "me-first" perspective on self-gratification that renders us vulnerable to such ostensibly sensible slogans as "Read my lips, no new taxes" and "Let's put an end to public job training programs; let's make [other] people take some responsibility for themselves."

This emphasis on self-gratification trivializes critical conceptions of citizenship, friendship and sexual relationships, as each impulse starts to focus on personal acquisitions. We now use testing both as a way of assessing the effectiveness of education and as a means of motivating students who have been taught to learn only for profit and success. But as we gain a meta-awareness of the construction of our postmodern consciousness, it becomes increasingly possible to reconstruct our understanding of the nature of individualism.

In this reconstruction of individualism, we can start with the nature of our changing relationships to others. Small, unchanging, geographically defined communities, with their comparatively small complements of significant others, are being rapidly supplanted by an expanding galaxy of relationships. The Andys, Opies, Barneys, Gomers, Goobers and Aunt Beas and the cohesive Mayberry they inhabit is only forty years old, yet it is light-years from the America of the twenty-first century. No matter how hard we try, hyperreality has fossilized Mayberry, and no one can go home again. We now know that a live presence is not necessary to a postmodern relationship. What does it say about us that Andy, Barney and Opie may be the best concrete example of community we can offer?

Moreover, they may actually have *become* our community. Radio commentator Paul Harvey discusses them as though they were real. For many individuals— our students in particular—media relationships provide the most emotionally evocative experiences of their lives. Hyperreality thus inverts "prehyperreality": The question is no longer whether television relationships substitute for "normal" relationships, but whether normal relationships can substitute for television relationships (Gergen, 1991). As these postmodern realities confront traditional conceptions of individuality and relationship, it seems obvious that our critical reconstruction of individualism must take up the new ways consciousness is constructed. To ignore the social and cognitive impacts of hyperreality is to bury our heads in the traditionalist sand. More specifically, it is to embrace a form of educational fundamentalism that seeks comfort in the education of a premodernist past as the world we know collapses around us.

DEFINING IDEOLOGY AND HEGEMONY: SHAPING CONSCIOUSNESS AND IDENTITY AS WE APPROACH THE FUTURE

While considering the ways education takes place in hyperreality and will take place in the future we need to understand the term "ideology" and its relation to this electronic media education we are all picking up. "Ideology" is traditionally defined as a system of beliefs, but our use of the term here goes beyond this definition. We see ideology as part of the process of protecting unequal power relations between different groups and individuals in society. For example, the *dominant ideology* sustains these unequal power relations through the process of making meanings—in a sense, by educating. Theories of ideology circulated after the beginnings of industrialization in the nineteenth century to explain why, in those industrializing societies, the poor continued to support the political and economic systems that exploited them, and later why so many women continued to accept egregious male domination. The concept of ideology we use here finds its grounding in this traditional progressive concern with oppression and its accompanying power disparity. Applying the concept of ideology as we explore education in hyperreality, we can begin to understand how powerful groups shape our consciousnesses for their own purposes (Thompson, 1987; Fiske, 1993; Steinberg & Kincheloe, 1997).

A second term we need to define in this context is "hegemony." Hegemony signifies the maintenance of domination and oppression less through actual force than by winning the consent of those being dominated. Hegemony, like ideological domination, implies a form of education. Hegemonic consent is never universally established; it is always contested by various groups with differing agendas. When combined with hegemony, ideology moves us beyond simplistic explanations that rely on terms such as "propaganda" to describe the way media, education and other cultural productions coercively manipulate citizens to adopt oppressive patterns of meaning. What we call "hegemonic ideology" denotes a much more subtle and ambiguous form of domination that discards propaganda's assumption that its subjects are passive and manipulable. In the complex realm of power and hegemonic consent, dominant ideological practices socially construct popular visions of reality. Thus, a social theory of hegemonic ideology is a form of epistemological constructivism buoyed by an understanding of power's complicity in the sense people make of the world and their roles in it (Kellner, 1990; McLaren, 1994).

As they gain new access to our private lives through the media in hyperreality, these hegemonic and ideological forces exert more and more influence as we determine *who we are*. "I am" includes the influences that have made me as I am; indeed, whenever knowledge is presented, an "I" is implicitly in it. In the context of our power-related analysis we can add this proviso: Wherever knowledge and the "I" go, there also goes the ideological. In our critical new paradigmatic context we use our understanding of hyperreality's media power, ideology and hegemony to explain the ways we become who we are in the new world unfolding before us. At the same time, we should point out that no matter how powerful the hegemonic ideological process becomes, the possibility always remains for individuals to resist (Mumby, 1989). Teachers can use the educational values we propose to help students protect their identities from the electronic information bombardment. But teaching to this end would force schools to abandon the goal of adjusting students to society and the demands of the dominant culture.

Once informed and organized, students can unmask hegemonic ideology's attempts to hide social conflict. The presence of agency (self-direction) serves to extend an individual's or group's domain of control. A sense of its absence—the absence of one's own influence—develops when gaps between various economic and cultural resources (power) become evident. Because perceptions of power differences can lead to conflict, the power bloc attempts to disguise or hide them and to project an illusion of consensus. Those with the power to tell society stories about itself—whether in the media, in school texts or in the political sphere—often reflect hegemonic ideologies in their social narratives. Consider the way newscasters comment on election results: "Well, now that the votes have all been counted and President Teasel has been elected, all Americans will unite behind their new president. Unlike any other country in the world, Americans believe that they are Americans first and then Republicans and Democrats. Our unity is one of our most valuable assets as a nation."

A narrative such as this, repeated over and over around election time, reassures Americans that although they may differ on the specific ways their country will reach the golden future, they are united around issues of substance. Sharing the same interests, Americans have no need to struggle over justice or fairness; no one has economic or political interests fundamentally different from those of the rest. In fact, America is a classless society, just as the dominant story tells us (Suvin, 1988; Fiske, 1993). As Doug Kellner (1990) noted, Americans are more likely to see nude bodies on television than to hear issues of socioeconomic class discussed or to see images of class conflict.

NOMADS IN POWER: LEGITIMATING KNOWLEDGE IN HYPERREALITY

Communications specialists often refer to the power groups that produce information in hyperreality for the media, schools and public consumption as "nomadic"—that is, constantly moving and changing their appearance in hyperspace.

Such nomadic power wielders circle the globe both physically and virtually, using their media access and influential connections to pursue their narrow economic interests. In other words, General Motors, for example, is no longer a Michigan corporation that makes cars and uses its capital in more or less traditional ways. In hyperreality General Motors spans the globe, moving constantly, reinvesting, influencing a wide variety and large number of markets, dealing in diverse goods and services in many nations.

Most of these nomadic corporations, like the Catholic Church during the Counter-Reformation, realize that a universal presence preserves power in an age of change and global colonization. The Church appeared on all the colonial frontiers with a universalized ritual, a grand architecture and the crucifix as ideological signifier. Wherever one traveled, the Church and its ideological symbols provided familiarity and security. In this later age of global colonization—with multinational corporations organizing the planet economically, electronically and ideologically in hyperreality—many of the same dynamics the Church faced in the sixteenth century are at work. Wherever an economic and electronic frontier opens, the multinationals arrive with their universalized rituals of profit making, the grand architecture of their corporate headquarters and outlets and such ideological signifiers as their corporate logos. Instead of gothic arches, the nomadic power of hyperreality raises golden arches, with all of their ideological capabilities. Wherever it occurs, this evangelism legitimizes the corporations and their worldviews in the public mind (Critical Art Ensemble, 1994).

Where are the social conflicts here when presumably everyone benefits from the global expansion of American business? What do these ideological symbols have to do with power interests and socioeconomic justice? Questions such as these illustrate the success of hegemonic ideology in the making of meaning and the education of the public. To gain a critical understanding of such power dynamics, one must first ascertain the realities of individual lives and identity formation vis-à-vis giant power wielders and with the meaning-making process of particular human agents vis-à-vis the practices of communication conglomerates.

Any analysis of power and ideology made from this perspective should also address their effects on the formation of human consciousness. One should extend traditional ideological studies of state and politics into lived social and educational worlds in which people barraged by the symbols of power can resist and sometimes even triumph over them. In educational settings a critical new paradigmatic perspective grants insight into how cultural backgrounds and ideological dynamics shape our students' experiences. Educators and other social agents need to recognize the ways hegemonic ideology constrains particular groups, thwarting their ability to use schooling for their personal benefit. Schools can become democratic spheres only when we expose these hidden ideological processes (Giroux, 1988).

Real students are crushed every day by power plays and ideological constraints; if we fail to address these oppressive realities, marginalized students will move further into the margins. As we come to recognize these insidious influences and notice their expression in the media curriculum and in the schools, we can see the process of oppression and how power inscribes inequality on the consciousnesses of students. As insightful observers, we understand how media representations of the working (lower socioeconomic) class, the underclass, women, gays and lesbians, the handicapped and minorities plant feelings of inferiority in the consciousnesses of all these people.

The prominent dynamics of the hyperreality education include the complex process by which the marginalized come to internalize the view of them held by power elites (some call this kind of inculcation "cultural pedagogy"). As we said in Chapter 1, when we discussed annihilation and assimilation, an aspect of the curriculum of hyperreality emerges here: the certification of unequal dominant-subordinate relations and the acceptance of inferiority. In both schools and cultural pedagogical sites, critical analysts labor to interrupt ongoing legitimation of unjust social relationships. Understanding the nomadic multinationals' unprecedented power to effect the internalization of inferiority among the dispossessed, critical scholars must share their disruptive work on this front with the victims of hegemonic ideology themselves. These people need access to our work to protect themselves from the sociopsychological dangers a hegemonic ideology poses. Critical analysts must open democratic communications with marginalized peoples in a *dialogue,* not a monologue, that edifies both groups (Musolf, 1992; Lincoln, 1995).

CONSCIOUSNESS AND POWER: THE PAIN ON THE PERSONAL LEVEL

The ability of power and ideology to position our poor and dispossessed students strengthens as we move into the future. Meanwhile, many teachers and students find these hard-to-define power issues too abstract to relate them to everyday life. How does "all of this" relate to schooling, they ask. A quick personal example may help us understand the fact that power and ideology exact a personal toll—that is, they hurt specific students and undermine their chances for a psychologically healthy and vocationally successful life. These sociocultural dynamics teach marginalized students that they are stupid and incapable of "making it" in the academic or professional culture.

Remember our carpenter friends Ronnie and Brandon, who did some renovation work on our house? Like many others "in the trades" they hated school, became convinced of their intellectual inadequacy and sought vocations that seemingly had little to do with what schools teach. Yet we saw them employ sophisticated math skills to solve unstructured problems.

"This isn't really math," Ronnie told us, "not like the math you do in school." As we explained how their math was in some ways more sophisticated than the math high schools teach they expressed first gratitude, then interest. Focusing on their facility with unstructured problems, as opposed to structured instructional problems, we convinced them that they were smarter than they thought.

As we explained our critical conceptions of ideology and class bias in education and the exclusionary, elitist discourse of educational psychology's view of intelligence, they began to understand the socially constructed nature of intelligence and how they had been victimized by an elitist viewpoint. The more we talked, the more interested they became. Initially reluctant to express their concerns with college professors who taught teachers, they began to voice the anger and resentment they felt toward formal education.

In conversations with other men and women in the trades, we have found similar anger. They, too, found school to be a place of embarrassment and hurt feelings, a place where one's failures and inabilities took center stage.

As long as we continue to demean poor peoples' forms of intelligence, many students like Ronnie and Brandon will suffer an irrelevant and humiliating school experience. Accordingly, we believe that critical teachers in the new paradigm should help students understand how a hegemonic ideology works to convince them of their incompetence. Then critical teachers can help them fight back and save themselves from marginalization and the personal pain that accompanies it.

THE CURRICULUM OF THE HIGH-TECH FUTURE: LEARNING FROM THE PROFUSION OF IMAGES

The culture of hyperreality has produced a new form of communication, a language of image that, according to Peter McLaren (1991), celebrates the look, the sign and the symbol. This language of image promotes a form of social amnesia that erases knowledge of the historical shaping of our consciousness as it engulfs us in a white-water river of signs and a torrent of changing images designed to dull our senses. Unlike many analyses of contemporary information culture, critical paradigmatic analysis recognizes a political dimension in these apparently random signs. For example, although advertisers call their advertising mainly informative, careful study suggests that it relies predominantly on image. Further, its images more than just market products by connecting them to desirable traits; they also sell an accompanying ideology, a system of values that furthers individuals' identification with a culture of consumerism (Kellner, 1991).

Miller Lite beer advertisements provide a good example of the use of signs and images to sell both a product and an ideology. After a series of failures to market diet beers, the advertisers who won the Miller account followed a new "game plan" for Miller Lite. Recognizing that a health-conscious culture might constitute a new market for a low-calorie beer, the advertisers also knew that the predominately male beer-drinking market would resist an effeminate image for a diet beer. Beer drinking is often a male bonding ritual and a feminine beer might compromise that association. Using this reading of masculine culture, the advertisers took the status position of sports and the new ethic of health and connected them to the culture of masculinity.

Enlisting the most recognizable macho sports figures available, they set out to prove that drinking a low-calorie beer could be masculine. Football players Dick Butkus and Bubba Smith, baseball legend Mickey Mantle, boxer Carlos Palomena, outdoorsman Grits Gresham, detective novelist Mickey Spillane and others were then unleashed to sell the ties that bind masculinity, sports, health and low-calorie beer. The marketers achieved great success selling Miller Lite, and they also sold a life-style. Specifically, they promoted images of a heterosexual (but homoerotic) culture of athletic men playing hypermasculine roles. Women were outsiders at least, decorations at best, and generally absent from the foreground except for Mickey Spillane's "doll," a vacuous "blond bombshell" with the looks but not the savvy of Roger Rabbit's "toon" wife, Jessica. Young males, principally Republican and antifeminist, welcomed the ads, which were wildly successful, judging from the sales of Miller Lite and the flood of low-calorie beer imitators Miller Lite launched.

From beer to cereal to cigarettes, the curriculum of hyperreality teaches all of us—young people in particular—to adopt particular identities and live particular life-styles. In this way corporate power wielders ideologically orient us to embrace particular modes of consumption that serve the interests of certain producers. Doug Kellner (1991) examined the ideological image of masculinity and the life-style choices embedded in Marlboro cigarette ads. He used his analysis to show how we can learn to read power and identity formation in the hyperreality curriculum. After integrating the Marlboro ads into his teaching, Kellner described the empowerment that results when students learn to critically analyze taken-for-granted features of their worlds. More often than not, Kellner found, students readily learn to decode the media's tacit meanings, uncovering in the process the way the larger culture constructs their consciousness. Unlike Marshall McLuhan, who maintained that those who live in a media culture develop a media literacy naturally, Kellner argued that such forms of reading and thinking must be taught. Once they learn the skills, however, students ride a straight highway toward understanding the ways oppression works. Indeed, deconstructing media often leads students toward important political understandings more quickly than critical readings of the traditional book culture. While both forms of reading hasten understanding, media reading does it faster because it engages students with forms close to their lived worlds that shape their subjectivities.

By engaging students at the level of emotion (remember the affective domain in Chapter 10) and with the formation of their subjectivities, the messages of hyperreality command a power rarely—if ever—felt before. Indeed, in the advertisements, political pronouncements and entertainment of much electronic information we find a postmodern version of a culture of manipulation. Hyperreality, then, often produces a climate of deceit. Just as the CIA produces "disinformation" designed to mislead the enemy and create conditions favorable to CIA interests, advertising and political discourse often distribute a form of disinformation designed to project a basic superficial idea while actually guiding people elsewhere. We believe the prevalence of this disinformation and the powerful images that illustrate it demand a teaching response that is part of a larger critical education exploring how we all see the world. It demands a form of teacher and student thinking capable of understanding how consciousness is constructed and then the use of this understanding to emancipate the disenfranchised.

The critical teaching for the future we envision shows teachers and students how to interpret electronic hyperreal images, to show how they shape consciousness and to explain what they mean in different circumstances. Using the critical hermeneutic research abilities we outlined in Chapter 8 to understand the power of images, we can study and interpret the power of television and how it constructs our ways of thinking. So doing, we find linear Cartesian-Newtonian logic having little to do with the construction of media political campaigns and television advertising. Neil Postman (1985a, 1995) encouraged the critical deconstruction of the electronic image when he observed that the traditional attempts to distinguish between "true" or "false" advertising claims follow a misguided assumption that the claims are couched in the language of logical propositions. Once we discard this language, in analyzing advertising we need to apply rules different from those we apply to other forms of communications. Advertisers on television appeal to a domain of symbols that can be neither validated nor refuted.

For example, a Levi's 501 jeans commercial makes no claims about the quality, durability or stylishness of the pants. The viewer is rushed through a barrage of shots of young people who are wearing 501 jeans and are indifferent to the camera. We can read the images as young, sensual, alive people choosing these jeans. But that is hardly the main point. In fact, it is: We, the people here at Levi's, are so engaged in the culture of "cool," marked by its flat affect and its knowing indifference, that we will not even appeal to you to buy our jeans; James Dean would never have done it that way. Now, associate *that* image with *these* jeans!

While other readings are possible, most involve at some level an emotional identification of Levi's 501 jeans with the culture of "cool." We "get it" because we are experts in the media culture of advertising. We are tired of those more blatant, less "cool" efforts to attract our attention.

Preparing our students to live in the twenty-first century requires of us a media literacy that not only allows us to analyze the effects of television, radio, popular music, computers and the like, but also teaches new paradigmatic forms of research such as semiotics, ethnography and the other forms of inquiry we analyzed in Chapter 9. Such analyses can start as early as elementary school, as students begin to wonder where adults get their information and their opinions about the world. Neil Postman (1985a) recommended that this media education involve both analyses of contemporary information forms and historical analyses of the origins and uses of ideographic writing; the etymology and sociopolitical consequences of the alphabet; the development and impact of the printing press, newspapers and magazines; and the technological origins of the computer and its present effects.

Postman's point is clear: media should be made problematic to our students in a way that encourages them to gauge the impact of information and its sources on their lives. Before such study becomes feasible, however, teacher education programs must prepare teachers for the role of media analyst. Also, critical educators must convince the public that, contrary to the pronouncements of educators such as William Bennett and Diane Ravitch, media education does not trivialize the curriculum.

Teacher education programs sensitive to the major elements of hyperreality and the postmodern condition require that prospective teachers study the nature of information. Historically information has come packaged in many forms. Long before the electronic image it came by way of speech, writing, print and paint. Our thinking has been partly shaped and twisted by the dominant discursive form for transferring information. To understand the way events are shaped and history flows, we must first understand the influence of information formats. We can talk at great length about the way politics has changed over the past decades, but we will never understand the reasons for the changes until we analyze politics in relation to forms of information. We are inattentive to abstract and ambiguous ideas, so television focuses our gaze on concrete images. Bill Clinton standing tall, smiling broadly and waving to the crowd *like a leader* is the issue—that is the image; now, what happened to the question of what government should do for the poor? Teacher education and schooling in general must address this change in information format as they prepare teachers and citizens in a democratic society to protect themselves from the epistemology of hyperreality. Indeed, such a social change demands a new form of literacy—a postmodern literacy—to "read" the effect of five thousand hours of television before kindergarten, of eight hundred television commercials a week and a cultural knowledge dominated by *X-Men, Animaniacs, Rocko's Modern Life, Spiderman, South Park* and *Ren and Stimpy.*

As we study information, we inevitably confront the ways media and popular culture shape the consciousnesses of teachers and students. Peter McLaren suggested that in this context we ask the following questions:

> *How are the subjectivities, dreams, desires and needs of students forged by the media, by leisure activities, by institutions such as the family and by cultural forms such as rock 'n' roll and music videos? How, for instance, is the practical ethics by which students engage everyday life inscribed within a contestatory politics of signification? How are images of male and female socially constructed? How do the politics of signification structure the problematization of experience? How are the subjectivities of students constituted by the effects of representations which penetrate the level of the body? (1991, p. 165)*

Without the critical thinking answers to questions such as these require and without the application of our media research strategies, we remain just as vulnerable to manipulators as those without educations.

As we analyze the way the various electronic media shape information, we learn that the leaders of hyperreality subsume natural ways of relating in the polished techniques of efficient communication. They suppress local dialects, eliminate idiosyncratic gestures, remove controversial topics, dress in a homogenized fashion and rehearse pleasant facial expressions. For example, before his careful media training, racist political activist David Duke was a fiery, rough-edged, often frightening Klansman. One of the authors remembers watching him march around the Louisiana State University campus in Nazi regalia spewing racist slogans at "Free Speech Alley" in the early 1970s. At the time most students just ignored him and considered him deranged. Later, after he learned the techniques of effective communication and cosmetic makeovers, Duke appeared on television as a soft-spoken, smiling, friendly, mainstream Christian with all the attending deference and courtesy the image entails. He hid his virulent racism in political policies said to protect traditional U.S. values and the Protestant work ethic. The political differences of the before and after Dukes were minimal, but the video-friendly image superseded the racist reality. Those with ingrained fears and distorted views of

African Americans could say, "I'm not a racist, but what Duke says makes an awful lot of sense."

In the novel *Brave New World* writer Aldous Huxley foresaw the danger to freedom emanating not from tyrannical threats of pain but from pleasure. In *Brave New World* citizens came to love the technologies that oppressed them and destroyed their cognitive abilities. To avoid living out Huxley's nightmare, we must learn the effects of the technologies we have grown to love. We must develop a media literacy that empowers us to subvert the invisible hyperreal empire by uncovering the codes behind its messages (Postman, 1985a; Gergen, 1991). As we learn to decipher the codes, we can use them to construct a democratic education and a participatory community in the midst of a disconcerting and confused postmodern world.

THE POPULAR CULTURE CURRICULUM: HOLLYWOOD AS TEACHER

It astonishes marketers, the motion picture conglomerates and critical educators that Americans, by and large, have yet to recognize the movies as a powerful educational influence. As apparent entertainment forms, movies and other manifestations of popular culture receive little serious attention in public schools or political forums. If it did little else, Senator Bob Dole's simplistic attack on Hollywood in his 1996 presidential campaign opened a tiny space for a public discussion of the influence of popular culture. The moral and political emptiness of traditional liberalism revealed itself in an inability to respond to Dole's critique other than by denying the social effects of movies: "They're just entertainment, after all." A social blindness to the power of movies and media culture in general to shape identities and behavior and to produce meanings undermines much of the current social analysis, in the process helping to stifle our ability to make sense of the world around us. The previous discussion of ideology in hyperreality informs our intention here both to address this social blindness and to convey the idea that all cultural products, media culture in particular, are historically inscribed (Smith, 1983; Kellner, 1995; Grossberg, 1992).

Such historical inscription has not used a permanent dye; inscriptions are open to reinterpretations from differing cultural locations and intersections of power and domination. Nevertheless, the inscriptions are clear enough to preclude someone's freedom to articulate any interpretation of a popular text he or she fancies. The reception of media takes place under conditions the viewer does not totally control. Such powerful cultural forces as neoclassical economic theory, nationalism and patriarchy make it difficult for audiences to entertain alternatives to the ideology they see inscribed. While many other readings are possible, it is certainly difficult, for example, to dismiss the racial inscription of D. W. Griffith's *Birth of a Nation* (1915). Swept up in the early twentieth-century romanticization of the Old South and plantation life, *Birth of a Nation* positioned the Ku Klux Klan as the savior of a South under the siege of radical—indeed perverted—Northern advocates of Reconstruction. To miss this inscription, even from the perspective of the early twenty-first century, would be difficult. Similarly, it is hard to ignore the historical inscription of post-*Exorcist* (1973) occult films. Portraying a society whose institutions are being assaulted by a plethora of forces, movies such as *Carrie, The Omen* and *The Shining* depict a crumbling culture unable to respond to social challenge. The task of critical educators is to reveal the inscriptions that provide insight into not only the nature of the culture, but also the forces that undermine its quest for democracy and social justice (Grossberg, 1989, 1992).

Cultural Studies as a Way to Look at the Future: Popular Culture as Cultural Pedagogy

As we discussed in our Chapter 12 analysis of youth culture, educators (even those sensitive to issues of power and social justice) have in general yet to confront the educational influence of popular culture. If pedagogy involves issues of knowledge production and transmission, the shaping of values and the construction of subjectivity, then popular culture is the most powerful pedagogical force in contemporary America. The pedagogy of popular culture is, of course, ideological in its production of commonsense assumptions about the world, its influence on our affective lives and its role in the production of our identities and experiences.

How, then, do progressives address the power of popular culture and the information environment of the present and, especially, the future? Only when progressives understand that individuals construct and transform themselves and their society at the crossroads of everyday lived reality, socioeconomic structures and popular culture, can they formulate strategies for a democratic education and a critical political practice in hyperreality. In this context, teachers and other cultural workers dedicated to social justice can begin to make sense of the ambiguous but influential activities that take place at the crossroads; they can begin to formulate strategies for making sense of the information overload (Collins, 1995). Thus, they prepare for a future certain to bring an exponential expansion of the social trends identified here.

Understanding the individual transformations, progressives begin to transcend the shock of the new and to take charge of various information technologies so as to gain a voice in the cultural pedagogical conversation. Their goal (it is *our* goal, really) is to rearticulate the chaos of hyperreality into a meaningful coherence with an inclusive democratic intent. This is the work of a critical media pedagogy bent on disrupting the narcissistic privatizing tendencies at work in contemporary popular culture.

But the ambiguous duplicity of popular culture, with its ability to both subject and empower, to inspire and discourage and to evade or resist, complicates the goals of democratic education. Such complexity and ambiguity often force progressives to retreat into more traditional methods of political work, which helps explain the failure of justice and diversity to gain a presence on the contemporary political landscape. It also partly explains why America has recently witnessed so much intolerance. Knowing that power works through popular media ambiguously, we must keep the ambiguity from clouding our realization that oppressive structures exist in everyday American life and will no doubt continue to exist there. Critical students must see this disturbing reality in relation to movies and other popular entertainment forms, exposing in the process the ways disempowerment can result from contact with cultural forms usually considered empowering (Collins, 1995; Smith, 1989; Grossberg, 1989, 1992).

Playing on their viewers' concerns, movies and other media become a part of a larger cultural loop that exerts a variety of mostly predetermined effects. Movies and video help individuals articulate those feelings and moods that ultimately shape their behaviors. Audiences use particular images to help them form and then rationalize their own tastes, images, styles and identities; indeed, they are the students of media pedagogy. These students connect to the popular culture curriculum by welcoming its production of desire, libidinal sensibility, affect and fantasy. Often providing an emotional catharsis, an escape from unpleasant circumstances, emotional support through identification with a character and the joy of personal investment in a story, the pleasure derived from movies and other media amounts to the production of subjectivity.

No other facet of the culture enjoys this much power to shape consciousness, as individuals grant affect-based popular culture the authority to help them organize their identities. Audiences allow popular culture to speak for them and to provide narrative structures that help them make sense of their lives. The emotional investment audiences make in movies can galvanize into affective alliances (fans of *Star Trek,* for example) with other individuals, texts and ideological viewpoints. Thus, the affect popular culture mobilizes can provide viewers with a sense of belonging, a sense that becomes progressively more compelling in the fragmented and alienated society we described in Chapters 1 and 2. Young people nowadays frequently are unable to find a sense of belonging in their families and schools, so they look to popular culture to fill the void.

Keeping the complexity of media and popular culture effects always in mind, remember that the affect produced differs depending on the historic and social contexts. Indeed, different forms of popular culture produce different affects and effects. These complexities suggest how serious the study of popular culture and its pedagogical and ideological implications can be. In fact, we need rigorous forms of analysis to study the production of media texts, their economic distribution, their reception by various audiences and the different processes audiences adopt in using them to make meaning and construct identities. The effort is, nevertheless, important because almost everyone in hyperreality lives within the pedagogical radar of popular culture. In traditional societies this cultural location generally included schools, churches, labor guilds and unions, political organizations and extended families. The construction of identity that traditionally took place around these cultural locations now occurs in the presence of popular culture, however. By default—because fewer and fewer alternative spaces seem to be available—movies and other media become the fields in which affective styles and ways of being sprout, flower and are harvested. Hyperreal identities are often more grounded on feeling and affect than on logic or rationality. Style, image, "cool"—they all relate to this notion of affective identity production.

In this context, cultural studies scholars search for the persuasive images that help shape identities of susceptible people. What we call here a persuasive image involves a representation that lingers in one's consciousness, continually shaping and reshaping one's affective subjectivity long after it originally appeared. Persuasive images of movie stars often help shape the cultural and subsequent responses. James Dean, John Wayne, Cary Grant, Gary Cooper, Sylvester Stallone, Clint Eastwood and many other male stars, for example, influence or have influenced the style, consciousness, self-image and behavior of many a man. Although the "narrative theme" of a movie may involve such unambiguous moral messages as "adultery is wrong and has negative consequences," the persuasive images of the movie may have little to do with, and may even contradict the narrative theme.

In *Body Heat*, for example, the narrative theme's emphasis on "adultery doesn't pay" pales in relation to the persuasive images of the passionate, steamy sensuality of the stars, William Hurt and Kathleen Turner. Much earlier, director Cecil B. DeMille understood well this dynamic in his lurid biblical epics with their ostensibly religious and moral narrative themes and their persuasive images of debauchery. Recently Mario van Peebles has produced films, such as *New Jack City*, with antidrug narrative themes that are accompanied by persuasive images of drug dealers living opulent and glamorous life-styles.

How young people read these films no one can preordain with certainty. Like any successful hegemonic production, movies attempt to maximize their audiences by providing something for everyone. DeMille's biblical epics, for example, provided moral themes for religious viewers and prurient material for the more lascivious. While DeMille's intentions were fairly blatant, all films incorporate a variety of elements—for example, different discourses, ideologies, narrative styles and images—that work against any single, discrete, unequivocable ideological effect. The complexity of the effects movies have on young people keeps us from finding simple connections between, for example, Steven Segal's violent movies and their causative effect on youth violence. Nevertheless, connections do exist. Persuasive images are profound educational tools with much more identity-producing power than educational scholars so far realize (Kellner, 1995; Grossberg, 1992). A teacher who walks into a contemporary (and especially a future) classroom without this understanding will have trouble appreciating why students act the way they do—not to mention in understanding what they are talking about. The hyperreal future demands this knowledge in those teachers who want to connect education to their students' identities and lived realities.

SCHOOLING AND PLEASURE: THE EDUCATIONAL EFFORT TO OSTRACIZE POPULAR CULTURE

Popular culture rarely attracts educators. Indeed, they tend to be uncomfortable with pleasure, especially the enjoyment their students express for popular culture. Stanley Aronowitz and Henry Giroux (1991) used the term "social imaginary," to describe the space popular culture creates in which young people locate their desires, uncover their emotional identifications and find pleasure. Specifically, young people see what it means to be socially mobile in situation comedies, in motion pictures' depictions of pleasure, in music video celebrations of style and in the emphasis on life-styles in advertisements. Thus, hyperreality is by no means simply oppressive; its imagery includes visions of pleasure and a better life.

In a culture still ambivalent about pleasure, some of us see threats in a cultural form—in this case, popular culture—that overtly promotes pleasure. Next to popular culture, we can easily see contemporary schooling as a vestige of a Victorian asceticism. In its denial of pleasure, school promotes a regime of discipline and devotion to the transference of play into labor. In this context school consistently devalues popular cultural forms and the pleasure they depict. Recognizing the power of popular culture at some tacit level, schools then work to detach students from it, reshaping them along the lines of such ascetic dominant cultural values as the work ethic and respect for authority. Yet the effort is doomed in a future in which the pursuit of pleasure in popular culture promises to occupy an even more prominent role in our lives. Thus a new "politics of pleasure," focused on the ways people identify with particular cultural forms and the ideologies they imply according to the kind of pleasure they provide, seems certain to emerge. Without an understanding of the use of pleasure in the social construction of individuals, our psychological insights into the personality formation, learning styles and motivational dynamics of young people will be shallow at best.

New Paradigmatic Educational Psychology: The Study of Consciousness Construction in the Hyperreal Future

Educators can learn from the disciplines of cultural studies and postmodern psychoanalysis that the formation of the self is never complete—it is always in the process of shaping and being shaped by the social realm. In this context, therefore, any interest in the development of identity and mental functions (in a word, intelligence) must take into account a wide variety of factors including the social dynamics of the unfolding future we have discussed in this chapter. Simply put, contrary to the pronouncements of fragmented and decontextualized modernist psychology, the mind does extend beyond the skin. Intelligence, memory and thinking are more than the possessions of particular individuals; they are always social processes. Therefore, we can appreciate the primitive nature of psychometric IQ testing with its confusion of intelligence (or its lack) with how familiar one happens to be with the culture of schooling and mainstream language patterns (Wertsch & Tulviste, 1992). Such social phenomena as popular culture and hyperreality's change of information production profoundly affect the way students come to think and learn. Typically modernist mainstream educational psychology "psychologized" the formation of identity, meaning that it views studies of consciousness construction as individual psychological processes, not as psychological, sociological, political and economic processes combined.

As we have argued, power groups in hyperreality achieve new access to individual consciousness, giving corporate and political elites new access to the formation of identities and worldviews. Social power now includes the ability to shape how an individual consciousness experiences the everyday dynamics of hyperreal social life. If the experiences are generally pleasant, the social structures with which people identify will encounter little pressure to embrace democratic reforms. Discontent at this level of experience, on the other hand, is potentially at least one of the most compelling catalysts for social change.

Thus the human psyche becomes the last frontier of domination. Power is manifested along a spectrum that ranges from the sociopolitical and economic formations, through education and other social institutions, to the complex subjectivities of individual members of the social order. A critical new paradigmatic psychology of education, while sensitive to the impact on all three levels, focuses much of its attention on the level of individual subjectivity (consciousness). Here the new psychology emphasizes the impact of power on (1) the intrapersonal—the domain of consciousness; (2) the interpersonal—the domain of relationships and social interactions; and (3) corporeality—the domain of the body and behavior and each person's physical presence in the social world. These domains of subjectivity, along with social formations and institutions, are subtly integrated in a way that produces cultural reality. As such, we cannot examine one aspect (for example, subjectivity) in isolation from the others—an assertion that forever changes the study of psychology (Fiske, 1993).

Modernist psychology has not only failed to study power relations and the interaction of the social and the individual, it has actually helped power shape subjectivity and individual perception. As Michel Foucault (1984) argued, contemporary power takes the form of disciplinary power, and disciplinary power means both the prerogative to punish and the ability to use human sciences—psychology in particular—to transform individuals into "subjects." Psychology—working together with medicine, criminology education and the other human sciences—has helped produce a "normalized society." In the name of caring and humanism the practitioners in these disciplines wield a "confessional power" to extract admissions, induce guilt, assert authority, pry into the deepest recesses of the mind and force people to consent to their own oppression. Deborah Britzman (1995) addresses this notion of "normalization" in her discussion of Queer Theory, a philosophy that investigates notions of identity by "refusing normal practices and the practice of normalcy," by "exploring those things that education either dismisses or cannot bear to know," and by "imagining a sociality unhinged from the dominant conceptual order" (pp. 66, 68). Britzman believes that this theory will not only help to liberate women, gays and lesbians, transsexuals and bisexuals, ethnic minorities and counterculture youth from the discrimination that is perpetuated in the name of "normalcy," but can support all human beings who face the guilt, shame, oppression and injustices of authorities and power elites who attempt to force people to be and act "normal" (Morris, 1997).

Using these disciplines of knowledge, elite interests manage the behavior of large numbers of people. The poor and the nonwhite in particular can be stabilized and routinized so as to make their responses predictable and reduce the need for overt displays of force. Hidden in the disciplinary language of concern, the elites deploy domination in a way that precludes the resentment and resistance of the people; they neutralize the emergence of counterpower and its inconvenient agitation, resistance, critical pedagogy and popular coalitions (Ball, 1992; Ferguson, 1984).

In hyperreality the stakes of the game rise as power develops new educational and industrial psychological strategies to control individual behavior. The need for a critical postmodern psychology and a critical education to go with it thus has never been greater, and in the coming years the need will increase exponentially. Few voices in American culture come conceptually equipped to critique this use of psychology for domination: Conservative analysts were blinded by their identification with power elites, liberals by their complicity with the fields of study and knowledge production. In such an uncritical context, the disciplinary techniques of management, surveillance and control developed unimpeded, as psychologists unabashedly bandied about and deployed labels such as "normality" and "abnormality." Operating with the imprimatur of the hard sciences, this scholarly activity became naturalized to the point at which its subjects remained unaware of its origins, assumptions and effects.

The late twentieth century brought the steady growth of these disciplines, especially during the emergence of hyperreality with its proliferation of electronic information, high-tech methods of surveillance and ubiquitous visual media that provide power wielders direct and private access to the formation of the individual consciousness. Cartesian-Newtonian science has turned against its inventors, just as science fiction writers feared, while "the authorities" have educated, cured, reformed and punished in compliance with the needs of the power bloc. In this context of "the cure," the problems and pathologies are located in the individual. Because the diagnoses reflect the abstract individualization of modernist science, they help shape the ideology produced by the power bloc with its need to justify and thus maintain the status quo—its education, its political economy, its social institutions and its scientific establishment (Cooper, 1994; Donald, 1993; Denzin, 1987; Wexler, 1996).

BEYOND POWER: NEW EDUCATIONAL HORIZONS

Modernism's scientific realism cites progress to justify the last several centuries of Western history. It defines "progress" as improved living conditions, conquest, a vague success and scientific achievement. Modernist education and psychology justify hyperreality's invasion of individual consciousness in much the same way, as a manifestation of technological progress. But when they examine progress from a critical perspective, educators often find that much of what the modernist and the postmodernist eras accepted as progress actually moved the culture backward. When labeling a particular outcome "progress," modernist observers occasionally hid the "side effects"—whatever fell outside the specific outcome achieved. What about the environmental contamination and storage problems created by nuclear power plants? What about new viruses and bacteria that are resistant to modern medicine? What about the overuse and misuse of "miracle drugs" such as penicillin that have led to a medical crisis? What about economic policies that triggered the global economic crisis in 1998 and destroyed the lives of millions of working-class and poor people throughout the world? What about the incredible loss of farmland, green spaces and life-supporting rain forests due to urban sprawl, clear-cutting of old growth forests and slash and burn practices precipitated by the greed of wealthy nations and corporate monopolies? Does anyone realize that we need an ozone layer, soil, fresh water and clean air to live? Do we understand the connection between the tons of unnecessary trash that we generate and the danger landfills pose to our water and soil? When we dump our toxic trash on the bottom of the ocean or in waterways do we really believe that the pollution will not come back to haunt us and our children? Has anyone taken note of the impact of global warming—and not just the personal inconveniences associated with El Niño in 1998 or the drastic changes in weather patterns at the end of the twentieth century? The "side effects" of modern "progress" are exacting a heavy toll on the Earth and her citizens.

The same is true in schools. When we claim that a school's standardized test-score improvement is a sign of progress, we focus only on numbers. If the scores stand as our irrefutable proof, we cannot explore any simultaneous deterioration in our students' sense of well-being or their inability to find significance in the classroom. Indeed, a postmodern critique of these scores might well find that the obsession with test-score improvement has destroyed a pleasant ambiance in the school. If so, the "improvement" would hardly be progress. Postmodern analysis uncovers how repressive modernist narratives come to be constructed and how they require particular epistemologic, political and cognitive perspectives (Gergen, 1991; Aronowitz & Giroux, 1991).

As critical educators struggle to make sense of the disconcerting aspects of hyperreality and the future it portends, we begin to explore what the new paradigmatic way of seeing holds for education, psychology, sociology and philosophy. No longer do we accept macho modernist proclamations such as "I am positive" and "I *understand* education and reality." With our awareness of the various filters the media and other power groups use, we begin to understand the construction process. Such knowledge leads to a postmodern humility, a realization, in the words of Julia Kristeva, "that at the deepest levels of my wants and desires [I] am unsure, centerless and divided" (1987, pp. 7–8).

This postmodern humility represents not a passing uncertainty but a critical resistance to all representations and interpretations that claim universal certainty. In rejecting modernism's reason as the supreme form of cognition, critical educators seek alternative historically and social contingent—partial, as opposed to total—forms of thinking and knowing. Postmodern teachers no longer appeal to some sacrosanct body of professional knowledge above all other bodies of information in value. The partial, historically and socially specific knowledge of the practitioner must be respected for its insight, not for its certainty. No longer can teachers and teacher educators observe a permanent chasm between professional and everyday knowledge (Ferguson, 1980; Aronowitz & Giroux, 1991; Feinberg, 1989). Literally, we must question not only the texts that we teach, but the very ground of our certainty that leads us to believe that we, as teachers, "know" the "truth." We must constantly deconstruct the things that we teach, examine multiple points of view from all sorts of political, historical, philosophical, gendered, religious and racial perspectives, and be open to multiple interpretations. Our teachings are never complete or final.

One method of examining postmodern ways of seeing is to think of an infinite game that mocks certainty and the fundamentalist excesses that accompany it. Whether the excesses be religious, political, pedagogic or cognitive, they all denote an epistemologic arrogance that impedes self-reflection and interpersonal communication. Prone to hyperbole and error themselves, postmodernists laugh at their own fallibility. No one wins the postmodern game, but all players benefit when it exposes the pseudocertainties that plague modernism. Inclusionary and nonhierarchical, the game invites us to challenge the traditional rules that penalize outsiders, the players on the sidelines and in the margins (Gergen, 1991). We constantly look for ways to engage all students in the pedagogical dialogue. We seek out the poor, the abused, the immigrant, the handicapped, the religious minority, the atheist, the gay or lesbian, the frightened, the racial or ethnic minority, the depressed, the silent, the belligerent, the artistic, the activist, the talented, the minor sport or female athlete, the non-athletic, the institutionalized, the runaway, the drop-out, the bored, the ostracized, the migrant—any of those in the school community who are marginalized—and we validate their voices and listen to their perspectives. We bring them into the educational dialogue; we become their allies; we learn from them. Postmodern teachers are not limited by the official knowledge of the textbook or the district curriculum; they are constantly looking for ways to expand their awareness of multicultural issues and to act on those insights to contextualize teaching.

The frightening power of the directors of GM, Disney, Mattel, IBM and General Electric rests in their ability to profit from the manipulative charades their advertisers and public relations experts produce. By adroitly exploiting the media, corporate and political leaders gain more and more power to shape educational, economic, psychological and political futures. The critical value of addressing our description of the futuristic hyperreality, the postmodern insights that help shape the new paradigm and the educational and curriculum proposition we advance is that they can help expose the methods power uses to oppress, how our identities are constructed without our conscious notice and how power can use education to cloud our understanding of the world and even make us complicit in destroying the ecosystem and the physical, psychological and spiritual health of students. Without the ability to research, to think critically, to analyze the complexity of the cosmos, to expose the influence of power, to recover our spirituality, to grow in our community and to make meaning in our lives, we remain at the mercy of the hyperreal illusion of the future, and our children stand to inherit a great human tragedy. We can avoid this dystopian future if we understand the contexts in which teaching operates and then act on that knowledge.

References

Abercrombie, N. (1994). Authority and consumer society. In R. Keat, N. Whiteley, & N. Abercrombie (Eds.), *The authority of the consumer*. New York: Routledge.

Adler, M. J. (1982). *The Paideia proposal: An educational manifesto*. New York: Macmillan.

Adler, S. (1991). Forming a critical pedagogy in the social studies methods class: The use of imaginative literature. In B. Tabuchnick, & K. Zeichner (Eds.), *Issues and practices in inquiry-oriented teacher education*. New York: Falmer.

Agger, B. (1991). Critical theory, poststructuralism, and postmodernism: Their sociological relevance. *Annual Review of Sociology, 17,* 105–131.

Ahlstrom, S. E. (1972). *A religious history of the American people*. New Haven: Yale University Press.

Alcoff, L. (1995). Mestizo identity. In N. Zack (Ed.), *American mixed race: The culture of microdiversity*. Lanham, MD: Rowman and Littlefield.

Allison, C. B. (1995). *Present and past: Essays for teachers in the history of education*. New York: Peter Lang.

Alvesson, M., & Willmott, H. (1992). *Critical management studies*. London: Sage.

Altrichter, H., & Posch, P. (1989). Does the 'grounded theory' approach offer a guiding paradigm for teacher research? *Cambridge Journal of Education, 19* (1), 21–31.

America 2000: An educational strategy. (1991). Washington, DC: U.S. Government Printing Office.

Amott, T. (1993). *Caught in the crisis: Women and the U.S. economy today*. New York: Monthly Review Press.

Amott, T. L., & Matthaei, J. A. (1991). *Race, gender, and work: A multi-cultural history of women in the United States*. Boston: South End Press.

Anderson, J. D. (1988). *The education of blacks in the south, 1860–1935*. Chapel Hill: The University of North Carolina Press.

Appiah, K. (1995). Straightening out *The Bell Curve*. In R. Jacoby, & N. Glauberman (Eds.), *The bell curve debate: History, documents, and opinion*. New York: Random House.

Apple, M. W. (1979). *Ideology and curriculum*. London: Routledge and Kegan Paul.

Apple, M. (1985). Teaching and women's work: A comparative historical and ideological analysis. *Teachers College Record, 86* (3), 455–473.

Apple, M. W. (1988). What reform talk does: Creating new inequalities in education, *Educational Administration Quarterly, 24* (3), 272–281.

Apple, M. W. (1992). *Constructing the captive audience: Channel one and the political economy of the text*. Unpublished manuscript.

Apple, M. (1999). *Power, meaning, and Lientity: Essays in critical educational studies*. New York: Peter Lang.

Apple, M. W., & Christian-Smith, L. (Eds.). (1991). *The politics of the textbook*. New York: Routledge & Kegan Paul.

Arlin, P. (1975). Cognitive development in adulthood: A fifth stage. *Developmental Psychology, 11* (5), 602–606.

Arnot, M. (1992). Schools and families: A feminist perspective. In K. Weiler, & C. Mitchell (Eds.), *What schools can do: Critical pedagogy and practice*. Albany, NY: SUNY Press.

Aronowitz, S. (1973). *False promises.* New York: McGraw Hill.

Aronowitz, S. (1983). The relativity of theory. *The Village Voice, 27,* 60.

Aronowitz, S. (1992). *The politics of identity: Class, culture and social movements.* New York: Routledge.

Aronowitz, S., & DiFazio, W. (1994). *The jobless future: Sci-tech and the dogma of work.* Minneapolis: University of Wisconsin Press.

Aronowitz, S., & Giroux, H. (1991). *Post-modern education: Politics, culture, and social criticism.* Minneapolis: University of Minnesota Press.

Ashburn, E. (1987). Three crucial issues concerning the preparation of teachers for our classrooms: Definition, development and determination of competence. In E. Flaxman (Ed.), *Trends and issues in education, 1986.* Washington, DC: U.S. Department of Education.

Ashley, D. (1991). Playing with the pieces: The fragmentation of social theory. In P. Wexler (Ed.), *Critical theory now.* New York: Falmer.

Axtell, R., & Epstein, J. M. (1996). *Growing artificial societies: social science from the bottom up.* Washington, DC: Brookings Institution Press.

Ayers, W. (1992). Disturbances from the field: Recovering the voice of the early childhood teacher. In S. Kessler, & B. Swadener (Eds.), *Reconceptualizing the early childhood curriculum.* New York: Teachers College Press.

Bahmueller, C. F. (Ed.). (1991). *Civitas.* Calabasas, CA: Center for Civic Education.

Baldwin, E. (1987). Theory versus ideology in the practice of teacher education. *Journal of Teacher Education, 38,* 16–19.

Ball, T. (1992). New faces of power. In T. Wartenberg (Ed.), *Rethinking power.* Albany, NY: State University of New York.

Balsamo, A. (1985). *Beyond female as variable: Constructing a feminist perspective on organizational analysis.* Paper presented at the Conference on Critical Perspectives in Organizational Analysis, New York.

Banfield, B. (1991). Honoring cultural diversity and building on its strengths: A case for national action. In L. Wolfe (Ed.), *Women, work, and school: Occupational segregation and the role of education.* Boulder, CO: Westview.

Banks, J. A., & Banks, C. A. M. (1997). *Multicultural Education: Issues and perspectives* (3rd ed.). Boston: Allyn and Bacon.

Barber, B. R. (1992). *An aristocracy of everyone: The politics of education and the future of America.* New York: Oxford University Press.

Barrow, R. (1984). *Giving teaching back to teachers.* Totowa, New Jersey: Barnes and Noble Books.

Baudrillard, J. (1988). *Selected works* (M. Poster, Ed.). Cambridge: Polity Press.

Bauman, Z. (1992). *Intimations of postmodernity.* London: Routledge.

Beard, C. A., & Beard, M. R. (1930). *The rise of American civilization.* New York: Macmillan.

Becker, C. L. (1932). *The heavenly city of the eighteenth-century philosophers.* New Haven: Yale University Press.

Becker, G. S. (1993). *Human capital: A theoretical and empirical analysis, with special reference to education* (3rd ed.). Chicago: University of Chicago Press.

Beed, C. (1991). Philosophy of science and contemporary economics: An overview. *Journal of Post-Keynesian Economics, 13* (4), 459–494.

Belenky, M. F., Clinchy, B. M., Goldberger, N. R., Tarule, J. M. (1986). *Women's ways of knowing: The development of self, voice and mind.* New York: Basic.

Bellah, R., et al. (1991). *The good society.* New York: Vintage.

Bennett, D. H. (1995). *The party of fear: The American far right from nativism to the militia movement.* New York: Vintage.

Bennett, W. (1987). *The James Madison elementary school: A curriculum for American students*. Washington, DC: U.S. Government Printing Office.

Bennett, W. (1994). *Book of virtues: A collection of great moral stories*. New York: Simon and Schuster.

Benson, S., Brier, S., & Rosenzweig, R. (1986). Introduction. In S. Benson, S. Brier, & R. Rosenzweig (Eds.), *Presenting the past: Essays on history and the public*. Philadelphia: Temple University Press.

Benson, G., Glasberg, R., & Griffith, B. (Eds.) (1998). *Perspectives on the unity and integration of knowledge*. New York: Peter Lang.

Berliner, D. C., & Biddle, B. J. (1996). *The manufactured crisis: Myths, fraud and the attack on the American public schools*. Reading, MA: Addison-Wesley.

Bernstein, B. (1994). *Statement of philosophy of art and education*. Ashland, OH: Coburn Gallery of Art, Ashland University.

Berube, M. R. (1991). *American presidents and education*. New York: Greenwood Press.

Best, J. H. (Ed.). (1962). *Benjamin Franklin on education*. New York: Teachers College, Columbia University.

Best, S. (1993). Perspectives on deregulation of schooling in America. *British Journal of Educational Studies, 41* (2), 122–133.

Best, S., & Kellner, D. (1997). *The postmodern turn*. New York: Guilford.

Bestor, A. (1985). *Educational wastelands: The retreat from learning on our public schools* (2nd ed.). Urbana: University of Illinois Press.

Block, A. (1995). *Occupied reading: Critical foundations for an ecological theory*. New York: Garland.

Block, F. (1990). *Postindustrial possibilities: A critique of economic discourse*. Berkeley: University of California Press.

Bluestone, B. (1988). Deindustrialization and unemployment in America. *The Review of Black Political Economy, 17* (2), 29–44.

Bluestone B., & Harrison, B. (1982). *The great American job machine: The proliferation of low wage employment in the U.S. economy: A study prepared for the Joint Economic Committee*. Washington, DC: The Joint Economic Committee.

Bluestone, I., & Brown, A. (1983). Foreword. In A. Wirth (Ed.), *Productive work—In industry and schools: Becoming persons again*. Lanham, MD: University Press of America.

Bobbitt, N. (1987). Reflective thinking: Meaning and implications for teaching. In R. G. Thomas (Ed.), *Higher-order thinking: Definition, meaning and instructional approaches*. Washington, DC: Home Economics Education Association.

Bogdan, R., & Biklen, S. (1982). *Qualitative research for education: An introduction to theory and methods*. Boston: Allyn and Bacon.

Bohm, D., & Edwards, M. (1991). *Changing consciousness*. San Francisco: Harper.

Bohm, D., & Peat, F. (1987). *Science, order, and creativity*. New York: Bantam Books.

Books, S. (1993). Literary journalism as educational criticism: A discourse of triage. *Holistic Education Review 5* (3), 41–51.

Books, S. (1994). *Social foundations in an age of triage*. New Paltz, New York: Unpublished paper.

Books, S. (Ed.). (1998). *Invisible children in the society and its schools*. Mahwah, NY: Lawrence Erlbaum.

Borgmann, A. (1992). *Crossing the postmodern divide*. Chicago: University of Chicago Press.

Boutros-Ghali, B. (1994, August 1). Boutros-Ghali speaks out. *Time, 144,* 37.

Bowers, C. (1982). The reproduction of technological consciousness: Locating the ideological foundations of a radical pedagogy. *Teachers College Record, 83* (4), 529–557.

Bowers, C., & Flinders, D. (1990). *Responsive teaching: An ecological approach to classroom patterns of language, culture, and thought*. New York: Teachers College Press.

Bowles, S., & Gintis, H. (1976). *Schooling in capitalist America: Educational reform and the contradictions of economic life*. New York: Basic.

Boycotts in Action. (1988). *Targets*.

Bozik, M. (1987, November). *Critical thinking through creative thinking*. Paper presented to the Speech Communication Association, Boston.

Brady, J. (1997). Multiculturalism and the American dream. In S. Steinberg, & J. Kincheloe (Eds.), *Kinderculture: The corporate construction of childhood*. Boulder: Westview.

Britzman, D. P. (1991). *Practice makes practice: A critical study of learning to teach*. Albany: SUNY Press.

Britzman, D. (1995a). What is this thing called love? *Taboo: The Journal of Culture and Education, 1*, 65–93.

Britzman, D. (1995b). Is there a queer pedagogy? Or, stop reading straight. *Educational Theory, 45* (2), 151–165.

Brosio, R. (1985). *A bibliographic essay on the world of work*. Paper presented to American Educational Studies Association, Chicago, Illinois.

Brosio, R. (1994). *The radical democratic critique of capitalist education*. New York: Peter Lang.

Buckley, W. F. (1957, August 24). Why the south must prevail. *National Review, 4*, 148–149.

Bullock, H. A. (1969). *A history of negro education in the south: from 1619 to the present*. Cambridge: Harvard University Press.

Bullough, R., & Gitlin, A. (1991). Educative communities and the development of the reflective practitioner. In R. Tabachnick, & K. Zeichner (Eds.), *Issues and practices in inquiry-oriented teacher education*. New York: Falmer Press.

Butler, J. (1990). *Gender trouble: Feminism and the subversion of identity*. New York: Routledge.

Button, H. W., & Provenzo, E. F., Jr. (1989). *History of education and culture in America*. Englewood Cliffs: Prentice Hall.

Butts, R. F., Cremin, L. A. (1953). *A history of education in American culture*. New York: Holt, Rinehart and Winston.

Caine, R. N., & Caine, G. (1991). *Making connections: Teaching and the human brain*. Alexandria, VA: ASCD Press.

Calinescu, M. (1987). *Five faces of modernity: Modernism, avant-garde, decadence, kitsch, postmodernism*. Durham, NC: Duke University Press.

Callahan, R. E. (1962). *Education and the cult of efficiency*. Chicago: University of Chicago Press.

Cannella, G. (1996). *Deconstructing early childhood education*. New York: Peter Lang.

Campbell, J. with Moyers, B. (1988). *The power of myth*. New York: Doubleday.

Capra, F., Steindl-Rast, D., & Matus, T. (1992). *Belonging to the universe: New thinking about God and nature*. New York: Penguin.

Caraley, D. (1992). Washington abandons the cities. *Political Science Quarterly, 107* (1), 1–32.

Carby, H. (1992). The multicultural wars. In G. Dent (Ed.), *Black popular culture*. Seattle: Bay Press.

Carlson, D., & Apple, M. (Eds). (1998). *Power/knowledge/pedagogy: The meaning of democratic education in unsettling times*. Boulder, CO: Westview.

Carnevale, A. (1992). Skills for the New World Order. *American School Board Journal, 179* (5) 28–30.

Caro, R. A. (1990). *The years of Lyndon Johnson: Means of ascent*. New York: Alfred A. Knopf.

Carr, W., & Kemmis, S. (1986). *Becoming critical.* Philadelphia: Falmer Press.

Carson, T., & Sumara, D. (Eds.) (1997). *Action research as a living practice.* New York: Peter Lang.

Cary, R. (1999). *Critical art pedagogy: Foundations for postmodern art education.* New York: Garland.

Case, R. (1985). *Intellectual development: Birth to adulthood.* New York: Academic Press.

Castenell, L., Jr., & Pinar, W. F. (1993). *Understanding curriculum as racial text: Representations of identity and difference in education.* Albany, NY: SUNY Press.

Center for a Postmodern World. (1990). John B. Cobb, Jr. (Ed.), *Position paper on postmodernism.* Claremont, CA: Claremont Graduate School of Theology.

Chamberlin, G. (1974). Phenomenological methodology and understanding education. In D. Denton (Ed.), *Existentialism and phenomenology in education.* New York: Teachers College Press.

Chesneaux, J. (1992). *Brave new world: The prospects for survival.* London: Thames and Hudson.

Christian-Smith, L., & Erdman, J. (1997). Mom, it's not real: Children constructing childhood through reading horror fiction. In S. Steinberg, & J. Kincheloe (Eds.), *Kinderculture: Corporate constructions of childhood.* Boulder, CO: Westview.

Chubb, J. E., & Moe, T. M. (1990). *Politics, markets and America's schools.* Washington, DC: The Brookings Institution.

Clifford, G. J. (1989). Man/woman/teacher: Gender, family, and career in American educational history. In D. Warren (Ed.), *American teachers: Histories of a profession at work.* New York: Macmillan.

Clough, P. (1998). *The ends of ethnography: From realism to social criticism.* New York: Peter Lang.

Clover, C. (1993). Falling down and the rise of the average white male. In P. Cook, & P. Dodd (Eds.), *Women and film: A sight and sound reader.* Philadelphia: Temple University Press.

Codd, J. (1984). Introduction. In J. Codd (Ed.), *Philosophy, common sense, and action in educational administration.* Victoria, Australia: Deakin University Press.

Cohen, S. (1999). *Challenging orthodoxies: Toward a new cultural history of education.* New York: Peter Lang.

Collins, J. (1995). Architectures of excess: Cultural life in the information age. New York: Routledge.

Collins, P. (1990). *Black feminist thought: Knowledge, consciousness, and the politics of empowerment.* New York: Routledge.

Condeloro, D. (1973). Undergraduates as historians: Recovering the history of a black community. *The History Teacher, 7*(1), 24–29.

Coontz, S. (1992). *The way we never were: American families and the nostalgia trap.* New York: Basic.

Cooper, B. S. (1988). School reform in the 1980s: The new right's legacy, *Educational Administration Quarterly, 24*(3), 282–298.

Cooper, D. (1994). Productive, relational, and everywhere? Conceptualizing power and resistance within Foucauldian feminism. *Sociology, 28*(2), 435–454.

Copa, G. H., & Tebbenhoff, E. (1990). *Subject matter of vocational education: In pursuit of foundations.* Berkeley, CA: National Center for Research in Vocational Education.

Cotton, J. (1992). Towards a theory and strategy for black economic development. In J. Jennings (Ed.), *Race, politics, and economic development: Community perspectives.* New York: Verso.

Counts, G. S. (1978). *Dare the school build a new social order?* Carbondale: Southern Illinois Press.

Courteney, R. (1988). *No one way of being: A study of the practical knowledge of elementary arts teachers.* Toronto: MGS.

Courts, P. (1997). *Multicultural literacies: Dialect, discourse, and diversity.* New York: Peter Lang.

Cremin, L. A. (1961). *Transformation of the school progressivism in American education.* New York: Knopf.

Cremin, L. A. (1970). *American education: The colonial experience, 1607–1783.* New York: Harper & Row.

Cremin, L. A. (1988). *American education: The metropolitan experience, 1876–1980.* New York: Harper & Row.

Critical Art Ensemble. (1994). *The electronic disturbance.* Brooklyn, NY: Autonomedia.

Cruickshank, D. (1987). *Reflective teaching: The preparation of students of teaching.* Reston, VA: Association of Teacher Educators.

Cuban, L. (1988). The persistence of reform in American schools. In Donald Warren (Ed.), *American teachers: Histories of a profession at work*, New York: Macmillan.

Cubberley, E. P. (1919). *Public education in the United States: A study and interpretation of American education history.* Boston: Houghton Mifflin.

Cuber, J. F. (1989). *Sex and the significant Americans: A study of sexual behavior among the affluent.* New York: Penguin.

Dalton, M. (1999). *The Hollywood curriculum: Teachers and teaching in the* movies. New York: Peter Lang.

Darder, A. (1991). *Culture and power in the classroom.* Westport, CT: Bergin & Garvey.

Darling-Hammond, L. (1995). Policy for restructuring. In A. Lieberman (Ed.), *The work of restructuring schools: Building from the ground up.* New York: Teachers College Press.

Daspit, T., & Weaver, J. (1998). *Popular culture and critical pedagogy: reading, constructing, connecting.* New York: Garland.

Davis, A.Y. (1981). *Women, race and class.* New York: Vintage.

Delany, S. L., Delany, A. E., with Hearth, A. H. (1993). *Having our say: The Delany sisters' first 100 years.* New York: Dell.

Deleuze, G., & Gauttari, F. (1986). *Kafka: Toward a minor literature.* (D. Polan, Trans.). Minneapolis: University of Minnesota Press.

Demos, J. (1986). *Past, present, and personal: The family and the life course in American history.* New York: Oxford University Press.

Denzin, N. (1987). Postmodern children. *Caring for Children/Society, 32–39.*

Derrida, J. (1976). *Of grammatology.* Baltimore: Johns Hopkins University Press.

Derrida, J. (1981). *Positions.* Chicago: University of Chicago Press.

Derrida, J. (1982). *Margins of philosophy.* Chicago: University of Chicago Press.

Dewey, J. (1908). *Ethics.* New York: Henry Holt and Company.

Dewey, J. (1916). *Democracy and education.* New York: The Free Press.

Dewey, J. (1929). *The sources of a science of education.* New York: Horace Liveright.

Dewey, J. (1934a). *A common faith.* New Haven, CT: Yale University Press.

Dewey, J. (1934b). *Art as experience.* New York: Minton, Balch & Company.

Dewey, J. (1938). *Experience and education.* New York: Macmillan.

Dewey, J. (1994). My pedagogic creed. In A. Sadovnick, P. Cookson, & S. Semel (Eds.), *Exploring education: An introduction to the foundations of education.* Boston: Allyn and Bacon.

DeVore, D. E. (1983). *The rise from the nadir: Black New Orleans between the wars, 1920–1940.* New Orleans: University of New Orleans.

DeYoung, A. (1989). *Economics and American education.* New York: Longman.

di Leonardo, M. (1994). White ethnicities, identity politics, and baby bear's chair. *Social Text, 41,* 5–33.

Diamond, S. (1995). *Roads to dominion: Right-wing movements and political power in the United States.* New York: Guilford.

Doll, W. E., Jr. (1993). *A post-modern perspective on curriculum.* New York: Teachers College Press.

Doll, M. A. (1995). *To the lighthouse and back: Writings on teaching and living.* New York: Peter Lang.

Donald, J. (1993). The natural man and the virtuous woman: Reproducing citizens. In C. Jenks (Ed.), *Cultural reproduction.* New York: Routledge.

Donmoyer, R. (1985). The rescue from relativism: Two failed attempts and an alternative strategy. *Educational Researcher, 14*(7), 2–7.

Donmoyer, R. (1987). Beyond Thorndike/beyond melodrama. *Curriculum Inquiry, 17* (4), 353–363.

Dorfman, A. (1971). *How to read Donald Duck: Imperialist ideology in the Disney comic.* Paris: International General.

Du Plessis, R. (1995). HOO, HOO, HOO: Some episodes in the construction of modern whiteness. *American Literature, 67*(4), 667–700.

Dubino, J. (1993). The Cinderella complex: Romance fiction, patriarchy, and capitalism. *Journal of Popular Culture, 27*(3), 103–118.

DuBois, W. (1973). *The education of black people: Ten critiques, 1906–1960.* H. Aptheker (Ed.) New York: Monthly Review Press.

Duckworth, E. (1987). *The having of wonderful ideas and other essays on teaching and learning.* New York: Teachers College Press.

Duke, D. (1979). Debriefing: A tool for curriculum research and course improvement. *Journal of Curriculum Studies, 9*(2), 157–163.

Duke, D. (1985). What is the nature of educational excellence and should we try to measure it? *Phi Delta Kappan, 66*(10), 157–163.

Edelman, M. J. (1974). The political language of the helping professions. *Politics and Society, 4*(4), 295–310.

Edelman, M. J. (1984). *The symbolic uses of politics.* Urbana: University of Illinois Press.

Edelman, M. J. (1988). *Constructing the political spectacle.* Chicago: University of Chicago Press.

Eisenman, R. (1995, October). Take pride in being white. Letter to editor. *Chronicle of Higher Education,* 134.

Eisner, E. (1984). Can educational research inform educational practice? *Phi Delta Kappan, 65*(7), 447–452.

Eisner, E. (1991). *The enlightened eye: Qualitative inquiry and the enhancement of educational practice.* New York: Macmillan.

Eisner, E. (1994). *The educational imagination: on the design and evaluation of school programs* (3rd ed.). New York: Macmillan.

Eliot, T. S. (1971). *The collected poems and plays of T. S. Eliot: 1909–1950.* New York: Harcourt, Brace, and World.

Elliott, J. (1989). *Studying the school curriculum through insider research.* Paper presented to the International Conference on School-Based Innovations: Looking Forward to the 1990s, Hong Kong.

Elliott, J. M. (1989). *Success indicators for elementary school counseling programs as perceived by maternal parents, teachers, students, administrators, and counselors.* Florida State University: Thesis.

Ellsworth, E. (1997). *Teaching position: Difference, pedagogy, and the power of address.* New York: Teachers College Press.

Ellwood, D. (1988). *Poor support: Poverty in the American family.* New York: Basic.

Elsbree, W. S. (1939). *The American teacher: Evolution of a profession in a democracy.* New York: American Book Company.

Emery, F., & Thorsrud, E. (1976). *Democracy at work.* Leiden: Martinus Nijhoff.

Fee, E. (1982). Is feminism a threat to scientific objectivity? *International Journal of Women's Studies, 4*(4), 378–392.

Feinberg, W. (1989). Foundationalism and recent critiques of education. *Educational Theory, 39*(2), 133–138.

Feinberg, W., & Horowitz, B. (1990). Vocational education and the equality of opportunity. *Journal of Curriculum Studies, 22*(2), 188–192.

Ferguson, A. (1991). *Sexual democracy: Women, oppression, and revolution.* Boulder, CO: Westview.

Ferguson, K. (1984). *The feminist case against bureaucracy.* Philadelphia: Temple University Press.

Ferguson, K. (1993). *The man question: Visions of subjectivity in feminist theory.* Berkeley: University of California Press.

Ferguson, M. (1980). *The Aquarian conspiracy: Personal and social transformation in our time.* Los Angeles: J. P. Tarcher.

Ferguson, S. (1994). The comfort of being sad. *Utne Reader, 64,* 60–61.

Fetterman, D. (1988). Qualitative approaches to evaluating education. *Educational Researcher, 17*(8), 17–23.

Fine, M. (1993). Sexuality, schooling, and adolescent females: The missing discourse of desire. In M. Fine, & L. Weis (Eds.), *Beyond silenced voices: Class, race, and gender in United States schools.* Albany, NY: SUNY Press.

Fine, M. (1998). *Off track.* [Film.] Markie Hancock (Prod. and Dir.). Markie Hancock Productions.

Finn, C. E. (1991). *We must take charge: Our schools and our future.* New York: Free Press.

Finn, C. (1982). A call for quality education. *American Education, 108,* 28–34.

Fischer, D. H. (1970). *Historians' fallacies: Towards a logic of historical thought.* New York: Harper Torchbooks.

Fiske, J. (1993). *Power plays, power works.* New York: Verso.

Fiske, J. (1994). *Media matters: Everyday culture and political change.* Minneapolis: University of Minnesota Press.

Fiske, D., & Shweder, R. (1986). *Metatheory in social science: Pluralisms and subjectivities.* Chicago: University of Chicago Press.

Flax, J. (1990). Postmodernism and gender relations in feminist theory. In L. Nicholson (Ed.), *Feminism/postmodernism.* New York: Routledge.

Floden, R., & Klinzing, H. (1990). What can research on teacher thinking contribute to teacher preparation? A second opinion. *Educational Researcher, 19*(5), 15–20.

Fosnot, C. (1988). *The dance of education.* Paper presented to the Annual Conference of the Association for Educational Communication and Technology, New Orleans.

Foucault, M. (1972a). *Power/Knowledge.* New York: Pantheon.

Foucault, M. (1972b). *The archaeology of knowledge.* New York: Pantheon.

Foucault, M. (1977a). *Language, counter-memory, practice.* Ithaca, NY: Cornell University press.

Foucault, M. (1977b). *Discipline and Punish: The birth of the prison.* (A. Sheridan, Trans.). New York: Vintage.

Foucault, M. (1979). *Discipline and punish: The birth of the prison.* NewYork: Pantheon.

Foucault, M. (1983). *This is not a pipe*. (J. Harkness, Trans.). Berkeley: University of California Press.

Foucault, M. (1984). *The Foucault reader*. (P. Rabinow, Ed.). New York: Pantheon.

Frankenberg, R. (1993b). *The social construction of whiteness: White women, race matters*. Minneapolis: University of Minnesota Press.

Franklin, B. (1986). Building the American community: The school curriculum and the search for social justice. In W. F. Pinar (Ed.), *Contemporary Curriculum Discourses*. Philadelphia: Falmer Press.

Franklin, B. (1998). *Whatever happened to social control?: The meaning of coercive authority in curriculum discourse*. Scottsdale, AZ: Gorsuch, Scarisbrick.

Fraser, J. W. (1989). Agents of democracy: Urban elementary-school teachers and the conditions of teaching. In D. Warren (Ed.), *American teachers: Histories of a profession at work*. New York: Macmillan.

Freire, P. (1970). *Pedagogy of the oppressed*. New York: Herder and Herder.

Freire, P. (1972). *Research methods*. Paper presented to a seminar entitled Studies in Adult Education, Dar-es-Salaam, Tanzania, *25*, 9–23.

Freire, P., & Shor I. (1987). *A pedagogy for liberation: Dialogues on transforming education*. South Hadley, MA: Bergin & Garvey.

French, W. M. (1964). *America's educational tradition: An interpretive history*. Boston: D.C. Heath.

Fried, R. (1995). *The passionate teachers: A practical guide*. Boston: Beacon Press.

Frisch, M. B. (1981). *The predictive validity of self-respect measures of assertiveness: and the external validity of role-play assessments of social skills as influenced by instructional demand*. University of Kansas: Thesis.

Fusco, C. (1992). Pan-American postnationalism: Another world order. In G. Dent (Ed.), *Black popular culture*. Seattle: Bay Press.

Gaines, D. (1990). *Teenage wasteland: Suburbia's dead end kids*. New York: Harper Perennial.

Gallagher, C. (1994). White reconstruction in the university. *Social Review, 24* (1–2), 165–187.

Gandhi, L. (1998). *Post colonial theory: A critical introduction*. New York: Teachers College Press.

Gardner, H. (1983). *Frames of mind: A theory of multiple intelligences*. New York: Basic.

Garman, N., & Hazi, H. (1988). Teachers ask: Is there life after Madeline Hunter? *Phi Delta Kappan, 60,* 670–672.

Garrison, J. (1988). Democracy, scientific knowledge, and teacher empowerment. *Teachers College Record, 89* (4), 487–504.

Garrison, J. (1989). The role of postpositivistic philosophy of science in the renewal of vocational education research. *Journal of Vocational Education Research, 14* (3), 39–51.

Gay, G. (1994). *At the essence of learning: Multicultural Education*. West Lafayette, IN: Kappa Delta Pi.

Gergen, K. (1991). *The saturated self: Dilemmas of identity in contemporary life*. New York: Basic.

Gilligan, C. (1981). *In a different voice: Psychological theory and women's development*. Cambridge, MA: Harvard University Press.

Gilligan, C. (1982). *In a different voice*. Cambridge, MA: Harvard University Press.

Giroux, H. (1986). Critical theory and the politics of culture and voice: Rethinking the discourse of educational research. *Journal of Thought, 21,* 84–105.

Giroux, H. (1988). *Schooling and the struggle for public life: Critical pedagogy in the modern age*. Minneapolis: University of Minnesota Press.

Giroux, H. (1991). Introduction: Modernism, postmodernism, and feminism: Rethinking the boundaries of educational discourse. In H. Giroux (Ed.), *Postmodernism, feminism, and cultural politics: Redrawing educational boundaries*. Albany, NY: SUNY Press.

Giroux, H. (1992). *Border crossings: Cultural workers and the politics of education*. New York: Routledge.

Giroux, H. (1993). *Living dangerously: Multiculturalism and the politics of difference*. New York: Peter Lang.

Giroux, H. (1995). White panic. In C. Berlet (Ed.), *Eyes right: Challenging the right-wing backlash*. Boston: South End Press.

Giroux, H. (1997). Are Disney movies good for your kids? In S. Steinberg, & J. Kincheloe (Eds.), *Kinderculture: Corporate constructions of childhood*. Boulder, CO: Westview.

Giroux, H. A., & McLaren, P. (1989). *Critical pedagogy, the state, and cultural struggle*. Albany, NY: SUNY Press.

Glickman, C. (1985). *Development as the aim of instructional supervision*. Paper presented to the Association for Supervision and Curriculum Development, Chicago.

Global Alliance for Transforming Education (GATE). (1991). Education 2000: A holistic perspective. *Holistic Education Review, 4* (4 [Supplement]), pp. 1–18.

Goals 2000: An Educational Strategy. (1993). Washington, DC: U.S. Government Printing Office.

Goldman, R. (1992). *Reading ads socially*. New York: Routledge.

Gomez, M. (1992). Breaking silences: Building new stories of classroom life through teacher transformation. In S. Kesller, & B. Swadener (Eds.), *Reconceptualizing the early childhood curriculum*. New York: Teachers College Press.

Goodlad, J. I., Soder, R., & Sirotnik, K. A. (1990). *The moral dimension of teaching*. San Francisco: Jossey-Bass.

Goodlad, J. I. (1992). *Toward educative communities and tomorrow's teachers*. Seattle: Institute for Educational Inquiry.

Goodman, J. (1986). *Constructing a practical philosophy of teaching: A study of preservice teachers' professional perspectives*. Paper presented to the American Educational Research Association, San Francisco.

Goodman, S. L. (1995). *Philosophy Statement*. Ashland University of Ohio: Unpublished Paper.

Goodson, I. (1997). *The changing curriculum: studies in social construction*. New York: Peter Lang.

Gore, J. (1993). *The struggle for pedagogies: Critical and feminist discourses as regimes of truth*. New York: Routledge.

Grady, H., & Wells, S. (1985–1986). Toward a rhetoric of intersubjectivity: Introducing Jurgen Habermas. *Journal of Advanced Composition, 6,* 33–47.

Gramsci, A. (1988). *An Antonio Gramsci reader*. (D. Forgacs, Ed.). New York: Schocken Books.

Green, J. (1984). People's history and socialist theory: A review essay. *Radical History Review, 28,* 169–186.

Greene, M. (1975). Curriculum and consciousness. In W. Pinar (Ed.), *Curriculum theorizing: The reconceptualist*. Berkeley: McCutchan Publishing.

Greene, M. (1978). *Landscapes of learning*. New York: Teachers College Press.

Greene, M. (1986). In search of a critical pedagogy. *Harvard Educational Review, 56* (4), 427–441.

Greene, M. (1988). *The dialectic of freedom*. New York: Teachers College Press.

Greene, M. (1995). *Releasing the imagination: Essays on education, the arts, and social change*. New York: Teachers College Press.

Greider, W. (1992). *Who will tell the people? The betrayal of American democracy.* New York: Touchstone.

Gresson, A. (1995). *The recovery of race in America.* Minneapolis: University of Minnesota Press.

Gresson, A. (1997). Professional wrestling and youth culture: Teasing, taunting, and the containment of civility. In J. Kincheloe, & S. Steinberg (Eds.), *Kinderculture: Corporate constructions of childhood.* Boulder, CO: Westview.

Griffin, C. (1993). *Representations of youth: The study of youth and adolescence in Britain and America.* Cambridge, MA: Polity Press.

Griffin, D. R. (Ed.). (1988a). *The reenchantment of science: Postmodern proposals.* Albany, NY: SUNY Press.

Griffin, D. R. (1988b). *Spirituality and society: Postmodern visions.* Albany, NY: SUNY Press.

Grimmett, P., Erickson, G., MacKinnon, A., & Tiecken, T. (1990). Reflective practice in teacher education. In R. Clift, W. Houston, & M. Pugach (Eds.), *Encouraging reflective practice in education: An analysis of issues and programs.* New York: Teachers College Press.

Grossberg, L. (1989). Pedagogy in the present: Politics, postmodernity, and the popular. In H. Giroux, & R. Simon (Eds.), *Popular culture: Schooling and everyday life.* Granby, MA: Bergin & Garvey.

Grossberg, L. (1992). *We gotta get out of this place.* New York: Routledge.

Grossberg, L. (1995). What's in a name (one more time)? *Taboo: The Journal of Culture and Education, 1,* 1–37.

Grumet, M. (1988). *Bitter milk: Women and teaching.* Amherst: University of Massachusetts Press.

Hacker, D. G. (1989). *Testing for learning outcomes.* Alexandria, VA: American Society for Training and Development.

Hacker, A. (1992). *Two nations: Black and white, separate, hostile, unequal.* New York: Ballantine.

Hafter, J. C., Hoffman, P. M. (1973). Segregation academies and state action. *Yale Law Journal, 82* (7), 1436–1461.

Hair, W. I. (1969). *Bourbonism and agrarian protest: Louisiana politics.* Baton Rouge, LA: Louisiana State University Press.

Hale, F. W., Jr. (1992). *Hale's inventory for assessing an institution's commitment to multicultural programming.* Columbus, OH: Technical Instructional Professional Support Services.

Hammersley, M., & Atkinson, P. (1983). *Ethnography: Principles in practice.* New York: Tavistock.

Hannam, M. (1990). The dream of democracy. *Arena, 90,* 109–116.

Haraway, D. (1991). *Simians, cyborgs, and women.* New York: Routledge.

Haraway, D. (1997). *Modest_witness@second_millenium.femaleMan_meet_oncomouse TM: Feminism and technoscience.* New York: Routledge.

Harding, S. (1986). *The science question in feminism.* Ithaca, NY: Cornell University Press.

Harding, S. (1996). Science is good to think with. In A. Ross (Ed.), *Science wars.* Durham, NC: Duke University Press.

Harred, J. (1991). *Collaborative learning in the literature: Old problems revisited.* Paper presentd at the Conference on College and Communication, Boston.

Harris, K. (1984). Philosophers of education: Detached spectators or political practitioners. In J. Codd (Ed.), *Philosophy, common sense, and action in educational administration.* Victoria, Australia: Deakin University Press.

Harvey, D. (1989). *The condition of postmodernity*. Cambridge, Massachusetts: Basil Blackwell.

Hassard, J. A. G. (1866). *Life of the Most Reverend John Hughes*. New York: Appleton.

Hauser, K. (1992). Unlearning patriarchy: Personal development in Marge Piercy's *Fly Away Home. Feminist Review, 42,* 33–42.

Hauser, J. (1991). *Critical inquiries, uncertainties and not faking it with students.* Paper presented at the Annual Conference of the Center for Critical Thinking and Moral Critique, Rohnert Park, California.

Hauser, M., & Jipson, J. (1998). *Intersections: Feminisms/early childhoods.* New York: Peter Lang.

Hayden, R. (1986). Comment. In D. Hine (Ed.), *The state of Afro-American history: Past, present, and future.* Baton Rouge, LA: Louisiana State University press.

Haymes, S. (1995). Educational reform: What have been the effects of the attempts to improve education over the last decade? In J. Kincheloe, & S. Steinberg (Eds.), *Thirteen questions: Reframing education's conversation.* New York: Peter Lang.

Haymes, S. (1996). Race, repression, and the politics of crime and punishment in *The Bell Curve.* In J. Kincheloe, S. Steinberg, & A. Gresson (Eds.), *Measured lies:* The Bell Curve *examined.* New York: St. Martin's.

Hebdige, D. (1989). *Hiding in the light.* New York: Routledge.

Hedley, M. (1994). The presentation of gendered conflict in popular movies: Affective stereotypes, cultural sentiments, and men's motivation. *Sex Roles, 31,* 721–740.

Hekman, S. (1990). *Gender and knowledge: Elements of a postmodern feminism.* Boston: Northeastern University Press.

Held, D. (1980). *Introduction to critical theory: Horkheimer to Habermas.* Berkeley: University of California Press.

Henderson, J. G. & Hawthorne, R. D. (1995). *Transformative curriculum leadership.* New York: Macmillan.

Herbst, J. (1989). Teacher preparation in the nineteenth century: Institutions and purposes. In D. Warren (Ed.), *American teachers: Histories of a profession at work.* New York: Macmillan.

Herrnstein, R. J., & Murray, C. (1994). *The bell curve: Intelligence and class structure in American life.* New York: Free Press.

Hillison, J., & Camp, W. (1985). History and future of the dual school system for vocational education. *Journal for Vocational and Technical Education, 2* (1), 48–56.

Hinchey, P. (1998). *Finding freedom in the classroom: A practical introduction to critical theory.* New York: Peter Lang.

Hindman, J. (1992). *Gestures? We don't need your stinking gestures!: Empowerment through radical teachers and cultural action for freedom.* Paper presented to the Conference on College Composition and Communication, Cincinnati, Ohio.

Hodge, R., & Kress, G. (1988). *Social semiotics.* Ithaca, NY: Cornell University Press.

Holstein, J., & Gubrium, J. (1994). Phenomenology, ethnomethodology, and interpretive practice. In N. Denzin, & Y. Lincoln (Eds.), *Handbook of qualitative research.* Thousand Oaks, CA: Sage.

Honan, W. H. (1994, July 24). At the top of the ivory tower the watchword is silence. *New York Times,* p. E5.

hooks, b. (1992). *Black looks: Race and representation.* Boston: Beacon Press.

Hossfeld, K. J. (1994). *Divisions of labor, divisions of lives: Immigrant women workers in Silicon Valley.*

House, E., & Haug, C. (1995). Riding the bell curve: A review. *Educational Evaluation and Policy Analysis, 17* (2), 263–272.

House, E. (1978). Evaluation as scientific management in U.S. school reform. *Comparative Education Review, 22* (3), 388–401.

Hudson, W. S. (1981). *Religion in America,* (3rd ed.). New York: Charles Scribner's Sons.

Huebner, D. (1975). Curriculum as concern for man's temporality. In W. F. Pinar (Ed.), *Curriculum theorizing: The reconceptualists.* Berkeley: McCutchan.

Huebner, D. (1988). The redemption of schooling: The work of James B. Macdonald. *Journal of Curriculum Theorizing, 6* (3), 28–34.

Hultgren, F. (1987). Critical thinking: Phenomenological and critical foundations. In R. G. Thomas (Ed.), *Higher-order thinking: Definition, meaning and instructional approaches.* Washington, DC: Home Economics Education Association.

Hunter, M. (1982). *Mastery teaching.* El Segundo, CA: Tip Publications.

Hunter, H. G. (1994, November 14). Did you hear the one about Plato? Students need stories of the past to experience the present. *Newsweek,* p. 20.

Husserl, E. (1970). *The crisis of European sciences and transcendental phenomenology: An introduction to phenomenology.* Evanston, IL: Northwestern University Press.

Hyun, E. (1998). *Making sense of developmentally and culturally appropriate practice (DCAP) in early childhood education.* New York: Peter Lang.

Jackson, P. (1968). *Life in classrooms.* New York: Holt, Rinehart & Winston.

Jackson, P. (Ed.) (1992). *Handbook of research on curriculum.* New York: Macmillan.

Jaggar, A. (1983). *Feminist politics and human nature.* Totowa, NJ: Rowman and Allanheld.

Jankowski, M. (1991). *Islands in the street: Gangs and American urban society.* Berkeley: University of California Press.

Jaros, D. (1973). *Socialization to politics.* New York: Praeger.

Jensen, A. M. (1998). *Philosophy statement.* Loraine, OH: Unpublished manuscript.

Jipson, J., & Reynolds, U. (1997). Anything you want: Women and children in popular culture. In S. Steinberg, & J. Kincheloe (Eds.), *Kinderculture: Corporate constructions of childhood.* Boulder, CO: Westview.

Johnson, W. (1991). Model programs prepare women for skilled trades. In L. Wolfe (Ed.), *Women, work, and school: Occupational segregation and the role of education.* Boulder, CO: Westview.

Jones, M. (1992). The black underclass as systemic phenomenon. In J. Jennings (Ed.), *Race, politics, and economic development: Community perspectives.* New York: Verso.

Jones, N., & Cooper, M. (1987). *Teacher effectiveness and education: A case of incompatibility.* Paper presented to the American Educational Research Association, Washington, DC.

Jordan, J. (1995). In the land of white supremacy. In C. Berlet (Ed.), *Eyes right: Challenging the right wing backlash.* Boston: South End Press.

Kaestle, C. F. (1983). *Pillars of the republic: Commons schools and American society, 1780–1960.* New York: Hill and Wang.

Kamii, C. (1981). Teacher's autonomy and scientific training. *Young Children, 31,* 5–14.

Kamin, L. (1995). Lies, damned lies, and statistics. In R. Jacoby, & N. Glauberman (Eds.), *The bell curve debate: History, documents, and opinion.* New York: Random House.

Karier, C. J. (1986). *The individual, society, and education: A history of American educational ideas,* (2nd ed.). Urbana: University of Illinois Press.

Kaye, H. (1987). The use and abuse of the past: The new right and the crisis of history. *Socialist Register,* 332–365.

Keating, A. (1995). Interrogating "whiteness," (de) constructing race. *College English, 57* (8), 901–918.

Kellner, D. (1989). *Critical theory, Marxism, and modernity.* Baltimore: Johns Hopkins University Press.

Kellner, D. (1990). *Television and the crisis of democracy.* Boulder, CO: Westview.

Kellner, D. (1991). Reading images critically: Toward a postmodern pedagogy. In H. Giroux (Ed.), *Postmodernism, feminism, and cultural politics: Redrawing educational boundaries.* Albany, NY: SUNY Press.

Kellner, D. (1992). Popular culture and the construction of postmodern identities. In S. Lash, & J. Friedman (Eds.), *Modernity and identity.* Cambridge, MA: Blackwell.

Kellner, D. (1995). *Media culture: Cultural studies, identity and politics between the modern and the postmodern.* New York: Routledge.

Kellner, D. (1997). Beavis and Butthead: No future for postmodern youth. In S. Steinberg, & J. Kincheloe (Eds.), *Kinderculture: The corporate construction of childhood.* Boulder, CO: Westview.

Kincheloe, J. L. (1989). *Getting beyond the facts: Teaching social studies in the late twentieth century.* New York: Peter Lang.

Kincheloe, J. (1991). *Teachers as researchers: Qualitative paths to empowerment.* New York: Falmer.

Kincheloe, J. L. (1993). *Toward a critical politics of teacher thinking: Mapping the postmodern.* New York: Bergin & Garvey.

Kincheloe, J. (1995). *Toil and trouble: Good work, smart workers, and the integration of academic and vocational education.* New York: Peter Lang.

Kincheloe, J. (1996). The new childhood: Home alone as a way of life. *Cultural Studies, 1,* 221–240.

Kincheloe, J. (1997). McDonald's, power, and children: Ronald McDonald (a.k.a. Ray Kroc) does it all for you. In S. Steinberg, & J. Kincheloe (Eds.), *Kinderculture: The corporate construction of childhood.* Boulder: Westview.

Kincheloe, J. (1999). *How do we tell the workers? The socio-economic foundations of work and vocational education.* Boulder, CO: Westview.

Kincheloe, J., & McLaren, P. (1994). Rethinking critical theory and qualitative research. In N. Denzin, & Y. Lincoln (Eds.), *Handbook of qualitative research.* Thousand Oaks, CA: Sage.

Kincheloe, J., & Steinberg, S. (1993). A tentative description of post-formal thinking: The critical confrontation with cognitive theory. *Harvard Educational Review, 63* (3), 296–320.

Kincheloe, J., & Steinberg, S. (1997). *Changing multiculturalism.* London: Open University Press.

Kincheloe, J., & Steinberg, S. (Eds.) (1998). *Unauthorized methods: Strategies for critical teaching.* New York: Routledge.

Kincheloe, J., Steinberg, S., & Gresson, A. (Eds.). (1996). *Measured lies:* The Bell Curve examined. New York: St. Martin's.

Kincheloe, J., Steinberg, S., Rodriguez, N., & Chennault, R. (Eds.) (1998). *White reign: Deploying whiteness in America.* New York: St. Martin's.

Kincheloe, J., Steinberg, S. R., & Tippins, D. (1999). *The stigma of genius: Einstein, consciousness and education.* New York: Peter Lang.

Kincheloe, J., Steinberg, S., & Villaverde, L. (Eds.) (1999). *Rethinking intelligence: Confronting psychological assumptions about teaching and learning.* New York: Routledge.

King, A. L. (1991). Richard M. Nixon, southern strategies, and desegregation of public schools. In L. Friedman, & W. F. Levantrosser (Eds.), *Richard M. Nixon: Politician, president, administrator.* Prepared under the auspices of Hofstra University. New York: Greenwood Press.

King, J. (1996). Bad luck, bad blood, bad faith: Ideological hegemony and the oppressive language of hoodoo social science. In J. Kincheloe, S. Steinberg, & A. Gresson (Eds.), *Measured lies:* The Bell Curve *examined.* New York: St. Martin's.

Kipnis, L. (1988). Feminism: The political consciousness of postmodernism. In A. Ross (Ed.), *Universal abandon? The politics of postmodernism.* Minneapolis: University of Minnesota Press.

Klahr, D., & Wallace, J. (1976). *Cognitive development: An information processing view.* Hillsdale, NJ: Erlbaum.

Klein, R. (1982). How to do what we want to do: Thoughts about feminist methodology. In G. Bowles, & R. Klein (Eds.), *Theories of women's studies.* Boston: Routledge and Kegan Paul.

Kliebard, H. M. (1986). *The struggle for the American curriculum, 1890–1958.* London and Boston: Routledge and Kegan Paul.

Kliebard, H. (1992). Constructing a history of the American curriculum. In P. W. Jackson (Ed.), *Handbook of research on curriculum* (pp. 157–184). New York: Macmillan.

Kneller, G. (1984). *Movements of thought in modern education,* (2nd ed.). New York: John Wiley and Sons.

Knobel, M. (1998). *Everyday literacies: Students, discourse, and social practice.* New York: Peter Lang.

Kolberg, W., & Smith, W. (1992). *Rebuilding America's workforce: Business strategies to close the competitive gap.* Homewood, IL: Business One Irwin.

Koller, A. (1981). *An unknown woman: A journey to self-discovery.* New York: Bantam Books.

Kozol, J. (1967). *Death at an early age.* Boston: Houghton Mifflin.

Kozol, J. (1975). *The night is dark and I am far from home: A political indictment of the United Sates Public schools.* New York: Continuum.

Kozol, J. (1991). *Savage inequalities: Children in America's schools.* New York: Crown.

Kristeva, J. (1987). *In the beginning was love.* New York: Columbia University Press.

Kroath, F. (1989). How do teachers change their practical theories? *Cambridge Journal of Education, 19* (1), 59–69.

Krug, E. A. (1966). *Salient dates in American education: 1635–1964.* New York: Harper and Row.

Kuhn, T. (1970). *The structure of scientific revolutions.* Chicago: University of Chicago Press.

Kunzle, D. (1992). *Dispossession by ducks: The imperialist treasure hunt in the Barks-Disney comics.* Unpublished paper.

Lakes, R. (Fall, 1985) John Dewey's theory of occupations: Vocational education envisioned. *Journal of Vacational and Technical Education, 2* (1), 41–47.

Lamphere, L. (1985, Fall). Bringing the family to work: Women's culture on the shop floor. *Feminist Studies, 11* (3), 519–539.

Langman, K. (1991) From pathos to panic: American character meets the future. In P. Wexler (Ed.), *Critical Theory Now,* pp. 187–221. New York: Falmer.

Lasch, C. (1984). *The minimal self: Psychic survival in troubled times.* New York: W. W. Norton.

Lather, P. (1991). *Getting smart: Feminist research and pedagogy within the postmodern.* New York: Routledge.

Lavine, T. (1984). *From Socrates to Sartre: The philosophic quest.* New York: Bantam.

Lawler, J. (1975). Dialectical philosophy and developmental psychology: Hegel and Piaget on contradiction. *Human Development, 18,* 1–17.

Layton, L. (1994). Blue velvet: A parable of male development. *Screen, 35* (4), 374–393.

Lerner, G. (1986). *The creation of patriarchy.* New York: Oxford University Press.

Leshan, L., & Margeneu, H. (1982) *Einstein's space and Van Gogh's sky: Physical reality and beyond.* New York: Macmillan.

Lesko, N. (1989). *Symbolizing society: Stories, rites, and structure in a Catholic high school.* New York: Falmer.

Lewin, K. (1946). Action research and minority problems. *Journal of School Issues, 2,* 34–36.

Lewis, D. L. (1993). *W. E. B. DuBois: A biography of a race, 1868–1919.* New York: Henry Holt.

Lewis, M. (1990). Interrupting patriarchy: Politics, resistance, and transformation in the feminist classroom. *Harvard Educational Review, 60* (4), 467–488.

Lieberman, A. (1995). Restructuring schools: The dynamics of changing practice, structure, and culture. In A. Lieberman (Ed.), *The work of restructuring schools: Building from the ground up.* New York: Teachers College Press.

Lincoln, Y., & Guba, E. (1985). *Naturalistic inquiry.* Beverly Hills, CA: Sage.

Lincoln, Y. (1995). *If I am not just one person, but many, why should I write just one text?* Paper presented at the American Educational Research Association, San Francisco.

Lind, M. (1995). Brave new right. In S. Fraser (Ed.), *The bell curve wars: Race, intelligence, and the future of America.* New York: Basic.

Lipsky, D., & Abrams, A. (1994). *Late bloomers, coming of age in today's America: The right place at the wrong time.* New York: Times Books.

Livingstone, D. (1987). Upgrading and opportunities. In D. Livingstone (Ed.), *Critical pedagogy and cultural power.* South Hadley, MA: Bergin & Garvey.

Livingstone, D., & Luxton, M. (1988). *Gender consciousness at work: Modification of the male breadwinner norm among steelworkers and their spouses.* Unpublished manuscript.

Loewen, J. W. (1995). *Lies my teacher told me: Everything your American history textbook got wrong.* New York: New Press.

Longman, L. (1991). From pathos to panic: American character meets the future. In P. Wexler (Ed.), *Critical theory now.* New York: Falmer.

Longstreet, W. (1982). Action research: A paradigm. *The Educational Forum, 46* (2), 136–149.

Lowe, D. (1982). *History of bourgeois perception.* Chicago: University of Chicago Press.

Lugg, C. A. (1996a). *For God and country: Conservatism and American school policy.* New York: Peter Lang.

Lugg, C. A. (1996b). Attacking affirmative action: Social Darwinism as public policy. In J. Kincheloe, S. Steinberg, & A. Gresson, III, (Eds.), *Measured lies:* The Bell Curve *examined.* New York: St. Martin's.

Lugg, C. A. (1996c). Calling for community in a conservative age, *Planning and Changing, 27,* 1–2.

Lugg, C. A., & Dentith, A. M. (1996). Workin' for a livin'. An essay review of Joe Kincheloe's *Toil and Trouble. Educational Researcher, 25* (1), 39–42.

Lugg, R. A., & Lugg, C. A. (1996). The reminiscences of Emily Knox Reynolds. *Pennsylvania History, 63* (3).

Lugones, M. (1987). Playfulness, world-traveling, and loving perception. *Hypatia, 2* (2), 3–19.

Luke, C. (1994). White women in interracial families: Reflections on hybridization, feminine identities, and racialized othering. *Feminist Issues, 14* (2), 49–72.

Luke, T. (1991). Touring hyperreality: Critical theory confronts informational society. In P. Wexler (Ed.), *Critical theory now.* New York: Falmer.

Luttrell, W. (1993). Working class women's ways of knowing: Effects of gender, race, and class. In L. Castenell, & W. Pinar (Eds.), *Understanding curriculum as a racial text: Representations of identity and difference in education.* Albany, NY: SUNY Press.

Lyons, R. (1988). Scarcity, conflict, and work: An essay on schooling. *Journal of Thought,* *23* (2/3), 6–27.

Lyotard, J. F. (1984). *The postmodern condition: A report on knowledge.* (G. Bennington, & B. Massumi, Trans.). Minneapolis: University of Minnesota Press.

Lyotard, J. F. (1992). *The postmodern explained to children: Correspondences 1982–1984.* London: Turnaround.

MacCannell, D. (1992). *Empty meeting grounds.* New York: Routledge.

Macdonald, J. B. (1974). A transcendental developmental ideology of education. In W. F. Pinar (Ed.), *Heightened consciousness: Cultural revolution and curriculum theory.* Berkeley: McCutchan.

Macdonald, J. B. (1981). Theory, practice, and the hermeneutic circle. *JCT: An Interdisciplinary Journal of Curriculum Studies, 3* (2), 130–138.

Macdonald, J. B. (1988). Curriculum, consciousness, and social change. In W. F. Pinar (Ed.), *Contemporary curriculum discourses.* Scottsdale, AZ: Gorsuch, Scarisbrick.

Macedo, D. (1994). *Literacies of power: What Americans are not allowed to know.* Boulder, CO: Westview.

MacLeod, J. (1987). *Ain't no makin' it: Leveled aspirations in a low-income neighborhood.* Boulder, CO: Westview.

Maher, F., & Rathbone, C. (1986). Teacher education and feminist theory: Some implications for practice. *American Journal of Education, 94* (2), 214–235.

Maher, M. (1992). *Men do and women are: Sixth grade girls, media messages, and identity.* Paper presented at the Center for the Study of Communications Mainstream(s) and Margins Conference, Amherst, Massachusetts.

Mahoney, M., & Lyddon, W. (1988). Recent developments in cognitive approaches to counseling and psychotherapy. *Counseling Psychologist, 16* (2), 190–234.

Malveaux, J. (1992). Popular culture and the economics of alienation. In G. Dent (Ed.), *Black popular culture.* Seattle: Bay Press.

Malveaux, J. (1994). *Sex, lies and stereotypes: Perspectives of a mad economist.* Los Angeles: Pines One Publishing.

Manning, P., & Cullum-Swan, B. (1994). Narrative, content, and semiotic analysis. In N. Denzin, & Y. Lincoln (Eds.), *Handbook of qualitative research.* Thousand Oaks, CA: Sage.

Marable, M. (1992). Race, identity, and political culture. In G. Dent (Ed.), *Black popular culture.* Seattle: Bay Press.

Marcuse, H. (1955). *Eros and civilizations.* Boston: Beacon Press.

Margo, R. A. (1990). *Race and schooling in the south, 1880–1050: An economic history.* Chicago: University of Chicago Press.

Marsh, M. (1992). Implementing antibias curriculum in the kindergarten classroom. In S. Kessler, & B. Swadener (Eds.), *Reconceptualizing the early childhood curriculum.* New York: Teachers College Press.

Martin, E. B. (1994, August 3). Left has its Zealots Too. Letters to the Editor, *Times of Acadiana,* p. 7.

Marshak, D. (1993, June 2). What employers know that educators may not. *Education Week,* pp. 25, 28.

Marzano, R. J. (1993, December/January). When two worlds collide. *Educational Leadership.*

McCallister, C. (1998). *Reconceptualizing Literacy Methods Instruction: To build a house that remembers its forest.* New York: Peter Lang.

McCarthy, S. (1995). *Why are the heroes always white?* Kansas City: Andrews and McMeel.

McCarthy, C., & Apple, M. (1988). Race, class, and gender in American educational research: Toward a nonsynchronous parallelist position. In L. Weis (Ed.), *Class, race, and gender in American education.* Albany, NY: SUNY Press.

McCaskill, J. L. (1956). How the Kelley bill was lost—and why. *NEA Journal, 45* (6), 363–366.

McCutcheon, G. (1981). The impact of the insider. In J. Nixon (Ed.), *A teacher's guide to action research*. London: Grant McIntyre.

McGinty, S. (1999). *Resilience, gender, and success at school*. New York: Peter Lang.

McIntosh, P. (1995). White privilege and male privilege: A personal account of coming to see correspondences through work in women's studies. In M. Anderson, & P. Collins (Eds.), *Race, class, and gender: An anthology*. Belmont, CA: Wadsworth.

McKernan, J. (1988). Teacher as researcher: Paradigm and praxis. *Contemporary Education, 59* (3), 154–158.

McLaren, P. (1986). *Schooling as ritual performance: Toward a political economy of educational symbols and gestures*. London: Routledge and Kegan Paul.

McLaren, P. (1989, 1994). *Life in schools: An introduction to critical pedagogy in the foundations of education*. White Plains, New York: Longman.

McLaren, P. (1991). Decentering culture: Postmodernism, resistance, and critical pedagogy. In N. B. Wyner (Ed.), *Current perspectives on the culture of schools*. Boston: Brookline.

McLaren, P. (1992). Literacy research and the postmodern turn: Cautions from the margins. In R. Beach, et al. (Eds.), *Multidisciplinary perspectives on research*. Urbana, IL: National Council of Teachers of English.

McLaren, P. (1993). Border disputes: Multicultural narrative, identity formation, and critical pedagogy in postmodern America. In D. McLaughlin, & W. Tierney (Eds.), *Naming silenced lives: Personal narratives and the process of educational change*. New York: Routledge.

McLaren, P. (1994). *Life in schools: An introduction to critical pedagogy in the foundations of education*. White Plains, NY: Longman.

McLaren, P. (1995). *Critical pedagogy and predatory culture: Oppositional politics in a postmodern culture*. New York: Routledge.

McLaren, P., Hammer, R., Reilly, S., & Sholle, D. (1995). *Rethinking media literacy: A critical pedagogy of representation*. New York: Peter Lang.

McLaren, P., & Morris, J. (1997). J. Kincheloe, & S. Steinberg (Eds.), Mighty Morphin Power Rangers: The aesthetics of macho-militaristic justice. Boulder, CO: Westview.

McLeod, J. (1987). The arts and education. In J. Simpson (Ed.), *Education and the arts*. Edmonton, Alberta, Canada: Fine Arts Council, Alberta's Teachers Association.

McMillen, L. (1995, September). Lifting the veil from whiteness: Growing body of scholarship challenges a racial norm. *The Chronicle of Higher Education*, p. A23.

McNamara, Robert. (1995). *In retrospect: The tragedy and lessons of Vietnam*. New York: Vintage.

Meisner, M. (1988). The reproduction of women's domination in organizational communication. In L. Thayer (Ed.), *Organization, communication*. Norwood, NJ: Ablex.

Merelman, R. (1986). Domination, self-justification, and self-doubt: Some social psychological considerations. *Journal of Politics, 48,* 276–299.

Merelman, R. (1995). *Representing black culture: Racial conflict and cultural politics in the United States*. New York: Routledge.

Merleau-Ponty, M. (1962). *Phenomenology of perception*. London: Routledge and Kegan Paul.

Metzger, E., & Bryant, L. (1993). Portfolio assessment: Pedagogy, power, and the student. *Teaching English in the Two Year College, 20* (4), 279–288.

Mies, M. (1982). Toward a methodology for feminist research. In G. Bowles, & R. Klein (Eds.), *Theories of women's studies*. Boston: Routledge and Kegan Paul.

Miller, R. (Ed.) (1993). *The renewal of meaning in education: Responses to the ecological crisis of our time*. Brandon, VT: Holistic Education Press.

Miller, J. L. (1990). *Creating spaces and finding voices*. Albany: State University of NY Press.

Morris, A. A. (1989). *Constitution and American public education*. Durham, NC: Carolina Academic Press.

Morris, J. B. (1996). *Assessment instruction in preservice teacher education at the University of South Carolina*. Thesis: University of South Carolina.

Morris, M. (1997). Ezekiel's call: Toward a queer pedagogy. *Taboo: The Journal of Culture and Education, I,* (Spring 1997), 153–166.

Morrison, T. (1993). *Playing in the dark: Whiteness and the literary imagination*. New York: Vintage.

Morrow, R. (1991). Critical theory, Gramsci, and cultural studies: From structuralism to post-structuralism. In P. Wexler (Ed.), *Critical theory now*. New York: Falmer.

Mullen, C., Cox, M., Boettcher, C., & Adoue, D. (Eds.) (1997). *Breaking the circle of one: Redefining mentorship in the lives and writings of educators*. New York: Peter Lang.

Mullin, J. (1994). Feminist theory, feminist pedagogy: The gap between what we say and what we do. *Composition Studies/Freshman English News, 22* (1), 14–24.

Mullings, L. (1994). Images, ideology, and women of color. In M. Zinn, & B. Bill (Eds.), *Women of color in U.S. society*. Philadelphia: Temple University Press.

Mumby, D. (1989). Ideology and the social construction of meaning: A communication perspective. *Communication Quarterly, 37* (4), 291–304.

Murray, C. & Herrnstein, R. J. (1994). *The bell curve: Intelligence and class structure in American life*. New York: Free Press.

Murray, R. (1992). Fordism and post-Fordism. In C. Jencks (Ed.), *The post-modern reader*. New York: St. Martin's.

Musolf, R. (1992). Structure, institutions, power, and ideology: New directions within symbolic interactionism. *The Sociological Quarterly, 33* (2), 171–189.

Nakayama, T., & Krizek, R. (1995). Whiteness: A strategic rhetoric. *Quarterly Journal of Speech, 81,* 291–309.

Nasaw, D. (1979). *Schooled to order: A social history of public schooling in the United States*. New York: Oxford University Press.

Nation at Risk, A (1983). Report of the National Commission on Excellence in Education. Washington, DC; United States Department of Education. New York: Macmillan.

NCRVE. (1992). *Vocational education: A special tip sheet for educational writers*. Berkeley: NCRVE.

Nelson, R., & Watras, J. (1981). The scientific movement: American education and the emergence of the technological society. *Journal of Thought, 16* (1), 49–71.

Nelson, C., Treichler, P., & Grossberg, L. (1992). Cultural studies: An introduction. In C. Nelson, P. Terichler, & L. Grossberg (Eds.), *Cultural studies*. New York: Routledge.

Newman, J. W. (1998). *America's teachers: An introduction to education,* (3rd ed.). New York: Longman.

News Notes, (1953). *Phi Delta Kappan, 35* (3), 156.

Nieto, S. (1996). *Affirming Diversity: The sociopolitical context of multicultural education*. New York: Longman.

Nietzsche, F. (1968). The birth of tragedy. In W. Kaufmann, (Trans. and Ed.), *Basic writings of Nietzsche,* (3rd ed.). New York: Modern Library.

Nightingale, C. (1993). *On the edge: A history of poor black children and their American dreams*. New York: Basic.

Noblit, G. (1999). *Particularities: Collected essays on ethnography and education*. New York: Peter Lang.

Noddings, N. (1984). *Caring: A feminine approach to ethics and moral education*. Berkeley and Los Angeles: University of California Press.

Noddings, N. (1989). *Women and evil.* Berkeley and Los Angeles: University of California Press.

Noddings, N. (1992). *The challenge to care: An alternative approach to education.* New York: Teachers College Press.

Noddings, N. (1995). *Philosophy of Education.* Boulder: Westview.

Nooteboom, C. (1991). *In the Dutch mountains.* London: Penguin.

Norris, J. (1998). *Phenomenology and action research.* Edmonton, Canada: personal communication.

O'Reilly, K. (1995). *Nixon's piano: Presidents and racial politics from Washington to Clinton.* New York: Free Press.

Oakes, J. (1985). *Keeping track: How schools structure inequality.* New Haven: Yale University Press.

Oakes, J. (1988). Tracking in mathematics and science education: A structural contribution to unequal schooling. In L. Weis (Ed.), *Class, race, and gender in American education.* Albany, NY: SUNY Press.

Obiakor, F. (1992). *The myth of socioeconomic dissonance: Implications for African American exceptional students.* Paper presented at the Council for Exceptional Children, Minneapolis, Minnesota.

Okin, S. M. (1979). *Women in Western Political Thought.* Princeton: Princeton University Press.

Oldroyd, D. (1985). Indigenous action research for individual and system development. *Educational Management and Administration, 13,* 113–118.

Oldroyd, D., & Tiller, T. (1987). Change from within: An account of school-based collaborative action research in an English secondary school. *Journal of Education for Teaching, 12* (3), 13–27.

Olesen, V. (1994). Feminisms and models of qualitative research. In N. Denzin, & Y. Lincoln (Eds.), *Handbook of qualitative research.* Thousand Oaks, CA: Sage.

Oliver, D. W., & Gershman, K. W. (1989). *Education, modernity, and fractured meaning: Toward a process view of teaching and learning.* New York: SUNY Press.

Orfield, G. (1969). *The reconstruction of southern education: The schools and the 1964 Civil Rights Act.* New York: Wiley-Interscience.

Orr, D. W. (1992). *Ecological literacy: Education and the transition to the postmodern world.* Albany: SUNY Press.

Ozmon, H., & Craver, S. (1999). *Philosophical foundations of education,* (6th ed.). Columbus, OH: Merrill.

Palmer, P. M. & Spalter-Roth, R. M. (1991). *Gender practices and employment: The Sears case and the issue of "choice."* Washington, DC: Graduate Institute of Policy Education and Research, Graduate School of Arts and Sciences, George Washington University.

Pagano, J. (1990). *Exiles and communities.* Albany, NY: SUNY Press.

Pascall, G., & Cox, R. (1994). *Women returning to higher education.* Bristol, PA: Open University Press.

Percy, W. (1954). *The message in the bottle: How queer man is, how queer language is, and what one has to do with the other.* New York: Farrar, Straus, and Giroux.

Percy, W. (1971). *Love in the ruins.* New York: Farrar, Straus, and Giroux.

Paul, W. (1994). *Laughing and screaming: Modern Hollywood horror and comedy.* New York: Columbia University Press.

Perez, L. (1993). Opposition and the education of Chicana/os. In C. McCarthy, & W. Crichlow (Eds.), *Race, identity, and reproduction in education.* New York: Routledge.

Perkins, L. M. (1989). The history of blacks in teaching: Growth and decline within the profession. In D. Warren, (Ed.), *American teachers: Histories of a profession at work*. New York: Macmillan.

Perkinson, H. J. (1991). *The imperfect panacea: American faith in education, 1865–1990*, (3rd ed.). New York: McGraw-Hill.

Phi Delta Kappan (1968), *50* (3), 151.

Phillips, K. P. (1969). *The emerging Republican majority*. New Rochelle, NY: Arlington House.

Phillips. K. P. (1990). *The politics of rich and poor: Wealth and the American electorate in the Reagan aftermath*. New York: Random House.

Piaget, J. (1973). *To understand is to invent: The future of education*. New York: Grossman.

Picasso, P. (1971). Conversations. In H. B. Chipps (Ed.), *Theories of modern art: A source book of artists and critics* (p. 268). Berkeley: University of California Press.

Pinar, W. F. (1975). *Curriculum Theorizing: The reconceptualists*. Berkeley: McCutchan.

Pinar, W. F. (Ed.) (1988). *Contemporary curriculum discourses*. Scottsdale, AZ: Gorsuch Scarisbrick.

Pinar, W. (1991). Curriculum as social psychoanalysis: On the significance of place. In J. Kincheloe, & W. Pinar, *Curriculum as Social psychoanalysis: Essays on the significance of place*. Albany, NY: SUNY Press.

Pinar, W. (1994). *Autobiography, politics, and sexuality: Essays in curriculum theory, 1972–1992*. New York: Peter Lang.

Pinar, W. F. (1997). Regimes of reason and the male narrative voice. In W. G. Tierney, & Y. S. Lincoln (Eds.), *Representation and the Text* (pp. 81–113). Albany, NY: SUNY Press.

Pinar, W. F., & Grumet, M. (1976). *Toward a poor curriculum*. Dubuque, IA: Kendall/Hunt.

Pinar, W. F., Reynolds, W. M., Slattery, P., & Taubman, P. M. (1995). *Understanding curriculum: An introduction to the study of historical and contemporary curriculum discourses*. New York: Peter Lang.

Pincus, F. (1980). The false promises of community colleges: Class conflict and vocational education. *Harvard Educational Review, 50* (3), 332–361.

Pioneer Planet. (1998). Big pay not always linked to top performance. http://www.pioneerpress.com/archive/ceopay/index.htm.

Piven, F. F., & Cloward, R. A. (1993). *Regulating the poor: The functions of public welfare, update edition*. New York: Vintage.

Polakow, V. (1992). *The erosion of childhood*. Chicago: University of Chicago Press.

Pollin, R., & Cockburn, A. (1991, February 25). The world, the free market, and the left. *The Nation, 252* (7), 224–236.

Popkewitz, T. (1981). The study of schooling: Paradigms and field-based methodologies in education research and evaluation. In T. Popkewitz, & B. Tabochnick (Eds.), *The study of schooling*. New York: Praeger.

Popkewitz, T. (1987). Organization and power: Teacher education reforms. *Social Education, 39*, 496–500.

Popular Memory Group. (1982). Popular memory: Theory, politics, and method. In Centre for Contemporary Studies, *Making histories: Studies in history-writing and politics*. Minneapolis: University of Minnesota Press.

Porter, A. (1988). Indicators: Objective data or political tool? *Phi Delta Kappan, 69* (7), 503–508.

Poster, M. (1989). *Critical theory and poststructuralism: In search of a context*. Ithaca, NY: Cornell University Press.

Postman, N. (1985a). *Teaching as a subversive activity.* New York: Vintage.

Postman, N. (1985b). Critical thinking in an electronic era. *Phi Kappa Phi Journal, 65,* 4–8, 17.

Postman, N. (1994). *The disappearance of childhood.* New York: Vintage.

Postman, N. (1995). *The end of education.* New York: Knopf.

Preston, J. A. (1982). *Feminization of an occupation: Teaching becomes women's work in nineteenth-century New England.* Unpublished doctoral dissertation, Brandeis University.

Provenzo, E. (1990). *Religious fundamentalism and American education.* New York: SUNY Press.

Provenzo, E. (1991). *Video kids: Making sense of Nintendo.* Cambridge: Harvard University Press.

Provenzo, E. (1997). Video games and the emergence of interactive media for children. In S. Steinberg, & J. Kincheloe (Eds.), *Kinderculture: The corporate construction of childhood.* Boulder, CO: Westview.

Pruyn, M. (1994). Becoming subjects through critical practice: How students in one elementary classroom critically read and wrote their world. *International Journal of Educational Reform, 3*(1), 37–50.

Pullin, D. (1994). Learning to work: The impact of curriculum and assessment standards on educational opportunity. *Harvard Educational Review, 64*(1), 31–54.

Pumroy, D. (1984). *Why is it taking so long for behavior modification to be used in the schools/or am I being too impatient?* Paper presented to the National Association of School Psychologists, Philadelphia.

Purpel, D. (1989). *The moral and spiritual crisis in education. A Curriculum for justice and compassion in education.* New York: Bergin & Garvey.

Purpel, D. (1999). *Moral outrage in education.* New York: Peter Lang.

Raizen, S. (1989). *Reforming education for work: A cognitive science perspective.* Berkeley: NCRVE.

Raizen, S., & Colvin, R. (1991, December 11). Apprenticeships: A cognitive-science view. *Educational Week, 26.*

Ramsay, C. (1996). Male horror: On David Cronenberg. In P. Smith (Ed.), *Boys: Masculinities in contemporary culture.* Boulder, CO: Westview.

Ravitch, D. (1974). *The great school wars: New York City, 1805–1973.* New York: Basic.

Rehm, M. (1989). Emancipatory vocational education: Pedagogy for the work of individuals and society. *Journal of Education, 171*(3), 109–123.

Reich, R. (1991). *The work of nations.* New York: Alfred A. Knopf.

Reinharz, S. (1979). *On becoming a social scientist.* San Francisco: Jossey-Bass.

Reinharz, S. (1992). *Feminist methods in social research.* New York: Oxford University Press.

Reisner, E. H. (1930). *The evolution of the common school.* New York: Macmillan.

Rendon, L., & Nora, A. (1991). Hispanic women in college and careers: Preparing for success. In L. Wolfe (Ed.), *Women, work, and school: Occupational segregation and the role of education.* Boulder, CO: Westview.

Ricci, M. (1996). Personal communication. Ashland, OH: Ashland University.

Richmond, S. (1986, December). The white paper, education, and the crafts: An assessment of values. *The Journal of Educational Thought, 20*(3), 143–155.

Rifkin, J. (1987). *Time wars: The primary conflict in human history.* New York: Simon and Schuster.

Rippa, S. A. (1969). *Educational ideas in America: A documentary history.* New York: David McKay.

Rippa, S. A. (1992). *Education in a free society: An American history*. New York: Longman.

Ritzer, G. (1993). *The Mcdonaldization of society: An investigation into the changing character of a contemporary social life*. Newbury Park, CA: Pine Forge Press.

Rivlin, A. (1971). *Systematic thinking for social action*. Washington, DC: The Brookings Institution.

Rizvi, F. (1993). Children and the grammar of popular racism. In C. McCarthy, & W. Crichlow (Eds.), *Race, identity, and reproduction in education*. New York: Routledge.

Roddick, A. (1991). *Profits with principles: The amazing story of Anita Roddick and The Body Shop*. New York: Crown.

Roditi, H. (1992, March, 16). High schools for docile workers. *The Nation, 254* (10), 340–343.

Rodriguez, L. (1994). Rekindling the warrior. *Utne Reader, 64*, 58–59.

Roediger, D. (1991). *The wages of whiteness: Race and the making of the American working class*. New York: Verso.

Rogers, V. (1989). Assessing the curriculum experienced by children. *Phi Delta Kappan, 70* (9), 715–717.

Rosenau, P. (1992). *Postmodernism and the social sciences: Insights, inroads, and intrusion*. Princeton: Princeton University Press.

Ross, E. (1988). *Teacher values and the construction of curriculum*. Paper presented to the American Educational Research Association, New Orleans.

Rouse, J. (1987). *Knowledge and power: Toward a political philosophy of science*. Ithaca, NY: Cornell University Press.

Rousseau, J. (1979). *Emile*. (A. Bloom, Trans). New York: Basic.

Rubin, L. (1994). *Families on the faultline: America's working class speaks about the family, the economy, race, and ethnicity*. New York: HarperCollins.

Ruiz, J. (1994, July 20). We Need Freedom from Religion. Letters to the Editor, *The Times of Acadiana*, pp. 8, 10.

Rumberger, R. W. (1984). *Is there really a shortage of mathematics and science teachers?: A review of the evidence*. Stanford, CA: Institute for Research on Educational Finance and Governance, School of Education, Stanford University.

Rury, J. (1989). Who became teachers? The social characteristics of teachers in American history. In D. Warren (Ed.), *American Teachers: Histories of a profession at work*. (pp. 9–48). New York: Macmillan.

Russell, M. (1983). Black eyed blues connections: From the inside out. In C. Bunch, & S. Pollack (Eds.), *Learning our way: Essays in feminist education*. New York: The Crossing Press.

Sadasvian, L. (1998). *A letter to educators*. Strongsville, OH: Unpublished document.

Scatamburlo, V. (1998). *Soldiers of misfortune: The new right's culture war and the politics of political correctness*. New York: Peter Lang.

Scholes, R. (1982). *Semiotics and interpretation*. New Haven: Yale University Press.

Schön, D. A. (1991). *The reflective turn*. New York: Basic.

Schön, D. A. (1987). *Educating the reflective practitioner*. New York: Basic.

Schön, D. A. (1983). *The reflective practitioner: How professionals think in action*. New York: Basic.

Schubert, W. H. (1986). *Curriculum: Perspective, paradigm, and possibility*. New York: Macmillan.

Sedlak, M. W. (1989). "Let us go and buy a school master": Historical perspectives on the hiring of teachers in the United States, 1750–1980. In D. Warren (Ed.), *American teachers: Histories of a profession at work*. New York: Macmillan.

The segregation decision. (1954, July). *The Nations's Schools,* (1) 27, 100.

Seiter, E. (1993). *Sold separately: Parents and children in consumer culture.* New Brunswick, NJ: Rutgers University Press.

Semali, L., & Pailliotet, A. (1999). *Intermediality: The teacher's handbook of critical media literacy.* Boulder, CO: Westview.

Semel, S., & Sadovnik, A. (Eds.) (1999). *Schools of tomorrow, schools of today: What happened to progressive education.* New York: Peter Lang.

Senge, P. (1990). *The fifth discipline: The art and practice of the learning organization.* New York: Doubleday.

Shannon, P. (1989). *Broken promises: Reading instruction in twentieth-century America.* Granby, MA: Bergin & Garvey.

Shapiro, A. (1999). *Everybody belongs: Changing negative attitudes toward classmates with disabilities.* New York: Garland.

Shapiro, S. (1990). *Between capitalism and democracy: Educational policy and the crisis of the welfare state.* New York: Bergin & Garvey.

Shea, C., Kahane, E., & Sola, P. (Eds.) (1989). *The new servants of power: A critique of the 1980s school reform movement.* New York: Greenwood Press.

Sherman, R., Webb, R., & Andrews S. (1984). Qualitative inquiry: An introduction. *Journal of Thought, 19,* 24–33.

Shipman, P. (1994). *The evolution of racism: Human differences and the use and abuse of science.* New York: Simon and Schuster.

Sholle, D., & Denski, S. (1994). *Media education and the (re)production of culture.* Westport, CT: Bergin & Garvey.

Shor, I. (1992). *Empowering education: Critical teachings, for social change.* Chicago: University of Chicago Press.

Shor, I., & Freire, P. (1987). *A pedagogy for liberation: Dialogues on transforming education.* South Hadley, MA: Bergin & Garvey.

Short, E. C. (1991). *Forms of curriculum inquiry.* Albany: SUNY Press.

Sidel, R. (1992). *Women and children last: The plight of poor women in affluent America.* New York: Penguin.

Silin, J. (1995). *Sex, death and children: Our passion for ignorance in the age of AIDS.* New York: Teachers College Press.

Simon, R. (1992). *Teaching against the grain.* South Hadley, MA: Bergin & Garvey.

Simon, R., Dippo, D., & Schenke, A. (1991). *Learning work: A critical pedagogy of work education.* Westport, CT: Bergin & Garvey.

Simpson, D., & Jackson, M. (1997). *Educational reform: A Deweyan perspective.* New York: Garland.

Sitton, T. (1981). Black history from the community: The strategies of fieldwork. *Jounal of Negro Education, 50* (2), 171–181.

Slattery, P. (1995a). *Curriculum development in the postmodern era.* New York: Garland.

Slattery, P. (1995b). Postmodern visions of time and learning: A response to the National Education Commission Report Prisoners of Time. *Harvard Educational Review 65* (4), 612–633.

Slattery, P., & Morris, M. (1999). Simone de Beauvoir's ethics and postmodern ambiguity: The assertion of freedom in the face of the absurd. *Educational Theory, 49* (1), 21–36.

Slaughter, R. (1989). Cultural reconstruction in the post-modern world. *Journal of Curriculum Studies, 3,* 255–270.

Sleeter, C. (1993). How white teachers construct race. In C. McCarthy, & W. Crichlow (Eds.), *Race, identity, and reproduction in education.* New York: Routledge.

Sleeter, C. (1995). Reflections on my use of multicultural and critical pedagogy when students are white. In C. Sleeter, & P. McLaren (Eds.), *Multicultural education, critical pedagogy, and the politics of difference*. Albany, NY: SUNY Press.

Smart, B. (1992). *Modern conditions, postmodern controversies*. New York: Routledge.

Smith, D. (1999). *Pedagon: Interdisciplinary essays in the human sciences, pedagogy and culture*. New York: Peter Lang.

Smith, J. (1983). Quantitative versus qualitative research: An attempt to clarify the issue. *Educational Researcher, 12*, 6–13.

Smith, G. (1996). Dichotomies in the making of men. In C. McLean, M. Carey, & C. White (Eds.), *Men's ways of being*. Boulder, CO: Westview.

Smith, P. (1989). Pedagogy and the popular-cultural-commodity text. In H. Giroux, & R. Simon (Eds.), *Popular culture: Schooling and everyday life*. Granby, MA: Bergin & Garvey.

Solomon, B. M. (1985). *In the company of educated women*. New Haven: Yale University Press.

Soltis, J. (1984). On the nature of educational research. *Educational Researcher, 13*, 5–10.

Spangler, J. L. (1998). Personal communication. Ashland, Ohio: Ashland University.

Spring, J. (1993). *Conflict of interest: The politics of American education*, (2nd ed.). New York: Longman.

Spring, J. (1994). *The American school, 1642–1993*, (3rd ed.). New York: McGraw-Hill.

Stack, C. (1994). Different voices, different visions: Gender, culture, and moral reasoning. In M. Zinn, & B. Dill (Eds.), *Women of color in U.S. society*. Philadelphia: Temple University Press.

Stafford, W. (1992). Whither the great neo-conservative experiment in New York City. In J. Jennings (Ed.), *Race, politics, and economic development: Community perspectives*. New York: Verso.

Stannard, D. E. (1992). *American holocaust: Columbus and the conquest of the new world*. Oxford: Oxford University Press.

Steinberg, S. (1997). The bitch who has everything. In S. Steinberg, & J. Kincheloe (Eds.), *Kinderculture: The corporate construction of childhood*. Boulder, CO: Westview.

Steinberg, S. (1997). Kinderculture: The Cultural Studies of Childhood. *Cultural Studies, II*, 17–44.

Steinberg, S., & Kincheloe, J. (1997). *Kinderculture: The corporate construction of childhood*. Boulder, CO: Westview.

Steinberg, S., & Kincheloe, J. (Eds.) (1998). *Students as researchers: Creating classrooms that matter*. London: Falmer.

Stewart, D., & McKunas, A. (1974). *Exploring phenomenology*. Chicago: American Library Association.

Stewart, M. (1993). *Ellen is home alone*. New York: Bantam.

Stowe, D. (1996). Uncolored people: The rise of whiteness studies. *Lingua Franca, 6* (6), 68–77.

Suvin, D. (1988). Can people be (re)presented in fiction?: Toward a theory of narrative agents and a materialist critique beyond technocracy or reductionism. In C. Nelson, & L. Grossberg (Eds.), *Marxism and the interpretation of culture*. Urbana: University of Illinois Press.

Suzuki, D. T., Fromm, E., & Demartino, R. (1960). *Zen Buddhism and psychoanalysis*. New York: Grove.

Swartz, E. (1993). Multicultural education: Disrupting patterns of supremacy in school curricula, practices, and pedagogy. *Journal of Negro Education, 62* (4), 493–506.

Taba, H. (1962). *Curriculum development: Theory and practice*. New York: Harcourt, Brace.

Tanaka, G. (1996). Dysgenesis and white culture. In J. Kincheloe, S. Steinberg, & A. Gresson (Eds.), *Measured lies:* The Bell Curve *examined.* New York: St. Martin's.

Tatum, B. (1994). Teaching white students about racism: The search for white allies and the restoration of hope. *Teachers College Record, 95* (4), 462–475.

Taxel, J. (1993). The black experience in children's fiction. *Curriculum Inquiry, 16* (3), 245–281.

Thernstrom, S. (1984). *A history of the American people, volume two: Since 1865.* New York: Harcourt, Brace Jovanovich.

Thiele, L. (1986). Foucault's triple murder and the modern development of power. *Canadian Journal of Political Science, 19* (3), 243–260.

Thompson, B. (1996). Time traveling and border crossing: Reflections on white identity. In B. Thompson, & S. Tyagi (Eds.), *Names we call home: autobiography on racial identity.* New York: Routledge.

Thompson, J. (1987). Language and ideology: A framework for analysis. *The Sociological Review, 35,* 516–536.

Toch, T. (1991). *In the name of excellence: The struggle to reform the nation's schools, why it's failing and what should be done.* New York: Oxford University Press.

de Tocqueville, A. (1838). *Democracy in America.* New York: The Classics of Liberty Library, Director of Gryphon Editions.

Torney-Purta, J. (1985). Linking faculties of education with classroom teachers through collaborative research. *Journal of Educational Thought, 19* (1), 71–77.

Tozer, S. (1993, Fall). Toward a new consensus among social foundations educators: Draft position paper of the AESA committee on academic standards and accreditation. *Educational Foundations.*

Tyack, D. (1974). *The one best system: A history of American urban education.* Cambridge: Harvard University Press.

Tyack, D., & Hansot, E. (1982). *Managers of virtue: Public school leadership in America, 1820–1980.* New York: Basic.

Tyack, D., & Hansot, E. (1990). *Learning together: A history of coeducation in American schools.* New Haven: Yale University Press.

Tyler, R. W. (1949). *Basic principles of curriculum and instruction.* Chicago: University of Chicago Press.

Ulich, R. (Ed.) (1954). *Three thousand years of educational wisdom: Selections from great documents,* (2nd ed.). Cambridge: Harvard University Press.

Urban, W. J. (1982). *Why teachers organized.* Detroit: Wayne State University Press.

Urban, W. J. (1989). Teacher activism. In D. Warren (Ed.), *American teachers: Histories of a profession at work.* New York: Macmillan.

Valli, L. (1988). Gender identity and the technology of office education. In L. Weis (Ed.), *Class, race, and gender in American education.* Albany, NY: SUNY Press.

Van Manen, M. (1991). *The tact of teaching: The meaning of pedagogical thoughtfulness.* Albany, NY: SUNY Press.

Van Manen, M. (1984). *Doing phemonological research and writing: An introduction.* Curriculum Praxis Monograph Series, No. 7. Edmonton, Alberta: University of Alberta, Faculty of Education.

VandeBerg, L. (1993). *China Beach,* prime time war in the postfeminist age: An example of patriarchy in a different voice. *Western Journal of Communication, 57,* 349–366.

Vattimo, G. (1991). *The end of modernity.* Baltimore: Johns Hopkins University Press.

Vaughn, A. T. (1989, July). The origins debate. *Virginia Magazine of History and Biography,* 311–354.

Ventura, M. (1994). The age of endarkenment. *Utne Reader, 64,* 63–66.

Verstegen, D. A. (1990). Education fiscal policy in the Reagan administration. *Educational Evaluation and Policy Analysis, 12* (4), 355–373.

Vidal, G. (1993). *United States: Essays 1952–1992.* New York: Random House.

Viruru, R. (1998). Exploring Indian constructions of the education of young children: A case study. Unpublished Doctoral Dissertation: Texas A&M University.

Vogel, J. (1994). Throw away the key. *Utne Reader, 64,* 56–60.

Walby, S. (1989). Theorising patriarchy. *Sociology, 23* (2), 213–234.

Walby, S. (1990). *Theorising patriarchy.* Oxford: Basil Blackwell.

Wallace, M. (1992). Boyz n the hood and jungle fever. In G. Dent (Ed.), *Black popular culture.* Seattle: Bay Press.

Wallace, M. (1993). Multiculturliasm and oppositionality. In C. McCarthy, & W. Crichlow (Eds.), *Race, identity, and representation in education.* New York: Routledge.

Warde, A. (1994). Consumers, identity, and belonging: Reflecting on some theses of Zygmunt Bauman. In R. Keat, N. Whiteley, & N. Abercrombie (Eds.), *The authority of the consumer.* New York: Routledge.

Warren, D. (Ed.). (1989). *American teachers: Histories of a profession at work.* New York: Macmillan.

Wartenberg, T. (1992). Situated social power. In T. Wartenberg (Ed.), *Rethinking power.* Albany, NY: SUNY Press.

Wax, R. (1971). *Doing fieldwork: Warnings and advice.* Chicago: University of Chicago Press.

Weaver, J., Slattery, P., & Daspit, T. (1998). Museums and Memories: Toward a critical understanding of the politics of space and time. *Journal of Curriculum Theorizing, 14* (4), 18–26.

Webster, F. (1985/1986). The politics of new technology. *Socialist Register,* 385–411.

Weil, D. (1998). *Towards a critical multicultural literacy: Theory and practice for education for liberation.* New York: Peter Lang.

Weiler, K. (1988). *Women teaching for change.* South Hadley, MA: Bergin & Garvey.

Weis, L. (1988). High school girls in a de-industrializing economy. In L. Weis (Ed.), *Class, race, and gender in American education.* Albany, NY: SUNY Press.

Weisman, J. B. (1991). *The Lowell mill girls: Life in the factory.* Carlisle, MA: Discovery Enterprises.

Wellman, D. (1996). Red and black in white America: Discovering cross-border identities and other subversive activities. In B. Thompson, & S. Tyagi (Eds.), *Names we call home: Autobiography on racial identity.* New York: Routledge.

Wells, D. (1987). *Empty promises.* New York: Monthly Review Press.

Wertsch, J., & Tulviste, P. (1992). L. S. Vygotsky and contemporary developmental psychology. *Developmental Psychology, 28* (4), 548–557.

West, C. (1993). *Race matters.* Boston: Beacon Press.

Westkott, M. (1982). Women's studies as a strategy for change: Between criticism and vision. In G. Bowles, & R. Klein (Eds.), *Theories of women's studies.* Boston: Routledge and Kegan Paul.

Wexler, P. (1996). *Critical social psychology.* New York: Peter Lang.

Wheatley, M. J. (1992). Leadership and the new sciences: Learning about organization from an orderly universe. San Francisco: Benett-Koehler.

Whitehead, A. N. (1933). *Adventure of ideas.* New York: Macmillan/Free Press.

Whitford, B., & Gaus, D. (1995). With a little help from their friends: Making change at Wheeler school. In A. Lieberman (Ed.), *The work of restructuring schools: Building from the ground up.* New York: Teachers College Press.

Whitman, D. (1995, November 6). Unfair cuts. *U.S. News and World Report,* 42–43.

Whitson, J. (1991). *Constitution and curriculum*. New York: Falmer.

Williams, S. (1992). Two words on music: Black community. In G. Dent (Ed.), *Black popular culture*. Seattle: Bay Press.

Willis, E. (1995). The median is the message. In R. Jacoby, & N. Glauberman (Eds.), *The bell curve debate: History, documents, and opinion*. New York: Random House.

Willis, P. (1977). *Learning to labour: How working class kids get working class jobs*. Farnborough, England: Saxon House.

Winant, H. (1994). Racial formation and hegemony: Global and local developments. In A. Rattansi, & S. Westwood (Eds.), *Racism, modernity, and identity on the western front*. Cambridge, MA: Polity Press.

Wingo, M. (1974). *Philosophies of education: An introduction*. Lexington, Massachusetts: D.C. Heath.

Wirt, F. M., & Kirst, M. W. (1992). *Schools in conflict: The politics of education*, (3rd ed.). Berkeley: McCutchan.

Wirth, A. (1983). *Productive work–In industry and schools*. Lanham, Maryland: University Press of America.

Wolfe, L. (1991). Introduction. In L. Wolfe (Ed.), *Women, work, and school: Occupational segregation and the role of education*. Boulder, CO: Westview.

Wolff, J. (1997). Women in organizations. In S. Clegg, & D. Dunkerly (Eds.), *Critical issues in organizations*. London: Routledge Direct Editions.

Wood, P. (1988). Action research: A field perspective. *Journal of Education for Teaching, 14* (2), 135–150.

Woods, P. (1983). *Sociology and the school: An interactionist viewpoint*. London: Routledge and Kegan Paul.

Woodson, C. G. (1919) *The education of the negro*. Washington, DC: The Associated Publishers.

Woodward, C. V. (1974). *The strange career of Jim Crow*, (3rd ed.). New York: Oxford University Press.

Woodward, C. V. (1966). *Reunion and reaction: The compromise of 1877 and the end of reconstruction*. Boston: Little, Brown.

Yeo, F. (1997). *Inner-city schools, multiculturalism, and teacher education: A professional journey*. New York: Garland.

Young, R. (1990). *A critical theory of education: Habermas and our children's future*. New York: Teachers College Press.

Yudice, G. (1995). Neither impugning nor disavowing whiteness does a viable politics make: The limits of identity politics. In C. Newfield, & R. Strickland (Eds.), *After political correctness*. Boulder, CO: Westview.

Yudof, M. G., Kirp, D. L., & Levin, B. (1992). *Educational policy and the law*, (3rd ed.). St. Paul: West Publishing.

Zeuli, J., & Bachmann, M. (1986). *Implementation of teacher thinking research as curriculum deliberation*. Occasional Paper Number 107. East Lansing: Michigan State University, Institute for Research on Teaching.

Zigler, E., & Finn-Stevenson, M. (1987). *Children: Development and social issues*. Lexington, MA: D.C. Heath.

Zinn, M. (1994). Feminist rethinking from racial-ethnic families. In M. Zinn, & B. Dill (Eds.), *Women of color in U.S. society*. Philadelphia: Temple University Press.

Zinn, M., & Dill, B. (1994). Difference and domination. In M. Zinn, & B. Dill (Eds.), *Women of color in U.S. society*. Philadelphia: Temple University Press.

Zweigenhaft, R., & Domhoff, G. (1991). *Blacks in the white establishment*. New Haven: Yale University Press.